20 March 1987

For Charles Robinson —

my fellow laborer in the

vineyards of Romanticism —

with admiration and respect,

And all best wishes —

Norman Fruman

COLERIDGE,
THE
DAMAGED
ARCHANGEL

COLERIDGE, THE DAMAGED ARCHANGEL

Norman Fruman

GEORGE BRAZILLER

New York

For information, address the publisher:
George Braziller, Inc.
One Park Avenue, New York 10016

Library of Congress Catalog Card Number: 71-148743
Standard Book Number: 0-8076-0607-3

First Printing
Printed in the United States of America by Ray Freiman & Company

For Doris

"[Coleridge] is at present under the medical care of a Mr. Gilman (Killman?) a Highgate Apothecary, where he plays at leaving off Laudanum. I think his essentials not touched: he is very bad, but then he wonderfully picks up another day, and his face when he repeats his verses hath its ancient glory, an Archangel a little damaged."

Charles Lamb to William Wordsworth,
26 August 1816

Acknowledgments

Anyone attempting to write comprehensively on Coleridge at present is faced with the difficult decision of when to call a halt. The first volumes of the collected works appeared recently, and it will be many years, perhaps decades, before this prodigious edition is complete. Eleven years have now passed since Professor E. L. Griggs brought out the indispensable third and fourth volumes of his projected six volumes of Coleridge's letters. The second volume of the notebooks bears the date 1961, and three more are envisaged. Obviously, in a finite lifetime, one must call a halt somewhere in tracking Coleridge, and perhaps it is fitting that the ingathering of his widely scattered writings should be colored with visionary hope rather than practical expectation.

The last chapter of this book was written in Highgate, London, in June 1969, and I have not taken note of any of the books and articles on Coleridge that have appeared since then, nor of a few titles published the previous year that I did not see until I returned to the United States. To have reopened discussion of certain problems in the light of new evidence would have been an almost endless task and would have protracted publication into an unforeseeable future.

During the writing of this book, I have accumulated professional and personal debts that defy adequate assessment. In the text I have cited the many scholars and critics whose work has made this one possible. But all Coleridgeans must acknowledge with special gratitude the magisterial achievement of Professor Kathleen Coburn and Professor Earl Leslie Griggs, whose editorial genius has so immensely broadened the scope of our knowledge.

The late Professor Edward L. McAdam, Jr., provided heartening support at a time when I had come to doubt the conclusions my research was producing.

To Dr. Sidney Levy, a dear friend and mentor, my obligations are profound, and personal in a way that defeats expression.

Thanks are due the staff at the British Museum and Dove Cottage, Grasmere. I remember with particular gratitude Mrs. Gosling, librarian of the Highgate Literary and Scientific Institution, who graciously provided me

ix

with unrestricted use of the Coleridge collection, a comfortable working area, and on many a cold and damp day, a cheerful fire and cups of hot tea. To Mary Isabel Fry and everyone connected with the Henry E. Huntington Library in San Marino, California, I owe a debt incurred over many years for all manner of courtesies, expert professional aid, and the maintenance of an atmosphere of peerless beauty and repose. To the entire library staff at California State College, Los Angeles, many thanks for prompt and skillful service, and forebearance in awaiting the return of overdue books. I gratefully also acknowledge a research grant from the California State College at Los Angeles Foundation, which paid for some clerical help and research materials.

I have had the great good fortune to have my manuscript read in turn by E. E. Bostetter, Elisabeth Schneider, and René Wellek. Though I was unable to act upon all their valuable suggestions, I did manage to adjust certain emphases and to expunge at least a few errors. The time and care these eminent and busy scholars have given a bulky manuscript by someone previously unknown to them reflect great credit on each individually and on the highest ideals of the profession. I am grateful also to Dean George Winchester Stone, Jr., not only for a careful and wise reading, but for sympathetic interest through the years.

Without the devoted and expert help of my former student, Mrs. Celia Almaguer, this book would be still unfinished. She typed almost the whole manuscript, rechecked most of the jungle of notes, and otherwise proved an ideal research assistant and friend. My colleague, Professor William G. Leary, has provided invaluable help in reading proofs and in resolving a variety of stylistic problems. I am grateful also to Mr. Edwin Seaver of George Braziller, Inc., a demanding and acute editor.

In writing *finis* to this long project, I cannot help but think of what I owe since childhood to my mother and father, to my sister and brother. To my young children, who may someday read this book, my loving apologies for having been sometimes distracted and impatient with interruptions. My greatest debt is to Doris, a wife of infinite resource and often a co-worker, whose energy, confidence, and loving support have never failed.

Los Angeles, 1971   N.F.

Contents

CONTENTS

xii

Introduction

"A big book is a big misfortune," complained Callimachus twenty-two hundred years ago, and he who undertakes to write at length upon a familiar subject must justify the risk of multiplying the world's misfortunes. Especially is this true of yet another book on Samuel Taylor Coleridge ("Logician, Metaphysician, Bard!"), whose minutest concerns have in recent decades become the subject of extended essays and spaciously proportioned monographs.

For many years past, devoted scholars everywhere in the English-speaking world have been collecting Coleridge's letters, notebooks, unpublished manuscripts, lectures, conversations, long-forgotten newspaper essays—in fact, the entire *oeuvre*, including the least scrap or partially obliterated note—and all is being assembled and prepared for publication with unsurpassed care and patience. This is not in the least surprising, for Coleridge today ranks among the heroes of thought, not only one of England's great poets, but a daring and profound speculator who fructified an astonishing diversity of intellectual realms.

To invite the reader into the company of so protean a mind hardly requires justification. And yet the instability of Coleridge's stature as a thinker is unique in world literature. No reputation of remotely comparable exaltation has been so consistently disparaged. From the year of his death to the present day the very basis of his claims on the attention of posterity—the independence of his ideas—has been regularly attacked. Not only has he been charged with being a derivative and fragmentary thinker, but one who purloined extensively from the writings of others, providing only misleading or obscurantist acknowledgments when these were provided at all.

Applying any of the conventional standards by which, historically, evidence has been measured, the case against Coleridge is very strong. Indeed, were it possible to submit the evidence bearing upon the question of his originality to a panel of experienced jurists in no way connected with the republic of letters, it cannot be reasonably doubted that the judgment would be decidedly unfavorable to his reputation. Yet scholars who have spent a lifetime with the evidence come to no such conclusion. Except for a few lonely dissenters, the overwhelming majority of authorities in the field dismiss the charges of plagiarism and intellectual dependence against Coleridge as mistaken, or, at best, so partial a truth as to be grossly misleading.

He has triumphantly survived the worst that his attackers have been able to muster against him. And as it is unlikely that the future will disclose unacknowledged borrowings of, say, the magnitude of those in *Biographia Literaria* or the lectures on Shakespeare, it would seem that his reputation is at last secure, though regrettably subject to harrassment. Still, it is legitimate to ask: On what basis has the overwhelming majority of scholars rejected the large number of serious charges of plagiarism against Coleridge?

Answers to this question abound in the voluminous literature on the subject. The commonest answer, by far—whether stated or unstated—is the simple and altogether understandable refusal of scholars to believe that a man so apparently honorable, so fundamentally decent and open-hearted, so generous and indifferent to personal reputation, could possibly have been guilty of deliberate misrepresentation and concealment. "I have not a single spark of the Love of Literary Reputation for it's own sake," Coleridge wrote to his brother Edward in the last decade of his pain-ridden life. "Could I be sure that the same good would be affected by any thing, I wrote, a very trifling sum would purchase from me the reputation of having written it."[1] To accuse such a man of deliberate and consistent plagiarism seems patently absurd.

Could it be shown, however, that Coleridge was by no means so guileless and disinterested a man of letters as is commonly supposed, were it even possible to imagine that he was cunning and deceitful, at times treacherous, vain and ambitious of literary reputation, dishonest in his personal relations, an exploiter of those who loved him, a liar—surely his own testimony on his intellectual history would not be so automatically accepted as true. To use such language of so beloved a figure as Coleridge, even in a hypothetical formulation, can give deep and widespread offense. And yet, even at the risk of affronting settled pieties, does not candor oblige us to consider a spectrum of possibilities where important issues are involved?

Plagiarism is often a complicated and always an explosive subject, and on a matter of this sort—where authorities sharply disagree—it is not only the average reader who is helpless to decide. Many who have written confidently about Coleridge's mind and contributions to thought are dismayingly ignorant not only of the issues but of the evidence that clamors to be considered. Nor is it likely that where controversy has long persisted, reexamination of the evidence from the usual perspectives will yield fresh results. Either new evidence must be brought forward that fundamentally changes the basis of judgment, or else, in the words of a distinguished historian, one must "take all the old well-known evidence, all the stale old clues, and try to think about them as if they were new, as if no one had written or thought about them before, in order to see whether they can yield new patterns, new hints, new solutions."[2]

In the present study much new evidence is brought to light, and all the old evidence is reconsidered. The pattern that emerges may not be wholly new, but it may well prove as startling to the reader as it was to the writer, struggling to make sense of masses of complex and contradictory facts. The resulting portrait of Coleridge the man, artist, and thinker is, I believe, clearer and richer, more internally consistent—and very much darker emotionally and morally—than has hitherto been drawn.

It is generally admitted that no adequate biography of Coleridge exists. This may be partly the result of the fragmentary materials all his biographers have worked with, for only now are his letters and acutely revelatory notebooks available for inspection. Yet even if we ignore this difficulty, we must admit that it is hard to imagine a biographer adequate to the subject. Still, Goethe and Leonardo have been well served by biographers. The crucial difficulty in writing of almost any aspect of Coleridge's career that involves judgment among conflicting pieces of evidence is the basic problem of his veracity.

Modern literary scholarship has good reason to be proud of the methods it employs to establish facts; former ages may well seem superstitiously credulous in comparison. Prodigious ingenuity and almost slavish patience are by no means uncommon scholarly attributes when a doubtful point remains to be settled. Vast warehouses of dusty records have been systematically scoured to fix a birthdate, and mouldy tombs exposed to the light of day to satisfy the historian's passion for certitude.

Because all this is true, it is readily assumed that the grain and texture of a man's life and personality that emerge from a modern scholarly biography can be relied on to be reasonably accurate. But this is not necessarily true. Facts derived from public records are, on the whole, what is least important in the life of a creative artist or thinker. It is the selection, ordering, and interpretation of facts that make a man's mind and personality take form. In Coleridge's case, much that is taken for ordinary fact about his life is false, and the detailed image of his character, mind, and art that has emerged from the tremendous surge of scholarly and critical studies of the past half-century is seriously askew.

It may well be doubted that any scholar has actually ever made an independent reading of every document he has quoted, or verified every fact, or fingered every available manuscript. The standards of modern scholarship are stringent in these regards, even punishing, but ultimately a sense of proportion prevails; despite occasional assertions to the contrary, it is usually taken for granted that the substance of an author's letters, his comments in conversation, and certainly the matter-of-fact statements in his published works are true. Of course, no memory is perfect, pens slip, and self-contradictory statements are readily enough made by a person after a lapse of time. But if it were necessary to validate every statement absolutely before accepting it as true, research would lose itself in innumerable bits of trivia having nothing to do with literature.

Unfortunately, the study of Coleridge is beset with special, perhaps unique difficulties. Wordsworth said of James Gillman's biography, published just four years after Coleridge's death, that it was "full of all kinds of mistakes. Coleridge is a subject which no Biographer ought to touch beyond what he himself was eye witness of."[3] This remark has simply not been understood. Charles Lamb, whose memory of Coleridge went back to schoolboy days, once wrote that as long as he had known Coleridge, so long had he "known him in the daily & hourly habit of quizzing the world by lyes."[4] Now much that is contradictory in the record may easily be written off to the natural excesses of an imaginative raconteur. Great men can hardly be expected to consider themselves perpetually on oath so as to simplify matters for subsequent admirers, and no doubt Coleridge was often too engrossed with matters of high intellectual import to trouble himself over mundane details. Let us also allow much to chance and simple error. Yet what remains is of enormous mass and consequence, sufficient to choke and misdirect the complex network of streams that makes up modern aesthetic and intellectual history. Revision of received opinion on a vast scale is rare and is never achieved without severe and acrimonious resistance. Yet if the conclusions that emerge from the following study are generally accepted, many chapters in the history of thought and letters in England for the past one hundred fifty years will need to be rewritten. With respect to the fateful transition in thought and feeling often called the "Romantic Revolution," the revisions called for are drastic.

Caution, it is easy to assert, is the hallmark of the scholar whose ideal is to take nothing for granted. But in practice—at least in Coleridge studies—this is not true. Everybody knows that Coleridge was often inaccurate and sometimes inconsistent, but neither the nature nor the magnitude of the problem is understood. E. H. Coleridge, for example, confronted with awkward improbabilities in his grandfather's writings, declares, "Coleridge's anecdotes about himself must be judged by the same standard which Charles Lamb applied to the morality of the characters in Wycherley's and Congreve's plays—the scene is laid in Arcadia." One reads such a comment with a merry smile and passes on undisturbed. EHC writes further: "and here it was that an incident which he related in the *Biographia Literaria with only a little expansion* actually did take place." One barely notices EHC's italics. At times an obvious fabrication will be passed over light-heartedly: such and such a story of Coleridge's must be taken "pro tanto."[5] One finds an occasional strained reference to his "deviousness" or "romancing," but on issues of consequence his veracity is simply assumed. Where lapses are unmistakable, they are assigned firmly to the pernicious influence of opium, or ill health, or disappointed hopes, or dejection, or transient infirmity of will, or they are numbered among the inconsequential droplets tossed up by the boiling sea of human vanity.

In the tenth chapter of *Biographia Literaria*, Coleridge tells how, during his early acquaintance with Wordsworth, the British government sent an observer down from London to keep the two young radicals under surveillance. The agent, who had a large nose, according to Coleridge, soon became alarmed because, from hiding, "he often heard me talk of one *Spy Nozy*."[6] Only later did the man realize that the reference was not to himself but to someone who had written a book long before. A distinguished biographer of Wordsworth finds that this story "throws an interesting light on Coleridge's pronunciation of the philosopher's name."[7] But need we start a train of such speculations? The story is surely most improbable, and Coleridge can be forgiven for an absurd pun as well as the next man. In a letter to Southey of 1801, he tells of entering a library in the town of Durham and asking the librarian "if he had Leibnitz. He answered—'We have no Museum in this Library for natural curiosities . . .' Heaven & Earth!—he understood the word '*live* Nits.' "[8] This tale has been solemnly reported by more than one scholar without a sign of skepticism.[9] Do we really need Clement Carlyon's contemporary report that Coleridge "was never above a pun when it crossed his mind opportunely"?[10]

These matters are in themselves embarrassingly trivial, and since they would seem to bear no possible relationship to literature, discussion of them could only be absurd. But the story of Spinoza and Spy Nozy has already led to speculation about Coleridge's pronunciation, and this in turn could influence the reading of a poem. It is easy to form the impression that critics wish to rule out of court only such biographical information as in some way seems to discredit the great men of literature. Surely this is excessively defensive. If men are to write biographies, study literary history, or analyze the relations among creative men, evidence will have to be weighed according to the same laws that govern any other kind of analysis. The sacredness of a text or the greatness of a reputation does not justify the introduction of *ad hoc* standards of truth. Poised and alert detachment are obligatory in dealing with Coleridge's Gordian accounts of his intellectual relations with such contemporaries as Schelling or Schlegel—and possibly even Wordsworth.

"Begin at the beginning, and when you get to the end, stop!" is one of the sagest bits of advice any author can take when undecided as to how to tell a complex tale. But this tested principle of organization will never do with Coleridge. To understand almost anything about him requires a variety of perspectives, and finally a basic orientation—or insight—which organizes masses of contradictory or even incomprehensible data into a coherent and self-consistent pattern of human motive and achievement.

The first part of the present work focuses, with a few exceptions, on the young Coleridge, and especially on the young man of letters. After he turned thirty many of his hopes went sour, and it is conventional to assign a date soon after 1802 as a decisive turning point in his personal and creative life. This is one of those partial truths about Coleridge that is consistently misapplied. "A Portrait in Mosaic" (Part I) gathers together a number of scattered or hitherto buried shards and attempts to fit their jagged edges into a coherent design. As is true of much archeological reconstruction, many fragments must be studied before a design suddenly reveals itself.

Part II begins with a detailed study of Coleridge's own literary self-portrait—*Biographia Literaria*—one of the most famous, controversial, and misunderstood books ever written. Almost the whole range of Coleridge's prose writings is traversed, and as those with even a rudimentary acquaintance with the subject know, many a bitter battle has been fought over the original proprietory rights to these fertile grounds; and the stinging odor of scholarly gunpowder still hangs heavy over those celebrated fields from which has sprung so much modern thought. It is Coleridge, of course, who today rules these vast domains, but not without repeated assaults on his titular legitimacy. The claimants, on the whole, speak German. How are they to be fairly heard in lands where their language is little understood?

Many historically significant studies of the subject have quoted only sparingly from German sources, sometimes without stooping to provide translations; others have consistently directed English readers to obscure German texts where, presumably, relevant comparisons with Coleridge might be made. I have assumed throughout that the reader knows no German and has only a rudimentary, if any, acquaintance with the host of German writers whom Coleridge knew and studied. Accordingly, I have directed the reader to English translations of the works in question, when they exist, so that he can test what might otherwise be mere assertion. Some of these works are of great worth in themselves. All are important in the context of Romanticism and the literary relations between England and Germany, in which Coleridge is incalculably the greatest mediating figure. However, what is important finally is the value of Coleridge's writings. The capstone chapter of Part II, "Coleridge as Critic and Aesthetician," may be read independently, but the judgments therein—many of which will seem extreme—are grounded upon the evidence provided in the preceding pages.

Understandably, Coleridge's achievement has been compartmentalized and demarked for study by specialists; obviously, it is desirable that his relations, say, with Kant or Schelling be studied by someone trained in the technical processes of philosophy, and especially of that period. But such a scholar is unlikely to have developed a similar expertise in the intricacies of late eighteenth-century English poetry or the history of Shakespeare criticism. Yet, unless we are to forego all hopes of synthesis, comprehensive studies must be attempted, however obvious the risks.

Coleridge's major poems have been subjected to scrutiny of almost unparalleled virtuosity and intensity. "The Ancient Mariner" and "Kubla Khan" provide the subject of John Livingston Lowes's *The Road to Xanadu,* one of the most important books of scholarship of this century and a work whose influence extends far beyond Coleridge studies. Elisabeth Schneider's brilliant (and underrated) *Coleridge, Opium, and Kubla Khan* concentrates on one poem, as does Arthur Nethercot's *The Road to Tryermaine* (a study of "Christabel") and Marshall Suther's *The Dark Night of Samuel Taylor Coleridge* (on "Dejection: An Ode"). Robert Penn Warren's book-length essay on "The Ancient Mariner" has been followed by scores of detailed articles by other writers on the rest of the Coleridge canon. But a comprehensive study of Coleridge's poetry remains to be done. Unfortunately, the assumptions and procedures that underlie the work of both Lowes and Warren extend beyond Coleridge studies; they are characteristic of modern literary scholarship and criticism. Part of the burden of the final division of this book is to challenge these formidable authorities, and to begin the task of synthesis.

"The Divine Artificer" (Part III) retravels the fabled roads to Xanadu and Tryermaine, but spends most of its time in the humble hills around Nether Stowey, where the mysterious poems were written. And mostly through the agency of the dreams Coleridge recorded in his turbulent notebooks, the poet's creative life is pursued into his nighttime world. The chapter on his dreams and the relationship of his emotional life to the form and meaning of his great poems—all of which is linked to the riven and sometimes tragic events of his external life—is undoubtedly the most controversial in the entire work. I have not sought provocative readings of "The Ancient Mariner," "Kubla Khan," "Christabel," "Ode to Dejection," or certain other poems; they have emerged from the pressure of evidence, and not from any eager striving for originality.

In the pages that follow it may appear at times that Coleridge has been thrust into the dock to be harried by a remorseless prosecutor intent upon diminishing a literary giant. But my purpose has been to understand, sympathetically understand, this infinitely complex man. The seemingly pitiless scrutiny of his letters and notebooks, the rude intrusion into his most private thoughts and feelings, all has but one end in view, to make some sense out of the riven life of this baffling genius. That attempt is made in the final chapters, toward which the whole work leads.

Finally, in view of some of my conclusions, let me say that I began this lengthy study with profound respect and a sense of deep personal affection for Coleridge. So have I ended, as I hope the reader will. Coleridge plain is a far more absorbing figure than the exalted seer fitfully glimpsed through the painted mists of illusion.

A Coleridge
Chronology

1772   (21 Oct.) Born at Ottery St. Mary, Devonshire, the last of ten children by the second marriage of his father, a rural vicar.

1781   (Oct.) Sudden death of father.

1782-91   At Christ's Hospital, London, a famous "blue-coat" charity school. Meets Charles Lamb. Friendly with Evans family.

1791   (Sept.) Enters Jesus College, Cambridge.

1793   (Dec.) Abruptly enlists in army under pseudonym after incurring large college debts.

1794   (Apr.) Back at Cambridge after army discharge arranged by brothers. Meets Robert Southey (b. 1774) at Oxford. Utopian scheme of Pantisocracy and emigration to America planned. With Southey writes *The Fall of Robespierre*, a tragedy (published Oct.). Period of radical political fevor. (Aug.-Sept.) Meets Thomas Poole, a prosperous tanner who becomes a steadfast friend. Engaged to Sara Fricker, the sister of Southey's fiancée. (Nov.) Declares love for Mary Evans and is rejected. (Dec.) Leaves Cambridge without degree.

1795   (Jan.-June) Lectures on political and moral subjects at Bristol. Quarrels with Southey during summer. Pantisocracy abandoned. Meets William Wordsworth (b. 1770). (4 Oct.) Marries Sara Fricker. *Conciones ad Populum* and *The Plot Discovered* published.

1796   (Mar.-May) Edits *The Watchman*, a periodical, which fails after ten numbers. (Apr.) Publishes *Poems on Various Subjects*, his first collection. (Had been publishing poems in various periodicals for previous three years.) Begins regularly to take laudanum (an opium compound) against physical ailments. (19 Sept.) Son Hartley born. Reconciles with Southey. (Dec.) Moves to Nether Stowey, to be near Poole.

1797   Writing *Osorio* and preaching before Unitarian congregations. (June) Visits Wordsworth, and close friendship begins. Start of *annus mirabilis*. In next year he will write "The Ancient Mariner,"

"Kubla Khan," "Christabel" (Part I), "Frost at Midnight," and almost all his other great poems. (July) Wordsworth moves to within three miles of Nether Stowey. (Oct.) *Osorio* finished.

1798   (Jan.) Accepts £150 lifetime annuity from Wedgwood brothers. (14 May) Son Berkeley born (dies 10 Feb. 1799). (Apr.) Publication of the novel *Edmund Oliver* (partly modeled on Coleridge) by Charles Lloyd (a highly unstable young friend) throws Coleridge into extreme agitation and leads to break with Lamb. Uses opium against mental distress. (Sept.) *Lyrical Ballads* published. Goes to Germany with William and Dorothy Wordsworth.

1799   (Feb.) At University of Göttingen. (July) Back with family in Stowey. (Oct.) First meeting with Sara Hutchinson, the sister of Wordsworth's future wife, with whom he falls into a long and hopeless love. (Dec.) Wordsworths move to Grasmere (Dove Cottage), in Lake Country. Resumption of affectionate friendship with Lamb.

1800   (July) Moves to Keswick, in Lake Country. (14 Sept.) Son Derwent born. Translates Schiller's *Wallenstein*. Superintends printing of second edition of *Lyrical Ballads*, with celebrated Preface by Wordsworth.

1801   Begins serious study of philosophy. Recurrent illness and deepening dependence on opium.

1802   Domestic friction intensifies. (Apr.) "A Letter to—" (becomes "Ode to Dejection"). (Sept.) "Hymn Before Sun-Rise" published. (Nov.) Unsuccessful attempt to break grip of opium. (23 Dec.) Daughter Sara born.

1803   (Sept.) Writes "The Pains of Sleep," an account of frightful nightmares, which now become almost daily affliction.

1804   (Apr.) Sails to Malta in hope of improved health. For seventeen months in employ of Sir Alexander Ball, governor of island.

1805   (Sept.-Dec.) In Sicily, Naples, and Rome.

1806   (Jan.) In Rome, Florence, and Pisa. (Aug.) Returns to England. (Nov.) Soon after arrival at Keswick, determines to separate from wife.

1808   Lectures on poetry in London.

1809   *The Friend* published. Frequent stays at Grasmere.

1810   Last numbers of *The Friend*. (Mar.) Sara Hutchinson leaves Grasmere. (Oct.) Goes to London. Bitter breach with Wordsworth.

1811   Lectures on Shakespeare and Milton.

1812   Last visit to Lakes. Reconciliation with Wordsworth, but without former deep bond. Further lectures on Shakespeare. Half of Wedgwood annuity withdrawn.

1813-14 *Remorse* (formerly *Osorio*) successfully produced. Lectures on literary and aesthetic topics. "On the Principles of Genial Criticism" published.

1816   (Apr.) Takes up residence with Dr. James Gillman of Highgate, with whom he will live as patient and friend for next eighteen years. "Christabel," "Kubla Khan," and "The Pains of Sleep" published; also *The Statesman's Manual.* Writes *Theory of Life.*

1817   *Biographia Literaria, Sibylline Leaves,* second *Lay Sermon,* and *Zapolya* published.

1818   Lectures on poetry and drama. *The Friend* rearranged and reissued. Lectures on literature and the History of Philosophy.

1818-34 Growing reputation and influence as "Sage of Highgate." Famed conversationalist. Publishes "Treatise on Method" (1818), *Aids to Reflection* (1825), and *On the Constitution of the Church and State* (1829). Major editions of his *Poetical Works* (1828, 1829, 1834). At work on *Opus Maximum.*

1834   (25 July) Death at Highgate.

I

A PORTRAIT
IN MOSAIC

1.

The Divine Afflatus

" 'FACTS—stubborn facts! None of your theory!' A most entertaining and instructive essay might be written on this text, and the sooner the better." Alas, this provocative jotting from one of the notebooks of Coleridge's middle years suffered the same fate as so many other plans that Robert Southey once said, the teeming mind of Coleridge "spawned like a herring." "O! it is the relation of the facts—not the facts, friend!"[1] the brief note vigorously concludes, and nothing more is heard of the project.

That the problem continued to interest Coleridge is demonstrated by a *Table Talk* entry dating from his last years. "To attempt to argue any great question upon facts only, is absurd," he said; "you cannot state any fact before a mixed audience which an opponent as clever as yourself cannot with ease twist toward another bearing, or at least meet by a contrary fact, as it is called. I wonder why facts were ever called stubborn things. . . ."[2]

Certainly the history of any of the bitter controversies that have swirled around Coleridge bears discouraging testimony to the seemingly infinite elasticity of evidence. If so, what end is served by the formidable thicket of quotations and references that lies just ahead of us? A partial answer is that great questions often consist of smaller ones, which, when adequately understood, provide the keys to unlock riddles of larger import. Instead of bewildering ourselves with problems of great magnitude, let us begin our inquiry with a limited, manageable, and—fortunately—often entertaining topic.

Coleridge asserted or implied that many of his poems were composed very quickly or under conditions of immediate inspiration and execution. The following list of such claims is culled from letters, prefaces, or the titles of the poems themselves:

"Happiness"—". . . I unwarily fell into Poetry. . . ." [Claimed for a portion of the poem][3]

"A Wish: Written in Jesus Wood, Feb. 10, 1792."[4]

"A Fragment Found in a Lecture Room"—"I wrote the following the other day. . . ."[5]

3

"Songs of the Pixies"—"On [that day] the following Irregular Ode was written. . . ."[6]

"The Rose"—"I immediately wrote the following little ode or song. . . ."[7]

"Lines Written at the King's Arms"—"I gave the window-shutter the following effusion. . . ."[8]

"Lines on a Friend"—"on the morning I received your letter, [I] poured forth these incondite Rhymes. . . ."[9]

"To a Friend" [Charles Lamb]—"I sent him these careless Lines which flowed from my Pen extemporaneously."[10]

"The Eolian Harp"—"Composed August 20th, 1795."[11]

"Religious Musings"—"Written on the Christmas Eve of 1794."[12]

"Ode to the Departing Year"—"written on the 24th, 25th, and 26th days of December, 1796. . . ."[13]

"This Lime-Tree Bower My Prison"—"One evening . . . [I] composed the following lines in the garden-bower."[14]

"The Wanderings of Cain"—"finished in one night!"[15]

"Kubla Khan"—"[composed] in a profound sleep. . . ."[16]

"Hexameters"—"When I was ill and wakeful, I composed some English hexameters. . . ."[17]

"Something Childish, But Very Natural"—". . . I wrote [it] one wintry night in bed. . . ."[18]

"Home-Sick"—"yesternight, I dittied the following hobbling Ditty. . . ."[19]

"The Snow-Drop"—"LINES WRITTEN IMMEDIATELY AFTER THE PERUSAL OF MRS. ROBINSON'S SNOW DROP."[20]

"On Revisiting the Sea-Shore"—"On my first emersion I composed a few lines. . . ."[21]

"Dejection: An Ode"—"Written April 4, 1802."[22]

"Hymn Before Sun-Rise, in the Vale of Chamouni"—"I involuntarily poured forth a Hymn. . . ."[23]

"An Ode to the Rain"—"Composed before daylight, on the morning . . ."[24]

"The Pains of Sleep"—"I do not know how I came to scribble down these verses to you—my heart was aching, my head all confused—."[25]

"To William Wordsworth"—"Composed on the night after his recitation of a poem. . . ."[26]

"For A Market-Clock"—"uttered . . . literally without a moment's premeditation—."[27]

"Fancy in Nubibus"—"almost without knowing it I composed the following. . . ."[28]

"Work Without Hope"—"Lines composed 21st February 1825."[29]

"Love's Apparition and Evanishment"—"[composed] without taking my pen off the paper."[30]

This list is not exhaustive. The catalog of titles that seem to imply rapid composition could be extended much further by the inclusion of the many poems Coleridge described as effusions, impromptus, or extempores.[31] Such titles, however, are easily accepted as dramatic conventions, as, doubtless, are such titles as "Lines Composed in a Concert-Room," or "Lines Composed While Climbing." The other poems in the list just given, however, make more specific claims to rapid composition, often under unusual circumstances. These matters were obviously important to the poet. In the Preface to "Christabel" he wrote: "In my very first conception of the tale, I had the whole present to my mind, with the wholeness, no less than the liveliness of a vision. . . ."[32]

A considerable proportion of all Coleridge's poems, therefore, would appear to have been sudden eruptions of the creative spirit, and so it is not surprising to find in his private correspondence reference to "the hot fit of composition."[33] But are these statements to be trusted? Whether they are facts or fancies, of course, has no bearing on the intrinsic value of the poems. Yet surely it is worth knowing whether we possess useful information about the creative process of a major poet, or face vexing problems as to how far we may confidently trust his statements, at least insofar as they pertain to certain aspects of his own compositions. Consequently, we shall examine some of these claims closely.[34] (Several poems passed over in the following discussion will be dealt with elsewhere.)

On 13 July 1794, when Coleridge was not yet twenty-two years old, he wrote to Robert Southey, whom he had met only a month before, "As I was meditating on the capabilities of Pleasure in a mind like your's [*sic*] I unwarily fell into Poetry."[35] The poem that follows in the letter reads:

> 'Tis thine with faery forms to talk,
> And thine the philosophic walk,
> And (what to thee the sweetest are)
> The setting Sun, the Evening Star,
> The tints, that live along the Sky,
> And Moon, that meets thy raptur'd eye,
> Where grateful oft the big drops start—
> Dear silent Pleasures of the Heart!
> But if thou pour one votive Lay,
> For humble Independence pray,
> Whom (sages say) in days of yore
> Meek Competence to Wisdom bore,
> So shall thy little Vessel glide
> With a fair Breeze adown the Tide—
> Till Death shall close thy tranquil eye
> While Faith exclaims 'Thou shalt not die![']

These lines, which Coleridge said had been produced "unwarily," are all but identical with lines in the poem "Happiness," which he had sent to his brother George almost three years before. Below is the relevant passage:

> 'Tis thine with Fancy oft to talk;
> And thine the peaceful Evening Walk;

And what to thee the sweetest are,
The setting sun, the evening star,
The tints that live along the sky,
And moon, that meets thy 'raptur'd eye,
Where oft the tear does grateful start—
Dear silent Pleasures of the Heart! ...
Once more to Heaven address the prayer.
For humble Independence pray,
The Guardian Genius of thy way;
Whom (sages say) in days of yore
Meek Competence to Wisdom bore.
So shall thy little vessel glide
With a fair breeze adown Life's tide ...
Till Death shall close thy tranquil eye,
While Faith proclaims, 'Thou shalt not die!'[36]

It is difficult to believe that when Coleridge said he had fallen unwarily into poetry while meditating on Southey's mind he was not being deliberately misleading. Of course, it can be argued that he really did "fall into poetry" in the sense that he was recalling and somewhat reorganizing some old verses for the occasion, but this seems like a desperate explanation. Flattery of a new friend is not, after all, a mortal sin.

Five months later Coleridge wrote Southey of the dangerous illness of Mary Lamb. "I sent him [Lamb] these careless Lines which flowed from my Pen extemporaneously."[37] The poem, "To C. Lamb," contains such lines as "I too a Sister *had*—an only Sister— / ... On her soft Bosom I repos'd my Cares / And gain'd for every wound an healing Tear. / ... O! I have woke at midnight, and have wept / Because she was not!" But these "careless Lines which flowed from my Pen extemporaneously" are strikingly similar to phrases in a letter written just three months before: "I *had* a Sister—an only Sister. ... Yea, I have woke at midnight, and wept—because *she was not*. ... he has still a gentle Friend, in whose soft Bosom he may repose his Sorrows, and receive for every wound of affliction the Balm of a Sigh."[38]

"Religious Musings," first published in 1796, carries the subtitle " A Desultory Poem, Written on the Christmas Eve of 1794." Coleridge's private correspondence shows, however, that he had toiled assiduously at the poem for some two years. In December 1794, he referred to the poem as in progress but unfinished. Ten months later it had grown to "not quite three hundred Lines—it has cost me more labor in polishing than any poem I ever wrote." In early March 1796: "The *Religious Musings* are finished. . . ." On 1 April: "I rest for all my poetical credit on the *Religious Musings*." On 11 April, Coleridge was awaiting his friend Thomas Poole's "critique."[39]

What, then, may he have meant by stating that the poem had been written in a single night? Some lines may possibly have been written on the Christmas Eve of 1794, but this would hardly justify the claim that a laboriously evolved work of over four hundred lines was completed within a few hours. The desire to associate theme and time perhaps led Coleridge to indulge in poetic license here, for in his early references to this poem it was called "The Nativity."[40] And it was possibly to anticipate by a few hours Milton's celebrated "On the Morning of Christ's Nativity" that Coleridge set his own "desultory" lines on Christmas Eve. The dramatic interest of composing a poem on the teachings of Christ in the hours immediately before the anniversary of his birth is apparent.

When he published the "Ode to the Departing Year" in 1796, it was signed "December. 27. S. T. Coleridge," but upon republication the following year he noted that the poem had been "written on the 24th, 25th, and 26th days of December, 1796."[41] However, he apparently considered stating that the Ode had been written in *one* day, on 23 December 1796, for he wrote this date under the title on one of the manuscripts prepared for the printer, and again after the last line of the poem.[42] The matter obviously had a nagging importance for Coleridge. In the 1803 edition of his works he still thought it worth noting that the Ode was a three days' effort; by 1817, however, he published it as "composed and . . . first published on the *last* day of that year." And thus it remained in all three subsequent editions of his work till his death in 1834.[43]

In 1799, while traveling in Germany, Coleridge wrote to his wife, Sara, "When I was at Ratzeburgh, I wrote one wintry night in bed but never sent you three stanzas which, I dare say, you will think very silly; & so they are." Since he provided Sara with a rather circumstantial account of the composition of "Something Childish, But Very Natural," it is somewhat surprising that he neglected to mention that the poem was actually a paraphrase of the German folk song *Wenn ich ein Vöglein wär'*. This material point he failed to mention in his many reprintings of the "silly stanzas."[44]

Just a few days later, he wrote to his friend Thomas Poole, "Yesterday, or rather, yesternight, I dittied the following hobbling Ditty." But the poem, "Home-Sick: Written in Germany," is another adaptation, this one from a poem by Samuel Gottlieb Bürde, which he copied in German that very month into his notebooks.[45] Coleridge neglected to acknowledge this not altogether trifling debt both in his letter to Poole and in his many printings of the "hobbling ditty."

In September 1803, he wrote to Southey of the frightful dreams and excruciating physical pain he had been suffering in trying to free himself from the opium habit. The letter abruptly breaks into a poem of some fifty-six lines ("The Pains of Sleep"), in which four lines are cancelled and recast, and one word struck out and replaced by another. At the end of the verses Coleridge wrote, "I do not know how I came to scribble down these verses to you —my heart was aching, my head all confused—but they are, doggrels as they may be, a true portrait of my nights." Twelve days later he wrote of these same nightmares to Sir George and Lady Beaumont: "Nine years ago I had a three months' Visitation of this kind. . . . these Dreams . . . formed *at that* *time* the subject of some Verses, which I had forgotten till the return of the Complaint, & which I will send you in my next *as a curiosity.*"[46]*

No evidence exists that Coleridge had composed "The Pains of Sleep" "nine years" before. In 1814 he said that the verses dated from 1803.[47] Why, then, two radically differing accounts within a fortnight of the genesis of the same poem?

We may begin by noting that Coleridge could hardly send the verses to Southey as schoolboy efforts, after ten years of intimate acquaintance during which we may be certain that little of early manuscript was held back by one from the other. The only motive Coleridge could have for such a fable—the meagerness of the poem's aesthetic quality—was amply covered by calling the lines "doggrels" and claiming that they were written in a confused state of mind.[48] Furthermore, Southey knew of Coleridge's desperate struggles with opium, and that "The Pains of Sleep" was an account of the dreadful nightmares Coleridge thought were directly related to his addiction.

Sir George and Lady Beaumont were certainly much less informed. Some of Coleridge's closest associates knew nothing of the grip opium had on him until many years later.[49] To send "The Pains of Sleep" to the influential Beaumonts with even the explanation given Southey would have been to reveal far more than was necessary. The poem could hardly impress them much as coming from the author of "The Ancient Mariner," but if he sent it as a poem written nine years before, when he was a mere stripling, some gratification might perhaps be wrung from the situation.[50]

Since, as we have seen, Coleridge frequently sent Southey poems as written extemporaneously or unwarily or as poured forth, it is not altogether improper to wonder whether similar claims may not often be unreliable. Why does he repeatedly make such statements if they are false? Some can be written off as harmless fun or the froth of human vanity. Wasn't Coleridge merely trying to impress his fellow-poet with the numerous visitations of his urgent Muse? Can similarly questionable statements, ceremoniously made in public, derive from the same motivation? If, as the examples thus far given suggest, he did not consider his titles or prefaces, or even personal letters dealing with his work, as pronouncements made in a court of law—even when they appear to convey specific and detailed information as to the time and circumstances under which a poem was written—that is a fact clearly worth noting. And especially is this true in connection with the many perplexing and contradictory statements he made about his major works.

Caution may be required in accepting Coleridge's statements literally even when these are recorded in solemn tones. In a long dedicatory letter to Thomas Poole, which prefaced the appearance of the "Ode to the Departing Year" as a pamphlet, he wrote, amid other moral reflections, "In general, when an Author informs the Public that his production was struck off in a

---

*Emphasis added. Hereafter, unless otherwise stated in the notes, italics in quotations are always mine.

great hurry, he offers an insult, not an excuse. But I trust that the present case is an exception, and that the peculiar circumstances, which obliged me to write with such unusual rapidity [that is, to complete the Ode in three days], give a propriety to my professions of it. . . ."[51] This declaration is odd, since earlier that year he had published "Religious Musings"—considerably more than twice the length of the Ode—as the production of a single night.[52] Why so much conscientiousness about this? Did the matter bother him?

Such "impropriety" as may exist, in any case, would appear to involve intentionally misleading one's audience. One does not publicly claim to have written a long poem in three days or on a Christmas Eve unless one desires such particulars to be known. Whether or not it is improper to proclaim the presence of the divine afflatus in one's compositions, the inspired poet has from ancient times been an object of awe and admiration. Criticism is to a certain extent disarmed by a prefatory declaration of writing under pressure; in such circumstances merits become the more remarkable.

On various occasions Coleridge expressed convictions as resting on points of personal principle that are difficult to reconcile with his actual practice. On 19 November 1796 he wrote to John Thelwall, "There have been two poems of mine in the New Monthly magazine—with my name—indeed, I make it a scruple of conscience never to publish any thing, however trifling, without it." But eight months earlier he had published an "Ode" in the *Watchman* over the signature "G.A.U.N.T."[53] Indeed, scholars are still laboring to identify Coleridge's many anonymous contributions to periodicals during this and later periods. (Even "The Ancient Mariner" and his other contributions to the now illustrious *Lyrical Ballads* were published anonymously.) In the course of his long literary career, he published over an extensive list of pseudonymns: Cordomi, Gnome, Cuddy, Siesti, Zagri, Bristoliensis, Nehemiah Higginbottom, Laberius, Aphilos, Cassiani junior, Nicias Erythraeus, and Demophilus Mudlarkiades, among others. This practice can hardly have been altogether dictated by modesty for, as we shall see, some of the poems published over pseudonyms were unacknowledged borrowings.

It may, then, be best to view Coleridge's statement, "I make it a scruple of conscience never to publish any thing, however trifling, without [my name]" as merely a bagatelle, the moral enthusiasm of high-spirited youth. Just three years later he was writing to Southey, "[I] am resolved to publish nothing with my name till my Great Work." And three years after this he was writing to Thomas Wedgwood, his gifted and generous benefactor, "Of this be assured, that I will never give any thing to the world in propriâ personâ, in my own name, which I have not tormented with the File."[54] For the moment it should be noted that Coleridge was not incapable of taking a strong moral stand on a matter inconsistent with his practice, a stand which he must have known to be insincere.

One of Coleridge's more endearing traits was that he quite regularly made disparaging remarks about his own work. We have seen that the verses in

"Lines on a Friend" were "incondite" and those in "To C. Lamb" "careless." "Home-Sick" was but a "hobbling ditty"; "Something Childish, But
Very Natural" was "silly"; and "The Pains of Sleep" were "doggrels."[55]
Respecting the development of Coleridge's critical faculties, it would be of
interest to know whether these comments represent his best judgment of the
poems mentioned or merely an affectation. One may be inclined to assume
that a major feature of his personality was a profound and perhaps self-
destructive modesty. Even "Kubla Khan," which had achieved a considerable
reputation in London literary circles long before its publication, and which
Coleridge was very fond of chanting in company, was introduced to the
world with a certain air of diffidence: "The following fragment is here
published at the request of a poet of great and deserved celebrity [Lord
Byron], and, as far as the Author's own opinions are concerned, rather as a
psychological curiosity, than on the ground of any supposed *poetic* merits."[56]
The Preface to "The Three Graves" states that it, too, was not being presented to the public "as poetry. . . . Its merits, if any, are exclusively psychological."[57] "The Pains of Sleep" was sent to the Beaumonts "as a curiosity."

Before adopting any point of view about Coleridge's repeated depreciation
of his own work, one should study the "Advertisement" to the 1797 edition
of his poems. Then twenty-five years old, he stated carefully here what he
considered an author's responsibility to his readers. Apologizing for the
inclusion in this edition of certain poems of which he presumably did not
have a high opinion, he wrote: "I . . . was fully convinced, that he, who gives
to the press what he does not thoroughly approve in his own closet, commits
an act of disrespect, both against himself and his fellow-citizens."[58] He
went on to explain very circumstantially what considerations led him to
reprint certain poems that his own strict conscience would have obliged him
to exclude. One of the poems, "Lines on an Autumnal Evening," he
insisted very specifically was being published contrary to his own poetic
conscience solely for the purpose of making a certain apology to the
renowned author of "The Pleasures of Memory," Samuel Rogers—for
reasons to be dealt with later. Nevertheless, the poem was republished in
1803, 1828, 1829, and 1834.

The 1797 edition also contains, without any apology, the "careless" "To
C. Lamb"; the "incondite" "Lines on a Friend"; and "The Rose," which
Coleridge had privately described as of the "namby pamby Genus."[59] Since
he evidently was not reluctant to publish and republish poems that, in his
own closet, he described as containing little or no merit,[60] one must assume
either that the 1797 "Advertisement" was not entirely sincere or that his
private comments were sufficiently postured as to be untrustworthy.

That caution is obligatory in accepting Coleridge's statements, even when
made with seemingly careful deliberation, is demonstrated by the large
number of false dates he assigned to his own works. The first version of the
"Monody on the Death of Chatterton" is in the book kept by the Reverend
James Boyer (the flogging Grammar Master of Christ's Hospital), into

which he had students copy their best compositions. The date given there is 1790. Coleridge was then eighteen years old. On the Ottery Copy-book version of the poem is a note: "written by the author at the age of sixteen." The poem was published for the first time in 1794, and reprinted, in ever-varying texts, in 1796, 1797, and 1803. In a letter of 27 May 1814, Coleridge sent his former publisher, Joseph Cottle, four lines that he emphasized had been written when he was "a *mere Boy*"; on 22 April 1819 he sent the same four lines to another correspondent with the statement that they had been written in his thirteenth year as "part of a School Exercise," emphasizing at the same time that the lines give "evidence of my very early Turn to meta-physics and speculative philosophy."[61] But these sophisticated lines appear for the first time in the 1829 version of the "Monody," standing at the poem's head. The work was published seven times during Coleridge's life-time, with extensive deletions, additions, and revisions in each case. In its final version it contained one hundred sixty-five lines, as compared to its original ninety. Nevertheless, Coleridge always referred to it as a "school-boy" poem.

"What is Life?" was actually written, according to Coleridge's own note-books, in August 1805, when he was almost thirty-three years old; but in 1819, as if with pinpoint certainty, he asserted that it had been written be-tween the ages of fifteen and sixteen.[62]

In the preface to *Sybilline Leaves* (1817) Coleridge stated that "Time, Real and Imaginary" was also a "schoolboy poem."[63] But only some six years before, when he was nearly forty, he had written into a notebook: "a just image of time real and time as felt, in two different states of being. The title of the poem therefore (for poem it ought to be) should be time real and time felt. . . ."[64] Even without this hard evidence, it would be realistically almost impossible to consider "Time, Real and Imaginary" a very early poem. A comparison of it with any of the productions of Coleridge's early period makes this quite clear. Yet he published the poem with a certain so-lemnity, as if solely "at the request of the friends of my youth," and he an-ticipated possible criticism with asperity: "Surely, malice itself will scarcely attribute [its] insertion [in this edition] to any other motive, than the wish to keep alive the recollections from early life."[65]

The brief poem "First Advent of Love" was included by Coleridge in a manuscript note, dated September 1827, under the heading "Relics of my Schoolboy Muse: i.e. fragments of poems composed before my fifteenth year." It was first published in 1834. Thirty-five years after his death it was pointed out that the ideas and imagery in the poem came from a passage in Sidney's *Arcadia*. Subsequently a note written by Coleridge in 1824 was found that clearly related the poem to Sidney.[66] It is a possible inference that attributing the poem to "schoolboy" days seemed to him more impressive than presenting it to the world as a mature composition of the Sage of High-gate, with or without acknowledgment to Sidney.

James Dykes Campbell has referred to the "light-hearted way in which

Coleridge affixed dates to his compositions."[67] Though the whimsy is not apparent, it may be that he really was amusing himself by affixing improbable, if not impossible, dates to his poems. But Campbell's explanation is not the only possible one, nor necessarily the most plausible. Another possibility is that Coleridge manipulated dates and settings to accomplish a certain purpose, namely, to be thought of as a poet with astounding creative powers who as a schoolboy had been a *Wunderkind*.

Surely both hypotheses deserve to be objectively evaluated in the light of facts and relevant circumstantial evidence. But this brings us back to the dilemma posed by Coleridge himself at the beginning of this chapter. What makes a deduction in the complex realm of human motive legitimate? Just three years before he died, Coleridge declared, "The truth depends on, and is only arrived at, by a legitimate deduction from *all* the facts which are truly material."[68] He could hardly have known that only a few months after his death, his old friend and fellow opium-eater, Thomas De Quincey, would publish an article that would embroil his reputation in controversies from which it has never since been wholly free.

In search, then, of all the facts that are truly material, we shall have to range far, wide, and deep into the Coleridgean labyrinth. Our journey must be directed toward trying to *understand* this immensely important and celebrated man of English letters. The riddles we face will not be much clarified by random flashes of insight or intuitive leaps of imagination. Like climbers inching up a treacherous mountainside, we can go forward only when our footing behind is secure. Panoramic views from the summit will not be vouchsafed us without our carefully traversing the precarious slopes below.

2.

The Parched Roots

FAR MORE than other complex personalities, Coleridge lends himself to characterization by extremes. He has been revered and scorned, canonized and damned, extolled for the essential nobility of his character, and condemned (especially in the nineteenth century) as an irresponsible, insincere, and self-indulgent sensualist.

The relevance of such controversies to purely literary concerns, abstractly considered, is itself a controversial subject. In practice, however, we are rarely purists. Certainly Coleridge himself did not normally question the existence of a profound correlation between moral character and genius. Shakespeare, Milton, Spenser, and Bacon were for him not only giants in the Pantheon of English letters, but men of great personal virtue. Conversely, Locke, Hume, Voltaire, Johnson, and Erasmus Darwin were condemned as pernicious in their works and otherwise disreputable. (Among other charges, at one time or another he accused each of plagiarism.) But there were literary figures in whom could be discerned a bleak gap between personal character and creative genius. It disturbed Coleridge, as it does many lovers of literature to this day. We feel, he wrote,

an uneasiness at a non-harmony, the wish not to see any thing admirable where you find, especially in the moral character, any thing low or contemptible, and the consequent wish to avoid the struggle within, this anti monadic feeling, this (what shall I say?) *knowing, feeling,* a man to be *one*, yet not understanding how to think of him but as two—in illustration of this I confess that it has cost & still costs my philosophy some exertion not to be vexed that I must admire—aye, greatly, very greatly, admire *Richardson* / his mind is so very vile a mind—so oozy, hypocritical, praise-mad, canting, envious, concupiscent /—but to understand & draw *him* would be to produce almost equal to any of his own, but in order to do this, "*down proud Heart down!*" . . . all hatred down!—Charity, Calmness, an heart fixed on the good parts, tho' the *Understanding* is surveying all.[1]

13

The feeling of uneasiness that Richardson provoked in Coleridge, he himself is capable of provoking in others. As his scattered letters and protean notebooks appear at last in substantially complete editions, his character grows increasingly complex and self-contradictory. At times, especially in his frequent bouts of despair, he was capable of the most bitter self-depreciation. Normally, however, as expressed to others, his self-image showed, depending upon one's point of view, a healthy self-respect, or a complacent sense of moral superiority. Thus we find in his personal correspondence:

I never feel anger—still less retain resentment—[2]

I have no mercenary feelings. . . .[3]

If I were capable of being tired with all these [advantages], I should then detect a Vice in my Nature, and would fly to habitual Solitude to eradicate it.[4]

I have . . . an utter dislike to all indirect ways of going about any thing. . . .[5]

. . . I have found, that I can not judge of other men by myself. I myself am *dead indifferent* as to *censures* of any kind—/ Praise even from Fools has sometimes given me a momentary pleasure, & what I could not but despise as *opinion* I have taken up with some satisfaction, as *sympathy*. But the censure or dislike of my dearest Friend, even of him, whom I think the wisest man, I know, does not give me the slightest pain. . . . All this looks very much like self-panegyric—I cannot help it—it is the truth.[6]

My opinions in Ethics are, if any thing, more austere than they ever were— . . . all I can say is that my moral system is more austere than your's—and I am sure that in this case your system is founded on Prudence of Men, & not on the Gospel of Christ.[7]

if it were at all in my character to set any price on my own compositions, I should be vexed that I had not taken a copy.[8]

When I cease to love Truth best of all things; & Liberty, the next best; may I cease to live—nay, it is my creed, that I should thereby cease to live. . . .[9]

I never had any ambition; & now, I trust, I have almost as little Vanity.[10]

from my childhood [I] have no avarice, no ambition—[11]

my Nature is too gentle & innocent. . . .[12]

to think meanly of what I have written, almost immediately after the hot fit of composition, is ever a disease of my mind.[13]

No human heart can retain anger for a shorter time than mine—[14]

I shall disgust many friends—but I do it from my *conscience*.[15]

By the bye, your book [Thomas Clarkson's *Abolition of the Slave Trade*], and your little map were the only publication, I ever wished to see my name in. . . .[16]

Self-panegyric, even when true, is unbecoming and lends itself easily to ridicule. In Coleridge's case, this has sometimes been recklessly exploited by rash critics. Yet his vulnerability derives from more than childlike innocence or guileless candor. An addiction to ethical postures at a substantial remove from demonstrable actions clangs stridently throughout his life. He was a man of exalted, indeed austere notions of personal honor and rectitude, and yet we find counterpointed in him a substantial range of impulses, which were repeatedly stronger than his conscious will. The gamut runs from trivial manipulations of strict truth to serious and deliberate breaches of standards of honesty and candor that he himself vehemently championed. As a sort of prolegomena to the study of Coleridge, it is worth examining a few concrete examples of posturing and insincerity that lend themselves to brief discussion. As a portrait, however, these should be considered as no more than a few charcoal strokes from a limited perspective in preparation for a comprehensive canvas.

It is generally believed that Coleridge's opium habit became fixed as early as 1801. In November 1802, he wrote to his wife that he had been trying hard to cut down on his massive consumption of the drug: "I take half a grain of purified opium, equal to 12 drops of Laudanum—which is not more than [an] 8th part of what I took at Keswick. . . ." The attempt to break the habit failed. Almost a year later came another effort. In September 1803, in the letter to Southey that included "The Pains of Sleep," he wrote, "I have abandoned all opiates except Ether be one . . . & when you see me drink a glass of Spirit and Water, except by prescription of a physician, you shall despise me." This attempt also failed. Between these two letters is the following comment to Southey about an old friend: "Your whole conduct to George Burnet has been that of a kind & truly good man. For myself, I have no heart to spare for a Coxcomb mad with vanity & stupified with opium."[17]

Barely two months after telling Southey he had abandoned all opiates comes this curious passage in a letter to Thelwall:

My Health is in a most distressful State; my Bowel & Stomach attacks frequent & alarming. But I bear Pain with a woman's Fortitude / it is constitutional with me to look quietly and steadily in it's face, as it were, & to ask it—What & whence it is?—

If this Letter reach you in time, you will oblige me by going to the best Druggist in Kendal for me, & purchasing an Ounce of crude opium, & 9 ounces of Laudanum, the Latter put in a stout bottle & so packed up as it may travel a few hundred miles with safety.[18]

The letters of the previous two years show Coleridge describing his stoic endurance quite regularly in similar terms. In September 1803, to Southey: "Bodily Torture! . . . I bear it, like an Indian / it is constitutional with me to sit still & look earnestly upon it, & ask it, what it is?"[19]

In February 1793, he wrote to the mother of Mary Evans (the girl forever identified as the "young Lady, whom for five years I loved—almost to madness")[20] of his failure to win a coveted scholarship at Cambridge. "The event of our examination was such," he wrote, "as surpassed my expectations, and perfectly accorded with my wishes." Perhaps he was still too upset by this very serious blow to his hopes to consider that Mrs. Evans would surely wonder why an impoverished student with no social connections would enter a long and arduous competition if losing accorded perfectly with his wishes. The real intensity of his feelings appears in the uncharacteristic outburst immediately following. In a sudden rage he condemns humanity as "a vile herd" and regrets that "some *Rich* man" did not "beget *me* for his *first born*." Writing to his brother George a few weeks earlier of losing the scholarship, he declared himself "perfectly satisfied both with the mode of the examination and the event of it," but hinted at exactly the opposite; in fact, one of the college masters had gone "so far, as to tell me in confidence, that I had not had fair play."[21]

The following year was to prove singularly distressing for the young Coleridge, leading to a crisis with ominous hints for the future. By the summer of 1793 he had run into debt at his college to the truly formidable sum of over £148. Although the relative value of money is always difficult to determine, we may judge the purchasing power of this sum by the fact that in 1796 Coleridge estimated his yearly income at £120, apparently enough to support himself, a wife, an infant, his mother-in-law, and his pupil, Charles Lloyd. In 1797 he wrote that in the country "you might live comfortably with an hundred a year." His yearly salary as a tutor for a wealthy family was to have been £150. The £150 that the enlightened Wedgwood brothers bestowed on him in 1797 was considered sufficient to maintain Coleridge and his family in moderate comfort without the necessity of his turning preacher.[22] It would therefore seem that running up a college debt of £148 in less than two years was no trifling achievement. At this crisis in Coleridge's life, in the words of Professor Griggs, "his brothers, apparently after censuring him, provided him with a sum of money; but he frittered away part of it on his way to Cambridge, and on his arrival at college he was confronted with a host of petty bills he had either forgotten or neglected to mention."[23] The size of the debt may be attributed to a lack of self-discipline, a failing common enough and perhaps not worth mentioning, but immediately frittering away "part" of the money provided by his family to settle the debt implies an uncommon degree of helplessness in the face of immediate temptation.[24]

A decade later, with all the bright hopes of youth corroded by ill health and opium addiction, with his career and marriage and self-confidence shattered, he wrote desperately in his notebook:

O great God! Grant me grace truly to look into myself, & to begin the serious work of Self-amendment—accounting to Conscience for the

Hours of every Day. Let me live in *Truth*—manifesting that alone which *is*, even as it *is*, & striving to be that which only Reason shews to be lovely—that which my Imagination would delight to manifest!—I am loving & kind-hearted & cannot do wrong with impunity, but o! I am very, very weak—from my infancy have been so—& I exist for the moment![25]

This bitter insight illuminates the impulsive behavior of the harrassed and despondent young university student. Overwhelmed by debts and anxiety, he cast his fate upon the drawing of a lottery ticket, lost, and ran away to join the army as a dragoon under the memorable pseudonym of Silas Tomkyn Comberbache.[26]

Several months later, the hapless recruit wrote his brother George a letter full of remorse. "I feel a painful blush on my cheek, while I write it— but even for the Un. Scholarship, for which I affected to have read so severely, I did not read three days uninterruptedly—for the whole six weeks, that preceded the examination, I was almost constantly intoxicated! My Brother, you shudder as you read." His letters home during this period are violently self-castigating: "My soul sickens at it's own guilt"; "Repentance may bestow that tranquillity, which will enable man to pursue a course of undeviating harmlessness"; "What an intolerable weight of guilt is suspended over my head. . . . Images of horror! They haunt my sleep."[27]

A certain caution should perhaps be exercised in accepting these con-. fessions and recriminations at face value. Besides some evidence showing that he was not altogether "a proverb in the University for Idleness," there are a few points worth considering. Coleridge now urgently needed his family's help to get out of the army. His previous conduct may have been a "strange Combination of Madness, Ingratitude, & Dishonesty,"[28] yet a skeptic dispassionately scrutinizing the motives for confessing more crimes than were actually committed might suppose that Coleridge thought his family would be more inclined to help a repentant sinner who had almost won a coveted scholarship with practically no preparation than one who had failed after normal effort. But this, perhaps, is to consider too curiously.[29]

Unreliability—an easy way with strict fact—is a common feature of Coleridge's letters. Attachment to particular metaphors or happy turns of phrase will cause him to shuffle ideas and events when writing to different correspondents. Thus, while on a walking tour of Wales during a college vacation, he wrote Southey of seeing "a most lovely Girl [gliding] along in a Boat—there were at least 30 naked men bathing—she seemed mighty unconcerned. . . . I stared—for she was elegantly dressed—and not a Prostitute. Doubtless, the citadel of her chastity is so impregnably strong, that it needs not the ornamental Out-works of Modesty." Within a fortnight, to another friend: "Walking on the sea sands—I was surprized to see a number of fine Women bathing promiscuously with men and boys—*perfectly* naked! Doubtless, the citadels of their Chastity are so impregnably strong, that they need not the ornamental Outworks of Modesty."[30]

Vanity of this kind is trivial in itself, and even rather charming in a young poet. But the interweaving of a certain coloring of imagination into presumably straightforward accounts of personal experiences can have more ominous implications. Still on this same walking tour in Wales, he wrote to Southey of the commotion that had taken place at an inn when, in the presence of "a Welsh Democrat," a clergyman, an apothecary, and a cluster of gentlemen, he proposed a toast to General Washington. In the tense political atmosphere of the time, such an act took courage, and we can understand why Coleridge took the trouble to set down the details to his ardent fellow pantisocrat:

> I [proposed] General Washington—The parson said in a low voice—(Republicans!)—After which the medical man said—damn Toasts! I gives a sentiment—May all Republicans be *gulloteen'd*!—Up starts the Welsh Democrat—May all *Fools* be gulloteen'd—and then you will be the first! . . .

Nine days later, writing to another college friend, he repeats enormous blocks of the former letter verbatim. But now, in the story of the altercation at the inn, instead of proposing General Washington, he names Dr. Priestley.[31] The discrepancy is odd, though perhaps to be accounted for by the force the respective names would have on the particular correspondents.

It turns out, however, that Coleridge should not have assigned the daring toast to himself at all. A walking companion in Wales, a Cambridge student named John Hucks, published a detailed account of the tour. Of the incident at the inn we learn that the scene began with a clergyman proposing a toast to "Church and King." Someone else thereupon toasted "General Washington," which created "a great commotion." The clergyman thereupon proposed a second toast, " 'May all *Democrats* be gullotin'd,' when the other, filling *his* glass, added, 'May all fools be gullotin'd, and then I knows [*sic*] who'll be the first. . . .' "[32]

Coleridge's invention would in itself perhaps be too inconsequential even for a footnote in a critical edition of Hucks's forgotten book, were it not that here as a youth he exhibits a tendency to attribute to himself ideas and experiences properly belonging to others. This penchant was to have agonizing consequences for himself and fateful ones for English literary history.

In early April 1804, Coleridge violently denounced his old friend and benefactor, Thomas Poole, for alleged niggardliness and general deterioration of character. At the same time, he extolled the manliness and kindness of a new friend, John Rickman. "*Never let him* [Rickman] *know*," Coleridge wrote urgently to Southey, "that I knew or had mentioned to you that he & Poole had had any unpleasant feelings towards [ea]ch other respecting a Blunder of Poole . . . which must have placed Rickman in a very awkward situation with the Speaker [of the Commons]."[33] Rickman, as the clerk to the speaker in the House of Commons, had franking privileges, and Poole had apparently blundered in the complicated but not uncommon practice of illegally franking through a privileged friend. At that period, it should be remembered, the recipient, not the sender of mail, paid the postage. Why should Coleridge warn Southey not to let slip that he, Coleridge, knew anything of this unpleasantness?

A glance at the correspondence immediately preceding reveals that only three weeks before Coleridge had found himself in precisely the same embarrassment because, to begin with, Wordsworth had sent *him* mail falsely addressed to Rickman. In the circumstances, Rickman would naturally assume that Coleridge had directed Wordsworth to do so. Coleridge immediately wrote Rickman of the "stinging Vexation" this situation caused him:

> Be assured, my dear Sir! I never meant, never gave permission, that any thing should be sent thro' you, save only that Copy of my Christabel for Lady Beaumont / and which I did not do merely to save myself any expence, but to do the thing in a handsome way to her Ladyship. So far the contrary, I had desired them [the documents] long ago to be sent me by the Coach . . . Lamb can tell you, how reluctantly & corntreading[ly] I ever avail myself of any privilege of a Friend or Acquaintance, as well knowing the Indelicacy with which many will use it, & the painful situations, it may involve & often has done. —I shall have impressed you very scurvily if you could believe me insincere, or not deeply sincere, when I say, that this circumstance disturbed in no small degree . . .[34]

Coleridge's candid admission of deviation from strict propriety in franking a copy of "Christabel" through Rickman (though not to save himself any expense) inclines one to take for granted the candor of the rest of the letter, which is very carefully dated—most fortuitously as will be seen in a moment—"Saturday Night, ½ past 10. March 17." It would appear that no sooner had Coleridge finished writing this self-originating apology and explanation than he had delivered to him a letter from Southey, also improperly franked, and this is accompanied by a note from Rickman himself bearing a reproof for what is now at least three pacquets of mail illegally addressed to him (from Wordsworth, a copy of "Christabel," and from Southey).

"Saturday Night—12 o'Clock," Coleridge writes, and states at once that he has broken open his former letter. "I certainly do feel a comfort that I had written to you before," he emphasizes with a certain naïveté, and then insists that he never gave Southey permission to send him mail through Rickman either. All this has resulted from a series of confusions in which "I cannot blame myself." Rather, he is "conscious of perfect innocence."[35] The next afternoon he dashes off still another letter to Rickman, containing further explanation and self-absolution. As to the pacquet of Wordsworth's poems, the illegal franking was entirely the fault of the Wordsworths, for his instructions as to mailing were such that "no human words tho' written with Light instead of Ink could have been clearer than mine: for I wrote out my Address . . . & specified too the Coach it was to go by, & how they were to send it to the Coach," and more, very particular and apologetic.[36]

Three letters on the same subject is perhaps too great a protest, even to the influential and irascible Rickman, and bespeaks some guilt. And indeed there was cause. Almost a month before, Coleridge had written the Wordsworths "most carefully to observe the following Directions" in mailing material to him, so as to avoid paying postage:

> Inclose the Packet in a cover directed to Mr. Coleridge. 2. Inclose this in a Cover directed to Jno. Rickman, Esqre. 3. Inclose this in a Cover directed to The Right Honble / The Speaker. . . . Be sure to be accurate in this. A correspondent of Poole's . . . neglected the *second Cover*—& when the Speaker opened the Letter, he found a letter to *T. Poole Esqre—the Speaker* made Letter-smuggler to an unknown *T. Poole Esqre.*[37]

A few weeks earlier still, Coleridge had written to the Wordsworths conveying very much the same information.[38] When Rickman proved to resent the number of letters being illegally franked through him by Coleridge's friends, instead of admitting his error, or at least some significant part of it, Coleridge admitted only enough to lend credence to his incrimination of the Wordsworths, who were completely innocent bystanders.[39]

To be on the defensive in any situation involving his moral character was not only acutely painful to Coleridge—as perhaps it is for most of us—; rather, it can be said that assaults upon his self-image, even in mild rebuke, could provoke nearly hysterical states of mind. And what he often said, and wrote, in such crises is unreliable in the extreme.[40]

Few men can have come by their weaknesses more honestly. Endowed by birth with intellectual gifts of the highest order, Coleridge was also destined to grow up amid circumstances cruelly scarring to his emotional security and general self-confidence. If the roots of his personality lay, as is said to be true of all of us, in his early years, those roots were put down in bitter soil and quickly parched for nourishment. Even the gross details of his boyhood and youth are grim. He was the last of ten children by his father's second wife. One brother died in infancy. Of the remaining eight siblings, four brothers and an only sister died before he was twenty. His father, a poor country clergyman, died very suddenly a few weeks before the boy turned nine.

Had the young Samuel Taylor Coleridge acquired during those first nine years of his life a rich fund of confidence either in himself or the basic goodness of the world around him, he might conceivably have survived the shattering blow soon to follow. "O the cruelty of separating a poor lad from his early homestead," he was to cry forty years later.[41] At this critically delicate juncture in the child's life, he was removed from whatever security was afforded by the familiar surroundings of his rural home in Ottery St. Mary, Devonshire, and installed in the grim confines of a huge charity school in London. There, in Christ's Hospital, a locus that was to enfever his dreams ever afterwards, he was to spend nine long years. Incredibly, he seems not once to have been visited by his mother during this whole time, and perhaps seldom by any other member of his family.[42] His vacations at home were few and brief. It is small wonder that he was to be on icy terms with his family for most of his life, often reproaching them for their cruelty, and describing himself as a "deserted Orphan."[43]

It is not our purpose now to explore Coleridge's childhood and youth in any detail. But something further must be said here to establish a context for the pervasive self-doubt and instability of character that we will encounter repeatedly in treating other subjects.

Most of what we know about Coleridge's formative years derives from the five famous "autobiographical letters" he wrote to his "best friend" at that time, Thomas Poole, between February 1797 and February 1798.[44] Coleridge was then twenty-five years old. The first two letters deal with genealogy and one or two obviously misty reminiscences of the first three years of his life. The third letter, written some seven months later, describes his years between three and six, and the psychological portrait that begins to emerge is already a destructive one.

"My Father was very fond of me," he writes, "and I was my mother's darling." But otherwise, at least in his recollections, he is surrounded by hostility. Molly, the family servant, "hated me"; Frank, an older brother, "hated me"; "Frank had a violent love of beating me"; "from Molly . . . I received only thumps & ill names."

So I became fretful, & timorous, & a tell-tale—& the School-boys drove me from play, & were always tormenting me—& hence I took no pleasure in boyish sports—but read incessantly . . . and acquired an indisposition to all bodily activity—and I was fretful, and inordinately passionate, and as I could not play at any thing, and was slothful, I was despised & hated by the boys.

An *Arabian Nights* story made so deep an impression on him that he was "haunted by spectres." This fearfulness culminates in the closing details of this third letter, in which we are told that he "most firmly believed" in an old prayer:

> Matthew! Mark! Luke! & John!
> God bless the bed which I lie on.
> Four angels round me spread,
> Two at my foot & two at my bed [head]—

> Frequently have I, half-awake & half-asleep, my body diseased & fevered by my imagination, seen armies of ugly Things bursting in upon me, & these four angels keeping them off.[45]

The diseased imagination here described was to foreshadow his lifelong struggle with nightmares, which were again and again to awake him screaming.

Coleridge's reference to having been his mother's "darling" needs a preliminary comment. Whatever may have been her attitude toward him in Ottery St. Mary, she seems to have cruelly ignored his existence ever afterwards. Coleridge, so openly affectionate toward those who showed him any kindness, was chillingly reserved toward her, wrote to her hardly ever, seems almost never to have spoken of her, and on sending regards in his few letters home, conveyed affectionate remembrances far and wide, but to his mother, pointedly, only his "duty": "You will give my duty to my Mother—& my love to my Brothers, to Mrs. J. & G. Coleridge."[46] He did not go home to her funeral or leave behind any comment on her death.

The emotional hunger experienced in those early years appears not only in direct reminiscences, but in the peculiar way the twenty-five-year-old Coleridge's memories of childhood are so consistently intermingled with vivid memories of food. The amount of space these details receive in the "autobiographical letters" seems extraordinary:

> After breakfast I had a halfpenny given me, with which I bought three cakes at the Baker's close by the school of my old mistress—& these were my dinner on every day except Saturday & Sunday—when I used to dine at home, and wallowed in a beef & pudding dinner. —I am remarkably fond of Beans & Bacon—and this fondness I attribute to my father's having given me a penny for having eat a large quantity of beans, one Saturday—for the other boys did not like them, and as it was an economic food, my father thought, that my attachment & penchant for it ought to be encouraged. . . . Frank hated me, because my mother gave me now & then a bit of cake, when he had none—quite forgetting that for one bit of cake which I had & he had not, he had twenty sops in the pan & pieces of bread & butter with sugar on them from Molly, from whom I received only thumps & ill names.[47]

Frank was dead when Coleridge wrote these words, and yet the old grudges involving food are called forth with undiminished intensity after almost twenty years.

The fourth autobiographical letter follows exactly one week upon the third and describes his life from seven to nine. Coleridge plunges directly into the most intensely described personal experience in these letters, one which he would refer to for the rest of his life and which would appear in various guises in his work. It begins with a vivid recollection of food:

From October 1779 to Oct. 1781. —I had asked my mother one evening to cut my cheese *entire,* so that I might toast it: this was no easy matter, it being a *crumbly* cheese—My mother however did it—/ I went into the garden for some thing or other, and in the mean time my Brother Frank *minced* my cheese, 'to disappoint the favorite'. I returned, saw the exploit, and in an agony of passion flew at Frank—he pretended to have been seriously hurt by my blow, flung himself on the ground, and there lay with outstretched limbs—I hung over him moaning & in a great fright—he leaped up, & with a horse-laugh gave me a severe blow in the face—I seized a knife, and was running at him, when my Mother came in & took me by the arm—/ I expected a flogging—& struggling from her I ran away, to a hill at the bottom of which the Otter flows—about one mile from Ottery. —There I stayed; my rage died away; but my obstinacy vanquished my fears—& taking out a little shilling book which had, at the end, morning & evening prayers, I very devoutly repeated them—thinking *at the same time* with inward & gloomy satisfaction, how miserable my Mother must be! . . . It grew dark—& I fell asleep—it was towards the latter end of October—& it proved a dreadful stormy night—/ I felt the cold in my sleep, and dreamt that I was pulling the blanket over me, & actually pulled over me a dry thorn bush, which lay on the hill—in my sleep I had rolled from the top of the hill to within three yards of the River, which flowed by the unfenced edge of the bottom. . . . In the mean time my Mother waited about half an hour, expecting my return, when the *Sulks* had evaporated—I not returning, she sent into the Church-yard, & round the town—not found!—Several men & all the boys were sent to ramble about & seek me—in vain! My Mother was almost distracted—and at ten o'clock at night I was *cry'd* by the crier in Ottery, and in two villages near it—with a reward offered for me. . . . About five in the morning or a little after, I was broad awake; and attempted to get up & walk— but I could not move—I saw the Shepherds & Workmen at a distance— & cryed but so faintly, that it was impossible to hear me 30 yards off —and there I might have lain & died—for I was now almost given over, the ponds & even the river near which I was lying, having been dragged. —But by good luck Sir Stafford Northcote, who had been out all night, resolved to make one other trial, and came so near that he heard my crying—He carried me in his arms, for near a quarter of a mile; when we met my father & Sir Stafford's Servants. —I remember, & never shall forget, my father's face as he looked upon me while I lay in the servant's arms—so calm, and the tears stealing down his face: for I was the child of his old age. —My Mother, as you may suppose, was out-rageous with joy. . . .[48]

This long letter concludes with the memorable account of the sudden death of his father, who had just taken the eleven-year-old Frank to Plymouth

Harbor to send him off to service in India. Returning home, the sixty-two-year-old clergyman had a premonition of death. All the family, except the youngest boy, were awake to greet him upon his return. But in the middle of the night, after his complaining of pains,

> my mother heard a noise in his throat—and spoke to him—but he did not answer—and she spoke repeatedly in vain. Her *shriek* awaked me—& I said, "Papa is dead."—I did not know [of] my Father's return, but I knew that he was expected. How I came to think of his Death, I cannot tell; but so it was.[49]

And so it was that this fretful and timorous child, despised and driven from play by other boys, already—for whatever reasons—engrossed with food, was sent to a large and overcrowded charity school in London, where the blue-coated boys slept two in a bed, were subjected to harsh and unrelenting discipline, and never adequately fed.

The final autobiographical letter to Poole takes us from rural Ottery to an uncle's home in London. From there, just before going to Christ's Hospital proper, Coleridge was sent for six weeks to a Junior School at Hertford, "a town 20 miles from London, where there are about 300 of the younger Blue coat boys—At Hertford I was very happy, on the whole; for I had plenty to eat & drink, & pudding and vegetables almost every day.[50] A detailed account then follows of the organization and daily routine of Christ's Hospital itself, which concludes:

> Our diet was very scanty—Every morning a bit of dry bread & some bad small beer—every evening a larger piece of bread, & cheese or butter, whichever we liked—For dinner—on Sunday, boiled beef & broth—Monday, Bread & butter, & milk & water—on Tuesday, roast mutton, Wednesday, bread & butter & rice milk, Thursday, boiled beef & broth—Friday, boiled mutton & broth—Saturday, bread & butter, & pease porritch—Our food was portioned—& excepting on Wednesdays I never had a belly full. Our appetites were *damped* never satisfied—and we had no vegetables.—
>
> S. T. Coleridge[51]

It seems curious for the letter to break off so abruptly, without even his usual affectionate compliments and regards. And it is with this pointed sentence, "Our appetites were *damped* never satisfied—and we had no vegetables," that the famous series of autobiographical letters comes so unexpectedly to an end, almost as if there was nothing more to be said.[52]

How strange that amid so many facts, and extraordinarily precise memories of what was eaten each day of the week and at each meal, there is scarcely a word about his own feelings, not a word of loneliness, no mention of missing mother or family at school, no mention of grief or longing for his dead father. In October 1801 Coleridge wrote to Southey, "I once said—that I *missed* no body—I only enjoyed the *present*,"[53] an insight borne out by these recollections. Just a few years later, we have seen, he was to cry out in his journal: "I am very, very weak—from my infancy have been so—& I exist for the moment!"[54] Those whose hopes in the future have been summarily shattered, may be forgiven for snatching the joys of the present. "I have been the Slave of Impulse, the Child of Imbecility,"[55] Coleridge confessed before he was twenty-two years old, and ten years later he wrote, "My Consciousness seems a faculty exclusively devoted to Love, and Pleasure, and general Thought; and Grief & Trouble link themselves on to those parts of my Being, which—as the blood & the secretions—are no parts of my Knowledge."[56]

Any comprehensive grasp of the later Coleridge's personality and character, it would seem self-evident, must come to grips with the appalling experiences of his youth.[57] He was to describe his boyhood in London as years in which he was a "Depressed, moping, friendless, poor orphan, half starved: (at that time the portion of food to the Bluecoats was cruelly insufficient for those who had no friends to supply them.)"[58] The posture of dependency that being the youngest child in a large family had already made all too natural was much reinforced by the harsh realities of a large charity school, where regimentation and bullying by the older boys was the basic system of discipline.[59] It is a melancholy fact that throughout his entire life, Coleridge was never really to be in charge of his own affairs.

At Christ's Hospital, only the boys with the most promise as scholars (or those few with social connections) could hope to escape being apprenticed to a trade or articled as a clerk by the age of fourteen or fifteen. This was the dreary destiny even of Charles Lamb, who was sent out as a clerk to the East India House in London and spent his life there. And several times a year bluecoat boys were recruited for the navy. The only way to escape any of these fates was by superior intellectual achievement. In such an atmosphere, intellectual competition derived less from mere vanity than grim reality.

Coleridge was in fact never to be secure for very long in anything, and in a crisis his fragile self-image might collapse completely. During a moment of hopeless despair in his love for Sara Hutchinson, he cried out to her in his notebooks, "O then pity, o pity me!"—and went on to flagellate himself with his "sense of my own small Worth & of others' superiority—my want of so much that must be lovely in the Heart of Woman, Strength, Manliness, & Manly Beauty. . . ."[60] "No one on earth has ever LOVED me," he wrote in another such crisis.[61] Coleridge's life, and his literary career, are simply not to be understood without reference to his lifelong struggle with this consuming sense of his own inadequacy, indeed of his own worthlessness.

3.

The Valley of Wonders

WHETHER an artist's statements are reliable or not is, at least theoretically, wholly irrelevant in assessing his creative stature. Coleridge's reputation today, however, is more than that of a major poet; he is widely esteemed as the greatest of English critics, and one of the most independent and profound minds in the long ages of recorded history. Whether his testimony is trustworthy is important if for no other reason than that his reputation has been dogged from the very year of his death by the charge of plagiarism. It has, in fact, been argued (though rarely) that the very ideas for which he has been most admired are those he adopted from others. What one thinks of the charges depends, to some extent, on one's estimate of Coleridge's character. He vigorously declared he had independently formulated certain influential concepts of Schelling, A. W. Schlegel, Kant, and others before he had ever seen their works. The coincidence extends to more than general ideas, for in the *Biographia Literaria*, Shakespearean criticism, and elsewhere, he frequently used the very words of other writers, their illustrations, their odd and original terminology, and their patterns of argument.

Coleridge's assertions of independence need not be automatically accepted. The problem seems rather to call for a minute examination of his actual practice as an author, in hope of achieving a comprehensive view of his personality and character. *Nil nisi bonum* is hardly a relevant banner to hoist before the inquiring scholar almost a century and a half after a man's death.

Mention of the "Hymn Before Sun-Rise, In the Vale of Chamouni" first appears in a letter to William Sotheby (10 September 1802), phrased in a manner by now familiar. Describing his poetic feelings in response to nature, he writes, "That this is deep in our Nature, I felt when I was on Sca' fell—. I involuntarily poured forth a Hymn in the manner of the *Psalms*. . . ."[1] Soon after Coleridge's death, De Quincey charged that Coleridge had plagiarized the work from Friederica Brun, a Danish-German poet.[2] Despite the obvious similarity of the two poems, the matter, if not explained away, was at

26

least placed in an acceptable light by Coleridge's numerous defenders, though the claim to immediate inspiration and execution was demonstrably false. After all, it was said, the poems were so similar that Coleridge could not possibly have intended a plagiarism so easily discovered. Friederica Brun was, however, scarcely known in England, and the fact is that no connection between the poems was noted until after Coleridge's death.

"Chamouni" was first printed in the *Morning Post* with an introductory note which begins with a description of Chamouni and the surrounding mountains and glaciers. Coleridge continues:

The beautiful *Gentiana major*, or greater gentian, with blossoms of the brightest blue, grows in large companies a few steps from the never-melted ice of the glaciers. I thought it an affecting emblem of the boldness of human hope, venturing near, and, as it were, leaning over the brink of the grave. Indeed, the whole vale, its every light, its every sound, must needs impress every mind not utterly callous with the thought— Who *would* be, who *could* be an Atheist in this valley of wonders! If any of the readers of the MORNING POST have visited this vale in their journeys among the Alps, I am confident that they will not find the sentiments and feelings expressed, or attempted to be expressed, in the following poem, extravagant.[3]

In a 1942 Lausanne dissertation, Adrien Bonjour demonstrated that this introduction, so weighty in solemn reflections, is frequently a paraphrase and sometimes a word-for-word translation of Brun's notes to her poem.[4] Bonjour prints the passages of German and English side by side and comments, "They [the notes] afford perhaps the best piece of evidence showing Coleridge's perfect consciousness and voluntary purpose when adapting the German poem. Much more even than in the text of the *Hymn* itself did he follow his original, some passages being no less than an actual translation with a few clever interpolations."[5] The *Gentiana major*, which Coleridge had found such "an affecting emblem of the boldness of human hope," was plucked from the notes of Brun,[6] while the valley "which must needs impress every mind not utterly callous" with the shallowness of atheism, had never impinged upon the retina of the devout moralist.

H. N. Coleridge and others have argued that Coleridge could not have had "any ungenerous wish . . . to conceal the obligation" to Brun because the use of her work was so bold and direct, whereas if he had really meant to plagiarize, some concealing arts would have been employed.[7] To these speculations Dykes Campbell has replied, "Had Coleridge been borrowing from Schiller or Goethe, this would have been a fair, though hardly a sufficient excuse; but the author borrowed from was obscure, or had merely a local reputation. See Wordsworth's *Prose Works* (iii. 442) for a proof that, even to him, Coleridge had never spoken of any source but his own imagination."[8]

Writing to William Sotheby about his feelings on Scafell, when "I involuntarily poured forth a Hymn," Coleridge said further, "afterwards I thought the Ideas &c disproportionate to our humble mountains—& accidentally lighting on a short Note in some swiss Poems, concerning the Vale of Chamouny, & it's Mountain, I transferred myself thither, in the Spirit, & adapted my former feelings to these grander external objects."[9] Mention of the "short Note" (actually several notes) of course proves that he consciously used Brun's notes as well as poem. May it be supposed it was for this reason that the poet's grandson suppressed this damaging portion of the letter to Sotheby in his 1895 edition of the *Letters*?[10]

As Brun's poem numbers only twenty lines and as Coleridge's is more than four times longer, it has been stated in various ways that "the dry bones of the German outline have been awakened by Coleridge into the fulness of life"; this was De Quincey's opinion,[11] although he held that in "mere logic . . . and even as to the choice of circumstances, Coleridge's poem is a translation."[12] Bonjour investigated possible sources of the poem apart from Brun. The discovery of substantial unacknowledged borrowings in a Coleridge composition has not, as a rule, led scholars to carry scrutiny of the same work further. Indeed, it is curious that more than a century passed between De Quincey's initial charges and Bonjour's thorough investigation of the subject.[13]

In a letter to Sara Hutchinson (Wordsworth's sister-in-law and the major passion of Coleridge's life), written at the beginning of August, Coleridge gave a very lengthy and minute account of his experience on Scafell, without mentioning a Hymn, involuntarily poured forth or otherwise. The same is true of the letter he wrote to Southey on 9 August. A letter of 26 August to Sotheby contains no hint that he had written a poem, and this was already three weeks after climbing the mountain. The retrospective mention on 10 September is, therefore, impossible to take seriously.[14]

In a notebook entry dated by Miss Coburn as having been written between 24 and 31 December 1802, and consequently shortly after the publication of the Hymn, Coleridge wrote; "A thief in the Candle, consuming in a blazinge the Tallow belonging to a the wick out of sight—/ Plagiary from past authors &c—"[15] It does not seem altogether unwarranted to believe that this entry adds something to the already decisive evidence that his plagiarism was perfectly deliberate.

In attempting to achieve a comprehensive view of Coleridge's character and actual practice as an author, we confront in the Hymn problems that transcend the specific issue of plagiarism. The facts disclose not only careful public misrepresentation but sedulous concealment even among his closest friends. Coleridge's thoughts on the Hymn some eighteen years later are of singular interest. In a letter, he wrote:

> Mr. Wordsworth . . . condemned the Hymn in toto . . . as a specimen of the Mock Sublime. It may be so for others; but it is impossible that I

should myself find it unnatural, being conscious that it was the image and utterance of Thoughts and Emotions in which there was no Mockery. Yet on the other hand I could readily believe that the mood and Habit of mind out of which the Hymn rose—that differs from Milton's and Thomson's and from the Psalms, the source of all three, in the Author's addressing himself to *individual* Objects actually present to his Senses, while his great Predecessors apostrophize *classes* of things, presented by the Memory and generalized by the understanding—I can readily believe, I say, that in this there may be too much of what our learned Med'ciners call the *Idiosyncratic* for true Poetry.[16]

Coleridge does not scruple to insist that his work differs from Milton's and Thomson's in that his was actually written with the "*individual* objects actually present to his senses." In appearing to assert the reality of personal experiences which had, in fact, never taken place, this statement is one of a large, disturbing cluster in Coleridge's later life.[17]

Why didn't he acknowledge his debt to Brun, and so free himself of the anxiety that fear of the discovery of plagiarism would surely arouse? In a note to "The Seven Sisters" Wordsworth wrote: "The story of this poem is from the German of Frederica [*sic*] Brun."[18] Could not Coleridge have handled his problem in some such way? Was it that he could not deprive himself of the approbation that a completely original composition would arouse? The answer to this question is entangled in a web of motives too complex and obscure for analysis at this point. But we may at least be sure that having let the initial moment for candor pass in his intimate circle, he would have found it extremely difficult to make a public acknowledgment later. Yet the risk involved seems too great for the gratification. That he was not found out during his own lifetime was fortunate enough, but Coleridge, one would imagine, must have surely felt some apprehension each time he reprinted the poem. The answer is perhaps not to be reached by using the processes of normal psychology in trying to understand Coleridge. Superficially he seems to have proceeded as if with the magical certainty that he was *not* going to be found out, or was oblivious to the risk he was taking with his reputation. Neither explanation is as tenable as that an imperious need for immediate gratification was a key feature of his personality. Unless we genuinely grapple with the hypothesis that Coleridge was often incapable of denying himself certain satisfactions, as one addicted, for example, cannot resist a drug, we may never be able to understand his baffling and tragic life.[19]

Without a comprehensive view of his character and personality, free of sentimentality and irrelevant allegiances, Coleridge's public career must forever remain a mystery. Bonjour has related the Chamouni plagiarism to what he called the poet's "dejection crisis," of which the "Ode to Dejection" is the most poignant expression. Bonjour assumes that an act of this kind was an isolated and atypical feature of Coleridge's literary practice and hence must be the result of some special emotional crisis.[20] But if we review

his activities as a man of letters both in earlier and later years we will find
attitudes toward the unacknowledged use of other people's writings ranging
from that of the stringent moralist to the cunning plagiarist, and finally to
the empyrean seer utterly indifferent to such gross, sublunary considerations.

4.

Souvenirs of Germany

Well, well, he shall not forfeit our regards—
The Eighth Commandment was not made for Bards!
Coleridge—"The Reproof and Reply"

Discussion of parallel passages involves hazards very difficult to avoid. What is word-for-word translation? What is paraphrase? What is adaptation and transcription? Terms like these, and many others, have no settled meanings. In the circumstances it is extremely difficult to be objective. The scholar who knows that Coleridge's English owes something to a foreign source is almost certain to translate with Coleridge's words directing his pen. This is a genuine dilemma, and a certain amount of misemphasis in discussions of this kind is probably unavoidable. Only the reader with a knowledge of German can compare the relevant texts and make his own judgments on controversial matters.

We have encountered thus far three unacknowledged German borrowings: "Something Childish, But Very Natural," "Home-Sick," and the "Hymn Before Sun-Rise." To these may be added many more. Coleridge first published "The British Stripling's War-Song" in the *Morning Post* in 1799. It was reprinted in 1800 but never thereafter. On neither occasion did Coleridge inform his readers that the poem derived from Stolberg's *Lied eines deutschen Knaben.* This was not an oversight, since the first draft of the poem was headed "The Stripling's War-Song, Imitated from Stolberg." Dropping the reference to Stolberg and changing the title to "The British Stripling's War-Song" suggests that Coleridge did not wish his audience to know that he was under any external obligations.[1]

In the same year and in the same newspaper he published the poem now called "Names" under the title "Song from Lessing." It was reprinted in the *Poetical Register* for 1803 as "From the German of Lessing," over a pseudonym. But in 1829 it was published simply as "Epigram," with no mention of Lessing—this not for a newspaper but in the collected edition of his poetry. In view of the earlier acknowledgments, commentators have been

quick to assume another careless oversight, but let us reserve judgment for
the moment.

On 21 October 1801 Coleridge sent Southey "a couple of Sapphic Verses
translated *in my way* from Stolberg"; he wrote that his "literal Translation"
was "more poetical than the original."[2] Six weeks later the effort was published in the *Morning Post* under the title "The Wills of the Wisp," with no
acknowledgment to Stolberg. A Latin epigraph accompanying the title reads
Vix ea nostra voco.[3] Readers with some Latin were perhaps puzzled at what
to make of the words, which may be translated as "I can hardly call these
verses mine." Neither Dykes Campbell nor E. H. Coleridge questioned the
matter; the letter to Southey seems to have escaped both.[4] Surely it is unlikely
that in just six weeks Coleridge had forgotten the origin of the poem in
Stolberg.

In 1834 Coleridge published a number of poems in the periodical *Friendship's Offering*. They were headed "Fragments from the wreck of Memory:
or, Portions of Poems composed in early manhood: by S. T. Coleridge." A
scholarly note was appended to the effect that these poems "attempt to adapt
the Greek metres to the English language."[5] Three of the poems in this group,
"Hymn to the Earth," "The Homeric Hexameter," and "The Ovidian Elegiac Metre" are, however, adaptations not of general Greek meters but of
specific German poems. After Coleridge's death, when these debts were
discovered, Wordsworth wrote, perhaps ironically, to Henry Crabb Robinson, "C. produced the lines to shew that he was a great discoverer in metre,
one who had for the first time found out and by these specimens exemplified
in a modern language & that his own, the spirit of these several constructions
of musical sound."[6]

"Hymn to the Earth" is a free translation of Stolberg's *Hymne an die
Erde*. The other two "experiments" are translated from Schiller. Sara Coleridge denied any ungenerous intent in her father because he did not supervise
the collected edition of his poems (1834) in which these verses appeared.
This is a frail argument, since Coleridge admitted poems of similar genealogy into editions of his work that he did supervise, sometimes providing
adopted poems with misleading notes. In any case, the three poems above
were originally published by Coleridge.

Since he often acknowledged even minute borrowings, it has often been
argued that his numerous failures to do so were merely oversights or carelessness. Candor, however, requires that we at least consider the possibility
that he acted deliberately. By sometimes providing acknowledgments he
made himself appear serupulous in this respect. As a purely practical matter,
the newspaper editors who accepted his verse would naturally suppose
that poems submitted by him under his own name were original and not
translations, as in other instances he carefully cited his sources. There
would, in fact, have been no reason for either his editors or readers even remotely to contemplate questions of authenticity. Only sixteen days after
giving the "Hymn Before Sun-Rise" to the *Morning Post*, Coleridge pub-

lished a two-stanza "Westphalian Song" in the same place. And this trifle was headed: "The following is an almost literal translation of a very old and very favourite song among the Westphalian Boors."[7] In view of the deliberate attempt to mislead the same readers as to the originality of the Hymn, the specific acknowledgment accompanying the insignificant "Westphalian Song" is not necessarily to be considered evidence of carelessness, but perhaps of a practice that acknowledges small debts and ignores major ones.[8]

"Catullian Hendecasyllables," first published in 1834, is a translation of part of Friedrich von Matthisson's *Milesisches Mährchen,* a fact first made public by F. Freiligrath in the Tauchnitz edition of Coleridge's poetry (1852).[9] "On a Cataract," first published in 1834, derives from a poem by Stolberg.[10] As both poems were printed in an edition not directly supervised by Coleridge, many commentators have refused to confront the question of plagiarism. This seems to take too simple a view of the facts. The 1834 edition came out during Coleridge's lifetime and was supervised by his nephew (and son-in-law), H. N. Coleridge. Though Coleridge may not have bestowed any personal labor on the edition, it is hard to believe that he was not informed of what was going to be included. HNC must have obtained these two hitherto unpublished poems from Coleridge himself. It seems improbable that he would have printed them without acknowledgment if he had known that they were indebted to German originals. Can one really suppose that HNC had access to manuscripts of his uncle and would publish poems for the first time without permission or discussion with the living poet? It should also be emphasized that E. H. Coleridge adopted the text of 1834 in preference to that of 1829—which had been used by Campbell—because of "the existence of conclusive proof that, here and there, Coleridge altered and emended the text of 1829, with a view to the forthcoming edition of 1834."[11] We must, therefore, assume that Coleridge gave at least tacit permission to publish the two poems.

Another poem published for the first time in the edition of 1834 is titled "From the German," but this happens to be Mignon's famous song from Goethe's *Wilhelm Meister.* F. W. Stokoe was the first to point out that Glycine's much-anthologized song from *Zapolya* is heavily dependent upon Tieck's *Herbstlied.*[12] To these German debts should be added the last five lines of "Fancy in Nubibus, or the Poet in the Clouds," silently compressed from Stolberg's *An das Meer,*[13] a poem that Coleridge declared he "let escape" from him in "a sort of lazy poetic mood . . . almost without knowing it."[14]

Of Coleridge's many epigrams, a large proportion are adapted or translated, without acknowledgment, not only from Lessing, but from Wernicke and other far less known German epigrammatists. Some of Coleridge's numerous debts may be followed in the appendices of the Oxford edition, where a score of borrowings have been identified.[15] Since 1912 further identifications have been made, a fact that naturally casts some doubt on the originality of the remainder. Coleridge not only did not specify his obligations but published some twenty-one epigrams under the heading "Original Epigrams," when in fact three were taken from Wernicke and one from a Latin epigram by George Buchanan.[16] In the circumstances one assumes that he was indifferent about specifying debts in what he may have considered ephemeral *jeux d'esprit*.

Taken in themselves, these failures to acknowledge sources are hardly mortal sins. Many were written under pressure of a burdensome newspaper contract.[17] It may also charitably be supposed that the pilfering from the Greek Anthology by western poets for centuries had established a tradition according to which works in a foreign language were fair game, particularly if the author was dead. Coleridge, however, borrowed from living foreign authors and silently borrowed epigrammatic material from obscure English poets, too.[18]

In any case, in 1828 he wrote swiftly enough to the editor of the *Berkshire Chronicle* protesting the theft of one of his *own* epigrams in the issue of the previous day.[19]

5.

The Watchman Observed

IF THE child is indeed father of the man, which is so easy to affirm in the abstract, then there is surely a basic continuity in the essential character and intellectual style of any man. Coleridge's literary oversights, when not attributed to mere carelessness or untidy habits, have often been ascribed to opium addiction or emotional crises deriving from despondency or thwarted hopes. It may not be amiss, therefore, to study his literary practice as editor of his first newspaper. He was then only twenty-three, at the sunrise of his career, not yet addicted to opium, and considered by nearly everyone a young man of dazzling promise.

The prospectus of the *Watchman* had promised only original essays and poetry, but Coleridge, understandably enough, failed to fulfill this ambitious pledge to his subscribers. At least three epigrams published in the *Watchman*, "On A Late Marriage," "On an Amorous Doctor," and "Of Smart Pretty Fellows" were, as Lewis Patton has disclosed, "borrowed, with some slight changes, from an Irish magazine, *Anthologia Hibernica* (Dublin, 1793). The first two . . . are ascribed to one John Brennan and the third . . . is in its original form the second stanza of a 'Song' by a Dr. McDonnell."[1] The last of these epigrams was signed by Coleridge.

Patton has also shown that "To a Primrose," published in the *Watchman* on 27 April 1796 over the signature "S," was also drawn from the *Anthologia Hibernica*. In a copy of the *Watchman* annotated by Coleridge there is in the margin opposite "To a Primrose" his own disclaimer: "N. B. Not by me." Curiously, Coleridge entered no such disclaimers in the margins next to other verses in the *Watchman* that were not his.[2]

As has been noted, the prospectus of the *Watchman* had promised original essays and poetry, but before many numbers had been issued, Coleridge, by his own statement, received an outraged letter from an articulate subscriber: "Alas! alas! COLERIDGE, the digito-monstratus of Cambridge, commenced Polit[ical] Newsmonger, Newspaper-paragraph-thief, Re-retailer of retailed Scurrility, keeper of [an] Asylum for old, poor, and decayed Jokes."[3] On 11 April 1796 Coleridge wrote to Poole that in London and Bristol the newspaper was read for its original matter, but that the people of Liverpool, Manchester, Birmingham, and elsewhere "regard the Essays & Poems [as in] truders unwished for & unwelcome."[4] Two days later, with the tenth number, the *Watchman* died at its post.

In an unpublished Yale University dissertation on the *Watchman*, Lewis Patton has identified unacknowledged borrowings in six of the ten issues. S. F. Johnson had provided a convenient summary of Coleridge's practice as an editor:

> In the first number twenty-eight of the thirty-two pages represent original writing or original summary of materials. Throughout the ten numbers, however, there is a steady increase in the amount of direct quotation, whether of letters to the editor, diplomatic and political documents, poetry, or accounts from other newspapers and journals, until, in the last three numbers, there is very little that is even apparently original.

Johnson carries this breakdown further:

> In the second number there are twenty original pages and twelve of borrowed material, all of it acknowledged. With the third number Coleridge's unacknowledged borrowings begin to appear; in this number there are only eighteen original pages. In the fourth number fifteen pages are original; in each of the fifth, sixth, and seventh numbers, ten pages; in the eighth number, six pages; and in the ninth only four.
>
> The tenth and last number (published on 13 May 1796) seems at first sight to contain a little more original work than its immediate predecessor, about five pages of the thirty-two. . . . The chief piece of apparently original writing is the opening essay . . . an ironic petition supposed to have been written in Denmark in 1660 on behalf of the oppressed populace. The essay is Coleridge's, but it represents, none the less, another unacknowledged borrowing, hitherto unnoticed by Coleridge scholars. With the exception of a very few minor changes, the essay is identical with the peroration of the last of the political lectures delivered at Bristol, *The Plot Discovered*, published in November 1795.[55]

Though the last number contains less than two pages of fresh matter, as Johnson points out, Coleridge in his farewell to the readers writes that some subscribers had complained "because it did not contain sufficient original composition; and still a larger number, because it contained too much." In the circumstances the last words of the *Watchman* seem unnecessarily sententious: "O, Watchman! thou has watched in vain!"

There is no need to wring one's hands over Coleridge's free appropriation of published materials as editor of the *Watchman* nor, conversely, ought one to dismiss the matter as inconsequential because the practice was common enough among his journalistic peers. Rural editors especially tended to treat copy in large newspapers as a kind of free wire service, and Coleridge was no exception. It is also well to remember that Coleridge was a novice at the trade, burdened with the responsibility of a recently acquired wife, and under the commanding necessity to provide bread and cheese. Even if this were not true, a very young man with thirty-two pages to deliver himself of every eight days can be forgiven for using forceps.

The problem with Coleridge, then as later, is that he deliberately puts forward borrowed material, including poetry, as *original,* and that he never admits at the time or later that deadline or copy pressures led him to make up about three-fourths of the *Watchman* from previously printed reports of various kinds.[6] Worse in some ways than this is that he could later find it in his heart twice to excoriate the busy William Cobbett for editorial practices much like his own.[7] In the *Biographia Literaria* he looked back on his first newspaper with deep moral satisfaction: "Oh! never can I remember those days with either shame or regret. For I was most sincere, most disinterested!" Surely it was unnecessary to leave readers of his literary life with the impression that the *Watchman* had failed because of its youthful editor's fearless crusading against the evils of the day.[8]

6.

On Imitation and Alteration

IN THE third issue of the *Watchman* (17 March 1796), Coleridge published a poem over the signature "T" and entitled simply "An Elegy." Two years before he had anonymously published the same poem with the same brief title in the *Morning Chronicle*. In modern editions the poem is given the title Coleridge provided in 1817, and in all the collected editions published during his lifetime: "Elegy Imitated from one of Akenside's Blank-Verse Inscriptions." The presence of the full title in the standard editions obscures significant information, which can be deciphered from the poetic variants provided by E. H. Coleridge.[1]

It is notable that Coleridge did not indicate in 1794 or 1796 that the poem owed anything to Akenside. He omitted the poem from the editions of his work till 1817, when the acknowledgment to Akenside was such that an interested party would be confronted with the prospect of searching through all of Akenside's blank verse inscriptions to satisfy his curiosity as to what extent Coleridge's poem was an imitation. He would find Coleridge's model in the third of Akenside's blank verse inscriptions, and might well conclude, upon studying the poems, that to term one an "imitation" of the other was somewhat misleading.

Comparison of Coleridge's twenty-four-line poem with Akenside's twenty-six-line effort[2] demonstrates the extent of Coleridge's debt, which went entirely unacknowledged in both printings of the poem before 1817:

AKENSIDE	COLERIDGE
Humbly walk,	O humbly press that consecrated ground!
O stranger, o'er the consecrated ground;	(1.4)
(ll. 7-8)	

. . . for there doth Edmund rest,	For there does Edmund rest, the learned
The learned shepherd. . .	swain!
(ll. 12-13)	(1.5)

38

           The faithless pride
Of fair Matilda sank him to the grave
In manhood's prime.
                  (ll. 15-17)

His manhood blossom'd; till the faith-
   less pride
Of fair Matilda sank him to the tomb.
                  (ll. 11-12)

        But soon did righteous Heaven
With tears, with sharp remorse, and
   pining care
Avenge her falsehood.
                  (ll. 17-19)

But soon did righteous Heaven her Guilt
   pursue! . . .
With keen regret, and conscious Guilt's
   alarms.[3]
Amid the pomp of Affluence she pined:
              (ll. 13, 17-18)

          Go, traveller; relate
The mournful story. Haply some fair
   maid
May hold it in remembrance, and be
   taught
That riches cannot pay for truth or love.
                  (ll. 23-26)

Go, Traveller! tell the tale with sorrow
   fraught:
Some tearful Maid perchance, or bloom-
   ing Youth,
May hold it in remembrance; and be
   taught
That Riches cannot pay for Love or
   Truth.
                  (ll. 21-24)

Other similarities appear, but these specimens will suffice. Though the term "imitated" admits of a wide latitude of definition, it can hardly be maintained that the parallels provided above constitute any legitimate imitation of one poet by another, however "imitated" is defined.[4] It seems rather more objective to say that Coleridge merely rimed Akenside. The curious fact that the only original lines in Coleridge's poem are the opening three, and that he changed the names of both of Akenside's lovers in his first printing of the poem, may suggest a certain effort to disguise further the work's origins. If we suspend our preconceptions as to the relative powers of Akenside and Coleridge, we may ask whether the latter has in any way improved the poem. Such a question, naturally, admits of no positive answer, but it can surely be argued that Coleridge, far from improving Akenside, has "imitated" with a notable loss of poetic force. The reasoning behind his slight changes seems less a matter of aesthetics than the necessity of finding rimes. The only apparent motive for this "imitation"—to confine ourselves first to the printings of 1794 and 1796—was the need to fill up space in the *Watchman* and to receive payment from the *Morning Chronicle* for the contribution of an apparently original composition.[5]

One wonders why Coleridge did not let the matter drop entirely after 1796. He could not, of course, have known that modern practices of textual collation would some day exhume his two youthful publications of the "Elegy" in which he had failed to provide any acknowledgment whatever to Akenside. And publishing the "Elegy" anonymously in the first instance and over the neutral letter "T" in the *Watchman* implies an anxious prudence in the young bard.

Of all Coleridge's curious "Adaptations," the history of his "Mutual Passion" is perhaps the most interesting. It was first printed in the *Courier* in 1811, where it was identified as "Altered and Modernized from an Old Poet."[6] Coleridge reprinted it in *Sybilline Leaves* as "a song modernized with some additions from one of our elder poets."[7] The poem appeared in Sara Coleridge's *Essays on his Own Times* (1850), and in Derwent Coleridge's 1863 edition of the poetical works.

Thomas Ashe was uncertain as to where to place "Mutual Passion" in his 1885 edition of Coleridge's poetry: "it certainly is not one of Coleridge's earlier poems," he stated; "at least, we feel convinced it is not."[8] The question of modernization and alteration from a previous model was completely ignored, and the poem was treated as an entirely original composition. In Campbell's edition of 1893 a special section is devoted to "Adaptations." "Mutual Passion," however, is not placed there but is again treated as an original work, even while retaining Coleridge's 1811 subtitle. Campbell affixed the date "?1799," despite Coleridge's implication that it was decidedly a very youthful work.[9] As for the reference to one of "our elder poets," Campbell noted that the phrase "would lead the reader to suppose an English poet, but Professor Brandl (*Life* of S.T.C. p. 248) says the poem is an 'imitation of the old-fashioned rhymes which introduce Minnesang's Frühling.' "[10] What could only have been an unlikely guess by Brandl, in view of Coleridge's reference to one of "*our* elder poets," became in Richard Garnett's *Muses Library* edition of 1898 an indubitable fact. "The 'old poet,' from whom ["Mutual Passion"] is 'altered and modernized,' is a German Minnesinger," notes Garnett knowledgeably, without even a by-your-leave to either Campbell or Brandl.[11] That the poem appeared at all in Garnett's selective edition was a tribute to the high repute in which it had come to be held.

It must, therefore, have come as a great shock to many people when W. E. Henley discovered that Coleridge's poem came from "A Nymph's Passion," by the illustrious Ben Jonson.[12] On the basis of this information E. H. Coleridge took "Mutual Passion" out of the speculative chronological position it had come to occupy in previous editions and placed it firmly in the appendices of his 1912 edition. On page 1118 of volume two it was out of harm's way and no longer contributing to Coleridge's reputation.[13]

Coleridge's misty reference to "an elder poet" implied someone so little known that mentioning the name would be superfluous. That on two occasions he failed to mention that his model was Ben Jonson is suspicious and suggests that he wished to discourage comparison between his own poem and Jonson's. Such a comparison at once demonstrates that Coleridge's claim to have altered and modernized, while technically true, is otherwise absurd. The alterations are trivial, arbitrary, and serve no purpose except to allow

Coleridge to publish the poem as a specimen of his own art. That it was so taken for a century is a fact worth pondering, especially by those who imagine that literary debts are easily discovered.

Below is Jonson's "A Nymph's Passion." Beside it, on the right, is Coleridge's "Mutual Passion," as printed in E. H. Coleridge's text (every word that differs in any way from its model is italicized). The reader may judge the extent of Coleridge's alteration and modernization, and the nature of his "additions."

A NYMPH'S PASSION

I love, and he loves me again,
  Yet dare I not tell who;
For if the nymphs should know my swain,
  I fear they'd love him too;
    Yet if it be not known,
    The pleasure is as good as none,
For that's a narrow joy is but our own.

I'll tell, that if they be not glad,
  They yet may envy me;
But then if I grow jealous mad,
  And of them pitied be,
    It were a plague 'bove scorn,
    And yet it cannot be forborne,
Unless my heart would,
    as my thought, be torn.

He is, if they can find him, fair,
  And fresh and fragrant too,
As summer's sky or purged air,
  And looks as lilies do
    That are this morning blown;
    Yet, yet I doubt he is not known,
And fear much more, that more
    of him be shown.

But he hath eyes so round and bright,
  As make away my doubt,
Where Love may all his torches light
  Though hate had put them out;
    But then, t'increase my fears,
    What nymph soe'er his voice but hears,
Will be my rival, though she have but ears.

I'll tell no more, and yet I love,
  And he loves me; yet no
One unbecoming thought doth move
  From either heart, I know;
    But so exempt from blame,
    As it would be to each a fame,
If love or fear would let me tell his name.

MUTUAL PASSION
Altered and Modernized from an Old Poet

I love, and he loves me again,
  Yet I dare not tell who:
For if the nymphs should know my swain,
  I fear they'd love him too.
    Yet while my joy's unknown,
    Its rosy buds are but half-blown:
What no one with me shares,
    seems scarce my own.

I'll tell, that if they not glad,
  They yet may envy me:
But then if I grow jealous mad,
  And of them pitied be,
    'Twould vex me worse than scorn!
    And yet it cannot be forborn,
Unless my heart would *like,*
    my *thoughts* be torn.

He is, if they can find him, fair
  And fresh, and fragrant too;
As after rain the summer air,
  And looks as lilies do,
    That are this morning blown!
    Yet, yet I doubt, he is not known,
Yet, yet I fear to have him fully shewn.

But he hath eyes so *large,* and bright.
  Which none can see, and doubt
That Love *might thence* his torches light
  Tho' Hate had put them out!
    But then to *raise* my fears,
    His voice—what maid so ever hears
Will be my rival, tho' she have but ears.

I'll tell no more! *yet I love him,*
  And he loves me; *yet so,*
That never one low which did dim
  Our love's pure light, I know—
    In each so free from blame,
    That both of us would gain new fame
If love's *strong fears* would
    let me tell his name!

This "alteration" can hardly have proceeded from a compelling poetic impulse. The changes in the last stanza are purely arbitrary and distinctly inferior to the original. Jonson's smooth "yet no / One unbecoming thought" creeps along in Coleridge's "yet so, / That never one low wish did dim,' and seems dictated solely by a desire to change at least one of Jonson's rime patterns, the only such change in the whole poem and a singularly infelicitous one.

Other adaptations of this kind, with similarly vague references to models— and sometimes with no references at all—may be found in Appendix V of E. H. Coleridge's edition. While these efforts perhaps matter only to scholars, they are of considerable psychological interest in providing insights into Coleridge's poetic mind.

7.

The Shrinking of the Canon

COLERIDGE'S numerous misdatings, oversights, unacknowledged borrowings, and the like may not be merely the inevitable slips and errors of a complex and stress-laden lifetime but the result, perhaps characteristically, of deliberate action.

It is a curious fact that over the years the Coleridge poetic canon has been steadily shrinking. On the evidence of a Wordsworth letter, to be considered in a moment, "Alcaeus to Sappho," always considered Coleridge's, was shown to have been originally Wordsworth's. In De Selincourt's great edition of Wordsworth's poems (1940), it was noted that "Inscription for a Seat" was also based on an early poem by Wordsworth. Most remarkable of all was the discovery that one of Wordsworth's juvenile pieces, "Beauty and Moonlight," was all but identical to the first draft of Coleridge's "Lewti."[1]

In 1950, Jane Worthington Smyser showed that at least three other early poems attributed to Coleridge were actually Wordsworth's: "To Lesbia," "The Death of the Starling," and "Morienti Superstes." She also provided compelling reasons for believing that "Moriens Superstiti" was Wordsworth's; this supposition was vindicated by the discovery of an early Wordsworth manuscript among the Dove Cottage papers. Finally, Mrs. Smyser doubted whether "The Old Man of the Alps" is really Coleridge's.[2] "To Lesbia" and "Morienti Superstes" were printed in the *Morning Post,* but never claimed by Coleridge afterwards. The same is true of "Alcaeus to Sappho" and "Inscription for a Seat." "The Death of the Starling" was never published by Coleridge, and its inclusion in the standard editions of his poems is the result of editorial error.

The history behind these somewhat surprising disclosures, as Mrs. Smyser suggests, is almost certainly connected with the fact that Daniel Stuart, the editor of the *Morning Post,* had engaged Coleridge to provide him with original poetry for a guinea a week in 1797. Coleridge, perhaps understandably, found it impossible to spur his Pegasus into so brisk and regular a canter. Wordsworth seems to have come to the rescue of his harassed friend on a few occasions by providing poems which he did not care to publish under

43

his own name. The existence of facts such as these raises difficult problems in establishing the Coleridge canon with any absolute confidence. In 1802, for example, Coleridge suggested to Lamb, who knew no German, the following plan: he would provide Lamb with prose translations of German poems, which Lamb would then versify. Lamb thought this offer "exceedingly kind," but not a "wise speculation," as he thought Coleridge might almost as quickly turn the German originals into poetry as prose. As speed of execution was clearly of some moment, the object behind this plan appears to have been financial. Lamb put forward his own offer:

> I dare say I could find many things of a light nature to suit that paper [the *Morning Post*], which you would not object to pass upon Stuart as your own, and I should come in for some light profits, and Stuart think the more highly of your assiduity. . . . But I will reconsider your offer, which is very plausible; for as to the drudgery of going every day to an editor with my scraps, like a pedlar, for him to pick out, and tumble about my ribbons and posies, and to wait in his lobby, &c., no money would make up for the degradation. You are in too high request with him [Stuart] to have anything unpleasant of that sort to submit to.

Unfortunately, all of Coleridge's letters to Lamb during this period are lost, so it is necessary to piece together the situation from Lamb's letters alone. He seems to have repeated his offer, for within a fortnight Lamb wrote: "Your kind offer I will not a second time refuse. You shall send me a packet and I will do them into English with great care."[3] Coleridge's verse contributions to the *Morning Post* appear to have stopped abruptly and completely at precisely this time. Since he was in far greater demand with editors than Lamb, and since Lamb had offered to have his own poems submitted under his friend's name, there exists the possibility that on some later occasion Coleridge did so. In that case it is possible that poems or portions of poems now circulating under Coleridge's name may not be exclusively his.[4]

To return to Mrs. Smyser's disclosures, the question is not being raised here of Coleridge's laying claim to a few works of Wordsworth, though there is of course a nice question as to the propriety of publishing poems as one's own, even for a single time, which are not. It is likely that Stuart had no idea he was in several instances getting Wordsworth's work instead of Coleridge's. It is very doubtful that Coleridge's public reputation was much advanced by the appearance of these poems, with the exception of "Lewti," but it is notable that he never wrote a scrap, public or private, to indicate the true authorship. It is surely significant that the first major collected edition of his poetry, in 1817, notes after the last line of "Lewti," "From the *Morning Post*, 1795." Since this antedates his intimacy with Wordsworth, the error suggests how treacherous and self-serving Coleridge's memory was on matters of this sort.[5]

Of the poems under discussion which were published, all bore pseudonyms, with the exception of "Alcaeus to Sappho." Only "Lewti" was ever reprinted, though this frequently and under his own name without any acknowledgment to Wordsworth. The history of "Alcaeus to Sappho" is worth discussing as providing an insight into Coleridge's mind and practice, for here it seems possible to show that he went out of his way to mislead Stuart and consequently the readers of the *Morning Post* into supposing that the poem was actually his own.

Toward the end of a letter to Stuart (7 October 1800) he wrote: "I shall fill up these Blanks with a few Poems."[6] E. H. Coleridge appended the following note to "Alcaeus to Sappho": "It is probable that these lines . . . were addressed to Mrs. Robinson, who was a frequent contributor of verses [in the *Morning Post*] signed 'Sappho'."[7] Probable enough, since Coleridge knew Mrs. Robinson and greatly admired her. "Alcaeus to Sappho" begins with the line: "How sweet, when crimson colours dart." As it happens, Wordsworth in a letter of February 1799 to Coleridge wrote of his own poem beginning "How sweet where crimson colours" for which he did "not care a farthing."[8] It appears, then, that Coleridge kept the poem for more than a year and a half before sending it to Stuart, perhaps when pressed for copy. The appearance of a poem in a letter from Coleridge would naturally lead Stuart to believe that he could go ahead and publish it as part of Coleridge's regular contributions. There was no reason whatever for him to imagine that the poem might be someone else's, although Coleridge did not directly claim it, as Professor Griggs points out, but merely stated, "I shall fill up these Blanks with a few Poems." But would it not be disingenuous to let the matter stand at that? When he included two poems by Wordsworth in a letter to Poole a year and a half later, he specifically identified them as such.[9] It also seems reasonable to suppose that the un-Wordsworthian title, "Alcaeus to Sappho," was provided as another way of appropriating the work, if only for just this one time.[10]

Is it possible that Coleridge published this poem without Wordsworth's permission? It is to be noted that if Wordsworth complained about the publication of "Alcaeus to Sappho" Coleridge would have been able to reply truthfully that he had not claimed the poem as his own but that Stuart had mistakenly assumed that it was. Speculation on this matter may seem grossly insulting to the memory of a great poet and to a famous literary friendship, certainly in the absence of adamantine chains of proof. Yet it must be noted that Coleridge was capable of borrowing even from Wordsworth without acknowledgment. Writing to Henry Crabb Robinson in 1840 of the recent charges of plagiarism brought against Coleridge, Wordsworth said: "Compare Chiabrera's epitaph upon Ambrosio Salinero, which I have translated, with Coleridge's tombless epitaph upon one he calls Satyrane and you will have another instance of how unadvised was his way in these little matters."[11] In 1809 Wordsworth wrote a series of epitaphs, translated from Chiabrera, several of which he contributed to Coleridge's *Friend*. In the same year

Coleridge published a forty-line poem in the *Friend,* now called "A Tomb-less Epitaph," but which originally had no title. A footnote read: "Imitated, though in the movements rather than the thoughts, from the viith, of *Gli Epitafi* of Chiabrera."[12] While providing an acknowledgement to Chiabrera, "though in the movements rather than the thoughts," he did not mention that Wordsworth had earlier translated the same piece and that his own effort was, to say the least, indebted to the former in the "thoughts" as well as the "movements."

The parallel passages below make this quite clear. The first is from Words-worth's fifth epitaph; the second is Coleridge's:

> . . . and full long,
> Fate harder still! had he to endure assaults
> Of racking malady. And true it is
> That not the less a frank courageous heart
> And buoyant spirit triumphed over pain;
> And he was strong to follow in the steps
> Of the fair Muses. Not a covert path
> Leads to the dear Parnassian forest's shade,
> That might from him be hidden; not a track
> Mounts to the pellucid Hippocrene, but he
> Had traced its windings. (ll. 3-13)

> Sickness, 'tis true,
> Whole years of weary days, besieged him close,
> Even to the gates and inlets of his life!
> But it is true, no less, that strenuous, firm,
> And with a natural gladness, he maintained
> The citadel unconquered, and in joy
> Was strong to follow the delightful Muse.
> For not a hidden path, that to the shades
> Of the beloved Parnassian forest leads,
> Lurked undiscovered by him; not a rill
> There issues from the fount of Hippocrene,
> But he had traced it upward to its source . . . (ll. 14-25).

Wordsworth waited till three years after Coleridge's death before publishing his own effort, written almost thirty years before.[13]

As we have seen, the appearance of unfamiliar poems in Coleridge's letters does not necessarily mean that they are his. In a letter to Mary Evans dated 13 February 1792 is a poem there titled "A Wish written in Jesus Wood Feb: 10th 1792."[14] The poem is preceded and followed by other verses of Coleridge. Though he never published the poem, both Campbell and E. H. Coleridge, for the most apparently compelling reasons, assigned the poem to him. After all, the title gives a very specific date for the composition of the poem, just three days before, and why doubt that the "wish" was actually made in Jesus Wood, since Coleridge was a student at Jesus College, Cambridge? But the poem turns out to be merely a translation of John Jortin's Latin "Votum" ["Wish"].[15] Why didn't he mention that fact to Mary Evans? Perhaps he didn't think the matter of consequence, or that the very young lady would be interested. However, the poem immediately preceding "A Wish" is titled "An Ode in the Manner of Anacreon." The conclusion is inescapable that if Coleridge wanted Mary Evans to know that "A Wish" was a translation he would have told her so. But to send her apparently original poetry, conceived and composed in Jesus Wood on a certain date, was no doubt more impressive than a mere translation.

Mary Evans also figures in the odd history of the poem "On Bala Hill," printed in both standard editions of Coleridge's poetry. The poem was found in his handwriting among Mary Evans' papers after her death. E. H. Coleridge notes that the "lines are all but identical with Southey's Sonnet to Lansdown Hill . . . dated 1794, and first published in 1797, and were, probably, his composition."[16] The poem is definitely Southey's. Its existence in the Coleridge canon is the result of a peculiar oversight on the part of his editors, since in a letter dated 18 September 1794 he wrote to Southey of this very poem and suggested certain changes to him.[17] A noteworthy fact is that in Mary Evans' copy of the poem some of the changes he suggested were incorporated. The change of title from Southey's "Lansdown Hill" to "On Bala Hill" seems confiscatory, since earlier in the year Coleridge had visited Bala Hill in Wales. The impression conveyed to Mary, therefore, might readily have been that the poem was an original composition written during his own travels. One would not choose, of course, to nag with the niceties of notation a youthful swain trying to impress his lady fair with specimens of his poetic art. But the unfeeling scholar may find himself noting in all this a certain precocious carelessness with respect to intellectual obligations.

In any case, no such defense is possible with respect to the poem Coleridge included in a letter to his friend, Josiah Wade, in February 1796. Again, it can be argued that he did not specifically claim the twelve-line effort as his own; he merely concluded a personal letter with it and put his initials below. The poem, reprinted in his *Poetical Works*, begins:

> The Fox, and Statesman subtile wiles ensure,
> The Cit, and Polecat stink and are secure . . .

In 1924, a German scholar identified all the lines as Robert Burns's.[18]

Almost precisely the same set of circumstances surrounds the poem called "The Faded Flower." In a letter of 1794 to Henry Martin of Jesus College (to whom Coleridge had dedicated *The Fall of Robespierre*), appear two poems in a postscript. The first is a portion of "Lines Written at the King's Arms"; the second, which follows immediately, is "The Faded Flower" sonnet. The first was published by Coleridge in 1794, the second not until after his death. None of Coleridge's major editors knew that Southey had published the poem as his own in 1795! The appearance of two poems in a personal letter by Coleridge, one of them often published, would quite naturally lead an editor to suppose that the second was also original. There is little reason to doubt that Coleridge's correspondent also thought so.[19]

A dubious rationalization led Coleridge into a breach of literary ethics when *The Fall of Robespierre* was published. He wrote the first act and Southey the last two. Nevertheless, the work was printed at Cambridge in 1794 under his name alone. In explanation he wrote Southey: "The Tragedy will be printed in less than a week—I shall put my Name—because it will sell at least an hundred Copies at Cambridge—. It would appear ridiculous to put two names to *such* a Work—But if you choose it, mention it—and it shall be done—To every man who *praises* it, of course I give the *true* biography of it—to those, who laugh at it, I laugh again."[20]

Since the work was published and advertised under Coleridge's name alone, it seems that Southey did not choose to put his name to a work two-thirds his. But of this we cannot be sure. Coleridge's letter is dated 19 September. The dedication on page 3 of *The Fall of Robespierre* is dated 22 September, and the work publicly advertised as published "this day" on 4 October and 11 October 1794.[21] Under the postal conditions in England in the late eighteenth century it is not certain that Coleridge could have sent a letter from Bath to Southey in Bristol and have gotten a reply so swiftly. No such letter is preserved. In later years Sara Coleridge twice mentioned *The Fall of Robespierre* in connection with her father being "too regardless in literary matters." In a private letter she wrote that he "published the Fall of Robespierre as by S. T. Coleridge though a large part was written by my Uncle Southey." She mentioned the subject again while defending her father in her edition of the *Biographia Literaria*.[22] It is not likely that she would have publicly chided her father had she any reason to believe that Southey had given his consent.

At all events, even if abetted by Southey, intentionally to mislead one's university friends and acquaintances for the sake of a greater sale is hardly a scrupulous act. This strangely capricious affair is still further evidence of Coleridge's indifference to conventional notions of literary ethics and the degree to which he was willing to be misleading for personal motives, pecuniary and otherwise.[23]

8.

The Pains of Memory

AT LEAST once in his early career—he was twenty-four at the time—Coleridge found himself sufficiently embarrassed by a charge that he had failed to acknowledge intellectual obligations to make a public reply. It is of particular interest to examine rather minutely his conduct in this awkward situation. The following note was appended by him to line 57 of "Lines on an Autumnal Evening" in the edition of 1796:

> I entreat the Public's pardon for having carelessly suffered to be printed such intolerable stuff as this and the following thirteen lines. They have not the merit even of originality: as every thought is to be found in the Greek Epigrams. The lines in this poem from the 27th to the 36th, I have been told are a palpable imitation of the passage from 355th to the 370th lines of the Pleasures of Memory Part 3. I do not perceive so striking a similarity between the two passages; at all events I had written the Effusion several years before I had seen Mr. Rogers' Poem.—It may be proper to remark that the tale of Florio in the 'Pleasures of Memory' is to be found in Lochleven, a poem of great merit by Michael Bruce.—In Mr. Rogers' poem the names are Florio and Julia; in the Lochleven Lomond and Levina—and this is all the difference.[1]

It is to be observed that before dealing with the major issue Coleridge takes the opportunity to apologize for having suffered "carelessly" written lines to be published. He then forthrightly admits that the lines aren't even original, every thought coming from the Greek Epigrams.

Since it seems unreasonable to suppose that the offending lines could not have been expunged before publication, a determinedly hostile critic might incline to the belief that Coleridge was here creating an occasion to present himself to the reader as a poet of scrupulous honesty and self-criticism, one, indeed, who will not suffer even the ideational content of previous works to pass into his own. And the purpose of this apology, it might ungenerously be argued, was to create in the reader a sympathetic frame of mind before discussing an alleged "palpable imitation" from a poem by Samuel Rogers.

That these conjectures are not wholly insubstantial is suggested by the fact that the fourteen lines of "intolerable stuff" which Coleridge had "carelessly suffered to be printed," were reprinted without the alteration of a single word in 1797, 1803, 1828, and 1834.[2] Still more suggestive of the possible insincerity of these opening remarks is the fact that "Lines on an Autumnal Evening" had been published in a provincial newspaper in October 1793, somewhat altered, under the title "Absence: a Poem."[3] In this earlier version the careless lines appear in almost identical form, only one line and two words differing. Thus Coleridge had at least three years to erase the intolerable verses from his poem but failed to do so, apparently preferring to draw attention to their worthlessness and unoriginality.

As to the "palpable imitation," he does not perceive so striking a similarity as had been alleged. Indeed, the "Effusion" had been written several years before he had seen Rogers' poem (which had, in fact, been published early in 1792, well before Coleridge was twenty years old). And since it has been called to his attention that he copied Rogers—though not by Rogers himself —Coleridge feels "it may be proper to remark" that Rogers is, in fact, a plagiarist. He then details a very particular instance of wholesale theft.

When Coleridge was preparing a new edition of his poems in 1797, the usually mild-mannered Charles Lamb wrote him most bluntly on the subject:

> I hope you expunge [a] great part of the old notes in the new edition. That, in particular, most barefaced unfounded impudent assertion, that Mr. Rogers is indebted for his story to Loch Lomond [sic], a poem by Bruce! I have read the latter. I scarce think you have. Scarce anything is common to them both. The poor author of the Pleasures of Memory was sorely hurt, Dyer says, by the accusation of unoriginality. He never saw the Poem.[4]

In the edition of 1797 Coleridge dropped the "impudent" note and apologized to Rogers. The apology occurs in the "Advertisement" we have noticed before. The first long paragraph of the "Advertisement" contains a solemn explanation of why the poet is permitting certain poems which fail to meet his own critical standards to be included in the edition. One is a poem dedicated to Cottle, which, though inferior, he is unwilling to exclude, for Cottle is a man to whom the author is indebted as "a Poet, a Man and a Christian."[5] On this morally satisfying note we are led immediately to a consideration of the second poem, which

> is entitled "An Effusion on an Autumnal Evening; written in early youth." In a note to this poem I had asserted that the tale of Florio in Mr. Rogers' "Pleasures of Memory" was to be found in the Lochleven of Bruce. I did (and still do) perceive a certain likeness between the two

stories; but certainly not a sufficient one to justify my assertion. I feel it my duty, therefore, to apologize to the Author and the Public, for this rashness; and my sense of honesty would not have been satisfied by the bare omission of the note. No one can see more clearly the *littleness* and futility of imagining plagiarisms in the works of men of Genius; but *nemo omnibus horis sapit* [no man is wise at all hours]; and my mind, at the time of writing that note, was sick and sore with anxiety, and weakened through much suffering. I have not the most distant knowledge of Mr. Rogers, except as a correct and elegant Poet. If any of my readers should know him personally, they would oblige me by informing him that I have expiated a sentence of unfounded detraction, by an unsolicited and self-originating apology.[6]

This performance proves as equivocal as the former. A "certain likeness" is still seen between Rogers' poem and Bruce's, an assertion which proves wholly groundless upon examination of the two works. Yet Coleridge applauds himself for making a public apology rather than silently removing the former note which, presumably, someone with a less fine sense of intellectual integrity would do. In any case, it is "little" and "futile" to accuse men of genius of plagiarism. The only reason he did so was that his mind was then sick and weary with suffering and anxiety. In later years, when, it is true, Coleridge was sorely afflicted both physically and mentally, he charged plagiarism against Hume, Schelling, Hazlitt, and Erasmus Darwin, men generally considered possessed of as much genius as Samuel Rogers. He chided Sir Walter Scott for a "pilfering imitation of Goethe's *Mignon*";[7] he also accused James Mackintosh, Horne Tooke, Voltaire, and many others of plagiarism.

As for the apology being "unsolicited and self-originating," one wonders what passed through Lamb's mind when he read the words.[8] One might suppose that Coleridge would have been slightly embarrassed at publishing "Lines on an Autumnal Evening" again and again in later years after stating that he disliked it and would consequently suppress it, and that only his sense of honesty required him to publish it, for the purpose of apologizing to Rogers, not to mention republishing word for word the fourteen admittedly unoriginal lines—"intolerable stuff"—which he had "carelessly suffered to be printed," without subsequently altering a single word.

Neither Campbell nor E. H. Coleridge appear to have thought it of sufficient interest to print lines 355-370 "of the Pleasures of Memory Part 3," so that the curious reader might determine for himself what basis, if any, there was in the charge that Coleridge had put forward a "palpable imitation." It seems also a reasonable inference that neither editor was especially curious about the matter, since had either examined Rogers' poem he would doubtless have discovered and noted that "The Pleasures of Memory" does not and never had a "Part 3," an error which may, and possibly may not, have been a careless oversight on Coleridge's part, or a printer's error. The reader who is undiscouraged by the faulty reference will find the passage Coleridge had in mind in Part II of "The Pleasures of Memory," which contains the story of Florio and Julia. Below are lines 354–370; there were no variants in any of the several editions of the poem before 1796 which Coleridge might have read.

> For ever would the fond enthusiast rove,
> With Julia's spirit thro' the shadowy grove;
> Gaze with delight on every scene she plann'd,
> Kiss every flow'ret planted by her hand.
> Ah! still he trac'd her steps along the glade,
> When hazy hues and glimmering lights betray'd
> Half-viewless forms; still listen'd as the breeze
> Heav'd its deep sobs among the aged trees;
> And at each pause her melting accents caught,
> In sweet delirium of romantic thought!
> Dear was the grot that shunn'd the blaze of day;
> She gave its spars to shoot a trembling ray.
> The spring, that bubbled from its inmost cell,
> Murmur'd of Julia's virtues as it fell;
> And o'er the dripping moss, the fretted stone,
> In Florio's ear breath'd language not its own.
> Her charm around the enchantress Memory threw,
> A charm that soothes the mind, and sweetens too!

Below, lines 27-36 of Coleridge's poem:

> I trace her footsteps on the accustom'd lawn,
> I mark her glancing mid the gleam of dawn.
> When the bent flower beneath the night-dew weeps
> And on the lake the silver lustre sleeps,
> Amid the paly radiance soft and sad,
> She meets my lonely path in moon-beams clad.
> With her along the streamlet's brink I rove;
> With her I list the warblings of the grove;
> And seems in each low wind her voice to float
> Lone-whispering Pity in each soothing note!

Comparison of the two passages seems to vindicate Coleridge completely, for the one hardly seems anything like a palpable imitation of the other. One of the verbal similarities is close—Coleridge's "I trace her footsteps on the accustom'd lawn," and Rogers' "still he traced her steps along the glade," but we can easily attribute this to coincidence. Ideational similarities between the two passages are more common than verbal ones, but these represent familiar themes in English poetry of the late eighteenth century.

If, however, one reads with unnatural attentiveness the whole of Rogers' poem, one may well be astonished to find that Coleridge was guilty of the very literary misdemeanor he had accused Rogers of in relation to Michael Bruce. The tale of Florio and Julia concerns a young man who has lost his lady love. Rogers' primary interest, however, was the thoughts and feelings of Florio when he visits the scenes which memory has made dear through association with his beloved. This latter portion of "The Pleasures of Memory" contains precisely the story in Coleridge's poem. In itself the plot is almost too commonplace to be worth mentioning. Nevertheless, a comparison of the poems reveals that Coleridge not only used Rogers' slight theme, but adoped many of the same images and reflections, and frequently the same words.

Early in Part II of "The Pleasures of Memory," Rogers suddenly speaks of "the captive bartered as a slave," who in his misery thinks of his dear departed climes. Memory leads the captive to yearn for death, from which he will wake on "Congo's distant shore," where he will renew the pleasures now past. The bereaved lover in Coleridge's "Effusion," reflecting on what has come and gone, breaks into a sudden and surprising analogy. His solace is now like that of a "Savage," who, having "bask'd beneath the Sun's unclouded flame," awakes amid a tempest and "sad recalls the sunny hour of sleep" (ll. 71-76). It is a singularly inept analogy, for the savage's loss—a temporary interruption of an afternoon nap—is frivolous compared to the loss of a dearly loved maid.

If one concludes from this that Coleridge's fancy was functioning rather strictly within the hints thrown out by Rogers' poem, one is given pause by information provided by Sara Coleridge that the passage just discussed is also indebted to the opening paragraph of Ossian's *War of Inis-thona.*[9] Here are Coleridge's lines as published in 1793:

> As oft, in climes beyond the western main,
> Where boundless spreads the wildly-silent plain,
> The savage hunter, who his drowsy frame
> Had bask'd beneath the sun's unclouded flame;
> Awakes amid the tempest-troubled air,
> The thunder's peal, and lightning's lurid glare;
> Aghast he hears the rushing whirlwind's sweep,
> And sad recalls the sunny hour of sleep. (ll. 71-78)[10]

Below, the first paragraph of *The War of Inis-thona:*

Our youth is like the dream of the hunter on the hill of heath. He sleeps in the mild beams of the sun: he awakes amidst a storm; the red lightning flies around: trees shake their heads to the wind! He looks back with joy on the day of the sun, and the pleasant dreams of his rest! When shall Ossian's youth return? . . . The song rises, like the sun, in my soul. I feel the joys of other times.

Can it be reasonably doubted that the lines of Ossian were refabricated in Coleridge's poem? In both passages we have an analogy dealing with a sleeping hunter. Coleridge's hunter basks "beneath the sun's unclouded flame"; Ossian's "sleeps in the mild beams of the sun." Both awake in a storm—in Coleridge, the air is "tempest-troubled," and there follows "lightning's lurid glare," which in Ossian had been "red lightning." Ossian's "trees shake their heads to the wind"; Coleridge's hunter "hears the rushing whirlwind's sweep." In both passages reflections follow dealing with the "joy" of former times.

Between 1793 and 1796 Coleridge altered the passage once more, but let it stand intact thereafter. The changes are slight, and almost all may be prompted by a desire to obscure Ossianic origins. The "hunter" now becomes more generalized as a savage; the "tempest-troubled air" is rather awkwardly changed to "troubles of the air," and the "tempest" reappears two lines later as "the tempest's sweep," taking the place of the "whirlwind's sweep," a phrase which has stood closer to Ossian's "wind." The "lightning's lurid glare," which had derived from Ossian's "red lightning," now appears as the "white lightning's glare." Where formerly the poet had "joy'd to rove" on the banks of his native stream, the line came to read, "When by my native brook I wont to rove," surely an awkward alteration, and a high price to pay for avoiding Ossian's word "joy." The 1796 edition of Coleridge's poems contains two acknowledged imitations from Ossian, both dated 1793, the year "Absence: a Poem" was first published.

The debt to Ossian is so clear that one may suppose that Coleridge owed nothing to Rogers' passage, which itself bears no verbal kinship with Ossian. But that this is not so is demonstrated by the lines which begin the analogy after the passage specifically dealing with the savage. Coleridge wrote:

> So *tossed by storms* along Life's wild'ring way,
> Mine eye reverted views that *cloudless day* . . . (ll. 77-78)

Rogers, a few lines after dealing with the captive, wrote:

> A little world of clear and *cloudless day*
> Nor *wreck'd by storms*, nor moulder'd by decay . . . (ll. 74-75)

Rogers had begun his passage thus:

> But pause not then—*beyond the western wave,*
> Go, see the captive barter'd as a slave! (ll. 51-52)

Coleridge, in the 1793 version, began the savage hunter passage:

> As oft, in climes *beyond the western main,*
> Where boundless spreads the wildly-silent plain . . ." (ll. 71-72)

He deleted both lines in all printings after 1796. That Rogers' phrases originally appeared at the beginning and end of the passage clinches the parallel.

But Coleridge's use of "The Pleasures of Memory" was far more subtle than indicated by these examples. Rogers, within a space of twelve lines (10-21), uses the words "vestal-lamp," "virtue," and "joy." Within six lines (87-92) Coleridge uses "Virtue," "Vestal's," and "joy." Within a single couplet Rogers has "immortal Friendship" and "tears" (387-388). Within three lines Coleridge has "Friendship's fixed star" and "tears" (87-89). Two lines later Rogers has "infant-years"; eight lines before Coleridge has "Infant Love."

Coleridge used many other bits and snatches and combinations of words and ideas in "The Pleasures of Memory" in various ways, often with considerable skill. Though most scholars are impressed only by clear verbal echoes in the citation of parallel passages, there is no reason to suppose that a skillful imitator would confine himself to the direct borrowing of words. The appropriation of ideas and images may imply the direct use of a model no less than words themselves. Thus, Rogers has his "Twilight" come "slowly on to meet the evening-star" (ll. 207-208); in Coleridge "Twilight stole across the fading vale" (l. 63). Rogers has "soft music on the ear of night" (l. 212); Coleridge has "far-off music, voyaging the breeze!" (l. 44). In Rogers: "the choral song; With rapt ear drink" (ll. 38-39); in Coleridge: "Yet sweet to Fancy's ear the warbled song" (l. 99).

In the passage cited as a "palpable imitation" there are resemblances which are more impressive after a large view of the two poems has been achieved than on first reading. Rogers' "still he traced her steps along the glade," and Coleridge's "I trace her footsteps on the accustomed lawn," now seem too close to attribute to coincidence. Immediately in Rogers there are "glimmering lights"; in Coleridge at once there is "glancing" and the "gleam of dawn." Rogers' lover then thinks he hears the "melting accents" of his departed beloved in the "breeze," which "sobs among the aged trees"; Coleridge's lover in imagination "seems" to hear "in each low wind" the "voice" of his beloved coming from the "grove."

And so the resemblances go.[12] Yet it would be difficult to find an instance which demonstrates more conclusively the danger inherent in assigning a specific and sole source for any given line in Coleridge than the very last example given. Though the image was doubtless started by Rogers' "melting accents" in the "breeze" which "sobs among the ancient trees," Coleridge's

> With her I list the warblings of the grove;
> And seems *in each low wind* her *voice* to float (ll. 34-35)

probably came more directly from William Lisle Bowles's "*In each low wind I seem thy voice* to hear," which appears in "On Leaving a Place of Residence" (l. 16); it is possible, however, that he (like Bowles) was remembering

Pope's "*In each low mind* methinks a Spirit calls," from "Eloisa to Abelard" (1. 305). Bowles was one of the youthful Coleridge's favorite poets, and many years later, in the *Biographia Literaria*, he paid him a very handsome tribute. In the 1793 version of the "Effusion," Coleridge had used the line "Where genius warbles sweet his gladdest strain" (1. 85), which was deleted in all subsequent printings. In Bowles's sonnet "On Resigning a Scholarship of Trinity College, Oxford," appears the line, "And Genius, warbling sweet her saddest song." Whether genius warbles sweet "his gladdest strain" or "her saddest song," it is obvious that Coleridge's line was a direct borrowing.

It is not at all surprising that a young poet as widely read as Coleridge should have been influenced by such diverse sources. "Lines on an Autumnal Evening" was modeled on "The Pleasures of Memory," and to account for the presence of Ossian and Bowles we need only make the plausible conjecture that when confronted with the analogy of the captured slave in Rogers longing for the happier days of yore, Coleridge thought of the analogy of the savage hunter in Ossian. The two ideas coalesced, resulting in the passage we now have, a loose mixture of varied materials. Similarly, the melting accents sobbing in the trees reminded Coleridge of the voice which seemed to float in each low wind. That he later deleted the verse suggests that he was uncomfortable with its closeness to Bowles, but such conjecture may be treacherous.

It is somewhat surprising that in the 1793 version he printed one line as follows: "No more shall deck thy 'pensive pleasures' sweet" (1. 95), thereby indicating that at least one phrase was not entirely original. Indeed, the phrase "pensive pleasures sweet" appears in Collins' "Ode to Evening," and the traditional acknowledgment of enclosing borrowings within quotation marks surely suggested a certain scrupulosity in these matters.[13] In all the printings of the poem in his collected editions, however, Coleridge deleted the quotation marks, as he did in the manuscript version of the poem given to Mrs. Estlin in 1795, entitled "An Effusion at Evening."

Yet he declared that he had written his "Effusion" several years before he had seen Rogers' poem, published, to repeat, when Coleridge was not yet twenty years old. At lines 17-18 of "Lines" there is a reference to coming from "the Muses' calm abode / . . . with Learning's meed not unbestowed." Thomas Ashe notes that if this refers to Cambridge and his college years, Coleridge's claim to have written the poem "in very early youth" is unlikely. Unlikely or not, we have his solemn assertion to contend with, together with the precise date affixed to a manuscript version of the poem. The evidence thus far considered might well prompt a skeptic to disregard Coleridge's assertion in this matter entirely. It happens, however, that still firmer evidence is available than what has thus far been offered.

The early draft of this poem, called "An Effusion at Evening," contains several points of singular interest which have not been previously noticed. Under the title Coleridge wrote, "Written in August, 1792." As Rogers' "The Pleasures of Memory" was published early in 1792,[14] Coleridge's date does not constitute evidence that his own poem was necessarily written before he could have seen Rogers'. The assertion, however, that he had written his "Effusion" *years* before he had seen Rogers' poem is seriously undermined.

E. H. Coleridge placed the date 1792 after the "Effusion," naturally following his grandfather's dating. But Coleridge was not telling the truth (or else not remembering) when he wrote the very specific "August, 1792" after his title, for in this draft of the poem, but never appearing in any other version, are the lines:

> *When link'd with* Peace I bounded o'er the *Plain*
> *And Hope itself was all I knew of Pain!* (ll. 19-20)

In Wordsworth's "An Evening Walk," published in 1793, are the lines:

> *When link'd with* thoughtless Mirth I cours'd the *plain,*
> *And hope itself was all I knew of pain.* (ll. 31-32)

As Coleridge's lines were privately sent to a friend, as they were never published, and as he and Wordsworth were not to meet for several years, they are conclusively shown to have been derived from Wordsworth, and were thus written *after* 1792.[15]

We may now confidently disregard Coleridge's assertion of priority over "The Pleasures of Memory" and examine realistically both his attack on Rogers and his "apology." What is noteworthy is the skill with which the young Coleridge handled what could have been a difficult situation. It is inconceivable that anyone told him that "the lines in this poem from the 27th to the 36th . . . are a palpable imitation of the passage from the 355th to the 370th lines of the Pleasures of Memory Part 3" (or Part II), for the similarity between the two passages is much less apparent than other parallels in the immediate vicinity. What he may have been told was that his whole poem was modelled on Rogers and that many of his lines, images, and ideas were clearly derivative. With remarkable coolness, he introduced his adroit diversion of limiting attention to a single passage which, taken in isolation, could not be seen as clearly dependent. One would have had to have been exceptionally hardened to impute such a scandalous motive to the author of a volume in which appeared the lengthy "Religious Musings" and other pious reflections.

It should be forcibly pointed out that Coleridge succeeded in limiting attention to a single, brief passage, despite obvious resemblances elsewhere, even in the very passage of "intolerable stuff" where all the thoughts presumably came from the Greek epigrams. His lengthy note was sufficiently obscurantist to deter Dykes Campbell and E. H. Coleridge from investigating further, and others have been similarly misled. Thomas Ashe did not even bother to print the full note of 1796 dealing with Rogers, innocently extracting only that portion in which the poet accused himself of carelessness and admitted an intellectual debt to ancient Greece. "The poem is redolent of Goldsmith and Gray," Ashe informs the reader, and does not mention Rogers.[16]

9.

"Nemo Omnibus Horis Sapit"

INTELLECTUAL dishonesty in a man of genius seems bizarre, as does petty greed in a man of great wealth. Yet compulsive acquisition of reputation or power derives from overmastering personal needs, the ultimate sources of which are always obscure. The broad outlines of Coleridge's profoundest intellectual aspirations are clear enough: above all he was driven by a desire to achieve a reputation for dazzling creative gifts and universal knowledge. At the same time, and in some ways far more destructive of his emotional security and peace of mind, he presented to the world, both in his private correspondence and in his public utterances, a personal portrait of childlike innocence and severe moral rigor. His letters in later life can be positively embarrassing, as when he writes, "I have never knowingly or intentionally been guilty of a dishonorable transaction, but have in all things that respect my neighbor been more sinned against than sinning," or, "I know the meaning of the word Envy only by the interpretation given in the Dictionaries. . . ." Not many men could bring themselves to write, even if they believed it true, "I can trace in my heart no envy, no malice, & no revenge," or refer to their "constitutional indifference to praise."[1]

"I cannot wholly approve of your Anthologizing," he wrote Southey in 1800. "My objections are various—& one of them of a moral nature."[2] Yet in Southey's *Annual Anthology* of that year Coleridge published "Something Childish, But Very Natural," "Home-Sick," and "The British Stripling's War-Song," all three silently adapted from German models. "My opinions in Ethics are, if any thing, more austere than they ever were," he wrote the following year to Thomas Poole, and then criticized systems "founded on Prudence of Men, & not on the Gospel of Christ."[3] He once wrote that he dreaded nightmares "as much as I dare dread a Thing which has no immediate connection with my Conscience."[4] A pure conscience, we are to suppose, was central to his scheme of things.

In 1811 he doubted whether he could "have endured to tell a deliberate falsehood."[5] The following year he wrote J. J. Morgan (another of those de-

59

voted friends who at crucial junctures in Coleridge's life was to show him extraordinary kindness and care) that he had broken with Wordsworth because the latter had, allegedly, told Basil Montagu that he was "A nuisance! —& then a deliberate Liar! O Christ! if I dared after this crouch to the Man, must I not plead guilty to these charges, & be a Liar against my own Soul?"[6] And on 13 April 1816, just before taking up what proved to be permanent residence at Highgate, he wrote to young Dr. Gillman: "You will never *hear* any thing but truth from me—Prior Habits render it out of my power to *tell* a falsehood. . . ."[7] In the *Biographia Literaria* he wrote of the "moral and intellectual importance of habituating ourselves to a strict accuracy of expression,"[8] and everywhere in that work projects himself as a triumphant example of such habituation. But this, it may be argued, is the later Coleridge, after the bright dreams of youth had corroded and turned to nightmare.

Yet, as we have seen, his literary ethics (to confine ourselves to that) were from early youth far from austere. He was only nineteen years old when he wrote to his brother George: "I have sent you a sermon metamorphosed from an obscure publication by vamping, transposition, &c—if you like it, I can send you two more of the same kidney."[9] This passage may shed some light on a mystifying reference in a letter of 1794 concerning the Reverend Fulwood Smerdon, who had been vicar at Ottery St. Mary, Coleridge's birthplace. "Poor Smerdon!" Coleridge wrote to his brother George upon hearing of Smerdon's untimely death, "the reports concerning His literary plagiarism (as far as concerns *my* assistance) are *falsehoods!*"[10]

It cannot be said that Coleridge was simply oblivious to mundane details of literary ethics. He had a special interest in the general subject, and among the countless plans with which he conjured was the following: "I have ample materials for a most interesting Historical & Metaphysical Essay on Literary Forgery."[11] Coleridge was fascinated by the career of Thomas Chatterton, the brilliantly gifted perpetrator of the Rowley fraud. The "Monody on the Death of Chatteron" is the earliest of his significant compositions, a work he laboured over throughout his lifetime and published seven times, often with extensive revisions. He defended Chatterton against detractors and expressed considerable rage at the treatment he had received.

There are some curious parallels between the two careers. The fatherless Chatterton had been sent to a "blue-coat" school in Bristol for eight years; the fatherless Coleridge had been sent to a "blue-coat" school in London for nine years. Chatterton sent what he claimed were genuine ancient manuscripts to the editor of *Felix Farley's Bristol Journal.* Coleridge spent an important part of his youth in Bristol and later published three essays in *Felix Farley's Bristol Journal.* These essays, "On the Principles of Genial Criticism," draw very heavily on Kant's *Critique of Judgment* without ever mentioning that philosopher's name.[12] Interestingly enough, Coleridge once even used the pseudonym "Bristoliensis," the name used by Chatterton in passing off one of the fraudulent Rowley manuscripts.[13]

Coleridge shifted his fundamental intellectual commitment from poetry to philosophy within a year or two after his return from Germany in 1799. He brought back to England with him a load of German metaphysical volumes and began to study philosophy in earnest. The first fruits of his researches are to be found in a series of letters on philosophical matters which he sent early in 1801 to his patron Josiah Wedgwood, the son of the famous potter. The major substance of these letters consists of a violent attack on Locke as an original thinker. In Coleridge's words: "the whole System of Locke . . . was to be found in the writings of Des Cartes." After carrying this attack through several letters, he concludes that from his researches "it would follow that the famous Essay on the human Understanding is only a prolix Paraphrase on Des Cartes with foolish Interpolations of the Paraphrast's."[14] These letters bristle with a lively sense of indignation at Locke's allegedly undeserved reputation for independent thought.

In the midst of one of these letters Coleridge writes:

In Mr. Locke there is a complete Whirl-dance of Confusion with the words *we, Soul, Mind, Consciousness,* & Ideas. . . . In short, the Mind in Mr. Locke's Essay has three senses—the Ware-house, the Wares, and the Ware-house-man.—What is the *etymology* of the Word *Mind?* I think that I could make it as probable as could be expected in a conjecture on such a subject that the following is the History of the Word—In a Swabian Poet of the 13th Century I have found the word *Min* (pronounced mein); it is used by him for Geist, or Gemuth, the present German Words for Mind.—The same poet uses the word Minen, which is only the old Spelling for the present German *Meinen*—the old signification of Meinen (& which is still in many parts of Germany the *provincial* use of the word) *exactly corresponds* with the provincial use of the verb 'To mind' in England. Don't you *mind* that?—i.e. Do you not remember it.—Be sure, you *mind* him of that—i.e. remind him of that.— Hence it appears to be no other than provincial Differences of Pronunciation between the words Meinen, & Mahnen—which last word retains the old (*present provincial*) meaning of the word Meinen—i.e. to *mind* a person (of his Duty for instance). But the insertion of the *n* in the middle of a German verb is admitted on all hands to be *intensive* or *reduplicative* / as the Dictionary Phrase is. In reality it is no more than repeating the last syllable as people are apt to when speaking hastily or vehemently. . . . But the oldest meaning of the word mähen is to move forward & backward, yet still progressively—thence applied to the motion of the Scythe in mowing—from what particular motion the word was first abstracted, is of course in this as in all other instances, lost in antiquity. For words have many fates—they first mean particulars, become generals, then are confined to some one particular again, & so forth—as the word 'indorse' for instance.—To mow is the same as the Latin movere which was pronounced mow-ere—& monere in like manner is only the reduplicative of mow-ere—mow-en—mow-enen—mow-nen, or monen. This word in the time of Ennius was *menere*, & hence *mens*—the Swedish word for Mind is Mon—the Islandic Mene. The Greek μνάομαι, i.e. μενάομαι, [1] from whence μνήμη, the memory, is the same word—and all alike mean a repetition of similar motion, as in a scythe. It is even probable that the word meh, ma, & moe, the old German and English Words for *more* is of the same Birth & Parentage. All infinitives are in my opinion Imperatives with or without some auxiliar substantive / in our language without, in Latin, German, etc *with*. What the Latin 're' and 'ri' are, I think I could make a bold guess at—and likewise at the meaning of the en, common to *all* the Gothic Dialects.—God bless you, my dear Sir! I would, I were with you to join in the Laugh against myself.[15]

As Josiah Wedgwood was not a trained philologist, it is doubtful that he was in any position to laugh at Coleridge's learned speculations. Like the rest of us, he was probably staggered at this demonstration of mighty erudition and philological daring in a young man only a few months past twenty-eight. As the "philosophical letters" to Wedgwood were first published in 1951, scholars have had relatively little time in which to consider the implications of the above passage, which seems to add still more spacious proportions to a mind widely acclaimed as the most profound and original of the whole nineteenth century, and to some, of all time.[16]

Admiration for this passage, however, is somewhat dampened by Miss Coburn's encyclopedic notes in her great edition of Coleridge's notebooks. After quoting the portion of the letter to Wedgwood given above, she comments:

The information given in this letter is practically all derived from the final note to the article *meinen* in the second edition of Adelung's Dictionary (1793 et seq), which Coleridge himself owned and admired. It was here that he found the reference to *Min*, used in the older language in the sense of Gemüth, and to the connexion of *meinen* with *mähen*, *meinen*, according to Adelung, being the transference to the mind of the bodily movement implied in *mähen*. Adelung also gives cross-references to *mahnen* and *Minne*, where *mahnen* is described as *Iterativum* or *Intensivum* (Coleridge's *reduplicative* or *intensive*) of *mähen*. Under *Minne* Coleridge would have found the suggestion that *minnen* is an intensive of *meinen* and the reference to the use of this word in Otfrid and in the Swabian poets. It was perhaps this latter remark which prompted Coleridge's reference to "a Swabian Poet of the 13th Century" using the form *Min* in the sense of Gemüth. A scrutiny of the two books of Swabian poetry which were the first books he ever borrowed from the Göttingen university library, 21 Feb 1799 . . . did not reveal any such apocopated form. But nothing in Adelung could have led him to think that this *Min* could ever be pronounced *mein* in any dialect, medieval or modern; being an abbreviation of *minne* its *i* was a short *i*, and it was only long *i* which underwent diphthongisation.[17]

It is notable that in presenting his etymological speculations Coleridge speaks of them as a "conjecture." Not only is there no mention of Adelung, or dependence on any authority outside his own brain, but he introduces such phrases as "in my opinion" and "I think I could make a bold guess at." And the letter ends on a gay note: he wishes he could join with Wedgwood in a light-hearted laugh at his daring notions. It is hard to believe that he did not deliberately exclude mentioning the existence in his own library of a German dictionary which had assisted his cerebrations.[18] What is especially dismaying about the whole passage is that it occurs during an attack on Locke, whom he charged with merely having paraphrased his ideas from Descartes with some "foolish interpolations."[19]

Of course it requires little ingenuity to explain all this away. A bit of exaggeration, after all, is hardly inexcusable in a young man writing to the patron who had only recently bestowed a lifetime annuity of £150 a year upon him as an earnest of the confidence in which he was held.[20] Having spent about a year abroad, Coleridge's display of Germanic learning was presumably incontrovertible evidence of his diligent study abroad.[21]

This explanation contains just enough truth to permit a student of Coleridge to maintain his flattering view of his subject intact. But Coleridge's misrepresentations to Wedgwood are only a small part of a much larger pattern of intellectual pretense. That he was a very learned young man is as certain as that he was extremely noisy about his knowledge. Whether, for example, he knew as much German as he claimed before going to Germany, whether he had read so widely in the English philosophers and especially the Cambridge Platonists, are matters of fundamental importance not only in his own aesthetic history but in that of the literary relations between England and Germany in the late eighteenth and early nineteenth centuries.

Calling into question Coleridge's learning may perhaps be the most foolhardy of enterprises in the world of scholarship today. Still, it can be shown that he often pontificated upon matters he knew little or nothing about. The misleading implications of his "etymological fancies" in a private letter to Josiah Wedgwood can be matched by several public pronouncements in the 1797 edition of his poems. "I have never been able to discover sense, nature, or poetic fancy in Petrarch's poems," he wrote; "they appear to me all one cold glitter of heavy conceits and metaphysical abstractions."

There is no evidence that Coleridge knew any Italian at the age of twenty-four, and indeed among the later marginalia is the following gloss on this passage: "A piece of petulant presumption, of which I should be the more ashamed if I did not flatter myself that it stands alone in my writings. The best of the joke is that at the time I wrote it, I did not understand a word of Italian, and could therefore judge of this divine Poet only by bald translations of some half-dozen of his Sonnets."[22] This "joke," such as it was, was not confined to a premature opinion about Petrarch. He might well have cited a later passage in the same 1797 edition of his *Poems*, wherein intimate knowledge of the Italian language is implied not merely by judgment upon an Italian writer, but by minute observations upon the language itself:

> A sameness in the final sound of its words is the great and grievous defect of the Italian language. That rule, therefore, which the Italians have established, of exactly *four* different sounds in the Sonnet, seems to have arisen from their wish to have *as many*, not from any dread of finding *more*. But surely it is ridiculous to make the *defect* of a foreign language a reason for our not availing ourselves of one of the marked excellencies of our own.[23]

In 1801, in the same series of philosophical letters we have been noticing, Coleridge wrote:

> I had read a multitude of out of the way Books, Greek, Latin, & German, & groped my way thro' the French of Malbranche; and there are men, who gain the reputation of a wide erudition by consuming that Time in reading Books obsolete & of no character, which other men employ in reading those which every Body reads; but I should be sorry to detect in myself this silly vanity. . . .[24]

As is so often true in Coleridge, his own writings provide the key clue to his own motives, conscious or otherwise. For there clearly was in Coleridge more than a little of the "silly vanity" of pretending to a wider erudition than he really possessed. In this very passage, for example, he writes: "I groped my way thro' the French of Malbranche." Perhaps. But would even a Coleridge be likely to tackle a complex philosophical work in a language he barely understood? Two months after writing this letter he borrowed from a library the first volume of Malebranche's *Search After Truth*, translated into English.[25] Of course this is not absolute proof that he had not already groped his way through the French philosopher, but it is strong presumptive evidence, especially in a man given to intellectual exaggeration.

In any case, it seems wise not to accept automatically such famous bits of Coleridgeana as that when he was three years old he could "read a Chapter in the Bible," or that before he was six he had read—in an *"every-thing* Shop" kept by an Aunt—"thro' all the gilt-cover little books that could be had at that time, & likewise all the uncovered tales of Tom Hickathrift, Jack the Giant-killer, &c &c &c &c &c. . . . At six years old I remember to have read Belisarius, Robinson Crusoe, & Philip Quarle—and then I found the Arabian Nights' entertainments. . . ." By the age of eight he had "read every book that came in my way without distinction."[26]

A month after he had turned twenty-four Coleridge wrote to Thelwall: "I am, & ever have been, a great reader—& have read almost everything. . . ." Of course, this kind of statement is not intended to be taken literally. Yet when he writes in the same paragraph, "I have read & digested most of the Historical Writers—; but I do not *like* History," one cannot help feeling that habitual exaggeration is operating equally with bravado.[27]

But it is in Coleridge's recollections of his early reading which he set down in later years for James Gillman—accounts which have been quoted again and again in biographies and studies of his intellectual development—that the necessity for sober appraisal of facts and probability must be weighed against the ceaseless flux of memory in the Sage of Highgate. After an astounding account of his reading as a little child at Ottery St. Mary, he goes on to recall the years at Christ's Hospital. In a note prepared at Gillman's urging, he wrote:

> From eight to fourteen I was a playless day-dreamer, a *helluo librorum* [devourer of books], my appetite for which was indulged by a singular incident: a stranger, who was struck by my conversation, made me free of a circulating library in King Street, Cheapside. [Here follows an amazing tale—repeated again and again in Coleridge biography without question —about the young blue-coat boy walking down the street while imagining himself swimming the Hellespont, accidentally sticking his hand into a stranger's pocket, being accosted as a thief, explaining himself, and thus delighting the learned gentleman. As to the King Street library:] I read *through* the catalogue, folios and all, whether I understood them, or did not understand them, running all risks in skulking out to get the two volumes which I was entitled to have daily. Conceive what I must have been at fourteen; I was in a continual low fever. My whole being was, with eyes closed to every object of present sense, to crumple myself up in a sunny corner, and read, read, read. . . . My talents and superiority made me for ever at the head in my routine of study, though utterly without the desire to be so; without a spark of ambition; and, as to emulation, it had no meaning for me; but the difference between me and my form-fellows, in our lessons and exercises, bore no proportion to the measureless difference between me and them in the wide, wild, wilderness of useless, unarranged book-knowledge and book-thoughts. Thank Heaven! it was not the age nor the fashion of getting up prodigies; but at twelve or fourteen I should have made as pretty a juvenile prodigy as was ever emasculated and ruined by fond and idle wonderment. Thank Heaven! I was flogged instead of flattered. . . .[28]

These passages bring us squarely back to a question raised in connection with the numerous misdatings of his compositions, some of which throw back to childhood or early youth the work of mature years: Was Coleridge driven by a commanding need to see himself as a *Wunderkind*? Not only did he obviously relish these recollections—be they true or not—but an indispensable condition of his intellectual superiority was its effortlessness and his total lack of ambition.

> Against my will [his recollections go on], I was chosen by my master as one of those destined for the university. . . . I became wild to be apprenticed to a surgeon. English, Latin, yea, Greek books of medicine read I incessantly. Blanchard's Latin Medical Dictionary I had nearly by heart. Briefly, it was a wild dream, which gradually blending with, gradually gave way to a rage for metaphysics [at age seventeen], occasioned by the essays on Liberty and Necessity in Cato's Letters, and more by theology. After I had read Voltaire's Philosophical Dictionary, I sported infidel! but my infidel vanity never touched my heart. . . .[29]

It is notable how great a proportion of Coleridge's childhood recollections these prodigious feats comprise. In themselves, the specific accuracy of this or that memory is of small consequence. But it happens—as we are about to see—that several momentous questions in English and European literary and intellectual history rest finally upon the credibility of his testimony.

Coleridge appears to have been pleased by his "philosophical letters" to Wedgwood. The next of his letters that is preserved was to Josiah Wade. "I have ill consulted the growth of my reputation and fame," he wrote. "But I have cheerful and confident hopes of myself. If I can hereafter do good to my fellow creatures, as a poet, and as a metaphysician, they will know it; and any other fame than this, I consider as a serious evil, that would only take me from out the number and sympathy of ordinary men, to make a coxcomb of me."[30]

And so it is to Coleridge's incomparable, later career as metaphysician, critic, aesthetician, and all-round thinker on men, the arts, and the physical world to which we must now turn. Our efforts thus far have been directed at providing a variety of early perspectives by which to approach the celebrated later man and, hopefully, to understand him. To this task of understanding, the resolute loyalties of the idolator or the malicious levelling of the debunker are equally destructive. The patterns of behavior and intellectual style we have been tracing, prominent as they are, have been consistently blurred and sometimes ignored in studies of Coleridge, so that what was always a most complex personality ends as an utterly incomprehensible one. The turbulence of his personal relations after 1800, the almost shattering anxieties brilliantly recorded (or guardedly hinted at) in his notebooks, and above all, for our present purposes, the bitterly disputed nature of his intellectual achievement—none of this can be understood without, as it were, rubbing between our fingers the arid emotional soils in which the ill-fated young Samuel Taylor Coleridge put down roots.

II

MONUMENTS, RUINS, AND SCATTERED LEAVES

10.

A Literary Life

THE RAMBLING structure of the *Biographia Literaria*[1] has frequently been attributed to the pressure under which it was written. The work's false starts and abrupt conclusions, the seemingly random digressions and transitions, have also been seen as a reflection of a mind teeming with too many ideas, insights, and learning to be limited or contained within any formal organization. For all its apparent faults, critics are nearly united in acclaiming it as one of the supreme works of literary criticism. To Arthur Symons it is "the greatest book of criticism in English."[2] Stanley Edgar Hyman hails Coleridge as "the first really great modern critic," and the *Biographia* as "almost the bible of modern criticism."[3] To Herbert Read, Coleridge stands "head and shoulders above every other English critic," because of his "introduction of a philosophical method of criticism."[4]

Coleridge's own record of his literary life assumes an extraordinary interest and value in view of the evidence thus far presented, and particularly insofar as it has been alleged that in the *Biographia* itself there are extensive and very important plagiarisms. Most scholars, however, have refused to accept the evidence afforded by a comparison of the *Biographia* and certain German texts as constituting deliberate plagiarism, or even as proof that its author's formulations were not original. Coleridge made certain general disclaimers, and maintained, again and again, that he could not honestly attribute to others ideas which he had achieved independently.

Though many attempts have been made to do so, no convincing evidence from his letters, notebooks, or conversation has ever been brought forward to show that he had these ideas developed in any systematic way, or even that he had them at all, before he read the German philosophers. Coleridge insisted that this was in fact the case, and that the concurrence of ideas with Friedrich W. J. von Schelling was a "genial coincidence." Though the conclusion may tax credulity, the inherent improbability of any single intellect independently arriving at a large number of important, diverse, and even peculiar conclusions that were available in foreign publications does not prove that it did not happen. Since Coleridge is considered a speculative genius of the first rank, even one of the seminal minds of history, we are certainly not disposed to accuse him either of literary theft or conscious deception. It has become distinctly unfashionable to speak of literary ethics where important writers are involved, especially poets. In fact, the case of Coleridge's extensive silent borrowings has gone far toward changing contemporary attitudes toward such practices. The word "plagiarism" itself is vaguely discredited.[5]

Viewed thus, the problem is brought to a standstill. The worst that Coleridge can be burdened with is failing to make a certain number of formal acknowledgments. This may disturb our ethical view of him, but it does not affect the profundity and originality of his achievement. To view the problem in such a way, however, requires us to believe that Coleridge was sincere in claiming these ideas as his own. Inevitably the question of his veracity and general trustworthiness is raised.

Scholars have been extremely reluctant to introduce personality into the problem, but it is hard to see how it can be avoided. The overwhelming majority have not doubted that Coleridge was a perfectly sincere and honest person, though it is widely granted that he was unfortunately careless and even eccentric in some ways. The extraordinary fact that many pages in the *Biographia* are silently translated out of a foreign language, from books either obscure or inaccessible or both, has been explained in a variety of ways. In due course these explanations will be considered.

The integrity of the *Biographia Literaria* should not be discussed in isolation from the rest of Coleridge's career. The multitude of unacknowledged obligations and the various forms of intellectual anxiety detailed in the previous pages provide important data in coming to a realistic view of this particular case. To say that the poetic borrowings (with the possible exception of the "Hymn Before Sunrise") were "trifling" and "hardly worth mentioning," even if true, is to argue that a host of petty borrowings is of no relevance in evaluating a truly serious charge. Any given instance of silent poaching may, of course, be explained away. But to dismiss *many* such instances as having no bearing on a major accusation seems not only naïve, but to disregard accepted canons of evidence. Nor should we confine ourselves to "trifling" borrowings in coming to a comprehensive view of what ideas in the *Biographia* may reasonably be assigned to Coleridge. For along with borrowings "hardly worth mentioning" are many major appropriations alleged and powerfully argued.

In Professor Wellek's recent examination of Coleridge's position in the history of criticism is the following useful summary of some of the more important scholarship of the past century which bears upon the subject:

At crucial points in his writings Coleridge used Kant, Schelling, and A. W. Schlegel, reproducing the very pattern of sentences and the exact vocabulary. . . . Much that has impressed I. A. Richards and Herbert Read—the discussion of the subject-object relation, their synthesis and identity, and the appeal to the unconscious—is simply the teaching of Schelling and cannot be made the basis of a claim for Coleridge's philosophical greatness. Coleridge's lecture "On Poesy or Art" (1818), which has been used by several expositors of his aesthetics as the key to his thought, is with the exception of a few insertions of pious sentiments little more than a paraphrase of Schelling's Academy Oration of 1807. . . . In discussing the contrast between ancient and modern literature Coleridge reproduces a crucial passage from Schiller's *Naive and Sentimental Poetry*. The manuscript notes for the lecture on "Wit and Humor" are a patchwork of quotations from Jean Paul's *Vorschule*. . . . A lecture on Greek drama is simply a translation from Schlegel and [according to Raysor] "ought not to be included in Coleridge's Works at all." Many crucial distinctions are derived from Schlegel. Thus the formula for the distinction between "mechanical regularity" and "organic form" is a literal translation. . . . *Theory of Life* is merely a mosaic of passages from Schelling and Steffens; the lecture on Aeschylus' *Prometheus* paraphrases Schelling's *Gods of Samothrace*. The big two-volume "Logic," still unpublished for the most part, is largely an elaborate exposition of the *Critique of Pure Reason* with all its architectonics, tables of categories, and antimonies taken over literally. . . . The newly published *Philosophical Lectures* draw most of their information and learning from Tennemann's *History of Philosophy*. . . . In all the cases cited Coleridge must have had the actual texts in front of him or used detailed notes taken directly from them. It seems to me a matter of intellectual honesty not to credit Coleridge with ideas distinctly derived and even literally transcribed from others.[6]

Surely the sheer volume of unacknowledged borrowings is of some value in judging Coleridge's intent where any particular case of plagiarism is alleged. Yet his intent is irrelevant in evaluating his credentials to a place among the important thinkers of his generation, let alone of history. Is it possible to believe that Coleridge had independently arrived at all the ideas in the many works listed above? Not even he claimed that. In practically every instance he simply put forward concepts and theories as his own without reference to sources outside his own private meditations. In every instance, with the exception of Schlegel, coincidence of ideas was not discovered till after his death, and in some instances not until recent years. As a result, many influential formulations have become attached, perhaps irrevocably, to his name.

A careful reading of the *Biographia Literaria* is profoundly revelatory of Coleridge's mind and literary practice. Critics have concentrated so intently on the critical and philosophical portions of the book that a major and actually quite prominent dimension of the work has been almost entirely ignored. That dimension is Coleridge's portrait of himself as a man of letters, which is, after all, what the title promises.

In Chapter XV of the *Biographia,* Coleridge set out to describe the attributes of the poet seen in "ideal perfection." Through the first thirteen chapters of the *Biographia,* without stating the intent directly, he builds up a picture of the *literary* man seen in ideal perfection. The man of letters thus described possesses a scrupulously strict literary conscience, deplores plagiarism and even much imitation, is meticulous in acknowledging even the smallest of intellectual obligations, is utterly without ambition or vanity, is uninterested even in the sale of his works (except as indicative of public sympathy), deplores personally motivated criticism, and derives "additional pleasure" in the discovery that his own thought actually came from the "conversation or correspondence of another."[7] This description of the ideal literary man is a mosaic of phrases used by Coleridge in the *Biographia* in describing his *own* mind and practice.

Early in the first chapter of the *Biographia* he discusses his early training at Christ's Hospital under the Rev. James Boyer and the later influence of William Lisle Bowles's sonnets on his poetic development. He then makes a long statement which, as it is the first of many such regularly introduced into the work, is worth quoting in full:*

Though I have seen and known enough of mankind to be well aware, that I shall perhaps stand alone in my creed, and that it will be well, if I subject myself to no worse charge than that of singularity; I am not therefore deterred from avowing, that *I regard, and ever have regarded the obligations of intellect among the most sacred of the claims of gratitude.* A valuable thought, or a particular train of thoughts, gives me additional pleasure, when I can safely refer and attribute it to the conversation or correspondence of another.[8]

Thus, almost at once, the author takes up a rigoristic position concerning the necessity of acknowledging intellectual obligations and fixes a definite attitude in the reader's mind concerning the moral character of the writer before him. Coleridge asserts that his credo is so singular as to be perhaps unique: "I shall perhaps stand alone in my creed." The final sentence of the passage almost strains the resources of credulity. Why should any man, and particularly an author, be pleased to learn that his ideas are not entirely original?[9]

Three pages later he quotes passages from Shakespeare and Gray, calling the first the "original," and the second an "imitation." Though the resemblance is extremely remote, he censures Gray for his "poor" imitation and goes on to state that he has been able to relate "various lines in Gray to their original in Shakespeare and Milton"; to Coleridge it is clear "how com-

---

* This is to remind readers that, unless otherwise stated in the notes, italics in quotations are always mine.

pletely all the propriety was lost in the transfer. . . ."[10] Almost immediately the subject becomes plagiarism:

> In the Nutricia of Politian there occurs this line:
> "Pura coloratos interstrepit unda lapillos."
> Casting my eye on a University prize-poem, I met this line:
> "Lactea purpureos interstrepit unda lapillos."

Now look out in the Gradus for *Purus*, and you will find as the first synonime *lacteus*; for *coloratus*, and the first synonime is *purpureus*. I mention this by way of elucidating one of the most ordinary processes in the *ferrumination* of these centos.[11]

Shawcross observes that "a reference to the *Gradus* shows that Coleridge's example is inaccurate. . . ."[12] It would be of interest to know how Coleridge fell into this error, since any of his comments on the subject of plagiarism, particularly here where he is providing an example of the technique of appropriation, has more than ordinary interest.[13]

Later in the first chapter of the *Biographia*, he tells an anecdote about a man who wanted to meet him but was hesitant because he, supposedly, had once published an epigram which had given Coleridge "great pain":

I assured my friend that, if the epigram was a good one, it would only increase my desire to become acquainted with the author, and begg'd to hear it recited: when, to my no less surprise than amusement, it proved to be one which I had myself some time before written and inserted in the *Morning Post*.

> To the author of the Ancient Mariner.
> Your poem must eternal be,
> Dear sir! It cannot fail,
> For 'tis incomprehensible,
> And without head or tail.[14]

Coleridge is here "inventing," as Shawcross notes, for the epigram actually appeared in the *Morning Post* not as directed against the author of "The Ancient Mariner," but with this heading: "To MR. PYE on his *Carmen Seculare* (a title which has by various persons who have heard it, been thus translated, 'A Poem an age long')."[15] The epigram quoted as his own was actually adapted, without acknowledgment, from Lessing's "The Eternity of the True Poem." [*Die Ewigkeit gewisser Gedichte*].[16]

The first chapter, often characterized as rambling and digressive, is actually unified by a single theme: Coleridge's moral disapproval of plagiarists, imitators, and otherwise intellectually dishonest persons, and his own singularity in professing scrupulously all intellectual obligations.

The second chapter, though nominally concerned with the "supposed irritability of men of Genius,"[17] deals with closely allied matter. In a long footnote Coleridge touches upon some of his ideas concerning Shakespeare which he had delivered in lectures: "The substance of these lectures I hope soon to publish;[18] and it is but a debt of justice to myself and my friends to notice, that the first course of lectures . . . was addressed to very numerous, and I need not add, respectable audiences at the royal institution, before Mr. Schlegel gave his lectures on the same subjects at Vienna."[19] Coleridge's claim to precedence of ideas is put forward in a way which appears to admit of no doubt. But, as we shall see, here and elsewhere he falsified the chronology of his knowledge of Schlegel's work.

In another footnote he speaks of a certain analysis of a few lines of poetry in one of his lectures which had created a great impression. He states that this analysis was conducted "much in the same way as has been since done, in an excellent article on Chalmer's British Poets in the Quarterly Review."[20] This may have been intended to suggest that an idea of his had been used without acknowledgment. But the article in the *Quarterly*, written by his brother-in-law Robert Southey in July 1814, "contains nothing corresponding to Coleridge's description."[21]

Before the chapter ends Coleridge attacks the low principles of reviewers and newspapers. He is personally, however, entirely indifferent to criticism:

> a tried experience of twenty years, has taught me, that the original sin of my character consists in a careless indifference to public opinion, and to the attacks of those who influence it; that praise and admiration have become yearly less and less desirable, except as marks of sympathy; nay that it is difficult and distressing to me, to think with any interest even about the sale and profit of my works, important as, in my present circumstances, such considerations must needs be.[22]

The attacks on critics which had preceded, and the more virulent ones to follow, therefore, are not to be taken as personally motivated. This is difficult to accept, especially in view of the truly merciless assault upon Maturin's play *Bertram*, reprinted in the *Biographia* from five articles contributed anonymously to the *Courier* in 1816.[23] Maturin's play had been presented at Drury Lane in 1816 after Coleridge had failed to get his own *Zapolya* accepted. Whether there is any connection between these events is uncertain. In any case, the twenty-seven-page review of *Bertram* brims with wrath. The whole play is "rant and nonsense," and Coleridge finds in some of the lines "a senseless plagiarism" from *Lear*, and a "no less senseless adoption" from Dryden, with echos from Milton.[24]

Only one page after declaring his indifference to public acclaim, he reveals once again his deep concern with the allocation of credit for intellectual achievement. So far as an author is concerned, what besides "all that relates to himself and his family, if only we except his moral character, can have fairer claims to his protection, or more authorize acts of self-defense, than the elaborate products of his intellect and his intellectual industry?"[25] On the same page appears one of his favorite metaphors: "I have laid too many eggs in the hot sands of this wilderness, the world, with ostrich carelessness and ostrich oblivion. The greater part indeed have been trod under foot, and are forgotten; but yet no small number have crept forth into life, some to furnish feathers for the caps of others, and still more to plume the shafts in the quivers of my enemies, of them that unprovoked have lain in wait against my soul."[26]

It is not easy to see how one's literary enemies may endanger one's soul, or even how they can be charged with such diabolic ends. Coleridge will not permit himself to say that critics had wounded his feelings, harmed his reputation, or hurt the sale of his books. Consequently the passage ends with an inflated rhetorical flourish.

We may pause to consider the picture drawn by Coleridge of himself in the first two chapters of the *Biographia*. He has told us that he considers intellectual obligations sacred, and that the products of the intellect deserve an author's protection before all things, save family and "moral character." So far as actual intellectual obligations go, he has cited his precedence over Schlegel and made a general statement as to how other men have battened on the richness and fertility of his mind. Thus, within thirty-three pages, a heavy concentration of firepower is directed at the twin themes of literary and moral rectitude.

Chapter III is a medley of themes, dealing with critics, modern criticism, and Southey.[27] Coleridge here devotes considerable space to the allegedly unceasing animosity of critics toward him, especially strange as he has never given any critic cause for personal offense. He had been careful, he says, even in his lectures to avoid comment on living writers. Although he had originally intended to deal with writers "from Cowper to the present day" in one of his lecture series, ". . . I changed my plan, and confined my disquisition to the two former eras [that is, earlier writers], that I might furnish no possible pretext for the unthinking to misconstrue, or the malignant to misapply my words, and having stampt their own meaning on them, to pass them as current coin in the marts of garrulity or detraction."

Shawcross notes: "This statement does not seem to be confirmed by the facts. In the courses both of 1808 and 1811-12, Coleridge's criticisms included living authors, whereas in neither of the courses of 1812 did he even propose (according to the prospectus) to deal with modern poetry."[28] Henry Crabb Robinson was sufficiently upset by Coleridge's treatment of a living poet in the last of the 1812 lectures to note in his diary: "he offended me by an unhandsome and unmanly attack upon Mrs. Barbauld. He ridiculed some expressions in her *Ode to Content.* . . . That he should select among the living authors, a woman, and that woman a lady who has been among his admirers formerly, and I believe always showed him civilities, is ungenerous and unworthy of his better feelings."[29]

Chapter III concludes with a long note dealing with the various good influences Coleridge derived from his meeting with Southey at Cambridge. These influences, he adds characteristically, did not extend to "moral or religious principles, for they had never been contaminated. . . ."[30]

With Chapter IV he begins to touch on the philosophic principles of art and criticism which contribute to the work's immense reputation. The chapter, however, is merely a prelude to the grand and difficult disquisitions to come—for which he apologizes to the reader. The topic is imagination and fancy. Wordsworth had discussed the matter generally; it is Coleridge's purpose to "investigate the seminal principal." But in this attempt "I shall be obliged to draw more largely on the reader's attention, than so immethodical a miscellany can authorize. . . . I would gladly therefore spare both myself and others this labor, if I knew how without it to present an intelligible statement of my poetic creed; not as my *opinions*, which weigh for nothing, but as deductions from established premises conveyed in such a form, as is calculated either to effect a fundamental conviction, or to receive a fundamental confutation."[31]

This is an excellent and fair statement. If the reader is to make the arduous effort of following an author through a new and difficult argument, it is worth assuring him that the author has found no other way to convey his creed and that the argument will be conclusive. Let us see, therefore, how well Coleridge fulfilled his side of the bargain.

Chapter V, "On the law of association—Its history traced from Aristotle to Hartley," is supposed to lead eventually to a statement on the true nature of fancy and imagination. To this end Coleridge surveys the history of association psychology. So far as sheer learning is concerned, this is a very impressive chapter. The range of names alone is weighty: Gassendi, Hobbes, Hartley, Newton, Kepler, Hume, Descartes, De la Forge, Pindar, Aristophanes, and St. Thomas Aquinas, among others.

"Long however before either Hobbs or Des Cartes the law of association had been defined, and its important functions set forth by Melanchthon, Ammerbach, and Ludovicus Vives; more especially by the last," says Coleridge knowledgeably, but fails to mention that with this sentence he begins to draw heavily upon J. G. E. Maass' *Versuch über die Einbildungskraft* [*Essay on the Imagination*] (1797), an annotated copy of which was in Coleridge's library.[32] J. C. Ferrier angrily drew attention to this debt in a *Blackwood's* article of March 1840:

> all the real information and learning put forth in *Biog. Lit.*, Chap. V., is stolen bodily from [Maass]. . . . a considerable show of learning is exhibited on the subject of the association of ideas; and of course the reader's impression is, that Coleridge is indebted for the learning here displayed to nothing but his own researches. But no such thing—he is indebted for it entirely to Maasz [*sic*]. He found all the quotations, and nearly all the observations connected with them, ready-made to his hand in the pages of that philosopher.[33]

Ferrier quoted the sentence above including the names Melanchthon, Ammerbach, and Ludovicus Vives to show that even the order of the names is precisely as in Maass.[34] He shrilly detailed a long series of such debts.

A close reading of Chapter V is most revealing. There are many quotations in Latin from obscure writers, which convey the impression of dazzling learning, but *all* of them (as well as several Greek terms) prove to have been originally searched out by Maass.[35] Coleridge claims to find "the fullest and most perfect enunciation of the associative principle" in the writings of Aristotle, more particularly in *De Anima*, *De Memoria*, and *Parva Naturalia*. Summarizing Aristotle's arguments, he writes: "As an additional solution of the occasional seeming chasms in the continuity of reproduction he proves . . ."[36] And he goes on to say what he thinks it is Aristotle has proved.

But he is mistaken. It is not Aristotle who has provided the "additional solution," but Maass.[37] Coleridge, it is obvious, became confused in following Maass's text as to when he was reading the arguments of the "wise Stagyrite" and when those of the obscure German.[38] In view of this fact, Coleridge's sweeping assertion but one page before rings rather hollow: "In as much as later writers have either deviated from, or added to his [Aristotle's] doctrines, they appear to me to have introduced either error or groundless supposition."[39]

Coming to the close of the formidable chapter, Coleridge has been, for three pages, taking from Maass his ideas, his interpretations, his learned quotations, all without indicating that the learning displayed is not entirely his own. Suddenly, for no particular purpose that is evident, we read:

> In consulting the excellent commentary of St. Thomas Aquinas on the Parva Naturalia of Aristotle, I was struck at once with its close resemblance to Hume's Essay on association. The main thoughts were the same in both, the *order* of the thoughts was the same, and even the illustrations differed only by Hume's occasional substitution of more modern examples. I mentioned the circumstance to several of my literary acquaintances, who admitted the closeness of the resemblance, and that it seemed too great to be explained by mere coincidence; but they thought it improbable that Hume should have held the pages of the angelic Doctor worth turning over. But some time after Mr. Payne . . . shewed Sir James Mackintosh some odd volumes of St. Thomas Aquinas. . . . the volumes had belonged to Mr. Hume, and had here and there marginal marks and notes of reference in his own hand writing. Among these volumes was that which contains the *Parva Naturalia*, in the old Latin version, swathed and swaddled in the commentary afore mentioned![40]

Coleridge has here blown up a false rumor into a full-scale charge of plagiarism in such a way as to take credit for immediate philosophical perspicacity later supposedly borne out by facts. Mackintosh himself subsequently pointed out in a very sharp note that the whole story was a grotesque farrago of errors: the book in question "was not a copy of the Commentary on the 'Parva Naturalia,' but of Aquinas' own 'Secunda Secundae;' and that, on examination, it proves not to be the handwriting of Mr. Hume, and to contain nothing written by him."[41]

Coleridge's accusation would in any case be baseless. Hume's "Essay on Association" contains nothing resembling the "main thoughts" of Aquinas' commentary on the *Parva Naturalia*. The "order" of the thoughts is not the same, nor are the illustrations similar.[42]

That Coleridge levels such a charge at Hume in the *Biographia* immediately after he has himself for several pages been translating and paraphrasing from a foreign writer without acknowledgment—from a book he had in his own library, annotated in his own hand, in which all the "main thoughts" are the same, and the "order" of the thoughts down to the order of obscure names within a sentence, in which the illustrations and quotations are the same—is to say the least, psychologically suggestive. It will be remembered that many years before, when accused of having "palpably imitated" Samuel Rogers, he had at once responded by charging Rogers with having perpetrated a major plagiarism in his most famous poem. In the previous chapters of the *Biographia* he had repeatedly affirmed his own belief in the sacredness of stating intellectual obligations. "If I may dare once more adopt the words of Hooker," he had said on the very last page before the fifth chapter began,[43] as if reluctant to draw too heavily on any one writer.

One can detect a rather clear pattern emerging in the *Biographia Literaria*: Coleridge will cite repeatedly, discuss intellectual obligations again and again, express severe contempt of imitators and plagiarists—and, during crucial passages of speculation or learning derived from little-known writers, suppress the source. He will, in fact, throw dust in the eyes of the reader, as he does at the close of Chapter V, by focusing attention on his own mental processes. Here, after pages of translation, he writes: "It remains then for *me,* first to state wherein Hartley differs from Aristotle; then, to exhibit the grounds of *my* conviction . . . ," and so forth.

Beginning Chapter VI, he declines to discuss a certain aspect of Hartley's thought, for this "has been already sufficiently exposed by the younger Reimarus, Maasse, &c."[44] The informed reader may be somewhat startled to find Maass mentioned at long last, but the name would, of course, have no special importance otherwise. The name appears within a statement which again brings us back to Coleridge's convictions about himself as an author which are being repeatedly presented to the reader. He is saying in effect that he will not trespass on matters which have already been dealt with elsewhere, certainly an odd claim in view of the facts as we have them. In the very next paragraph he touches upon a complex philosophical idea of which he disapproves:

From a hundred possible confutations let one suffice. According to this system the idea or vibration *a* from the external object A becomes asso-

ciable with the idea or vibration *m* from the external object M, because
the oscillation *a* propogated itself so as to reproduce the oscillation *m*.
But the original impression from M was essentially different from the
impression A: unless therefore different causes may produce the same
effect, the vibration *a* could never produce the vibration *m*: and this
therefore could never be the means, by which *a* and *m* are associated.

It is regrettable that Coleridge did not choose some clearer confutation
from the many others presumably available to him, especially as this one is
taken from Maass,[45] with no evidence of having been "imperfectly remembered." Coming as this passage does, after mentioning Maass in passing
(though after Reimarus, as if Coleridge found Maass of secondary importance), it would seem impossible to justify the lack of acknowledgment, no
matter from what point of view the matter is considered.[46]

Now occurs the first of several failures to pursue an argument to a conclusion. Coleridge has been dealing with a difficult subject, involving memory
and sensation, and though he remains *in medias res*, we read:

But not now dare I longer discourse of this, waiting for a loftier mood,
and a nobler subject, warned from within and from without, that it is
profanation to speak of these mysteries [a quotation from Plotinus
follows, translated as] "To those to whose imagination it has never been
presented, how beautiful is the countenance of justice and wisdom; and
that neither the morning nor the evening star are so fair. For in order to
direct the view aright, it behoves that the beholder should have made
himself congenerous and similar to the object beheld. Never could the
eye have beheld the sun, had not its own essence been soliform . . . .
neither can a soul not beautiful attain to an intuition of beauty."[47]

The reader who has been laboring after Coleridge may well feel both
cheated and insulted by this declaration. Surely an author entertaining such
an opinion of his audience ought not to have promised, fifteen pages before,
"deductions from established premises conveyed in such a form, as is calculated either to effect a fundamental conviction, or to receive a fundamental confutation."[48]

Considering the amount of space given to metaphysical disquisition in the
Biographia Literaria, it would seem that here was certainly the place to
attempt conclusive statements, and not to wait for a "loftier mood." This
tactic, as we shall see, was but one of several used at various crucial junctures in the *Biographia*.

Chapters VII and VIII range further over a variety of philosophical topics,
and Coleridge continues to show himself sensitive to the intellectual obligations of others. He refers to "Leibnitz's doctrine of a pre-established harmony, which he certainly borrowed from Spinoza, who had himself taken
the hint from Des Cartes's animal machines. . . ."[49] And on this very page

occurs the first of the major unacknowledged borrowings from Schelling.[50] Most of what Coleridge says for the following fifty lines is taken from Schelling, much of it word for word:

> How the *esse*, assumed as originally distinct from the *scire*, can ever unite itself with it; how *being* can transform itself into a *knowing*, becomes conceivable on one only condition; namely, if it can be shown that the *vis representativa*, or the Sentient, is itself a species of being; i.e. either as a property or attribute, or as an hypostasis or self subsistence. The former is, indeed, the assumption of materialism; a system which could not but be patronized by the philosopher, if only it actually performed what it promises. But how any affection from without can metamorphose itself into perception or will, the materialist has hitherto left, not only as incomprehensible as he found it, but has aggravated it into a comprehensible absurdity.[51]

Schelling's words, in Sara Coleridge's translation, read:

> Thus how an original Being can convert itself into a *Knowing* would only be conceivable in case it could be shown that even Representation itself . . . is a kind of Being; which is indeed the explanation of Materialism, *a system that would be a boon to the philosopher, if it really performed what it promises. But Materialism, such as it has hitherto been, is wholly unintelligible. . . .*[52]

To the reader unfamiliar with metaphysical speculation of this sort the borrowed passages make both impressive and demanding reading. However, the reader who has arduously followed Coleridge will again find himself disappointed: "I shall not dilate further on this subject; because it will, (if God grant health and permission), be treated of at large and systematically in a work, which I have many years been preparing, on the PRODUCTIVE LOGOS human and divine; with, and as the introduction to, a full commentary on the Gospel of St. John."[53]

The fate of this visionary work will be dealt with later. Meanwhile it is sufficient to observe that Coleridge has for the second time excused himself from pursuing a difficult subject. However: "To make myself intelligible as far as my present subject requires, it will be sufficient briefly to observe . . . ," and he goes on to make several points which again come from Schelling. The chapter closes with a figure of speech involving the phrase "self-complacent grin." Coleridge scrupulously draws our attention in a footnote to Pope's line: "And Coxcombs vanquish Berkeley with a grin," from where, presumably, he drew his figure.[54] The niceties of scholarly notation could hardly go further. But the large borrowings from Schelling are passed over in silence.

Chapter IX contains by far the most important statements Coleridge ever made that bear on the question of his plagiarisms. The famous passages, however, are by no means the only ones that should concern us, for practically the whole chapter deals with what Coleridge conceives to be his intellectual and literary obligations.

He begins by telling us how he had "successively studied in the schools of Locke, Berkeley, Leibnitz and Hartley, and could find in neither of them an abiding place for my reason. . . ."[55] In addition, the early study of Plato, Plotinus, Proclus, Pletho, and Boehme, among others, had contributed to the formation of his intellect.[56] Within the paragraph discussing Boehme occurs this famous passage:

> While I in part translate the following observations from a contemporary writer of the Continent, let me be permitted to premise, that I might have transcribed the substance from memoranda of my own, which were written many years before his pamphlet was given to the world; and that I prefer another's words to my own, partly as a tribute due to priority of publication; but still more from the pleasure of sympathy in a case where *coincidence* only was possible.
>
> Whoever is acquainted with the history of philosophy, during the two or three last centuries, cannot but admit, that there appears to have existed a sort of secret and tacit compact among the learned, not to pass beyond a certain limit in speculative science. . . .[57]

It is to be observed that Coleridge does not identify the "contemporary writer of the Continent," or his nationality, or give the name of the "pamphlet." One may well imagine the difficulty of identification were an author today to quote from some nameless work by a nameless "writer of the Continent." Since Coleridge nowhere uses quotation marks in the following pages, or citations of any kind, the reader has no way of knowing where the observations of the continental writer end and Coleridge's begin. The notes provided by Shawcross are inadequate guides for separating Schelling from Coleridge. From Sara Coleridge's 1847 edition it can be seen that for some eighty-five lines (almost three pages) following "Whoever is acquainted with the history of philosophy," the text is pure Schelling, with the exception of three or four scattered sentences. Coleridge's claim to be translating "in part" is thus an obscurantist qualification.[58]

At the conclusion of his present use of the nameless "writer of the Continent," he glowingly refers to George Fox, Jacob Boehme, and William Law: "The feeling of gratitude, which I cherish towards these men, has caused me to digress further than I had foreseen or proposed; but to have passed them over in an historical sketch of my literary life and opinions, would have seemed to me like the denial of a debt, the concealment of a boon."[59] It is surely strange that while distributing such accolades he has not yet found time even to mention the name of the man from whom he had just translated three pages. The expression of a delicate literary conscience at precisely this point is, moreover, not without significance, for, as we have seen, statements concerning intellectual integrity frequently occur in the vicinity of unacknowledged borrowings.

He then passes quickly to "the illustrious sage of Königsberg ... IMMAN-UEL KANT," whose works "at once invigorated and disciplined my under-standing . . . took possesion of me as with a giant's hand."[60] This tribute, though widely quoted by students of the development of Coleridge's mind, must be qualified. Kant did not "at once" impress him so strikingly; in 1796 the "illustrious sage" was still "the most unintelligible Emanuel Kant."[61] It was not until at least 1801, well after his return from Germany, that Cole-ridge began a thorough study of Kant.[62]

After various criticisms of the sage of Königsberg, several of which had been earlier made by Schelling, he passes to Fichte, who added the "key-stone" to the arch of his understanding. At last we come to Schelling by name, in two of whose works, Coleridge says, "I first found a genial coin-cidence with much that I had toiled out for myself, and a powerful assistance in what I had yet to do." He comments on this statement at length:

> I have introduced this statement, as appropriate to the narrative nature
> of this sketch; yet rather in reference to the work which I have announced
> in a preceding page [that is, the Logosophia] than to my present subject.
> It would be but a mere act of justice to myself, were I to warn my future
> readers, that an identity of thought, or even similarity of phrase, will
> not be at all times a certain proof that the passage has been borrowed
> from Schelling, or that the conceptions were originally learnt from
> him.[63]

All this background is directed to an as yet unpublished work, and not to the "present subject." "Future readers" are being warned. All this would certainly allay the suspicion of even the most cautious reader as to the possi-bility of Schelling appearing in the present work.

Coleridge now once again refers to the extraordinary coincidence of Schlegel's ideas on Shakespeare with his own, and his own alleged prece-dence. With respect to Schelling: "all the main and fundamental ideas, were born and matured in my mind before I had ever seen a single page of the German Philosopher; and I might indeed affirm with truth, before the more important works of Schelling had been written, or at least made public."[64]

This statement should be evaluated against the background of a long list of similar claims which stud Coleridge's career. A notebook entry of 1804 reads: "In the Preface of my Metaphys. Works I should say—Once & all read Tetens, Kant, Fichte, &c.—& there you will trace or if you are on the hunt, track me. Why then not acknowledge your obligations step by step? Because, I could not do in a multitude of glaring resemblances without a lie / for they had been mine, formed, & full formed in my own mind, before I had ever heard of these Writers. . . ."[65] The extreme exaggeration is signifi-cant. In a letter of 1801 we find: "I will now give you a literal Translation of page 49 of the celebrated Fichte's *Uber den Begriff der Wissenschaftslehre [On the Idea of the Theory of Knowledge]*."[66] Kant had been "heard" of as early as May 1796.[67] We find no statements by Coleridge about "genial" coincidences at the time he is first known to have read these philosophers. Besides Schelling, therefore, Coleridge claimed to have anticipated Kant, Fichte, and and uncertain "&c."

He asks, in a letter to his wife of April 1812: "Has Southey read Childe Harold? All the world is talking of it. I have not; but from what I hear, it is exactly on the plan that I myself had not only conceived six years ago, but have the whole Scheme drawn out in one of my old Memorandum Books."[68] No such scheme has yet to come to light.

Three weeks later he was writing to John Murray of certain political ideas then in print which he had anticipated by many years.[69] And in Henry Crabb Robinson's diary entry for 14 July 1816 we read:

> Coleridge talked about Goethe's work on the theory of colours: said he had some years back discovered the same theory, and would certainly have reduced it to form and published it had not Southey diverted his attention from such studies to poetry. On my mentioning that I had heard that an English work has been published lately developing the same system, Coleridge answered with great naïveté that he was very free in communicating his thoughts on the subject wherever he went and among literary people.[70]

Thus Coleridge claims to have anticipated Goethe in scientific speculation and suggests that his conversation had been plagiarized at home. These statements to Robinson were made between the time *Biographia Literaria* was written and published. Indeed, the period 1815-17 seems particularly rich in references to intellectual property. In a letter of 13 December 1817 to his disciple J. H. Green, after ranging widely across the field of German thought, Coleridge states, "As my opinions were formed before I was acquainted with the Schools of Fichte and Schelling, so do they remain independent of them. . . ." After alleging that one of Tieck's works "is too like an imitation of Heinse's Ardinghello," he goes on, "I have but merely looked into Jean Paul's Vorschule d. Aisthetic; but I found one sentence almost word for word the same as one written by myself in a fragment of an Essay on the Supernatural many years ago."[71]

In 1815 Coleridge had given Byron an account of a planned edition of his poetry, which was to include "a Particular Preface to the Ancient Mariner and the Ballads, on the employment of the Supernatural in Poetry and the Laws which regulate it."[72] At the conclusion of the thirteenth chapter of *Biographia Literaria,* he referred the reader to "the critical essay on the uses of the Supernatural in poetry, and the principles that regulate its introduction: which the reader will find prefixed to the poem of *The Ancient Mariner.*"[73] Despite this confident assertion, no glimmer of these projects has ever come to light. Thus even the "fragment" supposedly written "many years ago" may be only another estecean chimera.

Interestingly, Coleridge identified a single sentence in Richter's *Vorschule der Aesthetik* as almost identical with one of his own, but his own notes for a lecture on wit and humor are, as we shall see, mainly a patchwork of unacknowledged quotations from this very work.

In 1825 he wrote to John Taylor Coleridge:

> I can not only honestly assert, but I can satisfactorily prove by reference to writings (Letters, Marginal Notes, and those in books that have never been in my possession since I first left England for Hamburgh, etc.) that all the elements, the *differentials,* as the algebraists say, of my present opinions existed for me before I had even seen a book of German Metaphysics, later than Wolf and Leibnitz, or could have read it, if I had.[74]

No letters or marginal notes or notebooks in the voluminous Coleridgean materials have yet been discovered to substantiate this claim; and the claim, though widely quoted,[75] has value only if we believe Coleridge was, at least in matters of this sort, candid. He did not himself undertake to prove the assertion and there was no danger that his nephew would come forward to harass him with requests for documentation. It is suggestive that Coleridge should claim to be able to prove his case by reference to writings which had not been in his possession for more than twenty-five years, the only way of getting round the possibility of someone's abusively insisting that he might have faked letters and marginalia after the fact.

In a marginal note recorded in 1827, we read:

> This day I read the account of Faraday's Microphone and instantly recognized a fond and earnest dream-project of my own of 30 years' standing—with sundry other imaginations respecting what might be effected in the only embryo Science of Acoustics. The Walls of Jerico were to fall before my War-trumpet[s]. But where were the Hands, where the Tools of my Reason? I had not the *Organ* of all Sciences that respect Space and Quantity. My Dreams were akin to Reason: but I could not awake out of my prophetic Sleep, to effectuate their objectivization—for I was ignorant of the Mathematics![76]

Only Coleridge's most ardent enthusiasts will take seriously these acoustical pretensions. De Quincey, who was so far from underestimating Coleridge's intellect that he could describe it as the "most spacious . . . subtlest and the most comprehensive . . . that has yet existed among men," nevertheless wrote of that mind:

> it never gives back anything as it receives it. All things are modified and altered in passing through his thoughts; and from this cause, I

believe, combined with his aversion to continuous labour, arises his indisposition to mathematics; for *that* he must be content to take as he finds it.[77]

A *Table Talk* entry of 1833 records that Coleridge spoke at great length upon *Faust*: "Before I had ever seen any part of Goethe's *Faust,* though, of course, when I was familiar enough with Marlowe's, I conceived and drew up the plan of a work, a drama, which was to be, to my mind, what the Faust was to Goethe's. My Faust was old Michael Scott; a much better and more likely original than Faust."[78] Neither Coleridge's notebooks nor letters as thus far published give any hint of this scheme. Such evidence as we do have on the matter gives much reason to doubt his statement.

On 13 August 1812, more than twenty years before, he had spent "several hours" with Crabb Robinson alone, during which the latter read him "a number of scenes out of the new *Faust*." On this occasion Coleridge said nothing about any plan of his own on the subject. One week later, however, Robinson wrote: "Coleridge talks of writing a new *Faust*! He would never get out of a few barren, vague conceptions; he would lose himself in dreaming —his whole intellectual apparatus, employed by himself to no other purpose than to keep the different implements in exercise—I cannot say order."[79]

J. M. Nosworthy, in an interesting article on Coleridge's Faust project, draws a pertinent conclusion:

None of the incidents so expansively enumerated in 1833 appear to have been communicated to Crabb Robinson twenty years earlier. That the project at that time was vague in the extreme seems to emerge both from what Robinson says and the way in which he says it. I suspect, then, that the 1833 account was a resourceful, even a brilliant, piece of improvisation. Coleridge was now insistent that his "better *Faust*" had little in common with Goethe's play. He was unconscious, however, that most of the episodes he had planned, or thought he had planned, went deeply in debt to Marlowe's masterpiece.[80]

Now none of these claims promotes confidence in Coleridge's veracity when he insists in the *Biographia Literaria* that "all the main and fundamental ideas, were born and matured in my mind before I have ever seen a single page of the German Philosopher." But he goes further: "I might indeed affirm with truth, before the important works of Schelling had been written, or at least made public." This assertion can also be tested against facts.

Schelling published his first work in 1793, when he was only eighteen years old. By the age of twenty-five he had published several of his major works. The "Natur-Philosophy"[81] to which Coleridge refers in the *Biographia* was published in 1797, and the *System des transcendentalen Idealismus* in 1800. For Coleridge to have formulated the ideas in those works before their publication would mean not only that he possessed a formidably complex philosophy of which he made no mention in his letters, conversation, or notebooks, so far as we have a record of them, but that he possessed a philosophy very remote from the philosophical notions he *did* express during this period.

The development of Coleridge as a philosopher is a complex and confused subject, partly as a result of just such statements as this in the *Biographia.* We know that in 1796 he was so much a disciple of David Hartley that he named his first child after him. In 1794 he wrote: "I am a compleat Necessitarian—and understand the subject as well almost as Hartley himself."[82] In "Religious Musings" (1794-96) Hartley was "he of mortal kind / Wisest,"[83] which shows that for at least two years Coleridge was attached to the mechanistic, associationalist views he later inveighed against unceasingly. In a footnote to what might be taken as a mystical passage in "Religious Musings," he directs the reader to a commentary on Hartley by one Pistorius, where the reader will find Hartley "freed from the charge of Mysticism."[84]

On 31 December 1796 he wrote to Thelwall of Plato's "*gorgeous* Nonsense."[85] This brings us to within a few months of the publication of Schelling's *Ideas toward a Philosophy of Nature,* in which the transcendental notions expressed seem almost from another universe of discourse.

In 1797 Coleridge declared, "I am a *Berkleian*,"[86] and his next child is honored with the new master's name. In 1801, as we have seen, he began to study philosophy with a definite view to a philosophical career, but the "philosophic letters" to Wedgwood give no hint of the complex German formulations which were contemporary.[87]

It is therefore not possible to accept Coleridge's statement that he had arrived at Schelling's conceptions *before* they were published. And surely we are entitled to ask, as James Stirling did in the nineteenth century, "where in his [Coleridge's] works is that 'much that he had toiled out for himself'? where is that which, by Schelling's 'powerful assistance,' he afterwards did? where is this accomplishment that is like Schelling, and beyond Schelling, to be found represented?"[88]

That such a "genial coincidence" could exist was to Coleridge not at all surprising, for both he and Schelling had "studied in the same school," and both had admired Bruno and Boehme and Kant. In 1811 he had accounted for the "coincidence" of his ideas with A. W. Schlegel in much the same way:

For Schlegel & myself had both studied deeply & perseverantly the philosophy of Kant. . . . Suppose myself & Schlegel (my argument not my vanity leads to these seeming Self-flatteries) nearly equal in natural powers, of similar pursuits & acquirements, and it is only necessary for both to have mastered the spirit of Kant's Critique of the Judgment to render it morally certain, that writing on the same Subject we should draw the same conclusions by the same trains [of reasoning] from the same principles, write to one purpose & with one spirit.[89]

This explanation has a certain abstract plausibility, but sags under the pressure of concrete fact. For how could the study of Kant by two equally intelligent men make it even remotely probable, let alone "morally certain," that they would come to a large number of identical conclusions about the content, style, structure, and psychological motivation of Shakespeare's plays? The *identity* of Coleridge's and Schelling's views in this context cannot be related to having "studied in the same school," for Coleridge adopts many doctrines of Schelling which *diverge* from Kant.[90]

He continues: "The coincidence of SCHELLING'S system with certain general ideas of Behmen, he declares to have been *mere* coincidence; while *my* obligations have been more direct. *He* needs give to Behmen only feelings of sympathy; while I owe him a debt of gratitude."[91]

All this sounds as if Schelling had complained about Coleridge's use of his ideas, whereas there is no reason to believe that at that time Schelling even knew of his existence. Yet the passage above conveys the impression of nasty accusations muttered within the cloistered halls of philosophy. Coleridge, immediately before the passage just quoted, had written: "Schelling has *lately,* and, as of *recent acquisition,* avowed that same affectionate reverence for the labours of Behmen, and other mystics, which I had formed at a much earlier period."[92] Actually, Schelling had acknowledged debts to Boehme many times before.[93]

After these acrimonious comments, Coleridge bestows upon Schelling several high compliments and concludes with his famous disclaimer:

> To me it will be happiness and honor enough, should I succeed in rendering the system itself intelligible to my countrymen. . . . For readers in general, let whatever shall be found in this or any future work of mine, that resembles, or coincides with, the doctrines of my German predecessor, though contemporary, be wholly attributed to *him*; provided, that the absence of distinct references to his books, which I could not at all times make with truth as designating citations or thoughts actually *derived* from him; and which, I trust, would, after this general acknowledgment be superfluous; be not charged on me as an ungenerous concealment or intentional plagiarism. I have not indeed (eheu! res angusta domi!) been hitherto able to procure more than two of his books, viz. the 1st volume of his collected Tracts, and his System of Transcendental Idealism; to which, however, I must add a small pamphlet against Fichte, the spirit of which was to *my* feelings painfully incongruous with the principles. . . . I regard truth as a divine ventriloquist: I care not from whose mouth the sounds are supposed to proceed, if only the words are audible and intelligible.[94]

This is the crucial passage in all discussions of Coleridge's borrowings from Schelling in the *Biographia*. Since only his harshest critics consider this disclaimer wholly dishonest, while the rest accept it as more or less freeing

Coleridge of any deliberate intent to plagiarize, it seems obligatory to analyze this passage in some detail.

Three emotional responses are aroused in the reader by the total context.
First: "To me it will be happiness and honor enough, should I succeed in
rendering the system intelligible to my countrymen." All the author is claiming for himself is the honorable role of a mediator of ideas. This modest
statement may be coupled with the extremely high praise accorded Schelling
a few pages later: "With the exception of one or two fundamental ideas,
which cannot be with-held from FICHTE, to SCHELLING we owe the
completion, and the most important victories, of this revolution in philosophy."[95] This praise, however, is difficult to reconcile with a passage in Crabb
Robinson's diary for 3 May 1812, where it is recorded that Coleridge stated
that from "Fichte and Schelling he has not gained any one great idea." Again
in Robinson's diary, later the same year, Coleridge "maintains that from
Schelling he has gained no new ideas, all Schelling has said he having either
thought before or found in Jacob Boehmen."[96]

A charitable interpretation of these divergent opinions would be that Coleridge had much changed his mind on the subject when he came to write the
Biographia. However, within two years after publication of the Biographia
he had the opportunity to make Schelling's system intelligible to his countrymen. Yet in the series of philosophical lectures he delivered in 1818-19 he
excused himself from discussing the man who was responsible for "the most
important victories, of this revolution in philosophy" on the ground that his
time was limited. But there was time to remark: "in truth I should be puzzled to give you a true account [of Schelling's system]. For I might at one
time refer you to Kant, and then I should say what [Schelling] appears at one
time; another time to Spinoza, as applied to another aspect of his philosophy; and then again I should find him in the writings of Plotinus, and
still more of Proclus, but most in the writings of a Jesuit who opposed the
Protestants. . . ."[97]

He then charges Schelling with having turned Catholic and communicates
a slanderous statement allegedly reported from Schelling's mouth by one of
the German's "disciples": "I am teaching religion . . . but my bread is [the]
Roman Catholic Church, and I prefer that to the other doctrines because it
is more like the ancient pagans."[98] Schelling had not, in fact, become a Catholic.[99] In any case, what had all this to do with Schelling's ideas? One can
only conclude that Coleridge's statements in the Biographia Literaria and
elsewhere concerning his intellectual relations with Schelling were makeshifts
designed to meet the needs of specific situations. In the Biographia, obviously, it would have been ridiculous to attack the intellectual stature of a
thinker whom he claimed to have anticipated in all his capital pretensions.

The second emotional overtone raised in the "disclaimer" passage involves
the reference to limited financial means ("res angusta domi!"), which has
prevented the indigent author from procuring more than three works of
Schelling. It is faintly unseemly to challenge such a statement, but it should

be noted that in 1816, as we shall see, he was writing urgently to a bookseller for *all* the works of Schelling which he did not then own, and this was before the publication of the *Biographia.*[100]

Third, there is a vague accusation concerning the incongruity of Schelling's professed principles and some presumably mean-spirited attack against Fichte. The reader knows nothing about any of this, and it is irrelevant to the subject at hand. Nevertheless, the effect is somehow to prejudice us, however slightly, against Schelling.

So far as meeting any future charge of plagiarism, Coleridge in the "disclaimer" passage makes the following major points:

(1) He cannot always directly cite Schelling, even when he is quoting from his books, because to do so would be to suggest that he derived the thoughts from him, and this would be false. In any case, specific citation is unnecessary in view of the general acknowledgment he was now making.

If such a view became common in the kingdom of letters, a kind of chaos would at once prevail. Each man would decide for himself what ideas were original with him, even though they appear in print elsewhere. By stating somewhere in his works that a "genial coincidence" had occurred, any author could use the ideas and very words of any other writer without further acknowledgment. Credit for original insights and formulations is taken as a matter of course. Should such borrowings, which may include extended passages of direct translation, be discovered, our second author denies any intent to deceive, and points to the general disclaimer once made.

Coleridge's defenders have not seriously attempted to use this passage to mitigate the fact that later, in "On Poesy or Art," his *Theory of Life*, and his lecture on the *Prometheus* of Aeschylus, he silently paraphrased or directly translated from various works of Schelling; but they have maintained that the borrowed passages from Schelling in the *Biographia*, in a real sense, were acknowledged. Be that as it may, during Coleridge's lifetime no one suspected the presence of Schelling's ideas, let alone his very words, in the *Biographia*, and Coleridge received full credit for the ideas therein as original conceptions. Only after the discovery of the debt, after he had achieved a considerable reputation as a philosopher, was the existence of an acknowledgment to Schelling ferreted out of the book.

Coleridge himself modified the extreme view implied in using a general acknowledgment to cover all borrowings by stating that he could not "at all times" cite Schelling, because to do so would be to imply an original idea as a derivative. But Coleridge never in the entire book put a single page or sentence or idea of Schelling within quotation marks.

(2) He cannot always make citations because he does not own all of Schelling's books. He now possesses only two of them and a pamphlet.

If one is using notes or ideas from memory one can usually state the source, especially when they come from a specific, much studied, foreign author. The crucial point here is that many of the unacknowledged translations and paraphrasings from Schelling come from one of the books Coleridge here admits owning: the *System des transcendentalen Idealismus*. Consequently, this is a disingenuous argument, since actually owning the appropriate work of Schelling no more led him to acknowledgment than when he did not, supposedly, have the book in his possession.

But did Coleridge really not own all the books of Schelling which he used in the *Biographia*? On 13 August 1816 Coleridge wrote to a London bookseller, Thomas Boosey. The letter reads in part: "At present I should be glad to have, as speedily as possible, whatever catalogues you can lend me, for a few days. As soon as you can get them over, I am anxious to have *all* the works of Schelling, with exception of those, I already possess, of which I gave you the list in my last Letter, & to which you have now to add the *Denkmal*."[101]

Unfortunately, the previous letter in which Coleridge set down a list of Schelling's works he then owned has never been published.[102] But this letter of August 1816, written well before the publication of the *Biographia*, acknowledges the receipt of at least one of Schelling's works not mentioned in the *Biographia* passage in which he states that, "eheu! res angusta domi!", he has thus far been able to afford only the *Transcendental Idealism*, the first volume of Schelling's collected Tracts, and a small pamphlet. Yet the ninth chapter of the *Biographia* was written before 1816, so that we cannot be sure that Coleridge was definitely romancing.

Should the matter be allowed to rest at this point? Though we cannot be sure just how long the "list" of Schelling's works in Coleridge's possession in 1816 was, a few inferences are possible. He urgently asks for catalogues and is anxious to own "all" of Schelling's works just as soon as the bookseller can get them from Germany.[103] Now the *Denkmal* referred to above, which exists annotated in Coleridge's own hand, was published in Tübingen in 1812. The only work by Schelling of any consequence published after this date was *Ueber die Gottheiten von Samothrake* [*On the Divinities of Samothrace*] in 1815 (and in 1825 used without acknowledgment by Coleridge). A "list" of works seems to imply the possession of more than two or three. If Coleridge was able to obtain a work published in 1812 from his London bookseller in 1816, he certainly should have been able, over the years, to acquire several others. At least nine of Schelling's books were annotated by Coleridge, and he unquestionably read at least fourteen of them.[104]

The letter to Boosey shows that before the publication of the *Biographia* he owned a "list" of Schelling's works and was urgently trying to acquire the rest. It is not altogether reckless to suppose that Coleridge wanted Schelling's works before him for purposes other than experiencing repeated *déjà vues* and genial coincidences.

Finally, his statement about being too poor to buy books, even if true, ignores his ample opportunities to secure books from his many friends and literary connections, notably J. H. Green and Henry Crabb Robinson.[105] Since Coleridge's death, scores of German volumes annotated by him have come to light.

(3) Finally there is in the "disclaimer" passage Coleridge's often quoted statement that he considered truth a "divine ventriloquist" and did not care through whose mouth it spoke. This fine phrase surely expresses a noble ideal, however inapplicable to the soiled world of copyrights and royalties and the rivalries of ambitious authors. Apart from general considerations, however, the main question is whether Coleridge put forward the notion sincerely. Scholars have often quoted the phrase to account for his apparently dreamy indifference to such terrestrial activities as citing specific authorities. But they have displayed insufficient curiosity as to whether the divine-ventriloquist passage reflects a genuine conviction that can be supported by other statements of Coleridge, either public or private. Did he believe what he said and practice what he preached, or was the statement an isolated one, perhaps even anomalous in his writings? The following discussion, it is hoped, may help to repair a lacuna of too long standing in Coleridge studies. And since individual facts tending to undermine received opinion can often be dismissed as oddities or eccentricities, it will be necessary to cast our net wide in search of evidence.

Curiously, in the *Biographia Literaria* itself Coleridge repeatedly insisted upon precisely the opposite of what the divine-ventriloquist theory implies. He had written on page nine: "I regard, and ever have regarded the obligations of intellect among the most sacred of the claims of gratitude." We should also remember his care in pointing out his priority over Schlegel, and his statement that it was fortunate for his "moral character" that large and "respectable" audiences could be called upon to prove the reality of his claims.

If Coleridge was genuinely indifferent to matters of intellectual priority, nor cared through whom the voice of truth spoke, he behaved with strange rancor in so elaborately accusing Hume of plagiarism only a few pages before announcing the divine-ventriloquist theory and immediately after taking over whole pages without acknowledgment from Maass. A deep and long-standing antipathy to Hume appears to figure in this particular charge.

According to Hazlitt in "My First Acquaintance with Poets," Coleridge as far back as 1798 "spoke slightingly of Hume (whose Essay on Miracles he said was stolen from an objection in one of South's sermons—*Credat Judaeus Apella*!)." Hazlitt's skepticism is substantiated by George Sampson's statement that there "is no obvious resemblance between Hume's *Essay on Miracles* and any of South's sermons."[106] In 1801 Coleridge wrote to Southey: "As to Hume, was he not—ubi non fur, ibi stultus—& often thief & blockhead at the same time?" He was apparently fond of the Latin phrase ("where not stolen, there babbling"), for he used it almost fifteen years later for a similar purpose: "Ubi non Fur, ibi Stultus, is my character of his *Reverence*, Mr. Malthus."[107]

In 1796 Coleridge had accused Samuel Rogers of plagiarism, groundlessly, though he himself had extensively borrowed from "The Pleasures of Memory." At that time, when only twenty-four, he had apologized by saying that it was both "little" and "futile" to accuse men of genius of plagiarism, and he had done so only as a result of physical and mental distress.

But in 1801 he was at considerable pains to demonstrate that all that was of consequence in Locke had been taken from Descartes: "I think I have *proved* [Locke] to have gained a reputation to which he has no honest claim. . . . it would follow that the famous Essay on the human Understanding is only a prolix Paraphrase on Des Cartes with foolish Interpolations of the Paraphrast's."[108] This belief was no passing aberration with Coleridge. Very particular and detailed charges of this kind against Locke continued down the years.[109] In 1798 he told the young Hazlitt that James Mackintosh was "the ready warehouseman of letters, who knew exactly where to lay his hand on what he wanted, though the goods were not his own."[110]

In 1801 Coleridge wrote to Thomas Poole about the same Mackintosh: "I attended 5 of his Lectures—such a wretched patch work of plagiarisms from Condilliac [*sic*]—of contradictions, and blunders in matter of fact, I never heard from any man's mouth before."[111] Many years later he wrote in a book by Jeremy Taylor: "[Mackintosh is] imitating Jeremy Taylor—rather copying his semi-colon punctuation—as closely as he can."[112] He seems to have been particularly sensitive to borrowings from Jeremy Taylor,[113] whose *Holy Dying*, according to Crabb Robinson, he thought "a perfect poem, and in all its particulars, even the rhythm, may be compared with Young's 'Night Thoughts.' "[114]

Three years after writing that Mackintosh had plagiarized from Condillac, he wrote to William Godwin that Condillac's "Logic" was "basely purloined from Hartley."[115] The same assertion appears in the manuscript "Logic" which he left unfinished at his death: "In the far famed Logic of Condillac . . . the student may find the whole theory of *Materialism* (borrowed without acknowledgment from David Hartley)."[116] In Coleridge's *Theory of Life*, we find a similar remark: "the assumptions of the crudest materialism, stolen too without acknowledgment from our David Hartley's essay on Man, which is well known under the whimsical name of Condillac's Logic."[117]

In 1798 he praised a ballad-song in M. G. Lewis' *Castle Spectre,* in part because its "simplicity & naturalness is his [Lewis'] own, & not imitated," but in the same letter to Wordsworth he wrote that the serious style of the play was "Schiller Lewis-ized" and that he owned a certain book from which, "I suspect, Mr. Lewis has stolen all his sentimentality, moral & humorous. . . . The whole plot, machinery, & incident are borrowed—the play is a mere patchwork of plagiarisms."[118]

Claims by Coleridge that ideas from his essays and conversations were being widely adopted appear early, and persist throughout his life. In 1800, when he was a regular contributor to the *Morning Post*, he wrote Josiah Wedgwood that it was "not unflattering to a man's Vanity" to be able to trace from his own writings "a happy phrase, good image, or new argument running thro' the Town, & sliding into all the papers! . . . Then to hear a favorite & often urged argument repeated almost in your own particular phrases in the House of Commons—& quietly in the silent self-complacence of your own Heart chuckle over the plagiarism, as if you were the grand Monopolist of all good Reasons!"[119]

In 1814 he complained to Daniel Stuart that "I have never received from those in power even a verbal acknowledgment—tho' by mere reference to dates it might be proved, that no small number of fine Speeches in the House of Commons & elsewhere originated directly or indirectly in my Essays & Conversations."[120] Plagiarism among the orators in the Commons presumably persisted, for three years later he wrote of the ". . . *Plagiarisms* of [Southey's] Wat Tyler almost word for word from the Speeches of the opposition."[121] As for the unacknowledged adoption of his ideas by newspapers, in the *Biographia* itself he admitted, after a cluster of modest apologies, that he had derived some satisfaction

> from the republication of my political essays (either whole or as extracts) not only in many of our own provincial papers, but in the federal journals throughout America. I regarded it as some proof of my not having laboured in vain, that from the articles written by me shortly before and at the commencement of the late unhappy war with America, not only the sentiments were adopted, but in some instances the very language, in several of the Massachusetts state-papers.[122]

These interesting claims, for which no evidence has as yet been unearthed, appear only slightly modified a few years later in a footnote to his first *Lay Sermon.* Coleridge wrote that his essay on "Vulgar Errors in Taxation," which had originally appeared in the *Friend,* had been

> transferred almost entire, to the columns of a daily paper, of the largest circulation, and from thence, in larger or smaller extracts, to several of our Provincial-Journals. It was likewise reprinted in two of the American Federalist papers: and a translation appeared, I have been told, in the Hamburg Correspondenten.[123]

Since he was just fifteen years old when the "American Federalist papers" first appeared (in 1787-88), his essay on "Vulgar Errors" could hardly have been reprinted there.

In 1804 he called Erasmus Darwin—from whom he had taken without acknowledgment several poetic images and impressively learned footnotes, and was later to adopt an important theory of dramatic illusion—"a great *plagiarist*"; "He was like a pigeon picking up peas, and afterwards voiding them with excrementitious additions."[124] Coleridge's lifelong dislike of Darwin shows itself in one of Allsop's *Recollections* for 1821:

> Darwin was so egregiously vain [said Coleridge], that, after having given to his son a thesis upon Ocular Spectra, in itself an entire plagiarism

from a German book published at Leipzig, he became jealous of the praise it received, and caused it to be given out that he was the real author. Nay, he even wrote letters and verses to himself, which he affixed to his own Poems as being addressed to him, by (I think) Billsborough, a young admirer of his. He asked his friends whether they had not frequently heard him express opinions like these twenty years ago?[125]

In 1808 Coleridge delivered a lecture on education in which, according to Crabb Robinson, he "eulogised Dr. Bell's plan of education and concluded by a severe attack upon Lancaster for having stolen from Dr. Bell all that is good in his plans."[126] Coleridge's memory in this, as in similar charges, was tenacious, for he repeated it to Joseph Cottle six years later, adding: "Southey's Book is a dilution of my Lecture at the R. I. [Royal Institute]."[127]

Southey seems not to have escaped Coleridge's suspicious attentions. According to a charge twice made publicly by Hazlitt, he openly ridiculed Southey's talent and literary honesty:

[Coleridge] is troubled at times and seasons with a treacherous memory: but perhaps he may remember a visit to Bristol. He *may* remember (I allude to no confidential whisperings—no unguarded private moments— but to facts of open and ostentatious notoriety): he *may* remember *publicly*, before several strangers, and in the midst of a public library, turning into the most merciless ridicule 'The dear Friend' [Southey]. . . . Mr. Coleridge recited an Ode of his dear Friend, in the hearing of these persons, with a tone and manner of the most contemptuous burlesque, and accused him of having stolen from Wordsworth images which he knew not how to use.[128]

In 1811, according to Crabb Robinson, "Coleridge represented William Taylor as a retailer of German criticisms without having the honesty to confess his authorities."[129] Also in 1811, in a report of an evening's literary conversation by John Payne Collier, Coleridge noted that

Some of the best things in it [Campbell's "Pleasures of Hope"] were borrowed: for instance, the line—
    And Freedom shriek'd when Kosciusko fell
was taken from a much ridiculed piece by Pennis, a Pindaric on William III.,
    Fair Liberty shriek'd aloud, aloud Religion groan'd.
. . . Coleridge had little toleration for Campbell, and considered him, as far as he had gone, a mere verse-maker. Southey was, in some sort, like an elegant setter of jewels; the stones were not his own: he gave them all the advantage of his art—the charm of his workmanship (and that charm was great), but not in their native brilliancy.[135]

The image of the eclectic poet as an elegant setter of other people's jewels is itself hackneyed. The important point is that Coleridge rarely seems to go far in a literary discussion of any but the very greatest figures without introducing observations about borrowings, usually unacknowledged, and his tone is always disapproving in reports of his *conversation.*

In a letter of June 1814 to J. J. Morgan, after ridiculing some of Southey's poetry and asking, "Is he grown silly?", Coleridge continued: "The Courier for the last 2 years has been repeating me with a thousandfold Echo in it's leading [paragraphs]; & S.[outhey] has bedevilified into vilest Rhyme rhythmless the leading [paragraphs] of the Courier."[131]

Writing a few months later to the publisher John Murray of his translation of Schiller's *Wallenstein,* he charged that "my own remarks in the preface were transferred to a Review, as the Reviewer's sentiments *against* me, without even a Hint that he had copied them from my own preface."[132]

The very next month (September 1814) he wrote to Daniel Stuart of the ingratitude of other writers respecting their alleged obligations to him:

it would have asked no very violent strain of recollection for one or two of them to have considered whether some part of *their* most successful *Somethings* were not among the *Nothings* of my intellectual Nodoings.—But all strange things are less strange, than the sense of intellectual obligations. Seldom do I ever see a Review; yet almost as often as that Seldomness permits, have I smiled at finding myself attacked in strains of Thought, which would never have occurred to the Writer had he not directly or indirectly learnt them from myself. . . . [I can] prove— that there is not a man in England, whose Thoughts, Images, Words, & Erudition have been published in larger quantities than *mine*—tho', I must admit, not *by* or *for* myself.—Believe me, if I felt any pain from these things, I should not make this Expose—: for it is constitutional with me to *shrink* from all Talk or Communication of what gnaws within me.[133]

The following year Coleridge complained to Byron that the "richest and raciest clusters [of his poetry had been] carried off and spoilt by the plundering Fox."[134] In a letter to Byron later in 1815 we find him, somewhat surprisingly, complaining that even Wordsworth had improperly failed to acknowledge debts to himself: "I have not learnt with what motive Wordsworth omitted the original a[d]vertisement prefixed to his White Doe, that the peculiar metre and mode of narration he had imitated from the Christabel."[135]

Byron, the recipient of these statements, later came under attack himself. Among Coleridge's marginalia is the statement: "W. Wordsworth calls Lord Byron the Mocking Bird of our parnassian Ornithology; but the Mocking Bird, they say, has a very sweet song of his own, in true Notes proper to himself. Now I cannot say, I have ever heard any such in his Lordship's Volumes of Warbles. . . ."[136]

In September 1816 Coleridge wrote to Thomas Boosey a letter dealing largely with German literature. In it he discussed the distinction between genius and talent. Genius was an "originating, intuitive and combining Power," whereas talent was the "power of acquiring, arranging, illustrating, and applying the knowledge learnt from others." Delivering himself of one of those large generalizations of which he was so fond, he found the French nation since the latter half of the reign of Louis XIV so deficient in genius that the appearance of it in a French author "always suggests to my mind the suspicion of plagiarism or assistance from German or Italian Writers— (So *ex. gr.* whatever is solid and original in Mad. de Stahl was given her by Schlegel, & other Germans.)"[137]

Perhaps no writer, however, was so often the target of Coleridge's acute sensitivity in these matters as William Hazlitt. Hazlitt's first book was *An Essay on the Principles of Human Action* (1804). De Quincey in 1838 wrote: "Thirty years ago I looked into it slightly, but my reverence for Hartley offended me with its tone, and hearing that Coleridge challenged for his own most of what was important in the thoughts, I lost all interest in the essay." In 1845 De Quincey mentioned the book again, together with Hazlitt's "polemic essay against the Hartlean theory, supposing even that these were not derived entirely from Coleridge (as Coleridge used to assert)."[138]

We learn from De Quincey that Coleridge claimed yet another work of Hazlitt's as his own:

It is proper, by the way, that we should inform the reader of this generation where to look for Coleridge's skirmishings with Malthus. They are to be found chiefly in the late Mr. William Hazlitt's work on that subject [Anonymous Reply in 1807 to Malthus on his Essay on Population]—a work which Coleridge so far claimed as to assert that it had been substantially made up from his own conversation.[139]

The complaint that Hazlitt (and others) had plagiarized from his conversation was often made. Coleridge wrote to Daniel Stuart in 1813 of a recent published essay by Hazlitt: "I should have called [it] a masterly Essay on the causes of the Downfall of the Comic Drama, if I was not perplexed by the distinct recollection of having myself *conversed* the greater part of it at Lamb's."[140]

Crabb Robinson reports (21 December 1816) that Coleridge complained that Lamb was entertaining Hazlitt in his home, a man "who abuses the confidence of private intercourse so scandalously. He denies Hazlitt, however, originality, and ascribes to Lamb the best ideas in Hazlitt's article."[141] Three months earlier Coleridge had written to Hugh J. Rose that "almost all the *sparkles & originalities* of his [Hazlitt's] Essays are, however, echoes from poor Charles Lamb—and in his last libel the image of the Angel without hands or feet was stolen from a Letter of my own to Charles Lamb, which had been quoted to him."[142] In 1818 he complained to Morgan that Hazlitt had stolen a *phrase* of his, "mob-sycophancy."[143] In the *Table Talk* for 6 August 1832 he said: "compare Charles Lamb's exquisite criticisms on Shakespeare with Hazlitt's round and round imitations of them."[144]

If Coleridge really was dreamily indifferent to such sublunary concerns as acknowledging intellectual obligations, he was nevertheless unusually quick to note the failure in others. Quite apart from mere acknowledgment, he seems at times to have thought borrowing in itself unworthy of a man of genius. He wrote of *The Prophetess* by Beaumont and Fletcher: "Miserable parodies & thefts of fine lines in Shakespeare." Of a line in another Beaumont and Fletcher play: "It is strange that a man of Genius should have thought it worth while to steal, in this [?] parody line, the rants of Shakespeare's poisoned King John." He wrote of Beaumont and Fletcher: "*How* inferior would they have appeared, had not Shakespeare existed for them to *imitate?*—which in every play, more or less, they do, & in their Tragedies most glaringly—and yet—(O Shame! Shame!)—miss no opportunity of sneering at the divine Man, and sub detracting from his Merits"; "At all events, & in every respect, Jonson stands far higher in a moral Light than B. & F. He was a fair contemporary & in *his* way & as far as respects Shakespeare, an Original. But B. & F. were always imitators, often borrowers, and yet sneer at him with a spite far more malignant than Jonson, who has besides made noble compensation by his Praises."[145]

Even Samuel Johnson—so long famed for probity and moral rectitude—comes under Coleridge's lash. He severely objected to Boswell's three volumes of "Dr. Johnson's pilfered brutalities of wit." Next to a passage in Browne's *Religio Medici* Coleridge wrote: "Dr. Johnson adopted this argument and I think, gave it as his own." So sensitive was Coleridge to "imitation" that he was able to assert that "in the balance & construction of his periods Dr. Johnson has followed Hall: as any intelligent reader will discover by an attentive Comparison."[146]

Coleridge attacked even his divine Bacon for "his silence, or worse than silence, concerning the merits of his contemporaries," and wrote a beautiful tribute to Kepler (in the same essay) for so meticulously acknowledging his debts to former thinkers.[147]

In a marginal note in a volume of the German *Naturphilosoph* Oken, Coleridge wrote that Oken followed Goethe, Schelling, and Steffens in opposing Newtonian optics: "but stop! [Oken] waits till they are out of sight. Hangs out a new Banner (i.e., metaphors) and becomes a Leader himself."[148] This note is of particular interest in view of Coleridge's extensive borrowings from Schelling and Steffens in his *Theory of Life*.

In publishing his own epigrams he had neglected to identify sources over twenty times, and yet—we may remind ourselves—he quickly protested to the editor of the *Berkshire Chronicle* in 1828 that one of his own epigrams had been plagiarized by a Miss Mary Brown.[149] In a manuscript note to "Lewti," he improbably asserted that Joanna Baillie had borrowed a line from it, "as the dates of the poems prove,"[150] but, as we have seen, he never publicly acknowledged that the celebrated "Lewti" derived from a poem by Wordsworth.[151]

In 1816 he told Crabb Robinson "with great naïveté that he was very free in communicating his thoughts on the subject [his theory of colors] wherever he went and among literary people," and that his ideas had been plagiarized.[152]

He wrote to Allsop in 1819, "Have you see Cobbett's last number? . . . The self-complacency, with which he assumes to himself exclusively truths which he can call his own only as a Horse-stealer can appropriate a stolen Horse by adding mutilation and deformities to Robbery, is as *artful* as it is amusing."[153]

The image of the stolen horse may be related to a marginal comment in a volume of Tennemann's *Geschichte der Philosophie*, a work Coleridge used extensively, without acknowledgment, in his philosophical lectures of 1818: "The poor trick attributed to Aristotle (that of stealing his Master's black Horse, and then swearing that it could not be his Master's Horse because *that* was piebald) succeeded, I own, in the instance of Locke versus Aristotle and Descartes, and of Horne Tooke versus the Dutch Etymologists. . . ."[154] As to this charge, which Coleridge repeated, J. M. Robertson has pointed out:

> In regard to Horne Tooke, Coleridge echoed the earlier dictum of Hazlitt (in "The Spirit of the Age," 1825) that Tooke's "Letter to Mr. Dunning" contained everything of value that appeared in the later "Diversions of Purley;" but also went so far as to assert that "all that is true in Horne Tooke's book is taken from Lennep." Now, Lennep's book, as Dr. Richardson has pointed out, was not published till 1790, twelve years after the Letter to Dunning and four after the first part of the Diversions.[155]

In Chapter IV of *Biographia Literaria*, Coleridge provides a long, etymologically speculative note in his use of the word "desynonymize."[156] In a marginal note to this passage, hitherto unpublished, John Thelwall wrote:

> It is curious how freely persons of a certain cast of mind will borrow from those they affect to despise. What reader acquainted with the Diversions of Purley will not fail to discover that the fountain of all this reasoning is in that book—which indeed has given a new impulse to the grammatical speculations of mankind. Yet Coleridge in his conversations affects an utter contempt for Tooke & his grammatical philosophy, & scrupled [*d* written over *s*] not to apply to him in some discussions we had upon these subjects, with all the bitterness of rooted scorn, the epithet of *Charletan*.[157]

It is doubtful whether any other writer in the history of letters has accused so many writers of plagiarism, and so many so falsely. That this circumstance should coincide with the fact that Coleridge has been charged with having perpetrated the most extensive plagiarisms in the annals of literature (for a writer of any fame) is not without its own psychological interest.

But it is in the *Biographia Literaria* itself that we find the fullest and most detailed evidence bearing on the question of Coleridge's real attitude toward the whole question of *meum* and *tuum,* and consequently on the question of whether Coleridge put forward the divine-ventriloquist theory sincerely and was in fact wholly indifferent to these matters. On page thirteen of the *Biographia* he had thought it worthwhile to point out a plagiarized line in a "university prize-poem," and had even suggested how the plagiarist might have proceeded. Only a few pages before the divine-ventriloquist passage he had noted the resemblance of Schelling's thought to Boehme's and had sneered at the former's alleged avowal of "*mere* coincidence."[158] In a marginal note of uncertain date in one of Schelling's books he wrote: "How can I explain Schelling's strange silence respecting Jacob Boehme? . . . The coincidence in the expressions, illustrations, and even in the mystical obscurities, is too glaring to be solved by mere independent coincidence in thought and intention."[159]

In the *Biographia* he accused Maturin of plagiarizing from Shakespeare and Milton and took a disapproving attitude towards Gray's alleged "imitation" of Shakespeare. In dealing with Wordsworth in Chapter XXII he referred to those who "mimic" and "copy" his work, and to the "plagiarists" who "plunder" it.[160]

The evidence suggests persuasively that the divine-ventriloquist theory was a brilliant improvisation designed to meet a delicate situation. Only two pages before announcing it, Coleridge, while stating his intellectual obligations to Kant, Bruno, and others wrote: "It would be an act of high and almost criminal injustice to pass over in silence the name of Mr. RICHARD SAUMAREZ." It seems odd to bring in the name of this obscure man among such mighty thinkers, but if we read the long footnote we find Coleridge maintaining that the "germs" of Kant's philosophy existed in Saumarez, and that the latter's volumes "were published many years before the full development of these germs by Schelling"[161] —all of which makes Schelling still further a derivative thinker. To the original readers of the *Biographia Literaria*, all this must have seemed very confusing and rendered the whole question of who was obligated to whom rather obscure, and perhaps not terribly important.

In a very real sense all discussion of Coleridge's general acknowledgment to Schelling in the *Biographia* is self-defeating, for it gives brief and complicated passages a prominence which they simply do not have in the book. To concentrate so much attention on a cluster of sentences tends to fix them in the mind in such a way as to make the faults one is willing to attribute to Coleridge a matter of degree, on which opinion, by its nature subjective, is bound to vary. It cannot be too strongly emphasized that the general disclaimer to Schelling is a vague, hypothetical statement having no specific reference and quickly passed over. Finally, no one suspected that these statements were intended to shelter passages of translation and paraphrase, and when after his death, unacknowledged borrowings were discovered, the English literary world was astounded.[162]

The actual structure of the *Biographia Literaria* as it develops after the divine-ventriloquist theory is enormously significant. Coleridge at once quotes from Milton's *Reason of Church Government*:

> "Albeit, I must confess to be half in doubt, whether I should bring it [the Divine-Ventriloquist theory] forth or no, it being so contrary to the eye of the world, and the world so potent in most men's hearts, that I shall endanger either not to be regarded or not to be understood."
>
> And to conclude the subject of citation, with a cluster of citations, which, as taken from books not in common use, may contribute to the reader's amusement, as a voluntary before a sermon.[163]

Almost two pages of learned quotations in Latin and English follow, carefully cited.

Now it is crucial to observe that all these citations are not "a voluntary before a sermon." The next chapter, as Coleridge coolly informs us in the heading, is a chapter of "digression and anecdotes, as an interlude preceding that on the nature and genesis of the imagination or plastic power."[164] For some *forty-five pages* Coleridge returns to the past and deals with autobiographical material. Once more his own moral character is brought to the forefront of attention. We hear of his strenuous endeavors to raise the level of moral principles in England through his work in the *Watchman*, whose motto was "*that all might know the truth, and that the truth might make us free!*"[165] Rigid adherence to principles, according to Coleridge, offended his readers. He stresses his indifference to mundane considerations: "Thus by the time the seventh number was published, I had the mortification (but why should I say this, when in truth I cared too little for any thing that concerned my worldly interests to be at all mortified about it?) of seeing the preceding numbers exposed in sundry old iron shops for a penny a piece."[166] He continues to emphasize the great efforts made in the public behalf in his newspaper essays generally: "Yet in these labours I employed, and, in the belief of partial friends wasted, the prime and manhood of my intellect." "I do derive a gratification from the knowledge, that my essays contributed to introduce the practice of placing the questions and events of the day in a moral point of view. . . ."[167] And once again he returns to his fastidious avoidance in his writings of introducing the words or ideas of others:

> But my severest critics have not pretended to have found in my compositions triviality, or traces of a mind that shrunk from the toil of thinking. No one has charged me with tricking out in other words the thoughts

of others, or with hashing up anew the crambe jam decies cocta ["the mess warmed up ten times"] of English literature or philosophy. Seldom have I written that in a day, the acquisition or investigation of which had not cost me the previous labour of a month.[168]

I should dare appeal to the numerous and respectable audiences, which at different times and different places honored my lecture-rooms with their attendance, whether the points of view from which the subjects treated of were surveyed, whether the grounds of my reasoning were such, as they had heard or read elsewhere, or have since found in previous publications.[169]

At last the long digressive chapter ends, but the reader with an especially retentive memory who confidently expects the following one to take up the "nature and genesis of the imagination," which had been promised forty-five pages before, will again be disappointed, for now we have still another digression, this time addressed to budding authors and studded with advice and admonition as to how the honorable profession of letters should be conducted.

It is perhaps beyond the limits of normal human memory to recall, by the time one has reached the metaphysical disquisition in Chapter XII, that some sixty pages earlier Coleridge had made a vague, general acknowledgment of a hypothetical nature to a German philosopher named Schelling, a statement among many other announcements of intellectual obligations. An hour, a day, a week, or even longer may have passed between the reading of the two chapters. The reader has no way of knowing that, after a short preface, Chapter XII becomes almost pure Schelling. One would imagine that *this* was the place to make his obligations to Schelling known, however much there may have been a "genial coincidence" in ideas. All this was pointed out almost thirty years ago by Joseph Warren Beach:

how disingenuous his [Coleridge's] excuse, that he cannot at all times make with truth specific references to his original. Could he not, at least, in the course of a dozen or twenty close-printed pages, *all* derived from Schelling, and most of it a literal translation—could he not once state that, in this chapter, he has been making copious use of such and such works? . . . Instead of that, Coleridge here throws dust in our eyes with references to Plotinus, to Plato, to Pythagoras, and above all to his own visionary Logosophia. He uses the first person singular, in obvious reference to himself, where he is translating the very pronoun from Schelling. He sets forth his tremendous ten theses, all taken from Schelling, with the solemnity of Luther nailing his theses to the church door.

And then, having breathlessly unloaded tons of ill-digested metaphysics, all for the sake of "the deduction of the imagination," he suddenly breaks off without making that deduction—as if he realized that, after all, he had little to say on the subject. Instead, he offers a letter from an imaginary correspondent urging him not to go on with the subject, since it is so much over the heads of his readers. This imaginary correspondent addresses to Coleridge remarks about "your chapter on the Imagination," "your opinions and methods of argument," "the necessity *you* have been under to omit many of the links." There is not the faintest suggestion that these opinions and methods of argument are anyone's but Coleridge's.[170]

This stern (and uncharacteristic) judgment may be better understood if one analyzes the actual structure of Chapters XII and XIII of the *Biographia*. Though there has already been a grand build-up to the metaphysical disquisition about to commence, Coleridge opens the chapter with "requests and premonitions concerning the perusal or omission of the chapter that follows."[171] He asks that the reader "either pass over the following chapter altogether, or read the whole connectedly. The fairest part of the most beautiful body will appear deformed and monstrous, if dissevered from its place in the organic Whole."[172] This last sentence is most curious in that Coleridge actually composed his "own" disquisition, for the most part, by interspersing passages from two of Schelling's early works,[173] passages certainly "dissevered" from their place in the "organic Whole."

"But it is time to tell the truth," he states, drawing still closer to the disquisition.[174] Yet almost at once there is still another unfulfilled promise. This deals with the inadequacies of dictionaries: "What these are, me saltem judice, will be stated at full in THE FRIEND, re-published and completed."[175] This digression is not entirely irrelevant, for Coleridge's footnote on the subject, dealing in part with a Greek lexicon by Gilbert Wakefield, introduces this now-familiar declaration: "I was not a little gratified at finding, that Mr. Wakefield had proposed to himself nearly the same plan for a Greek and English Dictionary, which I had formed, and began to execute, now ten years ago."[176] The unwary reader may easily conclude that "genial coincidence" in the republic of letters is an everyday occurrence.

We now come upon a lengthy paragraph which describes human beings incapable of grasping philosophical ideas. Coleridge concludes: "To remain intelligible to such a mind, exclaims Schelling on a like occasion, is honor and a good name before God and man."[177] J. C. Ferrier's original comments on this passage may be allowed to stand here: "Exclaims Schelling on a *like* occasion!—why, this is the *very* occasion upon which Schelling utters that exclamation—the whole passage (with the slight exceptions mentioned) being a *verbatim* translation from him!"[178]

Coleridge's use of Schelling *en bloc* begins on page 171 of the first volume of Shawcross' edition and continues to the middle of page 173. This passage is taken from Schelling's *Abhandlungen zur Erläuterung des Idealismus der Wissenschaftslehre* (1796-97) [*Essays in Explanation of the Idealism of the Doctrine of Science*] with, as Sara Coleridge wrote, "only a few words here and there being added or altered by Mr. Coleridge." After an interlude of some twenty lines of his own, the Schelling transcription begins again, this time *en bloc* from the first four pages of the *System des transcendentalen Idealismus.*[179]

> It must be admitted [Ferrier wrote] that at the beginning of this extract Coleridge introduces the parenthesis ("see Schell, Abhandl, zur Erläuter. des Id. der Wissenschaftslehre.") But would not a reader naturally deduce, from this reference, merely the inference that Coleridge was here referring to Schelling in support of *his own* views, and not literally translating and appropriating the German's? Besides, if the reader had written to the Continent for this work, under the title here given to it, it is next to impossible that he could ever have procured it. For this title denotes a tract buried among a good many others in Schelling's *Phil. Schrift.*, which is the name that ought to have been given to the work referred to, if the reader was to derive any benefit from the information, or was to be put in the way of consulting the original source.[180]

It is difficult to speculate with confidence as to Coleridge's motives in providing this obscure reference. Needless to say, the reference itself has been seized upon to demonstrate that Coleridge's failure to acknowledge Schelling was not complete, but rather a matter of degree. This result itself suggests that the parenthetical and murky reference (which no one seems to have followed up for some twenty years) was intended precisely to blunt possible charges of plagiarism.

It is unnecessary to continue with a point-by-point citation of Coleridge's use of Schelling. The interested reader may trace Coleridge's obligations by carefully following the notes in Sara Coleridge's edition, which also contains several useful translations from Schelling.

A crucially important point overlooked by scholars is that after the statement about the "mechanism of the heavenly motions," Schelling proceeds, in Sara Coleridge's translation:

> The perfected theory of nature would be that, in virtue of which all nature should resolve itself into an intelligence. *The dead and unconscious products of Nature are only abortive attempts of Nature to reflect herself; but the so named DEAD nature in general is an unripe intelligence; thence through her PHENOMENA, even while yet unconscious, the intelligent character discovers itself.*[181]

Coleridge, immediately after "mechanism of the heavenly motions" proceeds:

> The theory of natural philosophy would then be completed, when all nature was demonstrated to be identical in essence with that, which in its highest known power exists in man as intelligence and self-consciousness;

when the heavens and the earth shall declare not only the power of their maker, but the glory and the presence of their God, even as he appeared to the great prophet during the vision of the mount in the skirts of his divinity.[182]

It can readily be seen that the first sentence in Schelling above is paraphrased down to the semicolon in Coleridge, after which there is a pious expansion not found in the German writer. The italicized sentence in Schelling is *omitted* by Coleridge. Next to this sentence in his copy of the *Transcendental Idealism* Coleridge wrote: "True or false, this position is too early. Nothing precedent has explained, much less proved it true."[183]

This damaging fact is silently passed over by both Sara Coleridge and Shawcross, but does not the existence of the marginal note prove that Coleridge was copying directly from Schelling's book, and not from notes made years before which he may then have later thought his own?

After his one-sentence interpolation, he continues mixing paragraphs from Schelling's *Transcendental Idealism* and *Abhandlungen* for almost four pages in the Shawcross edition. This joiner's work is interrupted by an anecdotal passage and then an impressive assertion: "In the third treatise of my *Logosophia*, announced at the end of this volume, I shall give (deo volente) the demonstrations and constructions of the Dynamic Philosophy scientifically arranged. It is, according to my conviction, no other than the system of Pythagoras and of Plato revived and purified from impure mixtures. Doctrina per tot manus tradita tandem in VAPPAM desiit."[184]

The "Logosophia," however, was not announced at the end of the volume, nor did Coleridge ever complete such a work, though he referred to it regularly during the remaining eighteen years of his life. The learned Latin quotation ("A doctrine passed down through so many hands ends as flat wine"), it is worth observing, was employed by Schelling in connection with Leibnitz.[185]

After almost interminable delays, warnings, parentheses, and misgivings, Coleridge at last comes to his "Ten Theses." The first six give the substance, and sometimes the actual language, of ideas in Schelling's *Transcendental Idealism*. (The fifth thesis is interrupted with another impressive reference, this time to "the critique on Spinozism in the fifth treatise of my Logosophia.") As for the remaining four theses, the substance of the seventh and eighth may be found variatim in three pages of Schelling's *Abhandlungen*; Theses IX and X again come from the *Transcendental Idealism*, with many sentences taken over verbatim.[186]

A few sentences after the tenth thesis there is a long quotation from Kant, and Coleridge meticulously provides not only the title of the work but even the year of publication. Immediately following, however, is a paragraph silently reworked from Schelling's *Abhandlungen*.[187] Coleridge continues to use Schelling without acknowledgment, but scrupulously identifies a Latin quotation taken from Bacon's *Novum Organum*. The chapter ends with a quotation, preceded by the words, "I will conclude with the words of Bishop Jeremy Taylor." The source is duly cited.[188]

Chapter XIII commences with three more quotations: (1) from *Paradise Lost*, (2) a quotation in Latin from Leibnitz, including volume and page numbers, and (3) a Greek quotation from the third Hymn of Synesius, including even a line reference. But the chapter itself commences with a paragraph freely translated from the *Transcendental Idealism*, which the reader may perhaps again be reminded Coleridge admitted owning while writing the *Biographia*. Again the ideas are put forward as exclusively his own.

Is it possible to believe that the edifice of citations surrounding plagiarized passages is not deliberately contrived?

Chapter XIII, confidently announced as being "On the imagination, or esemplastic power,"[189] proceeds to a brief discussion of Kant, which includes echoes from Schelling,[190] and then, just as we are deep in metaphysical matters, a row of asterisks abruptly terminates the formidable disquisition over which we have been laboring. Coleridge now intrepidly informs the reader: "Thus far had the work been transcribed for the press, when I received the following letter from a friend," and it is this letter which dissuades him from continuing with the subject, for the reason that it is too difficult for his readers![191]

Did Coleridge really expect his readers to believe that the letter indeed came from a friend, and that the work had actually been transcribed thus far for the press? Could not the preceding chapters, which it is now admitted do not get anywhere, at least so far as the oft-promised "deduction of the imagination" is concerned, have been expunged from the work?

It really makes little difference whether the "judicious" letter came from a friend or was written by Coleridge. But certainty provides further insight into the character of his literary ethics. Coleridge was himself the author, for in a letter to his publisher written in 1817 he referred to "that letter addressed to myself as from a friend, at the close of the first volume of the Literary Life, which was written without taking my pen off the paper. . . ."[192]

Since the origin of the letter is certain, it is easier to judge Coleridge's motives. Beach notes with his usual penetration that the letter waxes eloquent on the exceeding complexity of the preceding disquisition. The "friend" pointedly refers to "your opinions and method of argument," "your premises," "your conclusions . . . [which] you have so ingeniously evolved."[193] That most scholars still maintain that Coleridge had no deliberate wish to deny his intellectual obligations to Schelling is surely one of the marvels of literary history.

And then, immediately after all this, Coleridge penned one of the most-quoted pages in the literature of criticism, the celebrated distinction between imagination and fancy. It is presented as the "main result" of the foregoing disquisition, the details of which are "reserved for a future publication, a detailed prospectus of which the reader will find at the close of the second volume." And immediately after the two paragraphs on imagination and fancy, we are directed to "the critical essay on the uses of the Supernatural in poetry, and the principles that regulate its introduction: which the reader will find prefixed to the poem of THE ANCIENT MARINER."[194] With these promises—never to be fulfilled—the first book of *Biographia Literaria* comes to an end.

In the second volume, almost at once, something akin to a miraculous recovery takes place. It is as if, released from the viscous integument of metaphysics, he was free to beat his wings and take flight. The task which by intelligence, talent, training, and chance he was uniquely fitted to perform— the analysis of the poetry of his longtime friend and co-worker William Wordsworth, and the critical principles underpinning the poetic revolution that had taken place in the previous generation—this welcome task lay fresh and shining straight ahead. Like a man stumbling in the dust of a trackless desert, parched and expiring, he now sees the green oasis of those few glorious years of his youth looming before him. The famous fourteenth chapter of the *Biographia*, which opens the second volume, begins by recalling the background of *Lyrical Ballads*, one of the revolutionary volumes of poetry in English history. And with this discussion begins by far the best of Coleridge's prose works.

His main ideas as a critic both here and elsewhere are best dealt with comprehensively in a separate discussion. But it is imperative to notice that the issues that comprise by far the greatest part of the second volume of the *Biographia*—the distinguishing features of poetry, the nature of poetic diction, the characteristic virtues and defects of Wordsworth's poetry—these were controversies that had been regularly discussed for some fifteen years. The specific historical context of the *Biographia* has, for the overwhelming majority of its readers for the past century, simply vanished into the misty recesses of the past. A very great deal of what Coleridge had to say would not have appeared to his readers as particularly novel, and certainly not startling. Though Wordsworth's poems were, in 1815, by no means widely treasured among English readers, they were to perhaps all the important poets then flourishing, or to come into their own in the next decade (Byron, Keats, Shelley), the dominant force in nineteenth-century English poetry. Coleridge was reviving controversies which had raged more than a decade before, when the "Lake School" was under regular attack by such powerful molders of public taste as Francis Jeffrey of the *Edinburgh Review*.

Between the two volumes of the *Biographia* there is an almost complete break in philosophical continuity. Whatever the value of the literary criticism in the second part, it ought to be impossible to argue (in view of Coleridge's own termination of the discussion that was to elucidate the nature of the imagination and to provide a philosophical basis for criticism of the arts) that the force of his remarks on the nature of poetry in general and Wordsworth's in particular are of particular worth because of the philosophical foundation supporting them.

As an autobiography, the book almost ceases to exist after its fourteenth chapter. It is a curious fact that although Coleridge has much to say about his reading in philosophy, and the development of his philosophical intelligence, he has comparatively little to disclose about his development as a poet. In the very early chapters appear the often-quoted passages about the extraordinary instruction he received at Christ's Hospital from the Reverend James Boyer, and the influence of William Lisle Bowles on his youthful poetic consciousness. But we will search the whole of the two volumes through without finding much more than this. In the famous fourteenth chapter, of course, we are told how he and Wordsworth became neighbors, discussed the nature of poetry together, decided to publish a volume jointly to put their ideas before the public, and how he undertook, in such works as "The Ancient Mariner" and "Christabel," to familiarize the wonderful.

But we are told literally almost nothing about the many poems he wrote before becoming Wordsworth's neighbor, and though there is much detailed analysis of his great friend's poems he does not perform the same task for any of his own. Perhaps this was mere modesty. In any case it is a great loss. A detailed analysis of any of his own important poems, and especially of the great fragments "Kubla Khan" and "Christabel," would have been of incalculable value to later readers and critics. In fact, his remarks on those poems in other contexts have proven maddeningly contradictory and confusing.

Astonishingly, almost the only point about his aesthetic history that emerges with any clarity from *Biographia Literaria* is that his thinking about the nature of poetry began very early. It is from the evidence in this work that I. A. Richards confidently asserts that Coleridge, "from his fourteenth year, [had been] thinking about poetry with an assiduity and enterprise that cannot be matched in the biography of another critic."[195] How reliable Coleridge's reports of his youthful aesthetic meditations are, both in his reports of Boyer's instruction, and especially in his account of the genesis of *Lyrical Ballads* and the nature of his own poetic credo at the time he and Wordsworth became neighbors—matters which have rarely if ever been questioned in the form here proposed—these and other issues of crucial importance not only to Coleridge's autobiography but to English literary history must be dealt with later. From several points of view the necessity to truncate discussion of *Biographia Literaria* as a whole is regrettable. But a work so diffuse in itself is the occasion of a certain degree of formlessness in others. The attempt to achieve a comprehensive understanding of the *Biographia,* as is true of so many of Coleridge's other important works, can be the occasion for a full-scale biography and general intellectual history of his times.

11.

The Philosophical Lectures

IN 1818 and 1819 Coleridge delivered a series of fourteen lectures on the history of philosophy. Miss Kathleen Coburn first published the text of these lectures in 1949.[1] The editorial problems were formidable and brilliantly met; the work had to be pieced together for the most part from direct notes taken at the lectures by a professional shorthand writer, from Coleridge's one hundred twenty-three pages of lecture notes in one of his notebooks,[2] and from his copious marginalia on Wilhelm Gottlieb Tennemann's *Geschichte der Philosophie*. Tennemann's history, in twelve volumes, was published at Leipzig from 1798 to 1817.[3]

Coleridge provided his auditors with a *Chronological and Historical Assistant*, a work of some ten double-column pages which divides into three periods the area of philosophy under review, beginning with Thales and ending with philosophy during the reign of Justinian. The *Assistant* supplies a long series of dates (from 629 B.C. to 529 A.D.) in a column next to the names of the many philosophers. The parallel columns give concentrated information about the philosophers along with contemporary historical events. It is a detailed and systematic piece of work, and though it might readily be done by any diligent student of philosophy and history, it indicates rather more meticulous preparation and organization of materials than we are accustomed to associate with Coleridge.

It turns out, however, that the *Assistant* "is a translation, edited and added to, of Tennemann's historical tables."[4] In an article published some fifteen years before her edition of the *Philosophical Lectures*, Miss Coburn provided some parallel passages which are germane in this connection.[5] In the first volume of Tennemann, next to the date 608, the text reads, "Pythagoras geboren nach Larcher," and next to the date 584, the text reads, "Pythagoras geboren nach Meiners." In Coleridge's *Assistant*, beside the date 584, we find: "Pythagoras born, according to Meiners and others writers; but Larcher throws back the date of his birth to A.C. 608." Miss Coburn observes matter-of-factly: "Here Coleridge cites authorities. When Tennemann does not, neither does Coleridge." One further example may be useful. Tennemann writes next to the date 399: "Die Sokratiker begeben sich nach Megara." Coleridge, next to the same date, writes: "The disciples of Socrates betake themselves to Megara."[6] The translation here is, if anything, too literal. *Begeben sich* certainly suggested "betake themselves" rather than the more idiomatic "go."[7]

Miss Coburn informs us that the notebook Coleridge used in preparing the lectures mentions Tennemann several times, "and in the lectures Coleridge often makes use of him for dates and references." However, she finds, "plagiarism is not in the question" because Coleridge "was in fundamental disagreement very often" with Tennemann, because he was not "content in small details with Tennemann's inferences, but followed up footnote references for himself," and because "he often mixed with Tennemann's dry indigestible mass of documentation, lubricants from a deep uniquely Coleridgian well of information and insight."[8]

From Miss Coburn's own notes, however, it is possible to draw quite different inferences as to the extent of Coleridge's debt to Tennemann. Thus:

Tennemann, I, 87, gives the information in this sentence, except for the mariners. They are Coleridgian.[9]

Tennemann, I, 88, holds the same view and mentions the same names.[10]

Coleridge's presentation of Pythagorean cosmology is the same as Tennemann's.[11]

From here to the end of the next paragraph the facts come from Tennemann, I, 150-3.[12]

In his account of the Socratic daemon Coleridge is following Tennemann fairly closely. . . .[13]

Tennemann, II, 190 foll. provides the biographical facts.[14]

Tennemann, II, 197, f.n., gives the reference to Horace. . . .[15]

Tennemann, II, 197, f.n., gives a summary of Plato's words in the *Timaeus* . . . from which Coleridge has selected some phrases.[16]

Following Tennemann, III, 4 and f.n. . . . In fact the discussion of Plato's pupils that follows is largely based on Tennemann, III, 1-17.[17]

The facts of Aristotle's life here and on pp. 182-8 come largely from Tennemann, III, 21 foll.[18]

The names given in the lecture may or may not have been those in Coleridge's notes which, except for the insertion of Philon and the omission of Stilpo's son, follow Tennemann, I, 137. Tennemann was also used for the dates, the reference to Timon and the quotation of his words.[19]

Tennemann, II, 166-7, gives the substances of this sentence and the next one on Pyrrho.[20]

The discussion of the reputed atheism of Theodorus and his school follows Tennemann, II, 126-128.[21]

The sentences on Hegesias that follow are based on Tennemann, II, 128-9.[22]

The details of the biography of Epicurus are those given by Tennemann, III, 348 foll.[23]

Zeno. The biographical details and the account of the Stoics, are based closely on Tennemann, IV, 4-94.[24]

Apollonius of Tyana. . . . Coleridge is following Tennemann, V, 199-208.[25]

For these and other biographical data concerning J. Scotus Erigena, Coleridge is following Tennemann, VIII, 66 foll.[26]

Anselm.... The notes follow Tennemann, VIII, 115.[27]

It would be unbearably tedious to continue this demonstration of Coleridge's liberal use of Tennemann's history. Far from borrowing solely from a mass of inert facts, Coleridge surely seems to have been heavily in debt to Tennemann for that ordering of facts and selection of learned quotations which creates the impressive air of a vast and minute scholarship.[28] And yet he did not *once* cite his obscure contemporary in his lectures as the source of either ideas or information. On the contrary, the impression created is that of entirely original composition and reflection and encyclopedic accumulation of facts. In the *Prospectus* to the lectures Coleridge has emphasized the lack of a good philosophical history:

We have, indeed, a History of Philosophy, or rather a folio volume so called, by Stanley, and Enfield's Abridgement of the massive and voluminous Brucker. But what are they? Little more, in fact, than collections of sentences and extracts, formed into separate groups under the several names, and taken (at first or second hand) from the several writings, of individual philosophers, with no *principle* of arrangement, with no *method*, and therefore without unity and without progress or completion.[29]

It is notable that there is no reference to the existence of a German history superior to those cited, which the lecturer will, in fact, use continually.

In the published text of the lectures Tennemann's name appears just four times. Each mention occurs in a context which either damns him with faint praise or roundly discredits him. Thus in Lecture III:

Now this the writers of the history of these philosophers have clearly not mastered. . . . Thus the very best writer on philosophic history we have hitherto had, Tennemann, charges Pythagoras and the great men following him with having turned into objective different things that were purely subjective; but the very contrary appears to have been the object of Pythagoras himself and of those who immediately followed him. . . .[30]

The other references to Tennemann are uniformly disparaging:

the writing of Ocellus Lucanus the authenticity of which . . . I reject, not from the arguments brought against it by Tennemann . . . but because . . .[31]

The moral philosophy of Pythagoras, which Tennemann brings forward as exhibiting the infant state of thinking, seems to me rather to prove . . .[32]

It is easy to do as Tennemann has done, contrasting it, Neoplatonism, with those doctrines, but not so easy to know precisely in what respects particularly it varied from the doctrines of Plato and in what in coincided. As far as I have been able to discover, who perhaps have spent more time than I should be willing to acknowledge in reading the works of these men . . .[33]

Tennemann was mentioned in but two of the fourteen lectures. Since the name was doubtless unknown to practically the whole audience, there is no reason to suppose that it was remembered five minutes later or in any way related otherwise to the lectures. The references to Tennemann, if anything, would dampen any curiosity an auditor might feel to read the German's works for himself.

The notebook Coleridge used in preparing notes for his lectures frequently provides absorbing glimpses into his mental processess. For example, to his audience he said:

The most extraordinary man, perhaps, of his age, and the first philosopher that arose after the suspended animation of philosophy, was Johannes Scotus ERIGENA, of whom we know nothing but that he was an English-man. A wonderful man he must have been—who had travelled, according to his own account, into Greece, into Egypt, and from Egypt to Italy and thence through France.[34]

From Notebook 25 we learn that Coleridge at this point intended to add:

upon what authority a German historian has asserted that these travels were superfluous, and that Ireland was at that time the Athens of Christendom, especially in all Greek Literature, I am ignorant and somewhat incredulous.

The "German historian" was, of course, Tennemann.[35]

It is instructive to analyze these facts. Why, in his own notebooks, did Coleridge not state Tennemann's name but refer to him as a "German historian"? The inference is irresistible: he had intended to use the passage in a forthcoming lecture but did not wish to mention Tennemann by name specifically. We may even suspect that the passage was dropped because Coleridge may have cautiously considered that Tennemann was perhaps right, in which case his own uncharacteristic admission of ignorance and incredulity would be damaging to his reputation for encyclopedic knowledge. Coleridge's willingness to bring Tennemann into the discussion on a specific matter appears limited to this anxiously vague reference to a "German historian."[36]

It may perhaps be urged that while it was not entirely proper for Coleridge to have used Tennemann's facts thus freely without any acknowledgment, yet no more serious obligations of Coleridge to Tennemann may be entertained. Such a view is at least debatable, for it is often impossible to distinguish the simple use of facts from the deductions and inferences which often follow. For example, Coleridge expatiates upon

the ambiguity of Socrates's own doctrine, which split itself in his immediate followers into the Cynic sect under Antisthenes and the Cyrenaic or voluptuary sect under Aristippus. . . . Aristippus himself was not properly the founder of the school. He was a courtier, a man of fashion, a philosopher of the world, but his grandson Aristippus became, strictly speaking, a Master of Philosophy and the founder of a particular school. After him came Theodore, surnamed the Atheist, Hegesias, and Anniceris. And the tenets common to them all seem to be these: they all alike divided the movements of the mind into pain and pleasure, between which stood the stages of indifference; these movements, pain or pleasure, originate all in the body; they admitted however certain agreeable and disagreeable emotions—some of them at least did—that had their ground in the soul, such as the love of our country. But then what they gave with one hand they took away with the other, for they declared those emotions to be so faint and ineffective in themselves that unless they were accidentally associated by some bodily feeling they would have no weight and scarcely arrive at consciousness.[37]

Miss Coburn writes that "On Aristippus Coleridge follows Tennemann, II, 104, and also on his successors, Tennemann, II, 105-112."[38] Now many of these "facts" cannot be distinguished from ideas and interpretations. A comparison of what Coleridge actually said in the lectures with what Tennemann wrote demonstrates that Coleridge's debt is not limited to mere "facts," as, say, when a mathematician uses tables of logarithms and handbooks of formulae to produce original work. Similarly, in Lecture IV Coleridge discoursed learnedly as follows:

In the same spirit he [Plato] formed his intimate friendships with Archytas and Timaeus the Locrian. Both were and continued to be Pythagorean and both men of high rank and estimation in their country. The fame of Archytas as a mathematician we learn from Horace, and Plato himself speaks of Timaeus as a man of the profoundest philosophical insight and as the most distinguished in his native state for rank, property, and the magistracies he had borne. It is worth notice, too, that Plato brought back certain writings of the Scholars of Pythagoras with which Aristotle enriched his library. I mention these facts because I may as well say, if I were to give my conception of Plato's character, as far as any great man's character can be conceived of comparatively, I should say that . . .[39]

The whole of this passage, except for the last sentence, is pieced together from pages 197-198 of the second volume of Tennemann's history.[40] Was it not possible at least once to preface his remarks with, "according to Tennemann"? Is it just to speak of the "fame of Archytas . . . we learn from Horace," when in fact Tennemann gives the source in Horace? Further, when Coleridge mentions what Plato says of Timaeus he is actually selecting from certain phrases of Plato which Tennemann gives. This furtive appropriation of learning, which we have met repeatedly before in connection with Maass, is rampant throughout the *Philosophical Lectures*.

Miss Coburn's presentation of the evidence seems on occasion somewhat odd. Coleridge says, for example: "Each man's appeal is to his own incommunicable peculiarity of feeling. I have Cicero for my authority who says: *Praeter permotiones intimas nihil putant judicii.* . . ."[41] Miss Coburn points out that the "Loeb ed. gives *judici,*" and that "Tennemann . . . gives Coleridge's reading.[42] But is it certain that Coleridge made an independent reading at all? Is it not more reasonable to say that he gives Tennemann's reading of *judicii*, and not *vice versa*? It is also curious that when quoting Tennemann's quotation of Cicero he bypasses his direct source and announces, "I have Cicero for my authority." Is it possible to avoid the conclusion that he deliberately avoided mentioning Tennemann?

Yet Coleridge's debt to Tennemann may prove to have been the most easily handled of all the source problems posed by Miss Coburn's brilliant restoration of a very badly preserved text. What of Coleridge's debt to Kant, which we should surely expect to find in these lectures? It seems the process of identification has scarcely begun. For example, his confident statement about Aristotle in the fifth lecture: ". . . I will venture to challenge any scholars acquainted with the subject to show me, from the time of Lord Bacon to the present day, any one opinion not in itself too absurd for an Aristotle to have conceived, any one opinion upon which they themselves pride themselves, which is not to be found in Aristotle, with all the arguments which they have brought forward for it more ably and more systematically presented than it has ever been since that time," restates in an inappropriate context Kant's tribute to Aristotle's *Logic*: "since Aristotle it [the study of logic] has not required to retrace a single step. . . . It is remarkable also that to the present day this logic has not been able to advance a single step, and is thus to all appearance a closed and completed body of doctrine."[43] All this is merely a variant of a passage, as has been noted earlier in *Biographia*, where Coleridge asserts that with respect to the associative principle, Aristotle's enunciation of it was such that where "later writers have either deviated from, or added to his doctrines, they appear to me to have introduced either error or groundless supposition."[44] Many substantial passages from Schelling, especially in Lecture XII, which had already been used without acknowledgment in the *Biographia*, reappear in the *Philosophical Lectures*.[45]

One of the most widely quoted of Coleridge's philosophical statements is that all men are born either Aristotelians or Platonists. It was not Coleridge, however, who originated this catchy distinction, but Goethe. While delivering his *Philosophical Lectures*, Coleridge wrote J. H. Green urgently to borrow his copy of Goethe's *Farbenlehre* so that he could reread a passage in which Goethe "compares Plato with Aristotle, &, as far as I recollect, in a spirited manner."[46] Miss Coburn discusses this borrowing in detail, asserting that Coleridge "carried the distinction much further and to deeper levels than Goethe; he gave it philosophical content."[47] Goethe had argued that Plato and Aristotle "were the first to build up anything like real systems of thought," and that men had subsequently recognized "one or the other as Master, Teacher, Leader." Goethe noted specifically that this division could be found in the treatment of the Scriptures by commentators, in the transmission of knowledge; "in fact," in Miss Coburn's summary, "the centuries may often be characterized as dominantly Platonic or dominantly Aristotelean." Miss Coburn finds that "the development of his idea is casual, limited compared with Coleridge's"; as an example we find Coleridge's statement in the *Stateman's Manual* (1816), Appendix E: "Whether ideas are regulative only, according to Aristotle and Kant, or likewise Constitutive, and one with the power and Life of Nature according to Plato and Plotinus . . . is the highest *problem* of Philosophy, and not part of its nomenclature."[48]

Perhaps the question of at what point an idea assumes philosophic content is too subjective to be worth debate, but it may surely be argued that the division of the world's thinkers into Platonists or Aristotelians derives explicity from Goethe, and that Coleridge's application of this distinction in a variety of contexts, as for example in comparing Kant and Plotinus, remains application and not necessarily the transformation of a fundamental insight which, whatever its value, any honest history of ideas must necessarily assign to Goethe. In any case, the many commentators who regularly quote Coleridge as having divided the world into Platonists and Aristotelians do not appear to be thinking of distinctions between regulative and constitutive ideas, but rather between minds tending toward the abstract or concrete.[49]

Though we do not ordinarily view statements made in a public lecture as requiring anything like the specific citation that is mandatory in printed material, it is irresponsible to assert that no statement as to where ideas are coming from is in order. Intellectual integrity is not based on fussy details of citation but on a fundamental respect for the labors of others. What would we think, say, if a lecturer held forth knowledgeably on the minutiae of recent Russian science, without mentioning that most of his facts had come from a publication unknown to the audience? Further, would we not be inclined to judge very harshly if the same lecturer borrowed numerous interpretations of the facts, still from the same source? We would doubtless, and quite properly, feel that the man was attempting to dazzle us with his intellect. And if he refused to make any acknowledgments at all, even in a public lecture—did, in fact, sedulously *avoid* references when there were many opportunities to give them, and had in his own possession many notes in which the references existed, none given at the lecture—we would perhaps grow suspicious of everything the lecturer had said which purported to be original.

As a commentary on Coleridge's practice in the *Philosophical Lectures*, it is perhaps worth quoting again two brief passages from the *Biographia Literaria*, published less than two years before:

No one has charged me with tricking out in other words the thoughts of others, or with hashing up anew the crambe jam decies cocta of English literature or philosophy.

I should dare appeal to the numerous and respectable audiences, which at different times and in different places honored my lecture-rooms with their attendance, whether the points of view from which the subjects treated of were surveyed, whether the grounds of my reasoning were such, as they had heard or read elsewhere, or have since found in previous publications.[50]

Might not a harsh judge find in these words the hollow self-flattery of an uneasy conscience?

Like almost all Coleridge's prose works after *Biographia Literaria*, the *Philosophical Lectures* can scarcely be said to exist for any general audience. Whatever Coleridge may have added by voice and gesture in addressing the fashionable ladies and gentlemen who attended, these lectures on the page are dull, repetitious, diffuse, and flaccid.

As a survey of the history of philosophy and especially from what we know to have been Coleridge's own dominant philosophical interests, the most astonishing failure of the lectures is the gaping void where discussion of the German school of philosophy should be. Coleridge's abrupt and brutal dismissal of Schelling is shocking not only because of what had been promised in *Biographia Literaria*, but because we know how immense an influence Schelling had been. Professor Coburn, it will be remembered, suspected a lack of candor here, a suspicion that Coleridge was holding something back from the audience. This view, however, implies a certain degree of deception in one so often described as without guile and utterly open-hearted. Professor Bate provides another explanation of Coleridge's failure to discuss the Germans:

> on the whole, the *Philosophical Lectures* mark a decisive turn in the chronology of his thought. For here we are encountering a psychological block so complete, a censorship so strong, that at the moment he finds himself incapable even of summarizing the premises, aims, interests, of a form of thinking that for years had excited (and yet deeply disturbed) him more than any other. How could he start to explain these writers— to interpret what they meant and did—without surrendering to the overwhelming impulse to side with them, to say all that he could so easily begin to say about the "organic" and "dynamic" philosophy? But he was not yet ready. Better, in these lectures, this prefatory exercise to stay clear of the matter. He could so easily say the wrong thing. Given only another year or two, he would get his bearings.[51]

The source of this alleged profound psychological block is held to be religious; Coleridge was supposedly torn between his deep emotional commitment to the Anglican church and his intellectual attraction to the heterodox doctrines of German metaphysics. This useful explanation may also serve to account for other lacunae and inconsistencies in Coleridge's works which might otherwise be inexplicable or even embarrassing.

But a plainer account is possible, no less probable for being closer to home; namely, that Coleridge was hardly anxious to acquaint his auditors with the works of those Germans whose ideas, whose very words, he had been adopting in print, in his lectures (including the series he was then giving), and in his conversation. We have already seen that he discouraged his own disciple J. H. Green from reading Schelling.

The whole thorny subject of Coleridge's philosophical development obviously cries out for a full-length treatment by a professional philosopher with a thorough grasp of the Coleridge canon and above all of his biography. Too much of what has been written on Coleridge as a philosopher is utterly uncritical. Again and again the recollections of late years take precedence over the contemporary record.

In the second of Charles Lamb's two essays on Christ's Hospital appears this memorable description of its most famous student:

> Come back into memory, like as thou wert in the day-spring of thy fancies, with hope like a fiery column before thee—the dark pillar not yet turned—Samuel Taylor Coleridge—Logician, Metaphysician, Bard!
> —How have I seen the casual passer through the Cloisters stand still, entranced with admiration (while he weighed the disproportion between the *speech* and the *garb* of the young Mirandula), to hear thee unfold, in thy deep and sweet intonations, the mysteries of Iamblichus, or Plotinus (for even in those years thou waxedst not pale at such philosophic draughts), or reciting Homer in his Greek, or Pindar—while the walls of the old Grey Friars reechoed to the accents of the *inspired charity-boy!*[52]

The massive grandeur of Lamb's language reduces one to silence. When, at length, one recovers, and cold analysis begins, one finds much to question. Lamb was Coleridge's junior by two and a half years, and he left Christ's Hospital when he was but fifteen years old. Thus it was thirty-five years after the event that Lamb remembered hearing Coleridge discourse of Iamblichus and Plotinus and other such heady philosophic draughts. Perhaps, but it is easier to believe Coleridge's own statement in a letter to J. G. Lockhart shortly after Lamb's essay was published (in 1820) that the work had been "chiefly compiled from his [Lamb's] recollections of what he had heard from me. . . ."[53] If so, what we probably have in this famous passage is Coleridge on himself, in Lamb's inimitable accents. Let us inquire further.

Apart from Lamb's reference to Plotinus, as Richard Haven has shown, "there is no positive evidence of any further study until 1803,"[54] some fifteen to eighteen years after the events described by Lamb. In a letter to Ludwig Tieck, written in 1817, Coleridge wrote, apropos of the allegedly early development of some theories about light, that he had in his youth read "Behmen's Aurora, which I had *conjured over* at school";[55] but the evidence is overwhelmingly against this assertion, too, especially as it can be shown that Coleridge was reading Boehme in the months preceding his letter to Tieck.

In *Biographia Literaria*'s own account of his early philosophical development, Coleridge wrote:

> The early study of Plato and Plotinus, with the commentaries and the THEOLOGIA PLATONICA of the illustrious Florentine [Ficino];

of Proclus and Gemistius Pletho; and at a later period of the 'De Immenso et Innumerabili' and the *De la causa, principio de uno,'* of the philosopher of Nola [Bruno] . . . had all contributed to prepare my mind for the reception and welcoming of the 'Cogito quia sum, et sum Cogito.'. . . [56]

Haven acutely observes that

> if Coleridge was engrossed in the study of any or all of these authors before his departure for Germany [in 1798], and if he found or thought that he found suggestions of a philosophy superior to that of Hartley or Berkeley, it is strange that he was so silent about the discovery. He did not normally keep his enthusiasms to himself. But the letters of this period, apart from [one] to Thelwall . . . show not a single mention of the reading of any of these writers. He did, in 1796, ask a friend [Thelwall] to purchase for him a small volume containing selections from Iamblichus, Porphyrius, Proclus, and Plotinus, but if he received and read it, he said nothing about it. He borrowed Cudworth's *True Intellectual System* from the Bristol library twice, for three weeks in May of 1795 and for a month in November of 1796, but whatever ideas he found in it were kept a secret from his correspondents.[57] The notebooks do show a handful of Greek quotations culled from Cudworth including one from Plotinus, and the name 'Jacob Bohmen' appears without comment in a list of projected works. But this is all. And nowhere do we find mention of Pletho or of Ficino, the 'illustrious Florentine.' . . . and there is, again in the British Museum, Taylor's translation of *The Philosophical and Mathematical Commentaries of Proclus* with several notes by Coleridge clearly indicating a date between 1802 and 1812. One of these includes the remark that 'I have unfortunately never met with the original.'[58]

Of course, as Haven points out, none of this proves that Coleridge did not have an early acquaintance with any or all of the authors mentioned, but it should be sufficiently clear to all but the most stubbornly uncritical that Coleridge's own evidence as to his intellectual development is always colored, consciously or otherwise, by his *Wunderkind* compulsion.

Despite the bristling complexities and contradictions in the record of his philosophical development, and especially his relations with Germany, there are scholars—I. A. Richards is a notable example—who treat the entire problem with Olympian certainty. What Coleridge got from Kant, we are assured, he had really learned long ago from Plato and Plotinus.[59] But just how Plato and Plotinus are forerunners of Kant, and how—if they were—Coleridge saw them as such, this is left for the reader to determine. Southey, who appears to have read as much philosophy in his early years as Coleridge,[60] was obviously in a far better position to know what his close friend's and brother-in-law's thoughts were during the years under discussion (when he saw Coleridge constantly) than scholars a century and a half later groping through scraps of evidence and thickets of conflicting statements.

Southey wrote in 1808 of Coleridge's philosophical development that "Hartley was ousted by Berkeley, Berkeley by Spinoza, and Spinoza by Plato; when I last saw him Jacob Behmen had some chance of coming in. The truth is that he plays with systems, and any nonsense will serve him for a text from which he can deduce something new and surprising.[61] This contemporary evidence, possibly because of the obvious hostility in Southey's tone, is usually dismissed in favor of Coleridge's own later testimony. Thus R. L. Brett attacks those who deny the primacy of the English philosophic tradition and who

> associate Coleridge's philosophizing with German metaphysics. They
> assume that his role as a philosopher began only when he took up resi-
> dence in Germany; and for many, his achievement in philosophy is no
> more than that of introducing Kantian and post-Kantian metaphysics
> and aesthetics to his fellow countrymen upon his return. But his letters
> show how untenable this assumption is; they reveal clearly that his
> philosophy had already been formulated before he left the West Country
> for Germany in 1798.[62]

Despite this confident assertion, Coleridge's letters well past the turn of the century reveal nothing of the sort. Brett cites as evidence Coleridge's letter to his nephew John Taylor Coleridge, which was written in 1825 and has already been discussed.[63]

In general, it seems worth suggesting that the range of Coleridge's reading may have been considerably more restricted than generally assumed, not because he didn't read avidly but because there were only twenty-four hours in the day for him as well as for other human beings. One of the primary effects of Lowes's *Road to Xanadu* is not only to fix Coleridge in our minds as a library cormorant, but to mythologize him into a veritable cloud of cormorants, ranging over all the seven seas of books, with insatiable appetite.

" 'I have read almost everything,' said Coleridge, not without warrant, a year before he wrote 'The Ancient Mariner,' " Lowes repeats admiringly in the Preface of his famous book, "and he who sets out to track him through his reading leaves unread at his peril anything readable whatsoever that was extant in Coleridge's day."[64]

But nobody can have read as much as Coleridge is alleged to have. Slowly evidence is accumlating that Lowes and others have been too quick to assume reading in original and obscure volumes when the source was much nearer home.

In her commentary to the *Notebooks* Miss Coburn has shown that entries suggesting diverse reading sometimes come from a common secondary source. A note which Brandl and Lowes traced to *De oraculis Chaldaicis* actually came from Jeremy Taylor, a less recondite locus, and a quotation from Michael Psellus that Lowes too enthusiastically took as proof of far-ranging reading more probably came from Thomas Taylor's "A Collection of Chaldean Oracles," which appeared in the familiar *Monthly Magazine*. Again, it is Richard Haven who, in citing these points, sensibly observes that "such evidence suggests that Coleridge's acquaintance with complete and original works, especially during his early years, may have been less extensive than has sometimes been assumed."[65]

It would seem to follow, therefore, that that procedure is dubious which ransacks heaven and earth for sources from which the young Coleridge might conceivably have developed a philosophy something like the one he met with in Germany. For we *know* that Coleridge read, avidly read, the German school, and annotated their works, and used their ideas, their technical vocabulary, and sometimes page after page verbatim. And nowhere can one find in Coleridge's early writings a page which looks remotely like Kant or Schelling. Studies of Coleridge's philosophy are not likely to be much advanced by further insistence on the primacy of his English heritage, but rather by still more intensive study of the pervasive influence of Germany.

12.

Theory of Life and Coleridge's Writings on Science

COLERIDGE'S *Hints towards the Formation of a More Comprehensive Theory of Life* was published fourteen years after his death under the editorship of Seth B. Watson (London, 1848). An introduction by the editor spoke of Coleridge in reverential terms: "Everything that fell from the pen of that extraordinary man bore latent, as well as more obvious indications of genius, and of its inseparable concomitant—originality." The introduction concludes: "It is much to be regretted, that the estimable Author did not live to put a finishing hand to this Essay; but the part completed involves speculations of so interesting a nature, and presents such striking marks of deep and original thought, that the Editor, to whose hands it was committed, did not feel himself justified in withholding it from the judgment of the public."[1]

This essay, comprising some forty-five closely printed pages, is one of the most learned of all Coleridge's compositions. The exhibition of scientific knowledge, particularly of physics, chemistry, and biology, is breathtaking. We are confronted on almost every page with evidence that he was not only well abreast of advanced scientific thinking in practically every field, but that he had himself performed certain notable experiments in physics, chemistry, and biology, and differed sharply with some of the outstanding experimental and theoretical scientists of his time.

The essay begins with a reference to John Hunter, a leading figure in contemporary English science. Coleridge does not doubt that "the true idea of Life" existed in Hunter's mind, but he asserts that Hunter had failed to "unfold and arrange" his ideas "in distinct, clear, and communicable conceptions." He addresses himself to the task of stating Hunter's notions "with such modifications as the differences that will always exist between men who have thought independently, and each for himself, have never failed to introduce. . . ."[2] Coleridge at once asserts that all attempts "to explain the nature of Life" that have fallen within his purview fail. He will show why and then present his own theories on the subject. For some seven pages he reviews concepts and definitions of life previously held by others. All forerunners, it develops, had in one way or another failed to grasp the real nature of life.

121

Coleridge then gives his "own" definition of life: It is *"the principle of individuation,* or the power which unites a given *all* into a *whole* that is presupposed by all its parts." Life seems to inhere potentially in all matter, but becomes actual only when organized *ab intra* (from within), rather than *ab extra* (from without).[3] In support of this definition, Coleridge marshals evidence from physics, chemistry, and biology, not only such data as any up-to-date scientist might be able to provide, but, in some cases, wholly new experimental results. As his speculations unfold, we have the impression not only of an abstract theorist addressing us, but of a practical scientist who has peered long and hard into the microscope, washed the test tubes, and performed his own dissections. For example:

> The intropulsive force, that sends the ossification inward as to the centre, is reserved for a yet higher step, and this we find embodied in the class of *fishes.* Even here, however, the process still seems imperfect, and (as it were) initiatory. The skeleton has left the surface, indeed, but the bones approach to the nature of gristle. To feel the truth of this, we need only compare the most perfect bone of a fish with the thigh-bones of the mammalia, and the distinctness with which the latter manifest the co-presence of the *magnetic* power in its solid parietes, of the *electrical* in its branching arteries, and of the third greatest power, viz., the *qualitative* and interior, in its marrow.[4]

This conveys some idea of the tone in this discourse. Several pages later Coleridge reviews experiments in magnetism, and provides information about the difficulties encountered by a certain Brugmans in experimenting in this field. He cuts this discussion short with the statement, "So far Brugmans," and proceeds to describe an experiment presumably devised by himself:

> But the shortest way for any one to convince himself of this relation of the magnetic power would be, in one and the same experiment, to interpose the same piece of iron between the magnet and the compass needle first *breadthways;* and in this case it will be found that the needle, which had been previously deflected by the magnet from its natural position at one of its poles, will instantly resume the same, either wholly or nearly so—then to interpose the same piece of iron *lengthways;* in which case the position of the compass needle will be scarcely or not at all affected.[5]

Coleridge, as can be seen, is giving the reader experimental shortcuts which had apparently not been hit upon by professional scientific workers. After several further experiments of this sort, he states: "I can now, for the first time, give to my opinions that degree of intelligibility, which is requisite for their introduction as hypotheses. . . ."[6] These hypotheses concern the real nature of magnetism and electricity, previously misunderstood by scientists.

One hundred ten years after this amazing essay was written, and almost eighty years after initial publication, it was disclosed that *Theory of Life* incorporates some of Coleridge's most astounding plagiarisms. The facts in this case were initially set forth in an unpublished doctoral dissertation by the Swiss scholar Henri Nidecker.[7] Coleridge's borrowings from Schelling and his disciple Henrik Steffens, four of whose works annotated by Coleridge are in the British Museum, prove to be manifold.[8] Joseph Warren Beach, whose writings on the subject I shall quote extensively in the following pages, holds that "every leading idea of the essay, every turn in the argument, every ingenuity of metaphysical invention, is taken straight from either Steffens or Schelling!"[9] Beach continues:

But what is, if possible, more remarkable than the borrowing of ideas from these writers, is the taking over of long passages virtually, or entirely, without alteration. Thus M. Nidecker has called attention to a continuous discussion of three or four pages, detailing a series of experiments in magnetism and electricity, which are made up of a literal translation from Schelling's *Allgemeine Deduktion* [*General Deduction*]. . . . When it comes to the experiments in electricity, he makes one . . . significant change. He omits the references so carefully made by Schelling to the author, the work, and the very page, from which he takes his information.[10]

Beach then quotes a portion of one of Coleridge's more impressive experiments in *Theory of Life*:

That electricity, on the other hand, does not act in length merely, is clear, from the fact that every electric body is electric over its whole surface. But that electricity acts both in length and breadth, and *only* in length and breadth, and not in depth; in short that the (so-called) electrical fluid in an electrified body spreads over the whole surface of that body without penetrating it, or tending *ad intra*, may be proved by direct experiment. Take a cylinder of wood, and bore an indefinite number of holes in it, each of them four lines in depth and four in diameter. Electrify this cylinder, and present to its superficies a small square of gold-leaf, held to it by an insulating needle . . . and bring this square to an electrometer of great sensibility.[11]

Beach's discussion now crackles with indignation:

The reader will not care to go through the whole of this antediluvian experiment. But he can imagine its impressiveness for the ordinary reader of Coleridge's time. His vagueness in the matter of sources, where Schelling was precise, contributes to this impressiveness. In effect the experiment is presented not as one which has been devised by some historical investigator, but Coleridge seems to recommend it as if from his own laboratory experience. This is well calculated to impress the reader with the extraordinary learning, even in laboratory science, of the philosopher-poet; and the same effect is produced by Coleridge's complete failure to mention that *all* the scientific information here conveyed is from the same source, in Schelling—rather than collected from many sources by the widely-read scholar—his failure, indeed, ever to mention the name of Schelling in connection with the entire theory of which he was the originator.[12]

That electricity was a fluid which operated solely on the surface of objects seemed to early physicists a valid conclusion from the data yielded by experiments with the comparatively weak charges of static electricity. Later developments with respect to electrical *currents,* of course, revolutionized the whole subject. It was all too typical of the *Naturphilosophen* in general, and Coleridge in particular, to announce with amazing confidence fundamental theories embracing such phenomena as electricity and gravity (to which an Einstein devoted a lifetime), and for such theories to be based on woefully inadequate experimental data.

In Schelling the process of theory-spinning without regard to observable fact is nowhere more evident than in science. A passage from *On Human Freedom* fairly demonstrates the characteristic flavor of the *Naturphilosophen:*

Gravitation precedes light as its eternally dark basis which is itself not *actual* and flees into the night when light (which truly exists)[13] appears. Even light does not completely break the seal by which gravity is held. For this very reason gravity is neither the pure essence nor even the actual being of absolute identity, but it is only a consequence of its nature; or else it is this identity when regarded in a specific degree. For that which appears as existing with respect to gravitation, itself belongs to the basis. And nature in general is therefore everything that lies beyond the absolute being of absolute identity. With regard to the precedence [of gravity over light], moreover, this is to be thought of neither as precedence in time nor as priority of essence. In the cycle whence all things come, it is no contradiction to say that that which gives birth to the one is, in its turn, produced by it. There is here no first and no last, since everything mutually implies everything else, nothing being the 'other' and yet no being being without the other. God contains himself in an inner basis of his existence, which, to this extent, precedes him as to his existence, but similarly God is prior to the basis as this basis, as such, could not be if God did not exist in actuality.[14]

And so forth.

The reader with some German can draw much nearer to Coleridge's way with sources by studying the following passage in *Theory of Life,* and then comparing it with Steffens' earlier treatment of the same subject. Coleridge writes:

Naked and helpless cometh man into the world. Such has been the complaint from eldest time; but we complain of our chief privilege, our ornament, and the connate mark of our sovereignty. . . . In Man the centripetal and individualizing tendency of all Nature is itself concentrated and individualized—he is a revelation of Nature! Henceforward, he is referred to himself, delivered up to his own charge; and he who stands the most on himself, and stands the firmest, is the truest, because the most individual, Man.

Here is the relevant passage from Steffens' *Beyträge zur innern Naturgeschichte der Erde* (1801) [*Contributions to the Inner Natural History of the Earth*]:

Nackt und hülflos, klagte man von jeher, kommt der Mensch zur Welt —und gerade dieses ist seine grösste Zierde.—Es ist die *centripetale Tendenz* der ganzen Natur, die sich in ihm offenbaren will. Von nun an ist er an *sich* gewiesen, und wer *für sich* steht, und am *festesten* steht ist die *individuellste Bildung*—der wahrhafteste *Mensch*.

Is it not then clear that Beach is justified in emphasizing that Coleridge is not merely borrowing data (which presumably can be dismissed as of small consequence), but that he is also "borrowing an appreciable part of his eloquence, of the very moral sentiments with which he adorns his high abstractions"?[15]

The absence of the names of Schelling and Steffens throughout *Theory of Life* cannot reasonably be explained away on the ground that Coleridge did not put the finishing touches to his work. Such defenses only continue to ignore or distort facts. Throughout the essay he speaks of the ideas as his own. He underlines and emphasizes the point continually. He discusses or mentions in passing Bichat, Richerand, Black, Cavendish, Priestley, Scheele, Harriott, La Forge, Descartes, Lavoisier, Abernethy, Gilbert, Dalton, Ritter, Blumenbach, Brugmans, Bernoulli, Coolomb, and others. But there is no mention of Schelling or Steffens. Careful footnotes direct us to Lawrence's lectures. In the text Coleridge quotes "an admirable remark of Joh. Babt. a Vico," and tells us that it comes from "a Tract published at Naples, 1710." The tone of the paper throughout is extremely moralistic: "I have a rational and responsible soul," he writes, and refers to "the imperative voice of my own conscience." The last sentence of the essay hails "the Soul, as the principle both of Reason and Conscience."[16]

Everything in the essay from beginning to end shows the hand of the concealor at work: the pious tone that makes the thought of even a minor literary misdemeanor unimaginable, the extraordinarily large number of names and references, and the reiteration that the ideas present are not only the author's own, but different from anything that has previously been said on the subject.

The power to transform the deceptive light of common day into the celestial radiance of ultimate reality, which to some readers is the unique gift of Coleridge in the presence of the work of Shakespeare, or Milton, or Jeremy Taylor, often seems merely ludicrous when employed in behalf of a discredited by-way in the history of science. Coleridge's reputation as a profound thinker has profited by a process in which his absurdities are either reinterpreted so as to seem insightful, or simply ignored. Instead, a few concepts like that of "individuation," or his rejection of "mechanism," are isolated from their antiquated or embarrassing contexts and exhibited for approval. But Coleridge's whole approach to natural phenomena was by way of metaphysical abstraction, and thus it was possible for him to commit himself—with all his usual passionate attachment—to the most anti-scientific movement of his day. Since his ultimate aims were theological, it is not really surprising that his "organicism" should prove not to prefigure fresh ideas in biology, but rather to represent a free-floating mysticism. Precisely like Schelling, Coleridge never grasped the basic distinction between the amateur speculator and the professional scientist whose theories must be guided and tested by direct observation and experiment. He was unaware of the elementary fact that modern science is based on a structure of quantitative relations.

How unobjective he could be when his prejudices were aroused is well exemplified in the following passage from a letter to Ludwig Tieck, written in 1817:

I am anxious to learn the specific Objections of the Mathematicians to Goethe's Farbenlehre [Theory of Colors], as far as it is an attack on *the assumptions* of Newton. To me, I confess, Newton's positions, first, of *a Ray* of Light, as a physical *synodical Individuum*, secondly, that 7 specific individua are co-existent (by what copula?) in this complex yet divisible Ray; thirdly, that the Prism is a mere mechanic Dissector of this Ray; and lastly, that Light, as the common result, is = confusion; have always, and years before I ever heard of Göthe [*sic*], appeared monstrous FICTIONS!—and in this conviction I became perfectly indifferent, as to the forms of their geometrical Picturability. The assumption of the *Thing*, Light, where I can find nothing but *visibility* under given conditions, was always a stumbling-block to me. Before my visit to Germany in September, 1798, I had adopted (probably from Behmen's Aurora, which I had *conjured over* at School) the idea, that Sound was = Light under the praepotence of Gravitation, and Color = Gravitation under the praepotence of Light; and I have never seen reason to change my faith in this respect.[17]

Very shortly Coleridge was to claim Goethe's theory of colors as his own.[18]

Any sort of rounded picture of the development of his mind with respect to science will have to take into account that his attack on "mechanism" in all realms of thought led him to reject, with scorn, most of the central tenets of modern science. Writing to Lord Liverpool in 1817 (a letter far beyond the depth of the bewildered nobleman), Coleridge declared: "the atomistic scheme, and the almost unanimous acceptance of Dalton's Theory in England, & Le Sage's in France, determine the intellectual character of the age with the force of an experimentum crucis."[19] Dalton's atomic theory was thus to him a supreme example of the intellectual poverty of science in his day.

That Coleridge the poet, critic, and theologian became so deeply involved in these abstruse matters is another instance of his compelling need to see himself as a polyhistor. No realm of intellectual activity was foreign to him. And new ideas in science were ready to hand in the fantastic speculations of Schelling and Steffens. The year 1817, which immediately followed the composition of *Theory of Life*, is especially rich in Coleridgean scientific observations. In one of his letters, after several suggestions for scientific experiment to support the propositions he is putting forth, Coleridge goes on:

> So again Color is Gravitation under the power of Light, Yellow being the positive, blue the negative Pole, and Red the culmination or Equator; while Sound on the other hand is Light under the power or paramountcy of Gravitation. Hence the analogies of Sound to Light, and the adherence of Color to Bodies, and it's affectibility by Warmth.—N. B. Tho' I have placed Oxygen as East, and Hydrogen as West [referring to a weird diagram provided earlier in the letter], as the material Symbols of Contradiction and Dilatation, I am by no means satisfied that they really are so. Oxygen is probably E by North, while Chlorine, Iodine, and probably other indecomponibles not yet discovered are E. by S. and form a series of Links from Oxygen to Azote. In like manner, I doubt not [that many Substances are either] not yet discovered, or tho' known yet confounded under the common name of Hydrogen, forming a continuous chain of *Stuffs* from Azote. . . .[20]

And so on and on. At last, after pages of ever more fantastic rhapsodies extrapolated from Schelling and Steffens, Coleridge finds it necessary to make clear to his correspondent, C. A. Tulk, a Swedenborgian and a member of Parliament, the nature of intellectual property rights.

> Accept this very rude sketch of the very rudiments of '*Heraclitus redivivus*'[21]—One little presumption of their truth is, that as Words-worth, Southey, and indeed all my intelligent Friends well know & attest, I had formed it during the study of Plato, and the Scholars of Ammonius

[that is, the early Neoplatonists], and in later times of Scotus (Joan. Erigena), Giordano Bruno, Behmen, and the much calumniated Spinoza (whose System is to mine just what a Skeleton is to a Body, fearful because it is only the *Skeleton*)[22] long before Schelling had published his first and imperfect view.[23]

The reader may be forgiven the feeling that he has read this passage before. In contexts like these it is almost a paradigm of the Coleridge manner. First, he relates the system just provided, not to the thinkers whose works he has recently had at his elbow, but to an ancient, here Heraclitus, then grandly announces that all his intelligent friends know and attest that he had formed these concepts during the reading of . . . (a long list of learned sources follow), then a claim for intellectual eminence which is breathtaking (Spinoza's system is to mine as a skeleton is to a body), and at last the assertion of priority over Schelling, whose view was in any case imperfect.

Coleridge is here answering the charges of his own conscience, for surely in a private letter there was no reason to assert intellectual priority over Schelling (a question which we may be reasonably sure never came up in this form during his own lifetime). And then, lest his correspondent think that there is an unbecoming interest in matters of priority, he asserts how pleased he was to find Schelling coming to his ideas independently. It is the genial coincidence again: "If I had met a friend & a Brother in the Desart of Arabia, I could scarcely have been more delighted than I was in finding a fellow-laborer and in the only Country in which a man dare exercise his *reason* without being thought to have lost his Wits, & be out *of his Senses*."[24]

Coleridge's attitude toward Schelling and the *Naturphilosophie*, at least so far as statements to correspondents are concerned, very rapidly went from stages of admission of coincidence of ideas, to assertions of intellectual superiority, to outright condemnation of the co-worker whom he earlier would have hailed as a brother in the desert. In September 1818 he wrote to his disciple J. H. Green (a very important letter published for the first time in 1959), that Schelling's ideas in science had in fact led him astray: "from the tendency of my mind to confidence in others I was myself *taken in* by it, retrograding from my own prior and better Lights."[25] One month later, in another letter to Tulk, Coleridge admitted only that Schelling's "revival and more extensive application of the Law of Polarity" was "extremely plausible and alluring at a first acquaintance. And as far as the attack on the mechanic and corpuscular Philosophy extends, his works possess a permanent value. But as a *System*, it is little more than Behmenism, translated from visions into Logic and a sort of commanding eloquence. . . ." Coleridge then once again falsely asserts that "Schelling is a zealous Roman-Catholic" and relates this to the deficiencies of his intellectual system, which is a "defence of the Polytheism and Charms of the Church of Rome."[26]

His scientific rhapsodies appear everywhere in his later writings, his correspondence, marginalia and table talk. The *Friend* of 1818 bristles with thorny discussion of scientific topics much in the air at the time. Coleridge's tone towards contemporary scientists is that of a professional among equals, when he is not, as he often is, attacking physicists, chemists, zoologists, biologists, and ordinary physicians for their benighted convictions. Everywhere it is evident that despite his wide reading in the experimental scientists, his interest was primarily in theory. The absolute conviction that "all true and living knowledge must proceed from within" is not conducive to patient experimentation. Like Schelling, he assumed that the only way one could learn anything from nature was to have some theory to start with. The inner nature of all science was conceived of as an abstraction like mathematics, and all the principles of nature could be discovered by the pure reason alone. The latter half of Essay 11, Section 2 of the *Friend,* provides the transcendentalist position in brief. Taken seriously, it makes a mockery of science and provides endless justification for the wildest speculation.

A formidable display of scientific learning and speculation runs not only through the *Friend*, but also through *Aids to Reflection*,[27] and in neither work is Schelling or Steffens acknowledged. On the contrary, Coleridge's claims to originality are continually urged on the reader. The following passage from the *Friend* is especially interesting:

So long back as the first appearance of Dr. Darwin's *Phytologia* [1793], I, then in earliest manhood, presumed to hazard the opinion, that the physiological botanists were hunting in a false direction, and sought for analogy where they should have looked for antithesis. I saw, or thought I saw, that the harmony between the vegetable and animal world, was not a harmony of resemblance, but of contrast; and that their relation to each other was that of corresponding opposites. They seemed to me, *whose mind had been formed by observation, unaided . . . by partial experiment,* as two streams from the same fountain indeed, but flowing the one due west, and the other direct east, and that consequently, the resemblance would be as the proximity, greatest in the first and rudimental products of vegetable and animal organization. Whereas, according to the received notion, the highest and most perfect vegetable, and lowest and rudest of animal forms, ought to have seemed the links of the two systems, which is contrary to fact. Since that time, the same idea has dawned in the minds of philosophers. . . .[28]

Thus once again we have Coleridge explicitly claiming to have hit upon certain ideas (which had become popular) by "unaided" observation and "partial experiment." But it is to his letters we must go for his most incautious account of his scientific pretensions. In March 1801, in the midst of his study of the German philosophers which yielded the "philosophical letters" to Josiah Wedgwood, Coleridge wrote to Thomas Poole, in a tone wholly remarkable for him, in that his most grandiose personal aspirations are fully described:

The interval since my last Letter has been filled up by me in the most intense Study. If I do not greatly delude myself, I have not only completely extricated the notions of Time, and Space; but have overthrown the doctrine of Association, as taught by Hartley, and with it all the irreligious metaphysics of modern Infidels—especially, the doctrine of Necessity.—This I have *done*; but I trust, that I am about to do more—namely, that I shall be able to evolve all the five senses, that is, to deduce them from *one sense* & to state their growth, & the causes of their difference—& in this evolvement to solve the process of Life & Consciousness.—I write this to you only; & I pray you, mention what I have written to no one.—At Wordsworth's advice or rather fervent intreaty I have intermitted the pursuit—the intensity of thought, & the multitude of minute experiments with Light & Figure, have made me . . . nervous & feverish. . . .[29]

We would give much to examine even a few scraps of this "multitude of minute experiments with Light & Figure," but, alas, the record of notebooks and letters is blank. It seems best, therefore, to pass over these claims as merely a bubble occasioned by the "nervous & feverish" state Coleridge describes, and not as pointing to a lamentable loss to the world of knowledge. It is most unlikely that he was in any position to carry out "minute" experiments of any kind in science. Just six weeks before, he had written to Humphry Davy of his and Wordsworth's hope to commence "fellowstudent" in chemistry. He said then that for a long time he had "wished to initiate [himself] in Chemical science," but that for the present all he could do was "Sympathize blindly" with Davy's work.[30] And yet, five years before he had written to Thelwall, while providing a lengthy and important self-portrait: "Of useful knowledge, I am a so-so chemist, & I love chemistry."[31] Nothing came of these plans to build a laboratory and such knowledge of chemistry as Coleridge had may reasonably be supposed to have been altogether secondhand. At an 1817 evening at Lamb's, Crabb Robinson reports that "Coleridge was philosophizing in his rambling way to . . . Manning, who sometimes smiled as if he thought Coleridge had no right to metaphysicise on chemistry without any knowledge on the subject. . . ."[32]

Coleridge's intellectual claims during the early months of 1801 should be approached only with the greatest caution. He seems to have been in a state of intellectual euphoria, and was uncharacteristically grandiose in his claims both as to what he had done and hoped to do. In this letter to Davy he spoke of his hopes shortly to complete a work dealing with

the affinities of the Feelings with Words & Ideas under the title of 'Concerning Poetry & the nature of the Pleasures derived from it.'—I have faith, that I do understand this subject / and I am sure, that if I write what I ought to do on it, the Work would supersede all the Books of Metaphysics hitherto written / and all the Books of Morals too.[33]

Then, as if embarrassed by the breathtaking sweep of this claim, he added: "To whom shall a young man utter *his Pride*, if not to a young man whom he loves?"[34] He wrote similarly to Poole, six weeks later, of his having extricated the notions of space and time, etc., and of the waste of his talents in writing the long-promised book of travels through Germany, a work which he said was "*beneath me*—I say, *beneath me* / for to whom should a young man utter the pride of his Heart if not to the man whom he loves more than all others?"[35]

Coleridge's pretensions to original thought in science appear early, as does the pattern of unacknowledged borrowing and obscuring of sources which becomes so prevalent in his later career. In the first edition of "The Destiny of Nations" (1796), he had a long and ingenious footnote (ironically, to the lines attacking those scientists who cheat themselves "with noisy emptiness of learned phrase") attacking Newton's conception of the aether. The whole note, however (dropped from subsequent editions), was an unacknowledged condensation from Andrew Baxter's *An Enquiry into the Immateriality of the Soul.*[36]

Also very early in Coleridge's writings appears a violent antipathy to Isaac Newton and all his works, one of the effects of which was that any challenge to or modification of Newton's ideas was quickly adopted by him as an extension of his own thought. For this reason he was ready to hail the works of a Boehme or Goethe where it cast doubt on Newton's despised *Optics*. As early as 1801 we find him writing to Thomas Poole that the "Souls of 500 Sir Isaac Newtons would go to the making up of a Shakspere or a Milton." The fierce attack on Newton in this letter, and the unguarded arrogance of his assertions relative to his own intelligence (rare in Coleridge) obviously haunted him. More than two and a half years later he recanted, and pleaded with Poole to destroy the earlier letter and the present one, for "if I were to die and it should ever see the *Light* would damn me forever, as a man mad with Presumption." He wrote again for the same purpose a few months later.[37]

Coleridge's sense of his own presumption relative to Newton was very short-lived. For the rest of his life Newton's name appears in his work almost exclusively to be attacked. As one for whom the claims of philosophy and religion took precedence over the evidence of science, and for whom the phenomena of nature were observed within the framework of a preconceived position, Coleridge found the discoveries of Humphry Davy greater than those of Newton, "more intellectual, more ennobling and impowering human Nature."[38]

It would be easy to throw together a little anthology of Coleridge's absurdities and almost medieval credulity respecting scientific matters. At the beginning of Essay IV of the *Friend,* following "the celebrated Haller," he remarks that "we are deaf while we are yawning." No doubt he had much company in so automatically accepting a false statement as fact. The difference between Coleridge and most other mortals is that he not infrequently states impossibilities with the air of a man soberly declaring that he has seen a witch ride upon a broom-stick. Shakespeare's Antony may be forgiven for thinking that a horse-hair soaked in swamp water will become a worm or serpent. Coleridge complacently states: "This is, however, so far true that a horse-hair thus treated will become the supporter of apparently one worm, tho' probably of an immense number of small slimy water-lice. The hair will twirl round a finger and sensibly compress it. *It is a common experiment with the schoolboys in Cumberland and Westmorland.*"[39]

Underlying the violence of his objection to the whole tendency of experimental science after the Renaissance was the belief, widely held, that there was no room for an active God in the formulations of the "mechanists." Since controversy between the "Mechanists" and the "Vitalists" goes on vigorously to this day, it is not hard to find in the writings of Coleridge and the *Naturphilosophen* passages which appear to provide insightful objections to mechanistic interpretations of, for example, biological phenomena. But his standpoint is essentially metaphysical, not scientific.[40]

Persistent refusal among scholars in recent years to face this general fact has led to serious misinterpretations of his writings. For example, Coleridge's use of the term "individuation" has been treated as if he had a clairvoyant grasp of biological principles and would have been sympathetic to modern evolutionary concepts. For a long time, however, it was generally taken for granted that the contrary was true, namely, that he would have been unalterably opposed to the doctrines of Charles Darwin, if for no other reason than that they would tend to undermine the authority of the Bible as literal truth. After all, Coleridge repeatedly fulminated against "the absurd notion [held by] . . . all the countless Believers—even (strange to say) among Xtians of Man's having progressed from an Ouran Outang state—so contrary to all History, to all Religion, nay to all Possibility." This seems like a clear enough statement, and since it agrees with Henrik Steffens on the subject, there would seem to be little room for doubt.

Craig W. Miller, however, finds in Coleridge's views on evolution abundant proof of his scientific genius. In *Theory of Life* Coleridge wrote that there is a "wide chasm between man and the noblest animals of the brute creation, which no perceivable or conceivable difference of organization is sufficient to overbridge." How can this be reconciled with a belief in the evolution of forms? "Coleridge," according to Miller, "solves the problem in much the same way as do the modern geneticists, who see evolution in terms of a series of unexplained mutations." And the key piece of evidence for this astonishing insight is Coleridge's statement in *Theory of Life* that nature "does not ascend as links in a suspended chain, but as the steps in a ladder." Nothing is here said about mutation, it will be noted; what we have is a metaphor groping for a distinction between kinds of progress. And this metaphor is followed in the same sentence by another: "or rather she (nature) at one and the same time ascends as by a climax, and expands as the concentric circles on the lake from the point to which the stone in its fall had given the first impulse."[42] Does this clarify the first part of the sentence? Is the phenomenon of mutation at issue here?

And yet this passage has in recent years been used to explicate Coleridge's "true" position on evolution.[43] Ignored in these revisionary studies is the fact that Coleridge's pronouncements against evolution are perfectly clear whenever the question comes up in direct form. To counteract this seeming embarrassment, a passage such as that given above is offered. But this and one or two other such passages never confront the subject of evolution directly; they are culled from discussions on other or only dimly related topics. Thus Coleridge on the ascent of nature as being not like links on a chain but like rungs on a ladder, though really just another example of his favorite distinction between difference in kind rather than degree (as between fancy and imagination, reason and understanding, and various forms of mental functioning), is interpreted by Miller as a reference to mutation (as if the nature of mutation and its potential consequence for evolutionary theory was even remotely grasped by anyone at the time). And so the central problem of man's relation to the higher primates is made to seem as solved by Coleridge in some supersophisticated way.[44]

In tracing his sources it is almost always a poor procedure to seek for remote influences when there are available those much nearer at hand, sources known to him, existing in books he owned and annotated. Nidecker has, for example, sufficiently demonstrated the source of the idea of "individuation" in Schelling and Steffens. The reader with a command of German can easily satisfy himself as to the facts by consulting the relevant texts. But the student of Coleridge who knows no German, or not enough German to trouble himself with the intricacies of Schelling's often dark and oracular prose, is baffled in any attempt to find these texts in translation. Fortunately, there is much scientific discussion in two works of Schelling which have been translated—*Of Human Freedom*, and *On University Studies*. Both books contain ample evidence that Schelling characteristically held certain concepts and attacked others that English-speaking readers tend to identify as Coleridgean formulations.[45]

That *Of Human Freedom* was fresh in Coleridge's mind just about the time *Theory of Life* was written is suggested by a passage in a letter he wrote in September 1816 to Hugh J. Rose. In a brutal attack on Hazlitt's character, Coleridge referred to him as "a melancholy instance of the awful Truth—that man cannot be on a Level with the Beasts—he must be above them or below them"; Schelling had written, "wherefore Franz Baader is right in saying that it would be desirable if the rottennness in man could only go as far as animality; but unfortunately man can only stand above or beneath animals."[46]

Though the essential facts presented in the above discussion have been available to scholars for more than a generation, Coleridge's writings on science in general, and *Theory of Life* in particular, continue to grow in importance.[47] Scholars frequently refer to the *Theory of Life* in such terms as to avoid entirely the question of plagiarism. In M. H. Abrams' *The Mirror and the Lamp*, Coleridge's interest in "physiology and natural science . . . culminate[s] with his *Theory of Life*, which incorporates various concepts from the German *Natur-Philosophen* and from the discoveries and speculations of English 'dynamic' physiologists such as Hunter, Saumarez, and Abernethy."[48] Thus Coleridge's ideas are seen as related to a group of German thinkers, rather than taken from particular works of particular men, and these seem to be equated with his vague debts to English thinkers.

In a lengthy article, "Was *Theory of Life* Coleridge's 'Opus Maximum'?", Sam G. Barnes briefly touches upon the problem of sources: "Coleridge's plagiarism—extremely heavy in *Theory of Life*—is unimportant to this paper." Having thus dispensed with Schelling and Steffens, Barnes proceeds to analyze the concepts in *Theory of Life*, whether borrowed in essence or merely as to language, as nevertheless central to Coleridge's thought. The essay is finally seen as "the microcosm of the 'Opus Maximum' he often planned but never penned."[49]

Despite the work of Nidecker, the analysis of Beach, and the authority of Wellek, who describes *Theory of Life* as "merely a mosaic of passages from Schelling and Steffens,"[50] the most recent biographer of Coleridge can dismiss the charges of wholesale plagiarism in this essay as "one of those accusations that, when once made, are repeated without examination," and go on to write of Coleridge "clairvoyantly anticipating a central premise of modern science," and in general to deal with the essay as if, except for a three-and-a-half-page experiment lifted from Schelling and some pages adapted or translated from Steffens, the German background were irrelevant.[51]

Thus, we have little reason to be anything but gloomily confident that *Theory of Life* will receive further respectful attention from critics and scholars, and that it will increasingly constitute one of Coleridge's major claims to an important position among the world's original thinkers.[52]

13.

The "Opus Maximum"

OVER the last twenty years of his life Coleridge continually referred to a vast work in progress which was to be the foundation of his enduring reputation as a thinker. As early as 1799 he wrote of his great project to Josiah Wedgwood from Germany: "I shall have bought 30 pounds worth of books (chiefly metaphysics / & with a view to the one work, to which I hope to dedicate in silence the prime of my life). . . ."[1] He was far from silent on the subject, however, as Miss Snyder's partial list of references to it abundantly makes clear.[2] Coleridge referred to this work in various ways; usually it was his "Opus Maximum," sometimes his "Logosophia."

On 27 September 1815, he wrote that the project had employed his "best thoughts & efforts for the past twelve years and more"; ten days later he wrote Daniel Stuart that he'd been "collecting the materials for the last 15 years almost incessantly." The following April he wrote that the undertaking had occupied his "best Thoughts for the last 10 years & more," but by 6 February 1817 he had devoted to the work "all the Time and Thought in my power for the last fifteen years." Just three weeks later, the "sole Motive for the wish to live" was to prepare for the press "the results of twenty five years' hard study and almost constant meditation." By June of that year the time given to the project was "20 years' incessant Thought, and at least 10 years' positive Labor," which, he asserted, formed "a compleat and perfectly original system of Logic, Natural [Philosophy] and Theology."[3]

The existence of this immense work, it will be remembered, permitted Coleridge to defer completion of the "deduction of the imagination," which had seemed so central to the stated purpose of his *Biographia Literaria.* Almost ten years later, in *Aids to Reflection* (1825), he referred to the work again as "announced for the press," where the reader could find demonstrated that conscience "is the ground and antecedent of human (or self-) consciousness, and not any modification of the latter."[4]

In view of what actually remained at his death, his specific references to the project occasionally seem to have an almost hallucinatory quality. In September 1814 he wrote to Daniel Stuart:*

---

*Here, as elsewhere, unless otherwise noted, all italics are mine.

135

My morning Hours . . . I keep sacred to my most important Work, *which is printing at Bristol*, two of my friends having taken upon themselves the risk. . . . The Title is: Christianity the one true Philosophy— or, 5 Treatises on the Logos, or communicative Intelligence, Natural, Human, and Divine."[5]

In January 1821 he wrote to Allsop of

my GREAT WORK, to the preparation of which more than twenty years of my life have been devoted . . . must finally be a revolution of all that has been called *Philosophy* or Metaphysics in England and France since the era of the commencing predominance of the mechanical system at the restoration of our second Charles, and with this the present fashionable views, not only of religion, morals, and politics, but even of the modern physics and physiology. . . . Of this work, something more than a volume has been dictated by me, so as to exist fit for the press. . . .[6]

Less than a month before his death he spoke of his work in such terms as to arouse the greatest hopes:

You may not understand my system, or any given part of it; or by a determined act of wilfulness, you may, even though perceiving a ray of light, reject it in anger and disgust; but this I will say, that if you once master it, or any part of it, you cannot hesitate to acknowledge it as the truth. You cannot be sceptical about it.

The metaphysical disquisition at the end of the first volume of the *Biographia Literaria* is unformed and immature; it contains the fragments of the truth, but it is not fully thought out. It is wonderful to myself to think how infinitely more profound my views now are, and yet how much clearer they are withal. The circle is completing; the idea is coming round to, and to be, the common sense.[7]

At Coleridge's death his many philosophical manuscripts were turned over to Joseph Henry Green, his disciple and literary executor, with a view to preparation for publication. Green, after inspecting the papers, pronounced them unfit to publish.[8] For many years they have reposed in the British Museum, still largely unpublished, despite Coleridge's enormous reputation as a thinker.

Over the years many scholars have examined the manuscripts, described them, and published excerpts. Alice D. Snyder published an extensive description of the two-volume "Logic," together with copious excerpts. "Did Green exercise a 'sound discretion' in not publishing the manuscript?" she asks. Her answer is an unqualified affirmative:

It takes only a cursory glance to make one realize what would have happened if he had published it as it now stands. The bulk of the second volume, and parts of the first, would have been condemned as plagiarized from Kant, and (by those who knew him) from Mendelssohn. A *sympathetic* and *careful* reader would have discovered enough references to both these writers to make it *fairly clear* that there was no intention of taking credit for the work of other men, *but the references do not appear where one would expect to find them, and Kant's words are used so largely that only the most painstaking reading makes clear the extent to which Coleridge was doing his own thinking, and modifying the doctrines he was expounding.*[9]

The subject might be allowed to rest here with this sad commentary on Coleridge's great hopes, but the nagging, confused, and often tiresome problem of his plagiarisms obliges us to try to understand each appearance of it. The kindly interpretation of Miss Snyder is very common. Elsewhere she has been still more sympathetic: "Coleridge's manuscript was left in such an unfinished state by his amanuenses that no inferences regarding the moot question of plagiarism can fairly be drawn from the omission of specific references to sources."[10] This caution seems excessively rigorous. Why must a reader be "sympathetic" and "careful" to determine which ideas are original and which derivative in a given text, when the author is paraphrasing, or translating extended passages verbatim? Not all readers are scholars and it has already been sufficiently noted that even scholars have been repeatedly misled into assuming ideas, sentences, and whole pages to be Coleridge's which proved to be someone else's.

According to Miss Snyder, Coleridge appears to have followed his sources so closely that "only the most painstaking reading" reveals modification of the doctrines he was expounding. She describes the mass of manuscript in the British Museum (Egerton 2825 and 2826) as "unorganized, unfocused material, much of it professing to be little more than an exposition—often a translation—of the *Critique of Pure Reason....*"[11]

However Miss Snyder may have read what the manuscript "professes" to be, in conversation, letters, and writings Coleridge made far greater claims. In the *Biographia Literaria* he referred to the "Logosophia" at various crucial points as a work well under way which would complete the discussion of difficult topics left suspended. In the closing years of his life his hints as to the contents of his "Opus Maximum" because increasingly grandiose: "My system . . . is the only attempt, I know, ever made to reduce all knowledges into harmony,"[12] here showing an inexplicable disregard for the many attempts made by earlier thinkers to achieve such a harmony. Miss Snyder further says of Coleridge's "system": "Reduced to positive, formal statement, it is relatively arid, and, moreover, justifies the query as to whether it contained anything new or even deserved to be called a philosophy."[13]

In actually describing the contents of the two-volume "Logic," she provides evidence which organizes itself into a familiar pattern. Some excerpts from her comments and notes will make this sufficiently clear:

A parenthetical discussion of the rules and laws exemplified in nature
. . . proves to be a free translation of a passage in Kant's *Logik* (1800).[14]

In the "Logic" Coleridge takes over a number of Schelling's clauses
almost *verbatim*, but varies his argument by amplification and illustrations more than in the *Biographia*.[15]

Coleridge ends the chapter with an illustration taken, without acknowledgment, from Mendelssohn's *Morgenstunden*, of the logical relations
of superior and subordinate conceptions.[16]

the intuitive imagination (illustrated by an incident taken from Kirby
and Spence's *Entomology*). . . . For the illustration from Kirby and
Spence, in which Coleridge rather characteristically shows some confusion as to what is his own experience and what is that of the scientists
he cites, see below, pp. 111-112.[17]

In these rules Coleridge follows Kant closely, and such amplifications
as he indulges in add nothing of importance.[18]

The chapter called "Judicial Logic including the Pure Aesthetic" . . . is
essentially an epitome of Kant's transcendental aesthetic as it is developed in the *Critique of Pure Reason* and the *Prolegomena*. . . . Three
short chapters on analytic and synthetic judgements . . . do little but
restate Kant, drawing on the *Critique* and the *Prolegomena* for their
material.[19]

One page later in Miss Snyder's book we find Coleridge repeating the false
charge from *Biographia Literaria* that Hume had borrowed ideas from
Aquinas "without acknowledgement."[20]
    Miss Snyder cited other debts to Moses Mendelssohn elsewhere:

it is a surprise to discover, in the section of the "Logic" entitled "The
Criterion or Dialectic," that Coleridge had drawn freely on Mendelssohn's "Morgenstunden" for illustrative material and sometimes for
comment and interpretation. Discussing the problem of answerable and
unanswerable questions, he followed closely Mendelssohn's account of
the classification of questions given in Harris's "Hermes," and Mendelssohn's comments thereon. Of the four instances of supposedly unanswerable questions that Coleridge considered, two are instances that
Mendelssohn used in the same connection, and the other two are taken
from Mendelssohn's discussion of unrelated, or only loosely related,
points. The fourth instance is noteworthy, as it occurs in varying contexts in two published works but is attributed to Mendelssohn only in
the "Logic."[21]

Returning to Miss Snyder's outline of the unpublished philosophical manuscripts, we find:

> Coleridge first gives a chapter on "Mathematical and Logical or Discursive Synthesis a priori". . . . For the main points of his exposition he relies on Kant.[22]

> A chapter entitled "Of Transcendental Logic Positively" . . . continues the preparation of the reader's mind for the discussion of the categories. It includes . . . Kant's table of the judgments and his remarks thereon, modified and amplified to some extent.[23]

> The last chapter that the manuscript contains is an exposition of the categories. Coleridge gives Kant's table. . . . he offers six remarks. . . . Remark the second compares Kant's and Aristotle's tables of categories. . . . In this Coleridge follows Kant closely. . . . Remark the third follows Kant loosely on the reasons for not going into the matter of derivative conceptions. Remark the fourth follows Kant's first "observation," but gives more in the way of detailed exposition. Remark the fifth calls attention, again following Kant, to the fact that the mathematical categories have no correlatives. Remark the sixth, on trichotomy, is developed at much greater length than the corresponding comment by Kant. . . .[24]

These excerpts make melancholy reading and provide revealing glimpses of Coleridge's procedure in his "Opus Maximum," a work about which he wrote: "I chiefly rely for the proof that I have not lived or laboured in vain"[25]; "If Originality be any merit, this work will have that at all events from the first page to the last."[26]

Coleridge's dependence on Kant as a thinker has been intensively studied by René Wellek in *Immanuel Kant in England* and by Elisabeth Winkelmann in *Coleridge und die Kantische Philosophie*.[27] Wellek, taking a much sterner view of the borrowings than Winkelmann, has written of the manuscript "Logic" that "Coleridge, while reproducing even the most mechanical features of Kant's architectonics and terminology, criticized Kant from a point of view and with arguments substantially derived from the early Schelling."[28] The long chapter on Coleridge in *Immanuel Kant in England* is perhaps the most damning examination ever put forward by an acknowledged authority in the field. Wellek describes Coleridge's "system" as not a system at all, but "here a storey from Kant, there part of a room from Schelling, there a roof from Anglican theology."[29] Beach has been still more severe, at least insofar as indulging metaphor, in describing Miss Snyder's study of the "Opus Maximum": "This outline . . . proves to be mere abracadabra—nine-tenths theology of a highly fantastic and pretentious order, and one-tenth science almost as fantastic, with just a peppering of a metaphysics which is given a ridiculous turn by its strained application to science and theology."[30]

It must be noted that these opinions of Coleridge's stature as a philosopher are atypical. The overwhelming majority of scholars accept his claim to have achieved his philosophical position independently, and his use of the very words of others has been minimized in the many ways already described. J. H. Muirhead, rejecting Coleridge's dependence on the Germans as either significant or limiting, has argued that Coleridge is an important philosopher and that "this side of his multifarious and miraculous activity" is far more coherent than has hitherto been seen.[31] Coleridge's special achievement is seen by Muirhead as having been the founder of "the voluntaristic form of idealistic philosophy," of which he "remains to this day the most distinguished representative."[32] With the enormous growth of his reputation as a thinker, Coleridge has also been seen as a forerunner of Bergson, Kierkegaard, and the more recent existentialists.[33]

14.

The Shakespearean Criticism

COLERIDGE's writings on Shakespeare are among the chief glories of English literary criticism. Almost any history of Shakespearean criticism will assign to him the honor, not infrequently the exclusive honor, of having revolutionized the subject. Before him, understanding of Shakespeare's dramatic construction was without form and void; after him, order has been imposed upon chaos. The supremely high value placed upon this body of Coleridge's work has long been commonplace.[1]

His ideas have come down to us somewhat fortuitously and often in fragmentary form. One of the most famous and influential of the Shakespearean "lectures"—"Shakespeare's Judgment Equal to his Genius"—is actually a series of some six fragments written over at least a decade, and provided with an indeterminate amount of connecting material by Henry Nelson Coleridge, the poet's nephew, son-in-law, and first important editor (who also provided the title).[2] Most of the Shakespearean writings we owe to the reports of John Payne Collier, Henry Crabb Robinson's diary jottings, and Coleridge's own lecture notes. Between 1808 and 1819, he lectured frequently on Shakespeare. In all of the lectures after 1808 there are voluminous and striking similarities with the ideas of A. W. Schlegel, particularly those contained in his *Vorlesungen über dramatische Kunst und Literatur.* Coleridge claimed never to have "heard" of this work until after the eighth lecture of the 1811-12 series, given on the evening of 12 December 1811. Though this is untrue, as will be evident shortly, the first problem to confront is the fact that he had lectured on Shakespeare in 1808, before the publication of Schlegel's book. If, as Coleridge maintained again and again, this first course of lectures "differed from the following courses only, by occasionally varying the illustrations of the same thoughts,"[3] then the charge of having learned the principles of the new Shakespearean criticism from Schlegel would be baseless, unless it could be shown that he knew Schlegel's much earlier scattered essays on Shakespeare.

This subject has been intensively and repeatedly studied. The evidence is very complicated and does not admit of brief summary. All contemporary discussion must acknowledge the pioneering work of Anna Augusta von Helmholtz (Mrs. Phelan), and T. M. Raysor, among others. In this area critics have, on the whole, been least disposed to deprive Coleridge of his laurels as a brilliant original thinker, even while admitting that he may have borrowed many important concepts from the German, at least insofar as their verbal formulation is concerned. Even the very cautious conclusions of Mrs. Phelan as to Coleridge's debt to Schlegel have not been generally accepted.

Practically all discussion of this extremely vexed and often tiresome subject has bogged down in a quagmire of details and conflicting statements through a reluctance to face bluntly certain aspects of Coleridge's character and literary career. The cliché about not seeing the forest for the trees is singularly applicable. Coleridge's debts to Schlegel cannot be determined solely by a comparison of dates and texts and the general intellectual climate behind both men. The evidence suggesting deliberate plagiarism and obscurantism would be compelling even if this were an isolated instance in his life. But when the evidence is viewed comprehensively and dispassionately, there should, one would think, be no difficulty in concluding with confidence that without the aid of Schlegel's *Vorlesungen* the corpus of Coleridge's Shakespearean criticism would be radically different. The question indeed arises, would there be an extensive body of such criticism at all? Milton, after all, was one of Coleridge's supreme deities, and he often proposed a major study of Milton. But we have very little, and that little is not especially important. It would, of course, be unfair to prejudge the problem because the author has been elsewhere given to a lack of intellectual candor. But it would be equally false to prejudge in Coleridge's favor, as if great men were incapable of deception.

Perhaps the best way to approach this complex subject is to consider first a letter Coleridge wrote in December 1811 in which he discussed plagiarism in general and his relations with Schlegel in particular. For T. M. Raysor this document is "magnificent," a view echoed by Miss Coburn, who considers this "Coleridge's most important statement on plagiarism."[4]

The letter is too long to give in full. Its obstensible occasion was an offer made to Coleridge by some unnamed person to review Sir Walter Scott's poems injuriously. At the beginning he absolves Scott of any intent to plagiarize from "Christabel" in *The Lay of the Last Minstrel*. Scott acknowledged his debt to Coleridge in the introduction to the *Lay* in 1830 and said that he had made his obligations known previously in conversation. This was adequate enough in 1830, but an earlier statement of obligation to the meter in "Christabel" (and to a small number of phrases) would doubtless have helped Coleridge's reputation.[5]

In the circumstances, his attitude seems quite generous. This gist of his argument is that Scott was frank in praising "Christabel" to friends and that if he had any genuine intent to plagiarize he could readily have altered the few expressions which are obviously parallel in both poems.

The first mention in Coleridge's letters of his awareness that friends such as Southey, Lamb, and Dorothy Wordsworth were claiming that Scott's enormously popular *Lay of the Last Minstrel* was in debt to "Christabel" for its meter occurred in 1806, when Coleridge wrote to his wife that he did not believe the allegation.[6] By the following year he had read Scott's poem and wrote to Dorothy Wordsworth: "I . . . could not detect either in manner, matter, or metre, a single trace of dishonorable or avoidable Resemblance to the Christabel. I am puzzled, as to how such a notion could have arisen so widely & among persons unconnected with each other." One month later he wrote Southey that he "saw no likeness whatsoever to the Christabel, much less any improper resemblance." Shortly thereafter, he wrote that the *meters* of the two poems were different. However, when Scott's *Lady of the Lake* appeared in 1810, Coleridge shot off a violent attack to Wordsworth, charging the author with "peccadillos against the 8th Commandment." Particular instances cited are alleged borrowings from Wordsworth's "Ruth," from his own "Christabel," and rather excitedly, an unidentified borrowing: "I think, I have met with the same thought elsewhere!" We are told that "the Poem commences with the poorest Paraphrase-Parody of the [Wordsworth] Hart Leap Well," and that "in short, my dear William! —it is time to write a Recipe for Poems of this sort."[7]

Clearly, it is impossible to paddle one's way securely among the shoals and rapids of these many verbal cascades. As for Scott's debt to "Christabel" in *The Lay of ths Last Minstrel,* the passage of time has made more than a little obscure the reasons for so many of Coleridge's friends seeing not only a decided but even an improper connection. This is not to suggest that the connection was not there in the early nineteenth century, but rather that time has made the connections only barely noticeable, assuming that they were ever deeply etched.

Was Coleridge here strongly motivated to adopt a position much at variance with his many other utterances?[8] Two statements relative to Scott himself show quite clearly how quick he was to accuse others of pilfering on the basis of similarity in idea and expression: "A man so pre-eminent in literary and contemporary reputation as Sir Walter Scott, ought not to have transferred a character from Goethe at all; a man of such accredited frankness of temper as Sir Walter Scott ought still less to have transferred it *without acknowledgment*"; and again, "Unworthy of Sir Walter Scott was this pilfering imitation of Goethe's Mignon. . . ."[9]

Yet in this letter Coleridge strikes a much different posture: "Excuse me, if I say that I have ever held parallelisms adduced in proof of plagiarism or even of intentional imitation, in the utmost contempt."[10] His charges of plagiarism on precisely these grounds against Hume, Schelling, Condillac, and others indicate how flexible his convictions could be, depending on the situation in which they were uttered.

The main purport of this letter does not emerge for several pages. Though the subject appears to be the relation of Scott and "Christabel," it soon becomes clear that Coleridge is trying to show how complex is the problem of intellectual influence where two writers have similar backgrounds. In judging between two works where likenesses exist, he desires us to ask:

> is the general Likeness, or are the particular resemblances, such as a liberal and enlightened Reader could not with any probability consider as the result of mere Coincidence between two Writers of similar Pursuits, and (argumenti causâ loquor) of nearly equal Talent? Coincidence is here used as a negative—not as implying that Likeness between two Works is merely accidental, the effect of chance, but as asserting that it is not the effect of imitation.[11]

This is an enlightened position, one which any reader should keep in mind in attempting to judge "influences." In reading much late eighteenth-century poetry, for example, a casual reader might readily conclude that Poet B was indebted to Poet A for particular images or patterns of thought, whereas broader learning might readily show that certain ideas and forms of diction were merely the poetic furniture of the period. So far we can only concur with Coleridge. At once, however, he passes to the real subject of his letter.

> Now how far Coincidence in this sense and under the supposed Conditions is possible, I can myself supply an instance, which happened at my Lectures . . . only last week, and the accuracy of which does not rely on *my* evidence only, but can be proved by the separate testimony of some hundred Individuals. . . . After the close of my Lecture on Romeo and Juliet a German Gentleman, a Mr Bernard Krusve, introduced himself to me, and . . . said, Were it not almost impossible, I must have believed that you had either heard or read my Countryman Schlegel's Lecture on this play, given at Vienna: the principles, thought, and the very illustrations are so nearly the same—But the Lectures were but just published as I left Germany, scarcely more than a week since—& the only two Copies of the Work in England I have reason to think, that I myself have brought over. One I retain: The other is at Mr Boosy's —I replied that I had not even heard of these Lectures, nor had indeed seen any work of Schlegel's except a volume of Translations from Spanish Poetry. . . . A Friend standing by me added—This cannot be a question of Dates, Sir! for if the gentlemen, whose name you have mentioned, first gave his Lectures at Vienna in 1810 I can myself bear witness, that I heard Mr Coleridge deliver all the *substance* of tonight's Lecture . . . some years before.—The next morning Mr Krusve called on me & made me a present of the Work. . . .[12]

We must pause to notice that this morning visit would have taken place on 13 December 1811. But in Coleridge's lecture of 16 December 1811 he stated that he'd received the Schlegel volume from a friend "Yesterday afternoon."[13] We are not yet done with discrepancies on this single point. In an important letter-draft written three years later (published for the first time in 1959) Coleridge retold this story; now, however, a "German Gentleman just arrived from Germany," presented him with the "first Copy" of Schlegel to arrive in England not the next day, but had—fortuitously, one must say—brought it to the lecture hall and presented it to Coleridge on the spot. In this letter Coleridge declared that he'd delivered his lectures three years before Schlegel's in Vienna, whereas in other such statements he had been content to claim a priority of only two years.[14]

Assertions of independence and priority over Schlegel are very common in Coleridge's writings, and it would protract our discussion unconscionably to notice each of them. Worth comment, however, is his claim in 1818 that "16 or rather 17 years ago I delivered 18 lectures on Shakespear at the Royal Institution—three fourths of which appeared at that time startling Paradoxes."[15] Sara Coleridge was at great pains to explain away this impossible statement as either "momentary confusion of mind," or faulty copying from a manuscript then thought lost.[16] But Professor Griggs, who printed the letter from manuscript, notes: "The MS. *clearly reads* 16 or rather 17."[17] In general, it is misleading to account for inconsistencies in Coleridge by assuming momentary mental lapses: the problem is fundamental. In the letter just cited, he insists that his priority over Schlegel in all-important principles would be borne out by such "most adequate Judges, as Sir G. Beaumont, the Bishop of Durham, Mr Sotheby—and afterwards to Mr Rogers and Lord Byron. . . ." But no evidence from these or other people was ever brought forward in support, either then or later.

In 1819 Coleridge was to say that "it was fortunate for my moral reputation" that his lectures, allegedly given two years before Schlegel's, had not only been attended by "from five to seven hundred ear-witnesses," but that "notes had been taken of these by several men and ladies of high rank."[18] Regrettably, he appears not to have called upon any of those high-ranked ladies and gentlemen for a copy of the corroborative notes, which have not otherwise come to light, despite Sara Coleridge's efforts, and those of subsequent scholars.[19]

To return to Mr. Krusve and his volume of Schlegel: Coleridge goes on to say that upon perusing the German's lectures he discovered that the resemblances between his own thought and Schlegel's exceeded anything he had been led to expect:

> in all the Lectures that related to Shakespear, or to Poetry in general, the Grounds, Train of Reasoning, &c were different in language only—& often not even in that—. The Thoughts too were so far peculiar, that to the best of my knowledge they did not exist in any prior work of Criticism—Yet I was . . . more confirmed, than surprized. For Schlegel & myself had both studied deeply & perseverantly the philosophy of Kant. . . .[20]

The remainder of this chain of reasoning has been given earlier in relation to his explanation of the "genial coincidence" with Schelling in precisely the same way. Coleridge's conclusion is that two men trained in the philosophy of Kant, and with similar bent and intelligence will, it is "morally certain," when "writing on the same Subject . . . draw the same conclusions . . . write to one purpose & with one spirit."[21]

As the argument in this passage has already been considered,[22] we may pass at once to the core of this crucial document. If Coleridge's account is true, then the charges of having adopted the basic *principles* of Shakespearean criticism from Schlegel is absolutely refuted. Taken at face value, the defense is impregnable. Coleridge had just delivered a lecture which a gentleman from Germany affirms resembles even in small details the lectures of Schlegel published in Germany only a week before. The unlikely possibility that Coleridge had somehow secured a copy of the book in the brief interim is forestalled by Mr. Krusve's strange omniscience. He has "reason to think" that there are only two copies in England, one possessed by himself and the other by the London bookseller, Mr. Boosey. However, a further possibility (albeit most remote) remains. Coleridge may somehow have received a report of Schlegel's lectures as orally delivered. This avenue is at once shut off by a "friend," who announces that he can affirm that the "substance" of Coleridge's lecture on *Romeo and Juliet* was delivered "some years before" Schlegel's "Lectures at Vienna in 1810." All this, Coleridge says, can be supported by the testimony of "some hundred individuals" in the audience.

We have only Coleridge's word for it that such an event actually took place. No one undertook to interview the members of his audience and we have no further knowledge of the mysterious Mr. Krusve.[23] Henry Crabb Robinson's diary entry for the night of 12 December 1811 described the lecture as Coleridge's "worst," which hardly encourages us to believe that a revolutionary analysis of *Romeo and Juliet* had taken place. Curiously, Robinson scarcely mentions discussion of the play at all. He tells us that Coleridge began by "identifying religion and love, delivered a rhapsody on brotherly and sisterly love, which seduced him into a dissertation on incest. I at last lost all power of attending to him any longer."[24] Amid all these particulars, there is no hint of the interesting events which presumably took place immediately after the lecture.

In the circumstances, it seems worthwhile to examine with very great care each important point in Coleridge's often-quoted letter where external evidence does exist.

First: "I replied that I had not even heard of these lectures, nor had indeed seen any work of Schlegel's except a volume of translations from Spanish poetry." Coleridge's eighth lecture, a very small part of which dealt with *Romeo and Juliet*, was given on 12 December 1811, after which the meeting with Krusve presumably occurred.[25] However, more than a *month* before Coleridge had written to Crabb Robinson, "I am very anxious to see Schlegel's Werke before the Lectures commence."[26] This statement, as Wellek says, "can hardly be interpreted as a desire for first acquaintance with Schlegel's writings."[27] That Coleridge was "in Arcadia" when he said that he had never "heard" of Schlegel's *Lectures* before December 1811 we know from Crabb Robinson's diary entry of 29 January 1811. Speaking of Shakespeare, Robinson noted that Coleridge was "willing to censure . . . Schlegel's ideas concerning the German idea of the Greek chorus."[28] Coleridge thus knew at least some of the contents of Schlegel's first volume of *Lectures,* which had been published not in 1811—only a week before, according to Mr. Krusve—but in 1809. The second volume of Schlegel's *Lectures* had also been published in 1809, and the third, containing the lengthy discussion of Shakespeare, in December 1810, though the title page reads 1811.[29] Schlegel's oral lectures were in fact given in 1808 and not 1807 as Coleridge repeatedly stated.

Ignoring the usual canons of evidence, many scholars doggedly accept Coleridge's assertion that he had never "heard" of Schlegel's book before December 1811, had only read one of Schlegel's volumes, and that merely a translation of Spanish poetry. He had been in Germany for almost a year at the turn of the century, at a time when A. W. Schlegel was a major force in German literary life. Ludwig Tieck, who had edited Schlegel's tremendously influential translations of Shakespeare's plays, had spoken with Coleridge in Rome in 1806 on the subject of Shakespeare's doubtful plays.[30] At the same time Coleridge told Sophie Bernhardi, Tieck's sister, that he admired Schlegel's Shakespeare translations "unbelievably."[31]

In discussions of the revolution that took place in Shakespearean criticism in the nineteenth century it is often forgotten that what was revolutionized were the reasons for admiring Shakespeare, not the admiration itself. As T. S. Eliot has pointed out, "there is no period in which Shakespeare has not been treated with the greatest respect."[32] A mounting crescendo of enthusiasm for the Bard of Avon as a divine genius can easily be traced in eighteenth-century English criticism.[33] In what then did the revolution consist?

Any brief answer to this question involves simplification and inevitably some distortion. Yet we will not go far wrong to concentrate on the heart of the matter: the dilemma of Shakespeare's dramatic construction. Shakespeare as divine poet, as profound searcher of the human heart—these were commonplace views long before either Coleridge or Schlegel were born. But Shakespeare as superhuman architect of a unified dramatic form—this was an invention (or discovery) of the late eighteenth century. And the central locus of that revolution—intolerable as the thought may be—was not England, the Bard's own homeland, but Germany.

A. W. Schlegel's series of essays on Shakespeare began in 1796, in which the complexly organized dramatic structures of Shakespeare's plays, and the relevance of even remote details of character and language, were emphasized. The most renowned of these early essays was on *Romeo and Ju-*

liet, which appeared in Schiller's *Die Horen* in 1797 and later in *Characteristiken und Kritiken* (1801). Here is Schlegel's own summary of this seminal essay:

> In an essay on *Romeo and Juliet*, written a number of years ago, I went through the whole of the scenes in their order, and demonstrated the inward necessity of each with reference to the whole; I showed why such a particular circle of characters and relations was placed around the two lovers; I explained the signification of the mirth here and there scattered, and justified the use of the occasional heightening given to the poetical colours. From all this it seemed to follow unquestionably, that with the exception of a few witticisms, now become unintelligible or foreign to the present taste, (imitations of the tone of society of that day,) nothing could be taken away, nothing added, nothing otherwise arranged, without mutilating and disfiguring the perfect work. I would readily undertake to do the same for all the pieces of Shakespeare's maturer years, but to do this would require a separate book.[34]

These ideas, so strange at the time, did not make their way easily. R. Pascal, in his valuable little book *Shakespeare in Germany,* describes the subsequent activity of the Schlegel brothers thus:

> The Schlegels . . . in the face of opposition took their thesis of Shakespeare's artistry even further: not merely were all the parts of the plays subject to the whole, but further, they say, this is a conscious artistic process in Shakespeare. Shakespeare became for them an example of technical excellence due to reflection over aesthetics. In an aphorism of the *Athenaüm* of 1798 stands the challenging statement: no writer is more correct than Shakespeare, if by correctness, one means the conscious construction of all parts in the "spirit of the whole". He is more "systematic" than any other poet, his plays are extremely formal. . . . Shakespeare is for them in this period a supremely conscious artist; over and over again they refer to his "Absichtlichkeit" (deliberateness of construction).[35]

If Coleridge was familiar with these writings, published almost exactly at the time he was himself in Germany and mingling with students at a major university, we need go no further to identify the specific origin of the dictum almost universally attributed to him, namely, that Shakespeare's artistic judgment was equal to his genius—the rock on which all the basic principles of romantic Shakespearean criticism rests.

Can we be certain that Coleridge knew these writings? Between his own observations on *Romeo and Juliet* and those in Schlegel's early essay on the play are several connections. Both men discussed the mortal enmity between the Montagues and Capulets which provides the background of conflict in the play, but obviously this connection can be dismissed, since any discussion of the play might well proceed from this point. Both Schlegel and Coleridge, however, defended Shakespeare for having Romeo in love with Rosaline before meeting Juliet, and both emphasized the importance of the roles of Mercutio and the Nurse. On Juliet's suicide Schlegel wrote: "Her imagination falls into an uproar, so many fears confuse the tender mind of the maiden; and she gulps down the contents of the cup in her excitement—which would have shown a too manly resolution to empty deliberately." Coleridge analyzed the same scene in these words: "The taking the poison in a fit of fright . . . A girl of fifteen—too bold for her but for [this]."[36]

Raysor recognized that Coleridge could have seen Schlegel's essay when he was in Germany in 1798-99, but "in default of external evidence, it seems better to pronounce this case a striking coincidence rather than a proof of Schlegel's influence."[38] In view of the many similarities in the two treatments of the play, the fame of Schlegel's essay when Coleridge was in Germany, and the peculiar parallel in the analysis of the psychology of Juliet's suicide, this caution is perhaps in excess of the evidence.

If Coleridge knew Schlegel's essay early, however, it seems to have made little if any impression on him. He did not come back from Germany talking about new principles of literary criticism, nor is there any suggestion in his notebooks or letters of new trains of thought, though he was never slow in announcing intellectual discoveries, with or without reference to sources. Almost every firm piece of evidence about the development of Shakespearean criticism in England centers upon a date very close to about 1812 as the dividing line between old and new styles of thought. As far as Coleridge's contemporaries were concerned—those with a considerable knowledge of the subject—the intellectual impetus in this revolution came from Germany.

Crucial in this connection is the testimony provided by Wordsworth in his "Essay Supplementary to the Preface" (1815). Coleridge was so deeply hurt by a portion of this essay that in a letter he wrote three years later to William Mudford, in which he again asserted his priority over Schlegel, he burst out angrily against Wordsworth, who "has affirmed *in print* that a German Critic *first* taught us to think correctly concerning Shakespear." The following year, in a document solemnly recorded at Highgate, Coleridge wrote in anguish that although Wordsworth knew better, "from motives which I do not know or impulses which I *cannot* know, he has thought [it] proper to assert that Schlegel and the German critics *first* taught Englishmen to admire their own great countryman intelligently."[38]

Several difficult problems attend these statements. First, in the *Biographia Literaria* itself, in a passage which for all time must baffle any student of Coleridge, he wrote:

It was Lessing who first introduced the name and the works of Shakespeare to the admiration of the Germans; and I should not perhaps go too far, if I add, that it was Lessing who first proved to all thinking men, even to Shakespeare's own countrymen, the true nature of his apparent irregularities. . . . He proved that in all the essentials of art, no less than in the truth of nature, the plays of Shakespeare were incomparably more coincident with the principles of Aristotle, than the productions of Corneille and Racine, notwithstanding the boasted regularity of the latter.[39]

No satisfactory explanation of this astonishing passage has yet been made. Subsequent to his own statement, Coleridge twice harshly condemned Wordsworth for having said very nearly the same thing. But what is utterly mystifying is that he attributes to Lessing an influence on Shakespeare studies which is not only exaggerated in itself,[40] but if true would render almost meaningless the very questions of priority between himself and Schlegel over which he had defended himself so often and so vehemently.[41]

It is perhaps significant that in fact Wordsworth did not mention Schlegel by name (as angrily affirmed by Coleridge), or even refer to a "German Critic," but spoke rather of the Germans in general, as a nation: "In some respects they [the Germans] have acquired a superiority over the fellow countrymen of the Poet: for among us it is a current, I might say, an established opinion, that Shakespeare is justly praised when he is pronounced to be 'a wild irregular genius, in whom great faults are compensated by great beauties!'" Shawcross observes of this passage: "This is surely less of a concession to Germany than Coleridge's tribute"; but in fact Wordsworth's slight of Coleridge was very much more serious.

Immediately after the passage just quoted he asked: "How long may it be before this misconception passes away, and it becomes universally acknowledged that the judgement of Shakespeare in the selection of his materials, and in the manner in which he has made them, heterogeneous as they often are, constitute a unity of their own, and contribute all to one great end, is not less admirable than his imagination, his invention, and his intuitive knowledge of human Nature?" This passage, which sounds almost like a paraphrase of Coleridge's "Shakespeare's Judgment Equal to his Genius," is presented without any reference to Coleridge. Furthermore, this is immediately followed by a panegyric upon Shakespeare's sonnets in which Wordsworth acknowledges Coleridge as a tiller in the Shakespearean vineyard only to the extent of observing that "this flippant insensibility [to Shakespeare's Sonnets] was publicly reprehended by Mr. Coleridge in a course of Lectures upon Poetry given by him at the Royal Institution."[42]

Is it any wonder that Coleridge took offense? Whatever the public might suppose, to Coleridge and their intimate circle it could not have been anything but obvious that Wordsworth was honoring the Germans for their contributions to the understanding of Shakespeare's plays, and was ignoring Coleridge pointedly by bringing in his name in another connection. And it is to be noted that he does not praise Coleridge for any original contribution to the understanding of Shakespeare's sonnets, but merely announces public concurrence with his own opinion. Indeed, later in the essay he complains about the ranking of the English poets and asks: "where [is] he, whose rights as a poet, contradistinguished from those which he is universally allowed to possess as a dramatist, we have vindicated,—where Shakespeare?"

Of course it is possible to charge Wordsworth with gross ingratitude towards Coleridge and intellectual dishonesty to boot, but the charge is not likely to be urged, the more especially as very soon after speaking of himself and not Coleridge or any German as a vindicator of Shakespeare's claims as a poet, he says that "every author, as far as he is great and at the same time *original*, has had the task of *creating* the taste by which he is to be enjoyed. . . . This remark was long since made to me by the philosophical friend for the separation of whose poems from my own I have previously expressed my regret."[43] In a letter to Lady Beaumont eight years earlier Wordsworth had made the same remark, and again credited Coleridge with it.[44] In view of all this, can it be reasonably supposed that he would not have acknowledged Coleridge's priority if he had thought it justified? With respect to Shakespearean criticism, the "Essay Supplementary" demonstrates quite clearly that Wordsworth deliberately refused to accord Coleridge any honors as an original thinker in the field, but rather assigns such achievements to the Germans. As to Shakespeare as a poet, he does not recognize learning anything from Coleridge in this respect, but rather says that *he* has vindicated Shakespeare's claims, not as a dramatist, but as a poet. And then he does acknowledge Coleridge for the statement about original artists creating the taste by which they will be enjoyed.

Coleridge persistently misdated Schlegel's course of lectures as 1810,[45] while insisting that his own lectures of 1808 contained everything substantial as to the principles and conclusions he later elaborated. Further: "Mr. Hazlitt, whose hatred of me is in such an inverse ratio to my zealous kindness toward him . . . replied to an assertion of my plagiarism from Schlegel in these words: 'That is a lie; for I myself heard the very same character of Hamlet from Coleridge before he went to Germany and when he had neither read [n]or could read a page of German.' "[46]

These notes were not published till after the deaths of both Coleridge and Hazlitt, and, as Raysor comments, "it is not at all certain that Hazlitt would have given the necessary testimony, if he had been alive to do so. His Preface to *The Characters of Shakespeare's Plays* praises Schlegel and ignores Coleridge, and this could scarcely have been other than deliberate, coming from Hazlitt."[47] Hazlitt's words are rather more damaging than this suggests, for in his *Characters of Shakespeare's Plays* (1817), a volume dedicated to Charles Lamb, he pointedly wrote that Schlegel's lectures on drama

give by far the best account of the plays of Shakespear that has hitherto appeared. . . . We will at the same time confess [to] some little jealousy . . . that it should be reserved for a foreign critic to give 'reasons for the faith which we English have in Shakespear.' Certainly no writer among ourselves has shown either the same enthusiastic admiration of his genius, or the same philosophical acuteness in pointing out his characteristic excellences."[48]

In both Wordsworth's and Hazlitt's testimony, therefore, there was a deliberate and emphatic slight of Coleridge.[49] Both were surely in a far better position than later scholars to report on the intellectual climate of their own times and on intellectual influences. Lamb, Robinson, and other members of their circle also saw "the great obligations of Coleridge to the writer [Schlegel]."[50]

It is to be noted that Coleridge identified Hazlitt as a witness to his youthful views of the subject. Mrs. Phelan long ago called attention to what is often ignored in this connection, namely, the relevance of Hazlitt's detailed portrait of the early Coleridge in "My First Acquaintance with Poets":

Hazlitt visited Coleridge in 1798 at Nether Stowey, and reports the following conversation for that year. "Some comparison was introduced between Shakespeare and Milton. Coleridge said he hardly knew which to prefer. Shakespeare appeared to him a *mere stripling in the art*; he was as tall and strong, with infinitely more activity than Milton, but he never appeared to have come to man's estate; or, if he had, he would not have been a man, but a monster." This is quite in the manner of Pope and Johnson, and not at all in that of Lessing or Schlegel, the latter of whom had by this time written and published his excellent critique on *Romeo and Juliet*, in which he applies the same principles of criticism of which Coleridge so often discourses.[51]

However reasonable the assumption that Coleridge, before his first lectures in 1808, had known German Shakespeare criticism intimately, it is by no mean necessary to insist desperately that he did. For we know very little of the lectures. Coleridge insisted repeatedly in later years that all the principles and modes of thought of his later Shakespeare criticism were contained in these lectures. But assertions are not proof. Furthermore, in a letter to Wordsworth written just before the 1808 lectures were to come to an abrupt end, he referred to them as "disgusting," which hardly encourages the notion that they were revolutionary.[52] Reports of these lectures are extremely fragmentary. Mrs. Phelan had been able to adduce only three passages which seem to echo Schlegel's conceptions.[53] Raysor also cites three remarks from the 1808 lectures as similar to Schlegel's Lectures, which Coleridge could not then have known. Yet all these parallels are trifling and in no way touch upon principles. It was Schlegel's articulation of the organic-form formula, surely one of the most influential statements in the history of literary criticism, which proved the Rosetta stone to decipher the seeming hieroglyph of Shakespeare's dramatic construction. There is no hint of this in Coleridge's 1808 lectures.[54]

As an instance of the difficulties involved in assuming that he did *not* know Schlegel's *Lectures* before December 1811, we may consider Collier's reports of Coleridge's conversation during October of the year. Among many other observations are the following:

> Being asked whether he included the "Two Noble Kinsmen," among the doubtful plays, he answered, "Decidedly not: there is the clearest internal evidence that Shakespeare importantly aided Fletcher in the composition of it. Parts are most unlike Fletcher, yet most like Shakespeare, while other parts are most like Fletcher, and most unlike Shakespeare. The mad scenes of the Jailor's daughter are coarsely imitated from "Hamlet": those were by Fletcher, and so very inferior, that I wonder how he could so far condescend. Shakespeare would never have imitated himself at all, much less so badly."[55]

In Schlegel's *Lectures* we read:

> *The Two Noble Kinsmen* is deserving of more particular mention, as it is the joint production of Shakspeare and Fletcher. I see no ground for calling this in question. . . . But to find out how much of the *The Two Noble Kinsmen* may belong to Shakspeare, we must not only be able to tell the difference of hands in the execution, but also to determine the influence of Shakspeare on the plan of the whole. . . . I should say, that I think I can perceive the mind of Shakspeare in a certain ideal purity, which distinguishes this piece from all others of Fletcher's. . . . The part of the jailor's daughter, whose insanity is artlessly conducted in pure monologues, is certainly not Shakspeare's; for, in that case, we must suppose him to have had an intention of arrogantly imitating his own Ophelia.[56]

While Raysor agrees that "Schlegel gives almost exactly the same argument against the Shakespearean authorship of these scenes. . . . The dates preclude Schlegel's influence."[57] The dates, however, only preclude the German's influence if we accept Coleridge's account of his knowledge of the *Lectures*.

In the same conversation Collier reported Coleridge to have said:

> . . . Shakespeare was almost the only dramatic poet, who by his characters represented a class, and not an individual . . . while his eye rested upon an individual character, [he] always embraced a wide circumference of others, without diminishing the separate interest he intended to attach to the being he pourtrayed. . . . all Shakespeare's chief characters possessed, in a greater or less degree, this claim to our admiration.[58]

In discussing Shakespeare's characterization, Schlegel remarks:

A character which should be merely a personification of a naked general idea could neither exhibit any great depth nor any great variety. . . . The characters which Shakspeare has so thoroughly delineated have undoubtedly a number of individual peculiarities, but at the same time they possess a significance which is not applicable to them alone: they generally supply materials for a profound theory of their most prominent and distinguishing property.[59]

Collier continues:

Lamb led Coleridge on to speak of Beaumont and Fletcher: he highly extolled their comedies in many respects, especially for the vivacity of the dialogue, but he contended that their tragedies were liable to grave objections. They always proceeded upon something forced and unnatural; the reader never can reconcile the plot with probability. . . . Their comedies, however, were much superior, and at times, and excepting in the generalization of humour and application, almost rivalled those of Shakespeare. The situations are sometimes so disgusting, and the language so indecent and immoral, that is is impossible to read the plays in private society.[60]

On the same subject Schlegel had written:

. . . Beaumont and Fletcher bestow very little attention on harmony of composition and the observance of due proportion between all the different parts. They not unfrequently lose sight of a happily framed plot, and appear almost to forget it. . . . They are least successful in their tragic attempts. . . . they succeed much better in Comedy. . . . The indecencies in which these poets indulged themselves go beyond conception. Licentiousness of language is the least evil; many scenes, nay, even whole plots, are so contrived that the very idea, not to mention the beholding of them, is a gross insult to modesty.[61]

Despite this evidence, Raysor remains unconvinced of debt: "The supposed dates of Collier's reports preclude the possibility of an influence from Schlegel; and, in any case, the parallels are almost too general to be worth citing."[62] But these parallels may surely be seen as hardly so very general, and that so many should occur in so brief a space strengthens the probability that they came from Schlegel. In a report of conversation precise similarity of wording is not to be expected. That so much of it actually occurs is remarkable. No single parallel above is beyond the limits of coincidence—though what Coleridge says about the Jailor's daughter and the imitation of *Hamlet* is ideationally identical with Schlegel—yet when the number of parallels is considered, the dependence upon Schlegel seems persuasively indicated, particularly since within a few months Coleridge was to give at lectures long passages from Schlegel verbatim.

After 1811, as the parallel passages printed by Mrs. Phelan so clearly show, Coleridge's use of Schlegel's *Lectures* intensifies. This fact seems baffling. One supposes that he would have been most cautious in using Schlegel after the *Vorlesungen* became available in England; but we must remember that until 1815 the book was not available in English, and therefore few people read it. Even if an occasional auditor recognized Schlegel's ideas and words in Coleridge's lectures, there was no real danger of exposure. That could only come if he published his lectures. It is to be remembered that in the *Biographia Literaria* (1817) he announced: "The substance of these lectures [on Shakespeare] I hope soon to publish."[63] Though Coleridge lived till 1834, he never did publish his ideas on Shakespeare. This may be merely another of his unfulfilled projects, but it should be seriously considered that he shunned publication because it would expose him to the charge of plagiarism. He did, after all, publish several other works, of comparatively trifling consequence.

The following is a brief, representative selection of Coleridge's borrowings from Schlegel:

Schlegel	*Coleridge*
the word [Romantic] is derived from *romance*—the name originally given to the languages which were formed from the mixture of the Latin and the old Teutonic dialects. . . .[64]	I have before spoken of the Romance, or the language formed out of the decayed Roman and the northern tongues.[65]
most of the English and Spanish dramatic works are neither tragedies nor comedies in the sense of the ancients: they are romantic dramas. . . . Of the origin and essence of the romantic I treated in my first Lecture. . . .[66]	. . . I have named the true genuine modern poetry the romantic. . . . If the tragedies of Sophocles are in the strict sense of the word tragedies, and the comedies of Aristophanes comedies, we must . . . find a new word for the plays of Shakespeare. They are . . . a different genus . . . romantic dramas, or dramatic romances.[67]
Many productions which appear at first sight dazzling phenomena in the province of the fine arts . . . resemble the mimic gardens of children: impatient to witness the work of their hands, they break off here and there branches and flowers, and plant them in the earth; everything at first	The work of a true poet . . . is distinguished . . . as a natural from an artificial flower; or as the mimic garden of a child, from an enamelled meadow. In the former the flowers are broken from their stems and stuck in the ground; they are beautiful to the eye and fragrant to the sense,

Schlegel

assumes a noble appearance
. . . till the rootless plants begin
to droop, and hang their withered
leaves and blossoms . . . while
the dark forest, on which no art
or care was ever bestowed . . .
fills the solitary beholder with
religious awe.[68]

All that is most intoxicating [in
Romeo and Juliet] in the odour
of a southern spring,—all that is
languishing in the song of the
nightingale, or voluptuous in the
first opening of the rose, all alike
breathe forth from this poem. . . .
the echo which the whole leaves
behind in the mind resembles a
single but endless sigh.[70]

In the zephyr-like Ariel the image
of air is not to be mistaken, his
name even bears an allusion to
it; as, on the other hand Caliban
signifies the heavy element of
earth.[72]

If *Romeo and Juliet* shines with
the colours of the dawn of morning, but a dawn whose purple
clouds already announce the
thunder of a sultry day, *Othello*
is, on the other hand, a strongly
shaded picture: we might call it
a tragical Rembrandt.[74] In the
progress of the action, this piece
[*Macbeth*] is altogether the reverse of *Hamlet*: it strides forward with amazing rapidity,
from the first catastrophe . . . to
the last.[75]

Coleridge

but their colours soon fade, and
their odour is transient . . .
while the meadow may be visited
again and again, with renewed
delight. . . .[69]

In *Romeo and Juliet* all is youth
and spring . . . with Juliet love
has all that is tender and melancholy in the nightingale, all
that is voluptuous in the rose,
with whatever is sweet in the
freshness of spring; but it ends
with a long deep sigh, like the
breeze of the evening.[71]

Ariel has in everything the airy
tint which gives the name. . . .
Caliban, on the other hand, is all
earth, all condensed and gross in
feelings and images. . . .[73]

Of all Shakespeare's plays Macbeth is the most rapid, Hamlet
the slowest, in movement. Lear
combines length with rapidity. . . .
It begins as a stormy day in
summer, with brightness; but that
brightness is lurid, and anticipates the tempest.[76] Thus the play
of *Hamlet* offers a direct contrast
to that of *Macbeth*: the one
proceeds with the utmost slow-
ness, the other with breathless
and crowded rapidity.[77]

Were it not for the authority of so many eminent scholars, the average reader would surely conclude from the evidence of so many parallels that Coleridge's debt to Schlegel was enormous, and very probably larger than the sum of individual parts. Raysor finds some *forty* odd pages in Coleridge paralleled in Schlegel, not to mention, as he states, criticism suggested by Schlegel's ideas.[78] Mrs. Phelan prints fifty pages of Coleridge and Schlegel in parallel columns.[79] Despite all this, it is by no means accepted that the shape of Coleridge's Shakespearean criticism would in any important sense be different had Schlegel never existed. Where authorities disagree sharply, the layman is usually wise to reserve judgment.

And yet, taking into account only objective evidence, it is difficult to account for the reluctance of English and American scholars to draw seemingly obvious conclusions. Consider, for example, the lecture notes on *Macbeth* which Coleridge prepared for the second lecture of 1813 in Bristol. The evidence is profoundly revelatory, not only for its bearing on the debt to Schlegel but on Coleridge's plagiarisms in general. The notes were written well after Coleridge admitted knowing Schlegel's work. Among them are the following observations: "Excepting the disgusting passage of the Porter, which I dare pledge myself to demonstrate an interpolation of the actors, I do not remember in *Macbeth* a single pun or play or words." On puns Schlegel had written: "in *Macbeth*, I do not believe a vestige of it is to be found." Raysor thinks this parallel "so insignificant that it might easily be due to coincidence."[80] However, only a few lines below this observation Coleridge wrote:

The objection that Shakespeare wounds the moral sense by the unsubdued, undisguised description of the most hateful atrocity, that he rends the feelings without mercy, and even outrages the eye itself by scenes of insupportable atrocity. Now *Titus Andronicus* is admitted not to have been Shakespear's, I dare, with the one exception of the trampling out of Gloster's eyes in *Lear*, answer boldly in the name of Shakespeare, not guilty.

Immediately following this observation he wrote: "SCHLEGEL, p.67, [vol.] iii"!"[81] Here at last is conclusive proof that he had Schlegel's *Vorlesungen* before his eyes while preparing his own lectures, well after assertions of independence. His first sentence above is, in fact, reasonably close translation. Schlegel had written an extended passage on the visual and psychological horror in Shakespeare and had answered squeamish objections to it in almost precisely the same way:

The objection that Shakespeare wounds our feelings by the open display of the most disgusting moral odiousness, unmercifully harrows up the mind, and tortures even our eyes by the exhibition of the most insupportable and hateful spectacles, is one of greater and graver importance.

He has, in fact, never varnished over wild and blood-thirsty passions with a pleasing exterior—never clothed crime and want of principle with a false show of greatness of soul; and in that respect he is every way deserving of praise.[82]

That Schlegel's analysis of this feature of Shakespeare's work is far more temperate than Coleridge's is not the issue. The point is that the *order* of Coleridge's thoughts, so far as his notes go, is strictly within the pattern laid down by Schlegel: from the puns in *Macbeth* to the horror in Shakespeare—surely a most unusual progression.[83]

Coleridge's own notes continue: "How preparatory to the most horrid scene, the assassination of Lady Macduff . . ." At this point he writes: "For my conclusion, Schlegel, iii, 67-69."[84] Here again is proof of Coleridge's direct use of Schlegel.

Of the various assertions of independence of Schlegel, Sara Coleridge wrote that her father "could hardly have been aware how many of the German critic's sentences he had repeated in those latter lectures, how many of his illustrations had intertwined themselves with his own thoughts. . . ."[85] The lecture notes just quoted surely suggest that this conjecture is false. Indeed, one must suspect almost all defenses of Coleridge which assume that he was unaware of his sources. We have just seen him, in preparing his lectures, taking short cuts by specifying the very pages in Schlegel on which he will elaborate.

The notes just discussed were written for lectures delivered in Bristol in 1813. These lectures are a patchwork of ideas lifted from Schlegel, often hardly altering the words. It is possible to conjecture harshly that Bristol audiences, less sophisticated than those in London, might be imposed upon somewhat more grossly. Other notes for the Bristol lectures contain a series of twelve points with a gap for numbers 2-6. After this hiatus in the notes Coleridge wrote: "Schl[egel: vol. iii.] 69-71 for *Othello*."[86] All the other points, with the exception of two or three sentences, also come from Schlegel.

Scholars who proclaim not only the immense importance of Coleridge's Shakespearean criticism but its great originality not infrequently acknowledge the seeming embarrassment of so many parallel passages; nevertheless, they insist that the *essence* of the revolutionary approach to Shakespeare (and to literature generally) was an independent achievement, however often the absent-minded and busy Sage of Highgate may have adopted Schlegel in the verbal formulation of this or that notion.

Central to all such discussion is one of the most influential passages in the entire history of literary criticism, a *locus classicus* equal, perhaps, to anything in Aristotle: the distinction between organic and mechanical form. The general subject is best considered in a broad discussion of Coleridge as a critic and aesthetician. Here, however, it is imperative to emphasize that the formula, *though a literal translation from Schlegel*, is rarely attributed to him—often through mere ignorance—but even when Schlegel's priority is recognized, it is almost always done so grudgingly, defensively, and hedged round with obscurantist or altogether absurd qualifications. Below are the relevant passages[87]:

Schlegel	Translation	Coleridge
A. W. von Schlegels *Vorlesungen über dramatische Kunst und Literatur.* Kritische Ausgabe eingeleitet und mit Anmerkungen versehen von G. V. Amoretti (Bonn und Leipzig, 1923), II, lll.	A. W. Schlegel, *A Course of Lectures on Dramatic Art and Literature.* Trans. from the original German by John Black (London 1815), II, 94-95.	Egerton MS. 2800, fol. 24 verso (comp. Raysor, I, 197).
(1) Der dichterische Geist bedarf allerdings einer Umgrenzung, um sich innerhalb derselben mit schöner Freyheit zu bewegen . . . er muss nach Gesetzen, die aus seinem eignen Wesen herfliessen, wirken, wenn seine Kraft nicht ins Leere hinaus verdunsten soll . . .	(1) The poetic spirit requires to be limited, that it may move with a becoming liberty, within its proper precincts. . . . it must act according to laws derivable from its own essence, otherwise its strength will evaporate. . . .	(1) The spirit of poetry, like all living powers, must of necessity circumscribe itself by rules, were it only to unite power with beauty. It must embody in order to reveal itself. . . .
(2) Formlos zu seyn, darf also den Werken des Genius auf keine Weise gestattet werden, allein es hat damit auch keine Gefahr.	(2) The works of genius cannot therefore be permitted to be without form; but of this there is not danger.	(2) No work of true genius dare want its appropriate form; neither indeed is there any danger of this.
(3) . . . den Begriff der Form, der von der Meisten . . . nur mechanisch, und nicht, wie er sollte,	(3) . . . most critics . . . interpret it [form] in a mechanical, and not in an organic sense.	(3) . . . The true ground of this mistake, as has been well remarked by a Continental critic, lies

Schlegel	Translation	Coleridge
organisch gefasst wird.		in the confounding mechanical regularity with organic form.
(4) Mechanisch ist die Form, wenn sie durch äussre Einwirkung irgend einem Stoffe blos als zufällige Zuthat, ohne Beziehung aus dessen Beschaffenheit ertheilt wird, wie man z. B. einer weichen Masse eine beliebige Gestalt giebt, damit sie solche nach der Erhärtung beybehalte. Die organische Form hingegen ist eingebohren, sie bildet von innen heraus, under erreicht ihre Bestimmtheit zugleich mit der vollständigen Entwickelung des Keimes.	(4) Form is mechanical when, through external force, it is imparted to any material merely as an accidental addition without any reference to its quality; as, for example, when we give a particular shape to a soft mass that it may retain the same after induration. Organical form, again, is innate; it unfolds itself from within, and acquires its determination simultaneously with the perfect development of the germ.	(4) The form is mechanic when on any given material we impress a predetermined form, not necessarily arising out of the properties of the material, as when to a mass of wet clay we give whatever shape we wish it to retain when hardened. The organic form, on the other hand, is innate; it shapes as it develops itself from within, and the fullness of its development is one and the same with the perfection of its outward form.

Raysor notes that the "Continental critic" referred to in paragraph (3) above is "Schlegel, of course," and that "this acknowledgment was very unwisely deleted by H. N. C. [Henry Nelson Coleridge]."[88] Reference to a "continental critic" is, to be sure, some sort of acknowledgment, though we have seen that under such vague expressions as "writer of the continent," "continental historian," and the like, various writers were actually meant. The acknowledgment appears in the collection of fragments organized by Henry Nelson Coleridge into the famous essay now known as "Shakespeare's Judgment Equal to his Genius." The key sentences appear among notes headed by the word "Lecture." To a listening audience the reference could only be misty, and of course an auditor would have no way of knowing whether what was "well said" by the continental critic was the following phrase, sentence, paragraph, or entire lecture. Be that as it may, Coleridge did cite a source in enunciating at least part of the famous dictum. Other borrowings from Schlegel, however, are silently passed over.[89]

Beach tartly points out of some of the paragraphs cited that "the English is as close a rendering of the German as it could be made without sacrifice of idiom and elegance. And even so there is a sensible sacrifice of both."[90] His comparison of a few phrases of Schlegel's German and Coleridge's English would seem to make this altogether clear. And yet Raysor asserts that "Coleridge's eloquent phrases are undoubtedly an advance upon the passage from Schlegel.[91] It is hard to understand wherein Coleridge's superior eloquence lies (assuming this qualification were even relevant). Most readers will surely agree with Beach that Coleridge's "No work of true genius *dare* want it appropriate form," in paragraph (2), is an odd construction, and that the oddness probably derives from substituting the English "dare" for the German "darf" in "Formlos zu seyn, darf also . . ." in Schlegel's paragraph (2). Further, when Coleridge writes that form "shapes as it develops itself from within" in (3), the clumsy separation of the verb and reflexive pronoun results from too mechanical a translation of "sie bildet von innen heraus." Indeed, Coleridge's "The form is mechanic" in (4) is hardly English. Black's 1815 translation is perfectly natural and not slavishly tied to the German "Mechanisch ist die Form . . ." However, whether the translation is smooth or awkward, or more or less eloquent than its source, is hardly relevant. What matters momentously is that the formula is quoted again and again, often as a cornerstone of Coleridge's thought, without any mention of its origin in a foreigner's writings![92] And if scholars cannot bring themselves to acknowledge plainly the existence of a word-for-word translation, what may we expect by way of unclouded judgment where something less than identity is involved?

Considered without regard to problems of literary history or originality, the body of Shakespearean writings published under Coleridge's name is undoubtedly more valuable than Schlegel's, perhaps even by a wide margin. Coleridge wrote and lectured far more on the subject. On purely poetic matters—always crucial in any encompassing view of Shakespeare's art— Coleridge is a great authority where Schlegel is not one at all. But Schlegel is a much greater critic than English-speaking readers admit; indeed, it cannot be said that Schlegel is really known in the English-speaking world. As an analyst of Shakespeare's form Schlegel was brilliant. Despite Coleridge's repeated exalted tributes to Shakespeare's formal genius, he never achieved even in general outline an analytical demonstration of organic unity in one of Shakespeare's plays to be compared with Schlegel's—a fact which is almost always ignored.

Coleridge's value as a Shakespearean critic is consistent with his general critical powers. The net of learning and scholarship is cast wide across the

162 MONUMENTS, RUINS, AND SCATTERED LEAVES

world's literatures.[93] Analysis of particular points suggests again and again much broader concerns. Philosophy, politics, science, and theology are continually present in discussions of a particular play or character. And embracing aesthetic principles seem again and again on the verge of being brought into brilliantly sharp focus. Consider, for example, the following attack on earlier approaches to Shakespeare:

> It was, generally speaking, the prevailing tendency of the time which preceded our own, (and which has showed itself particularly in physical science,) to consider everything having life as a mere accumulation of dead parts, to separate what exists only in connexion and cannot otherwise be conceived, instead of penetrating to the central point and viewing all the parts as so many irradiations from it. Hence nothing is so rare as a critic who can elevate himself to the comprehensive contemplation of a work of art.

The relations here seen between art, science, philosophy, and literary criticism are, in their breadth of interest and intellectual confidence, quintessential Coleridge. But the passage is from Schlegel's now little-read *Lectures on Dramatic Art and Criticism.*[94] Coleridge's seeming intellectual self-assurance, despite continual protestations of modesty, is continually humbling to the reader, so that one is repeatedly reminded that one is in the presence of genius. "I was wont boldly to affirm," writes Coleridge early in *Biographia Literaria,* "that it would be scarcely more difficult to push a stone out from the pyramids with the bare hand, than to alter a word, or the position of a word, in Milton or Shakespeare, (in their most important works at least,) without making the author say something else, or something worse, than he does say."[95] And in the *Table Talk* we find Coleridge declaring:

> All I can say as to Beaumont and Fletcher is, that I can point out well enough where something has been lost, and that something so and so was probably in the original; but the law of Shakespeare's thought and verse is such, that I feel convinced that not only could I detect the spurious, but supply the genuine, word.[96]

These are astonishing claims to anyone who knows the actual history of the development of an accurate Shakespearean text. If there is a "law of Shakespeare's thought and verse" which is a certain guide to authentic creative provenance, it has never been discovered by the thousands of devoted Shakespearean scholars and editors who have labored patiently to distinguish Shakespeare's original text from its accretions and to repair its lacunae. The power of the naked aesthetic judgment to make determinations of the kind Coleridge means is not a belief founded upon either logic or experience but a persistent superstition among "philosophical" critics who want to believe that "severe" laws of artistic creation exist. The reader rarely pauses to consider soberly what is mere assertion in Coleridge and what can be supported by fact. His rhetoric, his eloquence, command their own assent. Yet it is noteworthy that the man so widely considered to have had the profoundest insight into Shakespeare's art should have been so wrong in his conjectures as to the order of Shakespeare's plays.

The problem of establishing a chronology for the plays from internal evidence (assuming that was all there was to guide us) would seem comparatively trifling compared to that of not only detecting a spurious word, but supplying the genuine one. Coleridge's final statement on the subject of Shakespeare's chronology was written in 1819, after the last of his lectures. *Troilus and Cressida, Julius Caesar* and *Timon of Athens* were placed among the last of Shakespeare's compositions, with *Cymbeline* and *The Winter's Tale* (both actually among the last of Shakespeare's works, and both written well after any of the others named) among the very earliest of his works.[97] What, really, is one to make of Coleridge's statement that in Shakespeare's "Fifth and last Aera . . . the energies of intellect in the cycle of genius were, tho' in a richer and potentiated form, becoming predominant over passion and creative self-modification."[98] Can anything be more impressive? But the last of the six plays he identifies as coming from this sublime era is *Coriolanus*—generally considered one of the Bard's lesser triumphs—and two others, *Julius Caesar* and *Troilus and Cressida,* are comparatively early plays. These opinions—for which no parallels have been found—are, to say the least, somewhat surprising coming from a man whose knowledge of Shakespeare's poetic development and judgment as a dramatist is supposed to be unrivaled.

Coleridge's reputation as a supremely gifted and original Shakespearean critic took hold long before there were systematic studies of the debt to Schlegel and others. The attitude taken by critics in the nineteenth century was frequently a compound of ignorance and misplaced jingoism. There can be no real doubt that to many English critics it was simply scandalous to believe that foreigners had first provided a reasoned basis for Bardolatry. This is well exemplified in the comments of H. D. Traill, one of Coleridge's early biographers:

Coleridge, *primus inter pares* as a critic of any order of literature, is in the domain of Shakespearian commentary absolute king. The principles of analysis which he was charged with having borrowed without acknowledgment from Schlegel, with whose Shakespearian theories he was at the time entirely unacquainted, were in fact of his own excogitation. He owed nothing in this matter to any individual German, nor had he anything in common with German Shakespearianism except its profoundly philosophising spirit, which, moreover, was in his case directed and restrained by other qualities, too often wanting in critics of that industrious race; for he possessed a sense of the ridiculous, a feeling for the poetic, a tact, a taste, and a judgment, which would have saved many a worthy but heavy-handed Teutonic professor . . .[99]

Traill here offers not facts, but xenophobia.[100] As an example of Coleridge's supremacy in psychological analysis, he quotes "the following acute but eminently sensible estimate of the character of Polonius."[101] This analysis will be found on page 217 of the second volume of Raysor, along with the editor's note that "this excellent character of Polonius is taken from Dr. Johnson's note on *Hamlet*."[102] The third and last of Traill's examples of Coleridge's unique genius is the passage beginning: "The fool is no comic buffoon to make the groundlings laugh—no forced condescension of Shakespeare's genius to the taste of his audience."[103] Schlegel, however, had described the Fool as Lear's "wisest counsellor," who "clothes reason with the livery of his motley garb."[104] He had also seen in Shakespeare's fools "an infinite abundance of intellect, enough indeed to supply a whole host of ordinary wise men."[105]

Of Traill's three examples of Coleridge's unparalleled insight as a Shakespearean critic, one is simply lifted from Johnson, and another clearly derived from Schlegel or, at the least, no advance on Schlegel's thought. The almost complete disaster of the point Traill was trying to make should give other critics pause in specifying particular passages as quintessential Coleridge.

Yet most recent discussions on the subject offer little hope for any early change in the general climate of opinion concerning his achievement as a Shakespearean critic. In an edition of Coleridge's Shakespearean criticism sure to be widely distributed, the editor, basing his text on Raysor's careful edition, informs us that he has "kept footnotes to a minimum, omitting all of Raysor's references to parallel passages in Schlegel."[106] This decision perpetuates the injustice to Schlegel, perpetuates a distortion of literary history, and gives still more momentum to Coleridge's ever-increasing reputation for profound originality. In an introduction written especially for this edition, Professor Alfred Harbage of Harvard takes up the question of Coleridge's debts to Schlegel and others. In the process he sharply censures Wellek for the latter's various strictures on Coleridge and even takes to task Raysor for using the word plagiarism too freely. "I believe there is no instance in Coleridge's Shakespearean criticism proper where the term is really appropriate," Harbage concludes.[107]

15.

Some Miscellaneous Prose

COLERIDGE left behind a vast and scattered body of prose writings. Some have never been published; many others can only be found in old and, by modern standards, inadequately prepared editions.[1] Over the last nineteen years of his life, Coleridge preserved a mysterious silence on most of the basic questions in criticism and aethetics which he had left unanswered or addressed in only the most fragmentary or elliptical way in *Biographia Literaria* and the lectures on Shakespeare. Instead he published moral and political tracts, such as his "Lay Sermons," *The Statesman's Manual,*[2] *Aids to Reflection,* and *On the Constitution of the Church and State.* On the whole these compositions have for generations remained unread outside of professional circles and, at least until recently, were generally considered sterile and irrelevant to any contemporary concern by those who thought about them at all.

It is not our purpose here either to survey or summarize in any detail the corpus of Coleridge's prose writings and lectures not dealt with already in separate discussions. It is relevant to ask, however, whether they demonstrate, as the works thus far considered do, a substantial dependence upon the ideas and often the very language of others, or are they more nearly independent performances, revealing a degree of original thinking and observation which justifies the exalted claims now being made for their value?

To this question, obviously, no conclusive answer can be given. It will not be possible to speak of Coleridge's originality as a journalist, for example, until his work is published in a modern edition and becomes available to the international community of scholars. And then, only when some considerable time has passed, will the problem of debt assume any firm shape. This is not meant to minimize the work of the present generation of Coleridge editors. Their labors have been as thorough and often heroically painstaking as the history of scholarship can show. But the task of establishing sources is one for the entire scholarly community, and it is a pursuit that never ends.

For many reasons it would be highly desirable to recover in their original form the several essays on moral and political subjects which the young Coleridge delivered in Bristol in the years immediately following his departure from Cambridge, during his early friendship with Southey, and in the first intense flush of enthusiasm for Pantisocracy and Aspheterism. The published text of so well known an essay as *Conciones ad Populum,* for example, may well differ substantially from the oral lecture, and there is in fact some reason to believe this is so. The uncertainty of the texts, and Coleridge's later insistence on the absolute continuity of his political credos from the seeming radicalism of his early youth to the decided conservatism of the Sage of Highgate contribute to the extraordinary difficulty of establishing both the chronology and color of his political opinions.[3]

But whatever his political, moral, religious, or literary views may have been at any particular time in his life, one aspect of his intellectual style remains constant: his repeated dependence in his lectures and publications upon unstated or misleadingly acknowledged sources. Coleridge's writings, at any point in his life—even in his earliest letters—disclose an anxious concern for intellectual appearances. The polymath and library cormorant is the earliest and most persistent of his self-projections.

The Bristol lectures on political and moral subjects, as John Colmer has said, "indicate an exceptionally well-stocked mind for so young a man." No doubt, by any comparative standard, Coleridge's mind was well stocked. Still, it is of some interest to learn that

the wealth of illustrative material and facts concerning British Constitutional history with which *The Plot Discovered* is adorned, came from a single source. Reference to Burgh's *Political Disquisitions,* which Coleridge had borrowed from the Bristol Library in November [1795] enabled him to amass a great deal of information at small intellectual cost.[4]

Since Colmer does not particularize, the reader is left to draw his own uncertain conclusions. The curious student can, of course, seek out the text of *The Plot Discovered* and compare it with Burgh's somewhat scarce work, and thus determine more precisely the extent of Coleridge's obligations. However, in the same year that Colmer's book appeared, Lucyle Werkmeister published a detailed article upon this very subject: "Coleridge's *The Plot Discovered:* Some Facts and a Speculation."[5]

Mrs. Werkmeister begins by wondering why Coleridge published his essay at all, since, she asserts, "the pamphlet laid no claim whatever to originality." We are reminded that the subtitle of Otway's *Venice Preserved* is *A Plot Discovered* and told that the play had been performed in Bristol in July 1795. Why Coleridge's title should imply a lack of originality in the contents of his political pamphlet is not altogether clear.

Mrs. Werkmeister prints in parallel columns some dozen direct borrowings, and recognizes that the twenty-three-year-old Coleridge may have leaned still more heavily upon Burgh, but she argues that it cannot be certainly known whether Coleridge's arguments for political reform (which tend not to change) derived from a study of the parliamentary debates themselves or from Burgh. After several examples of Coleridge's possible use of his source, Mrs. Werkmeister continues:

> The important thing is that not only did the pamphlet present material which was already available and to a large extent familiar to anyone who could read, but it made no attempt to disguise the fact. So far as the debates were concerned, Coleridge went out of his way to use a word or a phrase which would immediately identify the source, frequently making his points in precisely the same words as those in which they had already been made in Parliament. Although he did not perhaps acknowledge the whole of his debt to Burgh, he indicated something of its magnitude, for, having called special attention to the *Political Disquisitions*, he went on to say that the "whole work should be in the possession of every lover of freedom; its remarks on law and government are as profound as they are pointed, and it is an invaluable treasure to those, whose occupations allow them but little time for reading on account of the multitude and pertinence of historic facts collected. He who carefully peruses the 'Political Disquisitions' will meet with little new information in later writers."[6]

The reader who turns from this to Coleridge's address will perhaps be surprised to find that the author nowhere states or can reasonably be said to suggest that his work is unoriginal. Indeed, the paragraphs teem with facts and arguments which seem to result from the author's own assiduous industry among original and diverse materials. Consider the following typical passage:

> Burleigh, who lived in the reign of Elizabeth, said truly, "England can never be undone but by a parliament:" for Burleigh said it before the contract of the bill of rights had been entered into by the people and their governors. But now we cannot be *legally* undone even by a parliament: for (as Bolingbroke remarks) parliament cannot annul the constitution. The constitution is the law paramount, and prevents the supreme from becoming an arbitrary power. . . .[7]

One naturally assumes that the quotations from Burleigh and Bolingbroke derive from the author's wide reading. But in fact the quotations (and the remainder of the paragraph) are to be found in Burgh. Twenty-two pages into the thirty-three-page pamphlet there is a lengthy footnote in which several authorities are cited. Burgh's name is introduced for the first time parenthetically, "(as Burgh most sagaciously remarks)," and then, several lines still further down in the reduced type, there is a specific reference to Burgh, whose "whole work should be in the possession of every lover of freedom."

Let us consider the remainder of Coleridge's long note about Burgh's book again:

> its remarks on laws and government are as profound as they are pointed, and it is an invaluable treasure to those, whose occupations allow them but little time for reading, on account of the multitude and pertinence of historical facts collected. He who carefully peruses the "Political Disquisitions" will meet with little new information in later writers.

Would Solomon deduce from this that the author intended in any sense to announce an enormous debt to Burgh? After all, Coleridge cited many sources. Who would suppose that his references to Sir J. Hinde Cotton, to the eighth volume of debates in the Commons, to the fifth volume of the debates of the peers, all came from Burgh? Does his obscure reference to Burgh in a long footnote (which may not have formed part of his oral lecture) in any sense indicate the magnitude of his debt?

In fact, his citation to the third volume of Burgh, page 230, is wrong. (The reference should have been to pages 237 and 238.) Another slip of the pen? Perhaps. But it will be remembered that Coleridge gave a wrong citation to the passage allegedly borrowed from Rogers' *The Pleasures of Memory*. He directed readers with unnecessary vagueness to "one of Akenside's blank verse inscriptions," when it would have been just as easy to say which one. He published "Mutual Passion," as "Altered and Modernized from An Old Poet," when he might have acknowledged Ben Jonson directly, and thus have forestalled a century of editorial error.

We thus find, in one of Coleridge's first published works, that pattern of pretense and concealment characteristic of his writings and lectures to the end of his life.[8] Nowhere is this more apparent than in the series of miscellaneous essays and lectures on aesthetic topics which date from his middle years. These works are now widely acclaimed as among the chief glories of English literary and aesthetic criticism and speculation, despite at least the appearance of a decisive dependence upon German men of letters.

"On Poesy or Art," perhaps the most widely anthologized of these essays, contains scarcely a single idea which is not a direct translation or paraphrase from Schelling's oration "Concerning the Relation of the Plastic Arts to Nature." These debts, first generally noted by Ferrier, were considered in detail by Sara Coleridge, who cited some twenty parallels and the use of a few short sentences verbatim. "Mr. Coleridge seems to have borrowed from memory," she wrote, ". . . for the most part the thoughts of Schelling are mixed up with those of the borrower, and I think that, on a careful comparison of the Lecture with the oration, any fair reader will admit that, if it be Schelling's—and the leading thought of the whole is his, I freely own,— it is Coleridge's also."[9] Among some later critics, the deep bond between these two works is loosened to that of a dubious "resemblance." Others, convinced that Coleridge had been working out these ideas long before he had heard of Schelling, inevitably minimize the problem of intellectual debt.[10]

"On Poesy or Art" embodies Coleridge's most elaborate statement on the function of art (that is, painting, sculpture, music, architecture) as a "mediatress" between man and nature. This concept, together with famous passages on the unconscious, on art and the symbol, and much else, are best dealt with separately. But the question should be raised here how it is that Coleridge's independence in these formulations is so regularly insisted upon. All that one can find before Coleridge's departure for Germany are the vaguest and most contradictory hints on these topics, when they can be found at all. Is it not odd that a single Englishman—alone among his contemporaries—should develop ideas so like hosts of Germans, and only reveal them to the world long after a trip to Germany, and years after diligent study of their work, and then to present his ideas for the most part in the very words of these foreigners?

The unusual awkwardness and obscurity of both language and organization in this essay are readily attributed to the fact that Coleridge did not prepare his oral lecture for publication. In this instance we seem almost to glimpse the Englishman laboring over a foreign language, both to untangle complex grammatical constructions and to flavor the whole with his own style. "The wisdom of nature is distinguished from that in man, by the co-instantaneity of the plan and execution," Coleridge writes, availing himself of Schelling's godlike knowledge of cosmic processes. "What could be more pedantic," Beach justly inquires, "than 'the co-instantaneity of the plan and execution'?" Beach also strongly objects to Coleridge's phrase about the artist having to "eloign himself from nature." "Coleridge was often a clumsy writer," he notes. "But such cramp of style is generally a sign that he was building up his sentences on the model of a foreign tongue."[11] Less awkward but more characteristic of Coleridge's way with Schelling is his handling of the whole passage. Schelling had written that there are times when the artist must withdraw from nature, "but only in order to raise himself to the level of creative energy and apprehend it spiritually." In Coleridge the artist "absents himself for a season from her [nature], that his own spirit, which has the same ground with nature, may learn her unspoken language in its main radicals. . . ."[12]

It is symptomatic of a kind of critical xenophobia in English-speaking countries that Coleridge's unfinished and often awkwardly organized "On Poesy or Art" should be among those key essays regularly reprinted not only in collections of his own work but in anthologies of literary criticism, while Schelling's polished oration should have languished for generations available only in an old and obscure set of translations of German classics, until its appearance in 1953 in the appendix of a book by Herbert Read, a locus unlikely to provide wide circulation.[13]

Coleridge drew upon some of Schelling's ideas and especially his etymological and anthropological researches for the essay he read on 18 May 1825 before the Royal Society of Literature. In some places his "On the Prometheus of Aeschylus" paraphrases Schelling's *Gods of Samothrace*.[14]

Throughout the miscellaneous prose essays and lectures are scattered borrowings from Schlegel. The learned lecture on Greek drama, in Raysor's words, "is composed entirely of patches from different lectures by Schlegel, freely translated or paraphrased. . . . this lecture ought not to be included in Coleridge's works at all, if it had not in a sense established its right to a place there by long possession."[15] Sara Coleridge thought that the borrowings here, too, "were probably taken from memory, for they seldom follow the order of composition in the original, and no one paragraph is wholly transferred from it.[16] As other interpretations of facts such as these have already been explored, it seems unnecessary to challenge once again this improbable assumption.

In the lecture "General Character of the Gothic Literature and Art," ideas are again silently lifted from Schlegel. As for the lecture "Classical and Romantic Drama," which develops an influential distinction, it is for the most part a mosaic of unacknowledged borrowings from the same contemporary German.[17]

In the lecture on Dante, where several passages are "a reworking of the old ideas from Schlegel's first lecture," Coleridge suddenly adopts, with only slight paraphrase, a brilliant contrast between ancient and modern literature from Schiller's "On Naive and Sentimental Poetry." This learned and insightful analysis, replete with passages from Homer and Ariosto in Greek and Italian, is put forward without reference to any other human cogitation on the subject. It is instructive that despite the immense fame of Schiller's essay, it was not until 1922 that this "striking and complete parallel" was noticed.[18]

Demonstrating once again how the German *Zeitgeist* seems to have chosen himself as its English minion, Coleridge wrote to J. H. Green in 1817: "I have but merely looked into Jean Paul's Vorschule d. Aisthetic [*sic*]; but I found one sentence almost word for word the same as one written by myself in a fragment of an Essay on the Supernatural many years ago." Regrettably, no such essay or fragment exists.[19] What does, however, are the manuscript notes for a lecture on "Wit and Humor," which Coleridge delivered the following year (1818). They consist of jottings and quotations taken from the very work he had but merely looked into. Raysor cites some twenty-one borrowings in this lecture from the *Vorschule der Aesthetik*. Interestingly, Coleridge cited *one* of these as originating with Richter.[20]

The three essays "On the Principles of Genial Criticism" have been termed Coleridge's "most important single contribution to the general criticism of art."[21] Though Coleridge underscored to J. J. Morgan that the essays were "a bold Avowal of *my* sentiments on the fine Arts,"[22] their contents seem considerably less bold when the dependence on Kant is detailed. Shawcross' by no means exhaustive notes provide over a dozen references to Kant, whom Coleridge did not once mention throughout the whole series of papers.[23] There were, however, acknowledged quotations from such smaller fry as Sennertus, Burton, Scaliger, Hooker, and Porphyry, among others.

As is common in many of Coleridge's prose writings, these essays groan under the weight of formidable preliminaries. The difficulties of the subject are announced at large and the inadequacy of all previous discussions emphasized. The author has "carefully perused all the works on the Fine Arts known to him," and "much remains to be done."[24]

Throughout the first two essays the discussion of beauty draws heavily on Kant's analysis of beauty in the *Critique of Judgment*. At all times, however, the concepts are advanced as completely novel. In the third essay Coleridge even borrows an anecdote about an "Iroquois Sachem" who, Kant tells us, "was pleased in Paris by nothing more than the cook shops." Characteristically, Coleridge withdraws from a full discussion "because I am about to put to the press a large volume on the LOGOS," in which matters here left incomplete have been treated exhaustively. The essays conclude with the same quotation from Plotinus which shuts off discussion at a crucial point in *Biographia Literaria*, preceded by the same orphic accents: "I discourse not now, waiting for a loftier mood, a nobler subject, a more appropriate audience, warned from within and from without, that it is profanation to speak of these mysteries. . . ."[25] In fact, these fragmentary essays of 1814 mark the end of Coleridge's known meditations on the subject of the fine arts. The next twenty years are an almost total blank, but for those observations on the unifying function of the imagination which are of obvious relevance in any aesthetic discussion.

Despite the numerous and detailed borrowings from the *Critique of Judgment* in these essays, some scholars have been contemptuous of those who assert a decisive dependence on Kant. This is not so surprising as might appear. Coleridge undoubtedly knew far more about literature and poetry than was dreamt of in Kant's philosophy. Still, it is easy to go astray when pursuing the implications of this fact. We are not here discussing critical theory that derives from generalizations made after the study of particular works, but an abstract aesthetics which usually scorns to consider concrete works. Procedure here is from generalization to application. It is in any case a mistake to suppose that Coleridge was on home ground when discussing territories adjacent to, but outside the republic of letters. To dismiss him as a mere collagist, however, is not only a mistake in itself, it permits discussion to veer away to a minor and obviously sterile issue when the central question is what remains of Coleridge as an aesthetician after the debts are clearly identified, the stated and implied claims faced squarely, and the exalted atmosphere of discussion adjusted to. This question, however, must for the present be deferred.

If the failure to identify a heavily used source in an oral lecture is scarcely worthy of comment, it may perhaps be urged that the obscurity of the place in which these essays on "genial criticism" originally appeared, *Felix Farley's Bristol Journal*, is some mitigation of the awkward fact that Kant's name fails to appear among the numerous others cited. Neither argument is applicable to the *rifacciamento* of *The Friend*, which Coleridge published in

1818. Sixty years ago Shawcross denied any influence from the German idealists, but declared that the work "abounds in the fruits of Kant's teaching."[26] More particular accounts since then have established that *The Friend* was also nourished by Kantian foliage, limbs, and roots. Camouflage of particular groves in favor of—now and then—general celebration of the forest was but one of many odd devices employed to obscure the whole question of proprietary rights.

A characteristic example of these practices is to be found in a passage where Coleridge declares:

> The grand problem, the solution of which forms, *according to Plato*, the final object and distinctive character of philosophy, is this: for all that exists *conditionally* (that is, the existence of which is inconceivable except under the condition of its dependency on some other as its antecedent) to find a ground that is *unconditional* and absolute, and thereby to reduce the aggregate of human knowledge to a system.[27]

Beach observes that "in attributing the above formula to Plato, Coleridge gives no reference. It happens that the formula appears, almost literally, in Kant's *Critique of Pure Reason*." The passage, in Smith's translation, follows: "Obviously the principle peculiar to reason in general, in its logical employment, is:—to find for the *conditioned* knowledge obtained through the understanding the *unconditioned* whereby its unity is brought to completion." Beach comments: "Having in mind Coleridge's inaccuracy and his extreme want of candor in giving credit for his ideas, I venture to suggest that he has either forgotten that this is Kant's expression, or else that he found it more convenient to refer to the classic philosopher, by way of disguising the degree to which he was indebted to the Germans of his own day."[28] In fact, to have attributed so Kantian a formulation to Plato would be enchanting as a mere mistake; as a species of obscurantism the reference is grotesque.

Certain of Coleridge's conceptions on the laws of thought Beach believes derived from Kant's *Critique*:

> It is true that Coleridge finds this doctrine in Bacon (as well as Plato); and here he gives references and more or less pertinent quotations. But the very reference to Bacon he would have found in Kant's preface, together with an account of the relation between ideas (or laws) and experiments very like that which Coleridge gives as Bacon's. Here again, as in the case of Plato, Coleridge is very likely drawing a red herring across the trail of his German inspirations.[29]

In Section ii of Essay VI of *The Friend* is a thorny footnote that distinguishes between nature in the two senses of *forma formans* and *forma formata.* "This entire paragraph, except for the Latin terms, is a literal and unacknowledged borrowing from the opening sentences of Kant's *Metaphysische Anfangsgründe der Naturwissenschaft*, together with the accompanying footnote of Kant's (*Gesammelte Schriften*, IV, 467)."[30] Beach is unexpectedly charitable in not pointing out that immediately after this detailed borrowing Coleridge goes out of his way to take credit for the preceding analysis: "Having thus explained the term nature, I now more especially entreat the reader's attention to the sense in which here, and everywhere through this essay, I use the word idea. I assert . . ."[31] And the path away from Kant is turned more sharply by another reference to Bacon.

Tennemann's *History of Philosophy*, which had been culled from so liberally in the philosophical lectures, found its way into *The Friend* also:

> in the third essay of Section 2 he [Coleridge] had recourse to Tennemann. The quotation at the head of the essay . . . is from Heraclitus— and Tennemann. . . . Coleridge's first paragraph on the rise of the Sophists is Tennemann's wordier account in brief. . . . The quotation from the *Timaeus* in Coleridge's second paragraph is given by Tennemann, and the sentences that follow Coleridge's translation of it are, with variation, to be found among his Tennemann marginalia. The third and fourth paragraphs also have small points in common with Tennemann. . . . The fifth essay again echoes the *Geschichte der Philosophie*, as far as a long footnote in volume III, pp. 160-61 which is the *Assistant* condensed and is word for word part of the *Prospectus*.[32]

Miss Coburn cites the following sentence as verbatim from Tennemann: "Such were Protagoras, Gorgias, Prodicus, Hippias, Polus, Callicles, Thrasymachus, and a whole host of Sophists *minorum gentium*."[33] It is to be hoped that knowledge of the origin of this sentence will temper the assumption that Coleridge had minute knowledge of the dusty pages of these philosophic small fry.

Elsewhere in *The Friend* Coleridge introduces a series of reflections with the statement that the "leading thought . . . I remember to have read in the works of a continental philosopher." One may well ask, which continental philosopher? Schelling? Kant? Fichte? The thoughts turn out to be "practically a word-for-word translation" from Jacobi, though without any quotation marks to assist the reader to determine to what extent Coleridge is specifically indebted.[34]

As we have seen, many critics and scholars—often using a procedure whereby a remote parallel invalidates the near influence—minimize the German influence and insist that Coleridge developed his ideas from such English sources as the Cambridge Platonists and from ancient thinkers.[35] Yet again and again the *specific* borrowing proves to be from Germany, from books in Coleridge's own library, often annotated by himself, whereas the specific influence from antiquity or the Neoplatonists consists of scraps and tatters.[36]

The incorrigible deviousness of Coleridge's way with sources is vividly exemplified in two of the most famous passages of the *Friend*. The first sentence of Essay II of "The First Landing Place" (on Luther) begins: "Whoever has sojourned in Eisenach,* will assuredly have visited the Warteburgh, interesting by so many historical associations. . . ." A footnote reads, "*Durchflüge durch Deutchland, die Niederlande und Frankreich: zweit. Theil. p. 126."[37] If one knew some German, and thought about the matter at all, one would naturally suppose that the obscure title was some sort of chatty travel book, where we would find informative glimpses of the locales mentioned. Those few English readers who might have been inclined to pursue the matter would surely come to see that no author had been named, nor any indication of where or when the book was published. Even a scholar intent upon following in the track of Coleridge's reading would, in a world of numberless duties, assign a very low priority to so unpromising a reference. Time and chance, however, are the great allies of scholarship. Just a century after Coleridge penned the note, a German scholar, M. Eimer, published some surprising disclosures.[38]

The *Durchflüge* now swims into our ken as a work in seven volumes by one Jonas Ludwig von Hess, and Coleridge's celebrated essay on Luther proves to be vaguely connected not merely to page 126 of the second volume (as indicated with seeming respect to topographical details in Eisenach), but is actually a translation and amplification of some twenty-five pages more, dealing with Luther and related matters. Numerous learned quotations prove once more to derive not from Coleridge's wide researches, but from a single source; for example: "as appears from a passage in his [Luther's] letter to George Salatin, which I translate."[39] But the very pronoun "I" is adopted from the German. "Luther did not write, he acted poems," declares Coleridge. But this arresting conception is merely a translation of Hess's "Er schrieb nicht, er that Gedichte." And the memorable description of the young Luther, beginning: "methinks I see him sitting, the heroic student, in his chamber in the Warteburg, with his midnight lamp before him . . ." is literal Hess, including the personal pronoun: "Ich seh' ihn sitzen, den braven Luther, in seiner Stube auf der Warteburg, den Kopf gestützt, über eine Stelle brütend. . . ."[40]

As if all this were not sufficiently surprising, it turns out that the circumstances attending Coleridge's famous retelling of the tale of Maria Eleonora Schöning in the *Friend's* "Second Landing-Place" was very different from what he anxiously wished his readers to believe. In introducing the story, he wrote:

> The account was published in the city in which the event took place, and in the same year I read it, when I was in Germany, and the impression made on my memory was so deep that though I relate it in my own lan-

guage, and with my own feelings, and in reliance on the fidelity of my recollections, I dare vouch for the accuracy of the narration in all important particulars.[41]

Who would suppose from this that the publication referred to was not an ephemeral newspaper account but the fourth volume of Hess's *Durchflüge* (this time not mentioned by Coleridge)? As for the fussy preliminaries which call attention to Coleridge's prodigious memory and the intensity of his feelings, whole pages of the bitter tale of Maria Eleonora Schöning are precisely translated from Hess. As Eimer methodically places the parallel columns side by side, we are reminded of such Coleridgean phrases as, "in my own language," and "in reliance on the fidelity of my recollections." Surprisingly, one touching detail after the other, which we naturally assume is the work of Coleridge the poet, comes straight from the German source.[42]

The revised and augmented version of *The Friend* which Coleridge published in 1818 might have been one of the crowning intellectual achievements of his life. He was now forty-six years old. He had had almost a decade to hone and modify the loose materials of which the original *Friend* had been formed into a coherent embodiment of his diverse interests. Considered only with respect to external circumstances, here surely seems to have been a tremendous opportunity. And yet one's sense of *The Friend* from within is quite different. To the student of Coleridge, or the Romantic period generally, there are passages of absorbing interest. But one's overwhelming sense of the work is a mixture of boredom and frustration. Such an amalgam of preliminaries, promises, excuses, and anxious self-awareness. So many mighty columns of ideas sent marching toward formidable targets, only to have the commander-in-chief blow retreat so as to fight another battle on another day on another field.

Our frustration is not that *The Friend* is fragmentary, or elliptical. What disturbs us is that instead of at last beholding the vast flocks of intellectual fowl buried in the high grass bear themselves aloft on powerful wings, up comes—to borrow Coleridge's wonderfully disparaging comment about some of his own verse—"a metaphysical Bustard, urging it's slow, heavy, laborious, earth-skimming Flight, over dreary & level Wastes."[43] *The Friend* fails not for complex reasons but for a simple one: it is dull. All but the most persistent reader must finally lose interest in so clogged and sclerotic a performance.[44]

And in general this sad judgment can be made of most of the post-*Biographia* prose writings. It is our knowledge of Coleridge the poet, Coleridge the critic, which keeps us reading doggedly on. That he let his declining energies eddy into metaphysics and politics and theology and science constitutes a great loss to letters. Whatever one may think of Coleridge as critic or aesthetician, he is almost always interesting. But Coleridge on subjects other than literature is almost always boring, but for intermittent flashes of brilliant metaphor. And so, despite the substantial popularity in the nine-

teenth century of a moral guide like *Aids to Reflection*, the late prose
writings are today quite dead outside of professional circles. The same cannot be said of Charles Lamb's essays, or Hazlitt's, or De Quincey's, at least
in the judgment of the common reader, who, Dr. Johnson has told us, is the
final judge in these matters.

16.

Coleridge as Critic
and Aesthetician

COLERIDGE'S stature as a literary critic and aesthetician has never stood higher than it does today. As the acknowledged "father of modern literary criticism," his influence is incontestable and incalculable. Whether this influence is either desirable or deserved are wholly separate questions. What cannot be denied is that, taken in themselves, his writings comprise the most far-ranging, complex, and suggestive body of practical criticism and aesthetic speculation in English. As the letters, notebooks, marginalia, and other scattered leaves are gathered, Coleridge's influence magnifies; like the expanding universe, his reputation accelerates as it grows larger.

His achievement as a critic derives in part from two almost unique personal traits. The first is his intellectual range. He brought to criticism a vast knowledge of literature and an unparalleled combination of interests in philosophy, psychology, and the natural sciences, to which he added the invaluable experience of a practicing poet. And yet, as events were to suggest, perhaps more important than all this was the fact that, for all his destructive self-doubt, he also had—and had early—an exalted vision of his intellectual destiny. "I am not *fit* for *public* Life," he wrote to Thelwall in 1796, "yet the Light shall stream to a far distance from the taper in my cottage window."[1] Just four months later he described his hopes of writing an epic:

I should not think of devoting less than 20 years to an Epic Poem. Ten to collect materials and warm my mind with universal science. I would be a tolerable Mathematician, I would thoroughly know Mechanics, Hydrostatics, Optics, and Astronomy, Botany, Metallurgy, Fossilism, Chemistry, Geology, Anatomy, Medicine—then the *mind of man*—then the *minds of men*—in all Travels, Voyages and Histories. So I would spend ten years—the next five to the composition of the poem—and the five last to the correction of it.

So I would write haply not unhearing of that divine and rightly-whispering Voice, which speaks to mighty minds of predestinated Garlands, starry and unwithering.[2]

177

This immense project was nudged aside, after his return from Germany, by others of equal, if not greater, intellectual reach. In March 1801, as we have seen, he wrote to Poole that he had "completely extricated the notions of Time, and Space . . . overthrown the doctrine of Association," and that he was

> about to do more—namely . . . to evolve all the five senses, that is, to deduce them from *one sense*, & to state their growth, & the causes of their difference—& in this evolvement to solve the process of Life & Consciousness.[3]

Just six weeks before, in an extraordinary letter to the brilliant Sir Humphry Davy, he had outlined a project of more immediate interest to us: a book under the title

> "Concerning Poetry & the nature of the Pleasures derived from it."—I have faith, that I do understand this subject / and I am sure, that if I write what I ought to do on it, the Work would supersede all the Books of Metaphysics hitherto written / and all the Books of Morals too.[4]

The state of intellectual euphoria implied by these diverse and staggering projects suggestively coincides with his first serious excursion into German metaphysics, a time when he was reading, *inter alia*, Leibnitz, Lambert, Kant, and Wolff.[5] No man in England had so all-encompassing a vision of the interlocking fields of aesthetics, science, religion, and philosophy. And here lies Coleridge's greatest strength. For however cloudy, fragmentary, or indiscriminate his eclecticism was to prove in practice, he always had before him a fiery column, beckoning him toward that Promised Land in which all human thought and feeling would be grounded and operative in "universal logic" and Christian revelation.

It was Samuel Johnson who said of Bishop Hurd, "Hurd, sir, is one of a set of men who account for everything systematically; for instance, it has been a fashion to wear scarlet breeches; these men would tell you that, according to causes and effects, no other wear could at that time have been chosen."[6] Coleridge was one of this set of men. It could lead him into absurdities such as, "By the bye, the fact that Christianity in any genuine or ennobling form exists only in the Northern, or rather in the temperate climates, and degenerates in proportion to the increase of Heat—say from the 40 Deg. of N.L. to the Equator—is one of deep interest for a reflecting mind."[7] But it also led to positive results. All his life he strove to make intellectual connections. If the imagination was a unifying force, it was his lifelong dream to unify, and harmonize, all knowledge, all art, all thought, into a single embracing system.

To assess Coleridge as critic and aesthetician is, for this reason alone, a task of perhaps insuperable difficulty. Who can honestly claim the knowledge required to survey so vast a field? Coleridge left behind not only the familiar writings on Shakespeare and Wordsworth, but innumerable marginalia and notebook comments on writers of many periods and in various languages. He speculated on the nature of poetry and prose, the distinction between allegory and symbol, fancy and imagination, genius and talent. He wrote on the function of art as mediatress between man and nature, on classic and romantic literature; he theorized on the psychological origins of our ideas of taste and beauty, and promulgated a theory of dramatic illusion. Nor is this all. We have to contend with his theory of the imagination, with his ideas on the unconscious, on the reconciliation of opposites, with his formidable aesthetic terminology, and with his momentous emphasis on organic form as the emblem of genius.

Obviously, this is a task for a massive volume, not a chapter. But we need not therefore abandon ourselves to despair. Coleridge's main contributions to critical theory and practice can be identified and discussed with something less than exhaustive thoroughness without automatically guaranteeing superficiality. And the framework provided by the previous chapters makes it possible to treat certain aspects of his achievement, such as his intellectual independence, within a continuum of his lifelong professional interests and habits.

Only two years after the publication of *Biographia Literaria*, Coleridge wrote: "were it in my power, my works should be confined to the second volume of my 'Literary Life'."[8] Before turning to the second volume, which contains the critique of Wordsworth and much speculation on the language and nature of poetry, it is necessary to re-emphasize the break in continuity between the two halves of the work. The reason for this insistence upon what would otherwise be obvious is that again and again scholars treat the inconclusive Schellingian disquisition in the first volume with reverential respect and simply assume a logical connection between these chapters and the criticism and aesthetic analysis which follow. But there is no such connection. Nor has it ever been demonstrated that such a connection can exist, a point of no small importance. In *On University Studies*, Schelling confronted this very problem—the relationship between philosophy and practical criticism:

Now, granting that no one can understand the mystery of art, its absolute element, better than the philosopher, it may be asked whether the philosopher is equally capable of understanding its rational elements, of formulating the laws governing them. I refer to the technical aspect of art: can philosophy lower itself to consider empirical details of execution and the conditions under which the work is made?

Since philosophy is concerned solely with the Ideas, its task with respect to the empirical aspect of art is confined to formulating general laws of the phenomena, and these only to the extent that they express ideal forms. The forms of art are the forms of the things-in-themselves as they are in the archetypes. Consequently, the philosophy of art deals with these forms only insofar as they are universal and can be grasped in and for themselves, not insofar as they pertain to rules of execution or practice. What deals directly with the particular or with empirical means designed to achieve a given end is not philosophy but merely theory; philosophy is unconditioned, an end in itself. The objection might be raised that because the technical aspect of art includes the means by which an illusion of truth is created, the philosopher should deal with it. However, the truth the philosopher recognizes in art is of a higher kind, is identical with absolute beauty, the truth of the Ideas.[9]

If there is any bridge between a philosophical standpoint like this and practical criticism, it was not found by Coleridge. Neither in the Wordsworth chapters nor in his "Philosophic definitions of a Poem and Poetry with scholia," in the famous fourteenth chapter, does Coleridge even so much as glance back at the massive if skeletal foundations he had so laboriously patched together. Contemporary literary criticism is distinguished especially by its minute attention to particular texts, to concrete detail, to specific verbal relations within particular poems—procedures wholly foreign to Schellings's aesthetics. As a foundation for the practical discipline that is modern literary criticism, the formal philosophy of the first volume of the *Biographia* is therefore not only irrelevant because it is fragmentary, it is *conceptually* irrelevant.

Let us now go back to the point at which, *in medias res*, Coleridge interrupts his "deduction of the imagination" to take heed of the letter from the "judicious friend," a document which persuades the author to truncate his discussion abruptly and to content himself "for the present with stating the main result of the Chapter," which it is promised will eventually be written in full. Then follows one of the most famous and controversial pages Coleridge ever wrote:

The IMAGINATION then, I consider either as primary, or secondary. The primary IMAGINATION I hold to be the living Power and prime Agent of all human Perception, and as a repetition in the finite mind of the eternal act of creation in the infinite I AM. The secondary Imagination I consider as an echo of the former, co-existing with the conscious will, yet still as identical with the primary in the *kind* of its agency, and differing only in *degree*, and in the *mode* of its operation. It dissolves, diffuses, dissipates, in order to recreate; or where this process is rendered impossible, yet still at all events it struggles to idealize and to unify. It is essentially *vital*, even as all objects (*as* objects) are essentially fixed and dead.

FANCY, on the contrary, has no other counters to play with, but fixities and definites. The Fancy is indeed no other than a mode of

Memory emancipated from the order of time and space; while it is blended with, and modified by that empirical phenomenon of the will, which we express by the word CHOICE. But equally with the ordinary memory the Fancy must receive all its materials ready made from the law of association.[10]

The value of this distinction has been endlessly argued and little purpose would be served in summarizing the positions taken up by Lowes (contra) or Abrams (pro) or Lucas (contra) or Richards (ecstatic).[11] What may be emphasized, however, is that if the value of a critical idea bears any relation to its utility, Coleridge's distinction in practical criticism is of the most marginal worth. Such examples as he himself provided of texts showing Fancy and Imagination in action seem to suggest only that "imaginative" works are more complex than "fanciful" ones, which is not what Coleridge meant to say or imply.

Has any critic ever attempted to write a history of English poetry on the basis of this famous distinction? Can one imagine going through a play of Shakespeare's or a book of *Paradise Lost* and declaring that this is Fancy in operation and that Imagination?[12] Experimental psychology has yielded no data in the past one hundred fifty years to support any compartmentalizing of the mind's functions in this way. And in the same century and a half, although innumerable commentators have applauded Coleridge's formula, none that I know of has attempted to apply it systematically to concrete poems.

In the letter of 1802 where Coleridge first described Fancy as "the aggregating Faculty of the mind," and Imagination as the "*modifying*, and *coadunating* Faculty," he thereupon addressed himself to Greek and Hebrew poetry, and made several startling observations. One is not encouraged to believe in the formula's utility upon reading that in Greek poetry "all natural Objects were *dead*," but that "in the Hebrew Poetry you find nothing of this poor Stuff—as poor in genuine Imagination, as it is mean in Intellect—/ At best, it is but Fancy. . . ."[13]

The attempt to distinguish between Imagination and Fancy was a commonplace of eighteenth-century philosophy and criticism,[14] and it is not generally realized that Coleridge was working within a well-worn tradition. Of the many discussions on the subject, and of the many attempts to define and isolate various powers of the mind, it may suffice to confine ourselves to Arthur Browne's essay on "Fancy and Imagination" which appeared in his *Miscellaneous Sketches: or, Hints for Essays* (1798).[15] For our purposes, the central passage in Browne reads:

Fancy in the general meaning of mankind is the creative power, which is versed about things created by itself; whereas Imagination is employed only in discovering similitudes and relations not obvious, *among things existing*. . . . no two things can be more different: the subjects whose relations Imagination pourtrays and develops exist already and are not created by the mind, like the works of Fancy. Similes and comparisons are made between objects existing in nature—For example, the hero when compared to the lion, the mist on a long range of hills to to the army in array, or the sheet of spears to the waving ears of corn; the mourning fair to the melancholy nightingale, the comparison is invented, the subjects are prepared by nature, but fancy forms the character, it generates the scene, it models the group out of its native clay, and leaves to imagination the minuter office of analyzing, comparing or illustrating the beauties of mental creation, when it is satiated with those of corporeal nature.[16]

This is Coleridge's distinction with the terms reversed. In Browne's view the Fancy is *creative*, whereas the Imagination can only discover similitudes and relations "among things existing"; Coleridge's "Fancy, on the contrary, has no other counters to play with, but fixities and definites."

What has established Coleridge's formulation as a *locus classicus* is not only its eloquence, or even its key position as summarizing an intricate, weighty, and obscure argument, but rather the way the basically familiar ideas are invested with the weight of transcendental metaphysics and the technical jargon of the psychologists. Thus the Imagination itself may be either Primary or Secondary, the primary being "the living Power and prime Agent of all human Perception, and as a repetition in the finite mind of the eternal act of creation in the infinite I AM." The Fancy is "a mode of Memory emancipated from the order of time and space," and so forth. Clearly, the Arthur Brownes of this world have been left far below on this sublunary globe.

Discussions of the Imagination throughout the eighteenth and well into the nineteenth centuries seem essentially to be a by-product of the much larger question of how the flux of external stimuli is perceived by the mind, and secondly, how the mind orders, arranges, combines or adds to such data. The terms "Fancy" and "Imagination" were freely and often indiscriminately used to describe that Gordian complex of mental activities by which works of art come into being. As speculation, these writings are by no means without interest. Scarcely anything in all these writings, however, can be said to have added to the sum of human knowledge in any objective sense. Despite innumerable declarations by eighteenth- and nineteenth-century writers that certain aspects of mental activity can be subsumed under the headings of Imagination or Fancy, there is no agreement among aestheticians (let alone scientists) that this is so.

Descriptions of the operative *mode* of Imagination or Fancy (including Coleridge's) are merely assertions with no objective validation of any kind. As a poet Coleridge might have offered invaluable testimony to his own mental processes during composition. In fact he never did that, although Wordsworth's brilliant example in the 1800 Preface was there before him. Instead he offered still more abstract speculation in a field which cried out for solid experimental data. This is a key fact that is almost always ignored. Coleridge, Wordsworth, Schelling—indeed, it is safe to say all the poets and philosophers of the period—offered no verifiable evidence in support of their doctrines. They simply made assertions. It was an explicit cornerstone of Schelling's method (and implied everywhere in Coleridge) that the search for principles was of necessity a process of pure abstraction. A generalization built up from numerous concrete examples was not only irrelevant to the philosopher's concerns, it degraded them. The philosopher was never to stoop to peering through microscopes or patiently studying rats in a labyrinth. Such activities were purely for the corroboration of theory.

Yet quite apart from the problem of verifying hypotheses, is it not unwise on *a priori* grounds to posit mental functions that differ in their mode of operation not in degree but in kind? Coleridge was especially addicted to distinctions of this class, the paradoxical tendency of which is to destroy the organic unity of the mind—the last thing any organic critic would wish to do. That vast gulfs exist between the minds of a Shakespeare and a Shadwell it would be absurd to deny, but what is philosophically reckless and scientifically impossible to assert is that there are any absolute breaks in continuity in the operations of any particular brain. Yet it is one of the curiosities of Coleridge's intellectual history that he never grasped the mechanistic implications in his continual references to the separate faculties of the mind and his assertions of absolute distinctions in its operations, as if the skull sheltered mutually distinct compartments.

Whatever the philosophical or psychological difficulties inherent in the analysis of the Imagination, it certainly seems useful to distinguish between inventive powers ("The light that never was on sea or land") and powers of arrangement. But any attempt to go beyond these rough categories, which answer to the common experience of mankind, immediately breaks down and involves the aesthetician in a web of apparently insoluble difficulties. At what point does "mere" rearrangement become the sea change into something new and strange? There can be no absolute "fixities" and "definites," as F. L. Lucas has shrewdly observed, because of the "shifting winds of the unconscious."[17]

What then remains of the famous paragraphs on the Fancy and the Imagination, offered as the "main result" of the unfinished chapter leading to the "deduction of the imagination"? The gross distinction is certainly not original. As a tool to order works of literature in quality, the formula has proven barren, since even in Coleridge's terms there could be poor Imaginative works and fine but Fanciful ones. A reader keeping these categories in mind might be guided toward finding complexities within a work which lie below the surface of obvious mental association, but this is a considerable extrapolation from the text.

Yet if we reject the distinction—which surely seems long overdue—we are still left with Coleridge's description of what the Imagination does, and in a later passage of the *Biographia*, how it reveals itself in a work of art. These statements on the Imagination are generally considered his chief contribution to critical theory.

From where did Coleridge's strange (and transient) idea come that there are *two* imaginative faculties? We have seen that he later wished to expunge from the *Biographia* the baffling definition of the "primary" Imagination which, stripped of its jargon and pieties, states only that it is "the prime agent of all human perception."[18] The "secondary" Imagination is like the first, but it can *will* perceptions into mental existence, dissolve them, combine them, fuse them, and so forth.

The distinction here seems to me to be extrapolated from Kant, who wrote: "there are two stems of human knowledge, namely sensibility and understanding, which perhaps spring from a common, but to us unknown, root. Through the former objects are given to us; through the latter they are thought."[19] In Coleridge's definition of Fancy, objects "(*as* objects) are essentially fixed and dead," whereas the secondary Imagination is "essentially *vital*."

Has not Coleridge here simply misapplied Kant's distinction in an inappropriate context? It makes sense to distinguish between passive perception and active thought. To call both these functions parts of a single imaginative faculty is of interest, perhaps, to the technical philosopher. In an aesthetic discussion it causes havoc, for Coleridge's definition completely fails to distinguish between ordinary perception and a wide range of thinking patterns, to one of which he assigns extraordinary properties. Kant's definition is between passive perception and thought, Coleridge's between perception and the kind of imaginative activity we identify with the heroes of thought.

We shall, therefore, confine our attention to the "secondary" Imagination, for only this seems relevant to literary matters. In Coleridge this Imagination, it should be emphasized, is not only creative, but has an end in view: *to idealize and to unify*. The idealizing function of the Imagination has not had much influence on subsequent criticism, nor is it clear what Coleridge meant. But the unifying powers of some Imagination have had an incalculable influence. Indeed, the search for the unifying principle in literary works may in truth be considered the primary object of the contemporary literary critic.

At the conclusion of Chapter XIV, Coleridge took up the subject of the Imagination again, without reference to his former categories. The whole passage must be quoted:

> The poet, described in *ideal* perfection, brings the whole soul of man into activity, with the subordination of its faculties to each other, according to their relative worth and dignity. He diffuses a tone and spirit of unity, that blends, and (as it were) *fuses*, each into each, by that synthetic and magical power, to which we have exclusively appropriated the name of imagination. This power, first put in action by the will and understand-

ing, and retained under their irremissive, though gentle and unnoticed, controul (*laxis effertur habenis*) reveals itself in the balance or reconciliation of opposite or discordant qualities: of sameness, with difference; of the general, with the concrete; the idea, with the image; the individual, with the representative; the sense of novelty and freshness, with old and familiar objects; a more than usual state of emotion, with more than usual order; judgement ever awake and steady self-possession, with enthusiasm and feeling profound or vehement; and while it blends and harmonizes the natural and the artificial, still subordinates art to nature; the manner to the matter; and our admiration of the poet to our sympathy with the poetry.[20]

An extraordinary statement, and understandably famous. Let us address, in turn, several key points.

Coleridge begins by saying that "the poet, described in *ideal* perfection, brings the whole soul of man into activity, with the subordination of its faculties to each other, according to their relative worth and dignity." This strange and comprehensive statement has not received much attention, despite the immense prestige of the passage which it introduces. What is meant by man's "soul" in this context? Assuming that it can be reasonably defined, what are its "faculties"? And when we are clear as to this, on what philosophical or moral principles are the faculties of the soul graded as to "relative worth and dignity"? These answers having been supplied, we may at last ask, how does the poet (or his work) effect a *subordination* of these faculties to each other?

Have any of these questions ever been answered? In fact, the whole sentence is almost always passed over as quickly as possible to get at the description of the art product itself.

I. A. Richards, an exception to the above rule, has devoted a long discussion, in *The Portable Coleridge*, to the meaning of "faculties of the soul," stating that without such a gloss as he has provided the statement doesn't mean much, a rather damaging admission.[21] But this discussion, like the one in *Coleridge on Imagination*, seems to answer none of the questions posed above, and appears to rest satisfied with noting that Coleridge's doctrine as to the mind's "comparative rank and importance" is Plato's.[22] This may be, but the whole notion of the faculties of the mind was among the commonplaces of psychology after Locke. Milton referred to the "faculties of the soul" in *Paradise Lost*.[23] Addison in the *Spectator* had written, in a passage reminiscent of the *Biographia*:

Thus we see how many ways poetry addresses itself to the imagination, as it has not only the whole circle of nature for its province, but makes new worlds of its own, shows us persons who are not to be found in being, and represents even *the faculties of the soul, with her several virtues and vices*, in a sensible shape and character.[24]

The phrase when used by Coleridge himself in the *Friend* seems to mean no more than "that part of our nature" and "state of the mind,"[25] which suggests that the exalted atmosphere of *Biographia Literaria* may be implying far more than is really meant.

Schelling had continued to use the word "soul" in contexts where no religious or spiritual signification was intended. But his grasp of the unity of the mind was clear where Coleridge, most of the time, was simply a child of faculty psychology who altogether ignored Schelling's statement, "The essence of the soul is one. There are no faculties—these are assumed by a false psychological abstraction."[26]

It is significant that Coleridge nowhere attempts to explain what is meant in the sentence being discussed. At the very beginning of *Biographia Literaria* he wrote: ". . . I labored at a solid foundation on which permanently to ground my opinions, in the component faculties of the human mind itself, and their comparative dignity and importance."[27] That we here find the philosopher's activities described in almost the identical language ascribed to that of the artist suggests that we are dealing with a ceremonial formula, not a precise discrimination. Coleridge's statement about the ideal poet allows itself to be taken merely as a resonant celebration of the power of art. But something more seems to be involved. As with many other obscurities in Coleridge, a German source provides a clue to intended meaning.

In Schelling the "harmony of the subjective and objective" is possible only in art, not philosophy. So crucial is this conception to his whole philosophical system that it receives central emphasis in his "General Observation on the Whole System," which concludes the *System of Transcendental Idealism:*

> Absolute objectivity is given to art alone. If art is deprived of objectivity, one may say, it ceases to be what it is and becomes philosophy; give objectivity to philosophy, it ceases to be philosophy and becomes art. Philosophy to be sure, reaches the highest level, but it brings only, as it were, a fragment of man to this point. Art brings *the whole man*, as he is, to that point, namely to a knowledge of the highest of all, and on this rests the eternal difference and the miracle of art.[28]

It seems impossible reasonably to doubt that here is the origin of Coleridge's mysterious dictum. Schelling's statement, whether we agree with it or not, makes a kind of provocative sense. Coleridge's statement, however, is incomprehensible in itself and almost so in relation to its source. It is also to be noted that in the implied superiority of art over philosophy or science, or any other kind of intellectual activity, he was following Schelling's by no means typical position. Without philosophical underpinning, is not the statement absurd? It may be deeply satisfying for some of us to believe that the arts—music, literature, poetry, sculpture, architecture—bring "the whole soul of man into activity," but if we are asked to explain *how*, we must take refuge either in mysticism or silence.

Coleridge goes on to tell us that the poet "diffuses a tone and spirit of unity that blends, and (as it were) *fuses*, each into each [presumably the faculties of the soul], by that synthetic and magical power . . . Imagination. This power, first put in action by the will and understanding, and retained under their irremissive, though gentle and unnoticed, controul . . ." Again, the Imagination is a unifying power, put into action *first* by the will and understanding (the latter carries vaguely technical overtones), but what energizes the Imagination thereafter is left unsaid. Curiously, no room is left for the unconscious in this formulation, unless the idea is imported through the crack in the door left open by the phrase, "gentle and unnoticed, controul." In other contexts, however, Coleridge was to pronounce the unconscious "*the* genius in a man of genius."

We now come to how the Imagination reveals itself, and standing at the head of a long series of striking antitheses is the phrase "balance or reconciliation of opposite or discordant qualities." Considered as a basic source for certain modern views of the poem, the profound respect accorded this idea is understandable, since it is easy to hail it as the forebear of the whole panoply of paradoxes, ambiguities, tensions, and ironies which crowd the pages of today's critical journals.

Now it certainly appears that something very much more important is meant by "the balance or reconciliation of opposite or discordant qualities" than that much art (but not all) functions on the principle of contending forces, that without conflict there would be no tension, and that we are accustomed to demanding a resolution of the basic contending forces in dramatic conflicts.

Coleridge himself said it was Wordsworth's recitation of his "Salisbury Plain" that started him on the study of the Imagination, and that in that poem and Wordsworth's poems generally he found present a reconciliation of opposites. But, as F. W. Bateson has pointed out, he did not particularize.[29] Nor did he elsewhere provide an analytical demonstration of this principle in operation. The reader may well feel baffled trying to understand why the concept is placed in so important a position.

Again, the whole strange idea becomes explicable when identified against the intellectual background from which it derives. Coleridge's direct source, we may be confident, was once again Schelling, although the basic concept was familiar enough in German speculation. But we need not hunt far afield when we find this key idea studded throughout the very work of Schelling that Coleridge was using so liberally elsewhere in *Biographia Literaria,* namely, the *System of Transcendental Idealism*. There, in the formidable discussions of subject and object, philosophy and art, conscious and unconscious activity, the idea crops up again and again. The concept is, in fact, central in Schelling. In his "Deduction of the Art Product in General" (compare Coleridge's odd phrase, "deduction of the imagination" in *Biographia*), we find the following statements:

The whole productive drive comes to rest with the completion of the product; all contradictions are resolved, all riddles unraveled.

all aesthetic production rests on an opposition of activities. . . . it can only be given to art to satisfy our infinite striving as well as to resolve the ultimate and most extreme contradiction in us. Just as aesthetic production starts from the feeling of an apparently irresolvable contradiction, so, according to the testimony of all artists and of all who participate in their inspiration, it comes to a close in the feeling of an *infinite* harmony.

The organic product of nature will therefore also not necessarily be beautiful if beauty is exclusively the resolution of an infinite contradiction; and if it is beautiful, then its beauty will seem simply accidental, because the condition of its existence cannot be thought of as existing in nature.[30]

And so on and on, in scores of passages. These quotations make it perfectly clear what is only implied in the previous ones, namely, that we are dealing with technical terms and that their meaning is, at least in intention, strictly limited to certain problems in philosophy.[31]

English-speaking critics have imported, altogether inappropriately, these technical terms into literary criticism, where they make nonsense of our genuine aesthetic experiences. It is not that art does not often exhibit a profoundly satisfying resolution of conflicts and tensions. It does. But great art often does not. Certainly "Christabel" and "Hyperion" are highly imaginative works, but only a doctrinaire critic would think that they balance or reconcile anything (if only for the reason that they are both fragments). In fact, we are here in the presence of an act of uniformity against poets, the effect of which is to limit our openness and responsiveness when reading and to channel our attention toward polarities and resolutions which are often peripheral and sometimes nonexistent.

In the long list of antitheses which follows upon the reconciliation-of-opposites passage, one is particularly striking: "a more than usual state of emotion with more than usual order." Both ideas as such are ancient, deriving from Longinus and Aristotle, respectively, but the *connection* of the two in this way does seem to provide a sudden burst of insight into what is so extraordinary about particular works of art. One thinks of a Keats ode or Beethoven sonata. But the conjunction of intensity and order is rare. The properties are even to some extent antithetical, and it is not easy to see how either is a gift of the Imagination, rather than other physical or mental endowments one might name, such as organic sensibility or mathematical capacity.

If far too much were not consistently claimed for Coleridge's "theory of the imagination," it might be possible to value the famous passages for what they are, prose poems celebrating an abstraction: the complex of thoughts and feelings and desires through which works of art are brought into being. In the two key passages on the Imagination we have been considering, Coleridge condensed a very broad range of ideas from a variety of disciplines into a glorious hymn of praise to man's creativity, as he understood it, and as it was idealized by German metaphysics.

More cherished today than when they were written one hundred fifty years ago, his descriptions of the Imagination and the Ideal Poet are vitally alive, whereas the complex of ideas on which he drew are known only to scholars. This in itself is an extraordinarily ironical vindication of the claims of the Imagination to supremacy over the discursive reason. For in the world of *belles lettres* it seems to matter hardly at all whether Coleridge's ideas on this subject were original, or even whether they are internally consistent. What matters is that his words are enrobed in the rhythms and resonances of genius, and they command assent—or at the very least respect—by the majesty of their bearing.

The description of the Ideal Poet concludes what is for many the most important chapter of *Biographia Literaria*, the fourteenth, which in barely a half-dozen pages of "Philosophic definitions of a Poem and Poetry with scholia," has provided material for innumerable volumes of commentary. We may begin with Coleridge's "final definition" of a poem:

A poem is that species of composition, which is opposed to works of science, by proposing for its *immediate* object pleasure, not truth; and from all other species (having *this* object in common with it) it is discriminated by proposing to itself such delight from the *whole*, as is compatible with a distinct gratification from each component *part*.[32]

At the outset Coleridge distinguishes poetry not from prose but from a particular use of prose, namely, in works of science. This seems a strange procedure, and is partially explained by the fact that Wordsworth had made the same distinction, as had Lessing. And the central distinction is that the object of poetry is to give immediate pleasure, while the object of science is truth.[33] However, this distinction cannot with certainty be determined from the works themselves but only from dubious inference as to the intent of the author. In any case, the main distinction needed is that between works of poetry as a class and works of prose as a class, not between poetry and a narrow subdivision of works in prose.

Even if this were not true, however, the immediate objection arises that great poems have been written whose primary aim, it can readily be argued, is truth, not pleasure. Coleridge himself is at once worried that it is vaguely blasphemous to state that the primary intention of the biblical poets was pleasure, not truth, so he undermines his own argument only a page later by declaring: "[The] writings of Plato, and Jeremy Taylor, and Burnet's Theory of the Earth, furnish undeniable proofs that poetry of the highest kind may exist without metre, and even without the contradistinguishing objects of the poem." It is much to be doubted that contemporary critics and aestheticians would argue for Plato, Taylor, or Burnet as *poets*. If they are, and if their works constitute "poetry of the hightest kind," then Chapter XIV of *Biographia Literaria* and almost everything else written on the subject is quite useless.

Coleridge sees also that "pleasure may be the immediate object of a work not metrically composed; and that object may have been in high degree attained, as in novels and romances. Would then the mere superaddition of metre, with or without rhyme, entitle these to the names of poems? The answer is, that nothing can permanently please, which does not contain within itself the reason why it is so, and not otherwise."

This is one of a cluster of oracular pronouncements regularly treated with the respect accorded revealed truth. Where such truth is concerned, the proper attitude is perhaps awe and humility, but a statement in a system of aesthetic criticism presumably based on logical principles is meant to be subjected to the test of both logic and experience. From either point of view Coleridge's remark is one of the most misleading and mischievous he ever promulgated.

It is a hypothesis of science that nature functions according to universal laws, and an act of faith to believe that with sufficient knowledge man will come to understand how mutations happen, why one man has blue eyes and another brown, why tigers have stripes and leopards spots. It is a considerable remove from this to believe that tigers *must* have stripes and leopards spots, but lions neither, and that the reasons for this are discoverable by analysis of the quadrupeds themselves. Not only have terrestrial tigers permanently pleased without us knowing why they have stripes, but poetic tigers burning in the forests of the night have permanently pleased, without most of us having any idea why "the stars threw down their spears" at the sight.

Does a sonnet tell us why its structure of thoughts and feelings had to be embodied in precisely fourteen lines, neither more nor less? Why ten syllables to the line (with occasional variants of nine and eleven permitted, but not twelve or eight)? Why the overwhelming majority of such poems have rimes in the pattern of three quatrains and a couplet, or an octave in the difficult form of *abbaabba*, and a sestet in almost any variety of *c, d,* and *e*?

Why is it that Tudor and Jacobean plays run to five acts? Is it not queer that so many playwrights, whether writing tragedies or comedies, histories or farce, always worked within this rigid formula? Is the reason for this proclaimed within the plays themselves? Does Beethoven's great B-flat major quartet—a work which may be said to have permanently pleased—contain within itself the reason why its last movement is the second one Beethoven wrote for the work, and that its original last movement, the immortal *Grosse Fuge*, is almost always performed in lonely isolation from its parent stem, despite Beethoven's hopes to the contrary?

To believe that the structure of works of art is organically determined, not in a more or less useful metaphoric sense but literally, is a species of critical derangement. The assertion is so contrary to all reason and experience that the widespread belief in it is powerful testimony to a widespread desire to believe in something so flattering to the mystery and subtlety of the critic's art.

Again, knowledge of the source of a very peculiar idea in Coleridge, or queer formulation of an idea reasonable enough in itself, goes far to clear up the confusion. The origin of this particular dictum, I believe, is an amalgam of Kant and A. W. Schlegel. Early in the *Critique of Pure Reason*, Kant writes: "Experience tells us, indeed, what is, but not that it must necessarily be so, and not otherwise. It therefore gives us no true universality; and reason, which is so insistent upon this kind of knowledge, is therefore more stimulated by it than satisfied."[34] The first sentence is the origin of Coleridge's formula almost word for word; Kant's second sentence suggests why Coleridge might find in a work of art the kind of universal knowledge more appropriate to the operations of the pure reason as conceived by Kant. The binding link, therefore, between Kant's reason and Coleridge's work of art is that both deal with universal truths. But is it not ludicrous to attribute to works of art that kind of ordered reality which yields "universal" truths like those deduced by Kant's analysis of certain forms of mental functioning?

It would be easy to bypass Kant and go directly to Schlegel's *Vorlesungen*, so avidly studied by Coleridge, where he would have found the statement that "a work of art *should* contain, within itself, every thing necessary for its being fully understood."[35] The word "should," to which emphasis has here been added, makes all the difference between a sensible and an absurd statement. It would be *desirable* if we did not have to go outside a work to understand it. But of course we often do, and not always successfully. The Parthenon is undoubtedly a work of art; so are the Winged Victory and Venus de Milo, despite the fragmentary states of all three. None tells us why it is so and not otherwise.

Furthermore, it cannot be said in any strict sense that even *Hamlet*, to cite a supreme masterpiece, contains within itself everything necessary for its *comprehension*, let alone why everything in it is so and not otherwise. Of course, Schlegel's "comprehension" may not (and probably was not) intended to bear so heavy and precise a signification. The history of *Hamlet* criticism ought to have demonstrated beyond cavil that the play is comprehended in a bewildering variety of ways—by sensitive and knowledgeable readers—and that the belief in so rigorously objective a criticism as implied by Coleridge's statement is a pernicious superstition.[36]

The sensible approach here is not to make such adjustments as are necessary to preserve a great and influential statement. The problem is that the whole thrust of the idea is obscurantist. It enmeshes the critic in a web of falsehood at the start, and thus prevents him from seeing the work as it is, not as we would wish it to be.

We can now return to the problem in *Biographia* which we have left suspended. Why will the "mere superaddition of metre" to a novel or romance which has been written to give pleasure fail to result in a poem? We have seen how unsatisfactory was Coleridge's answer. He adds that other parts of the work would have to be made "consonant" with meter, but the reason for this is that poetry demands greater attention than does prose. The poem is, as a result, defined as a species of composition distinguished from others which have as their immediate end pleasure by "proposing to itself such delight from the whole, as is compatible with a distinct gratification from each component part." But this distinction proves useless too, for reasons that would have been less apparent in Coleridge's time. Coleridge did not forsee that novels could develop an aesthetic which met this criteria precisely. Joyce's *Ulysses* is more a poem in Coleridge's sense than Wordsworth's *Prelude* and perhaps even *Paradise Lost*.

Any reader can study Chapter XIV of *Biographia Literaria* with profit. It forces one to think, if only ultimately to disagree. It is interesting that Coleridge disposes almost contemptuously of the man who "chooses to call every composition a poem, which is rhyme, or measure, or both. I must leave his opinion uncontroverted." In fact, however, Coleridge's final definition does not leave one with even this clarity, for a poem, it turns out, can, like the Bible, have as its immediate end truth, not pleasure, and poetry of the highest kind can exist with or without meter. The only particle of definition which seems to distinguish poetry from prose is a kind of technical and ideational density which justifies in the reader "the perpetual and distinct attention to each part" of the composition, but this, curiously, is far more a distinguishing characteristic of a Euclidian theorem or any closely reasoned work of science than the real world of poems is likely to afford. In any case, there is nothing to distinguish this from the concentrated short story.

The trouble with Coleridge's definition, as with all definitions of this kind, is that the problem of aesthetic *value* is central but unexamined in the definition. Coleridge says that verses like

> Thirty days hath September,
> April, June and November . . .

"*may* be entitled poems," but he does not say why they should *not* be. It is clear enough, however, that he does not wish to consider these true poems not because they lack the "contradistinguishing objects of the poems," but because they are *worthless as literature*.

Wordsworth had confronted this problem with far greater clarity in his 1800 Preface. The question is, how is the critic to deal with the two stanzas below? The first is Dr. Johnson's famous parody of the ballad form. The second is "one of the most justly-admired stanzas of the 'Babes in the Wood' ":

> I put my hat upon my head
> And walked into the Strand,
> And there I met another man
> Whose hat was in his hand.
>
> These pretty Babes with hand in hand
> Went wandering up and down;
> But never more they saw the Man
> Approaching from the Town.

In both these stanzas [Wordsworth writes] the words, and the order of the words, in no respect differ from the most unimpassioned conversation. . . . yet the one stanza we admit as admirable, and the other as a fair example of the superlatively contemptible. Whence arises this difference? Not from the metre, not from the language, not from the order of the words; but the *matter* expressed in Dr. Johnson's stanza is contemptible. The proper method of treating trivial and simple verses . . . is not to say, this is a bad kind of poetry, or, this is not poetry; but, this wants sense. . . .[37]

Wordsworth is certainly right in identifying the essential difference between the two stanzas in the *matter* and not in the *form*. This is not calculated to make his argument popular in an era in which the distinction between the two is denied with messianic fervor. However, just on the verge of seeing that the problem in defining poetry inheres in *an assumption of value*, Wordsworth flinched. Below a certain thermal reading of value, the species of composition ceases to be poetry. Obviously, any definition of poetry which rests upon value is worthless as an objective definition, since value is inherently in the realm of the subjective.

What Coleridge fails to see throughout his discussion, and the point is persistently ignored to this day, is that "poetry" is not a fact that exists in nature in the same sense that light does. All definitions of poetry, or tragedy (an equally good example), that depend upon attitudes elicited in the reader must inevitably remain subjective. If tragedy, for example, must produce catharsis, and if catharsis is a purging of emotion (no matter what kind), then the determination of whether that has in fact happened must always be uncertain. Almost every sane and experienced reader has an acute sense of when he is reading poetry and when prose, when he is witnessing tragedy and when not. The problem arises purely as a matter of *definition*. Is the protagonist of high estate? If not, no tragedy. Ergo, neither the Willy Lomans nor Wozzeks of this world can figure in the tragic experience. But whether or not tragedy requires a figure of this kind is a matter of *definition*, not of actual experience in the theater (or one's study). It cannot be doubted that

Aristotle would have thought a tragedy about a slave impossible, no matter what the character of the slave. Feeling has changed very greatly since then, and Aristotle's particular definition in this one point is not likely to be urged today.[38]

It is perfectly obvious that Coleridge's idea of poetry is continually slipping between the problem of its form and the reservation of this term for the highest achievements of literature. The inevitable end of such a procedure is to call poetry anything in literature one thinks of as very great. In 1801 he gave a copy of Bartram's *Travels* to Sara Hutchinson and wrote in the fly-leaf: "This is not a book of Travels, *properly speaking*; but a series of poems, chiefly descriptive, *occasioned* by the Objects, which the Traveller observed."[39] So now we have a book of travels, written in prose, which is, "properly speaking," a series of poems, though surely it lacks the distinguishing features of poetry—a work, incidentally, which only a Solomon could decide had as its immediate object pleasure, and not truth.

In 1810 Jeremy Taylor's *Holy Dying* (over three hundred pages of densely figured, baroque prose, eddying about a cluster of pious themes) was hailed as "a perfect poem,"[40] a judgment typical both of Coleridge's absurd inflation of Taylor's merit and the looseness of his critical terminology. In Coleridge's usual discourse, the word "poet" could be indiscriminately applied to certain exalted *persons*. Thus in the *Friend*, when discussing Luther's dream of Satan, he writes: "[Luther] was a poet indeed, as great a poet as ever lived in any age or country; but his poetic images were so vivid, that they mastered the poet's own mind! He was possessed with them, as with substances distinct from himself: Luther did not write, he acted poems."[41]

The connection between the idea of poetry here and in the *Biographia* five years later seems to be nonexistent. We now have "images" as the center of the poetic process, about which nothing (wisely) is said in the *Biographia* definition. Furthermore, Coleridge now finds it is possible to "act" poems.[42] Clearly, poetry here is merely an honorific term.

In this whole supremely famous fourteenth chapter of the *Biographia* what we get are ideas, fragments of ideas, suggestions. The reader can pick and choose, accept, reject, think, sigh. But it is grossly mistaken to attribute to Coleridge some decisive contribution to the discussion of the poem. If he were not continually calling attention to the allegedly philosophical foundations of his argument, would anyone really suppose the chapter a radical departure even in method from previous discussion? "Philosophic definitions of a Poem and Poetry with scholia," the author announces in the headnote to the chapter, and as we read on we are constantly being lectured to: "The office of philosophical *disquisition* consists in just *distinction*. . . . In order to obtain adequate notions of any truth, we must intellectually separate its distinguishable parts; and this is the technical *process* of philosophy."[43] And so forth.

To all this one might, without going very far awry, oppose the response of the implacable Jeffrey, who complained of the Lake Poets: "Of the many contrivances they employ to give the appearance of uncommon force and animation to a very ordinary conception, the most usual is, to wrap it up in a veil of mysterious and unintelligible language, which flows past with so much solemnity, that it is difficult to believe it conveys nothing of any value."[44] Those who think that Coleridge had a genuine controlling conception of the poetic imagination or of the nature of poetry as such, should ask themselves how it is that after so much show of rigorously logical thinking and arduous attempts at precise and philosophical definitions of the Imagination and the Ideal Poet, he was capable of concluding his chapter as follows:

> Finally, GOOD SENSE is the BODY of poetic genius, FANCY its DRAPERY, MOTION its LIFE, and IMAGINATION the SOUL that is everywhere, and in each; and forms all into one graceful and intelligent whole.[45]

Apart from the shock of encountering so neo-classic and irrelevant an image at this point, what is one to make of the apparently casual introduction of two terms not hitherto mentioned, "good sense" and "motion," the first being the "Body" of poetic genius, whatever that may mean, and the other its "Life?" If motion really was this important, ought not he to have spared at least a few words to this subject?

With respect to the subjects thus far considered, *seminal* is surely the wrong word to apply to Coleridge as philosophical critic; aggregative and coadunative would appear to be much more precise. Is not the concluding paragraph all too typical an example of the easy eclecticism of Coleridge's mind, causing him to force together things much unlike each other because, taken individually, the units were "suggestive," or verbally attractive, or merely fashionable?

The discussion of Wordsworth comprises five substantial chapters of *Biographia Literaria*, each of which has been the occasion of voluminous commentary, none more so than the debate over the language of poetry, to which we will add our own increment later in a broad discussion of the Wordsworth-Coleridge relationship and the background of *Lyrical Ballads*. But it may be said at once that with respect to the issues *abstractly considered*, Coleridge has far the better of the argument. With what assurance does he seem to demolish point after point in Wordsworth's Preface! Poor, hapless Wordsworth! One wonders why he ever made such a fuss about restoring to poetry the language of real life. Does not Coleridge properly tell us that this rule does not have the force of universal law? But we are startled when he also tells us that where it *is* applicable, the rule "hath never by any one (as far as I know or have read,) been denied or doubted."[46] Can Coleridge really have been so ignorant as this? To judge by Chapter XVII of *Biographia Literaria*, one would never suppose that between Wordsworth's *Descriptive Sketches* of 1793 and "The Ruined Cottage" of 1797 anything of particular consequence had happened to the language of poetry. One would never imagine from Coleridge's entire discussion that Wordsworth was reacting against an *operative tradition of immense force.*

By setting up the terms of the discussion, Coleridge ignores the historical situation and argues about the language of poetry from an ivory tower. More dismal still, he devotes much of Chapter XIX to quotations from Chaucer and Drayton and Herbert, showing conclusively that a colloquial language was always present in English poetry. One would never suppose that Pope or Dryden or Gray, or that one hundred fifty years of neo-classicism preceded his own era.

But even in Coleridge's own terms, is it true that "the *best* parts of language [are] the product of philosophers, not of clowns or shepherds," or that "the best part of human language, properly so called [whatever that may mean], is derived from reflection on the acts of the mind itself "?[47] If he was right to insist that the language of poetry can be different from that of prose, or that meter does allow verbal licenses, was he not wrong to insist that there "ought to be an *essential* difference between the language of prose and of metrical composition"? And does he not misrepresent the poetic process when he argues, "I write in metre, because I am about to use a language different from that of prose"?[48]

Indeed, his whole argument seems a sterile one today. But this much can be said for Wordsworth: he argued for a poetic language which in the event liberated poetry from the bondage of tradition.

Elsewhere in Chapter XVII Coleridge writes:

> I adopt with full faith the principle of Aristotle, that poetry as poetry is essentially *ideal*, that it avoids and excludes all *accident*; that its apparent individualities of rank, character, or occupation must be *representative* of a class; and that the *persons* of poetry must be clothed with *generic* attributes, with the *common* attributes of the class: not with such as one gifted individual might *possibly* possess, but such as from his situation it is most probable before-hand that he *would* possess.[49]

There is not a syllable here that Sir Joshua Reynolds would not have approved, and scarcely one that would not have been anathema to Blake—or the Wordsworth of 1797-1805. And because Coleridge is so theory-ridden, he misrepresents what is extraordinary in poems like "The Brothers" and "Michael" and turns their central characters into representative "persons of a known and abiding class," as if that matters in the slightest to us. Why does he not say what was so obvious to readers like Hazlitt, namely, that Wordsworth had introduced common people into poetry in a way that had not been done before? And one of the extraordinarily fruitful results of this was to open up vast territories of thematic material either ignored previously or treated with comic scorn or idyllic patronization.

It should be remembered that Coleridge was dealing with an argument over fifteen years old and that he was in *Biographia* finally joining forces with men like Francis Jeffrey, whose strictures against Wordsworth are regularly decried as notorious. Coleridge wrote that

> a rustic's language, purified from all provincialism and grossness, and so far reconstructed as to be made consistent with the rules of grammar —(which are in essence no other than the laws of universal logic, applied to psychological materials)—will not differ from the language of any other man of common-sense. . . .[50]

This was precisely Jeffrey's position of 1802, as has been observed by J. A. Greig:

> The low-bred heroes and interesting rustics of poetry had "no sort of affinity to the real vulgar of this world." In serious poetry a man of this type had to lay aside grammatical errors and a considerable part of his vocabulary, and had, moreover, to speak in good verse and observe the graces of collocation. "After all this," Jeffrey declared, "it may not be very easy to say how we are to find him out to be a low man, or what marks can remain of the ordinary language of conversation in the inferior orders of society." This last passage contains, it will be observed, precisely the argument Coleridge was to use fifteen years later in the seventeenth chapter of *Biographia Literaria*.[51]

We might at this point note a cluster of similar agreements. Jeffrey had written that the works of the Lakers were characterized by "perpetual exaggeration of thought."[52] Coleridge complained that Wordsworth used "thoughts and images too great for the subject." "Is there one word . . . attributed to the pedlar in the EXCURSION,' " Coleridge asked, "characteristic of a *pedlar?*"[53] Jeffrey had more comically said that a man who spoke like the Pedlar would scare away customers or be taken for a madman or a gentleman who had assumed the character in a frolic.[54]

Mary Moorman has pointed out that Coleridge's criticism of "The Thorn," namely, "it is not possible to imitate truly a dull and garrulous discourser without repeating the effects of dullness and garrulity," is "almost quoting a sentence from Southey's review of the *Ballads* in the *Critical Review*, Oct. 1798."[55] Coleridge went on to say of some five stanzas in "The Thorn" that they "are felt by many unprejudiced and unsophisticated hearts, as sudden and unpleasant sinkings from the height to which the poet had previously lifted them, and to which he again re-elevates both himself and his reader."[56] John Thelwall, in a hitherto unpublished marginal note on this passage, wrote: "I am amused with these concessions. Some years ago, when C. & I had much talk about this poem in particular I could not wring from him any accordance with me upon the subject. The Thorn was then an object of unqualified panegyric with him."[57]

In assessing the chapters on Wordsworth, it is well to remember that *Biographia Literaria* is no longer a contemporary work, that we attribute to Coleridge ideas that were commonplaces in his time; and that we do not normally measure the *Biographia* against the stream of criticism from which it emerged.

In Chapter XXII, on the "defects" and "beauties" of Wordsworth's poetry, we return to the familiar mode of eighteenth-century criticism, despite the parade of philosophic principles. "I cannot here enter into a detailed examination of Mr. Wordsworth's works," Coleridge informs us, "but I will attempt to give the main results of my own judgement."[58] Well and good, but let us not misrepresent what is excellent in the chapter that follows. Coleridge does not analyze a *single* complete poem to demonstrate in action *any* of the key principles with which his name is identified. We hear nothing of organic unity, or of opposite or discordant qualities reconciled. What are the excellencies of Wordsworth's poetry?—(1) "an austere purity of language both grammatically and logically; in short a perfect appropriateness of the words to the meaning"; (2) "a correspondent weight and sanity of the Thoughts and Sentiments, won—not from books; but—from the poet's own meditative observation"; (3) "the sinewy strength and originality of single lines and paragraphs"; (4) "the perfect truth of nature in his images and descriptions, as taken immediately from nature"; (5) "a meditative pathos, a union of deep and subtle thought with sensibility; a sympathy with man as man; (6) Last, and pre-eminently, I challenge for this poet the gift of IMAGINATION in the highest and strictest sense of the word."[59]

By introducing Imagination, "in the highest and strictest sense of the word" (as if he had established a "strict" sense for this controversial term!), Coleridge at the very last moment bathes Wordsworth in universal aesthetic power, since we have already seen that the Imagination of the Ideal Poet is omnipotent. But it is not enough to be told that Wordsworth's Imagination is of the order of Shakespeare's and Milton's, and to have quoted "a few examples as most obviously manifesting this faculty." It is all much, much too easy. What was necessary was an analytical demonstration of the Imagination *operative,* revealing itself "in the balance or reconciliation of opposite or discordant qualities: of sameness, with difference; of the general with the concrete; the idea with the image; the individual with the representative," and so on through the series of resounding antitheses. Apart from the easy invocation of this all-purpose term, what is there either in the conduct of the Wordsworth criticism or the results arrived at which differs from what we would expect from Samuel Johnson? Without quibbling over this or that point, we may certainly allow that Coleridge is justified in what he identifies as "excellencies," just as he is, on the whole, right to find as defects in Wordsworth's poetry: (1) "INCONSTANCY of the *style*"; (2) *"matter-of-factness"*; (3) "an undue predilection for the *dramatic* form in certain poems"; (4) "occasional prolixity, repetition, and an eddying, instead of progression, of thought"; (5) "fifth and last; thoughts and images too great for the subject."[60]

There is nothing at all surprising in any of this, but organized and argued this coherently, it is impossible for an honest reader not to feel that his judgment has been more sharply focused and his sensibilities more finely honed. And yet, there is something oddly dissatisfying about the whole disquisition. Certainly the defect is not so much in what Coleridge has said, but in what is *unsaid*. As Coleridge deals with the Wordsworth canon, it is already being fixed in amber. We are in the presence of *safe* poetry. Its originality is wholly aesthetic, at a remove from political and social events, already set apart even from the stream of vital current ideas. Could one ever suppose from reading Coleridge that Wordsworth was a *revolutionary* poet, not only in his radical technical originality, but in ideational content? The poet addressed in Coleridge's analysis is already well on the way towards becoming the Daddy Wordsworth we all know, removed from history, his fangs drawn.

We can never, by reading Coleridge, recover or *understand* the intense excitement Wordsworth's poetry caused among the best of his contemporaries. Coleridge himself, in 1797, was simply overwhelmed by Wordsworth —as were Lamb and Southey, Thomas Poole and many others. If we turn from Coleridge's "defects" and "excellencies" to Hazlitt's noble tribute in *The Spirit of the Age,* we can see at once what is so seriously lacking in *Biographia Literaria*:

[Wordsworth's poetry] is one of the innovations of the time. It partakes of, and is carried along with, the revolutionary movement of our age: the political changes of the day were the model on which he formed and conducted his poetical experiments. His Muse (it cannot be denied, and without this we cannot explain its character at all) is a levelling one. It proceeds on a principle of equality, and strives to reduce all things to the same standard. It is distinguished by a proud humility. It relies upon its own resources, and disdains external show and relief. It takes the commonest events and objects, as a test to prove that nature is always interesting from its inherent truth and beauty, without any of the ornaments of dress or pomp of circumstances to set it off. Hence the unaccountable mixture of seeming simplicity and real abstruseness in the *Lyrical Ballads.* Fools have laughed at, wise men scarcely understand them. He takes a subject or a story merely as pegs or loops to hang thought and feeling on; the incidents are trifling, in proportion to his contempt for imposing appearances; the reflections are profound, according to the gravity and the aspiring pretensions of his mind.

His popular, inartificial style gets rid (at a blow) of all the trappings of verse, of all the high places of poetry: 'the cloud-capt towers, the solemn temples, the gorgeous palaces,' are swept to the ground, and 'like the baseless fabric of a vision, leave not a wrack behind.' All the traditions of learning, all the superstitions of age, are obliterated and effaced. We begin *de novo*, on a *tabula rasa* of poetry. . . .

Possibly a good deal of this may be regarded as the effect of disappointed views and an inverted ambition. Prevented by native pride and

indolence from climbing the ascent of learning or greatness, taught by
political opinions to say to the vain pomp and glory of the world, 'I hate
ye,' seeing the path of classical and artificial glory blocked up by the
cumbrous ornaments of style and turgid *commonplaces*, so that nothing
more could be achieved in that direction but by the most ridiculous bombast or the tamest servility; he has turned back partly from the bias of his
mind, partly perhaps from a judicious policy—has struck into the seques-
tered vale of humble life, sought out the Muse among sheep-cotes and
the peasant's mountain-haunts, has discarded all the tinsel pageantry
of verse, and endeavoured (not in vain) to aggrandise the trivial and add
the charm of novelty to the familiar. No one has shown the same imagination in raising trifles into importance: no one has displayed the same
pathos in treating of the simplest feelings of the heart. . . . The daisy
looks up to him with sparkling eye as an old acquaintance: the cuckoo
haunts him with sounds of early youth not to be expressed: a linnet's nest
startles him with boyish delight: an old withered thorn is weighed down
with a heap of recollections: a grey cloak, seen on some wild moor, torn
by the wind, or drenched in the rain, afterwards becomes an object of
imagination to him: even the lichens on the rock have a life and being in
his thoughts. He has described all these objects in a way and with an intensity of feeling that no one else had done before him, and has given a
new view or aspect of nature. He is in this sense the most original poet
now living, and the one whose writings could the least be spared: for they
have no substitute elsewhere.[61]

It is notable that Hazlitt almost contemptuously ignores Coleridge's arguments about poetic diction and drives right to the heart of one of Wordsworth's most revolutionary achievements in the real life of poetic events and
not in the often false arena of subsequent historical research. As to "sug-
gestiveness," are we not struck by Hazlitt's observations on the levelling
social implications of Wordsworth's poetry, a matter still hardly ever discussed? The claim that Wordsworth's poetic experiments were modelled on
the revolutionary movements of his time, namely in France, may be profound. Hazlitt's speculation as to what psychological sources within Wordsworth led him to discard former trappings of verse opens up a suggestive area
of study.
   The central fact is that the driving energy of Hazlitt's prose is directed at
a single point: Wordsworth's pervasive revolutionary style and message. Of
course one can dig around in Coleridge and find him praising "the sinewy
strength and originality of single lines and paragraphs," or Wordsworth's
"Thoughts and Sentiments,—won, not from books," and so forth.
   That he consistently minimized Wordsworth's originality is a psychological
problem, to be discussed hereafter. What needs to be emphasized now is that
in the familiar parade of defects and beauties Coleridge not only skipped over
the very categories by which his reputation as a critic is so esteemed today

(organic form, symbolism, the unconscious, etc.), but minimized, ignored, or actively denied the existence of properties in Wordsworth's poetry for which he was treasured in his own time and which worked one of the greatest changes in sensibility in the history of English poetry.

The range of Coleridge's intellectual interests was such that trying to encompass him is like trying to catch a whale in a net. To select from the multitude of concepts in his aesthetic essays, lectures, and marginalia those which are of substantial interest to contemporary critics and aestheticians is, inevitably, to some extent arbitrary. Most scholars would probably agree, however, that among his most influential statements are those on unconscious activity in art, the role of the symbol, the nature of organic form, and the function of art as "a mediatress" between art and nature.

The first and last in this series can be dealt with simultaneously, since the fullest discussion of each appears in "On Poesy or Art," an essay which has earlier been identified as a paraphrase of Schelling's "Concerning the Relation of the Plastic Arts to Nature." To the transcendental metaphysicians, notably Schelling, the relationship between art and nature was of momentous importance because—strange as it seems to the untrained intelligence—"the ideal work of art and the real world of objects are . . . products of one and the same activity." Schelling went on to say:

> The confluence of the two (conscious and unconscious activities) *without* consciousness gives rise to the real world, and *with* consciousness to the aesthetic world.
> The object world is only the primitive, as yet unconscious, poetry of the spirit; the general organon of philosophy—and the keystone of its whole arch—is the *philosophy of art*.[62]

Why such abstruse doctrines should be of interest to literary critics is by no means obvious. However, one realizes that if it is granted that art and nature derive from the same activity, then both have *equal* claims to representing *reality*. It may seem strange that the Sahara Desert and *The Brothers Karamazov* should be *real* in the same sense, but so it is, on these postulates. As a result, the artist can claim to be revealing *truth* of precisely the same ultimate order as the physicist.

Some such gloss as this is required to understand the meaning of Professor Whalley's statement, "Coleridge sees Poetry as a special kind of knowing: he sees it in its broadest sense as a peculiarly luminous reconciliation of the internal with the external."[63] And Professor Bate also argues that art is "a form of real knowledge and not an expression of something else less essential." Both art and nature, it is held, embody "universals" and "particulars." Explicating Coleridge's views, Professor Bate says:

> art presents an "abridgement" of reality itself. For "universal" and "particular" are mutually dependent in nature. Reality, that is, consists

in the manner in which value or form becomes definite and emergent in the particular: reality is the bridge between concreteness and value. Value becomes *real* at the same point where the concrete exemplifies the *ideal*. In this sense, therefore, the *ideal* and the *real* are one and the same, and "Idealism" is at the same time "the truest and most binding realism." This conception is crucial for the whole of Coleridge's thought. If his critical writings generally have a rather puzzling, hieroglyphic quality, this fundamental standpoint, when completely understood, can be used as something of a Rosetta stone, by the aid of which other principles and assumptions are seen to fall into place.[64]

If so, most of us will have to await another Champollion to decipher this Rosetta stone for us. In any case, whatever the ultimate truth of the matter, the basic ideas are all Schelling's and it is only simple justice that he should be credited with them.

One of the most famous passages in "On Poesy or Art" deals with the role of the unconscious. Coleridge wrote:

> In every work of art there is a reconcilement of the external with the internal; the conscious is so impressed on the unconscious as to appear in it. . . . He who combines the two is the man of genius; and for that reason he must partake of both. Hence there is in genius itself an unconscious activity; nay, that is the genius in the man of genius. And this is the true exposition of the rule that the artist must first eloign himself from nature in order to return to her with full effect. . . . He merely absents himself for a season from her, that his own spirit, which has the same ground with nature, may learn her unspoken language in its main radicals. . . .[65]

These are Schelling's words:

> It has long been perceived that not everything in art is the outcome of consciousness, that an unconscious force must be linked with conscious activity and that it is the perfect unanimity and mutual interpenetration of the two which produces the highest art. Works which lack this seal of unconscious science are recognizable by the palpable absence of a life which is autonomous and independent of their creator, while on the contrary, where it is in operation, art simultaneously imparts to its work, with the greatest lucidity of the intelligence, that unfathomable reality by virtue of which it resembles a work of nature.
>
> The dictum that art, to be art, must first withdraw from nature and only return to it in its final consummation, has frequently been offered as an elucidation of the artist's position in relation to nature. . . . Thus, he [the artist] must withdraw from the product or creature, but only in order to raise himself to the level of creative energy and apprehend it spiritually.[66]

It is extraordinary how at every point where Coleridge goes beyond paraphrase, we are confronted with obscurity and overstatement. Unconscious elements are present in all human activities, and Schelling is asserting (as usual scorning to provide any objective evidence) that in the highest art both conscious and unconscious activity are in perfect balance. Coleridge here garbles a clear if dogmatic statement and makes nonsense of it. "The conscious is so impressed on the unconscious as to appear in it," he says. But the appearance of the conscious in the unconscious has no meaning in relation to a work of art, though the opposite does. Further, when Coleridge says that the unconscious is *the* genius in a man of genius, he is adding an increment to Schelling which, as it stands, is either false or unprovable.[67] Surely every artist and work of art represents a unique combination of forces. The elements of conscious and unconscious activity certainly vary between Bach's *Art of the Fugue* and Stockhausen's *Momente,* between Tristan Tsara and Alexander Pope. Examples need not be multiplied.

How does it happen that "On Poesy or Art" assigns an absolutely dominant role to the unconscious in creative activity, but that the *Biographia* is mute on the subject? Surely the distinction between the Imagination and Fancy provided a perfect opportunity to introduce the topic. But all Coleridge says which in any way bears upon the matter is simply that the "secondary imagination" coexists "with the conscious will." This would imply that any creative role assigned to the unconscious would be left to the "primary imagination," "the prime agent of all human perception." In view of the exalted status later given to the unconscious, such a role for the primary imagination would be an embarrassment. The point, so far as I know, has never been pressed.

In the description of the Ideal Poet, the Imagination is "first put in action by the will and understanding, and retained under their irremissive, though gentle and unnoticed, controul (*laxis effertur habenis*)." Modern conceptions of the unconscious are not dreamed of here, and specifically, the kind of statements on the unconscious which we find in "On Poesy or Art," where the unconscious is crowned as "the genius in a man of genius." Surely this is at least a little hard to reconcile with a description of the Imagination so exalted that it is called a "magical power." But it is to be understood if one faces the embarrassing fact squarely that in "On Poesy or Art" Coleridge was working with Schelling's essay "Concerning the Relation of the Plastic Arts to Nature" open on his desk, and that the statements on the unconscious are paraphrases, and bad ones at that, of the material before him. In any case, speculation on the unconscious was a commonplace of German criticism and philosophy since well before the turn of the eighteenth century. It remains to be demonstrated that Coleridge added anything at all to the subject.[68]

The primacy of the Germans in original speculation about the unconscious is equally true of the idea of the symbol. Coleridge had very little to say about the symbol either as a literary device or as an aspect of mental functioning.

Nevertheless, his definition is immensely influential, to the exclusion of his predecessors:

> Now an allegory is but a translation of abstract notions into a picture-language, which is itself nothing but an abstraction from objects of the senses. . . . On the other hand a symbol . . . is characterized by a translucence of the special in the individual, or of the general in the special, or of the universal in the general; above all by the translucence of the eternal through and in the temporal. It always partakes of the reality which it renders intelligible; and while it enunciates the whole, abides itself as a living part in that unity of which it is the representative.[69]

This is indeed extraordinary language, and the reader will recognize the similarity between the middle sentence above and the description of the secondary Imagination. Since Coleridge did not provide concrete examples of the symbolic process in action, we are left again with abstract assertion. And since the major units of his definition are to be found previously in Goethe, Schiller, Schelling, Schlegel, and others, his contribution ought strictly to be limited to happiness of expression, the value of which derives from another order of achievement.

Patricia Ward has noted, significantly, I think, that "all of Coleridge's pronouncements on the distinction between the two [symbol and allegory] come after 1811; as late as 1808 he had not clearly recognized the difference. For example, in his lectures of 1808, he refers in passing to Dionysus as 'allegorically the symbol . . . of festivity.' " Ward quotes a relevant passage from Schlegel's *Vorlesungen*:

> The ancient mythology is in general *symbolical,* although not *allegorical;* for the two are *certainly* distinct. Allegory is the personification of an idea, a poetic story invented solely with such a view; but that is symbolical which, created by the imagination (*Einbildungskraft*) for other purposes, or possessing an independent reality of its own, is at the same time easily susceptible of an emblematical explanation, and even of itself suggests it.[70]

We may add the following from Schiller's "On Naive and Sentimental Poetry":

> If, on the one hand, the symbol and the thing symbolized remain forever foreign and heterogeneous, on the other, the speech issues from the thought as by an inward necessity, and is so entirely one with it, that the spirit seems exposed even under its material veil. In composition, it is expression of this kind, where the symbol entirely vanishes in the thing symbolized, and where the language still leaves the thought which it expressed naked, while another never can present without at the same time concealing it, that we style by eminence spirited and genial.[71]

What Schiller is here struggling to express is reasonably clear. Symbol and thing symbolized are separate entities, but in some compositions the symbol is obliterated by the thing symbolized. In Coleridge, however, what is a difficult idea to begin with is hopelessly muddied by a thick patina of transcendental mysticism, where the symbol is actually "a part of the reality which it represents, consubstantial with the truth, a living part in that unity of which it is representative." Those familiar with Coleridge's writings will recognize the Delphic accents of the seer upon the heights chanting divine truth. But is it the true oracle or merely the moaning wind we hear?

If one stops moving blindly in the world of abstraction and considers those works which mankind has determined as among its most sublime artistic achievements, we may perhaps put to a concrete test such a statement as this on symbols. What the White Whale in *Moby Dick* symbolizes has been debated for decades. Is it not absurd to maintain that a conception which is in the first place a *fiction* is part of the *reality* it represents? For anything to be "consubstantial with the Truth," we would have to agree that truth itself is real, rather than itself an abstraction, or, if you will, a symbol. What does water symbolize? It has been variously used as a symbol for creativity, for life, for death, for eternity, and much more. Does water partake of the "reality" it represents?

The problem, of course, is that statements like these are not meant to withstand logical analysis. They are "suggestive." But Coleridge was here only making an isolated borrowing from his German predecessors and contemporaries. What little he had to say on the subject shows how unstable, how learned *ab extra* his formulations were. In another context, as has been widely noted, he maintains that a symbol is always *part* of something else, a sail being a symbol for a ship![72]

His scattered and contradictory remarks on the symbol are a characteristic illustration of the way his transmission of ideas from Germany have become attached to his name as original formulations. And since the analysis of literary symbolism is one of the most vigorous branches of contemporary criticism, still more jewels are seen to be glittering in the crown of the greatest of English critics.

Of all the critical doctrines associated with Coleridge and the romantic movement, none rivals in importance that of organic unity. The idea of unity as a touchstone by which a work of literature was to be judged goes back to Aristotle and the very origins of literary criticism. Between Aristotle and the late eighteenth century, the idea of unity was developed into the complex of interlocking rules and regulations primarily associated with the French classical drama of Racine and Corneille.

The idea of the unities, however, was confined to the play; there was as yet no aesthetic of the novel, and the epic and ode and lyric and sonnet were thought to be governed by quite different rules. The idea of unity as a controlling law of *all* literary art simply did not exist. With respect to the drama,

however, the power of the classical unities was such that Shakespeare continued to be thought of as an irregular genius, one who rose above a Ben
Jonson by the sheer force of his native gift, but one whose powers of dramatic
construction were woefully undeveloped. Hence Coleridge's youthful remark
(though made after he'd had the practical experience of writing the play
Osorio) that Shakespeare was "a stripling in the art," who had never grown
to "man's estate."

It was into such an intellectual atmosphere that the Schlegel brothers, and
others, introduced their revolutionary doctrine that Shakespeare's plays
were masterpieces of dramatic construction, the key to the understanding of
which was not the "mechanical unities" of the French school, but an "organic" unity as defined by themselves. The first extensive analytical demonstration of this assertion, as we have seen, came with the Schlegels' early
essay on *Romeo and Juliet*. In introducing a translation of this seminal essay to an English audience in 1820, an anonymous English writer perfectly
identified the magnitude of what had been achieved, an insight subsequently
lost in the pages of a forgotten magazine:

> It is chiefly to them [the Schlegels] that posterity will be indebted for
> the power which it will possess of considering a mark of art no longer as
> an accumulation of fragments put together according to mechanical
> rules, but as a living organical individual, containing the conditions of its
> existence in its own seminal idea, and constituting on account of its very
> living individuality a member of a living universe. . . . [Henceforth the
> business of criticism will be] when it is employed upon a single work . . .
> to discover the seminal principle, the detection of which alone can make
> the whole poem intelligible, and then watchfully to follow the principle,
> as it gradually expands itself. . . .[73]

Testimony like this, coming from an obviously informed *contemporary* man
of letters, is usually of vastly greater consequence than the opinions of subsequent scholars who can only reconstruct, never experience a stream of
ideas forever past.

It was in his famous lectures on dramatic art that A. W. Schlegel used the
words which, in Coleridge's literal translation, have become a *locus classicus*
in English criticism. In the circumstances it seems somewhat unfair to
Schlegel to take for granted that Coleridge's earlier remarks on the subject
somehow add up to the very words he was later to borrow verbatim. In fact
no such case can be made.

Scrutiny of Coleridge's writings before his real familiarity with German
thought begins produces only negative evidence as to his independent grapplings with this idea. Before 1808 the word "organic" is used either neutrally
or in its physiological sense.[74] The organic-unity metaphor itself can be found
consistently in critical writings from antiquity to the present (pretty much
as the general idea of unconscious thought can be) without the concept hav-

ing much revelance to the sudden turn of meaning given it by the Schlegels. Immediately in the background of the Romantic critics, if one chooses to go ahunting, one can find Edward Young in his *Conjectures on Original Composition* using a "vegetable" image in describing art which issues "spontaneously from the vital root of genius; it grows, it is not made."[75] Kant, in the Preface to the second edition of the *Critique of Pure Reason,* held that

> pure speculative reason has a structure wherein everything is an organ, the whole being for the sake of every part, and every part for the sake of all the others, so that even the smallest imperfection, be it a fault (error) or a deficiency, must inevitably betray itself in use.[76]

In *On University Studies*, Schelling had asked, in approaching the problem of art:

> Can we define and subject to laws something that by its very nature recognizes no law but its own? . . . The rules of art that genius throws overboard are rules prescribed by a merely mechanical understanding; the artist of genius is autonomous—not in the sense that he is subject to no law, but in the sense that he is subject to no law but his own . . . . This is why true artists in every epoch have been serene, simple, great, and, like nature herself, acting in obedience to inner necessity.[77]

Obviously, Coleridge added nothing to the idea of organic form, and since he did not apply it in concrete instances, he cannot be said to have worked out implications unseen by others. Although this is not the place to argue the value of an idea which has had such immense influence, it can at least be pointed out that the Schlegel-Coleridge formula has become in practice every bit as rigid as the old dramatic unities. By insisting that genius always creates *laws* of its own, and that the analogy of the living organism with great art will *always* hold, the doctrine represents another act of uniformity against poets.

Bertrand Russell has somewhere written that given the mathematical powers of the human mind, some kind of web of mathematical relations could probably be thrown over any set of phenomena. Is this not true of the organic approach to art? Cannot ingenuity always find internal relations? Why must unity, coherence, organization be the touchstones of genius in the arts, any more than intensity, amplitude, originality? Should we not remind ourselves that we have unfinished symphonies, isolated quartet movements and piano rondos, innumerable broken statues—the Winged Victory, the Elgin Marbles—and that many of these are among the greatest works of man in their present fragmentary form? What of the glorious torsos of literature, *The Fairie Queen* and "Christabel," "Hyperion" and "Kubla Khan" —is it necessary to find in them the lineaments of a sublime organic form? Is this why they seem great to us? And when all is said and done, has not even Shakespeare suffered at the hands of the unifiers, who ferret out of the plays ever more recondite relations and ignore properties of his art that have—dare one say it?—no connection with unity? If the work of genius is embodied in an organic form, and if the unconscious is a potent force in the operation of genius (setting aside the extreme claims of the Romantics), how does it happen that the unconscious is almost totally ignored by critics in practice? Is it not also an important principle of modern criticism that we need not go outside the poem to understand it, certainly not to the private unconscious life of the artist, hidden even from himself? If so, our analysis of the organic form of any work of art must be radically defective, since our knowledge of any artist's unconscious is at best fragmentary. As to Shakespeare, we lack even a clear public personality, let alone an unconscious, to guide our study of the "organic" product of genius.

If we were not so dazzled by the Schlegel-Coleridge formula, would we accept the following as one of its central tenets?

> The form is mechanic when on any given material we impress a predetermined form, not necessarily arising out of the properties of the material, as when to a mass of wet clay we give whatever shape we wish it to retain when hardened. The organic form, on the other hand, is innate; it shapes as it develops itself from within. . . .

Does this square with the actual facts of the artistic situation? It may satisfy some mystical longings in us to suppose that Michaelangelo confronted numerous blocks of marble before deciding that this one contained within itself the *David* and that one the *Pietà*. But is it true in any but the most crude sense? Is not Plotinus, so often quoted by Coleridge, much more sensible on at least this single point?

> This form is not in the material; it is in the designer before ever it enters the stone; and the artificer holds it not by his equipment of eyes and hands but by his participation in his art. The beauty, therefore, exists in a far higher state in the art; for it does not come over integrally into the work; that original beauty is not transferred; what comes over is a derivative and a minor: and even that shows itself upon the statue not integrally and with entire realization of intention but only in so far as it has subdued the resistance of the material.[78]

Anyone who has listened repeatedly to Beethoven's *Thirty-Two Variations on a Theme of Diabelli* is unlikely to be persuaded that the incredible range of feeling and idea which Beethoven drew out of Diabelli's trivial tune were inherent in the material or that each variation could only be so and not otherwise. Is it useful to say that Keats's sonnet on Chapman's Homer or Milton's on his blindness are specimens of organic form? Has not the doctrine of organic form as it has been promulgated long since become a superstition? One of its most serious effects is to minimize or deny the immense influence of tradition in art, of the importance of well-understood laws of composition during certain historical epochs, of the aesthetic effects of familiar patterns in which the artist must create. This is not to say that genius may not always invent, however rigid the imposed form. But the assertion that genius inevitably reveals itself in *organic form* is quite often false. Geniuses have repeatedly been obliged to work within what Schlegel and Coleridge would have called "mechanical" form—and in recent decades artists have sometimes purposefully *avoided* the effect of unity.

The doctrine of organic unity was entrancing precisely because it imposed on art a body of law which seemed as complex and ultimately rational as that of science. The result has been grossly to overestimate the aesthetic force of unity in the arts as a whole and to minimize the whole range of subjective, emotional responses. It opened up a marvellously useful procedure for critics, but distorts our living experience of art.

In Coleridge's famous letter on plagiarism, in which he defended himself against the charges of unacknowledged borrowing from Schlegel, there is a passage the implications of which have been too little regarded. He tells us that when the mysterious Mr. Krusve left him the volume of Schlegel's lectures, he discovered that the resemblances between his own ideas and the German's exceeded anything he had been prepared to find:

> in all the Lectures that related to Shakespear, *or to Poetry in general,* the Grounds, Train of Reasoning, &c were different in language only— & often not even in that—. The Thoughts too were so far peculiar, that to the best of my knowledge they did not exist in any prior work of Criticism—Yet I was . . . more confirmed, than surprize[d]. For Schlegel & myself had both studied deeply & perserverantly the philosophy of Kant. . . .[79]

Is not Coleridge here granting, almost casually, that which English-speaking critics have never been willing to accept, namely, that Schlegel's and Coleridge's criticism do not parallel each other only on Shakespeare, but rather in the whole approach to poetry? This lends massive support to Professor Wellek's seemingly extreme insistence that the Schlegels through Coleridge transmitted to England and America the view of literature basically accepted today.[80]

If critics will not grant that the overall shape of Coleridge's Shakespeare criticism is crucially dependent upon Schlegel, how much less will the notion be entertained of still deeper and broader dependence! And yet if we quite ignore specific borrowings, we still find that the very spirit of Schlegel's lectures, its principles, its tone, its *Gestalt,* are all present in Coleridge's general criticism and aesthetic speculation. Here is a typical passage from the *Vorlesungen:*

the romantic delights in indissoluble mixtures; *all contrarieties:* nature and art, poetry and prose, seriousness and mirth, recollection and anticipation, spirituality and sensuality, terrestrial and celestial, life and death, are by it *blended together in the most intimate combination.* . . . Romantic poetry . . . is the expression of the secret attraction to a chaos that lies concealed in the very bosom of the ordered universe, and is perpetually striving after new and marvellous births. . . . The former [classic art] is more simple, clear, and like to nature in the self-existent perfection of her separate works. . . . For Conception can only comprise each object separately, but nothing in truth can ever exist separately and by itself; Feeling perceives all in all at one and the same time.[81]

This passage contains more than the mere germs of some of Coleridge's most famous dicta, including the contrast between romantic and classic art, the reconciliation of opposites, and the basic operations of the secondary Imagination.

Of Shakespeare's powers and attributes, Schlegel wrote:

As a profound thinker he had pretty accurately taken the measure of the circle of human capabilities. . . . Shakespeare, moreover, was a nice observer of nature. . . . To me he appears a profound artist, and not a blind and wildly luxuriant genius. . . . The activity of genius is, it is true, natural to it, and, in a certain sense, unconscious. . . . It is admitted that Shakespeare has reflected, and deeply reflected, on character and passion, on the progress of events and human destinies, on the human constitution, on all the things and relations of the world. . . . He unites in his soul the utmost elevation and utmost depth; and the most opposite and even apparently irreconcilable properties subsist in him peaceably together. The world of spirits and nature have laid all their treasures at his feet: in strength a demi-god, in profundity of view a prophet, in all-seeing wisdom a guardian spirit of a higher order, he lowers himself to mortals as if unconscious of his superiority, and is as open and unassuming as a child. . . . we therefore may perceive in the poet himself, notwithstanding his power to excite the most fervent emotions, a certain cool indifference.[82]

These ideas can be found all over Coleridge's writings, frequently expressed in very similar words. Once again we encounter the reconciliation of opposites, but here Schlegel also refers to the unconscious activity of the artist. In speaking of *Venus and Adonis,* Coleridge mentioned "the utter aloofness of the poet's own feelings."[83] This is surely a restatement of Schlegel's "a certain cool indifference." Moreover, Coleridge's statement occurs in a context discussing remoteness of subject. "No man was ever yet a great poet," he wrote, "without being at the same time a profound philosopher. . . . Shakespeare, no mere child of nature; no automaton of genius . . . first studied patiently, meditated deeply."[84] Schlegel's "all-seeing wisdom" is but one of the qualities he attributes to Shakespeare, and he elsewhere said that "no man can be a true critic or connoisseur without universality of mind,"[85] which is surely a more reasonable statement. In the *Biographia* Coleridge said: "To carry on the feelings of childhood into the powers of manhood . . . this is the character and privilege of genius."[86] And in his Shakespeare criticism: "the poet is one who carries the simplicity of childhood into the powers of manhood."[87] This is akin to Schlegel's statement that Shakespeare was "as open and unassuming as a child," a familiar idea in German criticism.

In discussing the "specific symptoms of poetic power," Coleridge observes: "A second promise of genius is the choice of subjects very remote from the private interests and circumstances of the writer himself."[88] It is possible that Coleridge was here projecting, since he had written "The Ancient Mariner" before setting foot on a ship. But the statement is otherwise bizarre, as the history of literature amply demonstrates. Wordsworth is a perfect example of the artist whose poetic power revealed itself at the full only when he wrote on subjects closest to his most personal interests.

We may suspect that Coleridge was influenced by what Schlegel had said of playwrights: "The distinguishing property of the dramatic poet who is great in characterization . . . is the capability of transporting himself so completely into every situation, even the most unusual, that he is enabled, as plenipotentiary of the whole human race, without particular instructions for each separate case, to act and speak in the name of every individual."[89]

All Schlegel is saying is that a great playwright understands human behavior so well that he can expose motivation in situations remote from his own direct experience. This is very different from arguing that specifically *poetic* power resides in such an attribute, for then a great poet must be a great psychologist. If this were true it would also have to be said that every great poet is potentially a great playwright, and this is obviously as absurd as the converse.

"Extraordinary situations," Schlegel wrote, "which intensely occupy the head and throw mighty passions into play, give elevation and tension to the soul: it collects together all its powers, and exhibits an unusual energy, both in its operations and in its communications by language."[90] Substitute Imagination for Soul and we find here "an unusual state of emotion," and implied in "collects together all its powers" the idea of "more than usual order." In any case, the basic ideas are those we identify with Coleridge's criticism.

When we consider how deeply the insights and principles of Schlegel are diffused throughout Coleridge's works, and when we remind ourselves further of the multitude of borrowings from German thought elsewhere in the prose writings, are we not forced substantially to modify the exalted claims made for Coleridge as an original critic and aesthetician?

At the turn of the century [writes E. M. Wilkinson] Germany, which for several decades had been taking with both hands from the rest of Europe, was ready to repay her debt with interest. Nowhere was spiritual and intellectual life so intense, and a mind as alert and omnivorous as Coleridge's could not but profit by it. His indebtedness is incalculable— incalculable in a qualitative rather than in a quantitative sense. Even where the evidence seems to point in a quite different direction, it may well turn out that Germany was the mediator.[91]

But should we not try to calculate the debt, soberly, without irrelevant loyalties and preconceptions? Is Professor Wellek not quite justified in maintaining that the

view of the relation between art and nature, the reconciliation of opposites, the whole dialectical scheme—comes from Schelling. The distinction between symbol and allegory can be found in Schelling and Goethe, the distinction between genius and talent in Kant, the distinctions between organic and mechanical, classical and modern, statuesque and picturesque in A. W. Schlegel. Coleridge's particular use of the term "Idea" comes from the Germans, and the way in which he links imagination with the process of cognition is also clearly derived from Fichte and Schelling.

Observing that many American and English critics minimize Coleridge's dependence on the Germans by showing that many of the leading ideas were foreshadowed by the English neo-Platonists and ancient writers, Wellek comments:

Coleridge was acquainted with Plato, Plotinus, Cudworth, Henry More, and others, but still he draws on the Germans, for only they use the same dialectical method as he, the same epistomology and the same critical vocabulary. The neo-Platonists remained essentially scholastic mystics.[92]

In a footnote to this passage Wellek reinforces the last points sharply:

All this is ignored by those who make Coleridge completely independent of the Germans, thus flying in the face of all evidence. . . . Coleridge introduced many terms and pairs of terms, common today, into English from the German: psychological, aesthetic, objective—subjective, organic . . . romantic, etc. . . . In a few cases others were picking up these terms a little earlier. Coleridge himself sometimes tried to trace them far back into history and argued that these distinctions existed in the schoolmen and English divines. But he produced no convincing evidence.[93]

Neither has anyone else. But even if one could, is it really fair to dig about in forgotten volumes to find the origins of ideas which we know were available to Coleridge in the rich current of ideas flowing from Germany? He had the volumes in his own library, and he systematically declined to acknowledge them in his own writing and lecturing. We should not continue to deny facts.

The checks and balances inherent in the concept of an international community of scholars, so crucial in the sciences, cannot really be said to exist in the disciplines of the modern languages and literatures, though the contrary is assumed with a casualness that can be startling. The brilliant work of an occasional foreign scholar on an aspect of American literature is the exception to the rule. This is not to say there are no scholars who command literatures in more than one language. Of course there are. But scholarly studies in modern literatures are overwhelmingly nationalistic. This is still more true of the initial training in lower schools on which the scholar's general attitudes are based.

Hence it is simply not true to say that the complex subject of Coleridge's relations with Germany has received a balanced, let alone an exhaustive hearing. The issue here is not the erudition of those great scholars who have already studied the subject; as to mere erudition we are not likely ever to see an improvement. The problem is rather that with the exception of a handful of scholars who come to Coleridge after a youth steeped in German literature and thought, the process has always been the other way. If English-speaking scholars are guilty of a frenzied xenophobia on the subject of Coleridge's debt to Germany, it can—and regularly has been—argued that Coleridge has been too often the victim of the "fury of the Germanist." It is truly astonishing that in a review of René Wellek's *A History of Modern Criticism*, T. M. Raysor, who has devoted a lifetime to editing Coleridge's miscellaneous and Shakespearean criticism, was able to write: "[Wellek] is the only student of Coleridge I know who has a full realization of Coleridge's profound indebtedness to German thought. . . ."[94]

Coleridge is, after all, an English writer. This simple fact explains why out of every hundred articles written on him, perhaps ninety-nine are written by English or American scholars. And for the overwhelming majority, the literature of Germany can scarcely be said to be more than a tangential concern. Coleridge's German background is something one reads about; it is not something imbibed as part of one's culture—the way we know that Pope derives from Dryden, or that Byron, Keats, and Shelley emerge from the immediate heritage of the eighteenth century as modified by the early Romantics.

Crucial in this connection is a fact hardly ever considered, namely, that modern literary criticism is an invention of England and America. It is hard to think of a single European critic in our century, until recently, who has made important and operative contributions to the body of critical theory now triumphant in American universities and (to a much lesser extent) in England. Coleridge's unparalleled reputation as a critic (rivaled only by Aristotle) has developed in the past two generations. This judgment has not been subjected to searching scrutiny by continental, especially German, scholars. Wellek, of course, is not only the key exception, he is the only exception with any important influence whatever. Month in and month out Coleridge's reputation is added to by books and articles written by scholars from his own linguistic community. These are not examined by German scholars in the abrasive and fruitful give and take of scholarly controversy. On the contrary, foreign scholars who presume to differ with current opinion are generally dismissed as incompetent to estimate the English heritage out of which Coleridge's ideas grew. We must remember also that modern literary criticism scarcely exists as a vigorous force even now in Germany.

Should the time come—and it is by no means inevitable—that German students turn their attention to their national literature from the general critical perspectives which have so intensely animated literary studies among ourselves, it is possible that the claims of the Schlegels, Schiller, Schelling, Lessing, Herder, and the scores of others who made up the astonishing German culture of the late eighteenth century will at last receive the attention they deserve, and in the process radically minimize the present emphasis on the uniqueness of Coleridge's original contributions or synthesis of these ideas. Until we have from Germany a counterweight to the month-in and month-out accumulation of scholarly celebrations of Coleridge's original genius, we are unlikely to see any fundamental change in the shape which the literary history of the Romantic period has assumed in the past forty years.

Should such a change actually ever come about, Coleridge would remain a giant, but rather in different guise. No man of his time had so exalted a vision of the shape of humanistic studies. He was a great pioneer in introducing German thought to England. If in his surreptitiousness he often muddied the current, he also bequeathed to us the classic language in which many a particular formulation is remembered. It is difficult to think of a single important idea from the early nineteenth century in which Coleridge was somehow not involved. It is impossible to study any area of English thought in the Romantic period which does not somehow either proceed from, or very quickly get round to him. He stands in the mainstream of English literary history like a colossus, often obstructing the view, often diverting the currents nearby from their true course, but indispensably *there*.

One final point—quintessential Coleridge. On the fourth page of his literary life, he paid glowing tribute to a "severe master" he had had as a schoolboy at Christ's Hospital, the Reverend James Boyer. From Boyer, he said, he had learned

> that Poetry, even that of the loftiest and, seemingly, that of the wildest odes, had a logic of its own, as severe as that of science; and more difficult, because more subtle, more complex, and dependent on more, and more fugitive causes.[95]

This statement is quoted again and again as a veritable cornerstone of modern literary criticism, as indeed it is. Richard Harter Fogle calls it as "exhilarating" as Sidney's "Defense of Poesy" and Emerson's "American Scholar."[96]

Coleridge did not learn this in his boyhood from a schoolmaster, but much later from the writings of musty old Edward Young. In a letter to William Sotheby of 1802, years after he had left school and fifteen years before the publication of the *Biographia*, he wrote: "Young somewhere in one of his prose works remarks that there is as profound a Logic in the most daring & dithyrambic parts of Pindar, as in the "Οργανον [logic] of Aristotle—the remark is a valuable one."[97] By 1802 Coleridge was already planning several *magna opera*, and it is easy to see why he was so drawn to a remark which established connections between literature and philosophy and hinted at laws underlying seemingly diverse phenomena. His notebooks for 1795 show that he was copying or paraphrasing passages from Young's essay "On Lyric Poetry," which he had taken out of the Bristol Library. Some were to appear, in various forms and transformations, in his later work.[98] At the time, however, he did not copy out Young's statement that "Pindar, who has much logic at the bottom as Aristotle or Euclid, to some critics has appeared mad. . . ." Only later, it would appear, did he perceive its significance, and of course this is to his credit. When at last he came to state the matter in the *Biographia*, he added several increments to Young's original idea, investing it with resonances and dubious implications, so that its origin in a suggestive statement by a neo-classic poet is scarcely recognizable.

Why should Coleridge have attributed to Boyer an influence which he might just as well have assigned to its proper source, Edward Young? The explanation, unfortunately, does Coleridge little credit. In the *Biographia* and elsewhere in his career he was most anxious to establish that he had from a very early age meditated upon just those concepts in philosophy, literary criticism, or science (depending upon the situation confronting him) which it might otherwise appear had come to his attention from the published work he had read in his maturity. In an account of his literary life it certainly seemed to establish his own claims to original thought—or at least Coleridge would have thought so—by writing that he had become aware of them in his early youth. And, indeed, subsequent critics almost to a man have snapped at the bait.

Gordon Mackenzie traces Coleridge's entire theory of poetry to "a life-long belief . . . that poetry had a logic of its own . . . the Rev. Bowyer instilled this precept in him."[99] And George Watson, in *The Literary Critics*, is still more confident:

We should hesitate long before denying Coleridge his originality as a critic; a reading of Kant, which he probably did not begin until his visit to Germany in 1798-9, only helped him to formalize his deepest intuitions concerning poetic creation. According to his own account of his school-days, he learned as a boy from his schoolmaster that "poetry . . . had a logic of its own as severe as that of science; and more difficult, because more subtle, more complex, and dependent on more, and more fugitive, causes."[100]

Most influential of all, however, is perhaps I. A. Richards, whose work has done so much to exalt Coleridge's reputation. From evidence such as the tribute to Boyer, Richards concludes that

> Coleridge's studies in this severe logic, his inquiry into these multiple and fugitive causes occupied the best years of his life. . . . [He] had been a preternaturally reflective schoolboy, in his early teens "delving into the unwholesome quicksilver mines of metaphysic depths." . . . I assume that Coleridge's great merit as a critic—a merit unique among English critics—is the strenuous persistence with which he had reflected philosophically upon criticism. [He had] gone on, from his fourteenth year, thinking about poetry with an assiduity and enterprise that cannot be matched in the biography of another critic.[101]

To the extent that all these weighty opinions rest upon the tributes to Boyer, they rest upon lilypads. And if it was Coleridge's intention to establish the image of a *Wunderkind*, for whom later learning only confirmed the schoolboy insights of the inspired charity-boy, he builded even better than he knew.

Coda

The "philosophical letters" which Coleridge sent to Josiah Wedgwood in 1801 related chiefly, in Coleridge's own words, "to the character of Mr. Locke, whom I think I have *proved* to have gained a reputation to which he had no honest claim. . . ."

> In my Biographical Dictionary the writer introduces Locke as "one of the greatest men that England ever produced.["] Mr. Hume, a much more competent Judge, declares that he was "really a great Philosopher." . . . three Germans . . . concur in pronouncing him to be "a truly original Genius." And Mr. Locke himself has made it sufficiently clear . . . that he did not regard himself as a Reformer, but as a Discoverer; not as an opposer of a newly discovered Heresy in Metaphysics but as an Innovator upon ancient and generally received Opinions.[102]

Coleridge heaped scorn on those who held Locke in high esteem: ". . . Mr. Locke has grossly misrepresented the ancient & received opinions, and . . . the Doctrines which he holds for Truths of his own Discovery are many of them erroneous & none original. . . . I cannot suppress my feelings of unpleasant doubt & wonder, which his frequent claims to originality raised in me; his apologies for new words as necessary in a system deviating so widely, as his, from the hitherto received Opinions. . . ."[103]

He insisted that Locke's system existed in Descartes "*actually, explicitly,*" and he underscored the last two words himself. After demolishing as best he could the foundations of Locke's reputation, he felt himself in the position of many another critic sensitive to being called a debunker:

> I feel deeply . . . what ungracious words I am writing; in how unamiable a Light I am placing myself. I hazard the danger of being considered one of those trifling men who whenever a System has gained the applause of mankind hunt out in obscure corners of obscure Books for paragraphs in which that System may seem to have been anticipated; or perhaps some sentence of half [a] dozen words, in the intellectual Loins of which the System had lain snug in *homuncular* perfection. This is indeed vile in any case, but when that System is the work of our Countryman; when the Name, from which we attempt to detract, has been venerable for a century in the Land of our Fathers & Forefathers, it is most vile. But I trust, that this can never be fairly applied to the present Instance—on the contrary I seem to myself as far as these facts have not been noticed, to have done a good work, in restoring a name, to which Englishmen have been especially unjust [that is, Descartes], to the honors which belong to it. It were well if we should rid ourselves of a fault that is common to us, in literary far more than in political Relations—the *hospitibus feros*, attributed to us of old. . . . Discoveries of these & similar Facts in literary History are by no means so unprofitable as might appear at the first view. They lessen that pernicious custom . . . of neglecting to make ourselves accurately acquainted with the opinions of those who have gone before us. . . . Life is short, & Knowledge infinite; & it is well therefore that powerful & thinking minds should know exactly where to set out from, & so lose no time in superfluous Discoveries of Truths long before discovered.[104]

Among the several reasons he advanced to account for the growth of so undeserved a reputation, Coleridge emphasized political and religious propaganda: "The effect, the Clergy have had in raising, extending & preserving Mr. Locke's Reputation cannot be calculated—and in the meantime the Infidels were too politic to contradict them." In view of the general cultural atmosphere surrounding Locke's name, he found, it was not surprising that this "undeserved" reputation grew:

> Those, who do read Mr. Locke, as a part of Education or of Duty, very naturally think him a great Man / having been taught to suppose him the Discoverer of all the plain preadamitical Common sense that is to be found in his Book. . . . his Errors & Inaccuracies are sometimes admitted . . . but more often as in other holy Books, are explained away —& the most manifest self-contradictions reconciled with each other / & on the plea, that so great a man has to be judged by the general Spirit of his Opinions, & not by the Dead Letters.

"But more than all," Coleridge wrote, still defending the rationale behind what was sure to be an unpopular indictment, "these little Detections are valuable as throwing [light] on the causes & growth of Reputation in Books as well as man."[105]

In taking a comprehensive view of Coleridge's character and his actual *biographia literaria*, it would be well to keep this attitude in mind.

III

THE
DIVINE ARTIFICER

17.

The Years of Apprenticeship

The parallel hunter inhabits one of the dreariest domains in the republic of letters. Rare is the quarter in which the learned journals do not carry articles establishing "sources." While we may complain at the dullness of it all, we respectfully read and duly account such articles contributions to scholarship. Unless, however, the source or parallels found are very similar in language or idea to the finished work, we are likely to feel a certain doubt, and perhaps impatience. We frequently wonder what difference it may make that Author A may have been indebted to Author B for such and such a line or concept. Unless the resemblance is overwhelming, we may readily attribute it to coincidence. Further, all too many "parallels" exist only in the mind of the article-writer. Dawns are likely to be pink and tempests frequently howl. Rivers run downhill and sometimes underground, and a summer in the sixteenth century may be very like a summer in the eighteenth century. Despite all such objections, "source" studies proliferate. Perhaps their worst feature is that in the vast majority, even when the source or parallel is clear, we do not feel that we have really learned anything. All minds are filled with the observation and reading of a lifetime. Inevitably, what one has heard or read will emerge in more or less altered form in one's speech or writing. What one knows has been learned from somewhere or is in some way the extension of the work of other men. Every artist, even the most dynamically original, inevitably takes far more from the past than he can give to the future.

On this basis it is easy to say that the borderlines between the original and the derived are blurred at best, and that it is only with the greatest caution that we can describe any given work as primarily one or the other. Yet, is there no qualitative difference between the original and the derived? Is not Dryden a more original poet than Shadwell? Pushed to philosophical extremes many a seemingly simple question becomes unanswerable. Clearly James Joyce is a more original novelist than Rudyard Kipling, but if one insists upon exploring the subject to the bottom one may readily become sub-

221

merged in matters which have nothing to do with Joyce, Kipling, or even novels.

Coleridge's poems are anthologized everywhere. He is widely considered one of the great and original poets in the English language. "When the eye or the imagination is struck with any uncommon work," wrote Dr. Johnson, "the next transition of an active mind is to the means by which it was performed."[1] It is the object of the present chapter to throw some light on the profoundly complex nature of Coleridge's poetic process.

The radical reestimation of almost every aspect of his career that has been so much a feature of modern literary scholarship and criticism has made contentious a large number of generalizations that not many years ago would have been taken for granted. To assert now that an unusual feature of Coleridge's poetry is that there is singularly little of any importance previous to the amazing flowering of 1797-98 (the *annus mirabilis*) would be to invite endless controversy. For well over a century Coleridge's coming-of-age as a poet has seemed so sudden as to be astounding. Indeed, many theories were put forward to account for so extraordinary, and brief, a flowering; earlier scholars, on the whole, hunted in vain for any steady growth in manner or matter leading up to the poetry of the great period.

A careful reading of the early poetry discloses isolated glimmerings of the later mastery, but noting them is a treacherous process.[2] One is likely to see in the verse of a poet with a great reputation much that would not be noticed in a lesser figure or thought significant. The tone and content of Coleridge's early poetry has, at least in the past, seemed characteristic of late eighteenth-century poetry in general. With the exception of, at most, two or three poems, nothing seemed to suggest the revolutionary work that followed upon the intimacy with Wordsworth.

Coleridge's development as a poet is forever connected with the name of William Lisle Bowles, to whom, in the *Biographia Literaria*, he paid a memorable tribute.[3] Bowles's sonnets, he said, had seized his imagination powerfully when he was but seventeen years old. This admiration for Bowles has long been known and to some extent studied. Over fifty years ago Lane Cooper noted that the "literary influence of William Lisle Bowles on Coleridge has often been exploited, although not always with enough discrimination and attention to detail."[4] But this influence has not been so much exploited as Cooper suggests. Dykes Campbell discusses it in general terms, noting that "the first breath of Nature, unsophisticated by the classical tradition, came to Coleridge from Bowles's sonnets; and he recognised it at once."[5] Coleridge presented Mrs. Thelwall with a copy of Bowles's poems, piously inscribed: "I entreat your acceptance of this Volume, which has given me more pleasure, and done my heart more good, than all the other books, I ever read, excepting my Bible." At the end of 1796, thus within a year of the *annus mirabilis*, he still wrote of Bowles as "the bard of my idolatry."[6] Toward the close of the preface to his *Poems* of 1796, he referred to Bowles's sonnets glowingly. The first of his "Effusions" was dedicated to

Bowles. Preceding the collection of sonnets in the 1797 volume was the half-title, "Sonnets attempted in the manner of the Rev. W. L. Bowles."[7] As we shall see, Bowles's influence extended far beyond the sonnets.

"How closely Coleridge would sometimes follow his model in subject, sentiment, and language," wrote Campbell, "may be seen by comparing his sonnet *To the River Otter* . . . with Bowles's verses *To the River Itchin, near Winton*."[8] The similarity between the two poems has often been noted. Yet, while subject and sentiments are nearly identical, there is practically no identity of language. Such imitation is, of course, not only perfectly natural in a young poet much under influence of another, but probably inevitable.

Garland Greever, who has written the standard biography of Bowles, invites us to compare the two river sonnets and also Bowles's "The Bells, Ostend" with Coleridge's "Pain."[9] He mentions resemblances in "mood" in other poems—limiting the influence to the poems written before 1797—but as he does not specify particular instances we are left to draw our own conclusions.

What has for more than a century been vaguely spoken of as an "influence" does not adequately describe the relationship between the two poets. Coleridge not only responded to the spirit, but incorporated passages from Bowles's poetry into his own, adapted ideas, images, and phrases, and built more than one whole poem on something of Bowles's without public reference to his model. The influence of Bowles often demonstrates Coleridge's dazzling power of imitation.

Lamb called "On a Discovery Made Too Late" the "most Bowles-like" of all Coleridge's effusions.[10] Though the mood of this poem is drenched in Bowles, I am unable to discover any significant *verbal* parallels between it and any work of Bowles. That one poet may enter deeply into the spirit of another without actually adopting words or unusual images raises difficult problems in determining influences. Scholars are most loathe to admit anything but verbal parallels into the company of proven sources. This tradition severely limits us in tracing debts, a subject which has considerable bearing on the question of originality.

Greever observed that the resemblances between Bowles's "The Bells, Ostend," and Coleridge's "Pain" are "marked," but he failed to say more. Let us inquire further. Bowles's sonnet begins*:

> How sweet the tuneful bells' responsive peal!
> As when, at opening *morn*, the *fragrant breeze*
> Breathes on *the trembling sense of wan disease*,
> So piercing to my heart their force I feel! . . .
> They fling their melancholy *music* wide . . .

---

*Throughout this chapter, in the quoted passages, all italics are mine unless otherwise stated in the notes.

Coleridge's sonnet begins:

> Once could the *Morn's* first beams, the healthful *breeze*,
> All Nature charm, and gay was every hour;—
> But ah! not *Music's* self, nor *fragrant* bower
> Can glad *the trembling sense of wan Disease.*
> Now that the frequent pangs my frame assail . . .

Had Coleridge not adopted a whole phrase of Bowles, "the trembling sense of wan disease,"[11] many readers might be inclined to believe that Bowles's poem, though recently read, had somehow dropped into his unconscious and emerged in a not too altered form. Only the most obviously related words have been italicized above, but it is apparent that many other words and images come just as directly from Bowles, though by way of synonym. Bowles's "opening morn" becomes "Morn's first beams"; "fragrant breeze" becomes "healthful breeze," with Coleridge using the word "fragrant" two lines later. Bowles's "piercing to my heart their force I feel" was surely the basis of Coleridge's "the frequent pangs my frame assail." The conclusion of Coleridge's sonnet is contrived from the conclusion of Bowles's in similar fashion: both compare the here and now with the happier days of yore. Bowles is melancholy about his lost youth, Coleridge about his lost health. Bowles's image of pain is borrowed practically intact to form the basis of Coleridge's poem, and it is from this that almost everything proceeds. On the manuscript Coleridge wrote, "Sonnet Composed in Sickness," thus perhaps implying that the lines were actually occasioned by personal experience.[12]

While still a student at Cambridge, he wrote into one of the prayer books in the college chapel a twelve-line poem which began:

> —I yet remain
> To mourn the hours of youth (yet mourn in vain)
> That fled neglected: wisely thou hast trod
> The better path—and that high meed which God
> Assign'd to virtue, tow'ring from the dust.
> Shall wait thy rising, Spirit pure and just![13]

The poem was published for the first time in *Literary Remains* (1836). Campbell noted that the lines given above were nearly identical with the last six lines of Bowles's "On the Death of Henry Headley."[14] These are Bowles's lines, with Coleridge's changes italicized:

> I, *alas!* remain
> To mourn the hours of youth (yet mourn in vain)
> That fled neglected,—Wisely thou has trod
> The better path; and that High Meed, which God

Ordained for Virtue, towering from the dust.
Shall *bless* thy *labours*, spirit! pure and just.[15]

Since Bowles was then a comparatively popular poet, Coleridge could not have published this effort without detection. However, to take an uncharitable view, some gratification might have been derived from writing Bowles's lines into a college chapel prayer book, thereby impressing both friends and faculty. But this, perhaps, is to speculate. Later, Coleridge was to borrow extensively from "On the Death of Henry Headley" in one of his important poems, without making any acknowledgment.[16]

One would suppose that all his major debts to so obvious an influence as Bowles would surely have long since been disclosed, but that it is no simple matter to detect resemblances between a poem and a skillful reworking is demonstrated by Mrs. Lucyle Werkmeister's discovery that Coleridge's "Anthem for the Children of Christ's Hospital" is an "adaptation" of Bowles's *Verses on the Philanthropic Society.*[17] It will be remembered that Coleridge was only nineteen years old when he wrote to his brother George: "I have sent you a sermon metamorphosed from an obscure publication by vamping, transposition, &c—if you like it, I can send you two more of the same kidney."[18] Mrs. Werkmeister's article provides much evidence that by "vamping, transposition, &c" Coleridge was capable of so transforming a model that his debt not only eluded notice for over a century and a half but remains difficult to perceive unless one studies the two poems very carefully. The results of such a scrutiny are of almost incalculable importance in coming to a rational view of the extent to which Coleridge may have used models in other poems where verbal similarities are remote but where one may legitimately suspect "vamping."[19]

Mrs. Werkmeister notes that the first four lines of the "Anthem" owe nothing to Bowles.[20] Only a slight difference exists in the viewpoint taken at the beginning of the two poems: Bowles stresses human benevolence while Coleridge stresses the benevolence of God. "Otherwise Coleridge's poem proceeds in much the same way as Bowles'."[21]

Both poets "hail the arrival of Compassion in the 'realms of woe' with exclamations. Bowles was perhaps more dramatic."[22] A personified "meek Compassion" (l. 109) shelters Bowles's orphans. Coleridge's "Compassion" (l. 15) is a "meek-eyed Power" visiting the "Children of Distress." "The parallelism of metaphor in the two poems is similarly striking. In the main, Bowles relied upon three comparisons, and Coleridge . . . evidently saw no reason to alter them. First, Bowles compares suffering and vice with a winter tempest. . . ."[23] At four different points Bowles refers to storms and tempests (ll. 17, 49-51, 88, 110-111), and Coleridge uses the storm image in the last four lines of the "Anthem." Mrs. Werkmeister finds Bowles's second metaphor in the comparison of "vice and suffering with clouds or darkness, virtue and happiness with sunlight or moonlight. . . . Finally, Bowles compared the effect of benevolence upon the poor with a cave suddenly penetrated by beams of light." In the final text of the *Verses* we find the lines Mrs. Werkmeister cites as one example of this idea:

> [They] have sought
> *Want's dismal cell*, and pale as from the dead
> *To life and light* the speechless orphan led. (ll. 174-176)

"In the 'Anthem' this comparison is implied," Mrs. Werkmeister notes, "rather than specified, but the implication is enough in the phrase, 'realms of woe' (l. 15), and in the lines:

> The beams that play around her head
> Thro' *Want's dark vale* their *radiance* spread:
> The young uncultur'd mind imbibes the ray,
> And Vice reluctant quits th' expected prey (ll. 21-24)."

Mrs. Werkmeister emphasizes that "it is clear from Bowles' account that Vice is frightened away by the radiance."[24]

In the 1790 text, however, the relevant passage in which the patrons of the Philanthropic Society are hailed as saviors, reads thus:

> . . . for ye who thus with wider scan,
> Prompt to relieve, have mark'd the woes of man!
> Who to *that dreary cave* where Misery lies,
> Nor hears her famish'd offspring's moaning cries,
> First pitying came, and pale as from the dead
> *To life and light* the speechless Orphan led.[25]

Interestingly, the seemingly close parallel between Coleridge's "Want's dark vales" and Bowles's "Want's dismal cell" declines to "that dreary cave" in the original *Verses*. But the loss is more than supplied by the original opening lines of the *Verses*:

> When Want, long bow'd with hopeless Misery,
> Retires forsaken to her cell to die . . .

The personified "Want" has returned, to be picked up also by Coleridge's "cheerless Want" (l. 13). A study of the "dreary cave" passage in the original *Verses* allows a variety of other connections to swim into view. In Bowles's poem, "Misery" does not "hear her famish'd offspring's moaning cries," but in the "Anthem," conversely, "Th' all-gracious Parent hears the wretch's prayer" (l. 9). Bowles's patrons "First pitying came," having "mark'd the woes of man!" In Coleridge it is a Lord who "beholds with pitying eye" the struggles of the oppressed, and bids Compassion "seek the realms of woe" (l. 15).

Coleridge so extensively reconstituted Bowles's poem that it is very difficult to convey the full borrowing without asking the reader to study both poems at length. I am indebted to Mrs. Werkmeister for the following points. In Coleridge there is a "child of Woe" (l. 7); in Bowles "children of woe" (l. 134). Coleridge has "Compassion seek the realms of woe" (l. 15); a footnote in Bowles hails the Philanthropic Society for "seeking out" vagrant children. Bowles describes a "Lost mother" (l. 156); Coleridge offers comfort to a "lorn mother" (l. 25). It would seem also that "morn," "sun," and "Love" in the last three lines of the "Anthem" owe something to the "morn," "sunbeam," and "Love," in Bowles's closing lines (ll. 180-187).

Verses on the Philanthropic Society was first published in 1790. Precisely when Coleridge wrote the "Anthem" is uncertain. Mrs Werkmeister thinks it may have been written before Coleridge left Christ's Hospital, and perhaps as early as March 1790, when he was seventeen years old. The "Anthem" was not published until the last year of Coleridge's life, and Mrs. Werkmeister suggests that he did not publish it sooner because he might have found its publication "embarrassing," for the reason that, "although the similarity to Bowles' *Verses* would have been unnoticed by most readers, for the *Verses* were not widely read, it would not have been unnoticed by Bowles himself."[26]

That the "Anthem" was written before he was eighteen years old shows a kind of astonishing ingenuity in Coleridge. A quite extraordinary skill is demonstrated in redistributing concepts, metaphors, and word-clusters into a new setting. The opportunity the poem provides to study Coleridge's developing poetic craft is thus of considerable value.

Keeping in mind how extensive were his borrowings from Bowles, we are in a better position to understand Coleridge's delight when, in later years, he came upon a line of his own in one of Bowles's poems. "[It] gave me great pleasure," he wrote, "from the thought, what a pride & joy I should have had at the time of writing it, if I had supposed it possible that Bowles would have adopted it."[27]

In a letter dated 13 February 1792, Coleridge sent Mary Evans' mother a poem called "To Disappointment." The poem so obviously derives from Milton that it may well serve as another example of the young Coleridge's way with models. "L'Allegro" and "Il Penseroso" are companion pieces describing two types of personality. As such, the poems have similar structures and development. "L'Allegro" begins:

> *Hence* loathed Melancholy
> Of Cerberus and blackest midnight born,
> In Stygian Cave forlorn
> 'Mongst horrid shapes, and shrieks, and sights *unholy,*
> Find out some uncouth *cell* . . .
> In dark Cimmerian desert ever *dwell.*
> But come thou Goddess fair and free . . .

Coleridge's "To Disappointment" begins:

> *Hence!* thou fiend of gloomy sway,
> That lov'st on withering blast to ride
> O'er fond Illusion's air-built pride.
> Sullen Spirit! Hence! Away!
> Where Avarice lurks in sordid *cell,*
> Or mad Ambition builds the dream,
> Or Pleasure plots th' *unholy* scheme,
> There with Guilt and Folly *dwell!* . . .
> Then haste thee, Nymph of Balmy gales . . .

Coleridge's poem is both a hasty and crude imitation of Milton, though the young Mary Evans may well have been unaware of that. He did not publish the poem, but it is nevertheless interesting precisely because it so much resembles the first quick draft of the kind of imitation he was later able to refine so subtly. We find in "To Disappointment" the same structure, some of the same words, and a succession of concepts identical to "L' Allegro." After ordering the fiend to depart, Coleridge invokes the "Nymph of *balmy gales*" and bids "sweet *May*" attend. Milton's goddess is at one point the daughter of Zephyr, "the *frolic Wind*," who met Aurora "a-*May*ing." There follows a Miltonic catalogue of joys, including a "treasures/Pleasures" rime (ll. 18-19), which is close to "L'Allegro's" "pleasure/measures" (ll. 69-70). Coleridge's "Illusion's air-built pride" and "mad Ambition builds the dream" echo the "idle brain" in "Il Penseroso" possessed of "fancies fond with gaudy shapes" (l. 6), after which, three lines later, Milton speaks of "dreams."

L'Allegro" and "Il Penseroso" haunt many of Coleridge's early poems.[28] "Happiness" seems clearly to derive from them and contains parallel situations. Coleridge writes, describing the joys of the reflective life:

> 'Tis thine with Fancy oft to talk,
> And thine the peaceful evening *walk;*
> And what to thee the sweetest are—
> The setting *sun*, the Evening Star . . . (ll. 80-83)

In "Il Penseroso" a similar catalogue begins:

> And when the *Sun* begins to fling
> His flaring beams, me Goddess bring
> To arched *walks* of twilight groves . . . (ll. 131-133)

The parallel here should not be confined to the words "sun" and "walk," for the whole passage following is identical in ideational content. Except for a moralistic conclusion, Coleridge's poem is "Il Penseroso" redone, containing the same theme within substantially the same structure. It is surely unnecessary to suppose that he used his model unconsciously, since shortly after the lines above quoted he refers to the "guardian genius of thy way":

> Whom (*sages* say) in days of *yore*
> Meek Competence to Wisdom *bore*. (ll. 98-99)

Milton had written:

> With two sister Graces more
> To Ivy-crowned Bacchus *bore;*
> Or whether (as some *Sager* sing) . . . ("L'Allegro," ll. 15-17)
> Thee bright-hair'd Vesta long of *yore*,
> To solitary Saturn *bore*. ("Il Penseroso," ll. 23-24)

Italics places a wrong emphasis on the extent of the parallel. In "Happiness" Coleridge uses Milton's contrast of two ways of life, comparing the life of philosophic "careless Quiet" (l. 79) with the riotous existence of "painted Pleasure," also termed an "Enchantress" (ll. 53-54).[29]

"Happiness" may also owe something to Bowles's poem "Music." Apart from general similarities in mood there are in Bowles's sonnet the words *sweet tints, eye, silent passions, tear* in that order. Within a six-line space in "Happiness" we find *sweetest, tints, eye, tear, silent pleasures* (ll. 82-87). The Bowlesian influence becomes rather more probable when one considers that Coleridge wrote a poem called "Music" at this time (1791), which, incidentally, also has elements in common with Milton. Coleridge's effort begins: "Hence, soul-dissolving *Harmony*," while Bowles's "Music" begins: "O *Harmony*! thou tenderest nurse of pain." After the Miltonic commencement, Coleridge establishes the lineage of the goddess Music in the Allegro-Penseroso manner:

> Born when earth was seiz'd with cholic;
> Or as more sapient *sages* say . . . (ll. 6-7)

and he rings one more variation on this theme with:

> Then if aright *old legendaries tell*,
> Wert thou begot by Discord on Confusion! (ll. 15-16)

Imitation, it has been often said, is the sincerest form of flattery. Coleridge, like almost every other poet, began his career with hardly any voice of his own and put his art to school with the masters he admired. But if the study of early poems tells us what we already know—that some young poets are parrots before they moult into eagles—it does not then follow that such studies are irrelevant. What one observes so clearly in Coleridge before the *annus mirabilis* is that the major experience of his poetry is the experience of reading other poets.

Some of his early poems are exercises in versification of a kind which permit us a largely unobstructed glance into at least one corner of Coleridge's youthful poetic workshop. One such specimen is his "Imitated from Ossian." Its first two publications carried in a note a brief excerpt from *Ossian:*

> The *flower* hangs its [heavy] head *waving* at times to the *gale.* "Why dost thou *awake me,* O *Gale?" it seems to say.* . . . "The time of my fading is near, the blast shall scatter my leaves. *Tomorrow shall the traveller come;* he that saw me in my beauty shall come. His *eyes* will *search* the field, but they will not find me. So shall they *search* in *vain.* . . .[30]

Coleridge's twenty-line poem reads in part:

> Beneath the dew the *Lily* weeps
> Slow-*waving* to the *gale.*
> 'Cease, restless *gale!' it seems to say,*
> 'Nor *wake me* with thy sighing!
> The honours of my vernal day
> On rapid wing are flying.
> '*To-morrow shall the Traveller come*
> Who late beheld me blooming:
> His *searching eye* shall *vainly* roam . . .
>   . . . the breeeze shall roll
> The voice of feeble power . . . (ll. 3-11, 17-18)

Comparison of the poem with its prose source demonstrates that the italicized words and phrases do not fully indicate their interdependence. Coleridge's "Who late beheld me blooming" owes as much to Macpherson's "he that saw me in my beauty" as any of the italicized passages, and "the breeze shall roll / The voice of feeble power" is obviously evoked by the "the blast that shall scatter my leaves," and so forth.[31]

Together with "Imitated from Ossian," Coleridge published a companion piece: "The Complaint of Ninathoma, From the Same." A note appended in 1796 and 1803 read in part:

> *How long will ye roll around me, blue-tumbling waters* of Ocean. My *dwelling* is *not always in caves; nor beneath the* whistling *tree.* . . . The youths *beheld* me. . . . *They blessed the* dark-haired *Nina-thoma.*[32]

Coleridge's sixteen-line poem reads in part:

> *How long will ye round me* be swelling,
> O ye *blue-tumbling* waves of the sea?
> *Not always in caves* was *my dwelling,*
> *Nor beneath the* cold blast of the *tree.* . . .
> The warriors *beheld Ninathoma,*
> And *they blessèd* the white-bosom'd Maid!

The "Complaint" as sent to Mary Evans contains a third stanza which never appeared in any published version. It reads:

> By my Friends, by my Lovers discarded,
> *Like the Flower of the Rock* now I waste,
> *That lifts it's fair head* unregarded,
> *And* scatters *it's leaves on the blast.*

Oddly, although this derives also from *Ossian*, the source is not *Berrathon* but a completely different book, *Oithona*, wherein a forlorn maid exclaims, "Why did I not pass away in secret, *like the flower of the rock, that lifts* its *fair head* unseen, *and* strews *its* withered *leaves on the blast.''*[33]

The poetic process here is similar to that of the first poem based on *Ossian,* and again is of interest because it permits us to put one of Coleridge's poems side by side with its direct source, and thus we can watch him learning to versify.[34]

Though we have seen several examples of what appears to be the direct influence of a single poet or poem, there are also from a very early age hints of a complex technique in working with a variety of sources in a single poem. In an earlier chapter we saw how extensively he was able to borrow from Rogers' "The Pleasures of Memory." "Absence: A Poem," was first published in 1793, a week after Coleridge's twenty-first birthday. In that youthful effort he deftly adapted Rogers' plot, and so thoroughly rearranged or modified ideas, images, and words, that were it not for a few incontrovertible verbal parallels, it might be almost impossible to assert absolutely that he had based his Effusion on Rogers. But the sources were not confined to one poem. A block of lines derived from the Greek Epigrams, according to Coleridge himself, at least two images stemmed from Bowles, and one couplet by way of an early Wordsworth poem. To the borrowings already discussed we may here add an image from the so-called "first draft" of "An Effusion At Evening," in which Coleridge wrote, "the *matin bird* with startling Song / *Salutes*" the morn. Bowles has "*the matin bird / Salute*" his lonely porch in "Hope" (ll. 3-4).[35] Further, Bowles has a description in "On Mr. Howard's Account of the Lazarettos" which Coleridge seems also to have recalled:

> Is aught so fair in *evening's* ling'ring *gleam,*
> As from thine *eye* the meek and pensive beam
> That falls like *saddest* moonlight on the hill
> And distant grove, when the wide world is still? (ll. 21-14)[36]

The closing lines of "Autumnal Evening" read:

> Like yon bright hues that paint the clouds of *eve!*
> Tearful and *saddening* with the *sadden'd* blaze
> Mine *eye* the *gleam* pursues with wistful gaze:
> Sees shades on shades with deeper tint impend . . . (ll. 102-105)

Since Bowles's "saddest moonlight" is an uncommon phrase, it seems probable that Coleridge's "sadden'd blaze" derives from it.

So far as the sources of the various versions of "Autumnal Evening" are
concerned, there are, clearly demonstrable, lines and images from Rogers,
Ossian, Bowles, and Wordsworth, which convey some idea of the difficulty
in tracing Coleridge's debts, and reveal the increasing diversity of sources
upon which he drew.

The song "Domestic Peace," from *The Fall of Robespierre,*[37] is scarcely
more than a snippet from the Effusion reset in another rhythm and context.
In the song, surrounding a personified Domestic Peace, can be seen

> Spotless Honour's meeker mien,
> *Love*, the sire of pleasing fears,
> *Sorrow smiling through her tears,*
> And conscious of her past *employ*
> *Memory,* bosom-spring of *joy*.

Any connection asserted between "Spotless Honour's meeker mien" above,
and the "blameless pleasures which dimple Quiet's cheek" in "Autumnal
Evening" (l. 85) would doubtless be thought fanciful, but surely less so when
it is observed that the line is soon followed by

> Where *Love* a crown of thornless Roses wears,
> Where soften'd *Sorrow smiles within her tears,*
> And *Memory*, with a Vestal's chaste *employ*,
> Unceasing feeds the lambent flame of *joy!*

We saw earlier that the passage beginning "As when the savage, who his
drowsy frame" in "Autumnal Evening" was derived from an analogy in
"The Pleasures of Memory" in which Rogers makes an almost identical
point involving a savage. Immediately after this analogy, Coleridge wrote:

> So *tossed by storms* along Life's wild'ring way,
> Mine eye reverted views that *cloudless day* . . . (ll. 77-78)

At a similar point Rogers had written:

> A little world of clear and *cloudless day*,
> Nor *wrecked by storms,* nor mouldered by decay. (ll. 72-73)

Coleridge used this whole passage in a poem called "Recollection," a work which he printed for the first and only time in the *Watchman*. "Recollection" begins with these eight lines developed from Rogers, then includes ten lines from the sonnet later published as "To the River Otter," and concludes with the last two lines of "The Gentle Look," which are also the last two lines of "Anna and Harland." "Recollection" is, therefore, almost entirely a collage of passages taken from the works of Rogers and Bowles. The twenty-eight lines of "Recollection" break down as having at least eight based on Rogers, ten modeled on Bowles's "To the River Itchin," and perhaps two more contrived from Bowles's "The River Cherwell" and "The Dying Slave."

This latter point may be discussed together with another feature of Coleridge's early poetry: its marked repetitiveness. "Recollection" concludes:

> Ah! fair tho' faint those forms of memory seem
> Like Heaven's bright bow on' thy smooth evening stream.

"Anna and Harland" concludes:

> For fair, tho' faint, the forms of Memory gleam,
> Like *Heaven's* bright *beauteous bow* reflected in the stream.

The last lines of "The Gentle Look" are:

> Yet fair, though faint, their images shall gleam
> Like the bright Rainbow on a willowy stream.

In "To a Young Lady" he wrote:

> Aye as the Star of Evening flung its *beam*
> In broken radiance on the wavy *stream* . . . (ll. 7-8)

These images are, of course, among the commonplaces of human experience. "Bright as a rainbow on streams, came Lulan's white-bosomed maid," appears in the very first episode of *Ossian,* which we know Coleridge had recently read.[38] Still, it is worth noting that Bowles in "The River Cherwell" speaks of "*Heaven's beauteous bow*" (l. 10), and in "The Dying Slave" a "golden *beam* / Glitter [s] on thy parent-*stream*" (ll. 9-10).[39]

The sonnet "Anna and Harland," reworks the Florio/Julia story from "The Pleasures of Memory," complete with the lorn lover roving the dear haunts of yore:

> Yet here her pensive ghost delights to stay;
> Oft pouring on the winds the broken lay—
> And hark, I hear her—'twas the passing blast.

The closing six lines of "Anna and Harland" were only slightly varied by Coleridge in the sonnet he addressed to Robert Southey in January 1795. In turn, the sonnet to Southey and the second version of the sonnet to Bowles are structural and ideational brothers and occasionally verbal twins.[40]

"To the Rev. W. J. Hort" was published in 1796 and never again during his lifetime. It is another collage of ideas, images, word clusters, and rimes, from "Autumnal Evening" and "Monody on the Death of Chatterton," with some slight salting from Milton and Gray.[41]

Before pursuing the relationship of Coleridge and Bowles further, it may be mentioned that when on 11 December 1794 Coleridge sent Southey "The Gentle Look" (whose final couplet contained the rainbow/stream image), he mentioned that the last four lines of the sonnet had been written by Lamb.[42] Subsequently he changed the last two lines to what we have seen above, which still leaves two lines by Lamb in the poem. It is hard to believe that Coleridge wrote the first ten lines of the sonnet and Lamb the last four without any further interdependence. With the sonnet to "Mrs. Siddons," Lamb and Coleridge took turns printing it as their own.[43] The existence of so much collaboration in Coleridge's early poetry creates particularly vexing difficulties in tracing his development.

In "Sonnet on Quitting School for College," he wrote:

> Adieu! adieu! ye much-lov'd *cloisters pale!*
> Ah! would those happy days return again,
> When *'neath your arches,* free from every stain,
> *I heard of guilt and wonder'd at the tale!*
> Dear haunts! where oft my simple lays I sang,
> Listening meanwhile to the *echoings* of my feet . . .[44]

The sentiment, manner, and matter of this poem derive, I believe, from Bowles's "On Leaving Winchester School," although there is no verbal identity. However, in "To a Young Lady" (1794), one of Coleridge's most synthetic compositions, one can see the further use of "On Leaving Winchester School." In this instance, since the announced subjects seem to have nothing in common, Coleridge perhaps felt freer in borrowing Bowles's images. The poem begins:

> Much on my early youth I love to dwell,
> Ere yet I bade that friendly dome farewell,
> Where first, *beneath the echoing cloisters pale,*
> *I heard of guilt and wonder'd at the tale.*

Here key phrases from his own "On Quitting School for College" are repeated almost intact. The "echoing cloisters pale," incidentally, is surely from "Il Penseroso's" "studious cloister's pale" (l. 156), which Coleridge had evidently misunderstood. But notice how "beneath the echoing cloisters

pale" recalls the earlier "much-loved cloisters pale . . . neath your arches
. . . echoing feet." After the image of the radiance of the evening star on
the stream, he continues:

> My soul amid the pensive twilight gloom
> Mourn'd with the breeze, O Lee Boo! o'er thy tomb. (ll 9-10)

Coleridge's footnote tells us who Lee Boo is, but does not mention that
Bowles also had written a poem on Lee Boo. In "To a Young Lady" Coleridge bids farewell to the "friendly dome" of college. In "On Leaving Winchester School" Bowles hears the "bell" from "yonder dome" of the school.
Coleridge hears a "knell that toll'd (l. 13). In both poems the time is evening. Coleridge has a "tear" (l. 12), and Bowles thinks he may drop some
"tears," (l. 13). These resemblances are, of course, trifling. Two people
writing on the same subject may surely hit upon the same words and
ideas. But as we happen to know that Coleridge read Bowles's poems repeatedly, the direct influence is more probable. Thus far his poetry seems
almost wholly contrived from books, and his young voice far more that of
a magpie than a nightingale.

The Gutch Memorandum book not only yields much information as to the
origin of some of the contents of the "Ode to the Departing Year," but, far
more important, tantalizingly illuminates Coleridge's habits and procedures
when composing at least some of his early work.[45] It is as if we had
glimpses of Coleridge's working brain by the stark light of intermittent
flashes of lightning. Thus it seems worth while to study this poem in some
detail before considering a few of the more important earlier ones.

Lowes's study of the Gutch notebook in *The Road to Xanadu* is justly
famous, but the infectious excitement of his style has tended to inhibit al-
ternative conclusions as to the nature of Coleridge's poetic process. The
reader is rare who can come away from Lowes without feeling that the notebook entries (so many of which appeared in Coleridge's poetry in forms ranging from verbatim to brilliantly transmuted) were entered without deliberate
system of any kind—the wildly creative mind, the hooks and eyes of memory
mysteriously linked.

"In the British Museum is a small manuscript volume of ninety leaves,
which is, in my judgment, one of the most illuminating human documents
even in that vast treasure-house." On such a note, Lowes began his first
chapter, dramatically called "Chaos." Our question is whether the notebook
really is "chaos without form and void." Lowes was convinced that "the
unique value of the Note Book lies in the insight which it affords us into the
polarizing quality of a poet's reading—a reading in which the mind moved,
like the passing of a magnet, over pages to all seeming as bare of poetic
implications as a parallelogram, and drew and held fixed whatever was
susceptible of imaginative transmutation."[46]

It is odd that Lowes seems not to have seriously considered the possibility that Coleridge was consciously on the hunt for images, lines, and ideas which could be used in his poetry, or that his voyages into so many obscure literary seas were not wholly without compass or sextant. Quite a different interpretation can be put on the evidence provided by the Notebooks. Let us consider the entry numbered 259:

                                        bowed spirit
[a]   Deep inward stillness & a bowed Soul—
[b]   Searching of Heart—
      Fancy's wilder foragings—
[c]   God's Judgment *dallying*—investiture.—
      retirement
[d]   feeble & sore-broken—
[e]   disquietness of my heart—
[f]   languishing—pour out my soul.
[g]   I will open my dark sayings on the Harp!
[h]   hasten my escape—
[i]   inhabit thou his praises—heritage—
[j]   Prevent the dawning of the Morn with prayers
[k]   My afflicted shouted for Joy—my Weak Ones cried aloud—
[l]   O Lord, thou Lover of Souls
[m]   The People of Perdition

This does indeed look like chaos. But the aura of bardic frenzy is somewhat dampened by the knowledge that the whole series of thirteen brief phrases comes from the Psalms and Apocrypha. Miss Coburn tells us that except for the first two words (a heading of sorts?) Coleridge wrote down his phrases "not always verbatim and with additions."[47] Some elaboration of this statement is necessary.

For example, the connection between his "Deep inward stillness & a bowed Soul" and Psalm 44:25, "For our soul is bowed down to the dust," is not certain. Similarly, Coleridge's second phrase, "Searching of Heart—Fancy's wilder foragings—" is not easily found in Psalm 64, to which Miss Coburn directs us. There, however, in Verse 6, we read, "They *search* out iniquities; they accomplish a diligent *search*: both the *inward* thought of every one of them, and the *heart*, is *deep*." This verse, therefore, would surely seem to be as much a "source" for Coleridge's "Deep inward stillness" as his "Searching of Heart."

But any doubt that the Psalms and Apocrypha are indeed the sources of these phrases disappears under the evidence of the following phrases:

Coleridge	*Source*
[c] "God's Judgment *dallying*" (STC's underscoring)	Wisdom of Solomon: 12:26: "wherein he dallied with them, shall feel a judgment worthy of God.

Coleridge	Source
[d] "feeble & sore-broken"	Psalms 38:8: "I am feeble and sore broken. . . ."
[e] "disquietness of my heart"	Psalms 38:8: "I have roared by reason of the disquietness of my heart."[43]
[f] "languishing—pour out my soul"	Psalms 41:3: and 42:4: "The Lord will strengthen him upon the bed languishing." ". . . I pour out my soul in me. . . ."
[g] "I will open my dark saying on the Harp"	Psalms 49:4: ". . . I will open my dark saying upon the harp."
[h] "Hasten my escape"	Psalms 55:8: "I would hasten my escape. . . ."
[i] "Inhabit thou his praises"	Psalms 22:3: ". . . O thou that inhabitest the praises of Israel."
[j] "Prevent the dawning of the Morn with prayers"	Psalms 88:13: "But unto thee have I cried, O Lord; and in the morning shall my prayer prevent thee."
[k] "My afflicted shout for Joy— my Weak Ones cried aloud"	Judith 16:11: "Then my afflicted shouted for joy, and my weak ones cried aloud. . . ."
[l] "O Lord, thou Lover of Souls"	Wisdom of Solomon 8:3: "yea, the Lord of all things himself loved her."
[m] "The People of Perdition"	Ecclesiasticus 16:9: "He pitied not the people of perdition. . . ."

The resemblance between Coleridge's phrases and the sources cited may be arguable in two or three instances. But the very fact that we can with certainty identify nine or ten of these phrases as coming from the Psalms and Apocrypha strengthens the supposition that the others, however remote as written from the literal sources, were suggested by them.

How did these phrases come to be written into Coleridge's notebooks in this way? Those inclined to view the activity in the mind of a poet as governed by the inscrutable "hooks and eyes" of association and imagination are content to suppose that Coleridge was at random jotting down phrases which his astonishingly retentive memory had retained from his reading. But this supposition requires a taxing degree of credulity. Consider the order of the "remembered" phrases:

    (1)   Ps. 44:25;
    (2)   Ps. 64;
    (3)   Wisdom of Solomon 12:26;
    (4)   Ps. 38:8;
    (5)   Ps. 38:8;
    (6)   Ps. 41:3 and 42:4;
    (7)   Ps. 49:4;
    (8)   Ps. 55:8;
    (9)   Ps. 22:3;
    (10) Ps. 88:13;
    (11) Judith 16:11;
    (12) Wisdom of Solomon 8:3;
    (13) Ecclus. 16:9.

An odd pattern of memory, surely. And if it were merely a matter of memory, why would Coleridge, or anybody else, remember from the vast tract of the Bible only bits and snatches from the Psalms and comparatively so much from the much more limited and obscure Apocrypha? It seems neither reasonable nor helpful to posit the preternatural flashings of the creative imagination as lying behind these entries. Much more reasonable is the supposition that in the cold light of common day Coleridge had his Bible and Apocrypha open before him and that he was flipping pages back and forth between them, pen in hand, picking up phrases which might prove useful. This practice seems somewhat more methodical than what is suggested in Lowes's happy phrase about "those unconsidered trifles which genius has the trick of filching as it goes."[49] The order of the entries from the Psalms is 44, 64, 38, 38, 41, 42, 49, 55, 22, 88, and these are interspersed with bits from Wisdom of Solomon, Judith, Wisdom of Solomon, and Ecclesiasticus, in that order. Considering the brevity and character of the entries, it would certainly seem that Coleridge was not reading consecutively at all but rather letting his eye travel through a verse or two on a page opened at random, and then, as soon as a possibly useful phrase had been found, turning at once elsewhere, going through precisely the same procedure. He may have used this method as a spur to his own powers of association. Certainly he appears to have been anxious not to use more than very brief phrases from any given psalm, and this is perhaps explicable on the assumption that he hoped to use some of the phrases in his work and did not wish their origin made obvious.

    The place occupied by these entries in the Gutch notebook seems to prove conclusively that Coleridge was purposefully storing up literary materials. This most famous of his memorandum books contains eighty-nine leaves. Those from number 64 through 72 are blank. Folio 73 contains a quotation from one John Haygarth, carefully identified by Coleridge. From here to the end of the notebook are several other quotations, from Josephus, Bayle's *Dictionary*, and so forth. Interspersed are a few unidentified quotations. One of them, from Jonathan Richardson's *Explanatory Notes and Remarks on Milton's Paradise Lost* (1734), was long printed as a specimen of Coleridge's youthful critical perspicacity.[50] The back of the notebook would seem to have been basically reserved for quotations from reading, bits and snatches of ideas, addresses to be remembered, and the like. Anyone keeping a commonplace book might do the same. Actually handling the Gutch notebook makes it perfectly clear that Coleridge worked from both ends, the back leaves being reserved for the purposes stated. The eight blank leaves between the two sections shows that he began using another notebook before he had completely used up this one. The entries from the Psalms and Apocrypha were obviously made at the time of reading—useful bits to be remembered and possibly employed, and changed in the noting as Coleridge wished.

The entries just discussed were made sometime during September or October of 1796. Coleridge wrote Poole on 26 December 1796 that at the beginning of the month the editor of the *Cambridge Intelligencer*, Benjamin Flower, had asked him to provide some verses for "the last day of this year"[51] Coleridge went on to say that the poem, "Ode to the Departing Year," had actually been written in the previous three days.

Apart from this statement there is no evidence that he had received his commission at the beginning of December 1796. The entries just discussed have the character of notes for a projected poem very like the one asked for by Flower. Be that as it may, Coleridge seems to have been planning some such poem as "Departing Year," and the commission, if it came early in December, provided a framework for the general lamentations on the state of the human enterprise that he was planning. Among the phrases from the Psalms and Apocrypha, and others to be discussed, were some which slid into the Ode.

After the jottings already given, the notebook contains four very brief entries on apparently unrelated matters. There are six entries from Ecclesiasticus, and their order—24:11; 25:1; 30:19-20; 40:6; 47:8; 51:15—suggests that Coleridge was now reading, or rapidly turning leaves, consecutively. He seems also to have been working far more carefully. Ecclesiasticus 47:8 reads: "In all his works he praised the Holy One most high with words of glory; and with his whole heart he sung songs, and loved him that made him." This was entered into the notebook as

> And with my whole heart sing the stately song
> Loving the God that made me.

The lines appear in "Fears in Solitude" as follows:

I walk with awe, and sing my stately songs,
Loving the God that made me! (ll. 196-197)[52]

The entry from Ecclus. 25:1, "In three things I stood up beautiful before God and man," appears in the "Ode to the Departing Year" as:

The Spirit of the Earth made reverence meet,
And stood up, beautiful, before the cloudy seat. (ll. 73-74)[53]

Similarly, Coleridge's dovetailing of phrases from the Psalms in his "Deep inward stillness & a bowed Soul" was used in the sixth line of the "Ode to the Departing Year" as "With inward stillness, and a bow'd mind." Another of Coleridge's entries reads: "and ever in his sleep, as in a day of keeping Watch, troubled in the Vision of his Heart; as if he were but even now escaped from a battle." Ecclus. 40:6 reads: "and afterward he is in his sleep, as in a day of keeping watch, troubled in the vision of his heart, as if he were escaped out of a battle."[54]

Miss Coburn believes that this verse "was used and expanded in the *Ode to the Departing Year* stanza vi." Since the only verbal connection in Stanza vi is "Wild is the tempest of my heart," not everyone will agree that the connection is certain.[55]

Following the six entries from Ecclesiasticus are two from Baruch. Then, in a single entry, are twenty-four brief and mysterious phrases. The first seven suggest their general character:

[a] Tame the Rebellion of tumultuous thought—
[b] ministration—
[c] sordid adherencies that cohabit with us in this Life—
[d] rolls round his dreary eye—
[e] outweighs the present pressure—
[f] Weigh'd in the balance of the Sanctuary—
[g] God's Image, Sister of the Cherubim—

Miss Coburn has identified these as "almost, perhaps all, from Jeremy Taylor's *Sermons*. . . . The variations from Taylor's actual words suggest that they were noted down from memory."[56] Since all twenty-four phrases come from five sermons (with the possible exception of the final three), and since Coleridge had borrowed Taylor's *Sermons* from the Bristol Library on 22 September 1796 and kept the volume until 12 October 1796, during which time these entries were made, it seems unnecessary to hypothesize that the slight differences in some instances between Taylor's and Coleridge's words imply imperfect memory, or that we are here in the presence of the strange fruit of fancy's wilder foragings. Surely Coleridge was reading with quill freshly sharpened, his falcon eye scanning the textual terrain for the poetic nutriment of striking images and word clusters. As with the material from the Psalms and Apocrypha discussed earlier, these bits were all entered at the back of the Gutch Memorandum book, among other quotations and literary gatherings.

Taylor, for example, had written that the soul was "an angelic substance, sister to a cherubim, an image of the Divinity. . . ." Into his notebook Coleridge wrote, "God's Image, Sister of the Cherubim." The last line of the "Ode to the Departing Year" reads: "God's Image, sister of the Seraphim." We see here how Coleridge seized upon a phrase-sequence in Taylor and re-fashioned it into a line he thought well enough of to place it as the final line of the poem, toward which a whole stanza builds.[57]

Whether an acknowledgment was due Taylor on the basis of the last line of the poem may be debated.[58] It may, of course, be said that anything from the Bible or Apocrypha is so familiar that citation would be unnecessary, if not fussy. Yet Coleridge cited Habakkuk and Revelation as sources of lines in "Religious Musings."[59] We are not concerned here, however, with ethics but with poetic process. When Coleridge wrote the "Ode to the Departing Year," did he remember the origin of the lines discussed? Since the notebook entries were made only a few weeks before, it smacks of the improbable to suppose that he had forgotten the origin of "God's Image, sister of the Seraphim." He could not have easily imagined that he had created such a line out of a void. Even if the specific source were forgotten, the origin of such an image would tend to tease the mind.

But we need not speculate in complete darkness. In the edition of 1803, Coleridge canceled the line and substituted another. Instead of "Cleans'd from the vaporous passions that bedim / God's Image, sister of the Seraphim," he substituted "Cleans'd from bedimming Fear, and Anguish weak and blind."[60] The alteration is sufficiently feeble to provoke the inference that Coleridge was so uneasy about adapting Taylor's line (for whatever reason) that he was willing to replace it even with a wretched one.[61]

"Ode to the Departing Year" was published four more times during Coleridge's lifetime (in 1817, 1828, 1829, and 1834), and on all these occasions Coleridge canceled the 1803 revision in favor of the original "God's Image, sister of the Seraphim." Until Miss Coburn's work, no one knew that the phrase derived from Taylor, so that the revision of 1803, if anyone had noticed it, would have been something of a stumbling-block to the common notion that Coleridge's poetic changes were always for the better.

All the entries just discussed were made in the weeks preceding the composition of the Ode. Are we justified in surmising that Coleridge opened his notebook to call upon phrases he had been collecting? If so, what inferences may we draw about his poetic process?

The facts, notwithstanding the immense influence of *The Road to Xanadu*, suggest that Coleridge accumulated images purposefully from his reading and wove them into his own compositions as a regular part of his poetic *modus operandi*. Scores of poets and novelists have, of course, kept commonplace books for the preservation and use of ideas and phrases they liked, and the practice in itself is surely no occasion for either moral or aesthetic judgment. What may be of substantial interest, however, is the degree to which Coleridge took his creative line of departure from books. Here, as elsewhere in the realm of aesthetics, we ought not to prejudge the relevance of evidence on theoretical grounds, for the whole subject of creativity is so obscure that no one can say with certainty what evidence may ultimately prove important in our understanding of creative activity.

Especially in Coleridge's case it seems important to bear in mind his dependence upon books when composing, for his creative process has come down to us as one of the most extraordinarily rich, spontaneous, and mysterious on record. In view of the immense difference in quality between the poems of the *annus mirabilis* and those of the rest of his life (with only a few exceptions), all evidence may be useful.

We may then properly ask why Coleridge entered brief phrases from Taylor into his notebooks, and in many instances altered them, if he did not hope to use them in his poetry? One need only examine the phrases to conclude that they could have no other purpose; for example: "rolls round his dreary eye," "outweighs the present pressure," "weighted in the balance of the Sanctuary," and so forth. Indeed, five of these phrases based on Taylor appear as Coleridge's own in the Appendix of poetic "Fragments from a Notebook" in the Oxford edition of his poetry.[62]

Coleridge had a very high regard for Taylor's works. He thought him "amongst the four great geniuses of old English literature," together with Shakespeare, Bacon, and Milton. "In mere eloquence, he thought the Bishop without any fellow."[63] We may, therefore, suspect that he would have thought Taylor's rhythmic and richly figured prose a mine to be diligently drilled for poetic gold.

"Religious Musings,"[64] more than four hundred lines long and, as we have seen, written over almost a two-year period, was publicly announced as the creation of a single night. The work draws upon many sources. That lines 14-22 derive from *Paradise Lost*, IV, 641-656 was pointed out long ago by R. D. Havens.[65] Milton is, of course, pervasive in the poetry of Coleridge before the *annus mirabilis*.[66]

The general philosophical influence of Hartley would naturally be suspected because of Coleridge's known discipleship during this period, and scholars have been busily employed in establishing links. Coleridge has himself drawn attention to the influence of Hartley early in "Religious Musings" in these lines on the loving soul:

> From Hope and firmer Faith to perfect Love
> Attracted and *absorbed*; and centered there
> God only to behold, and know, and feel,
> Till by exclusive consciousness of God
> All self-annihilated it shall make

God its Identity; God *all in all!*
We and our Father one! (ll. 39-44)

A footnote directs us to the page in Hartley where we can "see this demonstrated by Hartley."[67] The relevant passage concludes: "and *absorb* all other Ideas, and He himself become, according to the Language of the Scriptures, *All in all*."[68]

Lowes's prodigious researches turned up Darwinian debts and echoes in "Religious Musings." Late in Coleridge's poem "through the *tainted* noon / The *Simoom* sails, before whose purple pomp / Who falls not prostrate dies!" (ll. 268-270) and on the same page a lengthy note from Bruce's *Travels* identifies the origin of the purple simoom. But the direct source is Erasmus Darwin's *Botanic Garden*, where a *simoom* "rides the *tainted* air," and the identical paragraph from Bruce is given in a footnote.[69]

Thus the matter rested for some thirty years. Our understanding of Coleridge's sources for this motley work remained stagnant: the spirit of Milton hanging uneasily over the materials of Hartley. Then an important stride forward was taken by Herbert Piper in an article on "The Pantheistic Sources of Coleridge's Early Poetry,"[70] the main findings of which were incorporated in his subsequent book, *The Active Universe*. Of "Religious Musings", Piper writes:

The first half of the poem, down to line 191 does consist of religious musings, or rather religio-political preachings, largely drawn from a Unitarian pamphlet, Gilbert Wakefield's *The Spirit of Christianity compared with the Spirit of the Times* (1794). This pamphlet was an attack on the government for declaring war on France and its chief points were that Christ, 'the meek and lowly Nazarene', is the Prince of Peace (cf. *Religious Musings*, ll. 161, 169); that if one member of a community suffers, all suffer (cf. *Religious Musings*, ll. 119-121); that the Duke of Portland's speech, claiming that the war was in defence of religion, was unchristian (cf. *Religious Musings*, ll. 159-169); that the government supported the 'royal banditti' in their dismemberment of Poland (cf. *Religious Musings*, ll. 170-173) and also supported the slave trade (cf. *Religious Musings*, ll. 135-141); and that the clergy preaching war in their Fast-Day sermons were 'heathen ministers' and 'worshippers of Baal' (cf. *Religious Musings*, l. 185 'moloch priest') who 'call forth their congregations to desolate the globe with torrents of human blood' (cf. *Religious Musings*, ll. 185-192). When *Religious Musings* reaches this point, the subject matter changes: the second half of the poem turns abruptly away from present political issues to sketch the history of the world from the primeval age to the Millennium, and it attempts, by ideas drawn from Darwin and Priestley, to show the hand of God in the French Revolution.[71]

A concentrated summary of this kind can hardly convey to the reader the interrelations between "Religious Musings" and Wakefield's 1794 pamphlet. Wakefield had been a fellow at Jesus College, Cambridge, where Coleridge had been a student. He had been a vigorous supporter of the Mr. Frend at whose trial Coleridge had been a vocal supporter. Coleridge's interest in the writings of Wakefield (to whom he once wished to address a sonnet)[72] does not, therefore, need further explanation.

Let us examine more closely the influences suggested by Piper. Wakefield violently opposed British intervention in the French Revolution on Christian grounds, and it was with the utmost scorn that he quoted the Duke of Portland's statement that "the present war was necessary for the support and defence of the *Christian Religion!*"[73] The words that Coleridge puts into the Duke's mouth are that the war was "grounded on one principle—the preservation of CHRISTIAN RELIGION": Wakefield's italics have been changed to capitals.

Two pages further on in Wakefield's pamphlet a footnote directs the reader to a passage in Revelations for a lecture against the slave trade. Coleridge incorporates his tirade against the "hideous Trade" inside his poem itself, but several of his footnotes quote from Revelations.[74] Wakefield's "*meek and lowly Nazarene*" (italicized in the text) becomes Coleridge's "meek Galilean."

Comparison of the full texts adds considerable flesh to the influence Piper suggests between Wakefield's "worshippers of Baal" and Coleridge's "Moloch priest." Wakefield writes: "The worshippers of *Baal* have been always numerous. . . . could blow up the trumpet of war in *Sion;* could call forth their *evangelical* congregations to desolate the globe with torrents of human blood."[75] Coleridge's "Moloch Priest . . . bellows to the herd,"and

> In the fierce jealousy of wakened wrath
> Will go forth with our armies and our fleets
> To scatter the red ruin on their foes!
> O blasphemy! to mingle fiendish deeds
> With blessedness! (ll. 185ff.)

Finally, of Piper's specific comparisons, Wakefield's full text reads: "Thus our audacious ministry connive at the *royal banditti* in their dismemberment of Poland. . . ."[76] Coleridge confines his attack on the "iniquity in the plains of *Poland"* to a footnote, though the text itself refers to it indirectly.

Apart from general ideational debts to Darwin and Priestley in the second half of the poem, Piper unearthed several verbal borrowings from Darwin's *Botanic Garden* that had been missed by the remarkably exact eye of Lowes. Both Darwin and Coleridge mention Benjamin Franklin in related passages dealing with science. "In Darwin's poem the *sleeping giant*

> Starts up from earth, above the admiring throng
> Lifts his colossal form and towers along.

In Coleridge's the Revolution is portrayed as

> The Giant Frenzy
> Uprooting empires with his whirlwind arm
> Mocketh high Heaven; burst hideous from the cell
> Where the old Hag, unconquerable, huge,
> Creation's eyeless drudge, black Ruin, sits
> Nursing the impatient earthquake."[78]

Piper notes that Joseph Priestley had related the French Revolution to "those events prophesied in Revelations which were to follow the opening in heaven of the fifth seal"; Priestley "quoted scriptural prophecy by Newton and Hartley in support of this theory and hence both Newton and Hartley appear alongside Priestley in *Religious Musings*."[79] Coleridge, however, quoted the passage about the fifth seal from Revelations without mentioning that he got the idea for this association from Priestley, who elsewhere in the poem is honored as "patriot, and saint, and sage" (l. 371).

Despite the verbal relations suggested above, the overwhelming impression one gains from reading Darwin, Priestley, and especially Wakefield's pamphlet is not at all that Coleridge was borrowing words per se but rather following general ideas. British intervention in the French Revolution was surely of intense concern to every thinking Englishman, and there can be little doubt that these ideas must have been on everyone's lips. What is important is not, for example, whether Coleridge was rather closely following the organization and tone of Wakefield's pamphlet (which cannot reasonably be doubted), but rather that in a work on which he said he rested all his poetical pretensions the creative impetus should be so abstract, so much the product of dogged research among discursive books. We can now perhaps better understand his remark to Thelwall in late April 1796 that as to "Religious Musings," "I have studied the subject deeply and widely."[80] It is more than a little surprising that not only is there scarcely a hint in this long poem of the revolution in poetic diction and in the range of subject matter which was only a few short years off, but that the whole asethetic approach should be so rigid, so sunk in a kind of Miltonic *rigor mortis*.

I. A. Gordon's "The Case-History of Coleridge's *Monody on the Death of Chatterton*"[81] is a valuable study of the several versions of the poem, which when first written, probably in 1790, was ninety lines long. Gordon argues that Coleridge had Thomas Warton's ode "The Suicide" in mind while composing certain lines. "The *Suicide* describes with heavy moral condemnation a young poet of genius. . . . Overtaken by hopeless love and by poverty he stabbed himself." Warton had written:

> "Is this," mistaken Scorn will say,
> "Is this the youth whose genius high
> Could build the genuine rhyme?"

Gordon supposes that Coleridge was replying directly to Warton and other critics when he wrote:

> Is this the land of liberal Hearts!
> Is this the land, where Genius ne'er in vain
> Pour'd forth her soul-enchanting strain?

"Warton gives a picture of the poet's gloomy imagination" in a passage ending with:

> While misery's form his *fancy* drew
> In dark *ideal* hues, and horrours not its own.

Coleridge's poet has gay thoughts:

> And whilst *Fancy* in the air
> Paints him many a vision fair . . .
> With generous joy he views th' *ideal* gold.

The awkward "ideal gold" became in 1793 "rising gold," in 1794 and 1796 "ideal wealth," and in 1829 and 1834 "fancied wealth." "The original 'ideal gold' arose solely," Gordon supposes, "because Coleridge was writing with his eye on Warton and was attempting to rebut him in his own words."[82] Gordon also shows that the opening lines of Bowles's sonnet on poverty:

> O *Poverty*! though from thy *haggard eye*,
> Thy cheerless *mein*, of every charm bereft,

are clearly the origin of the following lines in the 1790 Monody:

> There, Death on every dear delight,
> Frowns *Poverty* of Giant *mein*!
> In vain I seek the charms of youthful grace,
> Thy sunken *eye*, thy *haggard* cheeks it shews.[83]

"How far these are deliberate echoes and how far unconscious memories from his extensive reading it is impossible to tell. A line like l. 68: 'And all her silent agony of Woe' with the physical structure and the one significant word of Goldsmith's: 'In all the silent manliness of grief' ["Deserted Village," l. 384] cannot have sprung to life independent of its predecessor."[84] Although, in Gordon's opinion, there is no way of telling what is conscious and what is not, he nevertheless concludes: "The original Pindaric *Monody* of 1790 is a patchwork of memories rather than a patchwork of debts."[85] How he can be so sure is not revealed, nor in what sense a memory is not a debt.

In 1794 "only seventeen of the original ninety lines reappear." Discussing some of the 1794 changes, Gordon shows how

> And whilst Fancy in the air
> Paints him many a vision fair,

was remodeled around "one of Gray's favorite words":

> And as floating high in air,
> *Glitter* the sunny *Visions* fair.

Gordon thinks that Coleridge was remembering from "The Bard":

> Descending slow their *glitter'ing* skirts enroll?
> *Visions* of glory . . .

Coleridge's poet is "attended by: *'Fancy hovering* round on shadowy wing.' Gray had written in the description of himself in *The Progress of Poesy*: 'Bright-eyed *Fancy hovering* o'er.'"[86] The last lines of the 1794 version read:

> *Ye Woods*! *that wave* o'er Avon's rocky *steep*.
> To Fancy's ear sweet is your *murm'ring deep*! . . .
> How *far from Men* amid this pathless grove,
> In solemn thought the Minstrel wont to *rove*,
> Like Star-Beam on the rude *sequester'd* Tide,
> *Lone-glittering*, thro' the Forest's murksome pride.
> And here in *Inspiration's eager hour* . . .
> With *wild unequal steps* he passed along,
> Oft pouring on the winds a broken song:
> Anon some rough *Rock's fearful Brow*,
> Would pause abrupt—and gaze upon the waves below.

We are assured that a "glance at Gray reveals the indebtedness":[87]

> *Woods, that wave* o'er Delphi's *steep* . . .
> [Isles, that crown the Aegean *deep* . . .][88]
> Ev'ry shade and hallow'd Fountain
> *Murmur'd deep* a solemn sound. ("Progress of Poesy")
> *Far from the madding crowd's* ignoble strife ("Elegy")
> Muttering his wayward fancies he would *rove* . . .
> Along the cool *sequester'd* vale of life ("Elegy")
> *Glittering* shafts of war ("Bard")
> *Glitter* in the Muse's ray ("Progress of Poesy")
> *Greece's evil hour* ("Progress of Poesy")
> Brushing *with hasty steps* the dews away ("Elegy")

Inevitably, some of these parallels are much more convincing than others. Gordon has perhaps overestimated a few of these debts, but he has shown incidentally that Coleridge's language was no advance on the poetic diction of fifty years before. Especially noteworthy is the heavy proportion of couplets. "Finally," says Gordon, "the whole conception of the Minstrel 'far from Men' and gazing distractedly from a precipice on the waves below is a blend of the melancholic recluse of the *Elegy* and the frenzied *Bard* standing

> On a *rock*, whose haughty *brow*
> Frowns o'er old Conway's foaming flood."[89]

Gordon suspects that Coleridge refrained from drowning his poet only because Chatterton had actually taken poison;[90] he might also have noted that Wharton's suicidal poet often went to "gaze with eager glance upon the tumbling flood."

Coleridge's "Monody" owes more to Gray's "Progress of Poesy" than Gordon noticed. Gray uses the phrase "thrilling Fears" (l. 93), Coleridge "thrilling tear" (l. 90). In Gray: "The living *throne*, the sapphire *blaze*" (l. 99); in Coleridge: "Eternal's *throne* . . . the *blaze* of Seraphim (ll. 104-105). Eight lines later Gray speaks of the "lyre" (ll. 107), and then of "words that *burn*" (l. 110). Coleridge, four lines after the throne/blaze passage speaks of a "*lyre*" and "*fire* divine to glow" (ll. 109-110). Gray's line: "Woods, that wave o'er Delphi's steep" is, of course, nearly identical with Coleridge's "Ye Woods! that wave o'er Avon's rocky steep." Yet in substituting *Avon* for *Delphi* Coleridge need only have adopted Gray's use of that place-name at line 85.[91]

Apart from "The Progress of Poesy," Coleridge was heavily indebted to Bowles's Monody "On the Death of Henry Headley," a work in itself saturated with Gray. Bowles's poem is forty-four lines long. It will be remembered that Coleridge was sufficiently familiar with the poem to use its last six lines as the beginning of a poem he wrote into one of the prayer books in his college chapel.

The passage given below is a patchwork of Bowles's lines. I have changed the order of the lines to show how very similar they are, thus rearranged, to the lengthy passage from Coleridge already cited by Gordon.

> The *waving wood*, high *o'er* the cliff reclined,
> The *murmuring* water-fall, the winter's *wind*,
> His temper's trembling texture seemed to suit;
> Like airs of *sadness* his responsive lute. (ll. 27-30)
> *Far from the murmuring crowd*, unseen, he sought
> Each charm congenial to his *sadden'd thought*. (ll. 19-20)
> Nor ceas'd he yet to stray, where, *winding wild*
> The Muse's *path* his drooping *steps* beguil'd,

> Intent to rescue some neglected rhyme,
> *Lone*-blooming, from the mournful waste of time. (ll. 13-16)[92]

Coleridge's passage reads:

> Ye *woods*! that *wave o'er* Avon's rocky steep,
> To Fancy's ear sweet is your *murmuring* deep!
> For here she loves the cypress wreath to weave;
> Watching with wistful eye, the *saddening* tints of eve.
> Here, *far from men*, amid this *pathless* grove,
> In *solemn thought* the Minstrel wont to rove,
> Like star-beam on the slow sequester'd tide
> *Lone*-glittering, through the high tree branching wide.
> And here, in Inspiration's eager hour,
> When most the big soul feels the mastering power,
> These *wilds*, these caverns roaming o'er.
> Round which the screaming sea-gulls soar,
> With *wild* unequal *steps* he pass'd along,
> Oft pouring on the *winds* a broken song. (ll. 114-127)

The passages seem strikingly close. In addition to the many verbal parallels, there is an almost complete identity of thought.[93]

Apart from the debts just discussed in Coleridge's "Monody," there is also a question as to how much of Samuel Favell appears in the poem. On 18 September 1794 Coleridge sent a sonnet to Southey with the following octave:

> No more my Visionary Soul shall dwell
> On Joys, that were! No more endure to weigh
> The Shame and Anguish of the evil Day,
> Wisely forgetful! O'er the Ocean swell
> Sublime of Hope I seek the cottag'd Dell,
> Where Virtue calm with careless step may stray,
> And dancing to the moonlight Roundelay
> The Wizard Passions weave on holy Spell. [94]

Except for the deletion of the word "Visionary," these lines appear intact in the "Monody." One month after receiving Coleridge's letter, Southey sent this sonnet to his brother Thomas, and attributed it to Favell.[95] This must give us pause, particularly as Southey was right, despite the skepticism of many scholars, in stating that "Lewti" had originally been a juvenile poem of Wordsworth's. Some dispute as to the authorship is suggested by Coleridge's letter of 11 December 1794 to Southey: "Of the Sonnet 'No more the visionary Soul shall dwell'—I wrote the whole but the second & third

Line.''[96] But this statement has a certain implausibility. Can Coleridge really have written: ''No more my Visionary soul shall dwell,'' and then had Favell continue with: ''On Joys, that were! No more endure to weigh / The Shame and Anguish of the evil Day,'' at which point Coleridge continued with ''Wisely forgetful! . . .''?[97] It is worth emphasizing that in a work heavily revised for publication through the 1790's, Coleridge was still able to publish, immediately before the *annus mirabilis*, a poem which simply bristles with personifications (Indignation, Pity, Affection, etc.). Even the original ''Neglect and grinning scorn and Want combin'd'' from the 1790 ''Monody'' (l. 77) survived, as did the basic heroic-couplet meter.

A brief discussion of the grandiosely conceived ''The Destiny of Nations'' (1795-96) will serve to emphasize certain recurrent, and in some respects dominant, features of Coleridge's early poetry. Diversity of materials collected from far and wide, looseness of structure bordering on complete formlessness, the ponderous influence of Milton, the hegemony of the ratiocinative over the emotional power of the poet—all are present in this abortive composition.[98] Most interesting, perhaps, is the glimpse one long passage affords into the cluttered workroom where a young poet, learning his craft, and writing under the twin distractions of time pressure and uncertain purpose, stumbled briefly into some of his best work:[99]

> . . . when, behold . . .
> An unattended team! The foremost horse
> Lay with stretched limbs; the others, yet *alive*
> *But stiff* and cold, stood motionless, *their manes*
> *Hoar with the frozen night-dews*: Dismally
> The dark-red dawn now glimmered; but its gleams
> Disclosed no face of man. The maiden paused,
> *Then hailed who might be near.* No voice replied.
> From the thwart wain *at length there reached her ear*
> *A sound so feeble* that it almost seemed
> Distant: and feebly, *with slow effort pushed,*
> *A miserable man crept forth: his limbs*
> *The silent frost had eat, scathing like fire.*
> *Faint on the shafts he rested.* She, meantime,
> Saw crowded close beneath the coverture
> A mother and her children—*lifeless all,*
> Yet lovely! *not a lineament was marred*—
> *Death had put on so slumber-like a form*!
> It was a piteous sight; and one, a babe,
> *The crisp milk frozen on its innocent lips,*[100]
> *Lay on the woman's arm, its little hand*
> *Stretched on her bosom.*

Among the multitude of Lowes's remarkable discoveries was the origin of these lines in the news columns of Coleridge's *Watchman*, dealing with the horrors of recent military campaigns. The eye-witness account tells how

> on the common, about half a mile off the high road, we discovered a baggage cart, with a team of five horses, apparently in distress; I galloped toward the spot, and found the poor animals were *stiff, but not dead; the hoar frost on their manes*, plainly shewing they had been there the whole night. Not perceiving any driver with them, I struck my sword repeatedly on the canvass tilt, *enquiring at the same time if there was any person in the cart; at length, a very feeble voice answered me, and someone underneath the canvass appeared to be making an effort to rise. A pair of naked frost-nipt legs were then advanced, and the most miserable object I ever beheld, sunk heavily upon the ground*; the whole of his clothing so ragged and worn, that I can scarcely say he was covered.

"The account of the horrors of the day's march proceeds," Lowes tells us, "and after a score of lines we read this":

> One scene made an impression upon my memory, which time will never be able to efface. Near another cart, a little further on the common, we perceived a stout looking man, and a beautiful young woman with an infant, about seven months old, at the breast; *all three frozen and dead*. The mother had most certainly expired in the act of suckling her child, as with one breast exposed, she lay upon the drifted snow, *the milk to all appearance, in a stream, drawn from the nipple by the babe, and instantly congealed*. The infant seemed as if its lips had but just then been disengaged, *and it reposed its little head upon the mother's bosom, with an overflow of milk, frozen as it trickled from the mouth; their countenances were perfectly composed and fresh, resembling those of persons in a sound and tranquil slumber.*

Lowes dismisses the passage not only because it is a detachable fragment from the main action of the poem, but because it is "retrieved and carried over bodily, undipped and unassimilated, from the miscellaneous wreckage of *The Watchman!*" With his eye on the Coleridge who wrote "The Ancient Mariner" and "Kubla Khan," Lowes finds that "the tragic figures in the snow are untouched by the finger of that plastic spirit which on occasion sweeps through chaos with imperial sway."

Be that as it may, Coleridge's lines are in some respects among the best he wrote before his great period, and their *diction*, though immeasurably below the heights of "The Ancient Mariner," is very much closer to that which was to metamorphose the language of poetry, and very shortly, than almost anything he had written up to this time. So astute a critic as Garrod, for example, sees in these lines an anticipation of Wordsworth's manner.[101] Thus treacherous is the task of tracing artistic development. Indeed, though these lines may be considered little more than a newspaper report run into verse, the essential naturalness of the report, energized and controlled by the rhythm of a loose blank verse, propelled Coleridge in the direction of Cowper, a poet whom he admired greatly. Cowper's blank verse, of course, often sounds—especially in brief extracts—like an anticipation of Wordsworth. Lowes's discovery of the origin of the passage just quoted in a straightforward newspaper article goes far toward solving what would otherwise be a substantial aesthetic mystery, namely, how in the midst of the declamatory turgidities of "The Destiny of Nations," he suddenly fell into so natural a manner.

Some notion of the range of Coleridge's excursions in search of materials may be provided by a grab-bag of observations.

One of the passages in "The Destiny of Nations" published by E. H. Coleridge, originally intended to form part of the finished poem, reveals quite clearly its origin in Milton. How the lines would have looked had Coleridge reworked them for publication is another matter. As they stand they are unmistakably contrived from the first hundred lines of *Paradise Lost*. Milton had invoked the Muse, who was present from the beginning of time:

> . . . and with mighty *wings* outspread
> Dove-like satst brooding *on the* vast *Abyss*. (ll. 20-21)

Coleridge wrote:

> When Love rose glittering and his gorgeous *wings*
> *Over the abyss* fluttered . . . (ll. 283-284)

Milton's "darkness visible" (l. 63) in Hell is echoed by the "Darkness Palpable" (l. 294) of Coleridge's "Desert of Death." Satan's "steadfast hate" (l. 58) and refusal to surrender is echoed by Coleridge's fiend's "Fierce Hate and gloomy Hope " (l. 298). The latter is also one of the "Rebels from God" (l. 314). Milton's "slaughtered saints" from the sonnet "On the Late Massacre at Piemont" appear in Coleridge as a "white-robed multitude of slaughtered saints" (l. 334). The following extract, though influenced by Milton's diction, actually derives from a much more remote source:

> As when the mad Tornado bellows through
> The guilty islands of the western main,
> What time departing from their native shores,
> Eboe, or *Koromantyn's plain of palms*,
> The infuriate spirits of the murdered make
> Fierce merriment, and vengeance ask of Heaven. (ll. 442-447)

Coleridge has a long footnote to this passage dealing with witchcraft among the slaves in the West Indies. Lowes discovered that

> Coleridge found Eboe and Koromantyn in Bryan Edwards. . . . And he twice used, almost verbatim, Edwards' phrases. "Koromantyn's plain of palms" (l. 445) is from a youthful poem of Edwards. . . . And the phrase in the footnote (which is Note Ninth in *Joan of Arc*): "The slaves in the West-India Islands consider Death as a passport to their native country," is Edwards': "the Negroes consider death . . . as a passport to the place of their nativity."

Coleridge did not mention Edwards, which again points up the extreme difficulty of establishing his sources.[102]

Herbert Piper has noted the detailed ideational relation between a thirteen-line passage in "The Destiny of Nations" and certain passages in Darwin's *Botanic Garden*.[103] Coleridge's handling of Darwin's specific images is worth some notice. In a description of the tasks undertaken by the "Monads," he tells us that

> Some nurse the infant *diamond* in the mine;
> Some *roll the genial juices through the oak*;
> Some drive the mutinous clouds to clash in air,
> And rushing on the storm with whirlwind speed,
> *Yoke* the red *lightnings* to their *volleying car.* (ll. 50-54)

Coleridge's Monads prove to be the counterparts of the Spirits of the four elements to whom Darwin addressed each of his four cantos. Darwin's nymphs of fire

> chase the shooting stars
> Or *yoke* the *vollied lightning* to their *cars*.

The nymphs of earth, Piper informs us, "among other duties, produce *diamonds*, while those of water bring 'the *genial shower*' for the roots of plants."

In a turgid passage following almost immediately, amidst a Miltonic catalogue of arctic place-names, we are told how

> The *Laplander* beholds the far-off *Sun*
> Dart his slant beam on unobeying snows,
> While yet the *stern and solitary Night*
> Brooks no alternate sway, *the Boreal Morn*
> With *mimic* lustre substitutes its gleam. (ll. 65-69)

and just a few lines further we read of "*rosy light*" (l. 79). Lowes has shown that this passage is a rearrangement of the first four lines of the sonnet to Godwin:

O form 'd t'illume a sunless world forlorn
As o'er *the chill and dusky brow of Night*,
In *Finland's* wintry skies the *Mimic Morn*
Electric pours a stream of *rosy light* . . .

Further, Coleridge here used the "electric streams" of Darwin's aurora in the *Botanic Garden*. Lowes, who tells us that he turned over the pages of the *Botanic Garden* perhaps twenty times, nevertheless—and inevitably so—missed some other debts.[104]

We may fittingly conclude our review of the early Coleridge canon by turning to the abortive play *Osorio*, which he began to write in February of 1797 and finished in October of the same year.[105] This work, therefore, engaged his attention for some nine months, at the end of which he was ready to stride magisterially into the pantheon of the immortals. Those nine months were, from an aesthetic point of view, the most fateful ones of Coleridge's life. They gave birth to his greatest poem thus far, "This Lime Tree Bower My Prison," and witnessed the transformation of a fitful and uncertain talent into a poetic force of immense power and range.

In view of the chronology of Coleridge's poetic development, *Osorio* might well serve as a key transitional document, straddling his *rite de passage* from poetic adolescence to potent manhood. But the play stubbornly refuses to accommodate itself to so tidy an approach. Apart from a very small number of scattered passages in which the mature Coleridgean voice can be heard, all seems echo, imitation, and patchwork. Lowes has observed that "the plot of *Osorio* is drawn freely from the Sicilian's tale in Schiller's *Der Geister-seher*," and in a lengthy and detailed note emphasized that although Brandl had pointed out the connection long before, "very little attention has been paid to this fact."[106] The plot parallels between *Osorio* and *Der Geisterseher* have been conveniently summarized by Frederic Ewen in *The Prestige of Schiller in England, 1788-1859*:

> *Osorio* shows evidence throughout of the impress of Schiller's *Ghost-Seer*. Its plot is drawn bodily from the incident . . . of the rivalry of two brothers for the hand of a woman, and of the murder of one of them by the other.
>
> Osorio is under the impression that he has done away with his brother Albert, and fervently presses his suit for the hand of Albert's betrothed. . . . Maria, however, is steadfast in her love. . . . She will not be persuaded by the blasting words of Osorio's and Albert's father, who cites Osorio's own testimony. . . . [Osorio] has spread the tale of the capture of Albert by pirates. This is exactly the situation in *The Ghost-Seer*, except that in the latter story, the murder has actually been committed.
>
> But Albert is not dead. He returns disguised as a Moresco, convinced that Maria herself had connived at his undoing and that she is already

the bride of his would-be murderer. In Schiller's tale it is the dead man who returns, in the garb of a Franciscan, at the very moment his former love is about to bestow her hand on the murderer.

Osorio, made desperate by Maria's exasperating fidelity to the dead, resorts to Albert, whom he believes, in his ignorance, to be a magician, and proposes to him a stratagem whereby Maria is to be fully persuaded that her lover has perished. The magician is to call up the dead man, and at the same time, as visible proof of the credibility of wonder, he is to produce an amulet, Maria's portrait, which had been taken from the presumably dead Albert. . . .

In the third act . . . the evocation of the spirit is consummated. With the trick practised by Albert—to wit, his substitution of a picture of the attempted murder in place of Maria's portrait—we have no concern at present. The more interesting matter is the similarity between this scene and the one in *The Ghost-Seer* where a parallel action takes place. Here, too, the dead man's ghost is invoked; the corroborative token, however, is a ring. In both instances, the mummery performed is accompanied with weird music from strange instrument. . . . In both cases, the vision is punctuated by a thunder-clap.[107]

In June 1797, the deep aesthetic intimacy between Wordsworth and Coleridge began. In a fragmentary letter, Dorothy Wordsworth has left behind a memorable portrait of her first impressions of Coleridge. The letter goes on:

The first thing that was read after he [Coleridge] came was William's new poem *The Ruined Cottage* with which he was much delighted; and after tea he repeated to us two acts and a half of his tragedy *Osorio*. The next morning William read his tragedy *The Borderers.* . . .[108]

The influence of Wordsworth's play on the second half of *Osorio*, which still remained to be written, has been observed by several scholars. Legouis has perhaps put the matter most succinctly:

Impressed by the character of the villain Oswald [in *The Borderers*], he [Coleridge] borrowed his pride and cynical philosophy for the traitor of his own work, a flagrant piece of imitation which begins at the very point in his tragedy where Coleridge had stopped before he became acquainted with *The Borderers*.[109]

At this point, upon the completion of a work which brought Coleridge to within a month of the beginning of "The Ancient Mariner," we may pause for retrospect and summary. In October of 1797 he turned twenty-five, and his apprenticeship was over. A full discussion of the early poetry would require a separate study, but the point which emerges clearly enough from the foregoing review is that Coleridge's early efforts were, surely to an extraordinary degree (both in prose and verse), heavily derivative and sometimes merely adaptation.

On 6 July 1794, Coleridge sent Southey a "Description of Heat from a Poem I am manufacturing."[110] The poem itself—"Perspiration. A Travelling Eclogue"—is inconsequential, but the word Coleridge used to describe his method of composition, "manufacturing," is not an entirely false way to characterize the process behind much of the poetry written through the middle of 1797.

What is particularly noteworthy in the early canon is its technical diversity. Not only is practically every one of the poems Coleridge wrote before he was twenty-five structurally different from the others, but no clear affinity is revealed for any particular line length or rime pattern. Tumbling over each other are anthems and monodies, sonnets and odes, epigrams and other *jeux*, imitations of Milton, Gray, Collins, Casimir, Anacreon, *Ossian*, Rogers, and Bowles, besides a sprinkling of translations and paraphrases from other sources. The canon is so diverse that one ought to be able to find in it an ancestor for almost everything attempted in the *annus mirabilis*. Yet between any of the apprentice works and the great triad of "The Ancient Mariner," "Kubla Khan," and "Christabel," a mysterious technical and conceptual gulf exists.

It is easy to see in the early Coleridge a gifted poet stuck on bad models, eddying and drifting in the sluggish tides of fashion. What was the intense young bard and pantisocrat trying to achieve?

"Religious Musings," both from internal evidence and by his own statement, represents the zenith of his youthful aspirations. The failure of the poem should not obscure the fact that it embodies the general shape of the poetic realm he hoped to conquer. Had he eventually written the great epic that ever floated before him in his waking reveries, both "Religious Musings" and the equally long and discursive "Destiny of Nations" would today be seen, not as inconsequential diversions from the mainstream of his genius, but as the inevitable stumblings of youth on the steep path up Parnassus. The steady and clear voices of "The Eolian Harp" and "Reflections on Having Left a Place of Retirement" are almost submerged among the collected poems by the strident torrents of grandiloquence that surround them.

"Ode to the Departing Year," which closes 1796, is—far more than is ever allowed—an altogether fitting projection of Coleridge's youthful self-image as a poet. Milton, both as poet and public figure, represents a central ideal. The inner tug of Coleridge's verse is toward philosophy, religion, and public affairs. The sonnets are almost all addressed to political figures; the longest poems and *The Fall of Robespierre* embrace political and theological themes. The Bristol period features—apart from the utopian plan of Pantisocracy— a succession of essays and lectures on political and moral subjects. The founding of *The Watchman*, the flirtation with a Unitarian ministry, the involvement with public affairs, all this testifies not only to the necessity of earning bread and cheese but to the broad range of his interests, of which poetry was only one. It is perhaps prophetic that nowhere in the early letters and notebooks do we find any bedrock commitment to the life of the poet.

18.

Spasms and Stagnation

I propose for the time being to skip over the *annus mirabilis* to consider, very briefly, the remainder of Coleridge's achievement as a poet. It seems worth forsaking chronology so as to isolate the great period for final discussion. Such a view of Coleridge's poetic career confirms quite forcefully what has often been asserted and too often ignored in recent years, namely, that with very few exceptions, all his important poems were written during a very brief period of his life, for which there appears to be little preparation in the early verse or much reverberation in the later.

After he departed for Germany in September 1798, Coleridge's self-originating inventive powers seemed to wane with startling suddenness. All the following poems were based upon German models, either directly translated or freely paraphrased, whole or in part, acknowledged and unacknowledged: "Catullian Hendecasyllables," "The Homeric Hexameter," "The Ovidian Elegiac Metre," "On a Cataract," "Tell's Birth-Place," "The Visit of the Gods," "From the German," "On an Infant," "Something Childish, But Very Natural," "Home-Sick," "The British Stripling's War-Song," "Names," "Westphalian Song," "Hymn to the Earth," "Hymn Before Sun-Rise," "The Picture, or the Lover's Resolution," and the famous "Song" from *Zapolya*.[1]

All but the last three titles derive from the German period of 1799. Several contain passages of considerable merit. Their particular interest, however, is the evidence they provide of Coleridge's thematic interests immediately following the *annus mirabilis*. "On a Cataract," "The Visit of the Gods," and "Hymn to the Earth" can all be related to the fountain and creativity themes of "Kubla Khan."[2] "Catullian Hendecasyllables" concludes with the image of a woman praying at night for her lover in a sacred grove. "On a Cataract" features a "slumberless fountain" from which voices are heard. It seems remarkable that in the presence of foreign poetry, a poet with so rich and varied an achievement just behind him should at once practically have abandoned the hard-won skills of his own apprenticeship and embarked upon the study and imitation of a whole new set of rhythms and stanza patterns

258

(none of which was to prove of any real value). In Malta, just a few years later, the same basic pattern was to emerge in relation to Italian, but with still more obviously flagging energy.

Among Coleridge's many paraphrases or translations after 1798 are: "Translation of a Passage in Ottfried's Metrical Paraphrase of the Gospel,"[3] "Water Ballad," "Hexameters, Paraphrase of Psalm xlvi," "Sonnet" (from Marini), "Faith, Hope and Charity" (from Guarini), and two translations from Hebrew poems by Hyman Hurwitz (of the Hebrew Academy in Highgate)—"Israel's Lament" and "The Tears of a Grateful People."[4] "A Tombless Epitaph," ostensibly translated directly from Chiabrera, was, as we have seen, heavily indebted to Wordsworth's earlier treatment of the same subject. Coleridge's notebooks are studded with translations and adaptations of German and Italian poets. Much of this work has the appearance of random eclecticism; more probably these endless experiments represent a flight from the disturbing personal themes that pressed from within for expression into the technical processes of poetry (in itself a kind of "abstruse research").

The pattern of taking a creative line of departure from reading, or leaning heavily upon the shape or substance of another's poem, shows itself repeatedly among the scattered poems of the last three decades. The last three of the six quatrains of "Separation" (written around 1805), derive from Cotton's "Chlorinda," with only minor alterations. Oddly, stanzas 11, 12, and 13 in Cotton's poem became stanzas 5, 4, and 6, respectively, in Coleridge's. "Separation" was first published in the year of Coleridge's death, without reference to any source.[5]

The 1806 sonnet, "Farewell to Love," is closely modeled upon one by Fulke Greville, and much is directly paraphrased. Coleridge begins: "Farewell, sweet Love! yet blame you not my truth"; the first line of Greville reads: "Farewell, sweet Boy, complaine not of my truth." Greville's concluding couplet,

> But *Cupid* now farewell, I will goe play me,
> With thoughts that please me lesse, and less betray me,

was adopted intact, but for the first six syllables, which Coleridge changed to, "O grief!—but farewell, Love!" The poem was published three times in Coleridge's lifetime without acknowledgment.[6]

The affecting "Work Without Hope" first appears in a journal entry dated 21 February 1825, in a draft of a letter to an unnamed friend. Immediately preceding the poem, Coleridge wrote: "Strain in the manner of G. HERBERT . . . N.B. The Thoughts and Images being modernized and turned into English." He subsequently drew his pen through everything following "N. B.," and when the poem appeared in 1828, 1829, and 1834, no mention was made of the debt to Herbert. The journal entry also contains the following reflection: "as we advance in years, the World, that *spidery* Witch, spins its threads narrower and narrower, still closing in on us, till at last it shuts us up within four walls, walls of flues and films, and windowless—and well if there be sky-lights, and a small opening left for the Light from above." The same date shows him shaping these lines into iambic pentameter, and adding the wonderful image:

> With viscous masonry of films and threads
> Tough as the nets in Indian Forests found . . .

What is poignantly apparent in such an entry is the residual power in the wreckage of a great talent.[7]

Despite the radical revaluation to which almost all of Coleridge's work has been subjected in the past generation, no substantial upward estimate of the later poetry has taken hold. His last genuinely productive year was 1802, the Indian summer of his creativity which witnessed not only the great "Ode to Dejection," but also "Hymn Before Sun-Rise" and "The Picture." "To William Wordsworth" and "The Blossoming of the Solitary Date Tree," both written in 1805, are able performances, and have been sufficiently admired. But "Phantom," an eight-line spasm of the same year, though often overlooked in anthologies, is probably better than either. Poems like "A Day-Dream" (1802) and "Recollections of Love" (1807) are among the best of the later poems, and especially moving to those aware of Coleridge's agonizing love for Sara Hutchinson. The isolation and despair described in "Limbo" (1817) and "Work Without Hope" (1825) are peculiarly modern in spirit. Though the poems are considerably diminished when considered solely in themselves, they take on a distinctly tragic quality in the context of his later life.

Except for scattered references to writing an epic upon the destruction of Jerusalem by Titus, there is nowhere in Coleridge's later writings or conversations any suggestion of the grandiose poetic aspirations so common in the early notebooks and letters. The poems themselves are almost all short, personal statements, often revealing a fitful energy quickly exhausted. His genius shows itself in flashes, but he seems to have no subject but a momentary spasm of feeling, and no secure or settled technique upon which to lean for support. The later poetry, whatever its value, is varied and eclectic in form, but the metrical experimentation seems aimless and restless rather than purposeful. The image comes to mind of a great artist adrift on a wide, wide sea, without sextant or compass or rudder, but still capable of moments of brilliant seamanship.

By rough page count in the standard Oxford edition, Coleridge wrote twice as much verse up to the age of twenty-six—a productive period of approximately eight years—than in all of the following thirty-six years of his life. The astonishing creative potency of 1797-98 was thereafter to elude him, except for brief and ever more fleeting encounters. And yet the resurgences of poetic power after 1798 may not be wholly inexplicable, any more than the abrupt failure of his art. Such works as "Love (1799), the second part of "Christabel" (1800), "Ode to Dejection" (1802), "To William Words-worth" (1805), and some other important poems written after 1798 may be seen as forming a revealing creative pattern. But this, and many allied mat-ters, is best discussed in relation to the almost miraculous flowering of Coleridge's poetic genius during the *annus mirabilis* itself.

19.

The *Annus Mirabilis* Begins

COLERIDGE'S brief period of masterful poetic achievement has long both fascinated and baffled critics and scholars. So little is known about the functioning of the creative process that we are readily disposed to account for the seemingly miraculous activity of 1797-98 as another instance of the inscrutable ways of the mind. To take cover behind the mysteries of the creative process is no doubt the safest shelter available to the cautious scholar. Yet, while the risks may be enormous and the chances of even partial success slight, the very human desire to flash a beam of light into darkness is not to be denied. Curiosity, in the ultimate scheme of things, may be the final virtue.

The intensity, power, and uniqueness of Coleridge's great poems are all the more remarkable when measured against the poetic practice we have just been studying. An important aspect of this "joiners work"—unexceptional in itself but with important bearings on our subject—is Coleridge's adoption for poetic purposes of emotions and attitudes remote from his own experience. When Wordsworth wrote, "When link'd with thoughtless mirth I cours'd the Plain / And Hope itself was all I knew of Pain," he was describing that which we have some reason to believe was genuine. But when Coleridge slipped the lines into his "Effusion at Evening" he was appropriating another's words to express something he had never experienced.[1] Coleridge was barely nine years old when he was taken from his country home and sent to a school in London. Thereafter he was a city boy, almost as much as Charles Lamb. He grew up in the heart of London and his associations must have been predominantly urban. If he had ever "cours'd the plain," it was before the age of nine, and this was not the period he was referring to in his poem.

Significantly, a substantial part of his early poetry is pastoral in character. In this he was, of course, merely following a literary convention, but what is remarkable is that we do not have from him a single important poem about the city, nothing remotely resembling a "Westminster Bridge." Except for two or three brief passages in the "conversation poems," the poetic record

262

is a complete blank as to what he really felt and thought during those crucially formative years of childhood. When he wrote as if retrospectively about his dear native rural haunts, and sunset over the peaceful village, he was not describing anything he could have personally experienced after the age of nine. A very substantial proportion of this early poetry manipulates emotions and "recollections" which were not and could not have been genuine.

Is the mystery of the *annus mirabilis*, then, completely inscrutable? Perhaps. But little as we know of creativity, we are not so completely chained in darkness as to be compelled to believe that the fickle Muse comes and goes with utter irrationality. Silk merchants do not suddenly write great poems, nor do novelists compose "Eroica" symphonies. The artistic process, however dimly we may trace its workings, is still clearly related to the total personality, training, and experience of a given human being. We do not have total breaks in continuity. Art no less than life is a process. There may be, of course, a sudden and dazzling maturity. An artist may stumble, grope, and take many false paths before finding what is true and right for him.

What happened during those months of 1797 and '98 which released in Coleridge his potential as a great artist? Was there some personal, moral, or artistic crisis which can be identified and made to serve as a Rosetta stone? The inquiry on which we are now embarked might well take as its motto the following passage from Johnson's *Preface to Shakespeare*:

> Every man's performances, to be rightly estimated, must be compared
> with the state of the age in which he lived, and with his own particular
> opportunities; and though to the reader a book be not worse or better for
> the circumstances of the authour, yet as there is always a silent reference
> of human works to human abilities, and as the enquiry, how far man may
> extend his designs, or how high he may rate his native force, is of far
> greater dignity than in what rank we shall place any particular perfor
> mance, curiosity is always busy to discover the instruments, as well as to
> survey the workmanship, to know how much is to be ascribed to original
> powers, and how much to casual and adventitious help.[2]

Although many critics have wondered at the baffling phenomenon of the *annus mirabilis*, only a few have ventured to explain it. Of these hypotheses, by far the most famous and long-standing has been that opium was the catalytic agent behind the quality of the great poems.

Late in the nineteenth century, J. M. Robertson stated this theory in its most powerful form. In a famous phrase he described "Kubla Khan" as "an abnormal product of an abnormal nature written under abnormal conditions."

> It may seem an extravagant thing to say [he wrote further], but I cannot
> doubt that the special quality of this felicitous work is to be attributed

to its being all conceived and composed under the influence of opium in the first stages of the indulgence—the stages, that is, in which he himself felt as if new-born, before the new appetite itself proved to be a disease.[3]

The arguments which may be brought against Robertson in particular and the theory in general are weighty. First, it is not true that Coleridge's initial indulgence in opium occurred in 1797 and 1798. He took opium, at least against physical ailments, as early as 1791. On many occasions before 1797 he wrote of using it, at times specifically against mental distress.[4] Secondly, and of vastly greater importance, there is almost no scientific basis for the popular belief that opium addiction of itself either in its early or later stages measurably changes the structure or form either of one's dreams or mental processes. Professor Elisabeth Schneider, in an exhaustive study of this subject, argues persuasively that whatever literary people may suppose to be the facts, modern scientific investigation demolishes many widespread and tenaciously held beliefs about the character and consequences of opium addiction.[5] The feeling of limitless space and timelessness, for example, is not peculiar to opium dreams but characteristic of dreams in general.

At this point a logical objection arises. It is simply not true to say that a dreamer with an opium derivative in his system has dreams in all respects identical with normal ones (assuming there were agreement as to what a "normal" dream is). Any foreign substance affecting the brain must in some degree affect dreaming, no less than waking perceptions. But to admit this is to concede hardly anything to those who would account for Coleridge's great poems on this basis. He took opium many times before the *annus mira-bilis*, and was almost continuously addicted to it for the rest of his life, but the great poems are confined to a limited period. Further, to say that opium affects states of mind is of no great consequence; so does tobacco, alcohol, fatigue, and emotions of every kind. A man under the direct influence of opium, if he did creative work at all, would certainly be affected by it, just as he would be if he were intoxicated, tired, or angry. Many artists have been drug addicts, without writing Ancient Mariners.

If, therefore, we cannot assert absolutely that opium had no effect on Coleridge's poetry, it is still more unwise to attribute any major effects in the poetry to it. Opium is surely not the key to understanding the great period. "The Ancient Mariner" was written over many months. "Christabel" was also the product of long and arduous work. To argue that opium liberated a great poetic ability in Coleridge for a brief time is to advance a theory for which there is, at present at least, scarcely any supporting scientific evidence and massive evidence against.

A second theory accounting for the briefness of the great period is that this was the only time in Coleridge's life that he was happy. The force of this theory, too, is enfeebled by objective analysis. Is it true that happiness liberates artistic power? One of Coleridge's most important poems, "Ode to Dejection," is about his personal despair, and was written, we may believe, when he was truly wretched. Is it possible to believe that over the last three decades of his life he was never for any space sufficiently content to write a great poem, while at the same time he went on correcting his earlier poetry, usually much for the better, showing that at least judgment and technique were still present?

Yet if this theory claims too much, it would be a mistake to discount altogether the possible effects of physical and mental well-being in someone so generally riven as Coleridge. The notebooks and letters of the whole Wordsworth-Coleridge circle for the 1797 and '98 period testify to the enormous enthusiasm—intellectual, aesthetic, and personal—that bound the two young poets together. Furthermore, in February 1798 Coleridge received an annuity of £150 a year, free of conditions, presumed sufficient for him and his family to live on in decent comfort. So great a windfall would surely go far to contribute to a general sense of content in any man, and certainly in so harrassed and desperately impecunious a young poet, husband, and father as Coleridge. In the months immediately following the magnanimity of the Wedgwoods, he completed "The Ancient Mariner" and wrote "Frost at Midnight," "France: An Ode," "Fears in Solitude," and "The Nightingale."

But we should remember that the force of this theory derives from the easy establishment of a cause-and-effect relationship between events that may have no other connection than that they coexisted in time. Gloom did not overtake Coleridge when he left Stowey for Germany. On the contrary, he seems to have been a very happy man (by Coleridgean standards) abroad, despite occasional and to-be-expected complaints of homesickness to his wife. Retreat from Sara was far from distasteful to Coleridge, even in 1798. In fact, he long overstayed his leave in Germany. There he continued to be free of pressing responsibilities, was as financially independent as he was ever to be in his life, and was surrounded by books, students, and impressive scenery. If he had recently been experiencing the first flush of opium addiction, or if joy was an indispensable condition of poetry, it would be straining credulity to maintain that both ceased to function the moment the cliffs of Dover faded into the distance. Yet in Germany he wrote no important poetry.

The last of the important hypotheses accounting for Coleridge's great period involves William Wordsworth. As usually stated, this theory holds that Coleridge and Wordsworth, both young and developing, found in each other a catalyst. The two men, it is held, inspired each other and liberated the tremendous creative power that was struggling for expression within both. "If Wordsworth learned from Coleridge how to *think*, Coleridge learned from Wordsworth what to *see*,"[6] is the sort of neat antithesis one often finds in discussions of the subject.

Superficially, at least, this appears to be the theory most solidly based on fact. It is certainly true that 1797 and 1798 were for both poets crucial years. Yet Robertson, interested only in Coleridge's development, has attacked this theory violently. The influence of Wordsworth alone, he argued, could not have resulted in Coleridge's great poems, as witness the "imbecilities" of "The Three Graves."[7] It is far more relevant, however, to recall that Coleridge knew Wordsworth for the rest of his life and yet the major poet in him went into seclusion early. It would seem, therefore, that Wordsworth could hardly have accounted for Coleridge's major achievement, however much his friendship may have been of moral and psychological value.

I would like to restate this last theory in another form, since I believe that the influence of Wordsworth on Coleridge's flowering as a great poet is vastly, perhaps incalculably, more important than has hitherto been allowed —not only as to the general contours and terracings of his poetic landscape, but in the minute texture and grain of his language. But even if this can be demonstrated, it would still remain palpably true that Coleridge's greatest poems proclaim a uniquely personal verbal music and moral vision. "The Ancient Mariner," "Cristabel," and "Kubla Khan" are very different from anything Wordsworth—or anybody else—ever wrote. Underlying the "magical" achievement of the great poems is a confluence of extraordinary events and influences, and an attempt to untangle them will be made. But it is still true that the intimacy with Wordsworth was absolutely crucial in Coleridge's development *as an artist*.

It is futile to discuss the influence of these two richly endowed young men on each other in terms of an occasional adopted phrase or image or general idea. Such influences will be found in the work of any artist who is not utterly shut off from the outside world. And such a relationship exists between Coleridge and every creative friend he ever had (for example, Lamb, Southey, Lloyd). As Synge wrote in the Preface to *The Playboy of the Western World*, "All art is a collaboration." It would be amazing were it otherwise.

What does matter are those fundamental and sometimes eccentric views of craft and content which sharply distinguish the Romantic poets from their predecessors, ideas about language and the proper subject matter of poetry. And it is here that influences *are* crucial, in that they can and do shape both the gross architecture and inner harmonies of a poet's work.

Coleridge's dazzling effect on friends and acquaintances is well known and easily understood. His brilliance was manifest. The combination of learning, extreme quickness of mind, and moral idealism was irresistible in a man so young, so accomplished, so blessed with enthusiasm, energy, and eloquence. The occasional skeptics among the crowds of admirers Coleridge left behind were few and inconsequential. He seemed to exude good nature, and his need for friendship and approval was such that his affections sometimes seemed to bubble up like a great fountain washing over those he loved or whom he wanted to love him.

Wordsworth, by comparison, seems almost dour. He did not hold audiences spellbound. He never lectured. In company he did not either by natural manner or determination hold the center of attention. There is no smack of the polymath about him. His genius does not always glitter in his recorded speech or letters.

And yet Wordsworth absolutely overwhelmed Coleridge—and not only Coleridge, but also Lamb, Southey, Poole, and many others. What was the basis of this awed admiration, if not the power, freshness, and *execution* of his ideas? On 8 June 1797, at the very beginning of their real intimacy, Coleridge wrote to Cottle:

> I speak with heart-felt sincerity & (I think) unblinded judgement, when I tell you, that I feel myself a *little man by his side*; & yet do not think myself the less man, than I formerly thought myself.—His Drama [*The Borderers*] is absolutely wonderful. You know, I do not commonly speak in such abrupt & unmingled phrases—& therefore will the more readily believe me.—There are in the piece those *profound* touches of the human heart, which I find three or four times in 'The Robbers' of Schiller, & often in Shakespere—but in Wordsworth there are no *inequalities*. T. Poole's opinion of Wordsworth is—that he is the greatest Man, he ever knew—I coincide.[8]

The following March he wrote:

> The Giant Wordsworth—God love him!—even when I speak in the terms of admiration due to his intellect, I fear lest tho[se] terms should keep out of sight the amiableness of his manners—he has written near 1200 lines of a blank verse, superior, I hesitate not to aver, to any thing in our language which any way resembles it. Poole (whom I feel so consolidated with myself that I seem to have no occasion to speak of him out of myself) thinks of it as likely to benefit mankind much more than any thing, Wordsworth has yet written.[9]

And in May he wrote:

> I have now known him a year & some months, and my admiration, I might say, my awe of his intellectual powers has increased even to this hour. . . . His genius is most *apparent* in poetry—and rarely, except to me in tete a tete, breaks forth in conversational eloquence.[10]

Coleridge's life is punctuated by his dependence upon some older, or stronger, or more stable personality: first his brother George, then Poole, for a time Morgan, and during the eighteeen long years at Highgate, his medical advisor, James Gillman. Wordsworth was the only such sheet-anchor who was at the same time his intellectual equal—and, to believe Coleridge, a giant by comparison.

Like Coleridge, Wordsworth had been orphaned early. The loss of both parents had been compounded by his separation from his sister and brothers, and by bitter financial problems. At the age of twenty, during a long vacation from Cambridge, he had gone on a walking tour through Switzerland and France. Two years later, again in France, he was caught up in the violent tides of the revolution. During this period he had the now well-known affair with Annette Vallon, which resulted in an illegitimate daughter. By the time he was twenty-seven, the beginning of his intimacy with Coleridge, his character had been tempered by the fires of conflict and crisis. Though continually subjected to emotional and physical stress (about which, like most things that concerned his purely private life, he was silent), he had determinedly organized his life and was passionately devoted to his work. All this, depending on one's point of view, can easily be characterized as fanatical, humorless, dogged, or tenacious. Whatever one's view, it cannot be disputed that William and Dorothy Wordsworth were living with extreme frugality on a small legacy so that he could pursue his art. For the rest of his days Wordsworth managed to have all the external routine of existence taken care of for him by slavishly devoted women, first his sister, Dorothy, then his wife, Mary, and her sister, Sara Hutchinson (Coleridge's beloved "Asra").

In Wordsworth's career there is a steady development from the early *An Evening Walk* and *Descriptive Sketches* (both published in 1793) towards the immense advance of 1797 and 1798 and, perhaps most crucial of all, a tremendous flowering of power *through* these years well into the next decade. What happened when the two men went to Germany together seems to provide an important clue to the mystery of the influence of each on the other. In Germany they separated, and *almost at once Coleridge abandoned original poetry*. What he did in Germany, as we have seen, was to translate folk-songs, epigrams, and comparatively obscure poems, and send them home to England as original compositions, in some cases as impromptus occasioned by specific personal experiences. Wordsworth, on the other hand, in the small town of Goslar and separated from Coleridge, wrote some of the most magnificent passages of the first two books of the *Prelude*, "The Fountain," "Ruth," and the finest of the "Lucy" poems, among much other verse of exceptional quality. Whatever else these facts may mean, they certainly suggest powerfully that, whereas Wordsworth was perfectly capable of writing superbly in complete isolation, Coleridge seems scarcely to have been able to write independently at all, after separating from Wordsworth.

Coleridge returned to England in July of 1799; Wordsworth had returned a few months earlier. In November of that year, without notifying his wife, Coleridge rushed off to visit Wordsworth. During this time or shortly afterwards he wrote another important poem, "Introduction to the Tale of the Dark Ladié," which finally became "Love." Late in 1799 he went to London and did newspaper work for Daniel Stuart. The verse of this period is ephemeral.

In the meantime "Christabel" remained with only one book written. Coleridge could not get on with it. In August of 1800, however, he moved his family from Stowey to Keswick, so as to be near Wordsworth. Here, after an agonizing effort, the second part of "Christabel" was finished. "Every line has been produced by me with labor-pangs," he wrote in September, and then he added: "I abandon Poetry altogether—I leave the higher and deeper Kinds to Wordsworth, the delightful, popular and simply dignified to Southey."[11]

In the following months Coleridge continued his newspaper work. Of poetry there was nothing. In 1801 his health turned ominously worse. He went to London again, and remained there from November to the following March. He then visited the Wordsworths at Dove Cottage, arriving on 19 March 1802.[12]

From December of the preceding year (1801) Wordsworth had been working with extraordinary productive energy. Almost forty of the poems which appeared in the edition of 1807 were written between December 1801 and December 1803, including much of the first two books of the *Excursion*. On 27 March 1802, at breakfast, he wrote the first four stanzas of his "Ode on the Intimations of Immortality."[13] Sometime during the next three weeks Coleridge wrote "Ode to Dejection,"[14] one of his greatest poems; it deals with the same subject as Wordsworth's Ode and in its original unpublished version echoed several phrases of it.

Once again proximity with Wordsworth had put a deep spur to Coleridge's sluggish Pegasus. And the same may be said of "To William Wordsworth," written in 1807, one of the last of Coleridge's poems to which importance has traditionally been attached. It was written in honor of the supposed completion of the *Prelude*, when the two poets were again in proximity. "A Tombless Epitaph" (1809), the much admired "imitation" of Chiabrera, closely followed an earlier translation of Wordsworth.

There is certainly a striking and suggestive pattern in this chronology of Coleridge's relations with Wordsworth. If, in fact, the latter's presence was somehow catalytic in the creation of Coleridge's great poems, are we justified in any inference other than that Wordsworth provided him with incentive or psychological strength or moral example, or something of this sort? Can Wordsworth's assistance have been more concrete?

Coleridge's familiar account of the genesis of the *Lyrical Ballads* has important bearings on our subject.

During the first year that Mr. Wordsworth and I were neighbours, our conversations turned frequently on the two cardinal points of poetry, the power of exciting the sympathy of the reader by the faithful adherence to the truth of nature, and the power of giving the interest of novelty by the modifying colors of the imagination. The sudden charm, which accidents of light and shade, which moonlight or sun-set diffused over a known and familiar landscape, appeared to represent the practicability of combining both. These are the poetry of nature. The thought suggested itself (to which of us I do not recollect) that a series of poems might be composed of two sorts. In the one, the incidents and agents were to be, in part at least, supernatural; and the excellence aimed at was to consist in the interesting of the affections by the dramatic truth of such emotions, as would naturally accompany such situations, supposing them real. . . . For the second class, subjects were to be chosen from ordinary life; the characters and incidents were to be such, as will be found in every village and its vicinity, where there is a meditative and feeling mind to seek after them, or to notice them, when they present themselves.

In this idea originated the plan of the "Lyrical Ballads"; in which it was agreed, that my endeavours should be directed to persons and characters supernatural, or at least romantic. . . . Mr. Wordsworth, on the other hand, was to propose to himself as his object, to give the charm of novelty to things of every day. . . .

With this view I wrote "The Ancient Mariner," and was preparing among other poems "The Dark Ladié," and the "Christabel," in which I should have more nearly realized my ideal, than I had done in my first attempt.[15]

This famous passage gives a picture of the genesis of *Lyrical Ballads* which in crucial particulars is false. Coleridge asserts that he and Wordsworth, after much speculation on the nature of poetry, had deliberately undertaken separate tasks so as to demonstrate "the two cardinal points of poetry" in a series of poems of two sorts. The first dealt with in his account are supernatural poems, and he says that "The Ancient Mariner" was written as his contribution to a mutually undertaken endeavor. But "The Ancient Mariner" was written before *Lyrical Ballads* had ever been conjectured by either poet.

Hazlitt, once again, provides an important clue in his retrospective account of Coleridge in 1798: "He said the *Lyrical Ballads* were an experiment about to be tried by him and Wordsworth, to see how far the public taste would endure poetry written in a more natural and simple style than had hitherto been attempted; totally discarding the artifices of poetical diction, and making use only of such words as had previously probably been common in the most ordinary language since the days of Henry II."[16] Nothing is said here of *two* kinds of poetry. And "The Ancient Mariner," as everyone knows, employs an archaic vocabulary and originally an archaic orthography ("The Ancyent Marinere").

Moreover, Coleridge wrote to Humphry Davy in October 1800 that "Christabel" was not going to appear in the second edition of *Lyrical Ballads* because it was too long, "& which was of more consequence—*the poem was in direct opposition to the very purpose for which the Lyrical Ballads were published.*"[17] That purpose, as Wordsworth stated much later in the Fenwick note to "We are Seven," was "to consist . . . of Poems chiefly on natural subjects taken from common life, but looked at, as much as might be, through an imaginative medium."[18] But it is the Preface to the *Lyrical Ballads* of 1800 that ought to be the central document in this discussion. And here, throughout a long and detailed essay, not a word is said about *any* of the poems which Coleridge in *Biographia Literaria* says were to be a fundamental part of their joint effort.[19]

Coleridge's distortions are important because they much obscure the fact that "The Ancient Mariner" was not conceived for any revolutionary poetic purpose. Indeed, the fact that the work was cast in the then modish ballad form much tended to obscure its uniqueness. Great work that it was, it provided only a minor impulse to the gathering momentum of the Romantic movement.

To Miss Isabella Fenwick, Wordsworth's friend and secretary during the closing years of his life, all students of Wordsworth and Coleridge owe much. Except for her insistence, the long series of remarks by Wordsworth on his own poetry now known as the "Fenwick" notes would probably never have been written. We have just seen Coleridge's account of the writing of "The Ancient Mariner." Nowhere else did he give further particulars. So far as we get the history from him, it was a completely independent venture which was to form part of a joint project, the *Lyrical Ballads*. Somewhere around 1843, when Coleridge was dead approximately a decade, the seventy-three-year-old Wordsworth reminisced about events of some forty-six years before:

In the spring of the year 1798, he [Coleridge], my Sister, and myself, started from Alfoxden, pretty late in the afternoon, with a view to visit Linton and the valley of Stones near it; and as our united funds were very small, we agreed to defray the expense of the tour by writing a Poem. . . . Accordingly we set off and proceeded along the Quantock Hills, towards Watchet, and in the course of this walk was planned the Poem of The Ancient Mariner, founded on a dream, as Mr. Coleridge said, of his friend, Mr. Cruikshank. Much the greatest part of the story was Mr. Coleridge's invention; but certain parts I myself suggested, for example, some crime was to be committed which should bring upon the Old Navigator, as Coleridge afterwards delighted to call him, the spectral persecution, as a consequence of that crime, and his own wanderings. I had been reading in Shelvocke's Voyages a day or two before that while doubling Cape Horn they frequently saw Albatrosses in that latitude. . . . "Suppose," said I, "you represent him as having killed one of these birds on entering the South Sea, and that the tutelary Spirits of those regions take upon them to avenge the crime." The incident was thought fit for the purpose and adopted accordingly. I also suggested the navigation of the ship by the dead men, but do not recollect that I had anything more to do with the scheme of the poem. . . . We began the composition together on that, to me, memorable evening. I furnished two or three lines at the beginning of the poem, in particular:

> 'And listened like a three years' child;
> The Mariner hath his will.'

These trifling contributions, all but one (which Mr. C. has with unneces-
ary scrupulosity recorded) slipt out of his mind as well they might.
As we endeavoured to proceed conjointly (I speak of the same evening)
our respective manners proved so widely different that it would have been
quite presumptous in me to do anything but separate from an undertaking upon which I could only have been a clog. We returned after a
few days from a delightful tour. . . . The Ancient Mariner grew and grew
till it became too important for our first object, which was limited to our
expectation of five pounds, and we began to talk of a Volume, which was
to consist . . .[20]

This passage will bear very considerable study. Wordsworth here was not
making a final statement for posterity. He had been talking of his early poem
"We are Seven," one of the poems in the original *Lyrical Ballads*, and by
association he wandered into the discussion of "The Ancient Mariner."[21]
If we remind ourselves that he was recalling events of some forty-six years
before, and how long a period that is in anyone's life, we may well feel that
the old man's impromptu recollections were far from complete. When he says
that he suggested certain parts of the story of "The Ancient Mariner," what
he goes on to talk about is prefaced with "for example." At length he says,
"I do not recollect that I had anything more to do with the scheme of the
poem." This is not a flat statement precluding the possibility that he had suggested more. He simply does not remember anything further. His use of the
word "scheme" implies that he was referring only to the *plot* of the poem, for
he immediately goes on to say that he "furnished two or three lines at the
beginning of the poem," and he remembers in particular two lines, which he
gives. However, at least for the first day and for part of the first evening
after "The Ancient Mariner" had been conceived, the two men worked at it
as if it were a joint project. In Wordsworth's account he withdrew because his
"manner" and Coleridge's were "different." The word "manner" does not
tell us anything specific. It may refer to their verbal styles, their ideas on
the point by point development of the story, or "manner" may mean their
whole personalities as poets. "Peter Bell," written in 1798 as a kind of counterweight to Coleridge's use of the supernatural in "The Ancient Mariner,"
contains the following pointed stanzas in its "Prologue":

> Long have I loved what I behold,
> The night that calms, the day that cheers;
> The common growth of mother-earth
> Suffices me—her tears, her mirth,
> Her humblest mirth and tears.
>
> The dragon's wing, the magic ring,
> I shall not covet for my dower,
> If I along that lowly way

With sympathetic heart may stray,
And with a soul of power.

These given, what more need I desire
To stir, to soothe, or elevate?
What nobler marvels than the mind
May in life's daily prospect find,
May find or there create?[22]

Thus Wordsworth rejects, as a subject for serious poetry, the whole universe of miracles in which the Mariner moves, and we can easily imagine why the two poets found it impossible to agree upon a detailed strategy for "The Ancient Mariner." Wordsworth's lines also invoke tangentially that very musical gift which seems so uniquely Coleridgean and which appears in Wordsworth's poetry almost exclusively in passages dealing with music itself, as in the description of the song of "The Solitary Reaper":

No Nightingale did ever chaunt
More welcome notes to weary bands
Of travellers in some shady haunt,
Among Arabian sands:

A voice so thrilling ne'er was heard
In spring-time from the Cuckoo-bird,
Breaking the silence of the seas
Among the farthest Hebrides.

In the criticism of "The Ancient Mariner" which Wordsworth printed in a note to the 1800 edition of *Lyrical Ballads*, he specifically objected to the vagueness of the Mariner's figure and his lack of a "distinct character." He also felt that the events in the story, "having no necessary connection do not produce each other."[23]

An absolutely cautious scholar would justifiably hesitate to assume that Wordsworth's contributions to "The Ancient Mariner" consisted of a jot more than is recorded in the Fenwick note. Coleridge has nowhere told us anything of all this. Wordsworth said his own "trifling" contributions had "slipt" out of Coleridge's mind, all but one. That "one" was Coleridge's acknowledgment in *Sybilline Leaves* (1817) that Wordsworth had written the lines: "And thou art long, and lank, and brown, / As is the ribbed sea-sand."[24] This, as Lane Cooper pointed out long ago, is "the clearest picture of [the Mariner's] outward physique" in the whole poem.[25] As the lines Coleridge acknowledged occur in Part IV of the poem, Coleridge had either transferred lines originally written for the beginning, or else when the poem was half finished Wordsworth was still offering close advice and suggestions.

In the edition of 1852, H. N. Coleridge published a note of great interest which had been communicated to him by the Rev. Alexander Dyce. Wordsworth had died in 1850. Dyce wrote:

When my truly honoured friend Mr. Wordsworth was last in London, soon after the appearance of De Quincey's papers in *Tait's Magazine*, he dined with me in Gray's Inn, and made the following statement, which I am quite sure, I give you correctly: "*The Ancient Mariner* was founded on a strange dream, which a friend of Coleridge had, who fancied he saw a skeleton ship, with figures in it. We had both determined to write some poetry for a monthly magazine, the profits of which were to defray the expenses of a little excursion we were to make together. *The Ancient Mariner* was intended for this periodical, but was too long. I had very little share in the composition of it, for I soon found that the style of Coleridge and myself would not assimilate. Besides the lines (in the fourth part)—

> 'And thou art long, and lank, and brown,
> As is the ribbed sea-sand'—

I wrote the stanza (in the first part)—

> 'He holds him with his glittering eye—
> The Wedding-Guest stood still,
> And listens like a three-years' child:
> The Mariner hath his will'—

and four or five lines more in different parts of the poem, which I could not now point out. The idea of "shooting an albatross' was mine; for I had been reading Shelvocke's Voyages, which probably Coleridge never saw. I also suggested the reanimation of the dead bodies, to work the ship.[26]

Exactly when the meeting between Wordsworth and Dyce took place is uncertain. Dyce says that it was "in London, soon after the appearance of De Quincey's Papers in *Tait's Magazine*." But these came out intermittently between 1834 and 1839, and Wordsworth visited London many times after 1834. In any case, the meeting took place *before* the Fenwick note was dictated in 1843. Superficially, the two accounts seem the same, but close inspection reveals important differences. In the later account Wordsworth remembered having written two or three lines near the beginning of the poem, and quoted two. In the earlier account he speaks of four lines, and quoted them, plus four or five more in different parts of the poem, which he could no longer point out, in addition to the two lines Coleridge had acknowledged.

Just a few years earlier, therefore, Wordsworth remembered some actual lines of verse which slipped out of his mind later or else he thought unnecessary to record. In the second account he said only that the poem was founded on a dream, but in the first he gives us a few fascinating details, especially that Cruikshank's dream was about "a skeleton ship, with figures in it."

In the earlier account, however, he does not say that he suggested that the shooting of the albatross was to be followed by "the spectral persecution, as a consequence of that crime and his own wanderings." Moreover, he did not in the earlier account say that the crime was to occur specifically when the ship entered the South Seas, or that "the tutelary spirits of those regions take upon them to revenge the crime."

That the two accounts should differ is not in the least surprising. Wordsworth was not at either time making a formal statement after searching his memory, which, after four decades, would be most unlikely to be precise. He was an old man, with a lifetime of poetry behind him. Memorable as the writing of "The Ancient Mariner" was, it may well be doubted that, after so many decades, he could have provided anything like a complete account of his contributions to the poem. What must be remembered, however, is that in each record there are important gaps filled by the other, and it is not unreasonable to suppose the two accounts, which have come down to us somewhat fortuitously, represent something less than Wordsworth's total contribution.

Yet, even as the facts now stand, what Wordsworth gave Coleridge by way of the plot alone is tremendously important. He has, in fact, suggested practically the whole plot. Curiously, scholars continually minimize this contribution. In both accounts Wordsworth carefully de-emphasized his own role: "Much the greatest part of the story was Mr. Coleridge's invention," he says, and "I had very little share in the composition." Lowes wrote that while "the signal importance of Wordsworth's contributions to the scheme of 'The Ancient Mariner' admits no question," yet Wordsworth was not so generous as just, when he declared that "much the greatest part of the story was Mr. Coleridge's invention."[27] It is hard to quarrel with this statement as it stands, except to note that, as Lowes proceeds to discuss the subject, Wordsworth's contributions are minimized at every point. While still granting "unreservedly" that Wordsworth contributed matters of importance, he insists that since the "skeleton ship, with figures in it," and the "Old Navigator" were clearly in Coleridge's mind from the beginning," Wordsworth's contributions supplied the "links" which "knit loose materials" already there into a story, "and fanned to flame a smouldering conception."[28] We really do not know that there was any "smouldering conception" there, or that the existence of smouldering conceptions tells us very much. Lowes continues: "it remains no less true that the magnificent imaginative elaboration of the jointly assembled ingredients of a plot is Coleridge's own, as truly as *Hamlet* and *Lear* and *Anthony and Cleopatra*, on grounds essentially the same, are Shakespeare's."[29] The invocation of Shakespeare's name need not terminate discussion. Had the Bard of Avon had at his side a Plutarch with dramatic and poetical powers equal to his own, ever ready to offer suggestions, advice, and criticism, as Coleridge had Wordsworth, we should all be most interested.

Lane Cooper, practically alone, has spoken up for Wordsworth strongly:

> most readers, and even students, of ["The Ancient Mariner"] have little notion how important Wordsworth's share in it really was. Actually, he gave Coleridge the very kernel of the plot, furnished him with a working basis, without which the author of the fragmentary *Kubla Khan*, the unfinished *Three Graves*, those scattered members entitled *The Wanderings of Cain*, and *Christabel*, it is conceivable, might never have brought *The Rime of the Ancient Mariner* to a conclusion.[30]

Wordsworth's own words can be brought to bear against this position. He had twice called his own contributions trifling. But surely we need not take this too emphatically in the context of their personal friendship and interfamilial ties. What is scarcely recognized at all in discussions of the two men is the range and specificity (as opposed to more insubstantial general influences) of Wordsworth's poetic aid. Indeed, Wordsworth's reticence about the whole subject is astonishing. But then, after Coleridge's death and de Quincey's scandalous plagiarism charges, Wordsworth was hardly inclined to stoke the flames of controversy by citing debts to himself.

It is illuminating that in defending the memory of his departed friend, Wordsworth did write to Crabb Robinson that on many occasions he had begged Coleridge to make proper acknowledgments, to no avail.[31] He casually mentioned in the same letter, by way of example as to how "careless" Coleridge was, that "A Tombless Epitaph" was based on his own translation from Chiabrera. Let us remind ourselves that he left no written or verbal record that "Lewti" had been based on one of his own poems, as was "An Inscription for a Seat," or that "Alceaus to Sappho," which was published under Coleridge's name, was based in part or entirely upon one of his own poems, and this may also be true of "The Mad Monk" and "The Old Man of the Alps." He seems to have given Coleridge a half-dozen or so of his poems to help him fulfill a contract with the *Morning Post*, but he left no record of this, either.

Coleridge published "The Three Graves," parts III and IV, without mentioning that Wordsworth (or anybody else) was in any way involved in formulating the scheme of the poem, though we now know that the first two sections are Wordsworth's. (When Coleridge published III and IV in the *Friend* [1809], he spoke of the poem "as consisting of six parts: the story of the first two he told in prose; of the last two he says they 'may be given hereafter, if the present should appear to afford pleasure,' but he never suggests that he would publish the first two.") Barron Field, in an unpublished life of Wordsworth, records that Wordsworth said to him: "I gave him [Coleridge] the subject of his *Three Graves*: but he made it too shocking and painful, and not sufficiently sweetened by any healing views."[32]

These facts would seem to form a clear pattern. Wordsworth assisted Coleridge frequently and materially, but Coleridge was singularly careless in acknowledging these debts. Such information as we have from Wordsworth on these and related matters is fortuitous and consists of rare, fragmentary comments made to certain friends and intimates over long periods of time.

Coleridge, a born editor, was also a born collaborator, to which his innumerable tinkerings and alterations with the poems of friends and others amply testify. *The Fall of Robespierre,* written with Southey in 1794 (and published under Coleridge's name solely), was but the first in a long series of joint efforts. Wordsworth, who had never collaborated with anyone on anything—and was never to do so again—in the months immediately following his intimacy with Coleridge was drawn into at least three mutual projects with him: "The Wanderings of Cain," "The Ancient Mariner," and "The Three Graves." Significantly, Wordsworth withdrew from all three undertakings. The benefits of publication, it would appear, were exclusively Coleridge's.

We must remember that in all the years before the intimacy with Wordsworth, Coleridge had drawn upon books and other poems for material. At the end of 1796 he was still a markedly derivative poet and his diction was, with rare exceptions, a polyglot language derived from Milton and a half-dozen eighteenth-century poets. In the "Ode to the Departing Year," written in the final weeks of December 1796, the second strophe begins:

> Hither from the recent Tomb;
> From the Prison's direr gloom;
> From Poverty's heart-wasting languish:
> From Distemper's midnight anguish;
> Or where his two bright torches blending
> Love illumines Manhood's maze;
> Or where o'er cradled Infants bending
> Hope has fix'd her wishful gaze:
> Hither, in perplexed dance,
> Ye WOES, and young-eyed JOYS, advance![33]

The strained and stilted diction orates for itself. Yet *within six months* he was writing such lines as the opening of "This Lime-Tree Bower My Prison," where the authenticity of the spoken voice in its natural rhythms is startling:

> Well, they are gone, and here must I remain,
> This lime-tree bower my prison! I have lost
> Beauties and feelings, such as would have been
> Most sweet to my remembrance even when age
> Had dimm'd mine eyes to blindness! They, meanwhile,
> Friends, whom I never more may meet again . . .

There is nothing less than a revolution in language and ways of feeling between these two passages. Somewhere between the end of 1796 and the summer of 1797 a profound aesthetic event took place. New and significant models had impinged on Coleridge's acute poetic intelligence, with momentous consequences. Where did these new ways of thinking, and feeling, come from? Where may we find the revolutionary poems Coleridge saw?

Between 1794 and the middle of 1797 Wordsworth had written, besides much else, "Guilt and Sorrow," "The Ruined Cottage," *The Borderers,* and "Lines Left upon a Seat in a Yew-Tree." An outstanding feature of this verse is its steady process of verbal purification. It was Wordsworth, and *only* Wordsworth, for whom simplicity of diction and concreteness of image were *idées fixes.* Driving impetuously to theoretical extremes, he wrote in 1798 the much abused lines in "The Thorn":

> This thorn you on your left espy;
> And to the left, three yards beyond,
> You see a little muddy pond
> Of water, never dry;
> I've measured it from side to side:
> 'Tis three feet long, and two feet wide.[34]

The only way to avoid wincing at such gaucheries is to recognize in them the inevitable detritus of aesthetic revolutionary ardor. Purity of language, infused with Wordsworth's intensely personal belief in the healing value and spiritual significance of nature, appears fully developed in the early "Lines Left upon a Seat in a Yew Tree":

> . . . and he would gaze till it became
> Far lovelier, and his heart could not sustain
> The beauty, still more beauteous! Nor, that time,
> When nature had subdued him to herself,
> Would he forget those Beings to whose minds,
> Warm from the labours of benevolence
> The world, and human life, appeared a scene
> Of kindred loveliness: then he would sigh,
> Inly disturbed, to think that others felt
> What he must never feel . . .

The specific image of the man "subdued" by the intensity of nature appears in precisely the same setting in Coleridge's "Lime Tree Bower," together with similarity of language:

> So my friend
> Struck with deep joy may stand, as I have stood,
> Silent with swimming sense; yea, gazing round

On the wide landscape, gaze till all doth seem
Less gross than bodily; and of such hues
As veil the Almighty Spirit, when yet he makes
Spirits perceive his presence.[35]

In the fifteenth chapter of the *Biographia Literaria* there is a singularly revealing passage which has not, I think, been much noticed. Coleridge quotes two lines in which "there is nothing objectionable, nothing which would preclude them from forming, in their proper place, part of a descriptive poem." The lines are:

Behold yon row of pines, that shorn and bow'd
Bend from the sea-blast, seen at twilight eve.

Coleridge notes that with "a small alteration of rhythm, the same words would be equally in their place in a book of topography, or in a descriptive tour." However, if the lines might quite readily be turned into prose, Coleridge proceeds to show how the "same image will rise into a semblance of poetry if thus conveyed:

'Yon row of bleak and visionary pines,
By twilight glimpse discerned, mark! how they flee
From the fierce sea-blast, all their tresses wild
Streaming before them.' "[36]

Some readers, especially those who misconceive the nature of Coleridge's genius, may find this a chilling glimpse into his poetic workshop. It can be argued—irrelevantly, I think—that everything deplorable in what is known as the "pathetic fallacy" is here paraded as an illustration of how to give "a dignity and a passion to the objects" which the poet represents. The original lines, "close to prose," are invested with meaning by a comparatively simple process. Any group of pines may be described as "bleak and visionary." That they should merely bend before the sea-blast is not enough. The image may be raised to a "Semblance of poetry" by having the pines "flee," with "all their tresses wild / Streaming before them." Curiously, we find in "France: An Ode," written early in 1798, a passage which Coleridge may here have been unconsciously remembering. This Ode has been excessively praised, partly, I think, because it was written during the *annus mirabilis,* but mainly (as with Shelley) because of its political sentiments. Nevertheless, the form and diction of the Ode mark a considerable step back from what had already been achieved. Despite scattered excellencies, its structure, personifications, images, and emotions are all conventional.

Then, as the poem seems in its conclusion about to blow apart from the pressure of its bombast, the poet invokes "Liberty," which speeds away

> Alike from Priestcraft's harpy minions,
> And factious Blasphemy's obscener slaves;

suddenly the Poet feels the presence of Liberty:

> —on that sea-cliff's verge,
> Whose pines, scarce travelled by the breeze above,
> Had made one murmur with the distant surge!
> Yes, while I stood and gazed, my temples bare,
> And shot my being through earth, sea, and air,
> Possessing all things with intensest love,
> O Liberty! my spirit felt thee there.

The conclusion is in every way the best part of the poem. And it is truly astonishing how abruptly Coleridge can shift from the declamatory "Priestcraft's harpy minions" and "Blasphemy's obscener slaves" to a passage that gives "dignity and passion" to the sea and air and pines and poet by fusing them all in a single image—One Life—a sequence which is pure Wordsworth, and so familiar in Coleridge through "This Lime Tree Bower My Prison" that we must appeal to the date of "Lines Left Upon a Seat in a Yew Tree" to establish Wordsworth's priority. More important, it is clear enough that for Coleridge the passage is a "Nature bit," "a set piece," dropped into a very different kind of poem.

What may well be suspected is that it is essentially to Wordsworth that we can attribute the remarkable change in Coleridge's poetry—both in the crucial medium of language and the general posture towards the natural world—which occurs after, and *only* after, the close friendship with Wordsworth.

That Wordsworth provided the stronger poetic impulse between the two men would appear to emerge from any impartial examination of the record. And it seems fair to say that throughout the whole nineteenth century and the first quarter of our own that this was the prevailing judgment. So radically has opinion changed in the past forty years, however, that a closer examination of the subject seems called for, not only to clarify literary history, but to illuminate the creative process in two accepted giants of English poetry. That prevailing opinion has changed radically is amply demonstrated in the following quotations from I. A. Richards, surely one of the best and most influential of modern literary critics and theoreticians:

> though no accountancy is possible with such deep interchanges and indebtednesses, Wordsworth seems undoubtedly the chief gainer from the strange poetic symbiosis which now began [in 1797]. It is arguable that as to many modes of excellence—by finding the style which Wordsworth was to advocate in the Preface to the *Lyrical Ballads*, by uttering a good half of the thoughts in that and in Wordsworth's later prose, by

designing Wordsworth's major poems for him, and by discovering the philosophic seas on which they float—Coleridge was Wordsworth's creator; or, since that is clearly too strong a word, that he first truly showed Wordsworth how to become his own poetic self.

The group of descriptive-reflective poems, of which "Frost at Midnight" is the best known and perhaps the best, needs little comment. He [Coleridge] is shaking himself free from the swelling, emphatic, declamtory diction of "Religious Musings," finding ways to make his language transparent to the sense and thoughts it has to carry, helping, in fact, to get a medium ready for Wordsworth's use in "Tintern Abbey". . . .

It is no paradox to say that what Coleridge most admired in Wordsworth was what Wordsworth could have learned from these poems ["Frost at Midnight" and "This Lime Tree Bower My Prison"].[37]

If Richards' views were lonely dissents, they could perhaps be dealt with summarily. But because they now represent almost received opinion, and since the subject has immense importance in itself, they may be cited in justification of the following excursus.

20.

The Background of
Lyrical Ballads, with
a Few Other Poems

FOR well over a century the Preface to the second edition of *Lyrical Ballads* (1800) has been esteemed as one of the chief masterworks of literary criticism in any language. This remarkable work not only promulgated a new set of aesthetic principles, but introduced a body of poetry which illustrated those principles in action, and successfully established not only the general shape, but the inner spirit of English poetry for the following century.

Perhaps the most extraordinary fact about the friendship between Wordsworth and Coleridge is that both men left behind not only a body of immortal verse, but literary criticism, by general consensus, of the highest order. Since the gift of poesy and that of genuinely original thought in criticism have only rarely co-existed in the same person, the fact that the two best poets since at least the death of Pope should have also been the best critics since Johnson, and perhaps the best that England had produced up to that time, is one of the truly amazing coincidences in English literature. Between the final works of Samuel Johnson in the 1770's and 1780's, and the publication of *Biographia Literaria* in 1817, the Preface to *Lyrical Ballads* stands like a great beacon. Without it, the immense transformation that occurred during that time in feeling and expression—and critical approaches to literature itself— would be still more obscure than it is.

It is a stubborn fact, and from some points of view an awkward one, that Wordsworth's name stands at the head of this indispensable composition. The shape of literary history, as it is now generally conceived, would be decidedly neater if Coleridge's did. After all, Wordsworth wrote so little criticism, and he does not easily grasp the weighty sceptre of critical majesty. A man who could write that "minute criticism is in its nature irksome, and as commonly practiced in books and conversation, is both irksome and injurious,"[1] is unlikely to arouse enthusiasm among practitioners of an art more minute than Wordsworth (or Coleridge, for that matter) would have thought possible. Worse still, Wordsworth seems to have held the critical faculty itself in contempt, at least compared to that of creation,[2] and main-

282

tained regularly that the only reason he ever wrote the famous Preface was that Coleridge continually urged him to do so.

Indeed, so indigestible is Wordsworth's authorship of this unique work, when present was one of the profound critical minds of all time—who was not to publish any criticism of consequence until some fifteen years later—that an exhaustive reexamination of the whole subject has long been vigorously pursued. The lineaments of gratified desire are clearly discernible in the conclusions which have thus far emerged in the flurry of papers on the subject. Closer scrutiny of the whole context of the Wordsworth-Coleridge relationship has made possible a reorganization of emphasis sufficient perhaps to oblige the next generation of students and scholars to apportion credit for the Preface to *Lyrical Ballads* in a mode more consonant with contemporary views of the relative powers of the two men. Henceforth, it appears, the Preface is not merely to be viewed as more of a joint product than hitherto supposed—or was dreamt of until our own more enlightened times—but we are in fact to assign the basic credit for the whole conceptual framework, if not the words themselves, to the mighty intellect of the younger of the two men.

Now there has always been a tendency to depreciate Wordsworth's philosophical powers in favor of Coleridge's, but why this has come to include general intellectual force is not easy to fathom.[3] The reasons for the former are obvious enough. Wordsworth showed little interest in philosophy as a formal subject, and seemed proud of the fact that he'd never, as he said, read a word of German metaphysics. The philosophical propensities of Coleridge are sufficiently well known. Wordsworth late in life gave it as his opinion that "Coleridge had been spoilt as a poet by going to Germany. The bent of his mind, which was at all times very much [given] to metaphysical theology, had there been fixed in that direction."[4] Apart from how little enthusiasm for philosophy this suggests, there is a satisfying neatness in assigning to Coleridge the philosophical end of the early partnership, with Wordsworth —at least in the past—providing the sturdy, if drabber, virtues of steadiness of purpose, firm grip on the tangible and concrete, and enormous self-confidence. That Coleridge's interest in philosophy was incomparably more intense than Wordsworth's is, of course, not to be doubted. The implications of that fact with respect to the powers of the two men as literary critics, however, are by no means so obvious as regularly assumed.[5]

Perhaps this is the major reason why it has become easy to assign Coleridge the role of prime mover in the 1800 Preface, namely, the prevailing conception of the critical powers of the two men. But that opinion was by no means shared by those who knew both Wordsworth and Coleridge intimately. De Quincey, for example, whose audacious praise of Coleridge's capacious intellect is regularly quoted, nevertheless declared that Wordsworth was the greatest critic he had ever known. He acknowledged Wordsworth as the originator of the central distinction in his famous essay on the literature of knowledge and the literature of power, as well as "for most of the sound criticism on poetry, or any subject connected with it that I have ever met with. . . ."[6] His description of Dorothy Wordsworth's intellectual powers is especially relevant in any discussion of the Wordsworth-Coleridge friendship. In praising Dorothy's strong native powers, De Quincey goes on to say that it would be strange indeed if, in such proximity with William,

> not only hearing the best parts of English literature daily read, or quoted by short fragments, but also hearing them very often critically discussed in a style of great originality and truth, and by the light of strong poetic feelings—strange it would have been that any person, though dull as the weeds of Lethe in the native constitution of his mind, failed to acquire some power of judging for himself.[7]

De Quincey's testimony, however, is regularly depreciated.

In 1965 appeared two major articles on the subject. Very early in Mark L. Reed's long essay, a significant theme is sounded: Wordsworth had the kind of character that "led him to devour, digest—but too seldom acknowledge—the loyalty and contributions of his small, diversely gifted group of satellites. His intolerance towards the personal weaknesses of Coleridge and his limited overt recognition of his debt to that great intellect are perhaps the most unforgivable of his failures in this respect." Soon we enter upon a discussion of an early stage of that "joint effort [the Preface] which Wordsworth so hastily began regarding as his own. . . ."[8] After this, it is perhaps unnecessary to add that Professor Reed is discontent with the traditional view as to who really wrote the Preface.

Max F. Schulz, in a similar inquiry, after paying "tribute to the inquiring originality of Coleridge's mind and to the sturdy intractability of Wordsworth's," goes on to remind us that "almost two years after the event, he [Coleridge] confided to Sotheby that 'it was first intended that the Preface should be written by me.'" Of this claim, for which there is no evidence elsewhere, Professor Schulz writes, with perhaps excessive confidence, "I see no reason to doubt Coleridge, whose unreliability extends mostly to dates and whose inclination at all times was to denigrate himself, especially when his god Wordsworth was involved."[9]

In George Watson's *The Literary Critics*, conjecture has become certainty. Coleridge's "first major critical essay (if one may so describe Wordsworth's 1800 Preface to the *Lyrical Ballads*) was written by somebody else. . . . The beginnings sound uncertain, but there can be little doubt that the inspiration of the 1800 preface was Coleridge's. . . ." What little doubt there might have been disappears three pages on, where Professor Watson finds Coleridge's attack on that very Preface in *Biographia Literaria* "positively graceless . . . the more so, when we remember that Coleridge had been its chief begetter."[10]

Perhaps it is foolhardy to try to swim against so heavy a tide of opinion. Still, before the current flows into new editions of the Cambridge and Oxford histories of English literature, a few caveats are in order, and a whole cluster of facts.

In the absence of other evidence, Coleridge's statements about his own intellectual history are not automatically to be credited. In general, when one man's name appears upon a published work and another man's doesn't, that is because the presence and absence of those names answer to the facts of composition. Any other explanation brings a very serious charge against him who deprives another of the recognition properly due him for intellectual achievement. We have seen that on several occasions Coleridge published under pseudonyms poems by Wordsworth, but there is no known similar instance of the reverse. And it was Coleridge who published *The Fall of Robespierre* under his own name, though Southey had written two of the three acts. There is no reason to suppose that Wordsworth was or could have been guilty of such an act.

What is surprising in these revisionary studies is how little hard evidence has been brought forward to substantiate the claim that Coleridge's contribution to the now-disputed Preface was of fundamental importance, let alone that Coleridge was a co-author and even its "chief begetter."

According to Dorothy Wordsworth's journal, the Preface was written between 13 and 30 September 1800. Coleridge's journals for all of July, August, and September are quite full, and show nothing whatever to support his later assertion that the Preface had actually been begun from "notes" of his own. The one entry, of highly uncertain date, that has a clear connection with the Preface reads in its entirety, as laboriously reconstructed,

[. . . . .]
    all savages should [?purpose/suppose/passive] imitation of [. . . . .] or [. . .] means of [. . . . . .], so poetry [. . . .] recalling of passion in tranquillity, or demands [. . .] [?disjuntion/distinction/dissociation] of poetry & [?painting/passion/prose] [. . .] [?real/great] [?divisive/ division] of music [. . . .] not separable [?poetic characters]—Metre distinct and artificial—till at length poetry forgot its essence in those forms which were only hieroglyphic of it. [?Different/Defence of] [?end/ aim] of poetry[11]

One would hardly think this promising, but much has been made of this scrappy and scarcely legible jotting![12] As for the phrase "passion in tranquillity," Coleridge might have set it down from Wordsworth's conversation, or originated it himself, or have transmitted it from his supposed reading of a Schiller review in a Germany periodical of 1791, as has been argued. And assuming this dubious point is granted? How odd that scholars are so ready to proclaim the great Preface at least a "joint product" on the basis of scraps like this, but to deny even a significant influence from Schelling or Schlegel, when confronted with dozens of pages of verbatim translation and close paraphrase!

Now it would be to skirmish on the wrong battlefield to deny that during all the time the Preface was actually being written that Wordsworth and

Coleridge were meeting almost daily, undoubtedly discussing all its main points, arguing, challenging each other—in short, doing all those things we would expect two close friends to do who were deeply immersed in writing and thinking about poetry. It would be surprising—unthinkable really—that Coleridge would not have given final shape to some of the sentences, and have provided the language for some of its ideas. A contemporary joint statement of precisely who was responsible for what in the essay would be immensely valuable to the world of scholarship. In its absence we ought to assume that Wordsworth would not have taken sole credit for a true joint product, and that insofar as he does, within the Preface, make clear at several points when ideas or knowledge were not self-originating, that the rest of the essay represents his own work.

One of the most extraordinary features of the Preface is its really amazing freedom from the inherited jargon of literary criticism. Whatever else one may praise in Coleridge's criticism, freshness of terminology is not one of them. In all of his lectures and published prose between 1811 and 1818, which comprise almost all the criticism we have, the basic German critical terminology is followed.

The Preface to *Lyrical Ballads* is as devoid of the commonplaces of criticism as any English literary history can produce. It is at least a little hard to believe that between Coleridge's many prefaces, notebooks, and letters through 1800, and all his writings thereafter, so great a gulf in tone and conceptual framework should exist in comparison with the *Lyrical Ballads* Preface. Yet if one scrutinizes the Preface with a view to Coleridge's possible contributions, one finds a few scattered sentences and phrases which certainly do smack more of Coleridge than Wordsworth.[13] In raising the question of Coleridge's participation in the 1800 Preface, George McLean Harper writes: "Of the following sentence, which is perhaps the most important one in that essay, we may assert with confidence that the second part, about the laws of the mind, is Coleridgean in substance and even in the very terms employed." Harper then quotes the following familiar extract:

The principle object, then, proposed in these poems was to choose incidents and situations from common life, and to relate or describe them, throughout, as far as was possible in a selection of language really used by men, and, at the same time, to throw over them a certain colouring of imagination, whereby ordinary things should be presented to the mind in an unusual aspect; *and, further, and above all, to make these incidents and situations interesting by tracing in them, truly though not ostentatiously, the primary laws of our nature: chiefly, as far as regards the manner in which we associate ideas in a state of excitement.*

"The hand which wrote those words may have been Wordsworth's," Harper goes on, "but the voice is that of Coleridge."[14]

This seems persuasive. But how little is added to Coleridge's credit thereby! For the portion of the sentence above to which emphasis has here been added is really one of the few pieces of intellectual cant in the whole essay. What on earth is meant? What are the "primary laws of our natures: chiefly, as regards the manner in which we associate ideas in a state of excitement"? A large claim, this, on which neither Wordsworth nor Coleridge would appear to have had much to say in their letters, essays, or recorded conversations. Is there a single poem in *Lyrical Ballads* in which the laws governing the association of ideas in a state of excitement is "traced"? When the lover sees the moon drop down behind Lucy's cottage, and is startled to think that she may be dead, we have an unusual association of ideas. But no laws of mental functioning are "traced" in that lyric, or in "Goody Blake and Harry Gill," "We are Seven," "The Last of the Flock," "The Thorn," "Anecdote for Fathers," or any of the other early poems for which the Preface seems to have been written. So if Coleridge was responsible for the second half of the sentence given above, that is small credit indeed. As for the first half, very possibly the crucial one in the whole essay—the central notion governing language—Coleridge in later years declared himself as always opposed to!

If recent scholars had been able to find in the record immediately before and after the publication of the 1800 *Lyrical Ballads* evidence supporting the contention of Coleridge's massive participation in the work, we may be sure that this would long since have been disclosed to the world. The record, however, is skimpy in that direction, whereas evidence tending to the contrary is massive. It deserves to be examined.

Coleridge's letters, prefaces, and notebooks before 1800 provide quite a full record of his literary beliefs, at least in comparison to what has been left behind by other poets and critics. And in this record there is scarcely a glimmer of those concepts which burst so suddenly upon the world in the 1800 Preface. It is true that almost from the first moment Coleridge became intimate with Wordsworth in 1797 there is a tremendous change in certain of his views, but, as we shall see, this tends rather strongly to support the thesis that Wordsworth was the more original of the two.

Coleridge's few early reviews and prefaces to the published editions of his poems are, at best, facile, and, at worst, surprisingly sterile performances. In 1797 he praised Ossian's "sweet voice" (an enthusiasm, significantly, never shared by Wordsworth), and gave it as his opinion that the charge of obscurity in poetry is a "heavier accusation" than that of turgidity.[15] In December 1796, after the often-quoted remark that we ought not to pass an "act of Uniformity against poets," Coleridge goes on to say that we can admire Akenside, Bowles, Milton, and Cowper almost equally,[16] surely a strange collocation of names. According to Hazlitt, Coleridge in 1798 spoke of Cowper as the "best modern poet," an unexceptional opinion for the time,[17] but one hardly sustained by the spirit of the 1800 Preface or by the letter of the "Essay Supplementary to the Preface" of 1815, where Wordsworth's review of the poets who had most influenced him contains just that combination of the unexpected and the conventional which clarifies much that would otherwise be obscure. And this is especially true of his handsome tribute to Percy's *Reliques*, which at once establishes its own sincerity and truth because of how much it illuminates. "I do not think that there is an able writer in verse of the present day," Wordsworth wrote, "who would not be proud to acknowledge his obligations to the Reliques; I know that it is so with my friends; and, for myself, I am happy in this occasion to make a public avowal of my own."[18]

Another passage in this essay of 1815 is germane to the question of who wrote the 1800 Preface:

> Of genius the only proof is, the act of doing well what is worthy to be done, and what was never done before: Of genius, in the fine arts, the only infallible sign is the widening the sphere of human sensibility, for the delight, honour, and benefit of human nature. Genius is the introduction of a new element into the intellectual universe: or, if that be not allowed, it is the application of powers to objects on which they have not before been exercised, or the employment of them in such a manner as to produce effects hitherto unknown.[19]

The emphasis on newness, novelty, independence, and originality could hardly be more pronounced. The passage very strongly suggests, coming from a poet, that he was altogether convinced that he, Wordsworth, commanded such powers. He may, of course, have been mistaken in that assumption. But that he never showed any external doubt of his own supreme gift is, however unbecomingly immodest, relevant. Wordsworth here allows relatively little to the synthesizer of other men's ideas, to those who work within a tradition whose possibilities are not yet exhausted. If Wordsworth's emphasis on radical orginality is excessive, as I think it is, it nevertheless reveals his sense of superiority over those who follow in the path of the plowman.

In Coleridge, conversely, as we have seen again and again, that emphasis on originality in Wordsworth's sense is rarely found. On the contrary, we hear of genial coincidences, of the moral certainty that two gifted men studying Kant would come to the same conclusions about Shakespeare's plays. We find Coleridge again and again citing intellectual precedent: Newton worked out the ideas of Kepler, who had "fully conceived" gravity; Kant was to be praised not as a metaphysician, but as a logician who had worked out what was "boldly conceived" by Bacon; the works of Schelling were a patchwork of borrowings from Fichte, and Boehme, and others. And so forth. Little purpose would be served in repeating here the masses of Coleridgean claims and *aperçus* of this kind.

If we go back to the 1800 Preface, then, we find that its primary concerns are not those which can be found in any of Coleridge's writings before he met Wordsworth. How to account for his silence even to his intimate acquaintances about his own share in the Preface? Of course, we may say that he was too given to prostration before his god Wordsworth, as has been alleged, and which has considerable truth in it. But not even to the privacy of his own notebooks?[20]

Let us consider first what is said about the subject matter of the poetry in *Lyrical Ballads*: "incidents and situations from common life." This is quintessential Wordsworth, and utterly alien to Coleridge. Now it is possible to argue, of course, that "The Eolian Harp," "This Lime Tree Bower My Prison," and "Frost at Midnight" all deal with incidents from "common life," as the term would be understood today. But the historical situation—so regularly ignored in discussions of the Preface (by none more than Coleridge himself)—puts an altogether different signification on the phrase. "Common Life" was that of the Simon Lees and Female Vagrants and even the mad Martha Rays, whose lives in another sense are anything but common. The introduction of ordinary folk into literature, *without patronization*, is one of the most original of Wordsworth's achievements. There is no hint of or even sympathy with this aim in any of Coleridge's writings.[21]

Wordsworth goes on to say that these incidents from common life are to be described "throughout, as far as was possible, in a selection of language really used by men." (The double qualification here—"As far as was possible," and "in a *selection* of language really used by men"—is inconvenient to those who think Wordsworth's theories of language "jejune" or otherwise absurdly simplistic, and are therefore quietly ignored.) It is in the practice of this theory, I believe, that the truly revolutionary element in *Lyrical Ballads* is to be found. Much of the psychological apparatus employed in the 1800 Preface (with the notable exception of the description of the creative process), is of small consequence to either English poetry or literary criticism. The attitudes toward nature, the convictions about its healing virtues which are found in the poems and implied in the Preface itself—all this, though important, would have had only slight, if any, effect on the subsequent course of English poetry. What matters fundamentally in *Lyrical Ballads* is the new *language* employed, for it is this language which subsequent poets down almost to the end of the first World War were able to employ successfully, although many did not find it necessary to adopt any other of Wordsworth's convictions. As T. S. Eliot said: "Sensibility alters from generation to generation in everybody, whether we will or no; but expression is only altered by a man of genius."[22]

Perhaps nothing has gone further to obscure the actual historical situation into which *Lyrical Ballads* was born than the subsequent writings of Coleridge on the subject. Again and again he maintained that as to the essential points of Wordsworth's theory, nobody else had ever held different views! But he himself held very different views at the time he met Wordsworth.

It is worth emphasizing that the continuity and interdependence of human thought is such that thoroughgoing analysis of the historical background of practically any set of ideas is likely to produce so many "sources" and "adumbrations" that one can easily be left with the impression that even those documents the world considers among its most original are scarcely more than rearrangements of pre-existing materials. F. W. Bateson, only a generation ago, could write that Wordsworth's Preface was "now generally recognized as perhaps the most original single document in the whole history of English criticism. . . ."[23] After serving for more than a decade as editor of the *Cambridge Bibliography of English Literature*, Bateson was perhaps uniquely qualified to make such a statement. Yet more recently E. D. Hirsch has found it necessary to warn readers that, although "the gross anatomy of the whole was new and strange,"[24] perhaps almost every idea in the Preface to *Lyrical Ballads* can be found in earlier writers. But this is misleading. That procedure is pernicious which finds in the writings of a Blake or a Nietzsche all the main insights of Freud, but lacking the later master's arrangement. This is simply not true. It is true that *some* of Wordsworth's most important ideas *seem* to be all over the place before him, but the congruence of ideas in the republic of letters is extremely difficult for those who live later to determine with any confidence. A mathematical proposition has a certain objective reality. But a statement in literary criticism derives not only from its own context, but from that of its whole period. Nothing is more deceptive than the appearance of congruence. Legouis and Beatty have long since produced platoons of writers, many almost invisible in their obscurity, from whom Wordsworth is supposed to have learned much. Perhaps so. But we may be permitted to doubt.

Thus, for example, on 8 November 1796 Lamb wrote to Coleridge: "Cultivate simplicity, Coleridge, or rather, I should say, banish elaborateness. . . ." This sounds as if Lamb and Wordsworth had a good deal in common on the idea of poetic diction. Of "The Eolian Harp," Lamb wrote the next month, "Write thus, and you most generally have written thus, and I shall never quarrel with you about simplicity."[25] But in fact Coleridge had only rarely written thus. And Lamb did not always praise him in this vein. In February of 1797 he wrote: "I was reading your Religious Musings the other day, & sincerely I think it the noblest poem in the language, next after the Paradise lost; & even that was not made the vehicle of such grand truths." He then identified a twelve-line passage as "without a rival in the whole compass of my poetical reading." It begins:

> There is one Mind, one omnipresent Mind,
> Omnific. His most holy name is Love.
> Truth of subliming import! . . .

Lamb continued: "The loftier walks of Pindus are your proper region. There you have no compeer in modern times. Leave the lowlands, unenvied, in possession of such men as Cowper & Southey."[26] The central problem is that poetic simplicity, a phrase probably on everybody's tongue, did not mean to Lamb what it meant to Wordsworth. In part this is the context behind Wordsworth's statement that "a practical faith" in these matters (that is, simple poetic diction) was almost unknown among men.

We see this truth operative in a letter of Lamb's written on 10 January 1797, still some six months before Coleridge and Wordsworth became close.

Lamb wrote to Coleridge thus about one of his own poems: "that it has no originality in its cast, nor anything in the feelings, but what is common and natural to thousands, nor aught properly [to be] called poetry, I see. . . ."[27] A statement like this, of course, is almost diametrically opposed to one of the central theses of Wordsworth's Preface. And it is clear that Lamb is writing to Coleridge as if on this matter there is complete congruity of thought— How could there not be, on so commonplace an idea?—almost as if on this point he is replying to a letter from Coleridge.

In January 1801, a few months after the second edition of *Lyrical Ballads* was published, Lamb wrote to Wordsworth specifically of the Preface: "All its dogmas are true and just, and most of them new, *as* criticism."[28] If most of the dogmas were new to Lamb, we can hardly suppose that they came from Coleridge, whom he had known since boyhood and with whom he had a voluminous correspondence. The next month Lamb wrote to his good friend Thomas Manning, specifically of the second volume of *Lyrical Ballads* (all Wordsworth's): "It is full of original thinking and an observing mind. . . ."[29] Again, Lamb was surely likely to know what was original in Wordsworth and what might have come from Coleridge. There is no hint of any debt from Wordsworth to Coleridge either in the poetry or the Preface, only powerful and direct testimony to Wordsworth's independence.

In 1803 Southey wrote to John May:

> I wish you would read the Lyrical Ballads of Wordsworth; some of them are very faulty; but, indeed, I would risk my whole future fame on the assertion that they will one day be regarded as the finest poems in our language.

To John Rickman the following year (30 March 1804):

> Wordsworth will do better, and leave behind him a name, unique in his way; he will rank among the very first poets, and probably possesses a mass of merits superior to all, except only Shakspeare.

And to William Taylor on 9 March 1805:

> soberly and solemnly I do believe, that of all the present generation he [Wordsworth] will leave behind him the most durable and valuable memorials: this I say knowingly of what he has written, hardly expecting credit even from you.[30]

What all this clarifies is the overwhelming effect of Wordsworth's poems on two of his sensitive contemporaries, men who were in an infinitely better position to judge of the relative claims of Wordsworth and Coleridge in original poetic and critical merit *up to that time* than any subsequent critic could possibly be. And for both these men, who for different reasons consider

Coleridge one of the titanic intellects of his or any generation, the question of precedence does not come up. There is no problem either for them or the rest of their contemporaries. The problem is part of the detritus of modern scholarship and the top-heavy reputation Coleridge is now bearing as the Da Vinci of literature.

Some part of the shock and wonder felt by Wordsworth's more sensitive contemporaries is still available to us. All we need do is spend several days exclusively with a thick anthology of English poetry of the eighteenth century, weighted heavily toward the poets in the last quarter of the century, especially the Akensides, Beatties, Charlotte Smiths, Erasmus Darwins, and Ossians. After several days of this, turn to the *Lyrical Ballads* of 1798 and 1800. The shock is intense. One feels oneself, even after all this time, in a startlingly fresh and strange world. The strangeness of it was widely perceived by contemporary critics, some of whom saw in its doctrines not merely a new departure in poetry, but, as the alarmed Francis Jeffrey, later the formidably powerful editor of the *Edinburgh Review*, put it, a "positive and *bona fide* rejection of art altogether. . . ."[31]

The testimony of De Quincey is also apposite. He noted that Wordsworth's early and basically traditional *Descriptive Sketches* would have been very popular with the public, had they been effectively brought to its attention; "on the other hand, his revolutionary principles of composition, and his purer taste, ended in obtaining for him nothing but scorn and ruffian insolence." And elsewhere, De Quincey records how in *Lyrical Ballads* he found "an absolute revelation of untrodden worlds." Repeatedly in his works he refers to Wordsworth's "exceeding originality," his "extraordinary power and originality,"[32] but nowhere is Coleridge credited even with being a co-partner in the invention of these principles.

But it is Hazlitt, I think, who has provided the most penetrating insight into what was most revolutionary in *Lyrical Ballads*. In "My First Acquaintance with Poets," he tells how on that memorable morning in 1798 Coleridge had read to him Wordsworth's ballad of "Betty Foy." The young Hazlitt saw in it "touches of truth and nature":

> But in the *Thorn*, the *Mad Mother*, and the *Complaint of a Poor Indian Woman*, I felt that deeper power and pathos which have been since acknowledged . . . as the characteristics of this author; and the sense of a new style and a new spirit in poetry overcame me.[33]

Now it is to be noted that Coleridge had by this time written "This Lime Tree Bower My Prison," and "Frost at Midnight." Yet it is not the meditative nature poem in which Hazlitt finds the revolutionary new spirit, but rather in these tales and ballads of ordinary human life, rich in concrete detail, precisely the sort of poem for which Coleridge had no gift and little sympathy. He was in this and similar attitudes much more a child of the eighteenth century than Wordsworth. "It is for the Biographer, not the Poet, to give the *accidents* of *individual* Life," he wrote Wordsworth in 1815. "Whatever is not representative, generic, may be indeed most poetically exprest, but is not Poetry."[34] Johnson would have been satisfied by this statement.

Interestingly, in the 1803 letter to John May quoted above, Southey identified those works of Wordsworth which would some day "be regarded as the finest poems in our language. I refer you particularly to 'The Brothers,' a poem on 'Tintern Abbey,' and Michael."[35] "Tintern Abbey" is perhaps the greatest of the three poems, but the other two constitute a radical break with the past in a way that "Tintern Abbey" does not. Bateson is surely right in emphasizing the rebelliousness in Wordsworth's whole approach to poetry: "Poems like 'The Idiot Boy,' 'We Are Seven' and *Peter Bell* are not merely outside the literary tradition—Blake's poems are outside it too—they are written in a deliberate defiance of it. The gross, offensive non-literariness is an important part of their meaning."[36]

Now in his noble tribute to Wordsworth's genius in "The Spirit of the Age," as has been observed earlier, Hazlitt actually says far more about the significance of *Lyrical Ballads* than does Coleridge in *Biographia Literaria*, where the revolutionary element in Wordsworth's poetry is consistently ignored or minimized. What was apparent to everyone by 1815, namely, that Wordsworth's Pegasus was the oddest beast to canter onto the poetic horizon in a century, was scarcely noticed by Coleridge. One would never suppose from his analysis of Wordsworth's "characteristic excellencies and defects" that the poet under review, whatever else one might think, was one of the most original, if perversely original, who ever lived.

Biographia Literaria, in fact, radically distorts the actual historical situation in which *Lyrical Ballads* appeared. By 1815, long after the bitter breach with Wordsworth, Coleridge was able to write in the confidence of a letter that Wordsworth attached too much importance to self-discovered ideas which the rest of the world consider commonplaces.[37] In the *Biographia* he went so far as to say, in his own peculiarly suggestive way, that the "main object of the Preface had been stated long before by Garve," and then proceeded to misconstrue what was offered as a "literal translation" from Garve in a way that, in Miss Coburn's words, "completely alters the meaning."[38] Finally, in asserting that nobody had ever held a theory of poetic diction different from the one Wordsworth was promulgating as his own, he was simply flying in the face of the whole history of the critical literature of the subject, from Aristotle to his own day.[39] And though in this, as in all other human affairs, there was dissent from prevailing opinion, it should always be remembered that Wordsworth destroyed once and for all the conviction that there *was* a standard poetic diction, a cornerstone of eighteenth-century critical belief.

It is curious that in the innumerable discussions of the Wordsworth-Coleridge relationship it has scarcely ever been noticed that at the very outset of his *Biographia Literaria*, Coleridge assigns to one of his teachers at

Christ's Hospital, and thus to his early boyhood, the revolutionary approach to poetic diction which the world had credited to Wordsworth. Coleridge's motives are not explicit, of course; in fact, they appear not to have been hitherto noticed. If he was offended by Wordsworth's statement that the Germans had first taught the world to think properly about Shakespeare's dramatic construction, consider what may have been Wordsworth's reaction to the following:

> In our own English compositions . . . he [Boyer] showed no mercy to phrase, metaphor, or image, unsupported by a sound sense, or where the same sense might have been conveyed with equal force and dignity in plainer words. Lute, harp, and lyre, muse, muses, and inspirations, Pegasus, Parnassus, and Hippocrene were all an abomination to him. *"Harp? Harp? Lyre? Pen and ink, boy, you mean! Muse, boy, muse? Your Nurse's daughter, you mean!* Pierian spring? *Oh aye! the cloister-pump, I suppose![40]*

If we choose to credit this account, we are obliged to conclude that Coleridge was an amazingly obtuse student not only at Christ's Hospital, but for a long time thereafter. His early poetry is studded with "garishness & swell of diction," of which Coleridge himself later complained.[41] Poem after poem before the *annus mirabilis* fairly bristles with lyres, muses, and divers personifications. Through many revisions of the "Monody on the Death of Chatterton," elegant circumlocutions of all sorts survive, including the "Neglect and grinning Scorn and Want" of the 1790 version. A passage from Coleridge's contributions to Southey's *Joan of Arc*, written in 1796, reads:

> A Vapor rose, pierc'd by the MAIDEN'S eye.
> Guiding its course OPPRESSION sate within,
> With terror pale and rage, yet laugh'd at times
> Musing on Vengeance: trembled in his hand
> A Sceptre fiercely-grasp'd. O'er Ocean westward
> The Vapor sail'd . . .

In a late manuscript note, Coleridge wrote: "These images imageless, these *Small-Capitals* constituting themselves Personifications, I despised even at that time; but was forced to introduce them, to preserve the connection with the machinery of the Poem, previously adopted by Southey."[42]

How does one account for so incredible a statement? Was he remembering his tribute to stern old Jemmy Boyer in his literary biography? There certainly appears to be an attempt in the later years to atone for the lacunae of the earlier years, which are utterly silent as to Boyer's pedagogical virtues. "Dura Navis," an iambic pentameter school-exercise, written under Boyer's presumably watchful eye, is nevertheless loaded with "images imageless," and here, too, Coleridge has provided a retrospective note for posterity:

I well remember old Jemmy Bowyer, the plagose Orbilius [Horace's schoolmaster, a flogger] of Christ's Hospital, but an admirable educer no less than Educator of the Intellect, bade me leave out as many epithets as would turn the whole into eight-syllable lines, and then ask myself if the exercise would not be greatly improved. How often have I thought of the proposal since then, and how many thousand bloated and puffing lines have I read, that, by this process, would have tripped over the tongue excellently. Likewise, I remember that he told me on the same occasion—"Coleridge! the connections of a Declamation are not the transitions of Poetry—bad, however, as they are, they are better than 'Apostrophes' and 'O thou's', for at the worst they are something like common sense. The others are the grimaces of Lunacy."[43]

Yet if Boyer ever chided Coleridge for the gaudy fabric of his poetic habiliments, he would have gone right on doing so up until the transformation of his poetic style around the middle of 1797, and intermittently ever after. If Southey was really to blame for his use of the despised neo-classic machinery in 1796, what of the poem Coleridge published in December 1797 in the *Morning Post*, when he was already working on "The Ancient Mariner"?

> Mother sage of Self-dominion
> Firm thy steps, O Melancholy!
> The strongest plume in Wisdom's pinion
> Is the memory of past folly.[44]

In the Supplement to his Poems of 1797 appear these stanzas:

> Thy mother's name, a potent spell,
> That bids the Virtues hie
> From mystic grove and living cell,
> Confess'd to Fancy's eye;
>
> Meek Quietness without offence;
> Content in homespun kirtle;
> True Love; and True Love's Innocence,
> White Blossom of the Myrtle![45]

Indeed, a first cousin to the "Pierian spring," of which Boyer is said to have complained, and, which was remembered so vividly by the forty-five-year-old Coleridge, actually appears in a poem published by him in 1798. In "The APOTHEOSIS, or the SNOW-DROP," we find such lines as,

"FAME unrebellious heard the charm, / And bore thee to *Pierian* climes."
And as if this—for which Southey can in no wise be blamed—were not bad
enough, as coming from someone so ably and corporally instructed, here is
the final stanza of this seventy-two-line poem:

> The LOVES trip round her all the night;
>   And PITY hates the morning's birth,
> That rudely warns the ling'ring SPRITE
>   Whose plumes must waft her back to earth!
> Meek PITY, that foreruns relief,
>   Yet still assumes the hues of woe;
> Pale promiser of rosy Spring,
> A SNOW-DROP mid the snow.[46]

It can be argued that these examples come from trifling poems, and that
as Coleridge was after all grinding out verses for badly needed guineas, he
is not to be held accountable for such stuff. But if this is true, it demonstrates how deeply ingrained the habit of such diction was. Can one imagine Wordsworth writing anything like this in 1798, under any kind of haste
or compulsion? The point is that this style came *naturally* to Coleridge when
he was working under pressure. It was not what the newspapers demanded.
Almost his whole apprenticeship was that of, so to speak, the studio painter
working from plaster casts rather than live models and rarely showing much
concern with natural light or objects in themselves.

No sooner, however, do Wordsworth and Coleridge become near neighbors,
when a radical change occurs in Coleridge's writings about poetry. In June
1797 he sends a long excerpt from Wordsworth's revolutionary "Ruined
Cottage" to a friend,[47] and the following month he writes Southey at
length of his present poetic credo. Now he does not wish to reprint his
"Monody on the Death of Chatterton," partly because it is "deficient in
chasteness & severity of diction." He cannot bear, upon examining the
poem now,

> to find such shadowy nobodies, as cherub-winged DEATH, Trees of
> HOPE, bare-bosom'd AFFECTION, & simpering PEACE. . . . A young
> man by strong feelings is impelled to write on a particular subject—
> and this is all, his feelings do for him. They set him upon the business
> & then they leave him.—He has such a high idea, of what Poetry ought
> to be, that he cannot conceive that such things as his natural emotions
> may be allowed to find a place in it—his learning therefore, his fancy,
> or rather conceit, and all his powers of buckram are put on the stretch—.
> It appears to me, that strong feeling is not *so* requisite to an Author's
> being profoundly pathetic, as taste & good sense.[48]

Does this not have the ring of new discovery, especially as written to his
closest confidant of the previous five years? Not much would seem to be

left to old Boyer's instruction. Yet it is notable that Coleridge here says nothing of Wordsworth's direct influence. In view of the general configuration of Coleridge's personality, it is not impossible to suppose that in later years, not necessarily consciously, he suppressed the near influence of Wordsworth and wildly magnified a remote and utterly ineffectual one from Boyer, assuming there was any at all.

Why should Coleridge have wished to do this? For the same reason that he suppressed the fact that he had learned about the "severe logic" of poetry from Edward Young in his maturity and not in his boyhood instruction under Boyer. It is not necessary to settle the question whether Coleridge was altogether conscious of these distortions. Especially in his later recollections, desire soon became reality. So loathe was he to credit living contempories with having taught him anything, whether Schelling or Schlegel or Wordsworth, that he simply threw back to his earliest instruction and continually self-advertised, preternaturally-wide reading the origins of his mature doctrines. Repeated recognition of intellectual debt to a forgotten schoolmaster only magnified the moral capital of the student.[49]

In the very brief preface provided to the printing of "The Three Graves" in *The Friend* (1809), Coleridge wrote not a word about the extreme simplicity of its ballad diction. But this was published before he and Wordswroth had quarrelled. When "The Three Graves" appeared in *Sybilline Leaves* (1817), however, the original brief note had now blossomed into a substantial preface which commences with some anxious observations about poetic diction:

[The language in] the following humble fragment [is] suited to the narrator; and the metre corresponds to the homeliness of the diction. It is therefore presented as the fragment, not of a Poem, but of a common Ballad-tale. [Can we imagine Coleridge having made such a statement about "The Ancient Mariner" or "Christabel" in previous years?] Whether this is sufficient to justify the adoption of such a style, in any metrical composition not professedly ludicrous, the Author is himself in some doubt. At all events, it is not presented as poetry, and it is in no way connected with the Author's judgment concerning poetic diction.[50]

It ought to be perfectly clear that Coleridge is here carrying on his battle with Wordsworth. Do these self-conscious defenses make any sense without reference to his strictures in *Biographia Literaria* on language? Having delivered himself there of his reasons for disagreeing with Wordsworth's views in the 1800 Preface, it was not sufficient to assert that now—some twenty years after the fact—he sharply differed with his old friend. No, he must give it out that he *always* had a different view. This of course is in keeping with Coleridge's inability to admit that he ever held a different opinion about any important matter at any time in his life. And just as his insistence upon the continuity of his political opinions from his early Jacobite days in Bristol to the present landed him, and his commentators, in innumerable, irresolvable difficulties, so his strictures on poetic diction hopelessly falsify the earlier record. For what possible reason would a poet with great works behind him undertake to write a lengthy poem in a meter "in no way connected with the Author's judgment concerning poetic diction"? Indeed, Coleridge almost makes it appear that "a common Ballad-tale" could not at the same time be "a Poem."

By widespread consensus, his two best poems before 1797 are "The Eolian Harp" and "Reflections on Having Left a Place of Retirement," both written in 1795, and thus well before proximity with Wordsworth. Certainly from the perspective of the revolutionary manifesto which the 1800 Preface to *Lyrical Ballads* represents, these two poems are the most easily identified as imbued with the new spirit. "The Eolian Harp" is especially noteworthy for its suggestion of the later Coleridgean music in such a passage as:

> And now, its strings
> Boldlier swept, the long sequacious notes
> Over delicious surges sink and rise,
> Such a soft floating witchery of sound
> As twilight Elfins make, when they at eve
> Voyage on gentle gales from Fairy-Land,
> Where Melodies round honey-dropping flowers,
> Footless and wild, like birds of Paradise,
> Nor pause, nor perch, hovering on untam'd wing! (ll. 17-25)[51]

There are conventional trappings here, to be sure, but the melody is unmistakable. Its presence has misled many critics, I think, into exaggerating the significance of the rest of the poem, in which appears perhaps the most natural of the young Coleridge's descriptions of nature. But we are reading meanings *back* into literary history when we unduly emphasize the importance of this poem. It is a lovely and essentially natural piece, and as such a rare specimen in the early canon.

"Reflections on Having Left a Place of Retirement," one of Coleridge's most neglected poems, is a crucial one in his aesthetic history. Written in a relatively chaste blank verse (though interspersed with such grimaces as "The sluggard Pity's vision-weaving tribe!"), these lines of 1795 really can be said to stand as an overture to all the good blank verse poems he was subsequently to write. C. G. Martin has shown that the "Reflections" owe much to William Crowe's "Lewesdon Hill," "a descriptive-meditative blank verse poem written in a relatively simple and un-literary style; and . . . voicing sentiments and discussing subjects which engrossed his [Coleridge's] own mind or echoed his own opinions." A few months before writing "Reflections," Coleridge had borrowed a volume which contained Crowe's poem.[52]

Perhaps the most memorable passage is that describing the panorama seen from the top of a high hill:

> Oh! what a goodly scene! *Here* the bleak mount,
> The bare bleak mountain speckled thin with sheep;
> Grey clouds, that shadowing spot the sunny fields;
> And river, now with bushy rocks o'er-brow'd . . . (ll. 29-32)[53]

Again, it is a mistake to exaggerate the significance of such lines. In 1795 appeared *A Pedestrian Tour Through North Wales*, written by Joseph Hucks, Coleridge's Cambridge friend and the companion with whom he had only recently toured Wales. Hucks celebrates nature's "inexhaustible sources, to a contemplative mind, of gratification and delight," from one end of the book to the other. In a description of the countryside around Bala in North Wales, he writes that

> few living creatures cheer these dreary scenes, but here and there a miserable hut . . . and a few poor sheep, thinly scattered over the steep sides of the mountain, or picking the short grass from the almost naked summit of the shaggy rock. . . . [54]

This is even better observed than in Coleridge, and in language as natural. Indeed, Hucks's "dreary scenes . . . and a few poor sheep thinly scattered over . . . the mountain," and "the shaggy rock" may have been in Coleridge's mind when he wrote of his own "bleak mountain speckled thin with sheep," and the "bushy rocks" o'er the river. In any case, the appearance of brief passages of straightforward blank verse do not of themselves testify to profound aesthetic stirrings. Lamb thought this poem "the sweetest thing to me you ever wrote."[55] And to us its language sounds, despite stridencies, very like what was soon to become the "true" voice of poetry.

This, however, was not Coleridge's contemporary view of the matter. In its first appearance in the *Monthly Magazine*, the poem was titled "Reflections on entering into active life. *A Poem which affects not to be Poetry.*"[56] Whatever Coleridge may have meant by the words here emphasized, it seemed to matter enough to him so that when he included the poem in his 1797 collection, he adopted the present title, and added "*Sermoni propriora*," a motto from Horace he kept ever after. He explained in a letter that the Latin tag meant "Properer for a Sermon"—that is, not of the highest poetical substance.[57] What could he possibly have meant other than that both the subject matter and the language, that very language we today so much admire, was unfit for the "highest" poetical works? "I rest for all my poetical credit on the *Religious Musings*," he had written in April 1796,[58] and had concluded the year with his turgid "Ode to the Departing Year." On a manuscript note to "Fears in Solitude," another poem of the *annus mirabilis*, Coleridge wrote: "N. B. The above is perhaps not Poetry,—but rather a sort of middle thing between Poetry and Oratory—sermoni propriora—Some parts are, I am conscious, too tame even for animated prose."[59] This is almost exactly what he had written of "Reflections on Having Left a Place of Retirement," and powerfully underscores the continuing uncertainty of his attachment to unadorned blank verse. The issue here, be it remembered, is not whether Coleridge was right or wrong on this matter, but rather that he never went through a self-directed period of revolutionary reexamination of his poetic style, and that the language used was acquired *ab extra*, with a quite astonishing power and brilliance and perhaps still more astonishing speed, after meeting Wordsworth.[60]

What is true of Coleridge's poetic style is almost certainly true of the transformation of his attitude toward nature as a result of the same friendship. The issue has nothing to do with fondness for or sensitivity to the beauties of the natural world. That subject was among the chief commonplaces of neoclassic verse, to go back no further. The crucial difference between the Romantic poets and their predecessors may be found in a letter from Coleridge to his brother George, written the month after he had composed "Frost at Midnight," and "France: An Ode": "I devote myself . . . in poetry, to elevate the imagination & set the affections in right tune by the beauty of the inanimate impregnated, as with a living soul, by the presence of Life." The formal stiffness of this statement suggests both recent formulation and the use of the idea as a kind of poetic myth. He goes on immediately:

I love fields & woods & mount[ains] with almost a visionary fondness—
and because I have found benevolence & quietness growing within me
as that fondness [has] increased, therefore I should wish to be the means
of implanting it in others—& destroy the bad passions not by combating
them, but by keeping them in inaction.

This is pure Wordsworth. And lest anyone doubt that not only the general ideas but some of the very words derive from that source, he sent along some eighteen lines from the conclusion of Wordsworth's unpublished "Ruined Cottage":

> Not useless do I deem
> These shadowy Sympathies with things that hold
> An inarticulate Language: for the Man
> Once taught to love such objects, as excite
> No morbid passions, no disquietude,
> No vengeance & no hatred, needs must feel
> The Joy of that pure principle of Love
> So deeply, that, unsatisfied with aught
> Less pure & exquisite, he cannot chuse
> But seek for objects of a kindred Love

> In fellow-natures, & a kindred Joy.
> Accordingly, he by degrees perceives
> His feelings of aversion softened down,
> A holy tenderness pervades his frame!
> His sanity of reason not impair'd,
> Say rather that his thoughts now flowing clear
> From a clear fountain flowing, he looks round—
> He seeks for Good & finds the Good he seeks.[61]

Coleridge's discovery of "Religious meanings in the forms of Nature"[62] comes in a sudden rush in the middle of 1797. All at once his letters are full of the subject, as are his poems. And as usual, what really seems to have burst upon him in his maturity is thrown back to his early years. Thus, in his "autobiographical letters" to Poole, we find him writing—some four months after daily intimacy with Wordsworth—that from his earliest childhood "my mind had been habituated *to the Vast*—& I never regarded *my senses* in any way as the criteria of my belief. I regulated all my creeds by my conceptions not by my *sight*—even at that age [that is, seven or eight!]." Never had he contemplated nature as "a mass of *little things*," but always as one indivisible whole.[63]

Whenever this subject is discussed two passages are sure to be quoted as "proof" of Coleridge's early pantheism. The first is from "The Eolian Harp" (1795):

> And what if all of animated nature
> Be but organic Harps diversely fram'd,
> That tremble into thought, as o'er them sweeps
> Plastic and vast, one intellectual breeze,
> At once the Soul of each, and God of all?

No sooner is this daring thought uttered, however, than the "beloved woman" at the poet's side darts with her "more serious eye a mild reproof" to reject such "unhallowed thoughts" and "walk humbly with my God." The poet accepts the reproof of the "Meek Daughter in the family of Christ!" and the poem concludes with familiar pieties.[64]

This passage has far less to do with moral meanings in nature than with the persistent deistic heresy into which Pope stumbled in his *Essay on Man.* Noteworthy is the complete absence of any suggestion of spiritual or therapeutic fallout in the contemplation of nature.

The second of the pre-Wordsworthian passages regularly quoted appears in "The Destiny of Nations" (1796):

> For all that meets the bodily sense I deem
> Symbolical, one mighty alphabet
> For infant minds; and we in this low world

> Placed with our back to bright Reality,
> That we may learn with young unwounded ken
> The substance from its shadow. (ll. 18-23)

The last three and a half lines, based on Plato's famous parable of the cave, should have forestalled critical confusion between the shadow of mysticism which flits over the "symbolic alphabet" of the senses and the homely reality of Wordsworth's daffodils and celandines. Coleridge's "symbolical alphabet" is part of the diverse philosophical materials he had laboriously culled, as we have seen, from so many sources, and contains no smack of either the personal commitment or emotional intensity of Wordsworth's celebrations of specific *things*.

By June of 1797 he begins "This Lime Tree Bower My Prison" by lamenting his inability to join his friends in their ramble into the fields and woods:

>   I have lost
> Beauties and feelings, such as would have been
> Most sweet to my remembrance even when age
> Had dimm'd mine eyes to blindness!

Thus brilliantly, naturally, the new voice, new diction, new feelings, new ideas, are all united in patterns we have come to take so much for granted, but were so novel then. Now we are told

> That Nature ne'er deserts the wise and pure;
> No plot so narrow, be but Nature there,
> No waste so vacant, but may well employ
> Each faculty of sense, and keep the heart
> Awake to Love and Beauty! (ll. 60-65)

Strange that so confident an assertion should be absent from his earlier verse, that an experience that seems so much a part of the poet's life should play no part in his former work and now, all at once, become a central theme, as if it had always been there.

However, barely two years later we find Coleridge writing:

>   . . . I had found
> That outward forms, the loftiest, still receive
> Their finer influence from the Life within;—
> Fair cyphers else . . .[65]

Fair cyphers else? If so, what moral meanings are left to nature? The issue here is not whether Coleridge was right or wrong in this—personally I think him quite right[66]—but rather that the earth which he was to describe in the "Ode to Dejection" as once having been "enveloped" in a "fair luminous cloud" (Wordsworth had already "apparelled" it in "celestial light")[67] was not something Coleridge had ever really seen in this way but was rather something he had learned from Wordsworth.[68] This is a matter of the utmost importance in understanding the relations between the two men and the subsequent course of Coleridge's career as a poet.

21.

Miracles and Rare Devices

IN February or March 1804 Coleridge copied into his notebook Pliny's tribute to his friend Pompeius Saturninus. The lengthy Latin passage reads, in translation:

> *His works are never out of my hands; and whether I sit down to write any thing myself, or to revise what I have already written, or am in a disposition to amuse myself, I constantly take up this same author; and, as often as I do so, he is still new. Let me strongly recommend him to the same degree of intimacy with you; nor be it any prejudice to his merit that he is a contemporary writer.* Had he flourished in some distant age, not only his works, but the very pictures and statues of him would have been passionately inquired after; and shall we then, from a sort of satiety, and merely because he is present among us, suffer his talents to languish and fade away unhonoured and unadmired? It is surely a very perverse and envious disposition to look with indifference upon a man worthy of the highest approbation, for no other reason but because we have it in our power to see him, and to converse familiarly with him, and not only to give him our applause, but to receive him into our friendship.[1]

Years later, Coleridge quoted the passage in the *Friend*, still in Latin, and applied it to Wordsworth. Significantly, this time he omitted the first two sentences. Yet those lines comprise, I believe, the best key we shall ever have to the essential nature of the influence of Wordsworth on Coleridge: "His works are never out of my hands; and whether I sit down to write any thing myself, or to revise what I have already written . . . I constantly take up this same author. . . ."

We have seen the immediate effects of that influence in the long letter Coleridge wrote Southey in the middle of July 1797, where we find a retrospective review of his past poetry much at variance with previous perspectives, and a sudden commitment to the kind of poetry brilliantly embodied by "This

Lime Tree Bower My Prison," sent along in this very letter, a poem which harvests the rich first fruits of his new friendship. In its carefully—perhaps too carefully—elaborated descriptions of the natural world, we can almost see the young poet tramping about the Quantock hills, gathering poetic materials. Of just this period in his life he later wrote in *Biographia Literaria*:

> My walks . . . were almost daily on the top of Quantock, and among its sloping combes. With my pencil and memorandum book in my hand, I was *making studies*, as the artists call them, and often moulding my thoughts into verse, with the objects and imagery immediately before my senses.[2]

Coleridge was writing here of his early preparations for a poem called "The Brook," a project which had in part grown out of what he said was "a defect in the admirable poem of the TASK."[3] This reference to Cowper's *Task* provides us with a link that much illuminates part of the creative process behind one of Coleridge's greatest poems, "Frost at Midnight." It was the next of the conversation poems to be written, in February 1798, during an interval in his preoccupation with "The Ancient Mariner." Between the influences of Wordsworth and Cowper, we here observe Coleridge at the very height of his transforming and synthesizing powers.

It was Humphry House who cited a twenty-five-line passage from Cowper's *Task* and established its connection with Coleridge's great poem:

> Me oft has fancy, ludicrous and wild,
> Sooth'd with a waking dream of houses, tow'rs,
> Trees, churches, and strange visages, express'd
> In the red cinders, while with poring eye
> I gaz'd, myself creating what I saw.
> No less amus'd have I quiescent watch'd
> The sooty *films that play upon the bars,*
> Pendulous, and foreboding, in the view
> Of *superstition, prophesying* still,
> *Though still deceiv'd, some stranger's near approach.*
> 'Tis thus the understanding takes repose
> In indolent vacuity of thought,
> And sleeps and is refresh'd. Meanwhile the face
> Conceals the mood lethargic with a mask
> Of deep deliberation, as the man
> Were task'd to his full strength, absorb'd and lost.
> Thus oft, reclin'd at ease, I lose an hour
> At ev'ning, till at length the freezing *blast,*
> That sweeps the bolted shutter, summons home
> The recollected pow'rs; and, snapping short

> The glassy threads, with which the fancy weaves
> Her brittle *toys,* restores me to myself.
> How calm is my recess; and how the *frost,*
> Raging abroad, and the rough wind, endear
> The *silence* and the warmth enjoy'd within! (IV, ll. 281-310)[4]

House begins his analysis by observing:

> When Cowper moves from the ordinary firegazing to the particular
> matter of the "stranger," the details are so similar that it is impossible
> to think that Coleridge did not have these lines in mind. Both use the
> superstition that Coleridge described in his note by saying: "In all parts
> of the kingdom these films are called *strangers* and supposed to portend
> the arrival of some absent friend"; the "extreme silentness" of the
> Nether Stowey cottage is paralleled by the "silence and the warmth en-
> joy'd within"; both stress the severity of the frost outside, though for
> Coleridge there is no freezing "blast". But the value of the comparison
> lies in the contrast between the moods of mind and two poetic methods.[5]

There is, however, considerably more to be said about the direct connection between the two poems. The passage above is drawn from the fourth
book of *The Task*, entitled "The Winter Evening." Coleridge's poem begins
with the familiar description of the inmates of his cottage all asleep, but for
the musing poet, for whom solitude "*suits* / Abstruser musings."

> . . . the thin blue *flame*
> Lies on my low-burnt fire, and *quivers* not. (ll. 5-6, 13-14)

For Cowper, the poet draws aside from the evening's pleasures to sit alone
by the "faint illumination" of his hearth, whose "*quiv'ring flame*" dances
uncouthly: "such a gloom / *Suits* well the thoughtful or unthinking mind."
These lines (272-279) occur immediately before the passage quoted by House
and were surely in Coleridge's mind also.

The cited passages deserve still closer examination. Cowper describes
"sooty films that play upon the bars"; Coleridge's "film . . . fluttered on
the grate" (l. 15). In Cowper we find "superstition *prophesying* . . . some
stranger's near approach." Coleridge's note tells us that these films, or
"strangers [are] supposed to *portend* the arrival of some absent friend."[6]
Cowper's "superstition" appears in the "superstitious wish" of the quarto
version of "Frost at Midnight." In Cowper "the fancy weaves / her brittle
toys." In the quarto version of "Frost at Midnight" we find the "curious
toys / Of the self-watching subtilizing mind."[7]

Coleridge's mind leaps to early school-days, when the films fluttering on
the grate raised thoughts of home amid his terrible loneliness. And now he
thinks of his "Dear Babe, that sleepest cradled by my side." How different
will the babe's life be from his own, for he had been reared

In the great city, pent 'mid cloisters dim,
And saw nought lovely but the sky and stars.
But *thou*, my babe! shalt wander like a breeze
By lakes and sandy shores . . .
     . . . so shalt thou see and hear
The lovely shapes and sounds intelligible
Of that eternal language, which thy God
Utters, who from eternity doth teach
Himself in all, and all things in himself.
Great universal Teacher! he shall mould
Thy spirit . . . (ll. 54-55, 58-64)[8]

These convictions can be found in several of Coleridge's poems of the period. In the fragment from the last act of *Osorio* called "The Dungeon," Nature is extolled for healing "thy wandering and distemper'd child: / Thou pourest on him thy soft influences (ll. 20-22). In "Fears in Solitude" we find a "spirit-healing nook" and "Religious meanings in the forms of Nature" (ll. 12, 24). And in "The Nightingale" the poet is advised to cease his laborious efforts and stretch his limbs amid the beauties of nature, open

                    to the influxes
      Of shapes and sounds and shifting elements
      Surrendering his whole spirit . . .

In this poem, too, the poet looks at his infant babe and declares: "I deem it wise / To make him Nature's play-mate" (ll. 27-29, 96-97).

How recent and unstable was the vintage of these beliefs we have seen. The sweet influences of nature were surely being powerfully intermingled with the vigorous convictions of Wordsworth. Years later, in the *Biographia* and elsewhere, Coleridge was to attack the whole notion that the rustic had any natural advantage over the city-bred.

. . . I will not conceal from *you* [he wrote to Allsop in 1818] that this inferred dependency of the human soul on accidents of birthplace and abode, together with the vague, misty, rather than mystic, confusion of God with the world, and the accompanying nature-worship, of which the asserted dependence forms a part, is the trait in Wordsworth's poetic works that I most dislike as unhealthful, and denounce as contagious. . . .[9]

In "Frost at Midnight," however, no cross-current of doubt mars the myth of nature's benevolence. Because the "Great universal Teacher" manifests himself in all things, "Therefore all seasons shall be sweet to thee," dear babe. And the poem concludes, in its final revised form, in the series of marvellous images:

> . . . while the nigh thatch
> Smokes in the sun-thaw; whether the eave-drops fall
> Heard only in the trances of the blast,
> Or if the secret ministry of frost
> Shall hang them up in silent icicles,
> Quietly shining to the quiet Moon.

How much this treads in the spirit of the meticulously observed real world so characteristic of Wordsworth's poetry may be seen in the thirty-five-line excerpt from "The Ruined Cottage" that Coleridge copied into one of his letters the previous June. A passage towards its conclusion reads:

> Meanwhile, her poor hut
> Sank to decay: for he was gone, whose hand,
> At the first nippings of October frost,
> Closed up each chink, and with fresh bands of straw
> Checquered the green-grown thatch; and so she sat
> Through the long winter, reckless and alone,
> Till this reft house by frost, and thaw, and rain
> Was sapped . . .[10]

This kind of devotion to the palpable object is one of Wordsworth's fundamental aesthetic principles. Coleridge, we have seen, was really always close to Johnson's injunction that it was not for the poet to number the streaks of the tulip, and though he triumphantly adopted quite another mode of procedure during his great flowering, it was almost wholly confined to the period of proximity with Wordsworth. We should remind ourselves that fundamentally he always believed in the principle he many years later set down in a letter to Wordsworth, in which he gave his reasons for disapproving of *The Excursion*, a passage we have quoted before: "It is for the Biographer, not the Poet, to give the *accidents* of *individual* life. Whatever is not representative, generic, may be indeed most poetically exprest, but is not Poetry.[11] In 1798 Coleridge was most unlikely to have brought himself, in a serious poem, to write of nigh thatch smoking in the sun-thaw, or perhaps even to have noticed such a phenomenon, without the example of Wordsworth's still more particularized fresh bands of straw checquering the green-grown thatch.

"A little *compression* would make it a beautiful poem," Coleridge wrote in October 1797 of one of Thelwall's compositions. "*Study compression!*"[12] That he was himself studying compression is apparent in all the work of the *annus mirabilis*, just beginning when he offered this sage advice. And it is "compression" which establishes the decisive difference between Cowper and Coleridge in the respective molds each gives his wandering thoughts in solitude on a cold winter's night. Coleridge must have had Cowper's poem more than vaguely in mind when he wrote "Frost at Midnight," for just a few weeks after finishing it he quoted thirteen lines from the fifth book of

The Task in a letter to his brother George, which included also some eighteen lines from "The Ruined Cottage," thus in one letter quoting extensively from the two poets who most decisively stand behind his own great poem.[13] "The Winter Evening" contains the elements of "Frost at Midnight" writ large and loose. Compression forms no part of Cowper's blank-verse landscape. And because "The Winter Evening" rambles through some eight hundred lines, Coleridge's larger debts to it have been overlooked. Far more than verbal similarity is involved. Even at this level there is more than House saw, was interested in, or cared to specify. In Coleridge's superb line, "The Frost performs its secret ministry," and creates "silent icicles." In Cowper the change being wrought by the snowfall is "silently perform'd" (l. 23). Coleridge can hear the descending drops "only in the trances of the blast" (l. 71). In Cowper there is both a "freezing blast," and a "chilling blast" (ll. 303, 331). Coleridge's use of the key word here, "*blast*," seems unlikely to be accidental.

But these parallels still do not exhaust the comparison. The whole last half of "The Winter Evening" contrasts the life of the town and the country, the central polarity of "Frost at Midnight." "Hail, rural life!" Cowper cries (l. 783),[14] extolling its virtues and bewailing the evil of cities, in which the heart of man still stirs for its natural home:

> What are the casements lin'd with creeping herbs,
> The prouder sashes fronted with a rage
> Of orange, myrtle, or the fragrant weed,
> The Frenchman's darling? are they not all proofs
> That man, immur'd in cities, still retains
> His inborn inextinguishable thirst
> Of rural scenes, compensating his loss
> By supplemental shifts, the best he may? (ll. 762-769)

"Frost at Midnight," then, reveals Coleridge as complete master of his synthesizing powers and in full control of poetic form. The major elements of Cowper's eight hundred lines are here compressed to a bare seventy-four lines, enriched with more concrete images and at every point enhanced by a pervasive sense of form, so lacking in Cowper. "Frost at Midnight" may be Coleridge's most successfully realized poem, the one that most fully exhausts its material and leaves the mind most satisfied. Here, more than in any other "conversation poem" ("This Lime Tree Bower My Prison" would be its only rival), he has achieved a perfect harmony of forces. From the beautifully described opening sequence the mind shifts naturally to memories of a lonely youth, thence to the sleeping babe, whose life it is supposed will be happier, and then a philosophical statement as to why this should be so, which grows naturally out of the situation, and at last a serene conclusion which brings the reader back to the opening sequence of the frost's secret ministry. And through all this, the mind's awareness of its own leaps and associations is objectified by the freaks and flaps of the dancing flames on the hearth.

By comparison, the creative process seen in "Lewti" is much less interesting, though we have four successive drafts to guide us, in addition to the early Wordsworth poem that provided the original foundation. Despite occasional charms, "Lewti" is an artificial and somewhat saccharine performance, of value in the study of Coleridge's art primarily because its stages of elaboration are so easy to follow. Without pretending to have unraveled the rainbow web of the creative act, we can at least accept with a certain confidence that "Lewti" and "Frost at Midnight" are paradigmatic of many of the poems of the great period. The skillful and intermittently inspired lapidary resetting stones, both precious and dross, culled from the poetic landscapes of many lands and ages, is not descriptive solely of the years of apprenticeship. The procedures characteristic of Coleridge's early years continue, though with strikingly superior results, into the *annus mirabilis*, certainly with respect to that small group of works he designated as "conversation poems." Coleridge twice referred to this aspect of his *modus operandi* in the important letter to Southey of July 1797. Of a passage in his recent poem "To the Rev. George Coleridge," he gave it as a fault that "the metaphor on the diverse sorts of friendship is *hunted down*," and he described, clearly with himself in mind, the young poet who "has such a high idea, of what Poetry ought to be, that he cannot conceive that such things as his natural emotions may be allowed to find a place in it—his learning therefore, his fancy, or rather conceit, and all his powers of buckram are put on the stretch—."[15] The circumlocution suggests how loathe he was to give his meaning straight out.

However arduously and ingeniously we may attempt to trace Coleridge in his exercise of "all his powers of buckram," we may be quite certain that we shall succeed only partially. In 1815 he began a long letter to Wordsworth about the latter's *Excursion* with the following significant preamble: "do what I would, it would be impossible in a single Letter to give more than *general* convictions. But even after a tenth or twentieth Letter I should still be disquieted as knowing how poor a substitute must Letters be for a vivâ voce examination of a Work with it's Author, Line by Line."[16] Precisely. We must never cease to remind ourselves that the documentary record of the relations between Wordsworth and Coleridge represents but a miniscule proportion of what passed between them. From the sea of books there is always hope of recovering still a few more grains of fact. But there is no hope of recovering from the insubstantial elements those innumerable conversations and working sessions on the Quantock hills and in the cottages of Racedown and Nether Stowey between two young poets who opened up to each other their hearts and minds and creative selves.

It was not until the fall of that busy and fateful year of 1797, some five months after the intimacy with Wordsworth, that Coleridge embarked on the work upon which his world fame was for so long to rest. Although "The Ancient Mariner" is "infinitely richer than the sum of its sources,"[17] one last aspect of the source problem needs to be considered. It has to do with the fact that in this work, a ballad, Coleridge was imitating a very old stanza pattern, one *not* represented among the scores of modes he had essayed in previous years.[18] That he should have succeeded so wonderfully in his first attempt at this form is truly amazing. This is part of the secret of Coleridge's genius—the extraordinary liberating effect on his poetic powers which resulted from giving himself over wholly to the imitation of a traditional, unpretentious style in which neither his intellectual aspirations nor personal emotions seemed to be involved.

The ballad tradition goes back to the dim origins of English poetry, but this does not explain why Coleridge chose to use the form to tell the Mariner's tale. Southey had already written ballads, as had Lamb, and Wordsworth was to acknowledge Percy's *Reliques of Ancient English Poetry* as a crucial influence on his theory and practice of poetry. But we find no mention of Percy in Coleridge's writings in this way; when he does refer to the ballads it is to emphasize, by no means approvingly, their artlessness. Since the natural bent of Coleridge's mind was sharply *away* from the artistic and intellectual naïveté the ballads then represented, his temporary interest in them would seem to be largely attributable to Wordsworth, for whom the ballad was, after all, central to his whole concept of what poetry should be. Whatever *Lyrical Ballads* may mean (it has often been said, too glibly, that most of the poems therein were neither lyrical nor ballads), it is obvious that Wordsworth envisioned poems like "Simon Lee" and "We Are Seven" and "The Thorn" as modern growths of the form and spirit of the medieval ballads.

During most of the eighteenth century the ballads had, in general, been despised for their alleged "rudeness," "uncouthness," and worse. But in the years immediately preceding the Wordsworth-Coleridge friendship, England had experienced an immense revival of interest in the form, and this had come to a head in the shower of German ballads which fell upon England during the 1790's. William Taylor's translation of Bürger's *Lenore* was extremely popular, and well known to Coleridge; from here, it is widely supposed, he drew the idea for the antiquated spellings of his Rime.[19] In 1796 the young Walter Scott translated *Lenore* under the title of "William and Helen," further testimony to Bürger's spreading influence. J. B. Beer cites the stanzas below in discussing the background of "The Ancient Mariner":

XLVII

Tramp! tramp! along the land they rode;
  Splash! splash! along the sea;
The steed is wight, the spur is bright,
  The flashing pebbles flee.

LXIV

The furious Barb snorts fire and foam;
    And with a fearful bound
Dissolves at once in empty air,
    And leaves her on the ground.

"Anyone who cares to read through *William and Helen*," Beer writes, "will find many echoes of this sort. . . . the exciting rhythms of Scott's version of *Lenore* had intoxicated Coleridge's imagination."[20] That may be so. But in the absence of any evidence it is easier to suppose that the two works often sound very much alike because the rhythms are inherent in the ballad form. Part of the power of any durable artistic form derives precisely from such common pulses and structures.

Far from having any revolutionary poetic purpose in mind when he began to write "The Ancient Mariner," Coleridge was—as Wordsworth's account tells us—acting upon a very modest impulse: to supply a newspaper with a poem in a mode then very popular and thus defray the expenses of a walking trip. For the first time in his life he was to employ his natively peerless and long-practiced gift of imitation upon a tale of some substance. This congruence of events is another remarkable feature of the *annus mirabilis*.

Southey's cruel dismissal of Coleridge's great ballad as a "Dutch attempt at German sublimity" has rarely been placed in its proper context. Today we are not wearied by the drumfire of ballads and ballad translations which had so blunted the ears of Coleridge's contemporaries that the unique achievement of "The Ancient Mariner" went almost wholly unnoticed. (Lamb was an honorable exception.)[21] But for our purposes here what must be kept in mind is that Coleridge was working in a tradition sufficiently well known for one of the early reviewers to remark that his poem had "more in it of the extravagance of a mad German poet, than of the simplicity of our ancient ballad writers."[22]

Because "The Ancient Mariner" is a ballad, it is possible to bypass the influence of Wordsworth entirely in discussing its verbal sources. But to do this is to commit a fundamental blunder. Before 1797 Coleridge had shown no interest in the ballads, and only a fitful and unsure concern with a chaste poetic diction—*sermoni propriora*. The basic language of "The Ancient Mariner" shows, in fact, far more the direct influence of Wordsworth than of the medieval balladeers or German contemporaries. When, in the 1798 version, Coleridge wrote:

The wedding-guest sate on a stone,
He cannot chuse but hear:
And thus spake on that ancyent man,
The bright-eyed Marinere (ll. 17-20)

he was writing Wordsworth's language. (The archaic spellings have no relevance to this discussion.) The stanza before read:

> He holds him with his glittering eye—
> The wedding guest stood still
> And listens like a three years' child;
> The Marinere hath his will.[23]

It may be doubted whether anyone suspected any difference in the *quality* of the language, though this stanza had been written not by Coleridge but by Wordsworth. Throughout "The Ancient Mariner" this simplicity of language is used with stunning effect.

Among the most striking differences between "The Ancient Mariner" and other ballads is that both tale and language are invested from beginning to end with that startlingly intense and half-mystical way of apprehending nature that was so peculiarly Wordsworth's. The supernatural machinery of "The Ancient Mariner" (with the exception of "The Night-mare Life-in-Death") is not especially compelling, and seems to provide little of its dramatic power. Coleridge himself recognized this by deleting so much of the miraculous in his brilliant revision of 1800. Yet an air of miracle and wonder hangs over almost the whole poem. Centrally operative in these effects is the attribution of portentous meanings to the forms of nature, in remote locales, and this was basically a reflection of the way Wordsworth was apprehending the known and familiar landscapes of England.

No discussion of the creative process out of which "The Ancient Mariner" emerged is possible without humble acknowledgment of the monumental work of John Livingston Lowes in *The Road to Xanadu*. (And yet this indispensable study, in so many ways beyond praise, has had—as will be seen hereafter—a most unfortunate influence on Coleridge studies.) To fill out the general framework elaborated by Wordsworth and Coleridge, we must now turn to the range of travel books upon which Coleridge drew so heavily for details and images of every kind in the writing of "The Ancient Mariner." It is true, of course, that he had a sterling eye for what was useful in the works of the many voyagers whom he so carefully read. But it would be a mistake to leave it at that. The focus of that sterling eye seemed to change abruptly around the middle of 1797. A stanza from the 1798 version of "The Ancient Mariner" may serve to draw together these several concerns:

> Listen, Stranger: *Mist and Snow,*
> *And it grew wond'rous cauld:*
> *And Ice mast-high came floating by*
> *As green as Emerauld.* (ll. 49-52)

One of Lowes's many remarkable achievements has been to locate practically every image in this stanza in the travel books Coleridge had been reading. In the pages of Frederick Martens, one of Lowes's chief sources, there are many descriptions of polar weather. " 'On the 2d of June . . . in the night we saw the Moon very pale, as it used to look in the day time in our Country, with clear Sun-shine, whereupon followed *mist and snow.*' Six pages later, '*the Ice came a floating* down apace . . . *and it was very cold.*' " Elsewhere in Martens is a description of ice "*as green as an Emerald.*" In Captain James the height of floating ice is recorded frequently: "We had Ice not farre off about us, and some pieces, *as high as our Top-mast-head*"; "many pieces being *higher than our Top-mast-head*"; another passage describes the ice as "full halfe *mast high.*" Another travel book records icebergs "*green as Emeralds.*"[24]

Now one can readily believe that the stanza above could have been written without the perusal of a single page of the voyagers. Mist and snow and fierce cold and tall icebergs can be easily enough *imagined* as characteristics of the polar seas, and it would not matter to many of us whether ice ever really looked green as emerald. In the circumstances of the Mariner's voyage, a green iceberg—let us say for the sake of discussion an impossibility—would be casually accepted by the reader as a supernatural phenomenon. However, we now know that Coleridge had been reading the voyagers in the months preceding and during the writing of "The Ancient Mariner," and thus the details of the poem are based on factual evidence. Coleridge's stanza is a remarkable achievement. From what must have been a multitude of impressions about the polar regions he chose with great economy precisely what he needed, and gave, within a few words, a brilliantly vivid description.

Significantly, he had not long before been writing poetry, also based on his reading, without any such effect. Much of "The Destiny of Nations" was composed in 1796. In January of 1797 Coleridge intended sending it to Wordsworth for criticism.[25] And here we find a description of another polar region:

> As ere from Lieule-Oaive's vapoury head
> The Laplander beholds the far-off Sun
> Dart his slant beam on unobeying snows,
> While yet *the stern and solitary Night*
> Brooks no alternate sway, *the Boreal Morn*
> With *mimic lustre* substitutes its gleam . . .
> Who there in floating robes of *rosy light*
> Dance sportively.[26]

Lowes gives this passage in a chapter called "Joiner's Work" and shows how directly dependent it is on Coleridge's reading, particularly in Erasmus Darwin.[27] Is it not astonishing that the author who offered the lines above for criticism in the first days of 1797 was, within the year, to write in "The Ancient Mariner" descriptions of polar regions which seem almost to come from a different intellect? In almost two years of writing poetry before "The

Destiny of Nations," there had been no advance in his depiction of such scenes. In a sonnet to William Godwin published on 10 January 1795, he wrote

> As o'er the *chill and dusky brow of Night*,
> In Finland's wintry skies *the Mimic Morn*
> Electric pours a stream of *rosy light* . . .[28]

This is practically identical with the lines in "The Destiny of Nations" given above. We may, therefore, feel that Coleridge's diction and whole approach to the description of natural grandeur, even in describing polar regions, remained stagnant and very stiffly neoclassic between 1795 and 1797. The poet's *feelings* about what he is describing remain cold and mechanical. The forms of nature described, though stupendous, are empty of spiritual meaning. But when Coleridge wrote "The Ancient Mariner" a revolution had occurred. In this crucial respect, "This Lime Tree Bower" and "Lines Left Upon a Seat in a Yew Tree" are far more the direct forebears of "The Ancient Mariner" than the *Reliques of Ancient English Poetry* or Bürger's *Lenore*. It is nearly impossible to imagine Coleridge, before meeting Wordsworth, writing anything so simple as

> Mist and Snow,
> And it grew wond'rous cauld:
> And Ice mast-high came floating by
> As green as Emerauld.

He would in all likelihood have continued to strive for impressive Miltonic effects, so commonplace at this time.

Before Lowes it had been generally assumed that the strange and striking images employed consisted, as it were, of the light that never was on sea or land. Yet when Coleridge wrote of "The hornèd moon, with one bright star / Within the nether tip," he was not imagining out of the void a supernatural occurrence, but masterfully reshaping a passage he had read in the *Philosophical Transactions of the Royal Society*: "a Star appear'd below the Body of the Moon within the Horns of it."[29] Shimmering behind other such images, Lowes has shown, are specific passages from Coleridge's known reading. Viewed *post facto*, this is not so very surprising. Coleridge had never *seen* any of the extraordinary sights he described so vividly. Until Lowes's work it was natural to assume that he had created them solely in the luminous crucible of the pure imagination. Now, however, it is clear that "The Ancient Mariner," for all its supernatural machinery, is for the most part based on solid and palpable fact. Coleridge committed himself to a subject about which he knew nothing at first hand and triumphed.

We are in the presence here of stupendous powers of purposeful reading and imaginative recreation. Sometimes the relationship between the source and its appearance in "The Ancient Mariner" is obvious. For example, the second stanza of Part VI reads:

> Still as a slave before his lord,
> The ocean hath no blast;
> *His great bright eye most silently*
> *Up to the Moon is cast—*

In Sir John Davies' *Orchestra: or A Poem on Dancing*, in a description of the sea, occur these lines:

> For his great chrystal eye is always cast
> Up to the moon, and on her fixed fast.[30]

The superiority of Coleridge's line derives from its dramatic context and smoother rhythm. On the other hand, "most silently" is surely a blemish. In any case, the use of the source is fairly straightforward. When, however, a source is genuinely transformed, used in a truly imaginative way, it is often impossible to assert with any confidence that it has in fact been employed. We have seen how long-practiced Coleridge was in these techniques. With the great development of his art in 1797, the problem of tracing debts becomes immensely complicated by the diversity of his sources and the skill with which he was now able to adapt them. The difficulty is well illustrated in the following example. In a poem as first published in the *Morning Post* in December 1799, entitled "To a Young Lady" (Miss Lavinia Poole), these lines appear:

> The breezy air, the sun, the sky,
> The little birds that sing on high, [later *warble high*]
> Their vernal loves commencing,
> Will better welcome you than I
> With their sweet influencing. . . .
> This World has angels all too few,
> And Heaven is overflowing![31]

In "The Romaunt of the Rose," which, as Lowes tells us, was accepted implicitly as Chaucer's in Coleridge's time, is the following passage. It occurs "in a description of the garden of Sir Mirth," and describes the birds therein:

> There mightin men so many flockes
> Of Turtles and of *Laverockes* . . .
> Thei *song ther song*, as faire and wel
> *As Angels doen* espirituell . . .
> Layis of love full wel souning
> Thei songin in their *jargoning*.[32]

The significance of the italics will, I trust, become clear shortly. For the moment it will surely be agreed that resemblances between the two passages just given are remote, assuming any resemblance is seen at all. In both cases we find birds singing and the words "love" and "angel," but there is no other identity of language. Furthermore, the word "angel" in Coleridge's poem does not occur in the context describing birds but in the last two lines which compliment the young lady. Anyone presenting the above description from the "Romaunt" as a source for Coleridge's "To a Young Lady" would, to say the least, be most intrepid.

However, "To A Young Lady" was dated by Coleridge as written on 31 March 1798, just eight days before, according to Dorothy Wordsworth's journal, "The Ancient Mariner" had been finished. In the latter are the following lines as they appeared in the *Lyrical Ballads* of 1798:

> Sometimes a-dropping from the sky
> I heard the *Lavrock* sing;
> Sometimes all little birds that are
> How they seem'd to fill the sea and air
> With their sweet *jargoning*.
>
> And now 'twas like all instruments,
> Now like a lonely flute;
> And now it is *an angel's song*
> That makes the heavens be mute.[33]

Here, as Lowes has shown, the italicized words clearly relate the famous stanzas with the one given from the "Romaunt." The appearance of "Lavrock," "jargoning," and the comparison of the birds' singing to "an angel's song" can hardly be accidental.[34] Now, these stanzas were written *before* those in "To A Young Lady," and represent an intermediate stage of transmutation. They show that the passage in "To a Young Lady" is also related to the "Romaunt," though now so remotely that we could not possibly establish the point without an earlier stage of the revision to guide us. Between the lines in "The Ancient Mariner" and those in "To A Young Lady" there is a decisive resemblance. The later poem is merely a crude rewriting of a far better group of stanzas. In both poems "little birds sing" in the "sky" and "air." "With their sweet jargoning" slides into "With their sweet influencing,"[35] and the "angel's song" which stilled the "heavens" now suggests to Coleridge, as if the key words were fixed by association in his mind, a pretty compliment urging the young lady to recover her health, for: "This World has *angels* all too few, / And *Heaven* is overflowing!"

After 1798 Coleridge changed "lavrock" to "sky-lark." His extremely repetitive use of images and metaphors is very evident in his attachment to the cluster now being pursued. In "Fears in Solitude," written in April 1798, only one month after "The Ancient Mariner" and "To A Young Lady," he wrote:

> While from the singing lark (that sings unseen
> The *minstrelsy* that solitude loves best),
> And from the *sun*, and from the *breezy air*,
> *Sweet influences* trembled o'er his frame; . . .
> In a half sleep, he dreams of better worlds,
> And dreaming hears thee still, O *singing lark*,
> That *singest* like an *angel* in the clouds! (ll. 18-21, 26-28)

We may relate these lines directly to "To A Young Lady," thence to "The Ancient Mariner," and finally to the "Romaunt."

The story is not yet complete. The cluster of images grouped around the idea of the skylark singing, minstrelsy, instruments, air, heaven, and the enrapt listener, appears two years earlier in "Reflections on Having Left a Place of Retirement":

> Oft with patient ear
> Long listening to the viewless *sky-lark's* note . . .
> Unearthly *minstrelsy*! then only heard
> When the Soul seeks to hear; when all is hush'd
> And the Heart listens! (ll. 19-20, 24, 26)

Here, in addition to the other connections, we find "all is hush'd" where formerly the heavens had been "mute."

Changes in the text of "The Eolian Harp" which Coleridge made for the edition of 1803 include one of the worst he was ever guilty of. Instead of the lovely comparison of the wind drawing from the harp

> Such a soft floating witchery of sound
> As twilight Elfins make, when they at eve
> Voyage on gentle gales from Fairy-Land,
> Where Melodies round honey-dropping flowers,
> Footless and wild, like birds of Paradise,
> Nor pause, nor perch, hovering on untam'd wing!

Coleridge substituted, as if desiring also a more "philosophical" statement:

> Methinks, it should have been impossible
> Not to love all things in a World like this,
> Where e'en the *Breezes* of the *simple Air*
> Possess the power and Spirit of *Melody*!

The derangement of aesthetic judgment extends to the annihilation of those wonderful footless birds of paradise and the desperate contrivance of the "simple air."

Happily, in *Sibylline Leaves* (1817), there is a magnificent recovery. The last two lines are revised to:

> Where even the breezes, and the *common* air,
> Contain the power and spirit of *Harmony*,

and in the *Errata* the footless birds are restored, to be followed by the great passage beginning "O! the one Life within us and abroad!" The whole now concludes with the perfect image:

> Where the *breeze warbles*, and the *mute still air*
> Is *Music* slumbering on her *instrument*.[36]

The whole cluster, we have seen, was more than twenty years in the making.

Perhaps the greatest difficulty in studying Coleridge's poetic process is that few of us are poets or can have studied poetry in the same way as he. On the hunt for sources and parallels we concentrate on words and ideas.[37] Yet one poet may imitate the *effects* of another no less than his ideas or images. This point may be illustrated by the following example. Miss Schneider believes that Coleridge's "Ode to Georgiana," written late in 1799,

> was obviously, and I think quite consciously, written under the influence of Milton's shorter poems. In one stanza Coleridge employed the most spectacular of all Milton's rhyme effects, that of the monotone *o*, which runs through the sonnet *On the Late Massacre in Piemont* with no relief *but the single ay*-rhyme at the end. Milton's rhyme-words were *bones, cold, old, Stones, groanes, Fold, roll'd, moans, sow, grow, wo*[*e*], and *they, sway, way*. The fourth stanza of Coleridge's *Ode to Georgiana*, though longer than a sonnet and mingling other rhymes, concentrates among twenty-two line-endings *those, owes, groans, tones, roll, soul, rose, woes*, and *day, away*, and reinforces these by other internal rhymes —*owe, growing, moment*. Milton's sonnet

> > *roll'd*
> > *Mother* with *Infant* down the Rocks.

> Coleridge's stanza half echoes this too, with

> > O'er the growing sense to *roll*,
> > The *mother* of your *infant's* soul![38]

It is noteworthy that no one before Miss Schneider observed this close imitation of a striking sound pattern from one of Milton's most celebrated poems.

The Gothic elements in the first version of "The Ancient Mariner" are related, of course, to the influence of the Gothic novel. Coleridge reviewed *The Monk* and had read, by his own statement, enough of such works to be "surfeited."[39] Yet even this characteristic cannot be held to be absolutely independent of Wordsworth. Coleridge wrote:

> His *bones* were *black* with many *a crack*, . . .
> A gust of *wind* sterte up behind
> And *whistled thro' his bones* . . .[40]

In the very early poem by Wordsworth called "The Vale of Esthwaite," written in 1787, we find:

> His *bones* look'd *sable* through his skin . . .
> But from his trembling shadow broke
> Faint murmuring—sad and hollow moans
> As if the *wind sigh'd through his bones.*[41]

It is possible, therefore, that Wordsworth assisted Coleridge considerably, either by direct suggestion, or indirectly by showing him his early verse. Even the striking image of light falling in flakes—"the elfish light / Fell off in hoary flakes"[42] —might have come from the description of morning at the beginning of Wordsworth's early "Descriptive Sketches," which "falls . . . In flakes of light."[43]

Significantly, the most exhaustive study of the sources of any single poet's work has been done on Coleridge. Lowes has devoted four hundred and thirty-four closely printed pages to the sources of "The Ancient Mariner" and "Kubla Khan," and more than one hundred fifty pages of encyclopedic notes and twenty pages of addenda and corrigenda. No other scholar has had anything remotely like Lowes's success in tracking down the reading of a poet as utilized in his work. Nor, we may with reason suppose, is this likely to happen, for all the facts thus far brought forward organize themselves around one clear fact: Coleridge worked primarily from books.

Do the origins of a literary work matter? Contemporary literary critics, almost to a man, would probably agree that knowledge of origins can have no bearing upon the *value* of a literary work. Perhaps the point is rather too easily conceded, for then an allied one, namely, that knowledge of origins may have considerable bearing on our estimate of the *artist*, a postulate which is almost self-evident, could not possibly be conceded. If so, a gulf would open between our judgment of the creator and the thing created, which is precisely where some tenets of modern literary criticism have led us.[44] In any case, it seemed to Lowes a crucial question to ask, after tracing elements of at least seven books Coleridge had read as they appeared in "The Ancient Mariner":

Did Coleridge have the seven books before him, or even definitely in his mind, when the stanzas were composed? Did he 'get up' his facts, and then deftly or laboriously dovetail them together? Or were there subtler processes involved?

The simple and obvious answer seems, at first blush, to be this: Coleridge, with that "tenacious and systematizing memory" of his, consciously recalled, through their strong associative links, the various details he had read, and no less consciously combined them. Some of them, that is—the luminous fishes, the multicoloured animalcules, the dolphins (who can say which?)—touched off the train of associations, and simultaneously or in succession the crowd of images rose as separate and distinct impressions consciously before him, this to be stripped of its colour, that of its shape, the other of its phosphorescent light, for incorporation in the new conception of the water-snakes. Now without much question we may at once assume, I think, that conscious recollection and recombination played their part in the complex operations which brought the diverse elements together. But the assumption that conscious reconstruction was *all* that was involved leaves us with a deeper mystery than ever on our hands. The explanation is more baffling than the fact explained. The discrepancy between the most consummate craftsmanship in joinery and the magical blending of sheer light and colour into moving forms remains, on the hypothesis of conscious combinings alone, inexplicable. . . . I do not believe that any conscious piecing together, however dexterous, of remembered fragments could conceivably have *alone* wrought the radiant forms which the Mariner saw.[45]

As Lowes has framed his reply it is impossible to dissent. No one has ever said that conscious recollection and effort are "all" that is involved in art, or that piecing together "alone" can account for anything. All human activity, all human perception and expression, involve unconscious as well as conscious elements. Even in the most seemingly mechanical joinery the unconscious functions. The unconscious participates in the very process of selection which the artist, no matter how mechanical and derivative, exercises.

In attempting to understand the processes of art, and specifically Coleridge's, we must not limit ourselves to sterile polarities. No creation is the result of conscious recollection and deliberate joinery "alone." But the emphasis of Lowes's enormously influential book may be radically misplaced. In describing Coleridge's mental activity he posits a "deep well," into which everything read and experienced sinks. In this deep well, scarcely more than a metaphor for the unconscious, mysterious links are formed between one image or idea and another. Lowes's suggestions as to how these links are formed almost entirely bypass the emotions in favor of the poet's literary and verbal associations. One idea somehow attaches itself to another because of this or that harmony or unity. At this point in his study of the imagination, Lowes becomes extremely vague. The very chapter titles provide a clue to his categories. There is a "shaping spirit," and a "magical synthesis," which organize the "sleeping images" by means of "hooked atoms," and finally "Imagination Creatrix" works its wonders over all.

We have seen how, in coping with the "prosy septuagenarian's" account of his contributions to "The Ancient Mariner," Lowes manages to limit its value merely to supplying the "links" which "knit loose materials" already present into a story, "and fanned to flame a smouldering conception." Similarly, only a few pages later in his exciting account, we come upon the relevance of the legend of the Wandering Jew to the eternally wandering Mariner. The obvious relation has long been noticed: the Wandering Jew and the Mariner are both doomed to roam the earth for committing cosmic crimes. In Lowes, however, the connection comes out this way: "the Wandering Jew haunted the frontiers of consciousness, waiting to be moved towards the light. . . . When Wordsworth proposed for the central figure *whom Coleridge already had in mind the commission of a crime to be expiated by the offender's wanderings*, the deeps were stirred."[46]

Even if the emphasized portion of the previous sentence were true, instead of a highly improbable supposition which flies in the face of Wordsworth's recollections, we would still be entitled to ask, is the elaboration of the Mariner's character as mysterious as all that? The Mariner, after all—and as Wordsworth ungraciously wrote—has no "distinct character." He scarcely acts at all, but is rather acted upon. What "deeps were stirred" when the Wandering Jew that had been haunting the frontiers of consciousness at last moved toward the light? The links between the Mariner and the Wandering Jew are, so far as Coleridge developed them, quite superficial and without much resonance.[47]

Perhaps it can be shown that the poetic process was not so mysterious as suggested. Lowes himself has drawn attention to the influence of Schiller's *Ghost-Seer* on "The Ancient Mariner," and other commentators have remarked upon the interruption of a wedding by a mysterious visitor that appears in both works. The connection would seem to be very much more significant and, in fact, probably provides the best explanation we shall ever have of why Coleridge *consciously* decided to have the Mariner tell his tale to a wedding guest. Below is the relevant passage from the *Ghost-Seer*. The Sicilian, a major character, is telling an important tale. We intrude in its midst:

> "The day arrived, and Lorenzo received his trembling bride at the altar. In the evening a splendid banquet was prepared for the cheerful guests in a hall superbly illuminated, and the most lively and delightful music contributed to increase the general gladness. The happy old marquis wished all the world to participate in his joy. All the entrances of the palace were thrown open, and every one who sympathized in his happiness was joyfully welcomed. In the midst of the throng"—The Sicilian

paused. A trembling expectation suspended our breath. "*In the midst of the throng,*" continued the prisoner, "*appeared a Franciscan monk,* to whom my attention was directed by the person who sat next to me at table. He was standing motionless like a marble pillar. *His shape was tall and thin; and his face pale and ghastly; his eyes were fixed with a grave and mournful expression on the new-married couple.* The joy which beamed on the face of every one present appeared not on his. His countenance never once varied. *He seemed like a statue among the living. Such an object, appearing amidst the general joy, struck me more forcibly from its contrast with everything around. . . . I frequently attempted to withdraw my eyes from this terrible figure, but they wandered back involuntarily, and found his countenance unaltered. . . .* his appearance struck every one with terror."[48]

Can anyone really doubt that this is the literary origin of the wedding setting in "The Ancient Mariner"? (Still deeper personal connections will be discussed later.) Of course all weddings have happy guests and lively music and heaping tables, but the remarkable similarity between the two passages is not to be disposed of this way. For the key features of Schiller's passage are the sudden interruption of wedding activities by an intruder (who also represents the Wandering Jew), tall and thin (the Mariner is "lean and lank"), with a pale and ghastly face. The speaker cannot withdraw his eyes from this terrible figure, to which they wander back involuntarily. Similarly, despite the wedding guest's efforts, the Mariner holds him with his glittering eye.

Now the parallel, particular as it is at many unusual points, does not, of course, account for the poetic power of Coleridge's scene. That is a separate matter and does not concern us at the moment. We are concerned now only with the way the basic *literary* materials got into the poem. Why Coleridge has the Mariner tell his tale to a wedding guest has long been debated. It is not a problem that the poem itself forces on us; the question derives from theories of criticism which require that every detail of a work of art be relevant—usually in intricately complex ways—to the meaning of the work. But the answer seems to be that the dramatic impact of Schiller's scene lingered with Coleridge and he adopted it when searching for a highly dramatic way to begin his poem. It is notable that Wordsworth has not a word to say about how this memorable beginning was brought to birth, although he says that they worked on the opening of the poem together. In fact, the opening sequence may not have been what Coleridge and Wordsworth worked on that first day; they may have worked on other passages. Let us remember also that Coleridge had only recently borrowed at large from Schiller's *Robbers* in *Osorio*, and that he spoke of Schiller in the most exalted terms.

Thus it would seem that we can identify the basic dramatic framework of "The Ancient Mariner," and account with what appears to be a high degree of probability for its famous opening wedding sequence, without recourse to sleeping images, hooked atoms, and the inscrutable workings of Imagination Creatrix. This is not to deny for one instant that the elements of the poems appealed powerfully to Coleridge for myriads of shadowy reasons. But to the extent that the workings of the Deep Well are emotional, Lowes has vigorously eschewed to deal with them. His interest is with a purely literary unconscious, one which deals with sleeping *literary* images, not the experiences of love, hate, guilt, and personal biography; with the shaping spirit of the imagination, not the pull, push, and cross purposes of the teeming unconscious of memories, frustrations, guilts, and, of course, books.

Yet Lowes's theory of the mind of the artist carries conviction by the force of his style alone. "Coleridge's imagination, at the period we are concerned with, was playing, like heat-lightning, about the remote horizons of the world"[49] is a fair example of the way Lowes pictures the poet's mental activity. We are told that, for Coleridge, "the pages of books had dissolved into a streaming interplay of images. And the central core of this study lies in the implications of that fact."[50] But it is not a "fact" that the pages of the many books Coleridge had read had "dissolved into a streaming interplay of images," in the sense that Lowes means. We have already considered much important evidence bearing on how he accumulated materials for his poetry and to what extent he was consciously aware of the uses to which he was putting his gathered materials.

It is significant that in early April 1797, just a couple of months before the great period began, Coleridge wrote to Cottle: "I should not think of devoting less than 20 years to an Epic Poem. *Ten to collect materials* and warm my mind with universal science." He then set down a breathtaking list of the subjects he would explore, concluding with "Travels, Voyages and Histories. So I would spend ten years—the next five to the composition of the poem—and the five last to the correction of it."[51] This is a most revealing utterance. Coleridge would give twice as much time to "collecting materials" as to writing the poem or its "correction."

In a valuable discussion bearing upon this subject, R. C. Bald cites two revealing entries from Coleridge's journals. The first was written on 26 October 1803: "Sadly do I need to have my Imagination enriched with appropriate Images & Shapes. / Read Architecture, & Ichthyology." The second was written "at least six years later": "To read most carefully for the purposes of Poetry Sir W. H.'s Account of the Earthquakes &c in the New Annual Register, 1783—or Phil. Trans. 73rd Vol."[52] In "The Ancient Mariner" and "Christabel," as Lowes and Nethercot have shown, the *Philosophical Transactions of the Royal Society* played important parts.[53]

Bald justly emphasizes that these journal entries, though written after "The Ancient Mariner,"

immediately suggest that the reading chronicled in *The Road to Xanadu* was not the desultory reading of an all-curious mind, with no definite plan or purpose in view; they suggest that Purchas and Captain Cook and Bruce, even Priestley on *Optics*, and the *Philosophical Transactions of the Royal Society*, were all "read most carefully for the purposes of Poetry."[54]

As to the recondite character of Coleridge's reading, "it must not be forgotten that this reading was part of a consciously formed plan"; also, *The Road to Xanadu*, "perhaps merely because he [Lowes] underestimated the stupidity of at least one reader . . . leaves the impression that many, if not most, of the finest effects of *The Ancient Mariner*, in a large part at least, owe their being to the workings of the subconscious—to 'the potency of the Well,' as he calls it." While granting that Coleridge may not have been aware of the extent to which all of his reading had contributed to a given passage—in this case the description of the water snakes is under discussion—yet, "he *must* have been conscious that he was reproducing in the poem impressions which had originally been created in his mind by the narratives of the voyagers."

Bald reminds us that one of the defects Wordsworth found in the poem was that "the imagery is somewhat too laboriously accumulated." Though Wordsworth's criticism "has never been taken seriously because of the apparent ease and perfection of *The Ancient Mariner* . . . yet it certainly records that Wordsworth's impression was not one of an almost spontaneous welling-up of imagery such as *The Road to Xanadu* suggests." We may perhaps go further and say that he was in a position to *know* that a "spontaneous welling-up of imagery" had not been the case for, as Bald immediately emphasizes, he "had been a spectator, almost a partner, of the throes of its production from the afternoon of 13 November 1797, when the poem was planned and begun, until the afternoon of 23 March 1798, when Coleridge 'brought his ballad finished.' "[55]

It is a most curious fact that Lowes almost never states unequivocally when he thinks Coleridge was consciously remembering and when the unconscious was at work. The overwhelming impression *The Road to Xanadu* leaves is that no "joiner's work" functioned in the poem but that everything beautiful had been wrought by "magical synthesis" of "the shaping spirit" in the "deep well."

A widespread Longinian prejudice concerning the mental processes at work in creation bedevils this subject. It somehow seems to denigrate art or reduce it to mechanism to suggest that an impressive effect was moulded with cold deliberation. "Again and again I must repeat," Wordsworth wrote in 1831, when the forces of neoclassicism were in full retreat, "that the composition of verse is infinitely more of an *art* than men are prepared to believe; and absolute success in it depends upon innumerable minutiae. . . ."[56] Many readers do not listen with patience to testimony like this, even when it comes from a practicing poet.

It would be absurd to deny the incalculable influence of the unconscious in all human affairs, and it may be that much of the power of art, so often utterly mysterious, derives from unconscious sources. But we need not be intimidated into granting that Coleridge's magnificent use of his reading, and especially the technical brilliance of "The Ancient Mariner," were processes basically carried on beyond the range of his awareness.

"The Ancient Mariner" was written over a period of four months. Coleridge could not have supposed when he was describing things he had never personally seen that he was conjuring them out of the void. When he wrote of green icebergs and a star within the tips of a hornéd moon, he was calling upon books either before him, or notes taken from such (as is so often the case in his notebooks), or searching his memory. He was probably always consciously on the hunt for materials which might be useful to him. There is no reason to be judgmental. Whether an artist borrows from books or from life is, in itself, irrelevant. In practice, however, it usually matters a great deal.

Evidence abounds showing how aware Coleridge was of this problem. In January 1798, in the very midst of his greatest period as a poet, he praised Monk Lewis for the "naturalness" of his poetry, "his own, & not imitated." As to Lewis' play *The Castle Spectre*, "The whole plot, machinery, & incident are borrowed—the play is a mere patchwork of plagiarisms."[57] In 1814, in a revealing passage which has not been sufficiently noticed, Coleridge wrote:

> From the time of Pope's translation of Homer, inclusive, so countless have been the poetic metamorphoses of almost all possible thoughts and connections of thought, that it is scarcely practicable for a man to write in the ornamented style on any subject without finding his poem, against his will and without his previous consciousness, a cento of lines that had pre-existed in other works; and this it is which makes poetry so very difficult, because so very easy, in the present day. I myself have for many years past given it up in despair.[58]

Perhaps, in some sense, he was a victim of his capacious memory. For if he wanted to describe the feelings of a man pursued by some dread, there was a passage from Dante or Blair available to him, and so forth. His mind seems to have been a vast card catalogue of images and metaphors, certainly a great many deliberately gathered from his reading. And they seemed continually to obtrude upon his own more personal responses to life. I think this goes far to explain the repetitiveness of many of his images, and why he was regularly so dependent upon books in order to write.

In coming to an understanding of Coleridge's achievement in the *annus mirabilis* we must, if we are to build upon a solid foundation, begin with his sources. Despite the voluminous proliferation of studies on the subject, we cannot confidently declare that such research is complete, or even that all Coleridge's major sources have been found. In recent years, for example, sweeping claims have been made about the origins of several of his major poems which, if true, would drastically alter our present views.[59] Of vastly more aesthetic consequence, we must try to account for the immensely superior *quality* of his verse during the brief months of 1797-98. As has been suggested, the presence of Wordsworth has been insufficiently emphasized. Of course this is not to imply that he wrote Coleridge's poems; but his direct hand in them is very much greater than has been supposed.

Many years later Coleridge wrote to a young friend, "If in a poem of 500 lines B. was known to have been assisted in 5 by his friend, A, it would in the verdict of credulous Malignity be soon altered from 005 to 500."[60] Yet we need be neither credulous nor malign to believe that Wordsworth's friendship was infinitely more valuable to Coleridge as a poet than ten lifetimes of diligent reading could have been. T. S. Eliot made the suggestive remark that without the example of Wordsworth, Coleridge would not have worked out his own poetry.[61]

Wordsworth possessed perhaps the finest poetic intellect England had produced since Milton, and this intellect listened attentively to Coleridge's recitations of "The Ancient Mariner" from its genesis to completion. Coleridge called him "a strict & almost severe critic."[62] Let us keep in mind their several collaborations, mutual enthusiasm, and often daily meetings. Coleridge was a man who welcomed the comment and suggestions of his friends, a habit which, in itself, is unexceptional.[63] It may well be imagined that he sought out Wordsworth's advice at every opportunity, solicited his opinion and criticism in scores of ways. Wordsworth himself may have had no idea of how much he was contributing to Coleridge's poems. In Germany, for example, Coleridge received from him the poem "Influence of Natural Objects" in a letter. In a description of ice skating Wordsworth wrote:

> The leafless *trees* and every *icy* crag
> *Tinkled* like iron; while far distant hills
> Into the tumult sent an alien *sound*
> Of *melancholy, not* unnoticed . . .[64]

Shortly thereafter Coleridge wrote his wife of the "pleasing circumstances" of "skating." Among them was "the *melancholy* undulating *sound* from the Skate *not* without variety; & when very many are skating together, the sounds and the noises give an imp[ulse to] the *icy Trees,* & the woods all round the lake *tinkle!*"[65] Lowes asserts in connection with these two passages that "recollection was again flowing in upon the impulses of immediate perception."[66] How much "immediate perception" there was is debatable. The key words in Coleridge's description come from Wordsworth. Since Wordsworth's poetic descriptions could be thus turned into prose by Coleridge, could not his observations and reflections during their many walks and excursions together have been turned into poetry by Coleridge? Wordsworth in such a case might have no conception of the degree to which he was contributing to his friend's poetry.

When Coleridge was in Germany he wrote to Thomas Poole, in the same letter which included the borrowed "Home-Sick": "my poor Muse is quite gone—perhaps, she may return & meet me at Stowey."[67] Could this not have been at least an unconscious recognition that the Muse who resided at Stowey was Wordsworth?[68] On 17 September 1800, soon after finishing "Christabel," Coleridge wrote: "Every line has been produced by me with labor-pangs. I abandon Poetry altogether—I leave the higher & deeper Kinds to Wordsworth, the delightful, popular, & simply dignified to Southey."[69] Three weeks later, apparently now resolved on a career as a metaphysician, he wrote Humphry Davy that he did not have a high opinion of "Christabel": "I would rather have written Ruth, and Nature's Lady than a million such poems."[70] Taking into account the many psychic strains he was then suffering, it is still very hard to account for this opinion purely on the grounds of temporary depression. Why should he have preferred to write one "Ruth" than a million poems like "Christabel"? Part of the answer is, of course, that he saw "Ruth" as one of the building blocks with which Wordsworth was erecting a great philosophical edifice. "Christabel," by comparison, was supposedly but a "common faery tale," as he put it in *Biographia Literaria*. But the main rent in his self-image as a poet, through which his confidence was draining, resulted from the agonizing strains of creation.

One of Coleridge's nephews recorded a conversation he had with Wordsworth in 1836:

He [Wordsworth] very much repeatedly regretted that my uncle had written so little verse. . . . He attributed, in part, his writing so little, to the extreme care and labour which he applied in elaborating his metres. He said, that when he was intent on a new experiment in metre, the time and labour he bestowed were inconceivable.[71]

"Christabel" had been brought forth with "labor pains" and left a fragment. There could have been little personal satisfaction for Coleridge in such a process, given his compelling need to be thought of as one from whom poetry flowed spontaneously. In December 1796 Lamb wrote him: "At length I have done with verse making. Not that I relish other people's poetry less,—theirs comes from 'em without effort, mine is the difficult operation of a brain scanty of ideas."[72] Coleridge must have read these lines with a certain bitterness. Lamb and others may have been convinced that his verse came from him "without effort"—he had in past years gone to extremes to convince his friends of precisely this—but he himself knew that writing poetry was too often an agonizing ordeal, the accumulation of materials laborious, and the resistence of the poetic medium increasingly heavy.

In October 1800 he wrote to Poole about "all the hell of an Author. I wish, I had been a Tanner." In December he wrote this revealing passage to Thelwall: "As to Poetry, I have altogether abandoned it, *being convinced that I never had the essentials of poetic Genius, & that I mistook a strong desire for original power.*" Two days later he wrote that Wordsworth was "a great, a true Poet—I am only a kind of a Metaphysician."[73]

On 25 March 1801 he wrote to Godwin: "If I die, and the Booksellers will give you any thing for my Life, be sure to say—'Wordsworth descended on him, like the Γνῶθι σεαυτόν (know thyself) from Heaven; by shewing to him what true Poetry was, he made him know, that he himself was no Poet'."[74] On 1 August 1803 he confessed to Southey that in him there had been "an instinct to have my power proved to me by transient evidences, arising from an inward feeling of weakness, both the one & other working in me unconsciously. . . ." Finally:

> A sense of weakness—a haunting sense, that I was an herbaceous Plant, as large as a large Tree, with a Trunk of the same Girth, & Branches as large & shadowing—but with *pith within* the Trunk, not heart of Wood /—that I had *power* not *strength*—an involuntary Imposter— that I had no real Genius, no real Depth / — / This on my honor is as fair a statement of my habitual Haunting, as I could give before the Tribunal of Heaven.[75]

Coleridge at once adds as to the "habitual Haunting": "How it arose in me, I have but lately discovered /—Still it works within me / but only as a Disease, the cause & meaning of which I know. . . ." Regrettably, he did not vouchsafe to disclose its "cause & meaning."

If only he *had* understood the destructive sources of his own cruel and fantastic self-doubts, he might have had a very different personal life and subsequent literary career. Yet even here, in a passage which gives every appearance of ruthless and unflinching self-analysis, the cunning processes of distortion and role-playing enter. The self-denigrating confessions provide some release from intolerable inner accusations, but contain their own defenses. Thus, the "instinct" to have his power proved to him by "transient evidences," that is, worldly fame, operated "unconsciously." No tincture of deliberate ambition is admitted.

But the crucial passage for us is that he has felt himself to be an "involuntary imposter." This may be as close as Coleridge ever came to confronting his most dreaded intellectual fear. The impostor, the usurper—these figures, as we shall see, haunt Coleridge's dreams and appear far more often in his poems than has been realized. He must, of course, have often seen himself as an impostor in relation to his friends and public. A man so basically religious in moral temper could not so often have imposed on guileless men like Wedgwood without deep inner distress. His distortions and prevarications would have in themselves caused him great pain, quite apart from the humiliating fear of exposure. Only the previous year (1802) he had published the "Hymn Before Sun-Rise" without mentioning Friederica Brun, and provided an elaborately false preface solemnly detailing the pious reflections aroused in him by a "valley of wonders" which he had, in fact, never seen.

Coleridge's seemingly merciless self-analyses are perhaps never completely candid. What man's are? Guilt and loathing and a genuine interest in psychological processes drove him to self-searchings which have all the appearance of confessions but served primarily to assuage overwrought mental states.

Yet in various statements about his poetic powers, he no doubt was grappling with what seemed to him the truth. In 1802 he wrote to Southey: "all my poetic Genius, if ever I really possessed any *Genius*, & it was not rather a mere general *aptitude* of Talent, & quickness in Imitation / is gone."[76] "Quickness in Imitation"—how revealing this is. How many poets can we name whom we could think of in such terms? Who but Coleridge returns again and again to the distinction between an imitation and a copy, between genius and talent? Who but Coleridge can we imagine making so odd a remark as:

Every one of tolerable education feels the *imitability* of Dr. Johnson's & other such's, style, the inimitability of Shakespeare &c / hence I believe arises the partiality of thousands to Johnson / they can imagine *themselves* doing the same / Vanity is at the bottom of it. The number of Imitators proves this in some measure.[77]

Surely this is untrue and a complete personal projection. Years later he wrote to Allsop: "The 'Ancient Mariner' cannot be imitated, nor the poem 'Love.' They may be excelled; they are not imitable."[78] Again and again his mind runs to the distinction between the self-originating artist and the one who works from books.[79]

"Quickness in Imitation." Was not this, in fact, Coleridge's "habitual haunting"? Was he not tormented by the conviction that an immense difference existed between himself and Wordsworth, that by the standards of the divine afflatus and self-origination Wordsworth was "a true poet," but that he was merely an artificer and "a Kind of Metaphysician"? Tragically, he seems to have thought that between the writing of a "Christabel" and a "Ruth" there was an immense gulf in psychic and creative processes, that his own poem was at best a technical *tour de force* on an inconsequential subject, whereas Wordsworth's had expressed thoughts and feelings drawn from his own heart and mind on matters of central human concern.

What a catastrophe for Coleridge, and for English poetry, that he should have thought in such terms. By 1802, it is true, he seemed to come to the end of the line as a poet if for no other reason that that he had run out of subjects. He no longer believed in the myth of nature's benevolence and religious meanings; that was, in any case, Wordsworth's province. The subject matter of Coleridge's conversation poems, be it remembered, was extremely limited. He had no capacity for inventing tales of ordinary human life. In that direction his sole subject was himself. And the vein from which "The Ancient Mariner" and "Christabel" had been mined proved thin, or else Coleridge feared—quite unconsciously—to descend into those turbulent depths again. And we too easily forget that both "Christabel" and "Kubla Khan" were fragments, testaments to the limits of his creative powers.

When Coleridge tried to flog his Pegasus, to whip and spur, he found himself turning to books, to new sources of images and metaphors. His own deliberate hoarding of bits and snatches from his reading, the anxious salting of the wings of his ideas in journal entries at all hours of the day and night, as if in fear they might otherwise fly away, all this may well have seemed to him proof that he was not gifted with the true poetic furor—certainly not in comparison to his friend Wordsworth, the scorner of notebooks, who believed that poetry took its origin from a spontaneous overflow of powerful feelings. How humiliating all this to the *Wunderkind* longings of Coleridge's nature! His whole future career might have been different if he had had the confidence to accept his own poetic *modus operandi* for what it was. Years later he paused over the following stanza of Milton's "Lycidas":

> But, O the heavy change, now thou art gone,
> Now thou art gone, and never must return!
> Thee, Shepherd, thee the woods, and desert caves
> With wild thyme and the gadding vine o'ergrown,
> And all their echoes mourn:
> The willows, and the hazel copses green,
> Shall now no more be seen
> Fanning their joyous leaves to thy soft lays.

He then wrote into the volume's margins the following observations:

There is a delicate beauty of sound produced by the floating or oscillation of assonance and consonance, in the rhymes gone, return, caves, o'ergrown, morn, green, seen, lays. Substitute flown for gone in the first line: and if you have a Poet's Ear, you will feel what you have lost and understand what I mean. I am bound, however, to confess that in the last five lines of this Stanza I find more of the fondness of a classical scholar for his favorite Classics than of the self-subsistency of a Poet destined to be himself a Classic,—more of the Copyist of Theocritus and *his* Copyist, Virgil, than of the free Imitator, who seizes with a strong hand whatever he wants or wishes for his own purpose and justifies the seizure by the improvement of the material or the superiority of the purpose, to which it is applied.[80]

How marvellous, how quintessentially Coleridge these observations are! We begin with an acutely sensitive intelligence studying the poetry of a master with a concentration and technical purposefulness reserved only for practical poets and publishing scholars. And then, characteristically, his mind turns to origins, to poets who imitate each other. Perhaps not one reader in ten thousand can feel what Coleridge finds as a blemish in Milton's last five lines. Without a profound knowledge of the classics, how can it matter? Yet granting even Coleridge's complaint, note the crucial point he goes on to make. If only he, Coleridge, had justified himself to himself this way, if only he had been able to seize with a strong hand what he needed for his own purposes, boldly and openly, and had justified his borrowings by improving on them! Instead, he disguised his sources, denied influences, pretended to spontaneous composition even when he had worked desperately hard—in short, he acted like a man unsure that any credit would remain to himself if he openly acknowledged his obligations. At bottom there was the Satanic voice whispering that instead of the solid wood of originality lying at the heart of his work there was the smashy pith of the gifted imitator.

For someone as destructively insecure as Coleridge, continual understanding, sympathy, encouragement, and praise were the fresh breezes of creative life. But this he did not receive from his wife, or from Southey, or—eventually—from the Wordsworths. It was not happiness as such that spurred him on during the *annus mirabilis*, but rather (among other influences) William and Dorothy's affection and admiration. Their love and approval served as a counterweight to that despondency which always threatened to pull him into the abyss. Yet self-confidence drained out of Coleridge—to use his own arresting image—like nectar in a sieve. Wordsworth's self-absorption inevitably came between the two friends. He had his own work to do, and he never doubted its supreme importance. Coleridge, conversely, did not even bring himself to publish "Christabel" and "Kubla Khan" until almost twenty years after they were written. How could he suppose that these fragments which mocked his capacity to carry through projects to completion were destined to be numbered among the golden pages of English poetry? He would have laughed with bitter derision had anyone suggested that someday his poems would be more popular than the sublimely self-confident Wordsworth's.[81] The younger poet saw himself, and quickly accepted the role, as satellite, shining with reflected glory. And he was continually distracted by other interests, tempted away from the demanding life of poetry by his more grandiose conception of his intellectual destiny.

No explanation of Coleridge's crisis in his self-image as poet will be satisfactory so long as only conscious factors are considered. His explanation of his failing powers in "Ode to Dejection" is an elaborate masquerade. In the very process of bewailing the loss of his "shaping spirit of imagination," he wrote one of his greatest poems. Marital unhappiness and loss of "joy" did not in themselves strip him of his creative power. That loss of joy was really a euphemism for a state of mind in which self-doubt, not only as a poet but as a man, had become absolutely shattering. The decade that followed the Dejection Ode was to be the blackest of his unhappy life, ten years of almost complete failure and personal demoralization.

Coleridge's most uniquely personal poems are "The Ancient Mariner," "Christabel," and Kubla Khan," and not those, like "Ode to Dejection" and "Frost at Midnight," where he speaks in his own voice of his own life. The intense emotional power of the great triad can never, of course, be accounted for by the study of literary origins alone. Thus our understanding of Coleridge's creative process can only be fragmentary so long as the nature of the appeal those works have upon our minds continues to be so elusive. It is to that problem which we must, at last, turn.

22.

"Kubla Khan"

BUT first, as Coleridge would say, a chapter of digressions. To discuss "Kubla Khan" as one might any other great poem would be an exercise in futility. For a century and a half its status has been unique, a masterpiece *sui generis*, embodying interpretive problems wholly its own. In a sense this work is an abstract of Coleridge's career: spectacular, mysterious, fragmentary, and intensely productive of controversy. The history of the poem furnishes, in some respects, an almost perfect summary of the character and growth of its author's reputation. And "Kubla Khan" itself raises questions of fundamental significance to poetry in general and Coleridge in particular. Before addressing interpretive problems, therefore, it seems necessary to try to dispel some of the luminous mists that have obscured the reality of the poem for a century and a half.

It would not be excessive to say that no small part of the extraordinary fame of "Kubla Khan" inheres in its alleged marvellous conception.[1] Its Preface is world famous and has been used in many studies of the creative process as a signal instance in which a poem has come to us directly from the unconscious.[2] Lowes found in "Kubla Khan" "the unconscious playing *its* game alone."[3] With rare exceptions, scholars have accepted Coleridge's Preface as fact, so that "Kubla Khan" provides conclusive "proof" of the amazing richness of the poet's creative unconscious. Coleridge told the story of the poem's genesis as follows:

> The following fragment is here published at the request of a poet of great and deserved celebrity [Lord Byron], and, as far as the Author's own opinions are concerned, rather as a psychological curiosity, than on the ground of any supposed *poetic* merits.
> In the summer of the year 1797, the Author, then in ill health, had retired to a lonely farm-house between Porlock and Linton, on the Exmoor confines of Somerset and Devonshire. In consequence of a slight indisposition, an anodyne had been prescribed, from the effects of which he fell asleep in his chair at the moment that he was reading

the following sentence, or words of the same substance, in 'Purchas's Pilgrimage': 'Here the Khan Kubla commanded a palace to be built, and a stately garden thereunto. And thus ten miles of fertile ground were inclosed with a wall.' The Author continued for about three hours in a profound sleep, at least of the external senses, during which time he has the most vivid confidence, that he could not have composed less than from two to three hundred lines; if that indeed can be called composition in which all the images rose up before him as *things*, with a parallel production of the correspondent expressions, without any sensation or consciousness of effort. On awaking he appeared to himself to have a distinct recollection of the whole, and taking his pen, ink, and paper, instantly and eagerly wrote down the lines that are here preserved. At this moment he was unfortunately called out by a person on business from Porlock, and detained by him above an hour, and on his return to his room, found, to his no small surprise and mortification, that though he still retained some vague and dim recollection of the general purport of the vision, yet, with the exception of some eight or ten scattered lines and images, all the rest had passed away like images on the surface of a stream into which a stone has been cast, but, alas! without the after restoration of the latter![4]

If this were the only information we possessed about Coleridge or "Kubla Khan," no one but a determined skeptic would insist that the passage above represents not reality but fantasy. Coleridge is so very circumstantial in his account, telling us in detail where the farmhouse was located, when the event took place, how long he slept, and so forth, that it simply never occurs to us to doubt the story, except as it sometimes seems incredible that a poem of such intricate craftsmanship should have been composed while asleep. We do not have any other such instance in all the long annals of time of any other poem remotely approaching such quality created in a dream. Instances of dream composition are quite rare, and such examples as we do have are pedestrian.[5]

In itself, of course, the extreme improbability of such an event does not prove that it did not occur. It must, however, be strongly emphasized that *the claim made for "Kubla Khan" was but one of a long series made by Coleridge concerning spontaneous composition.* In the first chapter of this study many such claims were examined. The results may be briefly reviewed: Coleridge sent Southey a poem with the statement that it had been composed when "I unwarily fell into Poetry," but the lines were actually only a portion of the poem "Happiness," which had been sent to his brother George some three years before; he said that "To a Friend" had "flowed from [his] Pen extremporaneously," though lines and images in it are almost identical with passages in a letter he had written a few months before. He claimed that "Religious Musings" had been written "on the Christmas Eve of 1794," but he had worked hard on the poem for almost two years. He said that the "Ode to the Departing Year" had been "written on the 24th, 25th, and 26th days of December, 1796," but on one of the manuscripts prepared for the printer he affixed the claim that he had written it in one day, December 23, 1796, and in later years he published the poem as having been written on the last day of the year. "I involuntarily poured forth a Hymn," he wrote Sotheby concerning the composition of "Hymn Before Sun-Rise," a poem derived from an obscure continental poetess. He sent "The Pains of Sleep" to Southey with the statement: "I do not know how I came to scribble down these verses to you—my heart was aching, my head all confused"; he did not, however, publish the poem with such a claim. Other poems, translated from German, were offered to intimates as compositions written on the spur of the moment.

The dates he gave to his compositions were very often wrong, and surely sometimes deliberately affixed so as to give the impression of his having possessed amazingly precocious poetic powers. We cannot, therefore, say that Coleridge was psychologically incapable of concocting such a story as he gave to the world in the Preface to "Kubla Khan." We need only read the Preface to "Hymn Before Sun-Rise" to realize that Coleridge was perfectly capable of making absolutely false statements in public, even in pious contexts.

If we examine the Preface to "Kubla Khan" with these facts in mind, we are at once confronted with a series of questions which, while not overwhelming in any separate instance, add up to a disturbing question mark.

The opening paragraph, half-apologizing for the publication of the poem which the author is not offering for its poetic merits, but as a psychological curiosity, is in keeping with Coleridge's typical manner of disarming criticism: the work is really being published at the request of others. But, as to the more important points: at a lonely farmhouse, who was in a position to "prescribe" an "anodyne"? We need not press this question, for no one takes this statement as it stands seriously. From another source, to be discussed shortly, we learn that the anodyne was opium, and self-prescribed. Coleridge goes on to say that he fell asleep at the moment that he was reading a certain sentence, "or words of the same substance," in Purchas. He had not, apparently, taken the slight trouble to check the sentence in Purchas, nor was it so indelibly burned in his memory that he could confidently quote it correctly. Psychologically, this is most curious. A man so interested in states of mind and psychological experiences would, one would think, closely compare the page he had been reading with the poem he had been so mysteriously "given." But he did not. He quoted Purchas very incorrectly, presumably from memory, and this may be significant. Coleridge says he then fell asleep, for something like three hours, in which the vision and the words to describe it rose up as "things" together. He is confident that he composed some two to three hundred lines. Upon awaking he began writing down "the lines that are here preserved." A somewhat mysterious visitor from Porlock interrupts this "eager" writing, and after the interval of an hour, the author was incapable of continuing. Why any man on business would be meeting Coleridge in a lonely farm house twenty miles from his home is baffling. There would have had to be an appointment, and Coleridge could not have been in the habit of meeting men on business in such places.

However, we may let all of this pass. The volume of Purchas is itself of some significance. Several commentators have pointed out that it was a rare book in Coleridge's time. It is most improbable that he would have found the volume in a lonely farmhouse, and a rare folio is not the sort of book one takes along on a very long walk. Miss Schneider points out that *Purchas His Pilgrimage* "in the edition of 1614 is a heavy and unwieldy *folio* of nearly a thousand pages."[6] All these questions would be troublesome had *any* poet written the Preface. Coming from Coleridge, the story simply becomes fantastic.

There never has been a shred of evidence supporting Coleridge's claim, outside of the poem itself. "Kubla Khan," as most readers have seen it, is a kind of phantasmagoria without any significant relation between its parts. "Nobody in his waking senses could have fabricated those amazing eighteen lines," says Lowes of the closing of the poem,[7] and the majority of readers have more or less accepted this opinion.

Of singular significance is the complete absence of any contemporary record dealing with "Kubla Khan." We do not even know with certainty when Coleridge wrote it. It seems incredible that he did not mention this extraordinary experience in a letter to *someone*. Yet in the voluminous correspondence of this period there is not a single reference to "Kubla Khan" or even to an unusual creative experience. Considering how often he wrote to friends, particularly Southey, of his spontaneous compositions, this gap in the record has a most suspicious air. It appears that only some time after the poem was written did he decide upon a magical origin for it. Some of his companions in Germany during 1799 made copies of poems he recited to them. Miss Schneider notes that these companions "mention some eight or ten [poems] that range in date back to early 1797, but *Kubla Khan* is not among them."[8] All this makes the origins of "Kubla Khan" still more uncertain.

Without doubting the basic truth of Coleridge's Preface, some scholars have wondered whether the words which we now have are precisely those written in the farmhouse. Coleridge said flatly that he there wrote down "the words that are here preserved." Though Lowes granted that Coleridge had made trifling changes in the text after 1816, he masterfully demolished all evidence suggesting that variants had existed before 1816. He admitted the possibility of variants, but he personally accepted as truth every word of the Preface and believed that "Kubla Khan" had never existed in any form different, in no matter how small details, from the published version.[9]

The disclosure in 1934 of the document now known as the Crewe manuscript should have thrown a bombshell into Coleridge studies.[10] The document was nothing less than an autograph manuscript of "Kubla Khan," so far as is known the only such in existence. This document proved that *many* variants existed in the poem before the 1816 publication. Furthermore, a note in Coleridge's handwriting at the bottom reads: "This fragment with a good deal more, not recoverable, composed in a sort of Reverie brought on by two grains of Opium, taken to check a dysentery, at a Farm House between Porlock & Linton, a quarter of a mile from Culbone Church, in the fall of the year, 1797." Now "a sort of Reverie," even if we take *this* at face value, is a very far cry from the 1816 Preface, with its account of a three-hour dream and the unconscious composition of a poem which was written down "eagerly." Had we only *this* note to guide us, who would suppose *unconscious* composition? Anyone suggesting that "a sort of Reverie" implied anything resembling the dream creation of the 1816 Preface would surely be considered extremely fanciful. The existence of two contrasting accounts, however, creates some embarrassment.[11]

Careful analysis of the Crewe manuscript seems to throw a flood of light into areas where formerly all was murky vapor or impenetrable night. Critics have generally considered the variants trifling, but that they are really not so will, I think, become sufficiently clear. The first lines of the published version read:

> In Xanadu did Kubla Khan
> A stately pleasure-dome decree:
> Where Alph, the sacred river, ran
> Through caverns measureless to man
> Down to a sunless sea.
> So twice five miles of fertile ground
> With walls and towers were girdled round . . .

Coleridge tells us that the sentence in Purchas, "or words of the same substance," read: "Here the Khan Kubla commanded a palace to be built, and a stately garden thereunto. And thus ten miles of fertile ground were inclosed within a wall." The passage in Purchase actually reads:

> *In Xamdu did Cublai Can* build a *stately* Pallace, *encompassing* sixteene *miles of* plaine ground *with a wall*, wherein are *fertile* Meddowes, pleasant Springs, delightfull Streames, and all sorts of beasts of chase and game, and in the middest thereof a sumptuous house of *pleasure*, which may be removed from place to place.[12]

These lines much more closely resemble "Kubla Khan" than those Coleridge published, a circumstance which may not have been entirely accidental.[13] More important, the lines which Coleridge wrote at the beginning of the earlier version were not those quoted above, but the following (apart from capitals, I have italicized all variants from the standard text):

In *Xannadù* did Cubla Khan
A stately Pleasure-Dome decree:
Where Alph, the sacred River, ran
Thro' Caverns measureless to Man
Down to a sunless Sea.
So twice *six* miles of fertile ground
With Walls and Towers were *compass'd* round . . .

These lines obviously stand still closer to Purchas and even more remarkably than the final version show how Coleridge could start from a model and transform it with the power reserved to genius. "So twice *six* miles" is doubtless suggested by Purchas' *six*teen miles. The reason for the change to *five* is not far to seek. *Five* alliterates with *fertile* later in the line, and the long *i* rings well against the vowel in *twice, miles*, and the English pronunciation of fert*i*le. Moreover, the phrase "So twice six miles" is grossly sibilant and immediately follows "sunless Sea." In reciting the poem Coleridge would have quickly discovered that the phrase could hardly be spoken without eliding "twice" and "six," apart from the harshness of the *s* sounds. Of course, he could have realized that before speaking it aloud, but at the time the Crewe MS was written the change had not yet occurred to him.

The same may be said of the change from "compass'd round" to "girdled round." The particular felicity of this phrase can only be fully measured against the previous line's "fertile ground," to which is now added the marvellous vowel series, "tow*ers* w*ere* g*ir*dled." "Compass'd," of course, came straight from Purchas' "encompassing sixteen miles of plaine ground." Sometime after writing the Crewe MS, the superior melody of "fertile ground / girdled round" occurred to Coleridge, and he did not hesitate to make the change, although in the Preface of 1816 he said that "the words here preserved" were the words he had written in the farmhouse, and he emphasized the total lack of effort in the composition. Words, images, and correspondent expressions had risen up before him as *things*, "without any sensation or consciousness of effort." Can we really believe that the dreaming unconscious conferred upon Purchas' "In *Xamdu* did Cublai Can" the necessary extra syllable to make the mellifluously iambic "In *Xannadù* did Cubla Khan"? Not only did the unconscious invent a wholly new place name, but provided the necessary accent over the *u* to forestall any garbling of the pronunciation!

Similar conclusions derive from another interesting variant in the poem. The 1816 version reads: "*And from* this chasm, with *ceaseless* turmoil seething"; this line obviously caused Coleridge some conscious decision, for when writing the Crewe MS he began the line "And from," then struck out the two words and wrote: "*From forth* this Chasm with *hideous* turmoil seething." Later he reverted to his first idea, apparently feeling that the extra alliteration was not worth the faintly stilted air of "From forth." However, the subsequent change from "hideous turmoil seething" to "ceaseless turmoil seething" enriches the line immensely by providing in one word both alliteration and assonance for "seething" and decisively improving the image itself.

For the 1816 version Coleridge wrote:

> But oh! that deep romantic chasm which slanted
> Down the green hill athwart a cedarn cover!

In the Crewe MS there are two very slight but interesting differences:

> But oh! that deep romantic Chasm, *that* slanted
> Down *a* green Hill athwart a cedarn Cover . . .

The important change here is not verbal but visual. When one thinks of "Kubla Khan" one thinks of *the* green hill, "a savage place!" *A* green hill is much less specific and ominous; "*that* deep romantic chasm *that* slanted / Down *the* green hill" would have been infelicitous. Yet if Coleridge's mind had been dominated by the remembrance of "*the* green hill" he would have written it. Later, when it occurred to him that he could change the second "that" to "which," it became possible to change "a" to "the." Hence, "that deep romantic chasm *which* slanted / Down *the* green hill" in the poem as we know it today.[14]

Still more interesting than any of the above concerning Coleridge's mental processes during the composition of "Kubla Khan" centers on what seem to be two insignificant variants still later in the poem. The Crewe MS (at this point neatly indented), reads:

> The Shadow of the Dome of Pleasure
> Floated midway on the *Wave* [later *waves*]
> Where was heard the mingled Measure
> From the Fountain and the *Cave*. [later *caves*]
> It was a miracle of rare Device,
> A sunny Pleasure-Dome with Caves of Ice![15]

The extreme familiarity of the poem much obscures the implications of these two changes. The "caves of ice," so central and dominating an image in "Kubla Khan," do not appear till line thirty-six, *after* the poem tells us of the "mingled measure / From the fountain and the *cave*." The Crewe MS variant startles us because we think of caves in this poem, and not of a single cave, which is how this crucial image is at first presented. Coleridge had to abandon the singular, for two lines after speaking very specifically of a single cave the poem exclaims about "caves," and in the closing lines exclaims again about "That sunny dome! Those caves of ice!" Why, then, "wave" and "cave" in the Crewe MS?

We can hazard a reconstruction of the technical problem confronting Coleridge. Both "wave" and "waves" are words which he used often in his verse. Yet the concordance reveals that throughout the entire corpus of his poetry Coleridge never uses "waves" as a synechdoche to mean ocean, sea, or river. The word "wave" is exclusively used in that context, as is true in poetic usage of the period generally. Furthermore, it is at least somewhat jarring to speak of "waves" in connection with a sacred river that "meanders with a mazy motion." Until it sinks underground "in tumult to a lifeless ocean," the river is placid, slow moving, still and serene, as probably befits a sacred river.

However, if we assume that the Crewe MS is a fairly early draft of "Kubla Khan," as I believe it is, then the disagreement in number between "cave" and "caves" two lines apart becomes explicable. Coleridge, in keeping with his normal poetic practice, would naturally speak of the "shadow of the dome of pleasure" floating "midway on the wave," when he meant the sacred river. He would then automatically rime "cave" with "wave," in the singular. But this presented a very difficult problem which in the poem *is not resolved*. Coleridge might have written:

> It was a miracle of rare device,
> A sunny pleasure-dome with *a* cave of ice!

in order to get his correspondences correct, but this strikes us as grossly inferior both rhythmically and visually to *caves* of ice. And such a change would have required a later change to: "That sunny dome! that cave of ice!" which, though not in itself intolerable, loses the richness of the long successive "o"s in "dome/those." Yet it would clearly not do to hear the mingled measure from a fountain and "a cave," and then speak of several caves. Had he left it at that, readers would have accepted it as part of the phantasmagoria of the dream, perhaps, but Coleridge, some time after the writing of the Crewe MS, became aware of the problem and made the change we now have:

> The shadow of the dome of pleasure
> Floated midway on the *waves*
> Where was heard the mingled measure
> From the fountain and the *caves*.
> It was a miracle of rare device
> A sunny pleasure-dome with *caves* of ice.

This pretty well solved the problem, but not completely, since the presence of waves on a meandering sacred river with a mazy motion is, at least to some readers, incongruous.

The last of the significant variants is by far the most interesting and powerfully illuminates Coleridge's mental processes while composing "Kubla

Khan." The variant corroborates conjectures made long ago as to the sources of the poem, and at the same time serves as a warning against certain scholarly and critical procedures which are unfortunately fashionable.

All this centers on the line "Singing of Mount *Abora*" in the 1816 version. Early in this century Lane Cooper published an article, "The Abyssinian Paradise in Coleridge and Milton,"[16] in which he suggested that Milton's "Mount Amara" possibly lay behind Coleridge's "Mount Abora." Lowes, confronting the problem of the form of the word "Abora," "unknown to any map, I think, since time began,"[17] used the same approach which had already yielded so many brilliant results. He noted the appearance of the word "Abola" in Bruce's travels, which Coleridge had read, and commented: "No reader of Bruce could reach the story of the fountains of the Nile without 'Abola' ringing in his ears. And 'Abola' was itself amply sufficient to suggest the dream-word 'Abora,' as 'Xamdu' or 'Xaindu' suggested 'Xanadu.' But there was another name in Bruce which with little doubt blended in Coleridge's memory with 'Abola,' to bring about the metamorphosis." That name, we learn, is "Astaboras." "Between '*Abola*' and '*Astaboras*,' accordingly, Coleridge's 'Abora' seems to have slipped into the dream." Lowes noted Cooper's suggestion, but felt it necessary to modify it: "In the sense in which 'the sacred river' at the same time is and is not the Nile, I think he [Cooper] is right; and in light of the facts already presented in this chapter takes on a new significance."[18]

Later, in commenting upon the sources of the name "Alph," Lowes wrote:

And by one of those puckish freaks of the dream intelligence which are often so preternaturally apt, 'Alpheus' has been docked of its syllabic excess, and dream-fashioned, as "Alph," into a quasi-equivalence with 'Nile.' The *artifex verborum* of the dream—witness 'Xanadu' and 'Abora'—was no less adept than the waking Coleridge in the metamorphosis of words.

Lowes then cited Havelock Ellis and a monograph by Kraepelin dealing with the "invention of new words in dreams."[19]

The Crewe MS throws a pitiless light on these conjectures, for it makes perfectly plain that "Abora" was not fashioned in the dream, nor was the word "Xanadu," as Coleridge finally spelled it, minted in a slumber of the senses. In the Crewe MS, where one would expect to find the Abyssinian maid singing of "Mount *Abora*," a singularly interesting double-variant appears. Coleridge first wrote either "Amara," and changed it to "Amora" by adding a stroke to the top of the middle *a*, or vice-versa by changing what had been a thin *o* with a light top-stroke, connecting it to the *r* by retracing the letter with greater pen pressure to form an *a*. In any case, at the time of the Crewe MS he had *not yet* decided upon "Mount Abora."

That Coleridge at any time wrote that the Abyssinian maid sang of

"Mount Amara" clamps home the parallel with one of the many false paradises detailed in the fourth book of *Paradise Lost*:

> Nor where *Abassin* kings their issue guard,
> *Mount Amara*, though this by some supposed
> True Paradise . . . (ll. 280-282)

That "Amara" could not remain in "Kubla Khan" will readily be granted. Again, the holograph text is neatly indented at this point:

> A Damsel with a Dulci*mer*
> In a Vision once I *saw*
> It was an Abyssinian Maid,
> And on her Dulcimer she played,
> Singing of Mount *Amára*.

In the 1816 version the line ending with "dulcimer" is the only unrimed line in the poem. To have left "Amara" stand unchanged would have given the poem a jarring note in one of its most lyrical passages. "Amara" does not rime with "saw" or "dulcimer," and if "Amara" was pronounced on the first syllable[20] the rhythm of the line would have been violently wrenched: "Sínging of Móunt Ámara." To pronounce the name "Amára" reestablishes the rhythmic pulse, but leaves us without a rime.

That all this was apparent to Coleridge is proved by his dallying with "Am*ora*," establishing a harmony of sound with "saw." Why, then, the final change to "A*bora*"? The reason is probably not far to seek. "Amora" as a substitute for "Amara" is obvious. The poet's work is too plainly seen as a disguise for "Amara." Anyone remembering Milton would recognize the word as an arbitrary change from a known place-name to a fictitious one made necessary by mere technical pressures. From "Amora" to "Abora" was a single brilliant step, perhaps suggested by the fact that *m* and *b* are both labials.[21] The changes, simple as they now appear, have been sufficient not only to disguise the poet's *conscious* work, but to bury the trail which might have explained the existence of the word "Abora," a topic much debated in Coleridge studies.[22]

These variants prove beyond question that Coleridge was "romancing" when he said that "the words here preserved" were the words he had written in the farmhouse (if indeed there is a farmhouse at all in the genesis of the poem). It was also untrue to say that "Kubla Khan," at least as he published it, had been composed "without any sensation or consciousness of effort," since many changes were made *after* he wrote the document now known as the Crewe MS. And may not this text be a reworked draft of perhaps many early attempts? What difference does it make? Once we abandon the notion that the words of "Kubla Khan" were "given" in a dream, then the question of whether they were composed with eager haste or laboriously—perhaps at many sittings—is not of unique interest.[23]

The source problems raised by "Kubla Khan" are, if possible, still more complicated than those related to "The Ancient Mariner."[24] And as regal splendors and earthly paradises are likely to provoke similar trains of sensuous thought in writers even very far removed from each other in time and place, the yearly flood of source studies on this poem is likely to continue with the regularity of the annual inundations of the Nile (which Lowes and others have identified with Coleridge's "sacred river").

Coleridge himself, though directing attention to Purchas, said nothing about drawing upon any other sources in "Kubla Khan," not even Milton. Yet he could not have supposed that Mount Amara as a place-name came out of the void. He certainly knew its origin in *Paradise Lost*, a poem that dominated his imagination for most of his life. The Abyssinian kings and Mount Amara appear in the fourth book of Milton's epic, and this book was particularly well known to Coleridge at least from his twenty-fourth year when, as we have seen, he imitated a portion of it in "Religious Musings."[25] Just sixty-five lines before the appearance of the Abyssinian kings and Mount Amara, Milton described Paradise thus:

> Out of the *fertile ground* he caus'd to grow
> All *Trees* of noblest kind for sight, smell, taste;
> And all amid them . . .
> Southward through Eden went a *River* large,
> Nor chang'd his course, but *through the shaggy hill*
> *Pass'd underneath ingulft* . . .
>
>   . . . which through veins
> Of porous Earth with kindly thirst *up-drawn*,
> *Rose a fresh Fountain*, and with many a *rill*
> Watr'd the Garden; thence united fell
> *Down the steep glade* . . .
> With *mazy* error under pendent shades
> Ran *nectar* . . .[26]

These and many other such "echoes" can be found in *Paradise Lost* and Milton's other poems.[27] But if Coleridge was actually remembering these lines, consciously or otherwise, he has surely with a mighty hand risen superior to his master. Despite the apparent connections, it is easy to remain unconvinced that they are genuine. Paradises in literature, no less than in painting, tend to be boringly similar. If the connections explain anything about "Kubla Khan" or Coleridge's creative process, the key to understanding them remains buried in quicksand. And this is true of the overwhelming majority of "sources" which have been found for this much-studied poem. They cease to be interesting because they illuminate nothing. Recognition that Milton's Abyssinian kings kept their issue under guard at an earthly paradise created upon Mount Amara at least provides some link, however mysterious, with the presence and song of Coleridge's Abyssinian maid. Such a link, besides revealing the poetic superiority of "Kubla Khan" to a definite source, offers a clue as to the meaning of the poem. But to ferret out of Coleridge's known or possible reading every stately mansion and underground river that may have provided a thread in the complex fabric of "Kubla Khan" is both a mechanical and futile exercise.[28]

Consider, for example, a letter Lamb sent Coleridge in February 1797. It may conceivably have an important bearing on the genesis of "Kubla Khan." In this letter Lamb referred to Coleridge's poem "The Raven" as "your dream," which may imply that Coleridge had offered it either as a real or as a "literary" dream. Further on Lamb put forward various poetic projects to him. One was to carry out a plan for a poem on the "Origin of Evil," which Coleridge had been speaking of. "Why not adopt it, Coleridge?" Lamb asks, "there would be room for imagination. Or the description (from a *Vision* or *Dream*, suppose) of an Utopia in one of the planets (the Moon, for instance). Or a Five Days' *Dream*, which shall illustrate, in sensible imagery, Hartley's 5 motives to conduct."[29] Thus the prospect of creating literary works in the form of "dreams" or "visions" was suggested by Lamb early in 1797, just a few months before the beginning of Coleridge's great year as a poet. On 15 April 1797 Lamb sent Coleridge a poem called "A Vision of Repentance." It begins:

> *I saw a famous fountain in my dream*,
> Where shady pathways to a valley led;
> A weeping willow lay upon that *stream*,
> And all around the *fountain* brink were spread
> Wide branching *trees*, with dark green leaf rich clad,
> Forming a doubtful twilight desolate and sad,
> The place was such, that whoso enter'd in
> Disrobed was of every earthly thought,
> And straight became as one that knew not sin,
> Or to the world's first innocence was brought;
> Enseem'd it now, he stood on *holy ground*,
> In sweet and tender melancholy wrapt around.

The poem goes on to describe how in "sweet *moonlight*" the dreamer sees "near the *fountain*" a "lovely lady" weaving garlands from stems of "*savage* thorn." She bends mournfully "o'er that sacred well." As the Lady begins to sing of her plight the verse form changes. Instead of iambic pentameter, the Lady's song is given in iambic tetrameters (the basic rhythms of "Kubla Khan"). Her song of sorrow ended, the dreamer prays for her deliverance. The poem concludes: "And thenceforth *all my dream was fled*."[30]

It seems odd that soon after Lamb twice suggested themes which might
be treated as "dreams" or "visions" Coleridge should proceed to dream the
most famous literary dream of all time; more curious still, that this dream
should in some ways resemble the poem Lamb sent him, in which there appear, in a dream, a "famous fountain," a "sacred well," "moonlight," and
"holy ground." Coleridge's woman wails for her "demon lover." Lamb's
Lady, betrothed to "Jesus, the son of Heaven's high King," had stained her
saintly honor by giving her heart to the world. Was not Lamb's Lady betrothed to a divine lover?

Obviously, one can conjure almost indefinitely with material like this.
And yet the danger of urging such connections too vigorously ought to be
manifest. Lamb's letter on dreams, visions, and poems, and "A Vision of
Repentance" satisfy many of the standard guidelines governing source
studies far better than most articles on the subject do. But it is hard to understand by what theory of creativity or mental functioning Lamb's poem can
be *shown* to have influenced Coleridge. He did not need Lamb to suggest
the musical uses of various line lengths; the verbal parallels can easily be
attributed to coincidence, and so forth. The only certitude left is that the
proposal to write poems in the form of dreams was discussed by Lamb and
Coleridge not very long before "Kubla Khan" was written.

If we ignore completely any genuine dream origin for "Kubla Khan,"
many long-standing interpretive problems disappear. The first thirty-six
lines of the poem, ending with "A sunny pleasure-dome with caves of ice!"
can easily be taken as the beginning of the long poem implied in its leisurely
development and extended description of the upwelling fountain. The break
in the poem at this point (and the only division in the Crewe MS) is then
seen as an absolute termination of the original intention. Coleridge presumably found that he could not continue in his former vein. This is Miss
Schneider's formidable opinion; she reads "Kubla Khan" as "a fragment
with a postscript added at some later time when it has become obvious to the
poet that he cannot finish the piece."[31] If so, the last eighteen lines are a
commentary on this very problem, with a bit of poetic licence involved in
claiming to have seen a damsel with a dulcimer in a vision. In any case the
maid was singing of Paradise so sweetly that if the poet could recapture her
song he could speak of that dome and those caves of ice so vividly that people
would call him demoniacally possessed and isolate him as a tabooed object, as someone who had experienced forbidden things.

Such a reading makes a great deal of sense. Without the 1816 Preface or
the Crewe MS note to complicate matters, some such reading would
probably long ago have been widely accepted. Readers have had their critical
faculties lulled into quiescence by the belief that they were reading a work
straight from the dreaming unconscious. Hence any interpretive difficulties
the poem offers, instead of being analyzed, are relegated to mystery. The
sunny pleasure-dome and the caves of ice are not in themselves mysterious.
Coleridge was after all describing the splendid palace of a barbaric king.

In the Gutch Memorandum-book he had copied a phrase from a travel book: "In a cave in the mountains of Cashmere an Image of Ice."[32] The ancestral voices prophesying war need not be taken as any more mysterious than the voices in the air in "The Ancient Mariner." What they were intended to mean we do not know, if only because—on this reading—the poem was never finished. The woman wailing for her demon lover is not necessarily present in the action of the poem but seems to be brought in by way of comparison: the "savage place" is as "holy and enchanted" as ever a place was that was haunted by a woman wailing for her demon lover. The poem does not say that there is such a woman on the premises.

And yet there is something disquieting about this explanation, sensible as it is. It is not just that one does not wish to reject completely so famous and so glorious a tale as Coleridge told in the 1816 Preface. There *is* something odd about this poem, it *is* different from anything else he (or anybody else) ever wrote. If readers have for too long blithely ignored the possibility that the poem makes a coherent statement because dreams are (supposedly) incomprehensible, there is now the danger of skipping over difficulties too glibly by falling back on the explanation that the poem is only a fragment with a commentary. This may be so. But I am not convinced.

If we reject the influence of dream or reverie in the *technical elaboration* of so delicate and masterful a composition, there is still the possibility that the poem owes something—and perhaps something very important—to states in which the poet was not fully in control of his thought processes. Coleridge has left behind many other fragments, including "Christabel," and none of them is remotely like "Kubla Khan," in a number of crucial ways. The absence of any reference to "Kubla Khan" until 1800 is a complex fact. It seems to knock out the possibility that he had ever actually planned to write a substantial poem on "Kubla Khan." Had that been his intention he would probably have made notes on the subject, as he did for so many other poems. But there is no mention even of Purchas in the notebooks until 1804.[33] When we consider the scores upon scores of projects Coleridge entered into his notebooks, it is possible to conclude that the subject of "Kubla Khan" did occur to him with some suddenness and that he never did any extensive reading to elaborate on whatever initial ideas he had. Conversely, had the poem been deliberately planned as a short composition (unless it was intended from the beginning to exude a "dream" quality), then it would seem well nigh impossible to understand it except as a themeless patchwork of unrelated images, carrying no significant weight of meaning, however ravishing it is to the ear.

Be that as it may, the poem does seem to embody a mysterious relationship between its several images, of a kind to be found nowhere else in Coleridge's poems. Nor is there any known model for the overall structure of "Kubla Khan." The ominous romantic chasm, the woman wailing for her demon lover, the strangely intense description of the fountain throwing up the sacred river, the caves of ice, the ancestral voices prophesying war, the

Abyssinian maid, the tabooed youth who has drunk the milk of paradise—
these are not the stuff of which Coleridge's other poems are made, not even
"The Ancient Mariner" and "Christabel," with which it is often linked.

Admittedly, such statements are highly subjective, but they are not therefore worthless. We ought not to minimize the interpretive problems of "Kubla Khan," as so many critics do. Lamb was certainly no fool, but he did
not think the poem made any sense.[34] If Coleridge deliberately set out to
write a "dream-poem" with which to astound people, he succeeded beyond
the dreams of egotism. But he did not go nearly so far in his initial claim
as given in the Crewe MS, where it is said to have been composed in "a sort
of Reverie." States between waking and slumber during which he had an
acutely active mental life are attested to repeatedly in the notebooks.

Years later, in the *Friend*, he tried to analyze the mental state of Luther in
his famous encounter with the devil. He saw "nothing improbable in the supposition" that Luther had experienced the hallucination "in one of those
unconscious half-sleeps, or rather those rapid alternations of the sleeping
with the half-waking state, which is the true witching time. . . ."[35] Coleridge
wrote down many dreams which had come to him during such states. They
are so totally different in quality from "Kubla Khan," as will be seen hereafter, as to render ludicrous the supposition that the poem owes either its
words or subtle rhythmical fabric to dream processes;[36] but the possibility
is not precluded that at least some of the major *images* in the poem derive
from dream- or reverie-states. Far from it. The whole conception of a barbaric conqueror and his dome of pleasure is utterly alien to Coleridge's other
poetry or stated aesthetic purposes, but they have much in common with his
dreams and waking fantasies. The experience of forbidden fruit ("the milk
of paradise") is radically atypical of Coleridge's thematic interests, but very
much a force in his fatal addiction to opium.

Over and beyond all this, he seems to have had *some* experience at a farmhouse between Porlock and Linton which he was to remember ever after
with intense feeling. In November 1810, soon after the events which caused
the long and bitter breach with Wordsworth, he poured out his thoughts into
a notebook:

> If ever there was a time & circumstance in my life in which I behaved
> perfectly well, it was in that of C. Lloyd's mad & immoral & frantic
> ingratitude to me. He even wrote a letter to D.[orothy] W.[ordsworth],
> in which he not only called me a villain, but appealed to a conversation
> which had passed between him & *her*, as the grounds of it—& as proving
> that this was her opinion no less than his—She brought over the letter to
> me from Alfoxden with tears—I laughed at it—After this there succeeded
> on his side a series of wicked calumnies and irritations—infamous lies
> to Southey and to poor dear Lamb—in short, conduct which was not
> that of a fiend, only because it was that of a madman—on my side,
> patience, gentleness & good for evil—yet this supernatural effort injured
> me—what I did not suffer to act on my mind, preyed on my body—

it prevented my finishing the Christabel—& at the retirement between Linton & Porlock was the first occasion of my having recourse to Opium; & all this was all well known to W. & D. W. as to myself.[37]

This was, of course, not the first time Coleridge had taken opium, even against mental distress. The entry is laden with other important distortions. What concerns us, however, is that he definitely does relate the retirement to the farmhouse with an opium experience. Now it is notable that although "Christabel" is mentioned in this entry, nothing is said of "Kubla Khan," hardly an encouraging point so far as upholding the dream origin of the poem is concerned. What is *possible*, however, is that at the farmhouse he experienced certain reveries and states of mind in which at least some of the major *images* of "Kubla Khan" floated through his consciousness: the great conqueror decreeing his house of pleasure, a mysterious woman wailing for a demon lover, the surging fountain, ancestral voices prophecying war, the Abyssinian maid, the tabooed youth. Some of these themes and images are clearly related to dreams and reveries in his notebooks and in letters to intimate friends.

If this hypothesis is correct, Coleridge intricately fashioned into verse the haunting substance of images which came to him from "a sort of Reverie," one or several, with or without opium, in a farmhouse or not (the matter is in itself unimportant).[38] Traces of the reverie involving Kubla Khan eluded Coleridge's capacity either to grasp clearly in his memory or to reduce to poetic form. Somehow connected with Kubla is an Abyssinian maid playing a dulcimer.[39] His memory here is vague, but he is convinced that if he could bring clearly back to mind her song he would be able to reconstruct before the reader's eyes so vividly the Khan's dome and caves of ice that he would be charged with having drawn upon forbidden powers or fruits.

If so, "Kubla Khan" should be seen as embodying themes and images not logically related by the waking consciousness but offered up by the mind of the poet in a state of reverie brought on by opium, or representing the familiar half-sleep, half-waking state, and subsequently written down, surely for all but perhaps a snatch of verse here and there, with all the conscious art and craft of a poet at the height of his powers. The impossibility of finishing the poem would then result not from the fact that the *words* were given in a dream, but that the *images* were provided in some such state. And when the shadowy insubstantiality of the images retreated with full consciousness, the words were helpless to embody anything but the scattered leaves the reverie had left behind.

Such an hypothesis, of course, rests upon the testimony of dreams and reveries actually recorded in Coleridge's notebooks. In any case, the question arises, "What does 'Kubla Khan' mean?" That problem, I am convinced, is inextricably bound up with the elusive meanings of "Christabel" and "The Ancient Mariner," and closely related to submerged and generally unnoticed themes throughout the body of his poetry.

Thus, to draw still nearer to understanding the causes and nature of the immense release in creative force during the *annus mirabilis*, we shall have to set sail upon seas perhaps no less dangerous than those of the accursed Mariner himself; and with no certainty that some kind saint will take pity on the voyager and, whatever his errors and transgressions along the way, bring him home safely to port at last.

IV

TRANSFIGURED NIGHT

23.

Themes

IN 1797-98 Coleridge and Wordsworth wrote many poems dealing with crime. So abundant is the evidence of their interest in the psychology of crime it has been assumed that this concern was essentially a manifestation of a general interest in the functioning of the mind and of the effect of the association of ideas on mental health. Discussions of this subject almost at once run into the arid wastes of Godwinism, Hartleyism, Associationism, and so forth. Coleridge's innumerable later elaborations on the subject provide inexhaustible fuel for this particular furnace of research. The result too often is a pall of smoke obscuring the crucial fact that Coleridge's important poems have almost literally nothing to do with purposeful explorations of human psychology; rather, the crimes are, with few exceptions, unmotivated, inexplicable to the criminal, and mystifying to the reader. In "Cain," *Osorio,* "The Ancient Mariner," "The Three Graves," "Christabel," and possibly "Kubla Khan," appalling crimes are committed against nature, God, or one's own family. Criminal psychology as a general subject is irrelevant to discussion of these works.

These poems have so many themes in common that the sources of their *emotional* intensity cannot fruitfully be discussed in isolation from each other. Thus to speak of the Mariner's "unmotivated crime" is not in itself to suggest anything unusual. Medieval ballads almost characteristically flash with violent actions for which no psychological reasons are specifically assigned. What the reader of the medieval ballads understands, however, is the background of general human malevolence that makes it possible for a maiden to poison her betrothed, for brother to kill brother, for a son to hate his mother. The crime of the Mariner, however, seems to be of another order. The reader wants to know why with his cross-bow he shot the innocent albatross. But he is never told. Only the most primitive auditor can listen to a tale without wishing to know why people act as they do.

Coleridge himself, in an often-quoted passage from his *Table Talk*, asserted that "The Ancient Mariner" would have been truer to its inner spirit without the summary moral imposed at the end:

Mrs. Barbauld once told me that she admired *The Ancient Mariner* very much, but that there were two faults in it—it was improbable, and had no moral. As for the probability, I owned that that might admit some question; but as to the want of a moral, I told her that in my own judgement the poem had too much; and that the only, or chief fault, if I might say so, was the obtrusion of the moral sentiment so openly on the reader as a principle or cause of action in a work of such pure imagination. It ought to have had no more moral than the *Arabian Nights'* tale of the merchant's sitting down to eat dates by the side of a well, and throwing the shells aside, and lo! a genie starts up, and says he *must* kill the aforesaid merchant *because* one of the date shells had, it seems, put out the eye of the genie's son.[1]

The problem of the Mariner's unmotivated crime can thus be seen as only one aspect of a larger pattern of doubt and uncertainty in the poem itself. Why, after all, is the Mariner saved and not one of the many others? He alone is responsible for slaying the albatross, yet eventually, by the intercession of "my kind saint," he survives to tell his ghastly tale. His shipmates, however, "four times fifty living men," die agonizing deaths and go, one cannot be sure which, to "bliss or woe." Surely that universe is morally bizarre in which two hundred superstitious medieval sailors die for their post-facto approval of the slaughter of a bird by another man. And why, after blessing the water snakes and thereby presumably experiencing moral regeneration, is the Mariner subjected to such a succession of frightful trials? And why must his penance go on and on? By what moral calculus is it fitting that he should wander from land to land, compulsively telling his tale over and over again? The more one attempts to fix this problem at a rational level, the more shadowy and insubstantial become the figures of the bird, the daemons, the whole chain of causation. Yet the power of the poem abides.

A completely irrational relationship between crime and punishment exists in Coleridge's "The Raven," a poem first published in March 1798, just as "The Ancient Mariner" was being finished.[2] In this simple tale a jet black raven plants an acorn which grows to a tall oak tree. The bird returns with a mate and together

> They built them a nest in the topmost bough,
> And young ones they had, and were happy enow. (ll. 21-22)

At length a woodman comes and chops the tree down, thereby killing the fledglings. The mother raven dies of a broken heart. The woodman floats the tree trunk downriver where it is used in the building of a new ship. Just after the vessel is launched a great storm arises; the vessel founders on a rock and all souls aboard perish. The raven flies round and round the scene, exulting:

> The Raven was glad that such fate they did meet.
> They had taken his all and REVENGE WAS SWEET! (ll. 43-44)

Thus the raven rejoices in the death of those who had nothing whatever to do with the loss of his mate and nestlings. But the woodman (and there is no indication that he was aware of an occupied nest in the tree) is not heard from again. Of course it can be said that it is not for a raven to make such nice distinctions, but this is hardly the point. The poem seems to suggest some connection between the severed tree, the ship, and guilt, but all the moral connections evaporate upon analysis. This vessel, like the one in "The Ancient Mariner," founders "in sight of the land," and an unpremeditated crime against a bird seems to figure in its destruction. The bird here is "Blacker than the blackest jet," while the albatross is noted for its whiteness. In a later revision of the poem Coleridge added the figure of "Death riding home on a cloud" (l. 42), whom the raven meets and thanks for the destruction he has wrought. The grim figure of Death, of course, appears in a central passage of "The Ancient Mariner."[3]

If we find motive and causation baffling in these poems, how much more complex and shadowy is Geraldine, the character in "Christabel" who provides the major impulse to the poem's action. What is her function? In fact, precisely what does she do? We do not know what crime has been committed, though we are led to believe it was a singularly horrible one. The reason the implications of these problems are not confronted is that it is always assumed that Geraldine is acting purposefully, and that we don't know what her motives are only because the poem is unfinished. But if Coleridge had any settled idea of why Geraldine acted as she did *at the time he wrote* "Christabel," he did not vouchsafe to entrust this information to his notebooks, or in any contemporary letter or conversation as they have come down to us. Neither Wordsworth, Southey, Lamb, Poole, nor the Wedgwoods nor Beaumonts managed to pry any explanation of the mystery out of the usually communicative Coleridge.

Through two substantial cantos of "Christabel" we are provided only the most fragmentary and contradictory clues as to what is actually happening. At every crucial point a curtain of secrecy descends. If this was Coleridge's intention—that "Christabel" should be a mystery that can never be unraveled—it would have been an amazing *tour de force*, but in fact to the very end of his life he kept talking of his hopes to finish the poem.[4] Gillman's biography contains two accounts of how, at least in later years, he proposed to do this. The shorter version says only:

> The story of Christabel is partly founded on the notion, that the virtuous of this world save the wicked. The pious and good Christabel suffers and prays for
> "The weal of her lover that is far away,"
> exposed to various temptations in a foreign land; and she thus defeats the power of evil represented in the person of Geraldine. This is one main object of the tale.[5]

Though this tells us nothing about how the "object" would be worked out in

action, we do at least have a straightforward statement that Geraldine embodies "the power of evil." Christabel thus represents innocence betrayed,
and many critics have interpreted the poem along these lines.

Late in Gillman's book is a detailed account, received from the poet's own
lips, as to how the story was intended to proceed from the end of Canto II:

> Over the mountains, the Bard, as directed by Sir Leoline, "hastes" with
> his disciple; but in consequence of one of those inundations supposed to
> be common to this country, the spot only where the castle once stood is
> discovered,—the edifice itself being washed away. He determines to
> return. Geraldine being acquainted with all that is passing, like the Weird
> Sisters in Macbeth, vanishes. Re-appearing, however, she waits the
> return of the Bard, exciting in the mean time, by her wily arts, all the
> anger she could rouse in the Baron's breast, as well as that jealousy of
> which he is described to have been susceptible. The old Bard and the
> youth at length arrive, and therefore she can no longer personate the
> character of Geraldine, the daughter of Lord Roland de Vaux, but
> changes her appearance to that of the accepted though absent lover of
> Christabel. Next ensues a courtship most distressing to Christabel, who
> feels—she knows not why—great disgust for her once favoured knight.
> This coldness is very painful to the Baron, who has no more conception
> than herself of the supernatural transformation. She at last yields to her
> father's entreaties, and consents to approach the altar with this hated
> suitor. The real lover returning, enters at this moment, and produces the
> ring which she had once given him in sign of her betrothment. Thus de-
> feated, the supernatural being Geraldine disappears. As predicted, the
> castle bell tolls, the mother's voice is heard, and to the exceeding great
> joy of the parties, the rightful marriage takes place, after which follows a
> reconciliation and explanation between the father and daughter.[6]

Now this synopsis, which certainly rounds out the story (however unsatisfying it may be otherwise),[7] still does not tell us what crime Geraldine
committed, nor from what regions of evil she comes, nor what the point of
Christabel's sufferings is. Whatever subtleties this account may hide, we
seem to be dealing essentially with a confrontation between good and evil
represented by Christabel and Geraldine.

Yet Derwent Coleridge, the poet's son, writing some fifteen years after the
publication of Gillman's book, flatly disputes this account of Geraldine:

> The sufferings of Christabel were to have been represented as vicarious,
> endured for her "lover far away"; and Geraldine, no witch or goblin, or
> malignant being of any kind, but a spirit, executing her appointed task
> with the best good will, as she herself says:—

> All they, who live in the upper sky,
> Do love you, holy Christabel, &c. (ll. 227-32)

In form this is, of course, accommodated to "a fond supersition," in keeping with the general tenor of the piece; but that the holy and the innocent do often suffer for the faults of those they love, and are thus made the instruments to bring them back to the ways of peace, is a matter of fact, and in Coleridge's hands might have been worked up into a tale of deep and delicate pathos.[8]

In support of Derwent, the poem itself provides substantial hints that Geraldine may not be entirely evil. She may be, at least in some sense, the person she claims to be, the daughter of Lord Roland de Vaux of Tryermaine, for Christabel's father "kenned / In the beautiful lady the child of his friend!" (ll. 445-446). The baron may, of course, be mistaken in noting the implied physical resemblance. We must also remember that when Christabel tells Geraldine how her mother had died the hour that she was born and sighs, "O mother dear! that thou wert here!" Geraldine at once adds, "I would she were!" A moment later the ghost of the dead mother seems to appear and Geraldine, "with altered voice," cries:

> "Off, wandering mother! Peak and pine!
> . . . this hour is mine
> Though thou her guardian spirit be,
> Off, woman, off! 'tis given me." (ll. 205, 211-213)

Finally, immediately after this passage, and just before the nameless crime, Geraldine says:

> "All they who live in the upper sky,
> Do love you, holy Christabel!
> And you love them, and for their sake
> And for the good which me befel,
> Even I in my degree will try,
> Fair maiden, to requite you well.
> But now unrobe yourself . . ." (ll. 227-233)

Of course, all this may be merely diabolical cunning in Geraldine, but it seems unlikely. Certainly no poem could have been reputably published in the nineteenth century in which Satanic forces have powers superior to benevolent ones, and Coleridge is the least likely of poets to have written such a work. In this apparent confrontation between Geraldine and the dead mother, it is Geraldine who has, as she herself says to the ghost, "power to bid thee flee." Geraldine twice drinks of the "wine of virtuous powers," which Christabel's own mother made "of wild flowers." She drinks for the second time just after she has banished the mother's ghost, and immediately after she drinks, "Her fair large eyes 'gan glitter bright."[9] It is hard to believe that Geraldine could twice drink of this virtuous wine and then go on to commit an act against Christabel the ultimate effect of which is intended by the author to be wholly evil. But this, like almost every other key plot point in the poem, acts like mercury as one tries to hold fast to its significance.

In 1816, almost two decades after the original versions, Coleridge added a seven-line passage at a crucial point in the famous disrobing scene. Christabel lies down on her couch and Geraldine reveals in

> her bosom and half her side—
> A sight to dream of, not to tell! (ll. 252-253)

But instead of having Geraldine, as before, stride forthwith to the helpless maiden's side, Coleridge now causes her to hesitate:

> Yet Geraldine nor speaks nor stirs;
> Ah! what a stricken look was hers!
> Deep from within she seems half-way
> To lift some weight with sick assay,
> And eyes the maid and seeks delay;
> Then suddenly, as one defied,
> Collects herself in scorn and pride,
> And lay down by the Maiden's side!—(ll. 255-262)

Surely it is difficult in the face of this to conceive of Geraldine as a purely malevolent spirit—all the more terrible because of her beauty. Why would Coleridge add this passage—after a hiatus of twenty years—to the other hints, if not to clarify that Geraldine commits her loathesome act—whatever it is—against inner resistance. She must be herself either the victim of malevolent forces, or at least the half-unwilling agent of forces ultimately tending toward good. Yet if this is so, how to explain the complete absence in both of Gillman's accounts— and we must remember that Coleridge lived under his roof for eighteen years—of any indication that Geraldine was not intended to be evil? On the contrary, Gillman regularly refers to her as such. Does it not appear that the poet himself was undecided?[10]

Thus, at several key points in Coleridge's poems, we find deep and inexplicable confusions, a world in which unmotivated or mysterious crimes are committed, in which the characters of the protagonists scarcely exist. Wordsworth was right to say that the Mariner "has no distinct character. . . . he does not act, but is continually acted upon . . . and that the events having no necessary connection do not produce each other. . . ." But the poem is not only not weakened as a consequence of these supposed faults, it seems to be strengthened as if by a mysterious power. The universe of both the Ancient

Mariner and Geraldine is all the more terrifying for the confusion as to whether they are as much victims as aggressors. And just as the Mariner's torments result not from premeditated malice but ominous impulse, so the curse upon him is lifted by an act of unconscious volition. He contemplates the once-loathesome water snakes, and

> A spring of love gushed from my heart,
> *And I blessed them unaware:*
> Sure my kind saint took pity on me,
> *And I blessed them unaware.* (ll. 284-287)

It is suggestive that redemption for the slaying of a bird is here made possible through the agency of snakes; Geraldine, the evil spirit who may be an agent of good, is again and again described as a reptile:

> [She] folded her arms across her chest,
> And couched her head upon her breast,
> And looked askance at Christabel—
> Jesu, Maria, shield her well!
>
> A snake's small eye blinks dull and shy;
> And the lady's eyes they shrunk in her head,
> Each shrunk up to a serpent's eye . . . (ll. 579-585)

Many connections swim into a kind of blurred focus in Bard Bracy's dream. He tells Sir Leoline that

> in my sleep I saw that *dove,*
> That gentle bird, whom thou dost love,
> And call'st by thy own daughter's name—
> . . . I saw a bright green *snake*
> Coiled around its wings and neck. (ll. 531-533, 549-550)

Bard Bracy's dream projects in crudely allegorical terms Geraldine as serpent and Christabel as dove, which Coleridge actually names Christabel, as if to be sure that the dullest reader will understand! And the dove, a white bird, symbol of innocence, thus establishes connecting links with the innocent white albatross killed by the Mariner.

The image of the bird and serpent locked in mortal struggle recurs in Coleridge. In *Cain,* finished the same year "Christabel" was begun, the tormented wanderer (as is the Mariner) comes to a hellish landscape where "the huge serpent often hissed . . . beneath the talons of the vulture, and the vulture screamed, his wings imprisoned within the coils of the serpent."[11] This can perhaps be dismissed as a conventional literary image, but recurrent images in an artist's work are rarely without autobiographical significance, however obscure the connection. In 1804, in a moment of terrible personal despair and self-loathing, Coleridge confided to his notebooks:

> ...I verily am a stout-headed, weak-bowelled, and O! most pitiably weak-*hearted* Animal! . . . but yet Charity! Charity! I have never loved Evil for its own sake; & ⟨no! nor⟩ never sought pleasure for its own sake, but only as the means of escaping from pains that coiled round my mental powers, as a serpent around the body & wings of an Eagle! ⟨My sole sensuality was *not* to be in pain!—⟩ [12]

And three years later, in a journal note on his hopeless love for Sara Hutchinson, he wrote:

> O God! forgive me!—Can ever the Eagle soar without Wings? And the wings given by thee to my soul—what are they, but the Love & Society of that Beloved. . . . [13]

In fact, we find Coleridge again and again, almost compulsively, referring to himself or to personal problems in bird images. Sometimes, as above, a bird of great natural range and power (and predatory instincts) is imprisoned by earthbound forces, or else crippled. The same idea appears in his famous description of himself as "a Starling self-incaged, & always in the Moult, & my whole Note is, Tomorrow, & tomorrow, & tomorrow." [14] The starling, perhaps not irrelevantly, is also a most aggressive bird, as is the insatiably voracious cormorant, which Coleridge described himself as being in a library. [15]

He can refer to his love for his children in an unhappy marriage as plucking out "the Wing-feathers of my Mind." [16] The thought of separating from his wife but leaving his young sons behind prompts this image: "If I go away without them I am a bird who has struggled himself from off a Bird-lime twig, & then finds a string round his leg pulling him back." [17] And elsewhere, a still more powerful metaphor: "indeed I am very, very hopeless & heartless! . . . decrease of Hope and Joy, the Soul in its round & round flight forming narrower circles, till at every Gyre its wings beat against the *personal Self*." [18] When we remember the ostrich eggs buried in the sands of oblivion, and the later self-portrait called "A Character," [19] built round the image of a bird, and the veritable aviary of similar references, [20] we may well feel that deeply personal and powerful meanings lie hidden in the description of the innocent dove-Christabel encoiled by a serpent, and in the tale of the Mariner, punished with eternal wandering for slaying a "pious bird."

It ought to go without saying that repetitiveness of theme in a writer strongly suggests the presence of personal concerns. As Wilhelm Stekel somewhere says, "Every artistic work is a confession." Thus it should not be at all surprising that a sensitive and fearful boy almost completely isolated from his family at the age of nine would henceforth in his life find a potent attraction in the theme of loneliness and human isolation. From this perspective alone, "The Ancient Mariner" would be one of the great poems in the language. Perhaps nowhere in English poetry before 1798 can be found so powerful and stark a series of images defining loneliness and despair. But the theme of loneliness appears again and again in Coleridge's major poems. The basic structure of the conversation poems is that of the poet thinking *alone*. In "This Lime Tree Bower My Prison," the poet is left behind with his thoughts while his friends ramble in the woods and fields. "Frost at Midnight" finds the poet alone at midnight in a sleeping house, and his thoughts take him to his interminable loneliness as a boy at school. The same theme appears in "To the Reverend George Coleridge," where the emotional consequences of removal from family are more explicitly treated. Loneliness and homesickness are prominent in the German poems of 1799. Such titles as "Fears in Solitude" and "The Solitary Date Tree" again reveal the centrality of the idea of separation from one's fellows in Coleridge's work. "Ode to Dejection," of course, is the key poem in this respect.[21]

Any comprehensive view of Coleridge's life and mind must, far more obviously than is true with other literary figures, take account of his wretched family relationships from childhood, and his quite considerable physical and psychic sufferings during his eight school years at Christ's Hospital in London, a locus that appears again and again in his persecuting nightmares. If we fully realize that Coleridge's early loss of the nurturing comfort of home and relatives was far more shocking and permanent than most orphans experience, we can perhaps begin to understand the terrible force and repetitiveness of this theme in Coleridge. Both as boy and man Coleridge was often thrown on the hospitality of the world. This may explain the peculiar intensity attached to the word "hospitality" in "The Ancient Mariner," where the albatross is at first "received with great joy and hospitality," only to be "inhospitably" slain by the Mariner. And in "Christabel" the Baron is wroth with his daughter for disgracing the laws of "hospitality" by urging that Geraldine be sent out of the castle forthwith.[22] For a boy who had himself been taken from his paternal home and thrown upon the callous indifference of the world, who had passed much of his loveless youth in the grim confines of Christ's Hospital—a name whose original meaning is firmly rooted in the very word hospitality—for such a boy, and man, crimes against the laws of hospitality might take on very personal and powerful meanings indeed.[23]

In the dramatic fragment from *Osorio* published separately under the title "The Foster Mother's Tale," the abandoned baby found under an oak tree reveals elements of self-portraiture. The boy grows to be a lover of nature, and then "a very learned youth":

> he read, and read, and read,
> Till his brain turn'd—and ere his twentieth year,
> He had unlawful thoughts of many things . . . (ll. 41-44)

In the same play, Maria is an orphan who has been brought up like a true daughter of a nobleman. The abandoned orphan Bethlen in *Zapolya*, raised by a mountaineer, proves in fact to be crown prince of Illyria, and Glycine in the same play proves a noble orphan also. Surely it is not entirely without interest that Coleridge dreamed of noble orphans (who metamorphosed themselves into himself) desperately trying to prove their true identity.

Wordsworth's "Salisbury Plain," *The Borderers*, and the abortive joint effort of "The Three Graves" all are carefully elaborated studies of recognizable human emotions inside credible, if unusual human settings. In Coleridge's great poems, however, the crimes themselves are no more comprehensible than the worlds in which they happen. The power of the poems seems to well straight up from the frightful deeps of demonic impulse in the human soul itself.

Yet none of this reveals itself at the surface of the poems by more than an occasional flash of mysterious light. On the contrary, dealing as they do in large, familiar human predicaments, loneliness, guilt, isolation, terror, the core of extraordinary irrationality at the heart of Coleridge's work is hidden from us, not consciously by the author, of course. Every complex dramatic invention is in some sense a projection of the artist's inner drama of tensions, desires, cross purposes, and moral censorship. Much of the enduring power of Coleridge's greatest poems may derive from this most primitive and powerful of sources.

Osorio, written just before "The Wanderings of Cain" and "The Ancient Mariner," concerns the attempted murder by Osorio of his older brother, whose place he wished to ursurp. (Both are in love with the same woman, Maria, an orphan raised like a sister in their household.) In the abortive fragment of "Cain," Coleridge tried to deal with the first and perhaps most sinister crime in history, the murder of Abel by his brother. (The name *Christ-Abel* can thus be seen as embracing the two archetypal victims of man's murderous impulses.) Like the Mariner, Cain must pass from land to land, the eternal wanderer, punished by God. The later *Zapolya* (1816) also deals with a fratricidal usurper, Emerick ("O curst usurper! O thou brother-murderer!").[24]

With respect to this theme, let us remember Coleridge's own account of his murderous rage towards his own older brother Frank, a hatred which persists long after Frank's death, as shown in a letter written on 16 October 1797, less than a month before "The Ancient Mariner" was begun. The following passage comes from one of the "autobiographical" letters to Poole, the series of which demonstrates that in the fall of 1797, just as the *annus mirabilis* begins, Coleridge was reviewing his earliest childhood:

I had asked my mother one evening to cut my cheese *entire*, so that I might toast it: this was no easy matter, it being a *crumbly* cheese— My mother however did it—/ I went into the garden for some thing or other, and in the mean time my Brother Frank *minced* my cheese, "to disap-

point the favorite." I returned, saw the exploit, and in an agony of passion flew at Frank—he pretended to have been seriously hurt by my blow,
flung himself on the ground, and there lay with outstretched limbs—I
hung over him moaning & in a great fright—he leaped up, & with a
horse-laugh gave me a severe blow in the face—I seized a knife, and was
running at him when my Mother came in & took me by the arm. . . .[25]

This hated brother Francis died of wounds suffered in battle in India in
1792, when Coleridge was twenty years old. It would be a serious mistake,
however, to confine the recurrent Cain theme in Coleridge to this single
relationship. For it was one of several tragedies in his life that he grew up to
hate most of the members of his immediate family, including his mother.[26]

That the story of Cain had struck deep tentacles into his mind appears not
only in his deliberate attempt to write a prose poem about his wanderings,
nor in the fact that the only two plays he wrote deal with fratricide; the same
story also figures in Coleridge's dreams. Among the several dozen dreams
recorded in Coleridge's notebooks is the following, entered under the date 6
December 1803: "Adam travelling in his old age came to a set of the descendants of Cain, ignorant of the origin of the world; & treating him as a Madman killed him. A sort of Dream, which I had this Night."[27]

When one examines the strange, baffling, and powerfully interlocking web
of themes in Coleridge's major poems, it is perfectly normal to ask what
connection may exist with the artist's own experience. It has always been a
respectable activity of scholars to relate themes, images, and language to
previous literary works. Yet it is a curious, and in some ways an utterly irrational fact, that many scholars adamantly refuse to cope with sources other
than purely literary ones. It is permissible to set down a passage from "The
Ancient Mariner" and suggest the remotest of parallels in Dante, or Blair, or
whoever, for this or that idea or turn of phrase.[28] But should another scholar
suggest a relation between the image, say, of a frightful fiend treading behind
one on a lonesome road, and the poet's known or possible fear of his past, at
once a great cry may go up: the whole procedure is viewed as improper, if not
wholly disreputable, beyond the pale of serious scholarship. Thus Lowes
ransacked with infectious zest the heaven and earth of great libraries for
literary sources but drew up abruptly in the presence of possible *emotional*
ones and soberly declared discussion of such connections improper, or premature in the light of current psychological knowledge. He was proceeding
upon impeccable scholarly principles when, in his lengthy discussion of
"Kubla Khan," he refused to consider any hidden personal meanings in a
work he had no doubt was a dream.

I wish to state with emphasis [he wrote] that I am dealing in this study
with what psychoanalysts call the material content of the dream, and
with that alone. With its so-called latent content—its possible symbolism
of wish-fulfilment or conflict or what not—I have nothing whatever to

do. Even granting one or another of the conflicting assumptions of modern dream psychology, I do not believe that after the lapse of one hundred and twenty-seven years the intimate, deep-lying, personal facts on which alone such an analysis must rest are any longer discoverable, and I doubt whether any trained psychoanalyst would venture an interpretation.[29]

The assumptions underlying this statement are less compelling than they seem. If a man regularly dreams that monsters are trying to devour him, it is not necessary to know the precise, personal meanings of the images to accept the general proposition that the dreamer feels threatened or fearful. It seems a bit odd that there should be such widespread agreement among literary scholars that the analysis of dreams is impossible without the personal associations of the dreamer to guide us, which is itself one of the "conflicting assumptions of modern dream psychology." *All* dream analysis is intellectually hazardous, and the further away the dreamer from us the more difficult is the procedure. But if we consider only difficulties we shall remain paralyzed. Examination of the relation between Coleridge's dreams and his creative life need not be avoided because the dividing line between evidence and conjecture is often muddy. Dreams, it is too often forgotten, are creations of the mind, and as such the dreams of poets ought to be especially important in literary studies, both as clues to the creative process itself and as possible information as to the meaning of consciously ordered works of art. Respect for the unity of the mind obliges us, if we are seriously interested in the nature of Coleridge's creativity, to grapple with the structure and meaning of his dreams.

Until the day comes that a trained psychologist and trained literary scholar converge in the same person, all studies of literary materials from a psychological point of view will be vulnerable to the charge of at least partial incompetence. This charge is no less serious for its being obvious, and often maliciously urged. Yet we should remind ourselves that if formal credentials, however necessary to the smooth functioning of a complex society, were the only standard of competence, Coleridge, who lacked a university degree—let alone a Ph.D.—would be unqualified to teach in most state-supported American universities. The broader the spectrum of intellectual concern, the greater the danger of superficiality. But this is no more inevitable than that professional expertise must always be narrow. Humanistic studies, above all, must not lose sight of its synthesizing ends in its stringently precise methods.

24.

Dreams

COLERIDGE'S emotional life is recorded for us, at once in its most chaotic and uncensored form, in the absorbing series of dreams that he confided to the pages of his notebooks and a few in letters to friends. Our concern will be with those elements in the dreams which seem to have some connection, however shadowy, with the world of his poems or with the general concerns of this entire study. Thus in connection with the mysterious universe of appearances in "The Ancient Mariner" and "Christabel," it must be emphasized at the very outset that at the heart of Coleridge's emotional life is a profound duality between his waking and sleeping worlds. It is not easy to think of any artist on whom sleep regularly inflicted such frightful torments. The intensity and duration of these nightmares are themselves so extraordinary as to cry out for study by specialists.[1]

Coleridge has left us no record of his youthful dreams, but that they were decidedly unpleasant seems likely. The matter is important because it is often assumed that the ferocious nightmares which he began recording regularly around 1803 were a new experience and the result of his deepening addiction to opium. Since these dreams occurred after the great triad with which we are now concerned, it may seem fatuous to discuss them as sources of those poems in any sense. But this argument is only superficially persuasive. The dreams themselves repeatedly deal with childhood, and Coleridge was to emphasize how recurrent was the basic material of his dreams. But even if no such record had been left behind, it is unlikely that anyone in the latter half of the twentieth century would seriously argue for a break in continuity between the thematic material of dreams from one year to the next.

The timorous Ottery child who was haunted by fear of specters in the dark was rarely to know restful sleep.[2] In 1794, when he was just past twenty-one years old, he wrote a friend about the pain he had caused to those who loved him by running away from Cambridge to join the army. Of the attendant guilt he felt, he wrote: "does it not plant my pillow with thorns, and make my dreams full of terrors?" Two days later he wrote contritely to his brother George of his guilts and sorrows: "Images of horror! They haunt

my sleep—they enfever my Dreams!" Later that year he sent Robert Southey a sonnet on Pantisocracy which included the lines:

> ye shall weep
> Tears of doubt-mingled Joy, like their's who start
> From Precipices of distemper'd Sleep,
> On which the fierce-eyed Fiends their Revels keep . . .

Very much the same image appears in a letter to Poole written five years
later: "my mind was thrown by your letter into the feelings of those distressful Dreams, where we imagine ourselves falling from precipices."[3]

In the "Songs of the Pixies," written in 1793, Night is invoked as the
"Mother of wildly-working dreams." In an early poetic autobiographical
statement (1794), Coleridge refers to the "dreamy pang in Morning's fever-
ous doze." In a sonnet written in 1796, addressed "to a young man who
abandoned himself to a causeless & indolent Melancholy," Coleridge bids
the youth heal himself: "O abject! if to sickly dreams resigned . . ."[4]

Other poems testify still more eloquently to his early experience with
bad dreams. The sixth stanza of the "Ode to the Departing Year" is unusually concrete in its nightmare images and thus seems to record personal
experience:

> The voice had ceas'd, the Phantoms fled;
> Yet still I gasp'd and reel'd with dread.
> And ever, when the dream of night
> Renews the vision to my sight,
> Cold sweat-damps gather on my limbs;
>   My ears throb hot; my eye-balls start;
> My brain with horrid tumult swims;
>   Wild is the tempest of my heart;
> And my thick and struggling breath
> Imitates the toil of death![5]

These details, especially the frightful struggles to breathe, are typical of
Coleridge's own later recorded dreams, as we shall shortly see. Velez, in
Osorio, says, "Yes, I am old—I have no pleasant dreams," and Osorio, his
wicked son, later refers to "a phantom of my sleep" and "a frightful
dream."[6] In "The Wanderings of Cain," the tormented protagonist "stood
like one who struggles in his sleep because of the exceeding terribleness of
a dream."[7] Sleep and dreaming figure crucially in the three unique poems of
the *annus mirabilis*. "Kubla Khan," allegedly composed in a dream, contains
within itself another dream. Christabel, in a key passage, dreams "fearfully," and Bard Bracy's dream is a symbol (or allegory) for Geraldine's
assault on the innocent maiden. And in "The Ancient Mariner," at the moral
turning point of the poem, when the Mariner blesses the water snakes and the

albatross falls from his neck into the sea, he is rewarded by sleep, "a gentle thing," and he praises Mary Queen who "sent the gentle sleep from Heaven, / That slid into my soul." It is doubtful that the word "gentle" has ever been asked to bear the emphasis which it did for Coleridge in this context.[8]

His comments on his own sleep and dreams do not become fully explicit until 1803, when his nightmares became a terror even to his waking hours. "I am tolerably well, meaning, the Day Time," he wrote to Southey in September of that year, "for my last night was just such a noisy night of horrors, as 3 nights out of 4 are, with me. O God! when a man blesses the loud Scream of Agony that awakes him, night after night; night after night!—& when a man's repeated Night-screams have made him a nuisance in his own House, it is better to die than to live."[9]

Almost the same heart-breaking description appears in another letter of the same year, with one significant and perhaps intuitive addition:

> God forbid that my worst Enemy should ever have the Nights & the Sleeps that I have had, night after night—surprised by Sleep, while I struggled to remain awake, starting up to bless my own loud Screams that had awakened me—yea, dear friend! till my repeated Night-yells had made me a Nuisance in my own House. As I live & am a man, this is an unexaggerated Tale—*My Dreams become the Substances of my life.*"[10]

Later that year, Coleridge described his dreams as "counterfeiting, as it were, the Tortures of Guilt, and what we are told of the Punishments of the spiritual World."[11] Just thirteen months after this he set down in his notebooks one of its most painful entries, in which he referred to the "almost epileptic night-horrors in my sleep /& since then every error I have committed, has been the immediate affect of the Dread of these bad most shocking Dreams—any thing to prevent them."[12] That he took massive quantities of both opium and alcohol at least partly in fear of these dreams is made manifest by a journal entry dated later that year:

> Friday Morning, 2 o'clock/ 7 September 1805.—Yes, a shocking recollection, that *years* have passed to a man in the prime of manhood/ on every night of which he has dreaded to go to bed or fall asleep/ & by that dread seduced again & again & again [to] poison himself.[13]

The question arises, how do we know that anything Coleridge has recorded about his dreams is true? Since on his own acts and motives he is never to be automatically trusted, how do we know that in the accounts of his dream life he was not writing for posterity and deliberately moulding the stuff of reality into the airy shapes of fantasy? May not his dreams, even when scrawled into the privacy of his notebooks (sometimes in code), be part of an elaborate charade, the ultimate intent of which was to enhance his intellectual or moral image?

These questions, abstractly considered, are deeply disturbing. Yet even the most determined skepticism must falter before the historical realities. Coleridge, as we shall see, repeatedly asserted that his dreams had no moral significance, and since—with the exception of "Kubla Khan"—there is not a single alleged dream that can be said to reflect credit of any kind on the dreamer, there appears to be no motive for deliberate distortion. Coleridge suppressed many of his dreams, or portions of them, because their contents seemed to him too wild or disgusting to commit to paper.[14] That he has left behind so much is proof that he had no conception of what their contents might signify, or the purposes dreams might eventually serve in character analysis. The dreams, moreover, are internally consistent over a long period of time in a way that could not be faked by anyone without a theory of dream symbolism and structure that simply did not exist in the nineteenth century. In any case, the skeptic is obliged to consider the evidence first, and subsequently to decide whether the question of spuriousness has substance.

The whole subject is perhaps best approached through the agonizing document entitled "The Pains of Sleep." Coleridge himself, with excessive harshness, called the verses "doggerels"; our concern, however, is not with the aesthetic value of the poem, but with what it may reveal. The poem first appears in an intimate letter to Southey, written on 11 September 1803. Just before the poem itself, this passage appears: "my spirits are dreadful, owing entirely to the Horrors of every night—I truly dread to sleep / it is no shadow with me, but substantial Misery foot-thick, that makes me sit by my bedside of a morning, & *cry*—. I have abandoned all opiates except Ether be one; & that only in *fits* . . . but still I can not get quiet rest."[15] Coleridge begins by telling us that he does not normally pray on bended knee before going to bed,

> But silently, by slow degrees
> My spirit I to Love compose
> In humble trust mine eye-lids close,
> With reverential resignation . . .

How horrible, after such preparations, the ferocious images that haunt the sleep which follows:

> . . . the fiendish Crowd
> Of Shapes & Thoughts that tortur'd me!
> Desire with Loathing strangely mixt,
> On wild or hateful Objects fixt: . . .
> Vain-glorious threats, unmanly Vaunting,
> Bad men my boasts & fury taunting[16]
> Rage, sensual Passion, mad'ning Brawl,
> And Shame, and Terror over all!

Deeds to be hid that were not hid,
Which all confused I might not know
Whether I suffered, or I did:
For all was Horror, Guilt & Woe
My own or others, still the same,
Life-stifling Fear, Soul-stifling Shame!

The huddled confusion here of guilt and innocence, of uncertainty as to who is criminal and who victim, who suffers and why, seems an extraordinary echo of the morally confused worlds of "The Ancient Mariner" and "Christabel." In the latter's memorable slumber sequence we are confronted starkly with the moral chaos of the nighttime world. Christabel, the *victim* of a nameless crime, is described as

With open eyes (ah woe is me!)
Asleep, and *dreaming fearfully*,
Fearfully dreaming, yet, I wis,
Dreaming that alone, which is—[17]
O sorrow and shame! Can this be she,
The lady, who knelt at the old oak tree? (ll. 292-297)

But Geraldine sleeps peacefully! The question here is very similar to the one asked at the end of "The Pains of Sleep." Why is the innocent Christabel tormented by fearful dreams, while the wicked Geraldine, this lady so lovely in outward shape,

holds the maiden in her arms,
Seems to slumber still and mild,
As a mother with her child. (ll. 299-301)

Toward the close of "The Pains of Sleep" the poet describes himself as awaking after three nights of

sufferings strange and wild,
I wept as I had been a child; ...
Such punishments, I said, were due
To natures deepliest stained with sin,—
Still to be stirring up anew
The self-created Hell within,
The horror of their crimes to view,
To know and loathe, yet wish to do!
With such let fiends make mockery—
But I—Oh, wherefore thus on *me*?
Frail is my soul, yet, strengthless wholly,

> Unequal, restless, melancholy,
> But free from Hate and sensual Folly.[18]

The last line provides one of the most significant of all keys into the labyrinth of Coleridge's mind. For someone to whom sensuality was peculiarly abhorrent, the existence of such outrageous passions in his dreams must have been morally unendurable. Sensuality is a human trait Coleridge not only condemns abstractly but recoils from in physical horror. "More than happy that Man," he wrote in later life, "who has never had occasion or an opportunity for noticing in himself a transition of pure and tender affection for a lovely object into a movement of concupiscence."[19] But from the very beginning, in the very prime of vigorous young manhood, Coleridge's use of the word "sensuality" reveals quite clearly how intimately connected it was with the mysterious currents of the mind and how frightened he was by it. In "Religious Musings" we read of

> . . . the inventive arts, that nursed the soul
> To forms of beauty, and by sensual wants
> Unsensualizes the mind . . . (ll. 208-210)

In "The Destiny of Nations":

> Fancy is the power
> That first unsensualizes the dark mind. (ll. 80-81)

In "France: An Ode":

> The Sensual and the Dark rebel in vain,
> Slaves by their own compulsion! (ll. 85-86)

"Sensual" and "dark" seem related ideas, alien, forbidding. In "Fears in Solitude" the French are condemned as "too Sensual to be free"[20] (l. 143).

These may be thought merely figures of speech natural to the heightened language of poetry, but Coleridge's letters and notebooks disclose a sensual repugnance of almost alarming intensity. In May 1796, just six months after his marriage, Coleridge wrote to John Thelwall:

> Great indeed are the moral uses of Marriage—It is *Variety* that *cantharidizes us*. Marriage, that confines the appetites to one object, gradually causes them to be swallowed up in *affection*. Observe the face of an whoremonger or intriguer, and that of a married man—it would furnish physiognomic demonstration. . . . the man who suffers not his hopes to wander beyond the objects of sense will, in general, be *sensual*—& I again assert, that a Sensualist is not likely to be a Patriot."[21]

Coleridge was a better logician than this. Yet again and again we find him relating sensual behavior to remote questions. More important, sexuality is repeatedly the subject of apologetics:

> The great business of real unostentatious Virtue is—not to eradicate any genuine instinct or appetite of human nature; but—to establish a concord and unity betwixt all parts of our nature, to give a Feeling & a Passion to our purer Intellect, and to intellectualize our feelings & passions. This a happy marriage, blessed with children, effectuates, in the highest degree, of which our nature is capable, & is therefore chosen by St. Paul, as the symbol of the Union of the Church with Christ; that is, of the Souls of all good men with God, the soul of the Universe. "I scarcely distinguish" said once a good old man, "the wife of my old age from the wife of my youth; for when we were both young, & she was beautiful, for *once* that I caressed her with a meaner passion, I caressed her a thousand times with *Love*—& *these* caresses still remain to us!"[22]

In Sir Thomas Browne's *Religio Medici* Coleridge came across the following passage:

> I could be content that we might procreate like trees without conjunction, or that there were any way to perpetuate the world without this trivial and vulgar way of coition.

In the margins of the volume he wrote:

> He says, he is a Batchelor, but he talks as if he had been a married man, & married to a Woman who did not love him, & whom he did not love. Taken by itself, no doubt, the act is both foolish, & debasing. But what a misery is contained in those words, "taken by itself." ? are there not thoughts, & affections, & Hopes, & a *Religion* of the Heart, that lifts and sanctifies all our bodily actions where the union of the Bodies is *but* a language & *conversation* of united Souls![23]

Of course these are lovely thoughts. But they should not blind us to the hesitancy that lies behind such a line as, "Taken by itself, no doubt, the act is both foolish, & debasing." The conjugal relation, needless to say, was a holy sacrament, and not to be attacked as such. A notebook entry of 1805 reads: "Of Uxoriousness & its extreme difference from conjugal Love / the latter is two eyes seeing one object ever/. The former, a horrible *Squint* in which the eyes look at each other."[24] Coleridge wrote this in Malta, during a three-year absence from his wife. During a protracted separation from her six years before, Coleridge had written to Thomas Poole from Germany of the strange, new customs he was encountering:

I am pestered every ball night to dance, which very *modestly* I refuse—They dance a most infamous dance called the Waltzen—There are perhaps 20 couple—the Man & his Partner embrace each other, arms round waists, & knees almost touching, & then whirl round & round, the whole 20 couple, 40 times round at least, to lascivious music. This they dance at least three times every ball night—There is no Country on the Earth where the married Women are chaste like the English—here the married Men intrigue or whore—and the Wives have their Cicisbeos. I entreat you, suspect *me* not of a Cicisbeo affair—I am no Puritan; but yet it is not customs or manners that can extinguish in me the Sacredness of a married Woman, or quench the disgust I feel towards an Adultress. . . .[25]

His Malta notebooks reveal that it was unendurable to him to suppose that a beloved female had even *contended* (albeit successfully) with sensuous thoughts in relation to another man.[26] And during the Highgate years he was to write that "a virtuous woman will *not* consciously feel what she ought not, because she is ever on the alert to discountenance & suppress the very embryos of Thoughts not strictly justifiable, so as to prevent them from remaining long enough in their transit over her mind to be even remembered."[27]

In 1801 Coleridge wrote Humphry Davy that for the past seven years he had been chaste, and that his "unchastities" had occurred solely between his nineteenth and twenty-second years.[28] In 1814 he was to report that "since my twenty second year [I] never had any illicit connection. . . ."[29]

In view of the evidence, it ought not to tax credulity that when Coleridge separated from his wife soon after he returned from Malta it was to embrace a celibacy that was to endure over the last twenty-eight years of his life. No breath of scandal attaches to Coleridge's name in this way, although indulgence in opium and brandy for mere pleasure, and general sensual excess, have been repeatedly charged against him. Coleridge was, to put the matter bluntly, repelled by sex, and much of his life is not to be understood without counterpointing this fact against the equally obvious truth that he was naturally endowed not only with the full range of desires and appetites, but with organic sensibilities more intense and complex than most other men.

A journal entry of 1805 refers to "a short-lived Fit of Fears from sex"[30] during adolescence, but these fears ran very much deeper than he realized. In December 1794, just having turned twenty-two years old, Coleridge found himself rejected by Mary Evans and engaged to Sara Fricker, whom he did not love. Faced with a rebuke by Southey for his delay and evasions in fulfilling his promise to Sara, he wrote:

To lose her [Mary]!—I can rise above that selfish Pang. But to marry another—O Southey! bear with my weakness. Love makes all things pure and heavenly like itself:—but to marry a woman whom I do *not* love—to degrade her, whom I call my Wife, by making her the Instrument of low Desire—and on the removal of a desultory Appetite, to be perhaps not displeased with her Absence!—Enough! These Refinements are the wildering Fires, that lead me into Vice.[31]

"Mark you, Southey!—" he concludes, "I will do my Duty!" and then goes on for several pages, with all apparent cheerfulness, on other subjects. The suggestion of a certain dramatic self-consciousness ought not to mislead us. For Coleridge, sexual relations were degrading—mere appetite—unless redeemed by an exalted love.[32] For such a man, dreams in which he regularly found

> Desire with Loathing strangely mixt,
> On wild or hateful Objects fixt,

were acutely demoralizing. And when sensual thoughts poisoned his waking fantasies he was forced to hypothesize that these ideas came from *outside* himself. For one who in his waking hours was so well defended against moral accusations, one who responded to any accusation touching upon his moral nature with almost hysterical defensiveness, the twilight realms before slumber and the visitations of the night were fearful indeed. The gulf between daylight ideals and the demon thoughts of darkness was dangerously broad and deep.

Convulsions of the known and familiar landscape, strange transformations of people and things, guilt, shame, fear—all these and more are the specters that stalked Coleridge's terror-laden nights. Of course the literature of dreams abounds in such images, but this does not make their appearance in the dreams of any particular individual any the less significant, unless of course we cling to a theory of dreams in which they arise solely from derangement of the black bile, or the position of the sleeping body, or to some other such primitive notion.[33] The abstract images just spoken of throng in concrete form through many of Coleridge's dreams, and at times shimmer into focus within his great poems.

And yet here, on the threshhold of his nighttime world, we must again pause to take note of the throng of caveats clamoring for attention. Let us remember how extraordinarily fragmentary is the record of dreams retained by the conscious memory. Ernest Jones reminds us that dreams are automatically domesticated to the "real" world upon awaking and being recounted. We usually forget that *all* experience recorded in words is fragmentary, and the less "verbal" an experience, the less tractable it is to the domestication of language. With respect to describing mental states, language is especially impoverished. Everybody knows how shadowy some dreams are, and how few are the dreams that are remembered at all. To extrapolate a detailed character study on the basis of sketchy reports of scattered and intermitted bursts of unconscious mental functioning is surely dangerous, if not wholly irresponsible. Conversely, we may also remind ourselves that the paleontologist is permitted to reconstruct complex animal forms from fossil imprints and eroded bones. But we need not court analogies in pursuit of procedural justification. Let the evidence be heard, and the rectitude of procedure determined by the value of the results.

Thus we shall now encounter and probe Coleridge's dreams, acutely conscious of our limitations and the shadowy guidelines of the whole subject, but convinced that they are a significant part of the poet's mental life, and continuous with the waking mind, about which we know (comparatively) so much.

Friday Night, Nov. 28, 1800, or rather Saturday Morning—a most frightful Dream of a Woman whose features were blended with darkness catching hold of my right eye & attempting to pull it out—I caught hold of her arm fast—a horrid feel—Wordsworth cried out aloud to me hearing my scream—heard his cry & thought it cruel he did not come / but did not wake till his cry was repeated a third time—the Woman's name Ebon Ebon Thalud—When I awoke, my right eyelid swelled.[34]

The danger of giving way to the mind's almost limitless powers of association becomes apparent when one finds a whole network of trails leading from this dream into Coleridge's life and work. Dorothy Wordsworth's journal entry for 28 November 1800 reads: "*Friday.* Coleridge walked over. Miss Simpson drank tea with us. William walked home with her. Coleridge was very unwell. He went to bed before Wm.'s return. Great boils on his neck."[35] Coleridge went to bed unwell: so much can be said with certainty. Beyond this lie the mirage-laden domains of speculation. Miss Coburn's notes include such suggestive comments as: "This dream-woman appears to have come out of the *Arabian Nights.* . . . In the story of the 185th Night, one of the main characters is a druggist, Ebn Thaher. . . . 'Thalud' was the name of an ancient Arabian people. . . ."[36] But the "Woman whose features were blended with darkness" surely does not derive essentially from a literary source, but rather from personal terrors. That Coleridge was unable to see the woman's features clearly may imply that she would otherwise be known to him; thus his unconscious may be protecting him from unwelcome knowledge. Shadowy, threatening females appear often in his dreams. Once "three old Women, the dim Apparitions of three, attacked me in [a] dark passage. . . ."[37]

It is tempting to ask the significance of the dream-woman's attempt to snatch his eye out. One thinks, perhaps too mechanically, of a castration fear and of Oedipus' self-punishment. Coleridge had intended his own Cain, who had a "fierce and sullen eye" that "glared," to end his wanderings by burning his eyes out.[38] Coleridge's own "right eyelid swelled" upon awakening from this dream. Two weeks before, he had written Josiah Wedgwood that his eyes were inflamed, "so blood-red, that I should make a very good

Personification of Murder."[39] In 1803 he wrote the same Wedgwood that he had "had a bad night, with distressful Dreams, chiefly about my eye. . . . in the morning my right eye was blood-shot, & the Lid swoln."[40] He often had trouble with his eyes.[41]

If already we feel ourselves circling aimlessly in a Sargasso Sea of weedy associations, consider the problem of the name Ebon Ebon Thalud. The Ebn Thaher of the *Arabian Nights* was a druggist—one thinks at once of opium as a connecting link. But Ebon Ebon Thalud is rather a man's name than a woman's. Is there here an undertone of the sexual confusion shimmering beneath the surface of "Christabel"? In an outline for a poem about Mohammed projected by Coleridge and Southey, the following notes appear in Coleridge's hand:

1st Book: The Deathbed of Abu Taleb—herein we develop the character of Mohammed—After the death of Abu Taleb the Tumult, & his escape by the heroism of Ali.[42]

Abu Taleb was an uncle of Mohammed. According to the Koran, he found the Prophet an orphan, poor and astray, and brought him up. Is there some personal association in Coleridge's unconscious? If Coleridge knew that "Thalud" was the name of an ancient Arabian people, its dream meaning might be that of "ancestor." That an ancestor could be responsible for so destructive an assault may even suggest the "ancestral voices prophesying war" in "Kubla Khan." Obviously, in the presence of so shadowy a series of possibilities, it is wisest to call a halt upon speculation and await more concrete evidence.

Two years later, in 1802, on the day before the seventh anniversary of his own unhappy marriage (and, by strange coincidence, the day before Wordsworth was to be wedded), Coleridge set down in his journal one of the most frightful and revealing dream descriptions he has left behind:

October 3—Night—my dreams uncommonly illustrative of the nonexistence of Surprise in sleep—I dreamt that I was asleep in the Cloyster at Christ's Hospital and had awoken with a pain in my hand from some corrosion / boys & nurses daughters peeping at me/ On their implying that I was not in the School, I answered yes I am/ I am only twenty—I then recollected that I was thirty, & of course could not be in the School—& was perplexed—but not the least surprised that I could fall into such error/ So I dreamt of Dorothy, William & Mary—& that Dorothy was altered in every feature, a fat, thick-limbed & rather red-haired—in short, no resemblence to her at all—and I said, if I did not *know* you to be Dorothy, I never should suppose it/ Why, says she— I have not a feature the same/ & yet I was not surprised—

> I was followed up & down by a frightful pale woman who, I thought,
> wanted to kiss me, & had the property of giving a shameful Disease by
> breathing in the face/
>   & again I dreamt that a figure of a woman of gigantic Height, dim &
> indefinite & smokelike appeared—& that I was forced to run up toward
> it—& then it changed to a stool—& then appeared again in another
> place—& again I went up in great fright—and it changed to some other
> common thing—yet I felt no surprize.[43]

The confusions of identity in this dream are remarkable. The dreamer is
unsure whether he is twenty or thirty, whether he may still be a student at
Christ's Hospital or not. Dorothy Wordsworth is "altered in every feature,
a *fat, thick-limbed* & rather *red-haired*." In another dream with a Christ's
Hospital setting of the following year (which we will deal with in detail
shortly), Coleridge is "insulted by a *fat sturdy* Boy of about 14, like a Bacchus / who dabs a flannel in my face."[44] Bacchus, the god of wine and pleasure, is often depicted as florid (red-haired). The overall description of Dorothy, as of the young Bacchus, strongly suggests elements of self-projection.[45]
In one of Coleridge's earliest poems he described his own "fat vacuity of
face," and he wrote on the manuscript, "The Author was at this time, *aetat.*
17, remarkable for a plump face."[46]
     It is to be noted also that the fat sturdy boy "dabs a flannel *in my face*."
In the "frightful dream" of 28 November 1800 the woman whose features
were "blended with darkness" tries to pluck out the eye in his face. When
Coleridge catches her arm, it has "a horrid feel." The dream of 3 October
1802 describes a "frightful pale woman who, I thought, wanted to kiss me,
& had the property of giving a shameful Disease by *breathing in the face*."
The flannel is in fact immediately described in Coleridge's notebook entry
as "rather soft hair brown Shawl stuff," suggesting again softness, perhaps
thus linked with breath.
     Immediately after the encounter with the frightful pale woman, in Cole-
ridge's journal entry, is another sequence: ". . . I dreamt that a figure of a
woman of gigantic Height, dim & indefinite & smokelike appeared."[47] This
may be another appearance of the "Woman whose features were blended
with darkness." The "gigantic Height" suggests a woman associated with the
dreamer's childhood, when adults loom so much larger in the mind. Startling transformation of people and objects is especially evident in this dream.
The gigantic woman turns into a "stool" and then into "some other common
thing," unidentified. Let us remember that "tall" and "lofty" Geraldine
was intended to transform herself into a man. A stool, being three-legged,
is occasionally a male dream symbol. Coleridge has "a pain in my hand
from some corrosion / boys & nurses daughters peeping at me." Again, the
threat in these dreams to his eyes, to his hand (and, as we shall see shortly,
to the penis itself), together with the associations inherent in the word "peeping," which may be a reversal of the actual memory, is acutely illustrative

of the intense guilt that had been instilled into so sensitive a boy as Coleridge in the stifling moral atmosphere of Christ's Hospital for acts and impulses perfectly normal to growing boys. But we must remember here that he wrote to Poole that as a child (well before his father's death and his subsequent removal to Christ's Hospital) he was fearful of the dark, dreaded specters, and "most firmly believed" in the old prayer:

> Matthew! Mark! Luke! & John!
> God bless the bed which I lie on.
> Four angels round me spread,
> Two at my foot & two at my bed [head].

"Frequently have I," he added, "half-awake & half-asleep, my body diseased & fevered by my imagination, seen armies of ugly Things bursting in upon me, & these four angels keeping them off."[48]

The "property of giving a shameful Disease by breathing in the face" may have much deeper meanings for Coleridge than the obvious suggestion of venereal disease. A few months earlier, he set down in his notebook an outline of a fantastic story about the inhabitants of the moon. These people were "exactly like the people of this world in every thing else except indeed that they eat with their Backsides, & stool at their mouths/ in consequence they are all sans-culottes, but then they are all cowled or veiled, a whole Planet of Nuns & Friars—their Breath not very sweet—but they do not kiss much & custom reconciles one to every thing."[49]

In this scatalogical tale, faces are "cowled or veiled," that is, hidden from view, shadowed in darkness. This particular idea, or fantasy, of the interchangeability of mouths and backsides, may be related to an entry Coleridge made in his journal near one o'clock in the morning in November of the following year. It had been a day of considerable excitement, and he had taken a massive dose of laudanum:

> for the first time in my Life felt my eyes near-sighted, & tho' I had 2 Candles near me, reading in my bed, I was obliged to magnify the Letters by bringing the book close to my Eye—I then put out the Candles, & closed my eyes—& instantly there appeared a spectrum, of a Pheasant's Tail, that altered thro' various degradations into round wrinkly shapes, as of ⟨Horse⟩ Excrement, or baked Apples—indeed exactly like the latter—round baked Apples, with exactly the same colour, the same circular intra-circular Wrinkles—I started out of bed, lit my Candles & noted it down, in order to state these circular irregularly concentrical Wrinkles, something like Horse dung, still more like flat baked or ⟨dried⟩ Apples, such as they are brought in after Dinner.— *Why those Concentric Wrinkles?*[50]

I am indebted to Dr. Sidney Levy for the suggestion that this experience and the story of the moon men who used their mouths and anuses interchangeable are related. "This is a kind of fantasy idea, daydream," Dr. Levy writes of the latter, "that is found in the very infantile, psychotic person-alities who experience the world through primary process perception. That is, the prelogical perceptions of the infantile or latent or overtly psychotic. His tendency to associate food and fecal matter is demonstrated in his reverie when he was not sure whether the object he was fantasying was an apple or horse manure."[51]

Just a month before these speculations about the concentric wrinkles, Coleridge wrote a long and agonizing entry into his journals at forty minutes past two in the morning. The date was 20 October 1803, the day on which he always celebrated his birthday: "I slept again with dreams of sor-row and pain, tho' not of downright Fright & prostration/ I was worsted but not conquered—in sorrows and in sadness & in sore & angry Struggles—but not trampled down/ but this will all come again, if I do not take care."[52]

Barely a week later came the following dream about his son Hartley (then six years old), in which hostility figures largely:

> Frid. Morn. [28 October 1803] 5 o'clock—Dosing, dreamt of Hartley as at his Christening—how as he was asked who redeemed him, & was to say, God the Son / he went on, humming and hawing, in one hum & haw, like a boy who knows a thing & will not make the effort to recollect it—so as to irritate me greatly. . . .[53]

Many of the entries of the following two weeks are fascinating in the in-tensity, brilliance, and confusion of the emotional and intellectual life they depict. Immediately after a lengthy entry which contains one of Coleridge's most fantastically grandiose lists of literary projects, he writes:

> It has long been my sincere wish, & (for that all our Habits partake of human Frailty) my *pride,* to try to understand in myself, & to make in-telligible to others, how great men may err *wildly*, yet not be mad—that all opinions that can be understood & are not contrad. in terms may have more to be said for them than Bigots & Scoliasts suppose.—Paschal!![54]

This entry is especially significant because it provides a rare example, how-ever obliquely stated, of Coleridge's belief in his own greatness, together with doubt about his sanity. We shall very shortly meet dream figures allegedly mad, or formerly so, who are certainly self-projections. Now, two entries later, and barely two weeks after the account of Hartley's christening, comes this far richer and more complex dream:

> Nov. 10th, ½ past 2 o'clock, Morning. Awoke after long struggles & with faint screaming from a persecuting Dream. The Tale of the Dream began in two *Images*—in two Sons of a Nobleman, desperately fond of shooting—brought but by the Footman to resign their Property, & to be

made believe that they had none/ they were far too cunning for that/ as they struggled & resisted their cruel Wrongers, & my Interest for them, I suppose, increased, I became they—the duality vanished—Boyer & Christ's Hospital became concerned—yet still the former Story was kept up—& I was conjuring him, as he met me on the Streets, to have pity on a Nobleman's Orphan, when I was carried back to bed, & was struggling up against an unknown impediment, some woman on the other side about to relieve me—when a noise of one of the Doors, strongly associated with Mrs. Coleridge's coming in to awake me, awaked me—the first thing, I became conscious of, was a faint double scream, that I uttered.[55]

Why this dream should have led to screaming is not obvious. The threat does not in itself seem so very terrifying. Yet at the dream's center is the unbearable sense of persecution; Coleridge begins by calling it a "persecuting Dream." It is easy to establish thematic links between this dream and the trials visited upon the Mariner and particularly Christabel. But something more than loose association seems involved when we read of "two Sons of a Nobleman" whose property is being taken from them. In the later *Zapolya* two noble orphans, Bethlen and Glycine, are deprived of their rightful inheritances. *Osorio* dealt with two sons of a nobleman, one of whom tries to usurp the other's property and betrothed.[56] Christabel and Geraldine ("My sire is of a noble line") are also the children of nobles; it will shortly be argued that both are projections of their creator, Coleridge, and that they represent his profoundly divided personality.

It is highly suggestive that these sons are "terribly fond of shooting"—which may well imply intense aggressiveness, if not something more specifically sexual—and they are also "cunning." The suspicion that the Nobleman in Coleridge's dream represents a father figure (the common fantasy of noble birth) and the *two* sons body forth in images *two* sides of the same nature, also a sense of being two people at once—and always the dreamer—is confirmed by what follows. The two sons actually become Coleridge! That he was shut off from grasping the possible significance of this is demonstrated by his immediate explanation to himself that as "my Interest for them, I suppose, increased, I became they." In his fantasies Coleridge was often a great and powerful personage. In later years he remembered how at Christ's Hospital it gave him pleasure to have visitors of rank.[57] Surely it is not surprising if the lonely boy fantasied himself not as the son of a poor rural vicar but as one of noble blood.

In the following month Coleridge recorded the reverie about the baked apples and horse excrement, and the dream about Adam being murdered by his descendants, which we may now examine more closely:

Dec. 6. 1803.—Adam travelling in his old age came to a set of the descendants of Cain, ignorant of the origin of the world; & treating him as a Madman killed him. A sort of Dream, which I had this Night.[58]

The phrase, "A sort of Dream," suggests how misty were the borderlines in his own mind between deep sleep, reverie, and fitful dozing.

The day before Coleridge had written a letter (perhaps in the hours just before going to sleep) to one Matthew Coates; the letter deals primarily with his own projected *travels,* following upon his decision to leave his wife and children to seek health abroad. Perhaps the guilt Coleridge was feeling towards his children over this decision (the letter describes his "many sore Struggles of mind from reluctance to quit my children") had something to do with the crime the dream records, committed against Adam (the first male sinner), "travelling," by his own descendants. It is possible too that the relation of his own plans to Adam (mistakenly thought of as a *mad*man) was jogged by his reference in his letter, twice, to a certain Dr. Adams, the author of *A Guide to the Island of MADeira* (1801), where Coleridge was planning to go.[59]

In this letter Coleridge wrote of his recent nightmares:

> After a time of Sufferings great, as mere bodily Afflictions can well be conceived to be, and which the Horrors of my Sleep, and Night-screams (so loud & so frequent as to make me almost a Nuisance in my own house) seemed to carry beyond mere Body—counterfeiting, as it were, the Tortures of Guilt, and what we are told of the Punishments of a spiritual World—I am at length a Convalescent—but dreading such another Bout as much as I dare dread *a Thing which has no immediate connection with my Conscience.*[60]

Coleridge saw no *moral* connection between his dreams and waking life. And forever afterwards he rigorously kept these two realms of his experience in separate compartments of the mind, thereby shutting off all possibility of achieving any revolutionary grasp of the meaning of dreams or any genuine understanding of himself. Such knowledge, of course, in men much less riven than Coleridge, has proven too much to bear.[61]

What significance has it that Adam is taken for a madman? We have seen that Coleridge wished to prove that "great men may err *wildly,* yet not be mad." A series of consecutive notebook jottings read: "Madness—Bulls— Self—God—Past Life + Present; or Conscience, &c."[62] Mental and physical taints or deformations, real or alleged, figure largely in his dreams—and poems. Since in his nightmares he is repeatedly and explicitly victimized, it is a reasonable assumption that other victims, like Adam, are surrogates for himself, especially when there are other reasons to think so. The same may well be true of victims in his poems. Suspicion that this dream about "the descendants of Cain" is linked with that of Hartley's christening by guilt and hostility toward his children is strengthened by a passage in a lecture of 1808, as thus summarized by Crabb Robinson:

> Mr. Coleridge met with an ancient M. S. at Helmstädt, in which God was represented visiting Noah's family. *The descendants of Cain* did not

pull off their hats to the great visitor, and received boxes of the ear for their rudeness. While the progency of Abel answered their catechism well, the Devil prompted the bad children to repeat the Lord's Prayer backwards.[63]

Hartley "as at his Christening . . . was asked who redeemed him, & was to say, God the Son/ he went on, humming & hawing, in one hum & haw, like a boy who knows a thing & will not make the effort to recollect it—so as to irritate me greatly. . . ."

This mixture of love and guilt, parental concern and unconscious hostility toward his children (intolerable to his waking mind) had long since taken the form of recurrent fear for their safety; soon it was to appear in the tormenting guise of compulsive fear of their imminent deaths.

Exactly one week after the dream of Adam's murder, Coleridge set down another dream, especially valuable for its concrete detail:

Wednesd. Morn. 3 'clock, Dec. 13, 1803. Bad dreams/ How often *of a sort*/ at the university—a mixture of Xts Hospital Church/ escapes there—lose myself/ trust to two People, one Maim'd, one unknown/ insulted by a fat sturdy Boy of about 14, like a Bacchus/ who dabs a flannel in my face, (or rather soft hair brown Shawl stuff) (was this a flannel Nightcap?) he attacks me/ I call to my Friends—they come & join in the Hustle against me—out rushes a university Harlot, who insists on my going with her/ offer her a shilling—seem to get away a moment/ when she overtakes me again/ I am not to go to another while she is "*biting*"—these were her words/—this will not satisfy her/ I sit down on a broad open plain of rubbish with rails & a street beyond/ & call out—whole Troops of people in sight—now [? cannot] awake.— Wind & the τα αιδοια πενσιλια [private parts] & somewhat painful/ but what wonderful wanderings thro' the Hall, with bad Portraits of the Emperor of Russia, the Hall belonging to the E.—the wanderings thro' Streets, the noticing the Complex side of a noble Building, & saying to my Guides—"it will be long before I shall find my way here—I must endeavor to remember this" / the turning up a Lane with wall & magnificent Trees (like a quiet Park-garden wall) In the early part of the Dream, Boyer, & two young Students, & R. Allen: Legrice & I quizzing/ N. B. arrogant sense of intellectual superiority under circumstances of depression, but no envy/—"*Obsonant*" The Harlot in white with her open Bosom certainly was the Cambridge Girl, ⟨Sal Hall⟩—One thing noticeable in an after Dream/ a little weak contemptible wretch offering his Services, & I (as before afraid to refuse them) literally & distinctly remembered a former Dream, in which I had suffered most severely, this wretch leaping on me, & grasping my Scrotum/—I therefore most politely assured him of the 3 guineas, but I meant only to get rid of him/—Again too the slight pain in my side produced a fellow knuckling

me there/—My determination to awake, I dream that I got out of bed,
& volition in dream to *scream,* which I actually to[o] did, from that
volition/ & the strange visual Distortions of all the bed Cloaths, some
lying as on a ~~form~~ frame toward the fire/ some one way, some another/
all which, I in my dream explained as the effects of ~~an~~ my eyes being
half-opened, & still affected by Sleep / in an half upright posture
struggling, as I thought, against involuntary sinking back into Sleep, &
consequent suffocation/ twas then I screamed, by will/ & immediately
after really awoke/ I must devote some one or more Days exclusively to
the Meditation on *Dreams.* Days? Say rather Weeks![64]

Of so lengthy and complex a dream, commentary and surmise could be
endless. Among the more obvious points is that Coleridge tells us he *often*
has bad dreams "of a sort" (surely a sign of deep, unresolved conflicts) about
his boyhood at Christ's Hospital and later university years, all somehow
huddled together. He mentions "escapes there—lose myself." He puts his
trust in "two People"—once again duality—"one Maim'd, one unknown"—
again deformation and disguise or mystery. If this is in any sense self-
projection—as it would certainly appear—we again have evidence of Coleridge's divided and destructive self-image. But a more important aesthetic
hint may be here buried. In an earlier Christ's Hospital dream he had felt
"a pain in my hand from some corrosion." Here a character is "Maim'd."
Pain and deformation often appear in his dreams. Now if we think of the
range of his poetry, do we find any maimed characters? At once we think
of Geraldine:

> Behold her bosom and half her side—
> A sight to *dream* of, not to tell!

How strangely the word "dream" now seems to leap off the page at us.[65] And
we may think also of Geraldine's tale of her kidnapping by strange men, who
took her on a long journey and once "crossed the shade of night" (l. 88).
Have we here an unconscious recognition that Geraldine herself comes from
over "the shade of night," that is, from his own dreams?[66] As for the specific
character of Geraldine's deformation, Coleridge wisely omitted the particularity of description present in some of the earlier manuscripts, wherein
her bosom and side "Are lean and old and foul of hue."[67]

The "fat sturdy Boy of about 14, like a Bacchus," has been discussed
earlier in relation to the red-haired Dorothy Wordsworth. What needs to be
noted now, however, is that in the grandiose list of literary projects Coleridge entered into his journal just two or three days before this "persecuting
dream," the last two read: "Destruction of Jerusalem.—Conquest of India
by Bacchus in Hexameters."[68] And those words appear in the journal immediately before the brief entry that states, "great men may err *wildly,* yet
not be mad." That these plans involve inner projections is suggested further

by a journal entry of the year before: "if ever I imagined myself as a conqueror, it was always to bring peace."[69]

Among Coleridge's notes for a lecture on "The Origin of Drama," given
in 1808, is the following: "In the devotional hymns to Bacchus the germ of
the first Tragedy. Men like to imagine themselves to be the characters they
treat of—hence dramatic representations."[70] The last sentence will bear very
considerable reflection. For we have here from Coleridge himself justification of a critical procedure which related dramatic representations to the
mind of the creator—a procedure so often disparaged in contemporary
criticism. And if we slightly rearrange his words, we can justify the present
pursuit into his dream and fantasy life: "Men like to imagine themselves the
characters they treat of—hence dramatic representations of themselves in
the form of other characters *in dreams*."

The god of wine, pleasure, and revelry, Bacchus, depicted as conqueror of
Asia, would thus seem to have deep affinities with the mighty Kubla Khan,
the oriental conqueror who builds a Pleasure Dome. If the connection seems
tenuous, let us remember that the two most certain sources for "Kubla
Khan" are Purchas and Milton, whose paradise "where *Abassin* Kings their
issue guard, / Mount *Amara*" figures so largely in the Abyssinian maid's
song. Immediately before these lines in *Paradise Lost* in a mention
of that earthly paradise where was hidden

> *Amalthea* and her Florid son
> Young *Bacchus* from his Stepdam *Rhea's* eye . . .

Thus the connection between Bacchus and the Abyssinian paradise appears in
Milton, who describes his Bacchus as *florid*, and as an orphan. Earlier it was
suggested that the red-haired, fat-limbed Dorothy Wordsworth who appeared in a dream is another embodiment of Coleridge's self-image, which
often projected itself as female, unattractive, and sensual. The Bacchana-
lian side of the dreamer's nature is constantly threatening ("he attacks me"),
just as a little later another self-projection, "a little weak contemptible
wretch," also assaults the dreamer. A measure of how terrifying this male
figure is compared to that of the "university Harlot" is shown in the fact
that the dreamer offers three guineas to get rid of the former but a mere
shilling to the latter.

When the Bacchus-like boy attacks, the dreamer calls to his friends, only
to have them "join in the Hustle against me"—revealing once again Coleridge's profound insecurity at Christ's Hospital (and, of course, at the time
of the dream). His statement that as a child he had been "despised & hated
by the boys"[71] bears affinities with this dream, and possibly with the experiences of the Mariner, cursed by each of the dying men, an eternal outcast—
and also with the isolation and contempt Christabel is condemned to at the
end of the second canto. In later years Coleridge said that the third part of
"Christabel" was to be "the song of her desolation."[72]

As if the "Hustle" against the dreamer were not bad enough, out rushes "a university Harlot," another terrifying woman connected with sex, who demands that the dreamer come with her. Coleridge almost buys her off, but she overtakes him again. He is "not to go to another while she is '*biting*.' " The dreamer seems baffled by the expression: "These were her words." What can "biting" mean?[73]

When we consider how destructive women are in Coleridge's dreams, and the aggressiveness of this harlot, we can hardly doubt that "biting" implies something especially frightening: more specifically, a sexual, castrating threat. The dreamer has already been attacked by the Bacchus-like youth, he will soon be leaped upon by a contemptible wretch; the harlot who wants the dreamer to come with her is "biting," a strange way to describe a state of sexual desire. Some overtone of the castrating woman (suggested earlier by the woman who tries to pluck out his eye) and the *vagina dentata* may certainly be present. Whatever the specific meaning, evidence of Coleridge's intense sexual fears of women, evident from more overt behavior, is here much reinforced.

Now, after several alarms and confusions, and two references to "wanderings"[74] (one of the major themes in Coleridge's poetry), we come upon another ferociously aggressive and physically deformed or feeble creature, a "little weak contemptible wretch offering his Services." And here, as with the harlot, the dreamer is "afraid to refuse." Another dream is remembered in which that same wretch appeared, "leaping on me, & grasping my Scrotum"; once more the dreamer is under physical attack, this time directed almost without distortion at his manhood itself.[75] And again the dreamer wants to "scream." Reality in the form of the "bed Cloaths"—nighttime reality?—is strangely askew.[76] There is a dreadful fear of suffocation.[77]

In passing we may note the suggestions of "Kubla Khan" at various points in this lengthy and complex dream. If Bacchus and the Khan are Asian monarchs, so is the "Emperor of Russia," who is shown in "bad Portraits" (another self-projection?).[78] The immediate reference to a "noble Building" can be linked with the stately pleasure dome, especially as almost at once we come upon "a Lane with wall and magnificent Trees (like a quiet Park-garden wall)," which contains more obvious overtones of

> fertile grounds
> With walls and towers girdled round
> And here were gardens bright with sinuous rills
> Where blossomed many an incense bearing tree.

The Legrice with whom the dreamer was "quizzing" was a school friend.[79] Quizzing meant "to make fun of (a person or thing), to turn to ridicule; occasionally, to regard with an air of mockery."[80] Lamb had once used this word to describe Coleridge: "As long as Lloyd or I have known Col so long have we known him in the daily & hourly habit of quizzing the world by lyes.--"[81] The word also appears in a dream of some six months before, "in which a Lecture I was giving, a very profound one according to my fancy, was not listened to/ but I was quizzed off."[82] Significantly, the use of "quizzing" in a context of failure to achieve intellectual recognition is paralleled precisely in the later dream, where immediately after the reference to "Legrice & I quizzing," Coleridge wrote, "N. B. arrogant sense of intellectual superiority under circumstances of depression." Somehow the word or idea of "quizzing" is connected with notions of intellectual achievement and recognition.[83]

The next month, January 1804, Coleridge set down one of his most suggestive dreams, all the more remarkable for its extreme condensation:

> My Dream—History of Scotus, deranged as a youth/ imagining himself in the Land of Logic, lying on the Road & in the Road to the Kingdom of Truth, falls into a criminal Intercourse with a Girl, who is in Love with him, whom he considers as the Daughter of the King of the Land/ —impersonation & absolute *Incarnation* of the most Abstract—. Detected he defends himself on this ground. O it was a wild dream, yet a deal of true psychological Feeling at the bottom of it.[84]

By 1804, of course, Coleridge had long since turned away from poetry to philosophy as his major concern. The previous November he had sent for one of Scotus' books.[85] In 1801 he was reading the comparatively obscure Scotus "to set the poor old Gemman on his feet again, & in order to wake him out of his present Lethargy, I am burning Locke, Hume, & Hobbes under his Nose."[86] That Coleridge was identifying with the philosopher is hardly to be doubted. Adam was taken for a madman; here Scotus was allegedly "deranged as a youth." We see Coleridge's fear of insanity recurring. It is in fact curious that the official reason given for his discharge from the army was insanity.[87]

The Mariner, of course, is taken for a madman ("gray-beard loon"), and his appearance and manner are those of one possessed. At the sight of the Mariner and the sinking of the ship, the pilot's boy "straightway doth crazy go." The poet at the end of "Kubla Khan" is very possibly possessed ("his flashing eyes, his floating hair"). But the most consequential manifestation of the irrational in Coleridge's work is not when he is deliberately trying to depict its real or supposed appearance, as in Osorio or the Mariner, but in the structural foundations of the three greatest poems of the *annus mirabilis*, in mysterious passages sprinkled throughout the canon, and most especially in his various grapplings with "the origin of evil."[88] Because he was a moral philosopher, these latter passages are not seen for what they are: skirmishings on the frontiers of incipient insanity. Just between the persecuting Christ's Hospital dream and that of Duns Scotus, he wrote the following into his notebooks:

I will at least make the attempt to explain to myself the Origin of moral Evil from the *streamy* Nature of Association, which Thinking = Reason, curbs & rudders/ how this comes to be so difficult/ Do not the bad Passions in Dreams throw light & shew of proof upon this Hypothesis?— Explain those bad Passions: & I shall gain Light, I am sure—A Clue! A Clue!—an Hecatomb a la Pythagoras, if it unlabyrinths me.—Dec. 28, 1803.

So this famous passage is almost always presented. But the publication of the complete notebooks demonstrates that the entry did not end thus but immediately continued with a reflection on the beauty of his pencil in the candlelight; this is followed at once by a very serious objection to the theory he has just put forward, a theory, obviously, comforting to a mind tormented with inexplicably horrible images:

But take in the blessedness of Innocent Children, the blessedness of sweet Sleep, &c &c &c: are these or are they not contradictions to the evil from *streamy* association?—I hope not. . . .

That the "bad Passions in Dreams" were in any sense part of his total consciousness, were—in his moralistic terms—connected with his conscience, all this was then and was to remain hidden in impenetrable mystery. It is fascinating to observe a brilliant man wrenched away from any insight into the truth because of a moral block in which he sees himself as basically virtuous, generous, self-effacing, without envy.

All is to be thought *over* and *into* [the note continues]—but what is the height, & ideal of mere association?—Delirium.—But how far is this state produced by Pain & Denaturalization? And what are these?—In short, as far as I can see any thing in this Total Mist, Vice is imperfect yet existing Volition, giving diseased Currents of association, because it yields on all sides & *yet* is—So think of Madness:—O if I live! Grasmere, Dec. 29. 1803.[89]

Delirium . . . madness . . . these terrors never lurk far from discussions of the origin of evil. As to those "diseased Currents of Association," Coleridge was to live for another thirty years without penetrating their significance.[90]

As time passed, religious perspectives came to obliterate psychological phenomena. Only three years later, he wrote to his brother George:

For the last six or seven years I have been more and more convinced, tho' I pretend not to *understand* much less *explain* the fact, that our *moral nature* is a power of itself; and not a mere modification of our common Intellect / so that a man may have wit, prudence, sense, &c &c, & yet be utterly destitute of a true *moral* sense. And when I observe the impotence of this moral sense, however highly possessed, unassisted by something still higher, &, if I may so express myself, still more extra-natural, I own, it seems to me, as if the goodness of God had occasionally *added* it to our nature, as an intermediate or connecting Link between that nature and a state of Grace.[91]

Coleridge, who could not admit to himself, except rarely, even the slightest faults of character, other than weakness of will and infirmity of purpose, must nevertheless often have reflected bitterly on his inability to fulfill contracts, his failure to provide adequately for his family, which his brother-in-law Robert Southey was toiling so unremittingly to do. When Coleridge thought about his addiction to opium and all the duplicities which followed from that, when he thought about many of the equivocal acts he had committed, just what could he make of his actions? He was a man with severe and exalted concepts of personal morality, but unless he was quite insane he of course knew, at least intermittently, of the gulf between his professed ideals and his accomplished acts. And so to posit a "moral sense" as something apart, independent of the intelligence, a power in itself, a biological endowment, a gift of God, one could take comfort in the thought that the lack of a moral sense as thus posited, was not in itself, by strange logical alchemy, a moral failing, any more than being tone deaf is a moral failing.

Coleridge's conviction that man was a fallen creature need not, therefore, be taken as an orthodox branch of the pious tree of his theology, something to be expected of the later Sage of Highgate—so far from the enthusiastic young Pantisocrat and idealist—but a conviction come to by bitter personal experience over the years. As such, seemingly pietistic conventionalities take on the dark colorings of personal confession, all the more revealing because they were surely unintended as such. So, for example, in *Aids to Reflection*:

> I profess a deep conviction that man was and is a fallen creature, not by accidents of bodily constitution or any other cause, which human wisdom in a course of ages might be supposed capable of removing; but as diseased in his will, in that will which is the true and only strict synonyme of the word, I, or the intelligent Self. . . . I utterly disclaim the notion, that any human intelligence, with whatever power it might manifest itself, is alone adequate to the office of restoring health to the will. . . .[92]

After the long and agonizing years of struggle with opium, and what must have seemed to him irrational acts of many kinds, the concept of man as a fallen creature with a diseased will in need of divine grace was surely necessary to his self-respect, perhaps even to his sanity.[93]

The rationalizing of extremely disturbing thoughts appears at several points in Coleridge's poetry. Significantly, such passages regularly deal with confused feelings towards members of one's family, eruptions of anger toward loved ones, thoughts of death about children. The villain Osorio can cry, "Love—love—and then we hate—and what? and wherefore? Hatred and love. Strange things! both strange alike." (III, 211). But Osorio is depraved and fratricidal: there is no bridge from such a mind to that of a normal man. In the famous conclusion to Part II of "Christabel," Coleridge attempts to account for cruelty in a loving father. We are told that the little child so

> fills a father's eyes with light;
> And pleasures flow in so thick and fast
> Upon his heart, that he at last
> Must needs express his love's excess
> With words of unmeant bitterness. (ll. 661-665)

These lines represent a kind of frantic distortion of the psychological realities inherent in what are, after all, common human experiences. But Coleridge's moral self-image was such that he could not consciously tolerate either aggressive or sensual thoughts in himself. The fearful crosscurrents of his unconscious appear in repeated dreads about the safety of his family. In February 1798, on a short journey away from home, he awoke at an inn

> at 5 in the morning, and was *haunted* by a strange notion that there was something of great importance that demanded my immediate presence at Stowey. I dressed myself, and walked out to dissipate the folly— but the Bridgewater Coach rattling by, & the Coachman asking me if I would get in—I took it for an omen—the superstitious feeling re- curred—and in I went—came home, & found—my wife & child in very good health![94]

In 1800, shortly after the birth of Derwent, he wrote: "My wife has given me another Son—but alas! I fear, he will not live."[95] The same fears appear in a sonnet Coleridge wrote in 1796, according to his own subtitle, "com- posed on a journey homeward: the author having received intelligence of the birth of a son."

> O my sweet baby! when I reach my door,
> If heavy looks should tell me thou art dead,
> (As sometimes, *through excess of hope*, I fear) . . .[96]

Is not the explanation of the strange and wayward thoughts afflicting Coleridge here explained in precisely the same way as the words of bitterness in "Christabel"? In both the poet deals with a psychological fact of his own experience in a way emotionally satisfying to himself. Of course, this is understandable. But it makes nonsense of the claim of one recent enthusiast that "there was no single psychological fact about himself which Coleridge did not know well before any of his commentators." Not only did Coleridge set down such thoughts (as most people do) to the supposedly meaningless flux of ideas, but he applied to them the Procrustes bed of the stringent morality that had been imposed upon him and from which he never escaped. As one had no control over dreams or the "diseased currents of association," they did not touch upon one's conscience. Yet if the thought that one's newborn son might be dead plagues the mind, and if an inner voice demands an explanation, the dreadful thought can be explained as coming from "excess of hope." And if one speaks bitter words towards a child, it is not because one has bitter feelings, but because it expresses "love's excess."

There is only one manuscript version of the conclusion to Part II of "Christabel." The lines appear in a letter to Southey and Coleridge's only comment upon them is: "A very metaphysical account of Fathers calling their children rogues, rascals, & little varlets—&c." Nothing introduces the lines. They appear abruptly after the following sentence:

Dear Hartley! we are at times alarmed by the state of his Health—but at present he is well—if I were to lose him, I am afraid, it would exceedingly deaden my affection for any other children I may have.[97]

The connection seems startling. The dream about Hartley's behavior at his christening, "so as to irritate me greatly," can now be seen against a richer background of emotional cross currents. Just a few days after this dream, Coleridge's journal discloses irritation with children in general and his son Derwent in particular:

remarkable disposition of all Children of his Age, who are any way kindly treated, to *contradict*—the pleasure they find in it/ when there is any plausibility in their own counterassertion it often rises into passion & self-willedness; when none, it is *fun*—& *wit*—. It hangs in a String with their love of calling white black, &c. as Derwent when he had scarce a score of words in his whole Tonguedom comes holding up a pair of filthy Pawlets, & lisps—Here's *clean white* Hands!—& then laughed immoderately.[98]

In Malta, where both Coleridge's fear and guilt towards his children much intensified, he had the following dream:

Had been playing with Souter's pretty children/ but went to bed with bad bowels—dreams interfused with struggle and fear, tho' till the very last not Victors—and the very last which awoke me . . . tho' a true Nightmair was however a mild one. I cried out early, like a scarcely hurt Child who knows himself within hearing of his Mother. But anterior to this I had been playing with Children, especially with one most lovely Child, about 2 years old or 2½—and had repeated to her in my Dream, "The Dews were falling fast" &c—and I was sorely frightened by the sneering and fiendish malignity of the beautiful creature/ from the beginning there had been a Terror about it, and proceeding from it/ —I shall hereafter read the Visions in Macbeth with increased admiration.[99]

"The sneering and fiendish malignity of the beautiful creature" at once brings to mind Geraldine[100] (and the reference to the "Visions in Macbeth" recalls a detail in the projected conclusion of "Christabel" given to Gillman: "Geraldine being acquainted with all that is passing, like the Weird Sisters in Macbeth, vanishes"). The poem Coleridge recites in the dream, "The Dews were falling fast," is Wordsworth's "The Pet Lamb," the story of a lost lamb brought home by a shepherd and treated with great kindness—the hospitality theme again. In one of the great stanzas added to "The Ancient Mariner" in 1817 there is a juxtaposition, four lines apart, of terrible fear and dripping dews:

> Fear at my heart, as at a cup,
> My life-blood seemed to sip!
> The stars were dim, and thick the night,
> The steersman's face by his lamp gleamed white;
> From the sails the dew did drip—(ll. 204-208)[101]

Such connections are extremely obscure, but what is apparent is a much more intimate connection between Coleridge's dreams and his poems than initially appears. For example, when the bodies of the dead men are animated to sail the ship, why the following detail?

> The body of my brother's son
> Stood by me, knee to knee . . . (ll. 341-342)

It is the only reference to the Mariner's family in the whole poem, and one wonders whether at this point unconscious personal associations have broken through the apparently seamless fabric of objective art. With Coleridge's journal to guide us, we can also take a fresh look at the powerful stanza in which the Mariner finds himself alone among the corpses on a rotting deck:

> I looked to heaven, and tried to pray;
> But or ever a prayer had gusht,
> *A wicked whisper came*, and made
> My heart as dry as dust. (ll. 244-247)

The psychological power of these lines derives precisely from the upwelling of evil thoughts from the depths of the unconscious, even when one speaks to

God. The Mariner provides no explanation of the "wicked whisper." It is simply given, a fact of the universe, as incomprehensible and inexplicable as the shooting of the albatross, the death of a ship's whole crew for the crime of one man, the pity which a kind saint inexplicably confers on the Mariner, so that he can bless the water snakes "unawares." But the "wicked whisper" takes on a peculiarly powerful personal meaning when we find that Coleridge later wrote into his notebook: "Those Whispers just as you have fallen or are falling asleep—what are they and whence?"[102] Were Coleridge and the Old Navigator psychic twins?

To return now to the dream of January 1804 in which Duns Scotus (another traveler) imagines himself "in the Land of Logic, lying on the Road & in the Road to the Kingdom of Truth." The polarity between the actuality (deranged as a youth) and the illusion ("imagines" himself in the Land of Logic) recalls the dream in which Coleridge imagines himself delivering a brilliant lecture, only to have his auditors not care and "quiz" him off. Intellectual insecurity trembles just below the surface of this dream. Even the name Duns Scotus is ambiguous, for this is the philosopher whose very name has given English the word "dunce."

Now again the dangers of sex appear. He "falls into a criminal Intercourse with a Girl, whom he considers as the Daughter of the King of the Land" (another noble child). The phrase "criminal intercourse" is sufficiently common; yet the phrase here bears more weight than that of a cliché. For in this dream, as suggested in others, sexual relations with women can have frightful results.

Reference to the King of the Land recalls the Emperor of Russia in another dream, the Nobleman who has two sons, and Adam, the father of us all. The appearance of Kings, Queens, Emperors, Noblemen, Giants, and so forth, represents the primary personages of dream experiences, as in the fairy tales of all nations. Whatever the ultimate significance of these archetypes as symbols, it can hardly be doubted that some part of what they represent are those figures from childhood who are most important to us, the great authority figures, toward whom we feel both love and dependence, security and fear, the adults of one's childhood, parents or their surrogates.

In this dream of Scotus (himself famed for his ingenious logical gymnastics), we come squarely upon the process of brilliant rationalization in action. The dreamer, detected in "criminal Intercourse," defends himself by asserting that the intercourse did not exist in reality but was rather the "impersonation & absolute Incarnation of the most Abstract"! How characteristic this is; how cunningly the dreaming mind copes with the sleeper's evasions, denials of reality, and pretenses. "O it was a wild dream, yet a deal of true psychological Feeling at the bottom of it." The true psychological feeling seems to consist in the extraordinary condensation of emotions ranging from grandiose intellectual ambition and destructive self-doubt, fears of mental derangement, and the cluster of incestuous implications inherent in sleeping as a youth with a girl in love with you who is the daughter of the king of the land.[103]

Having now examined a series of genuine dreams which Coleridge wrote into his notebooks, we are in a far better position to evaluate the claims of "Kubla Khan" as a dream poem. May we not now, once and for all, relegate to myth Coleridge's 1816 Preface? If there was any dream-origin for this famous poem, it surely resides in its *images*, certainly not in the glorious fabric of language. These images, however, most definitely do relate to his fantasies and unconscious life, and would seem far more to derive from "a sort of Reverie" than from the mind's deliberate aesthetic control.

If "Kubla Khan" were a genuine dream, it would represent the earliest one Coleridge recorded. Evidence as to the date of the poem, a point which may have unique importance, is circumstantial and most contradictory. Coleridge himself twice dated the poem in 1797, and the reasons for assigning any other date are not compelling. If there was a visit to a lonely farmhouse in the fall of 1797, during which there was an opium experience, there is considerable evidence for fixing an exact date. As Professor Griggs notes, Coleridge wrote John Thelwall on 14 October 1797 stating that he had been absent from home "a day or two."[104] This seems a slim point, but Coleridge's daily movements have been so intensively studied for 1797-98 that this remark is one of the very few concrete bits of evidence that he could have visited the farmhouse. "I should much wish, like the Indian Vishna [Vishnu], to float about along the infinite ocean cradled in the flower of the Lotos," he wrote, "& wake once in a million years for a few minutes—just to know that I was going to sleep a million years more."

Griggs supposes that this "suggests the effect of opium." In any case, several other references in this letter can be argued as having points of contact with "Kubla Khan": the reference to "rocks, or waterfalls, mountains or caverns" certainly is reminiscent of Kubla's landscape, and the phrase "in the fall of the year" seems to echo the Crewe manuscript's "written in the fall of the year, 1797." If "Kubla Khan," however, actually existed at this time, how to account for Coleridge's failure to mention it in this long letter to Thelwall, in which, after all, he quotes from his own "This Lime-Tree Bower My Prison" and *Osorio*? Why would Coleridge not communicate to his friend at least a few lines from the poem that he had so mysteriously been given in the previous days? Of course one can supply an answer to this question too, namely, that Coleridge was keeping his opium experiences to himself, but the answer is not convincing. It seems much better to assume that if the letter to Thelwall strongly hints at a retirement to a farmhouse and some sort of opium experience that there was as yet no "Kubla Khan" written, but that he may have brought away with him a few *images*, and perhaps a rough mental draft of some passages.

The letter Coleridge wrote immediately before this one is dated 9 October. It is the third of the famous series of autobiographical letters, and it provides a vivid account of his unhappy childhood at Ottery St. Mary, his harassment by his older brother Frank and the nurse Molly. The letter ends with his reference to the little nursery rhyme about Matthew, Mark, Luke and John.

> Frequently have I, half-awake & half-asleep, my body diseased & fevered by my imagination, seen armies of ugly Things bursting in upon me, & these four angels keeping them off.—In my next I shall carry on my life to my Father's Death.[105]

We can, therefore, say with absolute certainty that *if* Coleridge retired to a farmhouse between Porlock and Linton in the next few days and indulged in opium, his unconscious was then richly stirred with memories of child-hood, and most especially with the most intense memory a boy can have: the sudden death of a father, here combined with fierce hostility to an older brother and with memories of ugly things (forbidden and terrifying thoughts?) attacking him in bed.

Immediately upon returning from his brief excursion, Coleridge wrote to Thelwall (in reply to a letter waiting for him). The very next letter, two days later, is again to Poole, and this famous account begins with the memorable description of the murderous scene between himself and Frank, goes on to describe the night spent out of doors, and concludes with the vivid recollections of the father's death, with the nine-year-old boy rising out of slumber at the sound of his mother's shriek and saying, "Papa is dead," only to have this prove true.

No satisfactory reason has ever been given as to why Coleridge should have gone to a lonely farmhouse some twenty miles from his home. In an 1810 note about Charles Lloyd, he wrote that mental distress had driven him to this retirement when he first indulged in opium. This statement is so patently false as to be significant.[106] The bitter quarrel with Lloyd occurred in the summer of 1798. If Coleridge's 1810 account is to be credited, "Kubla Khan" could not have been written until then. But the 1810 note says nothing of "Kubla Khan," and since he was obviously deceiving himself about his early use of laudanum, we may justifiably ask whether he had not here displaced one anxiety which drove him to the farmhouse between Porlock and Linton for another, namely, the mental distress attendant upon recollections of childhood, of violent quarrels with his dead brother Frank, of the death of his father, and other unconscious stirrings not specifically mentioned. Could it not have been these memories which drove him to seek solace in laudanum, for which purpose he left home to be away from perhaps disap-proving eyes? If so, it is not at all unlikely that he would in time forget the specific reason for his "retirement." He would in all likelihood not even know at the time what was causing him such anxiety. The desire expressed in the letter to Thelwall for slumber in the flower of the lotus for a million years strongly suggests a bout of severe inner turmoil.

In later years, thinking about this experience, which was undoubtedly attended with a great deal of guilt, Coleridge would not improbably have assigned some other cause for the purposeful retirement. Such confusions are not at all uncommon, certainly not with Coleridge. In that case the "crime" committed at the farmhouse—indulgence in opium for the sake of sensual pleasure—would be buried or half-obliterated by assigning a far more acceptable cause for it (the allegedly mad behavior of Charles Lloyd), and a miraculous poem is offered as a result, "Kubla Khan," written in a dream, after taking an "anodyne" in consequence of a "slight indisposition," or —to Southey, with more directness of statement but perhaps no less false-hood of spirit—two grains of opium against dysentery.

If there was, then, a retirement to a farmhouse in October of 1797, Coleridge would have carried with him those painful memories of childhood. According to the classic texts of modern psychoanalysis, he would in fact have been carrying emotion-charged memories of primal intensity in our common psychological autobiography.

"Kubla Khan" has been so often cited as a dream specimen that a curious belief has grown up—accepted even in scholarly quarters—that the work now floats in a vast sea of psychonanalytic interpretation. But in fact scarcely more than an occasional Freudian or Jungian spray ever reaches the poem. In 1924 Robert Graves offered a silly and slipshod "Freudian" interpretation of "Kubla Khan," for which he was properly, and somewhat gleefully, roasted by Lowes.[107] Since then there have been few to rush in where scholars have feared to tread. Again and again discussions of "Kubla Khan" begin with ceremonial fanfares about the dangers of attempting to analyze a dream one hundred fifty years old; a few misty references follow to such "obvious" unconscious meanings in the poem as that the pleasure-dome may represent the female breast and the sacred river milk, and then the writer—more often than not—rejects the whole procedure as improper and proceeds to analyze "Kubla Khan" in ways that would have seemed laby-rinthine to Freud himself. Thus, for example, it is now practically an article of faith that "Kubla Khan" is a poem about poetry, that Kubla himself is a creator, the builder of a pleasure-dome, that the sacred river flowing under-ground is a symbol for the role of the unconscious in art. And so forth. Such interpretations are not in themselves absurd, however improbable. The problem is that the critic never states by what theory of mental functioning such a system of symbols is supposed to operate. In fact, "Kubla Khan" is regularly interpreted by the lights of contemporary literary criticism, mostly American in origin, in which a poem's structure of symbols is analyzed independently of the known facts of the artist's life (which are considered irrelevant).

It is possible to interpret *any* poem by using the standard conventions of dream analysis. But the results of such procedures are quite regularly gro-tesque. That this *seems* not to be true of "Kubla Khan" strengthens the con-viction that the poem does indeed carry an unusual weight of unconscious meaning. But the interpreter must never cease to remind himself that what may appear reasonable to one reader may be outrageous to another. One of the problems that so agitated romantic poets and philosophers is with us still, namely, what can be said to exist outside ourselves objectively, and what is subjective, a function of the way our minds are constructed? Do we perceive in a poem only what we have been trained to perceive, or are our perceptions really *there*? The critic who presumes to employ the insights of modern psychology is merely, according to some literary authorities, manipulating imaginary counters. In the circumstances, mere prudence would seem to dictate extreme circumspection in approaching such controversial materials.

What follows might well be relegated to the comparative obscurity of a note, introduced perhaps by an ironic gaiety so as to disarm criticism, the whole suggesting extreme tentativeness. But it is doubtful that such strategies would work, or are altogether honorable. Certainly what follows is not urged as *the* meaning of "Kubla Khan." Poems lend themselves—with often fatal facility—to every manner of symbolic reading. "Kubla Khan" is a poem embodying some ideas about the power of art. It is also about a pleasure-dome, an Oriental emperor, a wailing woman, an overflowing fountain—and much else. Every interpretation is in an important sense a catalog of the reader's interests (and that of his culture at any stage of history).

What follows, then, is *an* interpretation of "Kubla Khan," from a perspective authorized by the nature of the present discussion. We are concerned with Coleridge's dreams and reveries as they relate to his creative life. If, therefore, we suppose that "Kubla Khan" does in fact elaborate free-floating reveries (or any thoughts rising to the mind unsummoned), what would we then make of it?

Here is a notebook account of some of Coleridge's more pleasant "visions"; it was entered between 6 December 1803, when he dreamed of the murdered Adam, and 13 December 1803, the date of the terrifying Christ's Hospital nightmare about the university harlot:

When in a state of pleasurable & balmy Quietness I feel my Cheek and Temple on the nicely made up Pillow in Caelibe Toro meo [on my celibate couch], the fire-gleam on my dear Books, that fill up one whole side from ceiling to floor of my Tall Study—& winds, perhaps are driving the rain, or whistling in frost, at my blessed Window, whence I see Borrodale, the Lake, Newlands—wood, water, mountains, omniform Beauty—O then as I first sink on the pillow, as if Sleep had indeed a material *realm*, as if when I sank on my pillow, I was entering that region & realized Faery Land of Sleep—O then what visions have I had, what dreams—the Bark, the Sea, all the shapes & sounds & adventures made up of the Stuff of Sleep & Dreams, & yet my Reason at the Rudder/ O what visions, ⟨μαστοι⟩(breasts)as if my Cheek & Temple were lying on me gale o'mast on [large breasted] Seele meines Lebens! [soul of my life!]—& I sink down the waters thro' Seas & seas—yet warm, yet a Spirit.[108]

With these references to visions and sinking down through warm seas, we may look at "Kubla Khan" afresh:

> In Xanadu did Kubla Khan
> A Stately pleasure-dome decree:
> Where Alph, the sacred river, ran
> Through caverns measureless to man
> Down to a sunless sea.

Features of this kind, appearing in reveries or dreams, easily lend themselves to interpretation as sexual symbols. But why confine the pleasure-dome to a breast symbol? Breasts do abound in Coleridge's work, and the suckling babe is one of his most repeated images; but a pleasure-dome in the vicinity of "caverns measureless to man" suggests far more the *mons veneris*, especially as we hear at once of "fertile" grounds and "forests," almost classic symbols for primary sexual terrain. And is not such a reading much reinforced by the lines that follow?

> But oh! that deep romantic chasm which slanted
> Down the green hill athwart a cedarn cover!
> A savage place! as holy and enchanted
> As e'er beneath a waning moon was haunted
> By woman wailing for her demon-lover!

A pleasure-dome, fertile ground, forests, caverns, a deep romantic chasm slanting down a hill . . . surely the sexual details now seem overwhelmingly to point in a single direction. Perhaps in all this there is at last a clue to the strange ominousness of these lines. Why are they introduced with such a sense of awe? "But oh! . . . athwart a cedarn cover! A savage place!" The exclamation points beat like an ominous drum in a general atmosphere of dread. And why, after all, is the place "holy and enchanted"? "Holy" is an especially odd word in this context. What makes this particular locale sacred to God? Though the syntax does not make it certain that a woman is actually present wailing for her demon-lover, that does not strictly really matter if we are interpreting the poem as a dream, or a sequence of free-floating images.

The meaning and sources of this cluster of lines are among the most intensely studied problems in Coleridge, and as yet no really satisfactory explanation has been provided. Perhaps the explanation is after all a simple one. A demon-lover is either a supernatural lover (which accords well with a holy and enchanted spot) or someone towards whom the woman stands in such a relation that sexual love between them would be demoniacal. To state the matter plainly, a demon-lover might be an incestuous lover. Let us try to hold both these ideas in suspension as we proceed.

Patricia M. Adair, in a valuable discussion of "Kubla Khan," devotes a good deal of attention to the ancient cults of Bacchus (often connected with

Dionysus).[109] She notes that primitive legend involves many encounters between gods and mortals.

> The ecstasy which possessed the women who followed Bacchus was a fierce and blind desire to be lost in the daemon-god. Whether Coleridge imagined his worship at Delphi or Cashmere, both were "savage places," "holy and enchanted" by the presence of Dionysus. The original Crewe manuscript of Kubla Khan confirms this association by spelling the "demon-lover" of the 1816 version as "Daemon Lover."[110]

If there is a connection between the Bacchus who drives women (and his other followers) mad and Coleridge's woman wailing for her "Daemon Lover," then the meanings we have thus far been dallying with are strongly reinforced. For we have seen that Bacchus was to appear in Coleridge's dreams as a projection of himself and that this particular god, for a time a threatened orphan, so consistently connected in ancient legend with sensual excess, with madness and orgies ("bacchanalia" derives from his name), with music and poetry (Orpheus was one of his priests), was connected in Coleridge's mind with himself. As has already been observed, Bacchus, the conqueror of India, was not far removed from another great conqueror in the orient, Kubla Khan, who, like Bacchus, we encounter in his role as pleasure-seeker. The process by which a Kubla could slide into Bacchus is not at all uncommon in the mind's symbol-making powers.

Finally, to draw these several points together, the woman wailing for her demon-lover is calling for an incestuous lover or perhaps Bacchus, a projection of the dreamer (or reverie-er, to credit the Crewe MS account). In either case, this wailing takes place in the vicinity of a forbidding chasm, holy and enchanted, a savage place!—which confirms the suspicion of tabooed terrain.

> And from this chasm, with ceaseless turmoil seething,
> As if this earth in fast thick pants were breathing,
> A mighty fountain momently was forced:
> Amid whose swift half-intermitted burst . . .

Here again are lines of extraordinary visual and emotional power, the source of which seems wrapped in mystery. Nominally the description of a fountain welling up from underground, the lines have the capacity again and again to move us with an almost hypnotic force. "As if this earth *in fast thick pants were breathing*": considered as an image from the unconscious, without regard to what is specifically described, would we not rather quickly hit upon the supposition that some kind of sexual encounter is being described?

> A mighty fountain *momently* was forced:
> Amid whose *swift half-intermitted burst* . . .

In all the world's literature, is there a more precise description of sexual ejaculation?[111] The immediately preceeding reference to a woman wailing for a lover, and a fountain erupting from the chasm with a "swift, half-intermitted burst," seem to represent a sexual scene, especially if we suppose that the image arose in Coleridge's mind during some daydream or reverie state, and that it haunted him, as indeed the lines do most readers with their mysteriously evocative power.

The sacred river meanders through wood and dale, reaches the caverns measureless to man, and sinks in tumult to a lifeless ocean.

> And 'mid this tumult Kubla heard from far
> Ancestral voices prophecying war!

This is another of those key passages in the poem which is so extremely difficult to interpret. In themselves the lines seem utterly inconsequential. Lowes accounts for their presence by observing that "the last sentence Coleridge had read before his eyes rested on the words 'In Xamdu did Cablai Can build a stately Palace,' was a remarkable expression of the belief among the Tartars of the survival of the dead," and that within a page there was a passage about divining priests: "They foretell holy dayes, and those which are unluckie for enterprises. *No warres are begunne or made without their word.*"[112] Again, without being confined by any theory of mental functioning, conscious or unconscious—apart from a crude associationist psychology —one need only suppose that since a book Coleridge was reading contained references to the survival of the dead, and to the making of wars, we may more or less account for the mysterious presence in "Kubla Khan" of "ancestral voices prophecying war!" Why should these lines be remembered? What principle of selectivity is operating?

Yet if we consider the sequence of meanings thus far weaving through the series of images, tabooed sexual terrain, incestuous or demon lovers, orgasm, do not the threatening ancestral voices signify something much more precise, much more personally fearful? If "Kubla Khan" is in some way an incestuous dream, are not the ancestral voices prophesying war (conflict) those of the father?

"In my next I shall carry on my life to my Father's Death," Coleridge had written on the ninth of October, just a day or two before mysteriously leaving his home on a short excursion, perhaps to retire to a lonely farmhouse. And two days after returning he writes a long letter about a murderous assault on a hated older brother and the death of his father, an event he rather astoundingly says he *knew* had taken place ("Papa is dead") upon being awakened from slumber by his mother's shriek. Surely this is as classic an instance of oedipal stress as one is likely to encounter. In this reading, therefore, the threatening ancestral voices, so far from being another specimen of the inconsequence of the dreaming unconscious, actually confirms the oedipal conflict inherent in the poem and of course in Coleridge's life.

An extraordinary variant in the Crewe manuscript appears at this point. What Coleridge originally wrote was:

> And mid this Tumult Cubla heard from *fear* [113]
> Ancestral Voices prophecying War.

He crossed out the last three letters of "fear" and wrote "ar" above the line to make the word "far." Now "fear" is no worse a slant-rime for "war" than "far," so the change was hardly dictated by purely aural considerations. What seems probable is that the original "fear" was a slip of the pen, and particularly revealing if one agrees that the ancestral voices are issuing threats to the poet's unconscious: guilt causes the voices to be heard from fear.

> The Shadow of the Dome of Pleasure
> Floated midway on the Wave
> Where was heard the mingled Measure
> From the Fountain and the Cave
> It was a miracle of rare Device,
> A sunny Pleasure-Dome with Caves of Ice!

Thus the Crewe manuscript reading. And indeed it makes much more sense in terms of sexual terrain to have a pleasure dome and a fountain and a single cave rather than several. The atmosphere of the poem at this point is immensely lightened. In fact the change of mood is one of the miracles of Coleridge's art. Still, the startling contrast of a sunny pleasure-dome and caves of ice may well suggest the dual nature of the dome in the dreamer's mind. It is sunny and dedicated to pleasure, and yet there are caves of ice: cold, frozen, underground, perhaps forbidding. When we remember the caverns measureless to man and the lifeless ocean, the ominous chasm, and the ancestral voices heard from fear, it is not hard to suppose that the caves of ice reveal another crosscurrent in Coleridge's unconscious, his deep, intense recoil from an act which "taken by itself," he was to write later, was "both foolish, & debasing." [114]

> A Damsel with a Dulcimer
> In a Vision once I saw:
> It was an Abyssinian Maid,
> And on her Dulcimer she play'd
> Singing of Mount Amara [or Amora].

Thus, again, the Crewe reading. The image of an Abyssinian maid playing a real dulcimer seems impossible to credit, for reasons already discussed in the notes. The important feature of this image, however, is that the maid is Abyssinian, black. We have seen that Abyssinia slips into the poem via

Milton's Abyssinian paradise, but whence the Negro maid? Coleridge's poems abound with dark ladies and ladies with ebony tresses, but here is a lass altogether different: a bona fide African girl; to say the least, a very rare image in English poetry of this period. And the maid sings so beautifully that she can work wonders in the poet. What, if any, is her significance?

The appearance in dreams of beings from races different from that of the dreamer not uncommonly betokens forbidden sexual objects, especially where legal or social constraints upon miscegenation exist. A black girl in the dream of a white man may of course represent many things, depending upon the dreamer's private beliefs and associations. Yet as a generalization it is true that powerful interracial fears or yearnings suggest the problem of incest.

Whether such a generalization applies with equal force to eighteenth-century England or to Coleridge in particular is difficult to prove. In any case, the maid's song can induce a state of divine euphoria, a creativity akin to madness. And of what does she sing? Of Mount Amara, where the *younger sons* of Ethiopian kings were *banished*, never to see their homes again, and thus never to threaten the eldest brother with *fratricide*. (Was not Coleridge the youngest of several sons, and sent away from home in childhood, never to return?) Yet if there are underlying associations here, what do we primarily think of when we hear Mount Amara, or Amora? The nearest cognate words that at once occur are *amour. amor, amorous*—any one will do. The Abyssinian Maid is singing of the Mount of Love, which brings us back to the pleasure-dome and *mons veneris* at the beginning of the poem.[115]

If the dreamer can summon back that mental state in which he heard the maid sing of Mount Amara, he would be possessed of such a power to re-create an experience already past that others would be able to share its intensity. He would be taken for someone possessed with divine madness ("his flashing eyes! his floating hair!"), and he would be seen as someone fearful ("Beware! Beware! . . . Weave a circle round him thrice!")

> And close your Eyes in holy Dread:
> For He on Honey-dew hath fed
> And drank the Milk of Paradise.

Why "holy" dread? The word appears once before in the poem: the deep romantic chasm is a savage place, "holy" and enchanted. We seem forced to the conclusion that the word again has a religious significance: "holy" dread is fear of divine retribution. Does not this suggest some offense against the laws of God and nature? What crime has the dreamer committed? Against whom or what is it an offense to feed upon honey-dew and drink the milk of paradise? To create great works of architecture is no cosmic offense, nor great art of any kind. The gods inspire men to great work, they fill them with the divine breath, divine madness. All this is part of the commonplace mythology of the Muses. But many readers feel something very much more powerful and more dreadful here. The speaker seems to have committed a crime much more dire. We think here neither of art nor of food and drink reserved for the gods, but rather of acts and pleasures reserved only to the gods, whatever they may be. To drink the milk of paradise may hearken back to the suckling babe, but this again is part of the ordinary experience of mankind and no affront to nature or heaven. The poem leaves us with a nameless crime. The dreamer is tabooed because he has had a forbidden experience. The arrows all point in the direction of incestuous longings.

The honey-dew and milk of paradise may of course be laudanum and the whole tribe of stimulants. I am inclined to think a substantial part of the meaning does inhere in this connection, although this places Coleridge's awareness of opium as an evil influence and a forbidden pleasure several years earlier than most commentators are inclined to allow. Let us remember that in his 1810 retrospective account he does point to use of laudanum in 1798 against mental distress, and the tone overwhelmingly suggests attendant guilt. The final lines of the poem may well point to guilt about indulging in opium for pleasure. If any of the sensual images of the poem rose to Coleridge's mind as the result of opium, he could here be expressing awareness that the only way to recover the blissful state of mind that produces Kubla's dome would be to indulge again. In this case the visitor from Porlock in reality represents the snapping of the pleasurable state as the effects of laudanum wore off. As the mind returned to cold reality, the memory of the euphoric images receded. It would be hard to *feel* the pleasure which under laudanum had accompanied the fantasy of power and sensual joy, although the images might remain more or less intact. Thus, to recapture the *emotions* which accompanied the ideas, indulgence would be necessary again. To do so, however, would be to risk divine punishment.[116]

The dangers of analyses such as the foregoing should be self-evident. Without the dreamer's own associations to serve both as check and guide, one can easily veer off into private fantasy and association. And where association is concerned, the possibilities seem to be endless in any imaginative person, if he abandons his mind to it. The presence of pitfalls, however, need not forbid the attempt to transverse hazardous territory. We can be quite sure that the judgment and associations of other readers will act as powerful counterforces to identify gross blunders, to blunt thrusts down false trails, and in general to rebuke excessively fanciful speculation.

Was Coleridge, in view of the foregoing, telling the truth in the 1816 Preface to "Kubla Khan"? Was it, after all, a dream—presented to the world with a bit of poetic license? I think not. What matters to poetry, or to studies of the creative process, is whether the poem was *written* in a dream. We can be quite certain that the images did not rise up before Coleridge as *things* with the correspondent words. On the contrary, the words were elaborated with great skill and conscious judgment. The last part of the poem

may well have been written much later, but there is no possible way to decide
this with confidence from any evidence we have at present. The first thirty
lines of the poem in fact have a "conversational" quality. If Coleridge had
written no more and said nothing of dreams it would surely be taken as the
fragment of a longer poem never written. Still, for reasons given, this poem
does seem to derive from inner sources and aesthetic procedures so unusual
for Coleridge as to justify the belief that the major block of images in the
poem did derive from personal fantasies.

Finally, with respect to interpreting "Kubla Khan" as a projection of the
poet's mind, it does not absolutely matter whether the poem is a dream or
coldly conscious creation. In all activity of the mind there are unconscious
elements, and this is especially true in poetry. Perhaps everything that has
been said here about "Kubla Khan" would apply (assuming one is sympathetic to the interpretation) whether or not the poem is a dream in any
sense.

The question remains: Why should Coleridge have been able to transform
unconscious conflicts into enduring poetic images in 1797-98 and not thereafter? Though we should not pretend certitude when navigating without
stars and only rudimentary compasses, some illuminating buoys may be
seen bobbing on the dark sea. On the very eve of the great triad, in the fall
of 1797, *Coleridge was systematically reviewing his childhood.* For this
reason the date of "Kubla Khan" is especially important. The evidence
points to a genesis for the poem directly between the third and fourth autobiographical letters to Poole, written a week apart. These two letters form
the heart of the series: Coleridge's memories from the age of three to nine,
ending with his father's death. Enough has now been said of the third letter,
with its painful account of the lonely child, "hated" by a brother and family
servant, "haunted by spectres," "tormented" by the school-boys, sometimes
attacked by "armies of ugly Things."

The fourth letter, however, dealing with events between the ages of seven
and nine, one of the longest and most important he ever wrote, must be
looked at again. It begins by plunging into the memorable description of
Coleridge's brother Frank *mincing* the cheese which was to have been
toasted, the violent scene between them, the blow in the face, Frank's pre-
tence of death, the horselaugh and counter-blow, the seizing of the knife by
the young Coleridge, intercession by his mother, flight into the fields, and
the long night out of doors, and his rescue when close to death by a nobleman, Sir Stafford Northcote. After describing the rescue, Coleridge reflects
on the growth of his youthful mind, and then passes to what is, for our purposes now, the most crucial memory of his childhood:

Towards the latter end of September 1781 my Father went to Plymouth
with my Brother Francis, who was to go as Midshipman under Admiral
Graves; the Admiral was a friend of my Father's.—My Father settled
my Brother; & returned Oct. 4th, 1781—. He arrived at Exeter about

six o'clock—& was pressed to take a bed there by the Harts—but he refused—and to avoid their intreaties he told them—that he had never been superstitious—but that the night before he had had a dream which had made a deep impression. He dreamt that Death had appeared to him, as he is commonly painted, & touched him with his Dart. Well he returned home—& all his family, I excepted, were up. He told my mother his dream—; but he was in high health & good spirits—& there was a bowl of Punch made—& my Father gave a long & particular account of his Travel, and that he had placed Frank under a religious Captain &c —/ At length, he went to bed, very well, & in high Spirits.—A short time after he had lain down he complained of a pain in his bowells, which he was subject to, from the wind—my mother got him some peppermint water—and after a pause, he said—"I am much better now, my dear!" —and lay down again. In a minute my mother heard a noise in his throat —and spoke to him—but he did not answer—and she spoke repeatedly in vain. Her *shriek* awaked me—& I said, "Papa is dead."—I did not know [of] my Father's return, but I knew that he was expected. How I came to think of his Death, I cannot tell; but so it was.[117]

This is one of those texts which, from a psychological point of view, offers material for infinite exegesis. Most of the account is, of course, remembered from what was heard in family accounts of the father's death. And here the memory is exact, down to the name of Admiral Graves and the vivid detail of the peppermint water. Only his mother's shriek awaking him from sleep and his own sudden thought, "Papa is dead," is a direct memory. The oedipal force of this memory is genuinely startling, and reinforces almost irresistibly the contention that primal guilt glimmers behind the mysterious crimes and dreads of the "mystery poems."[118] (It is odd that the crucial thought, "Papa is dead," bears a period in the text, not an exclamation point, but that just two or three lines above the father's last words are, "I am much better now, my dear!")

Less than a month after this letter, "The Ancient Mariner" was begun. It is noteworthy that in Coleridge's account a long sea voyage is linked with the departure of his brother, who was to die fighting in India (which Bacchus conquered), and the death of his father—an event soon to be followed by his own departure from home, where he was never to live again and which marked the end of any close ties he was ever to have with his family. In the literature of dreams a sea voyage may symbolize one's journey through life, and the ship's crew may represent one's family. Before Coleridge reached twenty years old, a sister and four brothers had died. The Mariner's wanderings are punishment for an irrational, unconsciously willed act of murder. Did Coleridge's unconscious view his own sufferings and banishment from his family as punishment for some related act of diseased volition?

We must now remember back to Wordsworth's two accounts of the genesis of "The Ancient Mariner": "it was founded on a dream, as Mr. Coleridge said, of his friend, Mr. Cruikshank"; it was a "strange dream . . . [Cruik-shank] fancied he saw a skeleton ship, with figures in it." Apparently it was this detail which stuck in Coleridge's mind, and from which the poem was elaborated. The original "Ancient Mariner" also contains the grim figure of Death, described in stock Gothic terms; Coleridge's father is said to have dreamed of Death "as he is commonly painted," and was touched by Death with his "Dart."[119]

The albatross is killed with a cross-bow, and the souls of the dead crew, as they pass the Mariner by, sound like "the whizz of my cross-bow!" In a dream Coleridge had almost five years to the day after "The Ancient Mariner" was begun, two sons of a Nobleman appeared, "desperately fond of shooting." This phrase is never explained. The sons become Coleridge, who "awoke after long struggles & with faint screaming from a persecuting Dream."[120] In 1805 he dreamed "Of a Ship-wrecked Crusoe, who shot wild geese, swans &c for his food."[121] Is not the Mariner a projection of Coler-idge's unconscious, an outcast, wanderer, with intermittent "strange power of speech," guilty of crimes (thoughts) whose nature and motive he does not understand? "The Ancient Mariner," seemingly so "fertile in unmeaning miracles," yet has a primitive logic.[122] Precisely because no hint of causation explains the slaying of the albatross, it assumes the character of an arche-typal crime, springing from demonic evil in fallen man, "desperately fond of shooting."[123] The Mariner's sufferings are Coleridge's. The death of the crew and destruction of the ship may represent symbolically the loss of one's nur-turing environment. Surges of hostility, of murderous rage, against those with whom one competes for love—against siblings for the love of the par-ents, against the father for the love of the mother—this must be atoned for by rejecting all familial and fleshly comforts. In the 1798 "Ancient Mariner" Cruikshank's "skeleton ship with figures in it" became a specter-bark con-taining the figure of Death, and a woman, identified only as his mate.

> *His* bones were black with many a crack,
>   All black and bare I ween;
> Jet-black and bare, save where with rust
> Of mouldy damps and charnel crust
>   They're patch'd with purple and green.
>
> *Her* lips are red, *her* looks are free,
>   *Her* locks are yellow as gold:
> Her skin is as white as leprosy,
> And she is far liker Death than he;
>   Her flesh makes the still air cold.[124]

These are conventional images, but the skin "white as leprosy" brings to mind the "frightful pale woman" of the nightmares. The concept of death having a mate, however, is very far from conventional. And her features are surely those of the diseased harlot, another figure of Coleridge's dreams. The poem continues:

> The naked hulk alongside came
> And the twain were casting dice;
> "The game is done! I've won! I've won!"
> Quoth she, and whistles thrice. (ll. 195-198)

Precisely what has she won? If we do not cheat and look at later versions of the poem, we will find that we do not know what the dice game is about! Of course we soon learn that the entire ship's crew drops down dead one by one, and that the Mariner survives, but it is not easy to deduce just how the dice game figures in this. The harlotlike mate of Death is not yet given a *particular* function, nor does the great revision of 1800 clarify this mystery.[125]

In 1817, almost twenty years after his original conception of this scene, the nucleus derived from Cruikshank's strange dream, the blurred focuses are at last resolved. The elaborate description of Death is utterly expunged from the poem. He now exists only as a word. The entire emphasis of the dice game shifts to the woman, described without the change of a single word. But in the fourth line of this famous stanza, she is finally identified, in a chilling image:

> Her skin was as white as leprosy,
> The Night-mare LIFE-IN-DEATH was she,
> Who thicks man's blood with cold.

And the marginal gloss clarifies the action further: "Death and Life-in-Death have diced for the ship's crew, and she (the latter) winneth the ancient Mariner." Nightmares, a life of torment, punishment for a crime against God— all are inextricably interwoven in Coleridge's final conception. From the beginning the Mariner was spared only to know a lifetime of penance. But the fate later dealt him is appalling in a way the original version is not. When Coleridge in his own epitaph wrote that he had "many a year with toil of breath / Found death in life," was he not identifying with his Old Navigator? Perhaps only those who know his notebooks can fully share the horror of what this ghastly, leprous female meant for him. Below the level of consciousness, he must have perceived his nightmares as punishments for unconscious wishes.[126]

That the key role of horrible avenger is assigned to a demonic female provides the necessary clue which links "The Ancient Mariner" and "Christabel." If Coleridge's unconscious was roiled with oedipal or fraternal guilts, it was nevertheless the cruel mother who meted out the punishment, by banishment, by withdrawal of love. In all his subsequent crippled relationships with women, it was not a wife his longing spirit sought, but the sheltering love of the protective mother.

Dr. David Beres has provided an excellent summary of Coleridge's wretched relations with his mother and argues that childhood emotional deprivation was responsible for his later "never-satisfied, ever-demanding" need for love and admiration, and his repetitive pattern of dependence upon authority figures. For Beres, a professional psychoanalyst, the ambivalence of love and hate Coleridge felt towards his own mother is symbolized in the slaying of the albatross.[127] However, as students of literature, we need not confine ourselves to any single interpretive perspective. We live in a universe of abysmal error and demonic impulse in the human soul, and some crimes may finally be unforgivable. So much is the common experience of mankind, and the Mariner's fate answers to knowledge deep within us. The range of interpretation available to us without professional psychoanalytical training need rest only upon a simple fact of human experience: we have all known moments of hate towards the innocent, towards those we ordinarily love, and in our imaginations we have all been murderers.

Against the value of "The Ancient Mariner" Irving Babbitt has argued: "The fact that a fiction of any kind is enthralling is no sure proof that it has human substance. Otherwise certain detective stories would merit a high literary rating."[128] But surely if a work is enthralling after repeated readings, it must have human substance. More of the power of poetry inheres in the mysterious force of the arrangement of words than critics are generally willing to grant. But the extraordinary hold of a fable in many ways so silly as "The Ancient Mariner" testifies to its powerful unconscious meaning.

"Christabel," far more than "The Ancient Mariner," lends itself to interpretation as an expression of Coleridge's ambivalence towards his mother. Beres argues that the death of Christabel's mother in childbirth is a projection, like the slaying of the albatross, of the destruction of the mother in Coleridge's unconscious mind. The ambivalently conceived Geraldine thus embodies Coleridge's own feelings about his own mother, and Geraldine, like the Nightmare Life-in-Death, is the slain mother seeking vengeance. "Only the guilt-ridden child," Beres writes, "sees the beautiful mother also as a monster."[129]

The poem's manifest content, however, is the conflict between good and uncertain evil. Christabel, as we have noted, has not only Christ's name in it, but also Abel's; she is the archetypal victim. The critical assumption, natural enough, is that the protagonist is the innocent Christabel. But with our knowledge of Coleridge's dreams we can see that Geraldine is as much, probably much more, a projection of the complexity of Coleridge's psyche than the relatively flat Christabel. Together they embody the psychic duality we have encountered so often. "The Tale of the Dream began" he wrote of one of his persecuting nightmares, "in two *Images*—in two Sons of a Nobleman, desperately fond of shooting. . . . as they struggled & resisted their cruel Wrongers, & my Interest for them, I suppose, increased, I became they. . . ."[130] At a crucial point in "Christabel," Geraldine throws a glance of serpentine malice at the helpless maid. Christabel "Shuddered aloud, with a hissing sound":

> The maid, alas! her thoughts are gone,
> She nothing sees—no sight but one!
> The maid, devoid of guile and sin,
> I know not how, in fearful wise,
> So deeply had she drunken in
> That look, those shrunken serpent eyes,
> That all her features were resigned
> To this sole image in her mind:
> And passively did imitate
> That look of dull and treacherous hate! (ll. 597-606)

Christabel is becoming like Geraldine. Is not what is being expressed here Coleridge's fear of being overmastered by evil impulses and becoming the demon he feared and hated?[131] The poem remained a fragment because neither Geraldine nor Christabel could emerge as wholly victorious or defeated. The unresolved conflict in Coleridge's unconscious is mirrored in the unresolved poem, which breaks off just as Christabel, who has already lost one parent, seems to have lost the affection of the other. When, in later years, Coleridge gave it out that Christabel was wholly an innocent, suffering for the guilty of this world, he was projecting an inner wish that his own sufferings had been visited upon him, from outside, for some providential end.

Unresolved incestuous conflicts, hatred of women, divided personality, fear of sex, homosexual impulses, female demons issuing threats and punishments, and fiends in the guise of loved ones—all these figure in the confused amalgam of Coleridge's poems of crime and marriage. Death and marriage were fearful companions in his unconscious, underscored by genuine personal associations and projected in poem after poem.

In the detailed account of his father's sudden death, he pointedly notes that his father and brother went to Plymouth harbor in late September 1781, and that his father died on October fourth. More than twenty years later he told Gillman that the quarrel with Frank and the night out of doors had also taken place "in the first week of October," and that his father's death had occurred a year or so later "about the same time, if not the very same time, i.e., Oct. 4th." But in the letter to Poole the Frank incident is specifically assigned to "the latter end of October." Thus we see that with the passage of time the events had coalesced in his mind, suggesting how closely linked they were in his unconscious.[132] But other, more important, unconscious distortions are at work here, for Coleridge's father did not die on October 4th but on the 6th, as is clearly stated in the Ottery St. Mary contemporary church register.[133] An error of this kind in a man who always celebrated his own birthday a day too soon, October 20th instead of the 21st, would ordinarily be inconsequential. But it happens that Coleridge himself was *married* on the fourth day of October, just two years before the autobiographical letter to Poole.

Now if Coleridge's father had actually died on the same date it would be odd that the bridegroom did not remember it at the time. In fact, we have Coleridge's own description of his thoughts during his wedding ceremony, written just three days after the event, again to Thomas Poole: "On Sunday Morning I was *married*—at St. Mary's, Red Cliff—poor Chatterton's Church—/ The thought gave me a tinge of melancholy to the solemn Joy, which I felt. . . ."[134] Thus, he accounts for the feeling of melancholy at his wedding not because he had mixed feelings about it, but because the church was associated with Chatterton, "the marvellous boy," dead by his own hand at seventeen. If Coleridge's father had died on that date, would he not have remembered it? Thoughts of home and family would certainly be strongly in the minds of most persons getting married. St. Mary's Red Cliff in fact is similar in name to Ottery St. Mary. The displacement of October 6th to October 4th, remembered so tenaciously even afterward, is a memory distortion created by associating in his unconscious the catastrophe of his father's death with the unhappy marriage he had contracted.

That the date of October 4th loomed large in Coleridge's mind is, therefore, hardly surprising. The terrifying Christ's Hospital dream about "the frightful pale woman who . . . had the property of giving a shameful Disease by breathing in the face" (so reminiscent of the leprous Nightmare Life-in-Death) actually took place on 3 October 1802, the night before this fateful anniversary, and the day on which William Wordsworth and Mary Hutchinson (who figure in the dream) were to be married.[135] But we are not yet done with coincidence and the hooks and eyes of unconscious association. The neighbor Cruikshank, whose strange dream provided the springboard for the whole complex fabric of "The Ancient Mariner," had been—according to Coleridge himself—also married on the fourth day of October![136]

The Mariner's tale of crime, death, and wandering begins with a marriage, for reasons never convincingly explained from purely aesthetic perspectives. Is there some deep, underlying bond between the Mariner's tale and the world of brides and grooms? His penance makes him an outcast among men, and women. He must abjure the world of the flesh.

> O sweeter than the marriage-feast,
> 'Tis sweeter far to me,
> To walk together to the kirk
> With a goodly company!— (ll. 601-604)

Why? How do the pleasures of food and the flesh relate to the slaying of the albatross? Why the stark contrast between the sensuality of the wedding and the austere asceticism of the Mariner? Indeed, the learned wisdom of the wedding-guest after hearing the frightful tale is to turn away, forlorn, from the bridegroom's door.

Links between demonic crime and marriage reverberate throughout "Christabel," where there are reiterated interconnections between death bells and marriage bells. Christabel relates how her mother.

> died the hour that I was born.
> I have heard the grey-haired friar tell
> How on her death-bed she did say,
> That she should hear the castle-bell
> Strike twelve upon my wedding-day. (ll. 197-201)

The poem opens with the twelve strokes of midnight, to discover Christabel praying for her betrothed knight. And the second part begins with a matin bell, which "Knells us back to a world of death."

In the portions of the abortive "Three Graves" written by Coleridge, wedding scenes are crucial, and the wicked sexual longings of the widowed mother-in-law (which contain incestuous overtones) lead her to curse her own daughter.

> Beneath the foulest mother's curse
>   No child could ever thrive:
> A mother is a mother still,
>   The holiest thing alive. (ll. 256-259)

Here, in a single stanza, Coleridge's unconscious conflict of hate and guilt is embodied. The young wife's sorrows finally infect her husband, Edward, with gloom and mysteriously oppressive thoughts. In the climatic sequence, he has a nightmare in which he *murders* the mother.[137]

Another association between marriage and death is suggested by the permutations of a memorable detail in "The Ancient Mariner," that of the "nodding minstrels":

> The bride hath paced into the hall,
> Red as a rose is she;
> *Nodding their heads* before her goes
> The merry minstrelsy. (ll. 33-36)

The emphasized phrase also appears in a very early poem, the farcial "Monody on a Tea-Kettle," and here it is not merry minstrels at a wedding who nod their heads, but "funeral steeds / *nodding their heads* in all the pomp of woe." The phrase appears yet again in Coleridge's poetry, this time in the wedding procession imagined by the "Dark Ladié," where "First the nodding minstrels go." The appearance of this image in just two contexts, a wedding procession and a funeral procession, provides another suggestive unconscious link.[138]

The villainous rogue who attempts to force an unwilling maiden into marriage or illicit relations is one of the stock figures in the world's literature. Osorio and Emerick (in *Zapolya*), both fratricidal usurpers, are typical instances. But Maria's resistance to Osorio has unusual overtones. She steadfastly refuses to marry him, although many proofs have been given that Albert, her betrothed, is dead. Coleridge consistently emphasizes the extraordinary bond between the orphan Maria and the noble Albert in fraternal images, slightly grotesque to us, but obviously an ideal for him. Maria cries of her desire to remain true to Albert:

> Were we not
> Born on one day, like twins of the same parent?
> Nursed in one cradle? (ll. 97-99)

And Albert later cries of his love for Maria, "I lisp'd thy name ere I had learnt my mother's!" (II, 316). The incestuous overtones in this play are complicated by the fact that Maria is not only a sister in all but name, but a psychic twin of Albert, born on the same day, nursed in the same cradle.[139] A merging of identities, cognate to Christabel-Geraldine, is vaguely present in the bad-Osorio/good-Albert-Maria complex.

Another link between *Osorio* and "Christabel" may be perceived in the resistance of both Maria and Christabel to parental pressure towards unwanted marriages, a theme which has obvious personal meaning for the unhappily married Coleridge. But the form this problem takes in "Christabel" is extraordinary. In the projected conclusion recorded by Gillman, Geraldine was to transform herself into "the accepted though absent lover of Christabel. Next ensues a courtship most distressing to Christabel, who feels—she knows not why—great disgust for her once favoured knight."[140] Only at the altar itself is the reluctant Christabel saved, by the appearance of the real betrothed at the crucial moment. As thus conceived, the story really would have flirted with dangerous sexual matters. The demon who could change herself into a man would have thrown an intolerable homosexual light upon the earlier disrobing scene, which is disquieting enough as it stands. Coleridge's inner censorship acted very powerfully to screen that scene through the mother-child image:

> And lo! the worker of these harms,
> That holds the maiden in her arms,
> Seems to slumber still and mild,
> As a mother with her child. (ll. 298-301)

But analysis of the whole context now shows how closely that sentimental image was connected in Coleridge's unconscious with sinister longings. Christabel feels disgust for one who can fairly be described as a demonic lover; in "Kubla Khan" a mysterious woman was to wail for one.

Whatever unconscious meanings may be lurking beneath the surface of "The Ancient Mariner," "Christabel," and "Kubla Khan," the ordinary reader easily senses in them the presence of profound issues. When Lamb said that he had never been affected by any human tale as by "The Ancient Mariner," he was testifying to the direct experience of the emotions. From whence does this power derive? Surely not in any alleged crime against the imagination (even if this were not an absurd hypothesis for other reasons), or the presence of the doctrine of necessitarianism, of the "sacramental" view of life, or almost any of the many recent interpretations that are so widely held to have "ennobled" the poem. "The Ancient Mariner" does not need to be ennobled. It was experienced as a very powerful poem by most readers within Coleridge's lifetime, and so it has remained to this day.[141]

What every reader perceives at once in "The Ancient Mariner" is the intensity of the tale, which concerns a fabulous voyage into unknown portions of the globe, a mysterious and disturbing crime, frightful persecution, guilt, loneliness, delirium—and at last redemption. Is not the man rare who has not felt impelled in his imagination to commit a crime which he would be ashamed to carry out? These are among the primary experiences of men in all ages.

To the fortuitous cluster of happy chances which converge in Coleridge's *annus mirabilis*, we must now add the miraculous good fortune that in the three poems which readers have most cherished Coleridge addressed themes and fables far removed from any apparent personal concern. Indeed, we may be sure that if he had had any glimmering that these poems might be profoundly self-revelatory, he would have at once become self-conscious, defensive, declamatory. In the *Biographia Literaria*, we may recall, he said that one of the most significant indications of creative genius is the ability to write on topics and concerns far removed from the artist's direct experience. The remark is seemingly superficial and only to be understood as an attempt to account for the protean genius of Shakespeare, who presumably could not have had direct experience of the multitude of characters and states of mind he wrote so insightfully about. And it also looks back, perhaps, to his own feat in having written "The Ancient Mariner" before he ever set foot on a ship. But the remark has deeper implications. "Kubla Khan," "The Ancient Mariner," and "Christabel" were among his supreme achievements, and as far as Coleridge was aware, they were unconnected with his intellectual convictions or personal history. It is ironic that he was actually to put so much of his personal self into his work. By comparison, Byron is a secretive poet.

"The Ancient Mariner," "Kubla Khan," and "Christabel" are unique among Coleridge's important poems in being free of that posturing self-consciousness which disfigures so much of the remaining canon. Even "Ode to Dejection," a brilliant and moving poem, rings false as a *cri de coeur*, riddled too often with the intrusions of the self-conscious poet singing with his breast against a thorn, too obviously aware of dramatic posture and poetic balances. But into the great triad went the transfigured labyrinth of dread, confusions, guilts, and hopes, which characterize his dreadful nightmares. And because Coleridge was unaware of what his real subject was in these poems, they *could* become charged with the tension and turbulence of his own chaotic inner life, a nightmare realm normally screened not only from others, but from himself.

25.

The Unreconciled Opposites

HAVING followed Coleridge over so long and varied a public career, having intruded upon his private letters, rudely glanced over his shoulder at all hours of the day and night as he wrote his most personal thoughts into his journals, and finally, having pursued him even into the privacy of his dreams, we ask: what finally is the shape that emerges of this complex and riven personality?

During his own lifetime, he was an enigma to many of his closest friends, and there is little in their testimony to assist us. All Coleridge's mighty endowments, Wordsworth sadly declared in 1809, were "frustrated by a derangement in his intellectual and moral constitution. In fact he has no voluntary power of mind whatsoever, nor is he capable of acting under any *constraint* of duty or moral obligation."[1] He was "a man without a will," according to Hazlitt.[2] "One could almost believe that an enchanter's spell was upon him," wrote Mrs. Clarkson, "forcing him to be what he is. . . ."[3]

Such statements leave inexplicable the mystery of Coleridge's personality. Southey, for so many years his closest confidant, wearily wrote in 1812 of his brother-in-law's seemingly incomprehensible derelictions:

It is useless to grieve over these things. Coleridge will always sacrifice his own interests and the feelings of all belonging to him *rather than encounter the slightest temporary inconvenience*, though the neglect of duty is sure to bring with it its immediate punishment. We must take him as he is, alike unequalled for moral imbecility and intellectual strength.[4]

Dorothy Wordsworth, who had found the young Coleridge "so benevolent, so good tempered and cheerful,"[5] was later to write some of the harshest descriptions of him ever penned. A month after the failure of the *Friend*, she confided to a close friend:

With respect to Coleridge, do not think that it is his love for Sara which has stopped him in his work. Do not believe it: his love for her is no more

413

than a fanciful dream. Otherwise he would prove it by a desire to make her happy. No! He likes to have her about him as his own, as one devoted to him, but *when she stood in the way of other gratifications it was all over*. I speak this very unwillingly, and again I beg, *burn* this letter.[6]

Coleridge was appalled that anyone should think him sensually self-indulgent. On the contrary, "My sole sensuality was not to be in pain!" On those occasions when he tried to ferret out the reasons for behavior so alien to his ideals, he generally found them in causes beyond personal responsibility or control. He recognized, especially in his later years, that a terrifying gulf separated the "real" man he believed himself to be, and the untrustworthy, failed, and even irresponsible wretch he admitted he sometimes was. Given his subtle intelligence and philosophical training, it is characteristic that he was able to account for his behavior in a way at least intermittently satisfying to himself, and most useful in subsequent apologetics:

I know, it will be vain to attempt to persuade Mrs. Morgan or Charlotte [he wrote in 1814] that a man, whose moral feelings, reason, understanding, and senses are perfectly sane and vigorous, may yet have been *mad* —And yet nothing is more true. By the long long Habit of the accursed Poison i.e. opium my Volition (by which I mean the faculty *instrumental* to the Will, and by which alone the Will can realize itself—it's Hands, Legs, & Feet, as it were) was completely deranged, at times frenzied, dissevered itself from the Will, & became an independent faculty: so that I was perpetually in the state, in which you have seen paralytic Persons, who attempting to push a step forward in one direction are violently forced round to the opposite. . . . The worst was, that in *exact proportion* to the *importance* and *urgency* of any Duty was it, as of a fatal necessity, sure to be neglected. . . . In exact proportion, as I *loved* any person or persons more than others, & would have sacrificed my Life for them, were *they* sure to be the most barbarously mistreated by silence, absence, or breach of promise.—I used to think St. James's Text, "He who offendeth in one point of the Law, offendeth in all" very harsh; but my own sad experience has taught me it's aweful, dreadful Truth. What crime is there scarcely which has not been included in or followed from the one guilt of taking opium? Not to speak of ingratitude to my maker for the wasted Talents; of ingratitude to so many friends who have loved me I know not why; of barbarous neglect of my family . . . . I have in this one dirty business of Laudanum an hundred times deceived, tricked, nay, actually & consciously LIED.—And yet *all* these vices are so opposite to my nature, that but for this free-agency—annihilating Poison, I verily believe that I should have suffered myself to have been cut to pieces rather than have committed any one of them.[7]

"This one dirty business of laudanum." How satisfying to ascribe to a single omnipotent agency *all* his vices, otherwise "so opposite to my nature."

Is it any wonder that Coleridge desperately wanted to believe this tale, or that many later scholars have been quick to ascribe to the uncertain properties of opium demonic powers? Where the Devil has not existed, he has often been invented.

Yet, especially after 1802, Coleridge really did often feel himself the helpless victim of alien demons rioting within him, demons that he wished with all his heart to cast out. We confront the truly baffling spectacle of a man tortured by the dread not only of improper acts but of improper *thoughts*, who at the very time that his journals are scarred with his struggles and prayers for self-amendment was indulging in all manner of conscious lies and deceptions.

He abhorred hypocrisy, and was merciless in analyzing its manifestations in others. Of Mrs. Christopher Wordsworth's allegedly false piety and desire "to mortify the pomps & vanities of the World," he asked: "Are such People *conscious* of their Hypocrisy? Answer. No! They take good care, they shall not—& that is the worst sin of the two!"[8] Conversely, he wrote of Sir James Mackintosh: "he *means* to fulfil his engagements with you; but he is one of those weak-moraled men, with whom the meaning to do a thing means nothing. He promises with his whole Heart, but there is always a little speck of cold felt at the core that trans-substantiates the whole resolve into a Lie, even in his own consciousness."[9] Such uncompromisingly harsh moral attitudes are typical of Coleridge, especially on matters near allied to his own failings. But of moral judgment we have had far too much in Coleridge studies. What is now needed is understanding, understanding based on facts.

Coleridge liked to compose while walking over uneven ground. According to Hazlitt, he continually shifted from one side of the foot-path to the other while carrying on a peripatetic conversation: "He seemed unable to keep on in a strait line."[10] His celebrated conversation confounded many of his auditors, who found it mystifyingly disjointed and circuitous. Similarly, his handwriting is often broken and agitated, displaying extremely uneven pen pressure, and the words themselves are consistently blurred.

Such details, so easily dismissed as meaningless in themselves, take on a peculiarly suggestive relevance in a comprehensive study of this endlessly complicated man. From the vantage points provided by our long and arduous journey, not only the main avenues of inquiry, but many scattered and seemingly marginal observations should organize themselves into a vivid, internally consistent pattern of act and motive.

In the twilight realms of Coleridge's consciousness we have found starkly revealed the symbolic reflections of a tormented waking life. The dreamer who consistently projected himself as a child, or boy, continually threatened, fleeing from hostile pursuers, physically maimed, once mad (or believed so), unable to assert his true identity, and mocked in his intellectual pretentions —this was also the waking man, and these were his deepest fears.

The source of these crippling fears lies in the cruel sequence of early emotional disasters we have traced. At Ottery St. Mary the youngest of thirteen

children was already fearful, rejected by his playmates, and harrassed by
members of the household. The son of a poor and pious clergyman, he was
from his earliest years drilled in the catechism of a stern morality. At nine
he was to lose such fragile securities as home and family afforded. The harsh
charity-school far away greatly reinforced both the moralistic and intellectually competitive tendencies the timorous boy had already acquired. Only
two qualities fundamentally mattered at the school: moral rectitude and
intellectual promise. Discipline was extremely harsh, and sometimes took
humiliating forms. Coleridge later spoke with intense feeling about his
mental sufferings as a child from humiliating forms of punishment. In one
of his 1808 lectures, as reported by Crabb Robinson, he declared that
schoolboys

> lived in a state of civil war with their masters. They are disgraced by a
> lye told to their fellows; it is an honour to impose on the common enemy:
> thus the mind is prepared . . . for every falsehood and injustice when the
> interest of the party, when honour requires it. On disgraceful punish-
> ments such as fools-caps he [Coleridge] spoke with great indignation and
> declared that even now his life is embittered by the recollection of igno-
> minious punishments he suffered when a child; it comes to him in disease
> and when his mind is dejected. This part was delivered with fervour.[11]

Thus the pattern of falsehood and evasion began early. "Would'st thou
have pilfered from our school-boys' themes?" a character in *Zapolya* asks.[12]
At nineteen he wrote to his brother George: "I have sent you a sermon metamorphosed from an obscure publication by vamping, transposition &c.—if
you like it, I can send you two more of the same kidney."[13] Coleridge spent
nine long years under constant pressure to excel in an atmosphere where the
stakes were all too real. Failure to win a place at the university would have
been a disaster whose magnitude can be estimated only against the reality
of a rigidly class-ridden society. A life of drudgery as a copy-clerk or the
harsher destiny of seaman in the English navy were among the common fates
of boys who failed.

During all those years he was terribly lonely, and never had any reason
to doubt the simple truth that he was not loved. Indeed, he sometimes felt
altogether abandoned. His older brothers were busy with their own lives and
rarely looked in upon him. His mother seems to have been unspeakably
indifferent. The myriad deprivations of Christ's Hospital were to haunt him
for the rest of his days.

Coleridge's later tales of effortless academic victories distort the far less
spectacular reality. His early work in prose and verse is outstanding, but far
from astonishing, certainly not by the standards applied to genius. In the one
scholarship he competed for at Cambridge, he failed. He dropped out of
college early and never gained a degree. His brief army career was a disaster,
a circumstance that makes for much comedy in Coleridge biographies, but

ignores the sober fact that the clumsy recruit's ineptitudes did nothing for his shaky self-image as a man. The first girl he proposed to rejected him. He was not surprised. (Never in his entire life did he feel loved by a woman.) For a time Pantisocracy offered the hope of a new beginning, a kind of rebirth, in an ideal society where property and pride of birth were scorned, and intellect and goodness of heart exalted. But the Pantisocrats quarreled, and the dream faded.

The dependencies that featured his early life continued after his unfortunate marriage. At no point was he able to support himself through his own efforts. The *Watchman* collapsed after just ten numbers. His early poetry was well received, but the world was not dazzled. The explosive success that greeted the early publications of Samuel Rogers and Lord Byron was denied him. But he was still young, and hopeful, and much admired by intimates. His brain teemed with grandiose projects.

From the time he left Cambridge to the very end of his life, he was dependent upon the largesse of others. In Bristol various enlightened citizens helped him with small amounts of money. The Wedgwood annuity was an early godsend. Gifts from others followed, mostly small, to be sure, but symptomatic of Coleridge's inability to restrict his obligations. Gifts and loans were a way of life with him: Poole, Beaumont, Byron, Allsop, and many others, at various times supplied funds, sometimes in large amounts, as for example, £300 from De Quincey. The inability to manage money was, probably, not a matter of ineptitude. Coleridge was rather shrewd, all things considered, in financial matters. But he had no power of restraint. The reckless youth who squandered part of the funds provided by his brothers to pay his college debts is a resonant symbol of Coleridge at almost any time in his life. Here, as elsewhere, he was characteristically incapable of denying himself the pleasures of the moment.

He lived in the moment, and sufficient unto the moment were the solaces thereof. There is thus a partial truth in Coleridge's agonized cry, "My sole sensuality was not to be in pain!" It was, taken literally, quite false, but many of Coleridge's lies, evasions, and derelictions were responses to potential distresses, rather than active seeking after pleasures. A letter might contain bad news, demands, or—given the guilty feelings that were his lifelong companions—reproaches. Better not to open the letter at all. No matter that it was from an old friend, or son, or daughter, and that guilt would in time intensify. No matter. The next moment was taken care of, and that was paramount.

It was on Malta that he first experienced "the melancholy, dreadful feeling of finding myself to be a *man*, by a distinct division from boyhood, youth, and 'young man.' Dreadful was the feeling—till then life had flown so that I had always been a boy, as it were."[14] Coleridge was at least thirty-two years old when this thought first came to him; he had been married for almost ten years, and was the father of three children.

The inability to see himself as a fully-grown man is painfully evident in his fixed pattern of dependency, in the reflex posture of subservience he assumed in the presence of older, stronger, wealthier, or more assertive men. "I have felt in your society a feeling of confidence," he wrote in 1804 to John Rickman, shortly after their meeting, "which I never felt on so short an acquaintance, even in my younger days."[15] Soon Rickman was to complain of Coleridge's flattery and his "habit of assentation."[16] Crabb Robinson believed that Coleridge was often insincere, especially in his praise, because he feared to give offense. Coleridge's "anxiety to stand well with the lady disturbed his memory!" reports the implacable Cottle.[17] This anxiety to please, the habit of assentation, are facets of larger problems: his ceaselessly gnawing self-doubts and fear of rejection. Insincerity, flattery, even sycophancy in the presence of those whose approval he desired, heavily punctuate the records of his life. Here again, he simply could not believe that he could be liked for himself alone. Needing assurance so desperately, he went to extreme, embarrassing lengths to make others like him. Once in a large company he was sharply criticized by Sir Henry Englefield, who took strong exception to one of his lectures. Coleridge, according to Wordsworth, "instead of defending himself, burst into tears."[18] Such a response from an experienced public speaker and renowned conversationalist must be totally incomprehensible to those who have never stared open-eyed at the frightful web of fears that held Coleridge prisoner. Disapproval was tantamount to the approach of the devouring spider.

Vulnerable as a flayed man, never able to deafen himself to the inner voices that bore moral witness to his thoughts and actions, he was likely to respond with frantic anxiety to any direct charge of misconduct. At all costs the humiliating accusation had to be denied, his perfect integrity maintained.

The Coleridge who vigorously protested his perfect innocence to John Rickman in the matter of the falsely franked letters was lying, consciously, even though he solemnly affirmed his innocence upon his honor as a gentleman. But we will suspend useless moral dismay if we truly accept that a serious assault upon his self-image, especially as to his honor or intellectual stature, was literally unendurable. Adverse criticism in any form was neurotically painful to him, which is one of the many reasons why he submitted his work to the public with such anxious and misleading prefaces.

All this is indispensable to an adequate understanding of Coleridge. Praise was nectar, and he was an appallingly wide-meshed sieve that became increasingly frayed and battered with the passing years. All his life he drew nectar in that sieve, and so he could passionately affirm—undoubtedly believing it at the time he wrote—that he had never been adequately appreciated. The near-adulation of such men as Southey, Lamb, Wordsworth, Davy, Godwin, Hazlitt, and De Quincey—and hosts of lesser figures—was an insubstantial whisper drowned out under any kind of stress by the brass-throated inner demons who trumpeted that no one *really* admired him, or that all of them were deceived, and would one day find him out.

This kind of intellectual self-doubt is present throughout Coleridge's life, but deepens markedly after 1802. Such doubt is by far the major force in the shape of his literary career and subsequent reputation. He was a reader of out-of-the-way books early, but not merely because he possessed the avid curiosity of the all-encompassing intellect. In these remote or forgotten books he was always more or less on the hunt for useful matter. He was, after all, a professional man of letters, and from the beginning his need to don the mantle of universal knowledge was irresistible.

In this respect there is no essential difference between the Coleridge of twenty-three and sixty-three. And so the appropriations began, often with just enough ambiguity or oblique reference to the source to muddy any future charge of improper acknowledgment. The needs that drove him to risk public disgrace functioned with much less inhibition in private relations. How could he resist putting forward as the fruit of his own lonely meditation ideas derived from books unknown to his enrapt auditors? No real distinction existed for him between the gratifications of public acclaim and the warmer, more immediate approval of whatever listener happened to be about. It was, therefore, a keen insight of Carlyle to perceive that a man like Coleridge could mortgage the laurels of posterity for the stare of an idler. Testimony often rejected in Coleridge studies as mere animosity or error in those who knew him is sometimes acutely revelatory. Thus Southey wrote that the same things Coleridge said to him privately he heard "repeated,—repeated to every fresh company, seven times in the week if we were in seven parties. . . ."[19] The year Coleridge died, an Athenaem reporter interviewed two men, Underwood and Mackenzie, who had known him on Malta. The report, in part, reads:

> Underwood and Mackenzie say that there was more humbug in Coleridge than in any man that was ever heard of. Underwood was one day transcribing something for Coleridge when a visitor appeared. After the commonplaces, Coleridge took up a little book lying upon the table and said, "By the by, I casually took up this book this morning, and was quite enchanted with a little sonnet I found there." He then read off a blank verse translation, and the same critique was repeated five times in that day to different visitors, without one word being altered.[20]

Madame de Staël's famous remark that Coleridge was not a conversationalist but a monologuist is consistent with everything else we know of his public habits. He spoke compulsively, often with complete disregard for social propriety or the capacities of his auditors; the inner emptiness was too great, the hunger for approval too insistent for restraint.

Need we have any doubt as to what happened when this brilliant but intensely insecure young man providentially found himself in the flowering German culture at the close of the eighteenth century? Here was nourishment to satisfy the whole range of his restless literary appetites. What an incomparable feast of poetry, metaphysics, science, literary criticism, and

speculation on all manner of themes! Kant and Schelling, Schiller and Lessing, Jacobi and Schlegel, and more, many many more—all practically unknown in England!

Out of this fateful confrontation between a tormented genius, helpless in
the grip of overmastering impulses, and the abounding literary riches of
eighteenth-century Germany, has grown a unique reputation, one that has
massively distorted the shape of many chapters of modern literary history.
Could Coleridge have known that some of his poems would one day be
among the glories of English poetry, that his place would be secure as one of
the most searching intellects of his time, he might have been content to
add to his considerable laurels that of an incomparable mediator of ideas,
in which role his work was to be of immense historical importance.

But the self-doubts were too great. How was he who was haunted by the
conviction that he was an involuntary impostor, that he had "no real Genius,
no real Depth,"[21] to resist the temptation of his German experience? The
voracious library cormorant had come upon a sea teeming with unimaginable riches. Is it any wonder that he feasted?

The lifelong conflicts among Coleridge's various selves has resulted in a
personality and historical record of perhaps unparalleled complexity and
inner contradiction. Evidence abounds for almost any view one wishes to
take of him. The mercurial Coleridge, the protean fashioner of moral and
intellectual self-images, was simply not to be fixed in the pouncing grasp of
his detractors.

Only by the reflected lights and insights that every aspect of his career
casts upon every other can we make sense of this tragic and immensely
important life. Only by understanding the power and the tumult of the
forces contending for mastery within this tormented being can we cease to
be astonished at the spectacle of deception, evasion, and all manner of falsehood in a man with exalted moral principles. It is ironic that he who so
earnestly sought the principle of unity in all things should have been so
alienated from himself and so great a mystery to subsequent generations.

26.

Shipwreck and Safe Harbor

WHEN Coleridge set sail for Germany in September 1798, how fair were his prospects, how bright his hopes. His financial future seemed secured in a life-time annuity, supplied by enlightened and admiring patrons. Not yet twenty-six years old, he had already written "The Ancient Mariner," "Kubla Khan," the first canto of "Christabel," and a cluster of other brilliant poems. Who could have guessed that his poetic career was behind him?

Five and a half years later he set sail again, for the sun of Malta, driven by desperation, hopelessly enslaved by opium, incapable of sustained creative work, tormented by nightmares that woke him screaming night after night, enmeshed in every imaginable family trouble, plagued by money problems—a physical, and sometimes moral, wreck of a man.

It is a most instructive part of my Life [he wrote into his journal some months later] the fact, that I have been always preyed on by some Dread, and perhaps all my faulty actions have been the consequence of some Dread or other on my mind/ from fear of Pain, or Shame, not from prospect of Pleasure/—So in my childhood & Boyhood . . . imaginary fears of having the Itch in my Blood—/ then a short-lived Fit of Fears from sex—then horror of DUNS, & a state of struggling with madness from an incapability of hoping that I should be able to marry Mary Evans (and this strange passion of fervent tho' wholly imaginative and imaginary Love uncombinable by my utmost efforts with ⟨any regular⟩ Hope—/ possibly from deficiency of bodily feeling, of tactual ideas connected with the image) had all the effects of direct Fear, & I have lain for hours together awake at night, groaning & praying—Then came that stormy time/ and for a few months America really inspired Hope, & I became an exalted Being—then came Rob. Southey's alienation/ my marriage—constant dread in my mind respecting Mrs Coleridge's Temper, &c—and finally stimulants in the fear & prevention of violent Bowel-attacks from mental agitation/ then ⟨almost epileptic⟩ night-horrors in my sleep/ & since then every error I have committed, has

421

been the immediate effect of the Dread of these bad most shocking Dreams—any thing to prevent them/—all this interwoven with its minor consequences, that fill up the interspaces—the cherry juice running in between the cherries in a cherry pie/ procrastination in dread of this— & something else in consequence of that procrast. &c/—and from the same cause the least languor expressed in a letter from S[ara]. H[utchinson]. drives me wild/ & it is most unfortunate that I so fearfully despondent should have concentered my soul thus on one almost as feeble in Hope as myself.[1]

The emotional crisis which "Ode to Dejection" records has, of course, been the object of intense study. Nature devoid of spiritual meanings, frustration in love, these combine to banish joy and the shaping spirit of imagination. But the desperate notebook entry just cited, far more than the carefully ordered poem, scatters genuine clues towards an understanding of the spiritual dessication and ravenous despair that made creative work impossible.

So plenteous are the griefs in which Coleridge was enmeshed by the time he turned thirty that it seems unnecessary to cast about for others to explain the disaster which overtook him. And it would be a hard and ignorant man who would discount the influence of the Furies in human affairs. Nevertheless, although the pillars of his life had never been firmly rooted in either emotional security or a mature self-image, around 1802 almost everything seems to go to pieces at once. His marriage—never a satisfactory one, but for years apparently devoid of true bitterness—becomes intolerable. A kind of psychic storm explodes inside him. Self-doubt becomes poisonous. His nights are now to be given over to monsters.

In January 1804 he had a frightful dream while staying at Grasmere with the Wordsworths:

Rain, soaking Rain [he wrote to Southey]: and my two last Nights have been poisoned by it. Yesterday morning after a bad breakfast, having been almost wholly sleepless during the Night, I fell sound asleep—the weather, as I thought, promising to clear up. I hoped that I should awake in Sun shine. But in less than 10 minutes after I had fallen asleep, the Rain came down in a storm; & whether any way connected with this, I cannot say—but I dreamt among other wild melancholy Things, all steeped in a deep dejection but not wholly unmingled with pleasure, that I came up into one of our Xt Hospital Wards, & sitting by a bed was told that it was Davy in it, who in attempts to enlighten mankind had inflicted ghastly wounds on himself, & must henceforth live bed-ridden. The image before my Eyes instead of Davy was a wretched Dwarf with only three fingers; which however produced, as always in Dreams, no Surprize. I however burst at once into loud & vehement Weeping, which at length, but after a considerable continuance, awakened me/ My cheeks were drowned in Tears, my pillow & shirt collar quite wet/ & the hysterical Sob was lingering in my breast.[2]

We may well weep with Coleridge at this terrible dream, in which the Christ's Hospital locale establishes the first clue to the nightmare's personal significance. Sir Humphry Davy, Coleridge's friend, a young scientist of immense reputation (whom Coleridge thought a greater man than Newton), is here another screen for the tormented dreamer. Much is revealed of Coleridge's intellectual and psychological self-image in the phrase, "to enlighten mankind had inflicted ghastly wounds on himself, & must hence-forth live bed-ridden." For at least the past four months Coleridge had been living in dread of this fate for himself.[3] And now we come upon the dream-image so often met with in other dreams: duality and deformation. In place of the noble Davy, "a wretched Dwarf with only three fingers" appears. We think at once of the "contemptible wretch" in another Christ's Hospital dream, leaping upon Coleridge and grasping his scrotum. With the passage of two years, that threatening wretch has become bed-ridden and physically deformed.

Is it any wonder that Coleridge awoke screaming and weeping? Instead of the exalted surrogate of so great a genius as Davy, the dreamer is mocked by a pitiful dwarf, whose three fingers hint at the dreamer's fears of castration, impotence, and psychic deformation. Where in an earlier Christ's Hospital dream there are two people, "one Maim'd, one unknown," we now have terror.

In "Ode to Dejection" Coleridge writes that "afflictions bow me down to earth" and suspend "My shaping spirit of Imagination":

> For not to think of what I needs must feel,
>   But to be still and patient, all I can;
> And haply by abstruse research to steal
>   From my own nature all the natural man—
>   This was my sole resource, my only plan:
> Till that which suits a part infects the whole,
> And now is almost grown the habit of my soul. (ll. 87-93)

This presumably means that in order to suppress thoughts about a hopeless love, the poet buries himself in work unrelated to his lively physical sensibilities. Success in this endeavor, however, causes the catastrophic accompanying effect of numbing his whole "natural" being, thereby sus-pending his imagination and rendering poetry impossible.

This chain of ideas is so improbable, if not wholly specious, that one wonders what is being disguised. I suggest that Coleridge was actually grap-pling here with the experience of trying to suppress sensual thoughts (which dismayed and sickened him) about Sara Hutchinson, and that it was to this effort that in his innermost thoughts he attributed the shattering discovery symbolized in the dream of Davy and the dwarf: Coleridge was becoming sexually impotent.

In the longing, passive, earlier fantasy about Sara Hutchinson (large breasts, and sinking down through warm seas), he already referred to his "celibate couch." At no time in Coleridge's married life is there evidence of an ardent husband. Indifference toward his wife is too easily attributed to his dislike of her (about which he later wrote to almost everybody but Southey). But that indifference seems to have much intensified around 1800, when the passion (wholly distant) for Sara Hutchinson commenced. Yet well before this (aged twenty-five) Coleridge went off to Germany for ten months, leaving a young wife behind. Earlier long trips from home seem to have caused no personal distress. When he left England in 1804 he was to be separated from his wife for more than three years. And upon returning to England he delayed for over two months before going home. He arrived in Keswick on 30 October 1806, and within two weeks had prevailed upon the bitter and reluctant Sara to grant a permanent separation.[4] He was never to be reunited in the marital bond. At least the last twenty-eight years of his life passed in a rigid, self-imposed celibacy.

In the Maltese journal entry quoted earlier, Coleridge wrote of always having been "preyed upon by some Dread" which, in its various manifestations—including "a short-lived Fit of Fears from sex"—took the following mysterious form: "a state of struggling from madness from incapability of hoping that I should be able to marry Mary Evans (and this strange passion of fervent tho' wholly imaginative and imaginary Love uncombinable by my utmost efforts with ⟨any regular⟩ Hope—/ possibly from deficiency of bodily feeling, of tactual ideas connected with the image). . . ." What can this mean, if not a confession of at least imaginative impotence connected with a loved object? (The young Coleridge here "struggling with madness," strongly reinforces the recurrent fear of madness that appears in his dreams.) How fortuitous that he should have supplied the sequence of ideas within parentheses. How different the whole passage would read without it. "& I have lain for hours together awake at night, groaning & praying." For what? To marry Mary Evans—to be able to connect tactual ideas with her image—or both? It is impossible to know. Yet we can certainly perceive here not only sexual fears, which are common enough, but a block powerful enough to inhibit Coleridge from *imagining* physical contact with a loved object, or to fill him with dismay and loathing when such thoughts came unbidden.

On Malta he recorded with satisfaction that the night before he had had

a long Dream, of my Return, Welcome, &c. full of *Joy & Love*, wholly without *desire*, or bodily Inquietude, tho' with a most curious detail of Images, and imagined actions, that might be supposed absolutely to *imply* awakened Appetite. A Proof this of the little Power Images have over Feelings of Sensation, independent of the Will—compared with the power of Feelings over Images:—a proof too, one of a thousand, that by rigorous unremitting Purity of ~~my~~ our Thought, when awake, joined with the unremitting Feeling of intense *Love*, the imagination in Sleep may become almost incapable of combining base or low Feelings with the object of that Love.[5]

Similarly, in the famous letter of 1794 to Southey in which he announced his loss of Mary and said that he would marry Sara Fricker, he wrote: "When she [Mary] was present, she was to me only as a very dear Sister: it was in absence, that I felt those gnawings of Suspense, and that Dreaminess of Mind, which evidence an affection more restless, yet scarcely less pure, than the fraternal."[6] Surely all this is terribly prissy and hints at strong inhibitions in the presence of carnal promptings. When he looked back upon this period, in the midst of the crisis we are now discussing, he wondered, significantly, whether he did not *even then* suffer from some "deficiency of bodily feeling." In 1803 he speculated whether the "bad Passions" in his dreams were not "produced by Pain & *Denaturalization*."[7]

Relevant here are the effects of opium on the nervous system, a much debated subject. This much can be said with certainty: opium deadens tactile sensitivity in many users and can lead to impotence. More often, regular use of opium simply diminishes the sexual drive. In one of the later marginalia we find: "Opium is occasionally Aphrodisaic, but far oftener Anti-aphrodisaic. The same is true of *Bang*, of powdered Hemp leaves, and I suppose of the whole tribe of narcotic Stimulants."[8] Coleridge obviously knew whereof he spoke.

The symptoms of impotence that were annihilating what remained of his self-confidence as a man most probably took the form of frigidity rather than seriously crippled capacity. The very end of the long entry about Mary Evans and the tactile ideas reads:

the least languor in a Letter from S[ara]. H[utchinson]. drives me wild/ & it is most unfortunate that I so fearfully despondent should have concentered my soul thus on one almost as feeble in Hope as myself. 11 Jan. 1805.—

Important metaphysical Hint the influence of bodily vigor and strong Grasp of Touch in facilitating the passion of Hope: 5, 21, 14, 21, 3, 8, 19 [*cipher for* eunuchs]—in all degrees even to the full 5, 14, 19, 8, 5, 1, 20, 8 [ensheath(ment)] and the 2, 15, 20, 8 [both] at once.[9]

Taken by itself, this is a most baffling entry, especially in the way Coleridge uses the word "hope," which recurs so often in the journals and letters of this period, and at a crucial point in "Ode to Dejection" ("For hope grew round me, like the twining vine"). "*Eunuchs in all degrees—even to the full ensheathment and the both at once*": from whence such knowledge if not from bitter personal experience? The cipher disguises a shattering admission: full ensheathment is possible without feeling anything.

The suspicion that all this is hinted at in the reference to "bodily vigor and strong Grasp of Touch" is reinforced by the very next entry, in which Coleridge speculates on the "imperfections of the organs by which we seem to unite ourselves with external things." He goes on to describe "Touch with a sense of immediate power" as "mem. vi/Riley. inacts of Es*sex*," which Miss Coburn untangles as "virile-ly in acts of (Es)sex," and further notes that "Petronius glosses *virilia* as *membrum virile.*" Coleridge's meaning may not be "*virile-ly* in acts of sex" but "*mem.[brum] virile* in acts of sex." Either reading points to sexual problems. Coleridge's considerable interest in touch and "double-touch" very possibly derives less from the universal curiosity of the polymath than the impetus of urgent personal concerns.

The so-called "dejection crisis" of 1802 can therefore be seen against a much darker and more poignant background than that afforded by considering only the collapse of philosophical attitudes regarding nature and the misery caused by an unhappy marriage and hopeless love. More attention needs to be given to the organic implications of what it was that was stealing from Coleridge's nature "all the natural man." The problem we have been considering may well have appeared, if sporadically, considerably earlier. A 1799 journal entry reads: "Universities—Pox—Impotence—Lord Lonsdale." In 1803 he expanded on these notes as follows:

> The vices of tyrannical great men very closely connected with their vices as Striplings, at Schools & Universities.—Tiberius. Lord Lonsdale. P—x. Impotence.—Painful Sensation and Loss of Hope = castration of the self-generating Organ of the Soul/—Continuousness a true Foliation.[10]

It would require the Sphinx-reading powers of an Oedipus to untangle these riddles. What stands out clearly enough for us, however, are the further references to impotence, to which are now added "Painful Sensation and Loss of Hope"—surely having to do with himself and not Tiberius or Lord Lonsdale—all of which equals "castration of the self-generating Organ of the Soul." To attribute impotence to loss of hope is surely a strange guess at the etiology of the problem. What may conceivably be meant by "castration of the self-generating Organ of the Soul"?

If we substitute the word "body" for "soul," the mists begin to dispel at once. A notebook entry of 1807, almost frenzied in its anguish and despair, reads: "O God! forgive me!—Can even the Eagle soar without Wings? . . . I have, like the Exeter Cathedral Organ, a pipe of far-sounding Music in its construction, yet it is dumb, a gilded Tube, till the Sister ~~Tube~~ pipe be placed in correspondence/ O *Beloved!*—Beloved!"[11] Every phrase here is suggestive, from the Eagle unable to rise, to the useless "Organ." It is surely significant that Coleridge is desperately affirming to himself that his frigidity with his wife would vanish in the presence of the truly loved one. Significant also are the blurrings of the role of male and female. The long entry concludes with painful reflections on his lack of "manliness."

Having ventured thus far, it may be permissible to suggest that the connection in Coleridge's mind between his deepening frigidity and the loss of poetic power appears in a dream recorded on Malta:

> Wednesday Night—Dreamt that I was saying, or reading, or that it was said to me, "Varrius thus prophecied Vinegar at his Door by damned frigid Tremblings"—just after which I awoke—I fell asleep again, having in the previous Doze meditated on the possibility of making Dreams ⟨regular⟩, and just as I had passed on the other side of the confine of Dozing I afforded this specimen/" I should have thought it Vossius rather than Varrius—tho' Varrius being a great poet, the idea would have been more suitable to him, only that all his writings were *unfortunately lost in the Arrow*. Again I awoke. N. B. the Arrow Captain Vincent's Frigate, taken by the French, our Malta Letters and Dispatches having been previously thrown overboard, in Feb. 1805.—this illustrates the connections of Dreams.[12]

In the first dream the phrase "Vinegar at his Door by damned frigid Tremblings" may hint at narcoticized ejaculatory sensations. That the speaker is Coleridge appears in the subsequent doze, where Varrius is described as "a great poet" who (like Coleridge in fact) lost some letters and official papers at sea. (The phrase *"unfortunately lost in the Arrow,"* underscored by Coleridge himself, may nevertheless have a phallic significance.) There is a considerable play on names here. Varrius, a dream name so far as is known, strongly suggests to me its aural meaning—"various"—not an inapt cognomen for the many-sided Coleridge.

Loss of virility in any man—especially in one so young—can obviously have ruinous consequences. In so grievously insecure a person as Coleridge, the consequences could only be disastrous. In such a case opium would become a refuge, flight from the wife a necessity. The dreams of being attacked by vicious women, of having his eye plucked out, of being unable to escape from sexual demands, all may in part symbolize this crisis. Shortly before embarking for Malta, he wrote his wife of his hope that abroad, "I shall grow firmer & manlier," at which point some six lines have been cut off from the manuscript.[13] The word "manly" begins to appear regularly in his letters and notebooks.[14] *Aids to Reflection in the formation of a manly character* is part of the title of his most famous homiletic work.

The whole appalling complex of loneliness, frustration, despair, and self-loathing comes into terrifying focus in a single, lengthy journal entry of 1807.

Every thing, that has been known or deemed fit to win woman's Love, I have an impulse to make myself—even tho' I should otherwise look down upon it—I cannot endure not to be strong in arms, a daring Soldier—yet I know, I have no fear of Life or dread of Pain, & that I am not that because I cannot respect it—again, I must be the high Intellect, that despises it—& both at once. I must be graceful & a bold Horseman/I must sing & play on the Harp/I must be beautiful instead of what I am, and yet she must love me for what I now am, even for myself & my exceeding Love/& what then mean these vain wishes?[15]

The note passes to his tortured relations with Sara Hutchinson, and the fear that she will withdraw herself from his affections. A terrible, unidentified memory tears across his mind; it concerns his beloved and William Wordsworth, whom he wildly supposes has become his rival:

O agony! O the vision of that Saturday Morning—of the Bed/—O cruel! is he not beloved, adored by two [Mary and Dorothy]—& two such Beings—/& must I not be beloved *near* him except as a Satellite? —But O mercy mercy! is he not better, greater, more *manly*, & altogether more attractive to any the purest Woman? And yet, and yet, methinks, love so intense might demand love—otherwise who could be secure? Who could know, that his Beloved might not meet his Superiors?—W[illiam] is greater, better, manlier, more dear, by nature, to Woman, than I—I—miserable I!

The note grows still more frantic, and concludes:

I alone love you so devotedly, & therefore, therefore, love me, [Sara! —Sara!] love me![16]

Into one of the later notebooks Coleridge wrote the following (undated) mysterious lines:

Though veiled in spires of myrtle-wreath,
Love is a sword which cuts its sheath,
And through the clefts itself has made,
We spy the flashes of the blade!

But through the clefts itself has made
We likewise see Love's flashing blade,
By rust consumed, or snapt in twain;
And only hilt and stump remain.[17]

The sexual symbolism here seems unmistakable: a nexus of aggression and castration fear.

All this lies behind the near abandonment of poetry after 1802. The sense of worthlessness extends to an unconscious conviction not only of deformation but of contamination. In one dream Coleridge had suffered from "some corrosion of the hand." Now his once slovenly personal habits were to change markedly. "I cannot endure the least atom or imagination of dirt on my person," he confided to his journal, "but wash my body all over 20 times, where 8 or 9 years ago I washed half of it once."[18] More and more, his world was to become that of the Ancient Mariner, a catastrophe fated in the personality structure brought into manhood from too long a succession of scarring experiences.

Coleridge's lifelong dependency on older or more decisive men is a central fact of his biography. And its significance is too easily obscured by the obvious truth that such men were necessary to one so often ineffectual in practical affairs. But more is involved. The duality which appears in Coleridge's dreams also masks homosexual drives.

Few subjects are more treacherous to discuss or so easily misunderstood, or more wisely avoided. Yet understanding is not advanced by intellectual cowardice. It is plain that Coleridge was uncomfortable around women, that at times he hated and feared them.[19] Was not his whole adolescence spent almost completely shut away from them? Neither mother, sister, nor female friends shared his years of adolescence. His companions were the boys in the overcrowded wards of Christ's Hospital (where they slept two to a bed) or their stern preceptors. "The approbation & Sympathy of good & intelligent men is my Sea-breeze," Coleridge later wrote, "without which I should languish from morn to evening; a very Trade-wind to me, in which my Bark drives on regularly & lightly."[20] Yet at one time or another he quarreled bitterly with almost every one of these staunch supporters and sheet-anchors. It is suggestive that he married the sister-in-law of the closest friend and confidant of his early years, Robert Southey; and the sister-in-law of the next most important friend of his life, William Wordsworth, became the object of his most enduring, and utterly platonic, love.

His relations with various male friends was unusually intense, and often stormy. Without understanding how much emotion lay just below the surface of these otherwise normal friendships, certain crises in his life appear incomprehensible, and the larger shape of his personality unnecessarily mysterious. In December 1796 he wrote Thomas Poole two nearly hysterical letters.[21] They were in reply to Poole's late qualms about Coleridge's taking a cottage in Nether Stowey, where he lived. Coleridge's agitation, extreme as it was, can be attributed to the impetuosity of a youthful bard. But this is to misread the situation. Only a month before, he had written Poole of his hopes of retiring from the ills of the world to become a rural husbandman: "to enjoy these blessings *near you,* to see you daily, to tell you all my thoughts in their first birth, and to hear your's, to be mingling identities with you, as it were . . ." He concluded this long and "flighty" letter with the words, "God bless & protect you, Friend! Brother! Beloved!"—words affectionate far beyond conventional usage, arising perhaps from "the immediate inspiration of Laudanum," under which, Coleridge was soon to say, he had written.[22] The letter is perhaps all the more significant for that. He wrote affectionate letters to his wife from Germany, but none more than to this same Poole:

> O my God! how I long to be at home—My *whole Being* so yearns after you, that when I think of the moment of our meeting, I catch the fashion of German Joy, rush into your arms, and embrace you—methinks, my *Hand* would swell, if the whole force of my feeling were crowded there. —Now the Spring comes, the vital sap of my affections rises, as in a tree![23]

If we were to encounter these images in a modern poem, we should understand their meaning, deliberate or unconscious, well enough.[24]

"To be mingling identities with you"—we have many times in his dreams encountered this phenomenon, and it is to be suspected that the duality projected in the characters of Christabel and Geraldine reflect the feminine side of his nature. The mingling of identities appears in one of the entries made on the voyage to Malta:

> . . . I screamed in the night/. Mem. To examine whether Dreams of Terror & obscure Forms, ugly or not, be commonly preceded by Forms of Awe and Admiration with distant Love. Before three old Women, the dim Apparitions of three, attacked me in that dark passage I had seen a Lady, made up of Sir. C. Grandison's Lady & Sir P. Sidney's, talking with her Maid concerning Sir P. Sidney. . . .[25]

The two men are models of moral and manly virtue, and Sidney (whom Coleridge called "the paramount gentleman of Europe," and ranked with Shakespeare, Spenser, Milton, and Bacon)[26] was a poet, critic, nobleman, and brave soldier—almost an ideal projection of his deepest wishes. But it is the wife of this dual figure who speaks in the dream, after which he is attacked in a dark passage (another sexual symbol?). What meaning is embedded in these images?

Sir Charles Grandison, another heroic paragon (and like Coleridge a traveler to Italy) may also embody aspects of his creator, Samuel Richardson, whom Coleridge loathed. In extremely suggestive and revealing reflections on *oneness of character* and the mingling of "low and contemptible" traits in men of great ability, Coleridge wrote: ". . . I confess that it has cost & still costs my philosophy some exertion not to be vexed that I must admire—aye, greatly, very greatly, admire *Richardson/* his mind is so very vile a mind— so oozy, hypocritical, praise-mad, canting, envious, concupiscent."[27]

At no point in this severe but insightful analysis of Richardson did it occur to Coleridge that he might also be analyzing himself and thus be a deserving object of the anger and contempt so often visited upon him in his dreams.

That insight was not given to his consciousness. But in his nighttime world the mingling of the traits of Grandison and Sidney may really be that of Richardson and Sidney, which takes us back to the double-image of Davy and the wretched dwarf and all the other dualities we have encountered.[28]

Within a month, still on that magically described but spiritually and physically wracking voyage to Malta, Coleridge set down in a frenzy one of the most incandescently eloquent and heartbreaking passages in the entire range of his writings:

> for Sleep a pandemonium of all the shames & miseries of the past Life from early childhood all huddled together, & bronzed with one stormy Light of Terror & Self-torture/ O this is hard, hard, hard!—O dear God! give me strength of Soul to make one thorough Trial—if I land at Malta/ spite of all horrors to go through one month of unstimulated Nature—yielding to nothing but manifest Danger of Life!—O great God! Grant me grace truly to look into myself, & to begin the serious work of Self-amendment—accounting to Conscience for the Hours of every Day. Let me live in *Truth*—manifesting that alone which *is,* even as it *is,* & striving to be that which only Reason shews to be lovely—that which my Imagination would delight to manifest!—I am loving & kind-hearted & cannot do wrong with impunity, but o! I am very, very weak—from my infancy have been so—& I exist for the moment!—Have mercy on me, have mercy on me, Father & God! omnipresent, incomprehensible, who with undeviating Laws eternal yet carest for the falling of the feather from the Sparrow's Wing.—Sunday Midnight, May 13th, 1804.[29]

But it was not to be. Neither God nor any kind saint was to show either mercy or pity towards this haunted and humiliated spirit—not for many, many years. On Malta, where he hoped to find health and strength of purpose, he merely drifted, consuming vast quantities of brandy and laudanum every night, circling slowly deeper and deeper into the hell within.

In 1816 he betook himself to young Dr. James Gillman of Highgate for medical help, and luck at last was with him. After years of wandering, the deserted orphan more than ever needed the stability of deep and unflinching sympathy within the stable setting of a home. It is almost a miracle that this guileless young surgeon and his wife should have undertaken to treat Coleridge in their home. What was to have been a temporary arrangement proved permanent. At the age of forty-three Coleridge had at last found a snug harbor.

His creative recovery had begun a few years earlier. The lectures of 1812, for all their massive plagiarism from Schlegel, nevertheless reveal, in retrospect, a revived capacity to identify and organize thoughts, to carry assignments through to reasonable completion. And in 1815 an intended introduction to his collected poems grew to be the *Biographia Literaria.* A flurry of literary activity enriches 1815-18, but then barrenness again sets in, at least so far as publication is concerned (apart from *Aids to Reflection,* and a rare poem or moral pamphlet). The last decade is given over to the grandiose chimeras of the *Logosophia.*

   The story of those final years is a separate subject. Yet it is pleasant to record that those years were happy ones, at least by any comparative standard in Coleridge's life. There was still much heartbreak, especially the disaster of Hartley's university career and subsequent life.[30] The boy on whom so many hopes had been founded, the dear babe of "Frost at Midnight," was to prove as much a wanderer as his father, never to marry, never remotely to fulfill his promise. It is a mournful fact that after 1823 son and father were never to meet again. Hartley was thirty-eight years old when his father died. In all those thirty-eight years he did not live in his father's presence for as much as five years. Coleridge's brilliant daughter, Sara, who was to do so much for his after-fame, did not see him once between her tenth and twentieth years. The orphanhood which death had inflicted on the young Samuel Coleridge was in effect visited upon all his children.

   There were other troubles, especially ill health. The opium problem was brought under some kind of reasonable control. He was never able actually to break the habit, but this is hardly a matter for moral comment. There were financial troubles, but they were no longer acute, at least not as the years passed. The Gillmans were generous and the presence of so great a man in the house was more than sufficient compensation for the slight expense involved. The seventeeth-century stone house, with a wonderful view across Hampstead Heath, became famous. Visitor after visitor, many from America, respectfully made their way up to the attractive heights of Highgate to hear the dazzling and often mysterious monologues of the aging metaphysician and bard.

   More and more an austere defender of the faith, he must have seemed very much a minister himself, dressed as he habitually was now, in "a black coat, black breeches, with black silk stockings and shoes." Oddly, he once found himself wondering, "Without black velvet Breeches what is man?"[31] The abhorrence of dirt which marked so great a change in his early habits had long since become fixed. "He was *scrupulously* clean in his person," Gillman observes, "and especially took great care of his hands by frequent ablutions."[32] Only the compulsive imbibing of enormous quantities of snuff, which seemed to keep him perpetually engulfed in a kind of snowfall, betrayed the cormorant appetite within.

   The nightmares continued, but until the publication of the late letters and notebooks we shall not know their contents. "He had long been greatly afflicted with nightmare" writes Gillman, "and, when residing with us, was frequently roused from this painful sleep by any one of the family who might hear him."[33] While reading Sir Thomas Browne's *Religio Medici* Coleridge's eyes fell on the sentence, "I thank God for my happy dreams." In the margins of the volume he wrote: "I am quite different: for all, or almost all, the painful & fearful Thoughts that I know, are in my Dreams! So much so that when I am wounded by a friend, or receive a painful Letter, it throws me into a state very nearly resembling that of a Dream."[34] The pandemonium of nightmare thoughts rarely impinged upon his increasingly exalted daylight self-image. During the later years, among his friends and familiars, he sometimes went by the name of "Satyrane." He drew his self-portrait as follows:

> From his earliest youth, Satyrane had derived his highest pleasures from the admiration of moral grandeur and intellectual energy; and during the whole of his life he had a greater and more heartfelt delight in the superiority of other men to himself than men in general derive from their belief of their own. His readiness to imagine a superiority where it did not exist, was for many years his predominant foible; his pain from the perception of inferiority in others whom he had heard spoken of with any respect, was unfeigned and involuntary, and perplexed him as a something which he did not comprehend. In the childlike simplicity of his nature he talked to all men as if they were his equals in knowledge and talents, and many whimsical anecdotes could be related connected with this habit; he was constantly scattering good seed on unreceiving soils. When he was at length compelled to see and acknowledge the true state of the morals and intellect of his contemporaries, his disappointment was severe, and his mind, always thoughtful, became pensive and sad:—*for to love and sympathize with mankind was a necessity of his nature.*[35]

The door between reality and imagination was now permanently open.

Physical illnesses thickened around him, causing great and prolonged pain. More and more he came to trust in redemption through a merciful heaven and life in eternity. He was sixty-two years old when Death at last touched him with his dart. He gave up a life that profoundly wearied him.

In 1961, before a distinguished gathering of numerous descended relatives, poets, scholars, official dignitaries, and an admiring public, the bones of Samuel Taylor Coleridge were laid to rest for a second time. The simple grave in Highgate School Chapel had suffered abysmal neglect in preceding years, and it was only fitting that the remains of one of England's greatest literary men should be relocated with solemn ceremony. The visitor to St. Michael's Church in Highgate will find Coleridge's gravestone midway down the center aisle—a location of signal honor. Ironically, the vault below shelters in eternal proximity the remains also of Sara Fricker, the wife whom he could not abide in life. On a nearby wall a memorial plaque extols the virtues and graces of James and Anne Gillman, to be forever known for their patient and devoted service to the immortal bard buried nearby. Above

Coleridge's remains, his own epitaph is handsomely chiseled into a block of marble. The visitor inevitably pauses. Few, perhaps, can feel how much anguish and loss, and longing, the familiar words express:

Stop, Christian passer-by!—Stop, child of God,
And read with gentle breast. Beneath this sod
A poet lies, or that which once seem'd he.
O, lift one thought in prayer for S. T. C.;
That he who many a year with toil of breath
Found death in life, may here find life in death!
Mercy for praise—to be forgiven for fame
He ask'd, and hoped, through Christ. Do thou the same!

Table of Abbreviations

Allsop   [Thomas Allsop] *Letters, Conversations and Recollections of S. T. Coleridge.* 2 vols. (London, 1836).

Ashe   Thomas Ashe, ed., *The Poetical Works of Samuel Taylor Coleridge.* 2 vols. (London, 1885).

Asra   George Whalley, *Coleridge and Sara Hutchinson and the Asra Poems* (London, 1955).

Bate   Walter Jackson Bate, *Coleridge* (New York, 1968).

Beach   Joseph Warren Beach, *The Concept of Nature in Nineteenth-Century English Poetry* (New York, 1936).

Beer   J. B. Beer, *Coleridge the Visionary* (London, 1959).

Beres   David Beres, "A Dream, A Vision, and a Poem: A Psycho-Analytic Study of the Origins of the Rime of The Ancient Mariner," *International Journal of Psychoanalysis*, XXXII (1951), 97-116.

BL   S. T. Coleridge, *Biographia Literaria*, ed. J. Shawcross. 2 vols. (Oxford, 1907).

Carlyon   Clement Carlyon, *Early Years and Late Reflections.* 4 vols. (London, 1836).

CBG   Joseph Warren Beach, "Coleridge's Borrowings from the German," *ELH*, IX (1942), 36-58.

CHCR   *Correspondence of Henry Crabb Robinson with the Wordsworth Circle,* ed. E. J. Morley. 2 vols. (Oxford, 1927).

CL   *Collected Letters of Samuel Taylor Coleridge*, ed. E. L. Griggs. 4 vols. (Oxford, 1956, 1959).

CLL   *Coleridge on Logic and Learning*, ed. Alice D. Snyder (New Haven, Conn.: Yale University Press, 1929).

CSC   *Coleridge on the Seventeenth Century*, ed. R. L. Brinckley (Durham, N.C.: Duke University Press, 1955).

CT   *Coleridge the Talker*, eds. R. W. Armour and R. F. Howes (Ithaca, N.Y.: Cornell University Press, 1940).

DL   A. W. Schlegel, *Lectures on Dramatic Art and Literature*, trans. J. Black (London, 1815; revised by A. J. W. Morrison, 1846).

DQW   *The Collected Writings of Thomas De Quincey*, ed. David Masson. 14 vols. (Edinburgh, 1889-90).

DWJ   *Journals of Dorothy Wordsworth*, ed. Helen Darbishire (The World's Classics: Oxford, 1958).

EHC   Ernest Hartley Coleridge

EKC   E. K. Chambers, *Samuel Taylor Coleridge: A Biographical Study* (Oxford, 1938).

ER   Joseph Cottle, *Early Recollections; chiefly relating to the late Samuel Taylor Coleridge* . . . 2 vols. (London, 1837).

ERP   *The English Romantic Poets: A Review of Research*, ed. T. M. Raysor (New York, 1956, revised edition).

ES   Elisabeth Schneider, *Coleridge, Opium, and Kubla Khan* (Chicago: University of Chicago Press, 1953).

EY   *The Letters of William and Dorothy Wordsworth, The Early Years: 1787-1805*, ed. Ernest de Selincourt; second edition revised by Chester L. Shaver (Oxford, 1967).

Gillman   James Gillman, *The Life of Samuel Taylor Coleridge* (London, 1838).

Grosart   *The Prose Works of William Wordsworth*, ed. Alexander B. Grosart. 3 vols. (London, 1876).

GW   George Watson, *Coleridge the Poet* (London, 1966).

Haven   Richard Haven, "Coleridge, Hartley, and the Mystics," *JHI*, XX (1959), 477-494.

HCR   *Henry Crabb Robinson on Books and their Writers*, ed. E. J. Morley. 3 vols. (London, 1938).

HH   Humphry House, *Coleridge, The Clark Lectures: 1951-52* (London, 1953).

HNC   Henry Nelson Coleridge

H-P   Anna Augusta von Helmholtz (Mrs. Phelan), *The Indebtedness of Samuel Taylor Coleridge to August Wilhelm Schlegel* (Madison, Wisc., 1907).

HW   *The Complete Works of William Hazlitt*, ed. P. P. Howe. 21 vols. (London, 1930-34).

IS   *Inquiring Spirit: A New Presentation of Coleridge* . . . , ed. Kathleen Coburn (New York, 1951).

JAA   J. A. Appleyard, *Coleridge's Philosophy of Literature* (Cambridge: Harvard University Press, 1965).

JCF   J. C. Ferrier, "The Plagiarisms of S. T. Coleridge," *Blackwood's Edinburgh Magazine*, XLVII (March 1840), 287-299.

JDC   James Dykes Campbell

Kant   Immanuel Kant, *Critique of Pure Reason*, trans. Norman Kemp Smith (London, 1950).

KE   René Wellek, *Kant in England: 1793-1838* (Princeton, N.J.: Princeton University Press, 1931).

Letters *Letters of Samuel Taylor Coleridge*, ed. E. H. Coleridge. 2 vols. (Boston, 1895).

Life J. D. Campbell, *Samuel Taylor Coleridge, a Narrative of the Events of His Life* (London, 1894).

LL *The Letters of Charles Lamb, to which are added those of his sister, Mary Lamb,* ed. E. V. Lucas, 3 vols. (New Haven, Conn.: Yale University Press, 1935).

LP Thomas De Quincey, *Recollections of the Lake Poets*, ed. Edward Sackville-West (London, 1948).

LW *The Works of Charles and Mary Lamb*, ed. E. V. Lucas. 5 vols. (London, 1903-05).

MC *Coleridge's Miscellaneous Criticism*, ed. T. M. Raysor (Cambridge: Harvard University Press, 1936).

MM Mary Moorman, *William Wordsworth: A Biography*. 2 vols. (Oxford, 1957, 1965).

N *The Notebooks of Samuel Taylor Coleridge*, ed. Kathleen Coburn. 2 double vols. (New York, 1957, 1961). This edition is largely unpaginated and contains text and notes in separate volumes. References are to the number of the entry, e.g., *N*, 100 (text) or *N*, 100*n* (note).

Piper Herbert Piper, *The Active Universe* (London, 1962).

PL *The Philosophical Lectures of Samuel Taylor Coleridge*, ed. Kathleen Coburn (New York, 1949).

Poems *The Poetical Works of Samuel Taylor Coleridge*, ed. J. D. Campbell (London, 1893).

PPC Carl R. Woodring, *Politics in the Poetry of Coleridge* (Madison, Wisc.: University of Wisconsin Press, 1961).

PW *The Complete Poetical Works of Samuel Taylor Coleridge . . . ,* ed. E. H. Coleridge. 2 vols. (Oxford, 1912).

RW René Wellek, *A History of Modern Criticism: 1750-1950,* 2 vols. (New Haven, Conn.: Yale University Press, 1955).

RX J. L. Lowes, *The Road to Xanadu* (Boston and New York, 1927; revised 1930).

SC *Samuel Taylor Coleridge: Shakespearean Criticism,* ed. T. M. Raysor. 2 vols. (Everyman Library: London, 1960).

Shedd *The Complete Works of Samuel Taylor Coleridge*, ed. W. G. T. Shedd. 7 vols. (New York, 1853-54).

SSH *Coleridge: Studies by Several Hands on the Hundredth Anniversary of his Death,* eds. E. Blunden and E. L. Griggs (London, 1934).

STI F. W. J. Schelling, *System of Transcendental Idealism,* trans. Albert Hofstadter, in *Philosophies of Art and Beauty,* eds. Albert Hofstadter and Richard Kuhns (The Modern Library: New York, 1964).

TP Mrs. Henry Sandford, *Thomas Poole and his Friends.* 2 vols. (London, 1888).

TT	*The Table Talk and Omniana of Samuel Taylor Coleridge. With Additional Table Talk from Allsop's Recollections, etc.* [ed. H. N. Coleridge] (Oxford, 1917).
UL	*Unpublished Letters of Samuel Taylor Coleridge,* ed. E. L. Griggs. 2 vols. (New Haven, Conn.: Yale University Press, 1933).
US	F. W. J. Schelling, *On University Studies,* trans. E. S. Morgan; ed. Norbert Guterman (Athens, Ohio: Ohio University Press, 1966).
WJB	Walter Jackson Bate, ed., *Criticism: The Major Texts* (New York, 1952).
WLC	*Wordsworth's Literary Criticism,* ed. N. C. Smith (London, 1905).
WPW	*The Poetical Works of William Wordsworth,* ed. Ernest de Selincourt. 5 vols. (Oxford, 1940-49). Second edition (of Vols. I-III) by Helen Darbishire, 1952-54.

Abbreviations used to cite periodicals follow the table that precedes the annual bibliography in *PMLA*, the official journal of the Modern Language Association of America.

The ones most commonly used hereafter are:

BNYPL	Bulletin of the New York Public Library
E & S	Essays and Studies by Members of the English Association
ELH	Journal of English Literary History
JEGP	Journal of English and Germanic Philology
JHI	Journal of the History of Ideas
MLN	Modern Language Notes
MP	Modern Philology
N & Q	Notes and Queries
PMLA	Publications of the Modern Language Association of America
PQ	Philological Quarterly
RES	Review of English Studies
SP	Studies in Philology
TLS	(London) Times Literary Supplement

NOTES

INTRODUCTION

1. *UL*, II, 384.

2. J. H. Plumb, "The Historian as Detective," *New York Times Book Review* (9 November 1969), p. 56.

3. *The Letters of William and Dorothy Wordsworth: The Later Years* (Oxford, 1939), II, 942.

4. *LL*, I, 172. To "quiz" meant to ridicule or to mock.

5. *SSH*, pp. 15, 16, 17.   6. *BL*, I, 127.   7. MM, I, 33.

8. *CL*, II, 747. STC's underscoring.

9. For example, Maurice Carpenter, *The Indifferent Horseman: The Divine Comedy of Samuel Taylor Coleridge* (London, n.d.), p. 182.

10. Carlyon, I, 45.

1. THE DIVINE AFFLATUS

1. *Anima Poetae: From the Unpublished Note-Books of S. T. C.*, ed. E. H. Coleridge (London, 1895), p. 148.

2. *TT*, p. 165. 21 December 1831.   3. *CL*, I, 85.   4. *PW*, I, 33

5. *CL*, I, 34.   6. *PW*, I, 40. Headnote to poem.   7. *PW*, I 45, n. 1.

8. *PW*, I, 57, n. 1.   9. *CL*, I, 127.   10. *CL*, I, 147.

11. *PW*, I, 100, *app. crit.* See n. 52 below.   12. *PW*, I, 108.

13. *PW*, I, 160, n. 1.   14. *PW*, I, 178. Headnote to poem.   15. *PW*, I, 286.

16. *PW*, I, 296.   17. *CL*, I, 451.   18. *CL*, I, 488.   19. *CL*, I, 493.

20. *PW*, I, 356, n. 1.   21. *CL*, II, 752.   22. *PW*, I, 362.

23. *CL*, II, 864.   24. *PW*, I, 382.   25. *CL*, II, 984.   26. *PW*, I, 403.

27. *CL*, III, 236.   28. *CL*, IV, 779.   29. *PW*, I, 447.

30. *PW*, I, 488, n. 3.

31. For example, "The Language of Birds: Lines Spoken Extempore," "An Impromptu on Christmas Day," "Song, Ex Improviso." In the Preface to the 1796 edition of *Poems on various subjects*, Coleridge defended his use of the title "Effusion" thus: "I could recollect no title more descriptive of the manner and matter of the Poems." Lamb begged in a letter: "Call [them] Sonnets, for heaven's sake, and not 'Effusions' " (*Poems*, p. 538 and n. 1).

32. *PW*, I, 213, *app. crit.*   33. *CL*, II, 1075.

34. Elisabeth Schneider's *Coleridge, Opium, and Kubla Khan*, pp. 155-156, contains a brief but acute discussion of the problem of Coleridge's misdatings, which I gratefully acknowledge.

35. *CL*, I, 85. I have followed Coleridge's spelling and punctuation in quoting from E. L. Griggs's edition of the *Collected Letters*.

36. Quoted from *CL*, I, 13-14. A subtitle affixed to "Happiness" in one of the manuscripts reads, "Upon the Author's leaving school and entering into Life," which establishes still another context for the poem (*PW*, I, 30, *app. crit.*). Interestingly, the poem was not published till 1834, the year of Coleridge's death, though many slighter poems had been. As will be seen hereafter, the substantial debts to Milton, especially to "L'Allegro" and "Il Penseroso," may have had something to do with this decision.

37. *CL*, I, 147.   38. *CL*, I, 102.

39. *CL*, I, 147, 162, 187, 197, 203. See also *ER*, II, 51-53 for further evidence as to how "Religious Musings" was actually composed; this direct testimony comes from Joseph Cottle, Coleridge's Bristol publisher.

Despite all this evidence, scholars continue to declare that the poem was either entirely written in one night, or begun on Christmas Eve, 1794. Thus Sara Coleridge: "*Religious Musings* [was] written on Christmas Eve of 1794" (Shedd, III, 677); E. H. Coleridge: "*Religious Musings* [was] begun on Christmas Eve, 1794" (*PW*, I, 78, n. 1.); Carl Woodring: "begun on Christmas

Eve, 1794" (*PPC*, p. 166); Humphry House: "*Religious Musings* in its first form was written on Christmas Eve 1794" (HH, p. 64).

In attempting to account for the many strange discrepancies between Coleridge's statements about his own work and the factual record, I have studied his use of the words "written" and "composed" with reference to his own compositions, suspecting that some important distinction might be involved. But in fact he used the terms interchangeably.

40. *CL*, I, 147, 162.

41. *PW*, I, 160, n. 1; David V. Erdman, "Unrecorded Coleridge Variants," *SB*, XI (1958), 150.

42. *Coleridge's Poems, Facsimile Reproduction of the Proofs and MSS. of some of the Poems*, eds. J. D. Campbell and W. H. White (Westminister, England, 1899), pp. 87, 98.

43. *PW*, I, 160, n. 1. A similar indecision seems to have gripped Coleridge in determining precisely when he wrote "To William Wordsworth." It was published in 1817 and thereafter as "Composed on the Night After his Recitation of a Poem on the Growth of an Individual Mind." But on two of the manuscripts we find that it was composed "for the greater part" not on the night after the recitation, but "on the same night" (*PW*, I, 403, and *app. crit.*).

44. *CL*, I, 488; *PW*, I, 313, n. 1; *PW*, II, 1129 (where the German poem is reprinted). Coleridge's poem follows the source very closely in its first two stanzas; the concluding stanza is essentially an original composition.

45. *CL*, I, 493; *N*, 407 and n. The poem was first published in 1800 over the pseudonym "Cordomi." Clement Carlyon, for a time one of Coleridge's traveling companions in Germany, reports that Coleridge dictated parts of the poem at a little inn on the Brocken. He seems not to have known that the poem was not entirely original. See *PW*, I, 314, n. 1, and Carlyon, I, 66.

46. *CL*, II, 984, 993.   47. *CL*, III, 495.

48. When Coleridge published "The Pains of Sleep" in 1816 he said nothing about the extraordinarily interesting circumstances under which the poem was allegedly written. In the same thin volume, however, was "Kubla Khan," also published for the first time. And the Preface to the latter makes what is perhaps the most famous claim to marvelous unconscious creativity in the annals of literature. A comprehensive analysis of many vexing problems attending "Kubla Khan" appears in a separate chapter.

49. Joseph Cottle, for example, learned of it only in 1814. See *ER*, II, 149.

50. "He was obviously eager at this time to make a favorable impression upon the Beaumonts, who were recent acquaintances, and was probably unwilling to own the poem as a product of his mature years. He was no doubt merely protecting his poetic flank with the date 'nine years ago' " (ES, p. 317, n. 63).

51. *CL*, I, 289.

52. "The Eolian Harp," also published earlier that year, carried the information: "Composed August 20th, 1795" (*PW*, I, 100, *app. crit.*). An early draft of this poem, titled "Effusion 35," bears the same date (*PW*, II, 1021). This draft, however, is less than one-third the length of any of the published versions. Furthermore, since Coleridge was not married until 4 October 1795, it would seem highly improbable that he wrote a poem about his married life in August.

53. *CL*, I, 259; *PW*, I, 35, n. 2.   54. *CL*, I, 535; II, 877.

55. At other times he called his poem "The Raven," "this doggerel"; "Fears in Solitude" was "perhaps not Poetry"; a sonnet on the birth of a son "puts in no claim to poetry"; "Reflections on Having Left a Place of Retirement," which was published in every edition of Coleridge's poetry from 1797 onwards, appeared originally with the subtitle, "A Poem which affects not to be Poetry"; "Ode to Georgiana" was "somewhat dullish"; the "Introduction to the Tale of the Dark Ladie'" was offered to the world as a "silly tale"; even "Christabel" was depreciated as "nothing more than a common Faery Tale" (*PW*, I, 170, n. 1; 257, n. 1; 153, n. 2; 106, *app. crit.*; *CL*, I, 552; *PW*, II, 1053; *BL*, II, 211).

56. *PW*, I, 295. Italics in text. "For me to discuss the *literary* merits of this hasty composition were idle and presumptuous"—Coleridge on the "Ode to the Departing Year" (*CL*, I, 289. STC's underscoring).

57. *PW*, I, 268.   58. *PW*, II, 1147.

59. "The Rose" was another poem supposedly tossed off in a trice. It was sent to George Coleridge with the following background: "A piece of Gallantry. I presented a moss rose to a Lady—Dick Hart asked her if she was not afraid to put it in her bosom as perhaps there might be Love in it. I immediately wrote the following little ode or song or what you please to call it. It is of the namby pamby Genus" (*CL*, I, 57-58). Sara Coleridge said she thought "The Rose" was "from the French," but she gave no details (Shedd, III, xxxviii).

60. "Lines Written in the Album at Elbingerode," described by Coleridge as containing not "a grain of merit as Poetry" (*CL*, I, 504), was given to the press shortly thereafter, in 1799, and again in 1800, 1817, 1828, 1829, and 1834.

61. *Poems*, p. 562, No. 14; *PW*, I, 13, *app. crit.*; *CL*, III, 499 (STC's underscoring); *CL*, IV, 937 and n. 1.

62. *CL*, IV, 937, n. 1.

63. J. D. Campbell comments: "This, I have little doubt, is one of the many instances in which Coleridge amused himself and his friends by affixing impossible—or, at all events, highly improbable—dates to his compositions. . . . it is necessary to warn the student that the favourite epithet 'schoolboy' attached by Coleridge to any poem of his is of no value as evidence" (*Poems*, p. 638, No. 197).

64. *PW*, I, 420, n. 2. Henry Nelson Coleridge, the poet's nephew, son-in-law, and early editor, confidently cites this poem as the "first decided indication of his [Coleridge's] poetic and metaphysical genius together, and was written in his sixteenth year" (Shedd, III, 152*n*).

65. *PW*, II, 1151. Two years before his death, Coleridge spoke with "positive satisfaction [of this] very youthful poem . . . as proving a truly remarkable advance of his own mind (and perhaps of his poetical powers) towards maturity" (*CT*, p. 233).

Sibylline Leaves (1817) was the first edition in Coleridge's lifetime to contain the main body of his work. "Time, Real and Imaginary" is the first poem in the volume and is followed by "The Raven" and "Mutual Passion," all three given as specimens of Coleridge's schoolboy muse. Only after this alleged juvenilia (paginated in roman numerals) does the main text begin. As will be seen hereafter, both "The Raven" and "Mutual Passion" were written long after Coleridge left college. The edition of 1828 prints "Time, Real and Imaginary" and "The Raven" among Coleridge's "Juvenile Poems."

66. *PW*, I, 443, n. 2. "I have little doubt," says Campbell, "that it was in 1824 that he composed [First Advent of Love], and that he was dreaming when he wrote the memorandum of 1827" (*Poems*, p. 641, No. 207). George Ridenour has argued persuasively that there are two sources for this little poem, the first line in Coleridge ("O fair is Love's first hope to gentle mind!") being "an unmistakable reminiscence of the opening line of the famous canzone of Guinicelli, 'Al cor gentil ripara sempre Amore.'" Ridenour also quotes the relevant passage in Sidney ("Source and Allusion in Some Poems of Coleridge," *SP*, LX [1963], 76-78.). For lists of incorrect datings of poems and some other inaccuracies, see *RX*, p. 584, n. 3, and ES, pp. 331-332, n. 3.

67. *Poems*, p. 641, No. 207.   68. *TT*, p. 165. 27 December 1831.

2. THE PARCHED ROOTS

1. *N*, 2471. Italics in text.   2. *CL*, I, 132.   3. *CL*, I, 241.

4. *CL*, I, 271.   5. *CL*, II, 755.   6. *CL*, II, 761-762. STC's underscoring.

7. *CL*, II, 772-773.   8. *CL*, II, 899.   9. *CL*, II, 954.

10. *CL*, II, 991.   11. *CL*, II, 1000.   12. *CL*, II, 1057.

13. *CL*, II, 1075.   14. *CL*, III, 59.   15. *CL*, III, 75. STC's underscoring.

16. *CL*, III, 78. These examples are from Coleridge's correspondence through March 1808, when he was thirty-five years old. Remarks of a similar kind, to confine ourselves to Griggs's edition of the letters as thus far published, may be found at *CL*, II, 881, 948, 1044, 1054, 1202; III, 48, 80, 108-109, 118, 157, 171, 216, 231, 232, 249-250, 277, 334, 337, 381, 382, 408, 428, 450, 472, 523, 530; IV, 554, 582, 585, 604, 630, 638, 665, 669, 673, 674-675, 678, 680-681, 699, 705-706, 716-717, 720, 736, 749, 803, 819, 827, 865-866, 870, 888. This sort of self-portrait appears also at numerous points in the poetry and prose.

17. *CL*, II, 884, 982, 910. That Coleridge could write in such a tone at a time when Southey knew of his own fitful struggles with laudanum confirms the melancholy truth that it is all too easy to despise one's own weaknesses in another. Just five months later, Coleridge wrote to another correspondent, who knew nothing of his own addiction: "I met G. Burnet this morning. It made my heart feel almost as if it was going to ake, when I looked at his Eyes—they seemed so thoroughly those of an Opium-chewer" (*CL*, II, 1068). Burnet had been one of the idealistic youths who had helped hatch the original scheme of Pantisocracy.

18. *CL*, II, 1019.

19. *CL*, II, 990. For other expressions in the same vein, see *CL*, II, 739-740, 772, and 774. For Coleridge in different circumstances insisting upon his *cowardice* of pain, see *CL*, III, 491.

20. *CL*, I, 121.   21. *CL*, I, 46-48. STC's emphasis.

22. *CL*, I, 273, 305, 228. See also *CL*, I, 155, 270, 361, 363, 365 for financial needs and purchasing power. According to Cottle, Coleridge rented a house in Bristol shortly after his marriage for £5 a year; Coleridge's house at Stowey cost £7 a year (*ER*, I, 60, 187). Mary Moorman asserts that £100 a year, though meager, would have enabled Wordsworth to live without a profession (MM, I, 167). In fact, William and Dorothy Wordsworth lived on some £60 to £70 a year for a long period.

23. *CL*, I, 59, n. 1.

24. How this massive debt came to be is the subject of one of the many vivid fictions Coleridge communicated to his credulous host, Dr. James Gillman of Highgate, who subsequently incorporated them with great solemnity in his hagiographic biography:

> On [Coleridge's] arrival at College he was accosted by a polite upholsterer, requesting to be permitted to furnish his rooms. The next question was, "How would you like to have them furnished?" The answer was prompt and innocent enough, "Just as you please, Sir!" —thinking the individual employed by the College. The rooms were therefore furnished according to the taste of the artizan, and the bill presented to the astonished Coleridge. . . . Thirty years afterwards, I heard that these College debts were about *one hundred pounds*! (Gillman, pp. 41-42. Italics in text.)

Although there is no shred of evidence in the contemporary record to support this improbable fable, it has been passed on from biographer to biographer for more than a century.

25. *N*, 2091. Italics in text.

26. *CL*, I, 61, and *PW*, I, 54-55 ("To Fortune"). Gillman dutifully records that Coleridge emptied "his pockets of his remaining cash" among the poor of London just before joining up (Gillman, p. 57).

27. *CL*, I, 67-68, 65, 74, 63.   28. *CL*, I, 67, 45, n. 2, 65.

29. In any case, Coleridge's "confession" should not be accepted as a true account of his life at Cambridge without verification from external sources. Taken in isolation it contains little more authority than the letter he wrote to his son Derwent some thirty years later. Derwent, who eventually became a minister, was a student at Cambridge, and Coleridge thought his habits "morally ominous":

> I know by experience what the social recreation is that does an under-graduate good. In my first Term . . . I read hard, and systematically. . . . Six nights out of seven, as soon as Chapel was over, I went to . . . Middleton's (the present Bp. of Calcutta) Rooms—opened the door

without speaking, made and poured out the Tea and placed his cup beside his Book—went on with my Aeschylus, or Thucydides, as he with his Mathematics, in silence till 1/2 past 9—then closed our books at the same moment—the size and college Ale came in—and till 12 we had true Noctes Atticae which I cannot to this hour think of without a strong emotion. With what delight did I not resume my reading in my own rooms at Jesus each following morning. Think you a Ball or a Concert or a Lady Party, or a Literary Club, would have left me in the same state . . .? (*UL*, II, 299)

A letter like this, of course, is something of a classic joke between the generations. But Coleridge seems not to have confined such posturing to paternal duties. Gillman emphasizes the hard reading and industry of his subject's college years (without reference to moral error of any kind). And it may be suspected that even Wordsworth knew no more about the subject than Derwent or Gillman did, when he wrote in *The Prelude* of Coleridge's college years:

> From the heart
> Of London, and from cloisters there, thou camest,
> And dids't sit down in temperance and peace,
> A rigorous student. (VI, 278-281)

30. *CL*, I, 83, 93. Italics in text.   31. *CL*, I, 89, 91. Italics in text.

32. John Hucks, *A Pedestrian Tour through North Wales in a Series of Letters* (London, 1795), p. 25. Italics in text. The discrepancy could conceivably be accounted for on the desperate supposition that Hucks was trying to protect Coleridge by changing the story. But Hucks nowhere mentions any of his companions by name, and it is very hard to believe that he was too timid to write, "One of my companions proposed a toast to General Washington." In fact he attributes the toast to a Welshman, and underscores the point by quoting his rustic English, "May all fools be gullotin'd, and then I *knows* who'll be the first." Surely such hypotheses are unnecessary when we are confronted with contradiction in Coleridge's two accounts, which, incidentally, go on with a variety of other details reflecting upon his own wit and presence of mind, none of them mentioned in Hucks.

33. *CL*, II, 1124. STC's emphasis.   34. *CL*, II, 1094-95. STC's emphasis.

35. *CL*, II, 1095-96.

36. *CL*, II, 1096-97. These letters are worth reading carefully in their entirety. Among other strange assertions, Coleridge claimed that he had misread Rickman's "prohibition" for "permission." Rickman was soon to become one of Coleridge's harshest critics. "I am a little annoyed by a habit of *assentation*," he once wrote to Southey, "which I fancy I perceive in him; and cannot but think that he likes to talk well, rather than to give or receive much information." On another occasion he wrote to Poole: "As usual in his conversation, so in his writing, he does the devil's work—flattery,—without hope of reward" (Orlo Williams, *Lamb's Friend the Census-taker: Life and Letters of John Rickman* [London, 1912], pp. 88, 151. Italics in text).

37. *CL*, II, 1065. STC's underscoring.

38. *CL*, II, 1060. Relevant related material can be found at *CL*, II, 1117, 1121.

39. Just a few months before, Coleridge had written rather smugly to Poole (who was himself very shortly to fall from grace) of the moral dangers besetting Wordsworth: "I saw him more & more benetted in hypochondriacal Fancies, living wholly among *Devotees*—having every the minutest Thing, almost his very Eating & Drinking, done for him by his Sister, or Wife—& I trembled, lest a Film should rise, and thicken on his moral Eye" (*CL*, II, 1013. STC's emphasis).

40. One of the more comic features of Coleridge's defensiveness was his lifelong difficulty with returning borrowed books on time. We find him apologizing to Mrs. William Sotheby for his unintentional "and almost hopelessly long detention" of her husband's copy of Petrarch (*CL*, III, 364). Almost exactly a year later he writes urgently to his wife to send off "instantly" the volume to Sotheby (*CL*, III, 364, 431). A letter of 1814 to J. J. Morgan reveals the anxious

lengths to which Coleridge went to find several borrowed books which he had owed for a long time, and the extraordinary degree to which they were scattered about (*CL*, III, 496). On apparently the same affair, more than a year later Coleridge returned a volume with apologies: "the truth is, I had quite forgotten it, in consequence of Hartley [his son] having had the volumes in his Bed Room" (*CL*, IV, 596). Six months later he wrote with much sense of grievance at the failure of a mutual acquaintance to lend him a book:

> With regard to the cause of the [book] being denied to me, I can only say, on *my Honor* that it is founded in pure Slander which owes it's only Color to a *Mistake*—I have been sinned against most grievously in respect of my own books; but have never sinned—and the only instance, that approached to the resemblance of retaining a Book, was that of having in the languor of Sickness aggravated by the Bustle of Departure left Mr Sotheby's Petrarch at Keswick when I went to Malta. . . . With this one exception (if exception it can be called) I solemnly and on my honor as a Man & a Gentleman declare the charge to be utterly false, & unsupported by one single fact.—If I have in one or two instances detained Books not to be procured in this Country for a length of time, it has been with the permission of the owner. (*CL*, IV, 635. STC's emphasis.)

Coleridge was surely stung to the quick by this charge, and three months later, in requesting the loan of some books from John Murray, the publisher, he added, "you may depend on my giving the practical Lie to the cruel calumny concerning my carelessness in returning Books lent to me" (*CL*, IV, 648). We may well agree with Coleridge that this "seeming trifle [had] both wounded and injured" him, for three months later he unburdened himself on the same topic to John Hookham Frere, repeating the account of how he failed to return Sotheby's book. How recklessly Coleridge could counterattack when he felt himself accused of any failing of character is shown by what follows:

> Likewise, some 10 years ago poor Charles Lamb took it into his head, that he had lent me a Volume of Dodsley's old Plays—I thought him in joke at first; but hearing, that he talked it off whenever he was tipsy (an effect, which 3 glasses of wine will produce at any time) I begged him to let me have the other volumes and I would send him a new set. This he refused with oaths, that he would never speak to me again if I attempted it—At length, however, I was lucky enough to procure the odd volume from Southey, & gave it to Lamb—. His wild Speeches, (half joke, half dream) had it seems been caught up by Robinson, who had talked (and O ye Gods! how he does talk!) at the Westminster Library, & elsewhere. Yesterday I had an opportunity of cross-questioning him. Robinson! I have borrowed more Books from you, than from all my acquaintance collectively: because I could not procure German Books elsewhere. Have I ever lost one? No!—Have I ever retained your Books beyond the given time without obtaining your permission?—No!—Then you ought in justice to do your best to contradict the calumny, which your knowledge of poor Charles Lamb's Character ought to have prevented you from helping to spread. (*CL*, IV, 655-656)

Crabb Robinson's voluminous *Diaries*, so detailed in references to Coleridge, provide no hint of this uncharacteristically vigorous face-to-face reproach.

Four years later Coleridge apologized to an unknown correspondent for the excessively long detention of borrowed books, for which not he but Mrs. Gillman was to blame (*CL*, IV, 846). The following year leaves us a painfully strained letter of apology to John Murray—the recipient of Coleridge's former letters on the subject of book borrowing—for the long detention of "Lightfoot's Works, &c, &c" (*CL*, IV, 945). See also *CL*, I, 97, 258, 265.

41. Gillman, p. 15.

42. Many familiar stories appear in biographies of Coleridge about this period which are, to say the least, dubious. A particularly famous one derives from Crabb Robinson, who passes on from two unnamed women that it was a Judge Buller, a friend of the family, who secured the boy's place at Christ's Hospital. Robinson goes on as follows:

> Coleridge was accordingly sent to town. Buller sent him to the Bluecoat School. The family were proud; thought themselves degraded by this; and refused to notice the boy in the school.

He was, as it were, discarded for his misfortune. His brothers would not let him visit them in the school dress, and he would not (when he could) go in any other. The judge (whether he was judge then I cannot tell) invited him to his house to dine every Sunday. One day, however, he had company, and the Bluecoat boy was sent to dine at the second table. Coleridge was then but nine years old, but he would never go to the house again. Thus he lost his only friend in London, and having no one person to care for him or show him any kindness, his childhood passed away wretchedly; but he says he was thus led to become a good scholar, for he had his book always in his hand that he might forget his misery. (*HCR*, I, 106)

It is hard to think of anyone who could or *would* put such a story abroad, apart from the later Coleridge himself. His brothers may have been neglectful, but it is difficult to believe in such cruelty, especially as it belies their known actions in many other situations. The tale about the young boy's pride is a patent invention, for this is precisely the kind of self-assertive act against authority and established social position which Coleridge was quite incapable, at any time in his life, of carrying out.

43. *CL*, III, 103.

44. In Griggs's edition, these are numbered 174, 179, 208, 210, and 234.

45. All quotations are from *CL*, I, 347-348.

46. *CL*, I, 398. Coleridge's wretched relations with his mother have been explored from a psychoanalytic perspective in a neglected article by Dr. David Beres, who also notes the intense emphasis on food in Coleridge's childhood recollections. (See "Beres" in the Table of Abbreviations.)

47. *CL*, I, 347. Those who impinge upon the lives of the great, especially by way of conflict, whether friends, relatives, or mere acquaintance, all too often receive short shrift at the hands of biographers. Frank Coleridge and Molly are no exceptions.

Another perspective on these relationships is afforded by the letters Francis wrote home after he'd gone to India. To his sister Nancy in 1785 (when he was fifteen), Francis wrote:

I hope my dear Mother still continues to enjoy a good state of health. . . . And now for my good, my dear, and faithful Molly ("what, before Brothers and Sisters? For shame, Frank!" I think I hear you say. Yes, Nancy, for I am sorry to say that I lay under more obligations to that good woman than I do to all the Brothers and Sisters I have got, except my secundum Pater, John, assure her of my unutterable affection and love towards her; that she is still as dear to me as ever; who else would ever wipe the tear off little Frank's cheek, and comfort him in any little distress of sickness? Poor as she was, she never refused me any little money I might have wanted. No; her generous soul gave ever before I asked. Desire my Mother to give her five guineas out of the Hundred pounds I have sent, that is, if she can conveniently spare them, for when poor Molly has had but a penny in the world she would divide it with me, and doth not gratitude demand something in return? . . . the man that can be guilty of Ingratitude—let him die the death of a Dog, and even that, in my opinion, is too good for him!) ([Bernard] Lord Coleridge, *The Story of a Devonshire House* [London, 1905], pp. 46-47)

Francis, in some respects at least a most admirable fellow, died in India in 1792 at the age of twenty-two, after distinguishing himself for bravery in battle. When STC ran away from Cambridge and joined the army under the alias Silas Tomkyn Comberbache, he may have chosen the last name not only as a whimsical suggestion of his horsemanship, but through some obscure association with the middle name of this now dead brother, Francis Syndercombe Coleridge.

48. *CL*, I, 352-354. STC's emphasis.

49. *CL*, I, 355. Again the underscoring is Coleridge's.

50. *CL*, I, 388.   51. *CL*, I, 389. STC's underscoring.

52. Coleridge's recollections in Gillman's biography contain the same interweaving of culiary detail, for example:

Conceive what I must have been at fourteen; I was in a continual low fever. My whole being was, with eyes closed to every object of present sense, to crumple myself up in a sunny corner, and read, read, read; fancy myself on Robinson Crusoe's island, finding a mountain of plum-cake and eating a room for myself, and then eating it into the shapes of tables and chairs—hunger and fancy! (Gillman, p. 20)

53. *CL*, II, 767. STC's underscoring.   54. *N*, 2091.   55. *CL*, I, 106.

56. *CL*, II, 1049.

57. It is precisely at this early point that most biographies of Coleridge go astray. Thus, to the question, "Was Coleridge unhappy at school?" Lawrence Hanson replies:

Lamb, Wordsworth, and Coleridge himself, seem to have been at some pains to draw a pathetic picture of the "liveried schoolboy," the "poor friendless boy" whose few acquaintances soon tired of his visits and neglected him. Coleridge, at a later date and in his best conventional manner, bewails the fate of his "weeping childhood, torn By early sorrow from my native seat." But it is difficult to believe that this "depressed, moping, friendless, poor orphan, half starved" represents more than a phase through which most of the boys had to pass. The conditions at the school must indeed have seemed grim to a newcomer: the brutality of some monitors, the fearsomeness of the punishments, the inadequacy of the food, were alone sufficient to chill the stoutest heart. But they were not the whole of school life, they did not even form the major part of it; and to set against them, Coleridge had the wonders of a great city, access to unlimited books, and above all, a capacity which he quickly revealed of drawing to himself, first friends and later disciples also. (*Life of S. T. Coleridge* [Oxford, 1938], p. 17)

If there was ever any warrant for flying in the face of all Coleridge's public statements on this subject (and, one might add, the general experience of mankind), it has long since been dispelled by the publication of Coleridge's notebooks. "N.B. The great importance of breeding up children *happy* to at least 15 or 16," he wrote, "illustrated in my always dreaming of Christ Hospital and when not quite well having all those uneasy feelings which I had at School" (*N*, 1176. STC's underscoring). One need only read the terrifying nightmares recorded at *N*, 1250 and 1649 to realize that the "pathetic picture" of the liveried schoolboy was far from overdrawn.

Despite this now voluminous evidence, the latest biography of Coleridge simply follows Hanson on this crucial point: "In later years, he [Coleridge] (and even more his friends Charles Lamb and Wordsworth) romanticized the friendless youth torn from his native village to the great city of London ('pent 'mid cloisters dim, / And saw nought lovely but the sky and stars'). But he soon found friends. . . ." (Bate, p. 5)

58. Gillman, p. 12. This last point is confirmed by Lamb (see below). Suggestive reminiscences of "Coleridge at School," written by a fellow bluecoat-boy, may be found reprinted in an article by John Beer (*N & Q*, NS, V [1958], 114-116).

59. The key document here is Charles Lamb's "Chirst's Hospital Five and Thirty Years Ago" (*LW*, II, 12-22). The whole should be read carefully. On the single point of the discipline imposed by the older boys, here is Lamb's account:

The oppressions of these young brutes are heart-sickening to call to recollection. I have been called out of my bed, and *waked for the purpose*, in the coldest winter nights—and this not once, but night after night—in my shirt, to receive the discipline of a leathern thong, with eleven other sufferers, because it pleased my callow overseer, when there has been any talking heard after we were gone to bed, to make the six last beds in the dormitory, where the youngest children of us slept, answerable for an offence they neither dared to commit, nor had the power to hinder.—The same execrable tyranny drove the younger part of us from the fires, when our feet were perishing with snow; and, under the cruelest penalties, forbade the indulgence of a drink of water, when we lay in sleepless summer nights, fevered with the season, and the day's sports. (II, 14. Italics in text.)

Alois Brandl's account of Christ's Hospital in *Samuel Taylor Coleridge and the English Romantic School,* trans. Lady Eastlake (London, 1887), pp. 10 ff. is still worth reading. See also Edmund Blunden, "Coleridge and Christ's Hospital," in *SSH,* pp. 53-69.

60. *N*, 2998.   61. Quoted from *Asra*, p. 87.

3.   THE VALLEY OF WONDERS

1. *CL*, II, 864. The Hymn was first published on 11 September 1802.

2. *Tait's Magazine* (September 1834).

3. *PW*, I, 377. Italics in text.

4. *Coleridge's "Hymn Before Sunrise,"* pp. 218-219. Below is the first part of Coleridge's introductory note, with the relevant Friederica Brun note printed beside it. Passages which Coleridge translated word for word, or nearly so, are italicized in the German text:

Chamouny is one of the highest mountain valleys of the Barony of Faucigny in the Savoy Alps; and exhibits a kind of fairy world, in which the wildest appearances (I had almost said horrors) of Nature alternate with the softest and most beautiful. The chain of Mont Blanc is its boundary, and besides the Arve it is filled with sounds from the Arveiron, which rushes from the melted glaciers . . . and forms other torrents of snow-water, having their rise in the glaciers which slope down into the valley.

Chamounix ist eins der höchsten Bergthäler der Baronie Faucigny in Savoyen. Es wird seiner romantischen, im Kontrast der wildesten Naturszenen mit den sanftesten Schönheiten abwechselnden Lage wegen, vorzüglich von Reisenden besucht: die Kette des Mont-Blanc begrenzt es; und ausser der Arve wird es von den Gletscherwassern des unaufhaltsam *tobenden Arveiron,* und vier andern, aus den sich *ins Thal senkenden Gletschern entstehenden, Schneewassern* durchrauscht.

To avoid the influence of Coleridge's English, I asked a German colleague for a literal translation of Brun's text, without showing him Coleridge's note. The translation reads as follows: "Chamounix is one of the highest mountain valleys of the Barony of Faucigny in Savoy. It is favored (visited) by travellers on account of its romantic location, abruptly changing from the wildest natural scenery to one of mild (soft) beauty. The chain of Mont-Blanc forms its border; and in addition to the Arve, the glacier waters of the incessantly raging Arveiron roar through it, as well as four other streams, snow-fed from glaciers that extend towards the valley."

Coleridge's poetic "snow-water" proves to be a precisely literal translation of Brun's *Schneewassern*. Here, as elsewhere in Coleridge, a distinctly unidiomatic English phrase or construction may suggest the influence of a foreign source.

5. Bonjour, p. 218. The quotation misleadingly suggests a certain asperity of tone in Bonjour towards his subject. In fact Bonjour continually identifies opium and emotional depression as the sole causes of Coleridge's failure to acknowledge Brun, which Bonjour views as nearly unique in Coleridge's career. He repeats that Coleridge's failures to acknowledge sources are in general not only "very small," but that the contrary practice, the specification of even minute acknowledgments, is "overwhelming." A "fine instance" of Coleridge's "characteristic" care in citing even "recondite" sources is an acknowledgment to the Italian poet Chiabrera for the "movements" of the verse in Coleridge's "A Tombless Epitaph" (*ibid.*, p. 94 and n. 1). Bonjour is quite unaware, however, that Coleridge neglected to mention his immense debt to Wordsworth's own translation of the Chiabrera poem. (See the discussion in "The Shrinking of the Canon," pp. 45-46).

6. Brun: "Ich pflückte am Gletscher du Bosson, *wenige Schritte vom ewigen Eise, die schöne Gentiana major in grosser Menge*" ("At the du Bosson glacier, a few steps from the eternal ice, I plucked great quantities of the beautiful *Gentiana major*").

Reprintings of the "Hymn Before Sun-Rise" from 1809 onwards contained the following brief preface: "Besides the Rivers, Arve and Arveiron, which have their sources in the foot of Mont

Blanc, five conspicuous torrents rush down its sides; and within a few paces of the Glaciers, the Gentiana Major grows in immense numbers, with its 'flowers of loveliest [liveliest, *Friend*, 1809] blue.' "

It seems not to have been observed by anyone that the last four words are set off as a quotation. What was Coleridge trying to do? I suggest that here, as often elsewhere, Coleridge left himself a tiny escape hatch in the event of a plagiarism charge during his lifetime. He *could* have argued (as many after him have in this and other connections) that the indication of a quotation surely demonstrated no intent at ungenerous concealment, but rather oversight.

7. *TT*, p. 20.   8. *Poems*, p. 630.   9. *CL*, II, 864-865.   10. *Letters*, I, 405.

11. But this opinion, which is in any case somewhat beside the point, is far from universal. Thomas Ashe, one of Coleridge's most enthusiastic editors, thought the German original "much superior to the paraphrase" (Ashe, II, 87). Brun's German text is printed in *PW*, II, 1131.

12. *LP*, p. 24.

13. In two letters to the *Times Literary Supplement*, however, A. P. Rossiter has carried the work still further and related the Hymn to other sources (28 September and 26 October 1951). In a footnote to Griggs's edition of the letters, he has summarized his findings thus:

> I believe that these [sources] include echoes from Stolberg's poem on a cataract . . . possibly others from Brun's alpine verses, and that both form and substance are strongly influenced by Bowles's *Coombe Ellen*—a rhapsodic blank verse nature-poem, in which (lines 16 f.) will be found the *point d'appui* of the inconsequent disquisition in this letter [to Sotheby] on the Greeks, Numina Loci, etc. S.T.C. leaves this poem unmentioned, in a way suspiciously like his silence on the Brun poem. The inference is, that the involuntary hymn story was an estecian myth, an imposition on the guileless Sotheby. (*CL*, II, 865)

14. But the letter of 26 August proves that Coleridge had very recently read Bowles's *Coombe Ellen*, for he there mentions "perusing the second Volume of Bowles," and quotes a line from the poem (*CL*, II, 855).

A reading of *Coombe Ellen* lends some support to Rossiter's conjecture that Coleridge was "strongly influenced" by it. Form and substance *are* similar and there are more than a few verbal echoes. Compare especially "Hymn Before Sun-Rise," ll. 15-16, 49-50, 54-63, and *Coombe Ellen*, ll. 5-6, 17-19, 272-286.

15. *N*, 1316.

16. *CL*, IV, 974. STC's underscoring. It is not known to whom this letter was written.

17. "It is worth noticing," wrote H. W. Garrod, "that Coleridge says far less in this poem ["Lines written in the Album at Elbingerode"], about the Brocken, which he *had* seen, than in the lines on Mount Blanc about that mountain, which he *never* saw" (*Coleridge: Poetry and Prose*, ed. H. W. Garrod [Oxford, 1925], p. 181. Italics in text).

This idea might well bear considerable development, for it is one of the mysteries of Coleridge's genius that his imagination seems to have been encumbered by his personal experience and the light of common day but rather took wing in the realm of "pure imagination." He wrote infinitely better of sailing ships and polar seas before he ever set foot on a vessel than he ever wrote of his innumerable voyages among books and philosophical ideas.

18. As he did in 1809, 1817, 1828, 1829, and 1834 (*PW*, I, 376, n. 2).

19. One such gratification, as we have seen, was to be thought of as a poet who often wrote under conditions of immediate inspiration. That Coleridge claimed to have written the "Hymn Before Sun-Rise" involuntarily is partly explained by the fact that he was trying to impress him correspondent, Sotheby, a considerable figure in the literary world. Coleridge had met him earlier in the year and had already written him two letters dazzlingly rich in learning and speculation (*CL*, II, 808-819). He sent Sotheby a substantial block of the unpublished "Ode to Dejection" as if he were offering a trifle. In the third letter to Sotheby there is evidence everywhere of Coleridge's unrelenting need to overwhelm the older man with his intellectual power and moral depth. "I can with truth say," wrote Coleridge, "that from those, I love, mere general

praise of any thing, I have written, is as far from giving me pleasure, as mere general censure—in any thing, I mean, to which I have devoted much time or effort" (*CL*, II, 863). Such detachment cannot often have appeared in human affairs, and it was never characteristic of Coleridge. The letter proceeds to a variety of weighty aesthetic matters, ranging far and wide over the world's literature for illustrations. Coleridge wishes to demonstrate that in poetry there can be a logic as profound as Aristotle's. It is at this point that, almost by way of casual illustration, Coleridge offers as proof a certain "Hymn in the manner of the *Psalms*" which he had "involuntarily poured forth" when on Scafell. However, the poem, which was to be published the next day in the *Morning Post*, was not about Scafell, but about Mount Blanc and the Vale of Chamouni, replete with glaciers, eternal ice, and Alpine scenery utterly remote from what England had to offer. We can almost see this problem flash through Coleridge's mind as he hastily covers his tracks: "afterwards I thought the Ideas &c disproportionate to our humble mountains—& accidentally lighting on a short Note in some swiss Poems, concerning the Vale of Chamouny, & it's Mountain, I transferred myself thither, in the Spirit, & adapted my former feelings to these grander external objects."

How tortuous and anxiously careful an explanation this is. Why didn't Coleridge assert that he'd poured forth the Hymn in the vale of wonders itself? This solution seems to have been forestalled by the fact that Sotheby and all Coleridge's friends knew that he had returned from abroad long before. It was simply not probable that he had kept a substantial poem in his desk for more than two years while frantically publishing so much other verse, including the merest *jeux*. Thus, for the momentary gratification of being thought the author of an "involuntary" poem, Coleridge landed himself in the difficulty of having to account for an Alpine locale. (There is no evidence that he repeated this story to anyone else.) And how simple he makes it seem to convert a poem written in the English mountains to the Alps. Clearly, Coleridge had no wish to identify Friederica Brun herself, and certainly not to Sotheby, the translator of Wieland's *Oberon* and thus presumably well versed in German poetry. But why mention at all a "short Note in some swiss Poems, concerning the Vale of Chamouny"? Of course this was meant to explain the change in locale, but the reference, though hopelessly obscure, may have provided a safety valve, however small, for the anxiety Coleridge was perhaps feeling about the intellectual debt he was so carefully suppressing.

20. A commonly held view. Cf. "Coleridge's loss of hope . . . was a chief cause of his plagiarism" (T. M. Raysor in *ERP*, p. 108).

4. SOUVENIRS OF GERMANY

1. See *Poems*, p. 617, and Stolberg's German text in *PW*, II, 1129-30.

2. *CL*, II, 769. STC's underscoring.

3. *PW*, II, 979-980, *app. crit.*

4. Three days later the *Morning Post* published Coleridge's "Ode to Tranquillity" without his signature, together with the same Latin tag, which, Carl Woodring notes, Coleridge got from Sir Philip Sidney (*PPC*, p. 188).

5. *Poems*, p. 614, No. 127.

6. *CHCR*, I, 402. It is sometimes suggested that Coleridge's friends knew of these debts, though there is no such evidence. Lamb did not know that "The Ovidian Elegiac Metre" was from Schiller. He quoted the lines in a letter to Samuel Rogers as a "happy exemplification" (*LL*, III, 394). Schiller's German lines are in *PW*, II, 1125. The reader should consult Appendix VI in Vol. II of EHC's Oxford edition for the German originals of many of the poems discussed in this section. See also Kathleen Coburn, "Original Versions of Two Coleridge Couplets," *N & Q*, NS, V (1958), 225-226.

7. *PW*, I, 326.

8. But cf. Max Schulz, "Coleridge's 'Debt' to Dryden and Johnson," *N & Q*, NS, *X* (1963), 189: "Because of his ingenuous acknowledgment of debts to others, however, source hunters

have usually focused on what he borrowed, avid to trace a trail of obligations (which he rarely bothered to cover up) and content to imply intellectual compromise where there was none and, consequently, to pass up the more absorbing and illuminating study of how, with integrity and originality, he was for ever making other men's material his own."

9. *PW*, I, 307, n. 1; II, 1125. This pretty poem, seventeen lines long, renders seventeen lines from Matthisson's poem, which goes on for some ninety-five lines more. George Ridenour finds it "striking" that Coleridge should have omitted all of Matthisson's proper names except Cytherea, including the name of the lover. He supposes that Coleridge was striving for "inexplicitness." This may be so, but Coleridge's poetic creed, by the time he had learned to read German, usually emphasized concreteness and specificity. The excision of Matthisson's proper names would, naturally, contribute to the difficulty of identifying the contemporary German source, especially when the reader's attention is directed to Catullus in the title. (See "Source and Allusion in Some Poems of Coleridge," *SP*, LX [1963], 75.)

10. *PW*, I, 308, n. 1. The German original is thirty-five lines longer than the version printed in *PW*, II, 1126. Stolberg's title is "Der Felsenstrom" and not "Unsterblicher Jüngling," as given by EHC. Coleridge's poem begins with translation but then expands substantially on the source lines used. After the first nine lines of "On a Cataract," as Marshall Suther points out, "Coleridge's 'translation' is only in the vaguest way related to Stolberg's poem, which is just under twice as long" (*Visions of Xanadu* [New York, 1966], p. 135, n. 2).

11. *PW*, I, iii.

12. *German Influence in the English Romantic Period* (Cambridge, 1926), pp. 123-126. Coleridge's translation is indeed very brilliant. His sometimes remarkable power as a translator is related generally to his editorial gifts and his peculiar dependence upon books for his creative line of departure. See *post*, "The Years of Apprenticeship."

13. *PW*, I, 435, n. 1. The eight lines of Stolberg's German verse are given in *PW*, II, 1134. As has been said, terms such as "taken from," "adapted," or "borrowed" are only loosely descriptive of Coleridge's specific practice, which varied from poem to poem.

14. *CL*, IV, 779.

15. *PW*, II, 951-969.

16. *PW*, II, 963, No. 40; 964, No. 44; 965, No. 46; 966, No. 51.

17. *CL*, II, 876: "The Poetry, which I have sent [to the *Morning Post*], has been merely the emptying out of my Desk. The Epigrams are wretched indeed; but they answered Stuart's purpose better than better things—/. I ought not to have given any signature to them whatsoever / I never dreamt of acknowledging either them or the Ode to the Rain." Coleridge was here writing to his patron Thomas Wedgwood and thus anxious to account for the appearance of bad poetry over his name.

18. *PW*, II, 952, Nos. 2 and 3 (ascribed to John Brennan), and No. 4 (by a Dr. McDonnell). See Lewis Patton in *TLS*, 3 September 1938, p. 590; *PW*, II, 957, No. 19 (from a Latin epigram by John Owen); and *PW*, II, 966, No. 51 (adapted from a Latin epigram by George Buchanan).

19. *N*, 646*n*.

5. *THE WATCHMAN* OBSERVED

1. *TLS*, 3 September 1938, p. 590, and *PW*, II, 952. The three epigrams discussed were all published on 2 April 1796, just five days after Coleridge borrowed the *Anthologia Hibernica* from the Bristol Library. This suggests the desperate haste with which the inexperienced young editor was hunting for material to make copy for the voracious *Watchman* (see Paul Kaufman, "The Reading of Southey and Coleridge: The Record of their Borrowings from the Bristol Library, 1793-98," *MP*, XXI [1924], 317-320).

2. Since "To a Primrose" does not belong in the Coleridge canon, some doubt is cast as to the pure originality of "On Observing a Blossom on the First of February 1796." It is printed in

PW, I, 148 immediately before "To a Primrose" and seems like a companion piece to it. Both poems are variations on the same theme and have some verbal dependencies. Lamb thought Coleridge had in mind Burns's "poem on the ploughed up daisy" while writing "On Observing a Blossom" (*LL*, I, 9). This proves a shrewd observation. Both "On Observing a Blossom," and "To a Mountain Daisy" particularize upon the threat of the north wind to the tender early bud, but this can easily be dismissed as a poetic commonplace. What seems most unlikely to be accidental, however, are the two identical analogies which follow. Both Burns and Coleridge compare the doomed flower with the death of a young girl and an unappreciated "bard."

3. *CL*, I, 191-192. Before the first number of the *Watchman* had appeared one of Coleridge's friends made the following prognostication to another: "You know how subject Coleridge is to fits of idleness. Now, I'll lay any wager . . . that after three or four numbers the sheets will contain nothing but Parliamentary Debates, and Coleridge will add a note at the bottom of the page: 'I should think myself deficient in my duty to the Public if I did not give these *interesting* Debates at *full* length' " (*Ill. London News*, 15 April 1893, p. 463. Quoted from *CL*, I, 192, n. 1. Italics in text).

4. *CL*, I, 202.

5. "Coleridge's *The Watchman:* Decline and Fall," *RES*, IV (1953), 147-148.

6. "He [Coleridge] ransacked many . . . sources for scraps to imitate, adapt, or plagiarize. . . . The scramble for copy banished joy, creativity, and honesty" (*PPC*, p. 21). Lewis Patton has shown that "in addition to at least four unacknowledged borrowings from the *Monthly Magazine*, there are three from William Tooke's *Varieties of Literature* (London, 1795), six from *Anthologia Hibernica*" ("Coleridge and the 'Enquirer' Series," *RES*, XVI [1940], 188-189).

7. *CL*, III, 142-144.   8.   *BL*, I, 115, 120.

6.   ON IMITATION AND ALTERATION

1. *PW*, I, 69-70, n. 2, and *app. crit.*

2. *PW*, I, 69; II, 1123.

3. Coleridge's "conscious Guilt's alarms" above is echoed by "the sore wounds / Of conscious guilt" in Akenside's *fourth* blank verse inscription (ll. 6-7).

4. "The Visit of the Gods" first appears in *Sibylline Leaves* (1817), with the acknowledgment "Imitated from Schiller." But Coleridge's poem is almost a word-for-word translation from Schiller's *Dithyrambe*, reprinted at *PW*, II, 1127. Coleridge's changes consist of altering the German third person to first and introducing a very slight shift in the request the poem makes. Since practically everything else is verbatim translation, "imitated" seems a misleading designation for the poetic process involved. The poem was among three "Songs of my composition" that Coleridge sent to the composer John Whitaker in 1811 with the hope that they would be set to music. No mention was then made of the poem's origin in Schiller (*CL*, III, 320).

5. Both Dykes Campbell and E. H. Coleridge note that the poem was omitted from the edition of 1852 prepared by the poet's daughter. Campbell thought there was "a doubt in the editor's mind as to whether it was Coleridge's" (*Poems*, p. 570, No. 49). E. H. Coleridge declares that the poem was "omitted in 1852 as of doubtful origin" (*PW*, I, 69, n. 2). This seems a very strange supposition by both editors. Sara Coleridge would not have omitted a poem from her 1852 edition as of doubtful origin when it had already appeared in four editions during her father's lifetime. She certainly knew of the poem's appearance in the *Watchman*. In the Preface to the 1852 edition Sara clearly stated on what grounds certain poems were being omitted, and these were solely "certain sportive effusions of Mr. Coleridge's later years" which had lost their novelty, and juvenile works which had not been sealed by the poet's own approval (*PW*, II, 1170). On this basis the "Elegy Imitated from Akenside" should have been printed in 1852. Nevertheless, it was not. It seems obvious that Sara Coleridge was very far from doubting that her father had actually written the poem. But she also may have observed, as neither Campbell nor EHC did, that the appearance of the poem in the *Watchman*, not to mention the *Morning Chronicle*,

which she may not have known about, constituted a plagiarism. In 1847 Sara Coleridge had been at great pains to defend her father's reputation in connection with alleged plagiarisms in the *Biographia Literaria*. It is possible to suppose that she banished the "Elegy" from the 1852 edition so as to protect her father's reputation. Sara Coleridge's other omissions from the 1852 edition are of extraordinary interest for similar reasons.

6. *PW*, II, 1118-19.   7. *PW*, II, 1151.

8. Ashe, I, clxxxii, n. 1.   9. *PW*, II, 1151.

10. *Poems*, p. 619, No. 137.   11. Page 298.   12. *PW*, II, 1119.

13. Why the "Elegy Imitated from Akenside" is not also placed in the appendix containing adaptations is not easy to understand.

7.   THE SHRINKING OF THE CANON

1. Compare *WPW*, I, 263 ("Beauty and Moonlight"); WPW, II, 531; and *PW*, II, 1049-1052 ("Lewti").

2. "Coleridge's Use of Wordsworth's Juvenilia," *PMLA*, LXV (1950), 419-426; hereafter cited as Smyser. On the origin of "Moriens Superstiti," see David V. Erdman, "Unrecorded Coleridge Variants," *SB*, XI (1958), 154. Stephen M. Parrish and David V. Erdman, in "Who Wrote The Mad Monk?" *BNYPL*, LXIV (1960), 209-237, have debated the problem of authorship. To Parrish's seemingly irrefutable arguments, Erdman opposes ingenious replies, the necessity for which suggests their inherent weakness. For example, the massive internal evidence for Wordsworth's authorship is turned aside with the argument that Coleridge was *parodying* Wordsworth's style. Neither author considers the crucial implications of the fact that Coleridge never *republished* the poem, which he surely would have done had he had any real claim to the work.

R. S. Woof discusses the evidence as to the "The Old Man of the Alps" (*PW*, I, 248) at some length and concludes that "the poem, undoubtedly, is mainly Coleridge's" ("Wordsworth's Poetry and Stuart's Newspapers: 1797-1803," *SB*, XV [1962], 167-168). Nothing in Woof's evidence justifies the word "undoubtedly." The poem appeared over the pseudonym "Nicias Erythraeus," the same one Coleridge was to use five weeks later for "Lewti," but he never republished the poem, for which the implications are the same as those for "The Mad Monk." JDC omitted the poem from his meticulous 1893 edition, where the merest scraps were, quite properly, gathered. Whatever his reasons, they were probably strong ones.

3. *LL*, I, 321-322, 324-325.

4. In one of Lamb's commonplace books there is a paraphrase of a song from Schiller, stated by E. V. Lucas to have been prepared for Coleridge (*LL*, I, 31). Oddly, Lucas has omitted a relevant sentence from a Lamb letter of 1800 (*LL*, I, 182), where after the words "R. Burton Peccator," the following should appear: "To this I will add a little Song, which I paraphras'd for Coleridge from Schiller—(which by the bye, is better than Schiller's ballad a huge deal)" (George Leonard Barnett, "A Critical Analysis of the Lucas Edition of Lamb's Letters," *MLQ*, IX [1948], 308). In 1800 Coleridge had also tried to get Lamb to write for the newspapers. "He has lugged me to the brink of engaging to a newspaper," Lamb wrote his friend Thomas Manning, "and has suggested to me for a first plan the forgery of a supposed manuscript of Burton, the anatomist of melancholy" (*LL*, I, 178).

5. Lamb sent a letter to Coleridge in 1800 praising "Lewti," and it seems clear that he knew nothing of Wordsworth's hand in it (*LL*, I, 204). In a notebook entry of 1810 addressed to Sara Hutchinson, Coleridge referred to "my little poem on *Lewti*, the Circassian" (George Whalley, "Coleridge Unlabyrinthed," *UTQ*, XXXII [1963], 327). On a MS note to line 47 of the poem, Coleridge had the effrontery—perhaps forgetting Wordsworth altogether—to write: "This image was borrowed by Miss Bailey in her Basil as the dates of the poems prove" (*PW*, I, 255, n. 1).

The first hint of Wordsworth's connection with "Lewti" came in a copy of the *Annual Anthology* annotated by Southey. On the title page next to "Lewti" Southey wrote: "A school poem of W. W. corrected by S. T. C.," and below the poem itself he added, "W. Wordsworth when a boy, corrected by S. T. C." Despite the twin statement, Lowes was certain that the poem's "rhythm, diction, mood, and imaginative quality is as unmistakably Coleridge's as it is unmistakably not Wordsworth's" (*RX*, p. 516, n. 76). Events were to demonstrate Lane Cooper's acuteness in suggesting that Lowes had not fathomed the young Wordsworth (*PMLA*, XLIII [1928], 591). E. K. Chambers, who is regularly criticized for insufficient respect towards Coleridge, is the only other scholar who seems to have taken Southey seriously (*E&S* [1933], 103).

6. *CL*, I, 629.   7. *PW*, I, 353, n. 1.

8. *EL*, p. 256. Since the rest of Wordsworth's poem is lost, there is no way of knowing how closely Coleridge followed it. Wordsworth included another poem among those for which he did not care a farthing; all that remains of that one is a first line, "One day the darling of my heart." It is not absolutely certain that Coleridge did not use this latter poem in some way also. If for no other reason but this, Chester Shaver, the editor of the revised standard edition of the early letters, might have restrained himself from referring to the poem as "fortunately lost" (*ibid.*, n. 2).

9. *CL*, II, 800.

10. Mrs. Smyser feels that in connection with her disclosures there is "no need to take up the dull, unrewarding, and unpleasant problem of Coleridge's 'plagiarisms'" (p. 426). In this context the question of plagiarism need not be taken up, although there is, perhaps, a certain dubiety in publishing as one's own the work of someone else. The pained reluctance to confront without prejudice unpleasant problems in Coleridge is lamentably typical.

11. *CHCR*, I, 402.   12. *PW*, I, 413, n. 1.

13. In a repeatedly incautious appendix celebrating "Coleridge's Knowledge of Italian" (*N*, p. 403 of the second volume of notes) Professor Beatrice Corrigan has described Coleridge's translation of Chiabrera's seventh epitaph as "a most ingenious improvisation on a theme, with only a few lines of the original surviving." May it not be allowed that Coleridge's effort owes less to Chiabrera than it does to Wordsworth, who is not even mentioned?

14. *CL*, I, 28.

15. See John Sparrow's letter, *TLS*, 3 April 1943, p. 163. John Jortin, the distinguished ecclesiastical historian, had himself been educated at Jesus College, Cambridge.

16. *PW*, I, 56, n. 3.

17. Noted by Bertram R. Davis, *TLS*, 10 September 1938, p. 584.

18. From the second "Epistle to Robert Graham, Esq., of Fintry" (O. Ritter, "Coleridgeana," *Englische Studien*, LVIII [1924], 372-373). As always, it is instructive to study Coleridge's revisions of others' work. The borrowings from Burns come from between lines 17 and 36 of the Epistle. Coleridge condensed these twenty lines to twelve, mostly by dropping whole couplets. Coleridge's poem is at *PW*, II, 1089.

19. See E. L. Griggs, "Notes Concerning Certain Poems by Samuel Taylor Coleridge," *MLN*, LXIX (1954), 27-31; *CL*, I, 95; *PW*, I, 70. At this point in Coleridge studies it would seem prudent to treat with considerable caution unidentified poems in Coleridge's letters or notebooks which he never published.

20. *CL*, I, 106. STC's underscoring. Carl Woodring acidly observes that Coleridge "may have practiced just the opposite" (*PPC*, p. 198).

21. See the article by Griggs cited in note 19. An advertisement by STC at the end of *The Fall of Robespierre* is dated 2 September 1794 (*BNYPL*, LXII [1959], 448).

22. E. L. Griggs, *Coleridge Fille, A Biography of Sara Coleridge* (Oxford, 1940), p. 147, n. 1. Shedd, III, xxxvii.

23. The desire to obscure intellectual obligations seems to lie behind the vague titles Coleridge provided for two of the poems included in the collection of verses he presented to Mrs. Estlin of Bristol in his own handwriting ca. 1795. EHC refers to this collection as MS. E (*PW*, I, xxv).

Coleridge changed the title "Imitated from Ossian" to "Ode"; "Imitated from the Welsh" became simply "Song" (*PW*, I, 38, *app. crit;* 58, *app. crit.*). The Estlins would have been justified in assuming that these were completely original compositions. Estlin was an admirer of Coleridge and apparently was the treasurer of a fund created by a group of Bristol friends to assist the promising poet (EKC, p. 40; *Life*, p. 66).

"In one of the Prayer Books in the Chapel of Jesus College, Cambridge," a twelve-line poem in Coleridge's handwriting, was found and published after his death (*PW*, II, 1124). The first six lines, however, came from a poem by Bowles (*Poems*, p. 474). See *post*, "The Years of Apprenticeship."

8.   THE PAINS OF MEMORY

1.   *PW*, I, 52-53, n. 1.

2.   *PW*, I, 51, n. 1.

3.   Robert Mayo, "Two Early Coleridge Poems," *The Bodleian Library Record*, V (October 1956), 311-318.

4.   *LL*, I, 96.

5.   After this handsome tribute, Coleridge neglected Cottle for the remainder of his life and failed even to mention the name of this important early friend and publisher anywhere in his literary autobiography. To such slights has sometimes been attributed the unusual candor and often sharply critical tone of Cottle's now neglected *Early Recollections, chiefly relating to the late Samuel Taylor Coleridge . . .,* 2 vols. (London, 1837).

6.   *PW*, II, 1147. Italics in text.   7.   *MC*, p. 335.

8.   Alfred Ainger, the editor of the standard Victorian edition of Lamb's works, managed to conclude that Coleridge made "a handsome apology" to Rogers. (See the Modern Library reprint of Lamb's *Complete Works*, p. 1035.)

9.   Shedd, III, xxxviii, n. The reader should see the whole long note beginning on page xxxvi.

10.   Mayo, "Two Early Coleridge Poems," p. 315.

11.   Mayo, p. 315.

12.   "Domestic Peace" (*PW*, I, 71-72) from *The Fall of Robespierre*, is a reworking of a small part of this "Effusion."

13.   In the brief Preface to the *Poems* of 1796, Coleridge acknowledged a debt to Samuel Favell, a former Cambridge schoolfellow, for merely a "rough sketch" of a sonnet (*PW*, II, 1137). And he acknowledged "the Author of 'Joan of Arc' " as having written "the first half of Effusion XV." But of the large debt to Rogers, all was silence.

14.   P. W. Clayden, *The Early Life of Samuel Rogers* (London, 1887), p. 212.

15.   In a footnote to "Lines Written at Shurton Bars" (1795), Coleridge acknowledged that the expression "green radiance" was "borrowed from Mr. Wordsworth" (*PW*, I, 97, n. 1). Under this note in a copy of the *Poems* of 1797 Coleridge wrote, "This note was written before I had ever seen Mr. Wordsworth" (*Poems*, p. 577, No. 82). The expression, "green radiance," appears in "An Evening Walk" (1793) at line 178.

16.   *The Poetical Works of Samuel Taylor Coleridge* (London, 1885), I, 12n. All this throws some light on Coleridge's almost unceasing animosity to Rogers for the rest of his life. In 1803 Coleridge wrote to the influential Sir George and Lady Beaumont, friends of Rogers: "On Tuesday Evening Mr. Rogers, the author of the Pleasures of Memory, drank Tea & spent the evening, with us at Grasmere—& this had produced a very unpleasant effect on my Spirits. Wordsworth's mind & body are both of a stronger texture than mine; & he was amused with the envy, the jealousy, & the other miserable Passions, that have made their Pandaemonium in the crazy Hovel of that poor Man's Heart—but I was downright melancholy at the sight. . . . Forgive me, dear Sir George! but I could not help being pleased, that the Man disliked you & your Lady—& he lost no time in letting us know it. If I believed it possible that the man liked

me, upon my soul I should feel exactly as if I were tarred & feathered." [Five days before, Coleridge had written in his notebook of a visit to a condemned prisoner: "Then visited Hatfield . . . *vain*, a hypocrite / It is not be mere Thought, I can understand this man" (*N*, 1432. STC's underscoring).] At other times Rogers was "the drivelling Booby," and a "Contemptible." In 1811, during a public lecture at which Rogers was present, Coleridge attacked various "Pleasures" poems (*CL*, II, 964-965, 676, 1098; III, 353, n. 1). Coleridge's malicious tattling does not seem to have disturbed the friendship between Rogers and the Beaumonts. "Sir George and I were always excellent friends," said Rogers years later (*Recollections of the Table-Talk of Samuel Rogers, first collected by the Revd. Alexander Dyce*, ed. Morchard Bishop [Lawrence, Kan., 1953], p. 21).

As to what Rogers himself or Coleridge's friends may have thought about the accusations and counter-accusations, with the exception of the letter of Lamb quoted, the record appears entirely silent. There is the barest hint in the first canto of Byron's *Don Juan*, written more than 20 years later, that the issue may not have been entirely dead. Byron was both a friend and admirer of Rogers. In the 205th stanza of *Don Juan*, Byron attacked several living poets, among them Coleridge, whom he called "drunk," and three lines later, having in the meanwhile lashed out at Crabbe and Campbell, Byron wrote, in an apparently vague rebuke to all the poets being lampooned, "Thou shalt not steal from Samuel Rogers. . . ."

9. *"NEMO OMNIBUS HORIS SAPIT"*

1. *CL*, IV, 705, 720, 803, 888.   2. *CL*, I, 585.   3. *CL*, II, 772, 773.

4. *CL*, II, 1021.   5. *CL*, III, 337.

6. *CL*, III, 382. According to Coleridge, it was during a quarrel with Montagu in 1810 that the latter said something like: "Wordsworth has commissioned me to tell you that he has no hope of you, that you have been a rotten drunkard and rotted out your entrails by intemperance, and have been an absolute nuisance in his family." The effect of this upon anyone, let alone so volatile and grievously insecure a person as Coleridge, may well be imagined. The rupture with Wordsworth which followed was bitter, protracted, and never truly healed. Almost everyone who has written on the subject has been partisan toward one or another of the principals. The interested reader will find most of the basic materials in the letters of Wordsworth and Coleridge, and Crabb Robinson's diaries.

7. *CL*, IV, 630. STC's underscoring.

8. *BL*, II, 115.

9. *CL*, I, 34.

10. *CL*, I, 127. STC's emphasis.

11. *CL*, I, 585.

12. See *RW*, II, 152, Shawcross' notes in *BL*, II, 241, 311, and *post*, p. 171.

13. *PW*, II, 951. Joseph Cottle, two pages after telling of a strikingly ingenious but dishonest publication proposal by Coleridge, writes, "In certain features of their character, there was a strong resemblance between Chatterton and S. T. Coleridge," but he does not particularize (*ER*, I, 145-147).

14. *CL*, II, 686, 699. Ten years later Coleridge was still sticking by this position, but now maintaining that he'd convinced Sir James Mackintosh (*CT*, pp. 157-158).

15. *CL*, II, 696-697. STC's underscoring.

16. Portions of the editorial headnote to the first of these philosophical letters can be read as quite damaging to such extraordinary estimates of Coleridge's intellectual stature, though doubtless they were not intended to be. Griggs admits that Coleridge "overstated Locke's dependence upon Descartes and failed to recognize the fundamental differences between the two philosophers." Far more significant that this, however, is the opinion of Professor R. I. Aaron, a great authority on Locke, that while "Coleridge gives evidence of having studied Book I and

the opening chapters of Book II of the *Essay, he does not seem to have read the rest of the work with much care" (CL,* II, 678). This judgment is all the more surprising in that Locke's *Essay on the Human Understanding* was, after Newton's *Principia,* the most important book studied at Cambridge at the time Coleridge was a student there. "Nearly all of the moral questions asked of degree-candidates on examination Wednesday dealt with subjects of the Essay" (Ben Ross Schneider, *Wordsworth's Cambridge Education* [Cambridge, 1957], p. 106). In 1794, a month after he had turned twenty-two, Coleridge wrote his brother George that he had made "a diligent, I *may* say, an intense study of Locke, Hartley and others who have written most wisely on the Nature of Man" (*CL,* I, 126. STC's emphasis). Possibly apropos here is De Quincey's opinion that with respect to Malthus' book, Coleridge "probably contented himself *more suo* with reading the first and last pages" (*DQW,* IX, 17). Of course, this kind of remark is usually dismissed with De Quincey's other "petty rancours." As we shall see, however, Coleridge repeatedly claimed far more knowledge that he had.

17. N, 378*n.*

18. Miss Coburn does not comment on her facts except to state, in connection with the many factual blunders in the passage, that Adelung "must bear the blame for some at least of Coleridge's etymological fancies" (*N,* 378*n*).

19. Next month, writing to Godwin, Coleridge added Hobbes and Hume as among those with unmerited reputations for originality (*CL,* II, 787).

20. It is in this light that much that would otherwise be noisome in Coleridge's letters to the Wedgwood brothers is to be understood. "I should think your judgment," Coleridge wrote to Thomas Wedgwood, "on the sentiment, the imagery, the flow of a Poem decisive / at least, if it differed from my own, & after frequent consideration mine remained different—it would leave me at least perplexed. For you are a perfect electronomer in these things" (*CL,* II, 876-877). Few will suppose that Coleridge really entertained so high an opinion of Thomas Wedgwood's critical faculties, especially as less than a year before he had written to his wife: "it is of the first importance to me to make the connection with the Wedgwoods one of Love and *personal* attachment, as well as of moral & intellectual Hope" (*CL,* II, 776. STC's underscoring). Much in Coleridge's letters to the Wedgwoods is simply incomprehensible without facing squarely his anxiety to please them. His need to flatter a conservative patron helps explain how he could refer to Gibbon and Johnson as among "our most esteemed modern writers," just two months after dismissing them, when writing to a radical like Godwin, as "Trash" (*CL,* I, 619, 644, and *PPC,* pp. 84-85, where Woodring has observed these and other "outrageous discrepancies"). It is not without interest that Josiah Wedgwood's daughter Emma wrote in the privacy of a letter to her own daughter, many years later, upon the publication of Mrs. Sanford's biography of Thomas Poole: "The Tom Poole book is pleasant except that every word of Coleridge's letters revolts me, they are a mixture of gush and mawkish egotism, and what seems like humbug. . . . I can't imagine how my father ever liked and admired Coleridge. I believe Dr. Darwin would have been more acute" (*Emma Darwin: A Century of Family Letters, 1792-1896,* edited by her daughter Henrietta Litchfield [New York, 1915], II, 283-284).

21. This is the more especially true when one remembers that one of Coleridge's major purposes in going to Germany was to write a life of Lessing. But despite his repeated assurances that he had amassed "very large collections" of materials for this purpose, all that he seems to have done was to make "a brief summary *of a German summary* of the standard biography by Lessing's brother" (*N,* 377 and *n.* See also p. 452 in the Notes volume). George Watson incautiously seizes upon the existence of this *précis* to account for Coleridge's failure to complete some of his many writing projects: "at times he would write himself out of an idea in a first draft, lose interest in it and never publish it; the biography of Lessing, for example, which he visited Germany in 1798-9 to write, was fully drafted in some thirty manuscript pages before being abandoned forever" (GW, p. 5). These thirty manuscript pages run to eight in the printed edition, whose notes throw a bleak light on this particular fancy.

22. *Poems,* p. 542 and n. 1.

23. *Poems*, p. 543. In the surrounding passages, Coleridge shows a very surprising ignorance of the sonnet, and his very confident critical assertions make dismal reading. Late in 1797 Coleridge was claiming a very extensive knowledge of German. "I am translating the Oberon of Wieland," he wrote to Joseph Cottle, "—it is a difficult Language, and I can translate at least as fast as I can construe" (*CL*, I, 357). Coleridge's knowledge of German is a subject of great importance and will be dealt with later. Suffice it to say for the moment, however, that this statement is probably a wild exaggeration, assuming there is any truth to it at all, and that it has led later scholars badly astray.

24. *CL*, II, 679. Interestingly, in Hazlitt's recollections of the young Coleridge he says of his reading: "Coleridge somehow always contrived to prefer the *unknown* to the *known*" (*HW*, XVII, 113. Italics in text).

25. On 4 April 1801 Coleridge borrowed some fourteen books from the Carlisle Cathedral Library, among them the translation of Malebranche. See Paul Kaufman, "Coleridge's Use of Cathedral Libraries," *MLN*, LXXV (1960), 395-399. More than four years before this, Coleridge had written to Thelwall: "I am just about to read Dupuis' 12 octavos, which I have got from London. I shall read only one Octavo a week—for I cannot *speak* French at all, & I read it slowly" (*CL*, I, 260. STC's emphasis). Beyond the single word "Dupuis" in Coleridge's notebooks, there is not a scrap of evidence that the twenty-four-year-old Coleridge, with no demonstrable grounding in French to fortify him for so arduous a task, undertook to read what Lowes has called "a mad performance"—in twelve octavo volumes at that. Nevertheless, Lowes automatically assumes that "Coleridge was painfully going through [Dupuis], a volume a week, in French" (*RX*, p. 233). Professor Coburn rather noncommitally directs the reader to Lowes for a discussion of Coleridge's reading of Dupuis (*N*, 327*n*), but that the discussion is entirely surmise. According to one of Coleridge's travelling companions on the continent in 1828, "Coleridge did not understand French at all" (T. C. Grattan, *Beaten Paths and Those who Trod them* [London, 1865], p. 120).

26. *CL*, I, 312, 347, 359. STC's underscoring.

27. *CL*, I, 260. For another example of Coleridgean intellectual grandiosity, see his letter to Charles Lloyd, Senior, sent just a few days before. Among "that knowledge and those powers of Intellect" which Coleridge proposed to impart to the younger Lloyd were "the *elements* of Chemistry, Geometry, Mechanics, and Optics," apart from metaphysics, history, languages, and "a thorough examination of the Jewish and Christian Dispensations" (*CL*, I, 256. STC's emphasis). As to Coleridge's knowledge of the sciences mentioned (to confine ourselves to more demonstrable matters), he did not at twenty-four command the *elements* of these subjects, and since he never got beyond a rudimentary grasp of mathematics, or acquire any practical laboratory experience, it is doubtful that he was ever in a position to teach the subjects. (But see *post, "Theory of Life* and Coleridge's Writings on Science.")

28. Gillman, pp. 20-21. Italics in text.

29. Gillman, p. 23. As an example of how these recollections are passed along as fact, see *CT*, p. 15. "When Coleridge reached the age of eight he had absorbed everything in his father's library, and at fourteen he had read through the entire stock of a circulating library . . . devouring two books a day, folios and all, whether or not he understood them—all this in addition to his required studies at Christ's Hospital, in which he excelled."

30. *CL*, II, 705.

10. A LITERARY LIFE

1. References to the *Biographia Literaria* throughout this chapter are to the edition of John Shawcross (Oxford, 1907), 2 vols. Reference to an editorial note is preceded by Shawcross' name, for example, Shawcross, I, 200. Reference to the 1847 edition of Sara Coleridge is to the reprint in the third volume of the *Works* edited by Shedd.

2. *Biographia Literaria* (Everyman ed.), p. x.

3. *The Armed Vision: A Study in the Methods of Modern Literary Criticism* (New York, 1948), p. 11.

4. *Coleridge as Critic* (London, n.d.), p. 18. Reprinted in *Lectures in Criticism* (New York, 1949), and *The True Voice of Feeling* (New York, 1953).

5. Eliot, Auden, Lowell, and scores of contemporary poets have ransacked the world's literatures for images, lines, stanzas, and more, and have often—playfully, arrogantly, or as a matter of principle—kept their sources to themselves. "Allusiveness" has become a virtue, and the silent incorporation into one's art of this man's wit and that man's trope is in some quarters modernity itself. The aesthetic problem involved is a massive one and far beyond our present concerns. In general, a very sharp distinction is made between the borrowing of concepts, propositions or theories, on the one hand, and purely artistic materials, on the other. That Eliot lifted a "stiff, dishonored shroud" from James Russell Lowell, for example, seems of much less consequence than that the influential phrase "objective correlative" was actually first enunciated by Washington Allston (see Stanley Burnshaw, *The Seamless Web* [New York, 1970], p. 75, n. 23). A rough common sense stands behind these distinctions, but once the matter is challenged nothing short of a substantial demonstration of the reasons behind them will suffice. As to the problem of poetic borrowings, see hereafter.

6. RW, II, 152-153. Needless to say, Wellek's writings on Coleridge have been heatedly attacked. As Wellek's facts are indisputable, his opponents contest his interpretation of them.

7. *BL*, I, 9.   8. *BL*, I, 9.

9. Compare his letter to Poole of 1799: "you will believe me, when I say, that I have few feelings more pleasureable than to find myself in intellectual Faculties an Inferior" (*CL*, I, 491). Coleridge continued to assert this as true of himself. In March 1815, just a few months before most of the *Biographia* was written, Coleridge wrote: "I have often heard of the Pain of Inferiority: this I could never understand. I have often enough met my superiors, some in all things, many in many things—and God knows! the feeling was so delightful, that it has not seldom tempted me to overrate persons—but the pain of *Superiority!* THAT I *have* felt, and *do* feel it almost as often as I read a Speech or composition of my Contemporaries." Coleridge continued in this vein in a letter to Lord Byron later that year: "To think of myself at all except *representatively* & for psychological purposes was new to me; but to think of myself comparatively was not only new but strange" (*CL, IV*, 554, 604. Italics in text).

10. *BL*, I, 12. One of Coleridge's notebook entries of 1804 reads: "Gray's Orient Forms from Smallwood's Verses." But Gray had in fact written "orient hues" (in "The Progress of Poesy"). One wonders why Coleridge was so quick to fire in these matters. See *N*, 1919 and *n*.

11. *BL*, I, 13. Italics in text. *Ferrumination* does not appear in Johnson's *Dictionary*. The word, which is defined as "the action of cementing together," was obsolete in Coleridge's time.

12. *BL*, I, 209.

13. In a notebook entry dated fourteen years before the publication of the *Biographia*, Coleridge had written: "Lactea purpureos interstrepit unda lapillos / Pura coloratos." There was no reference to obtaining it from a university prize-poem or any further comment. As it happens, the passage in the notebook is vaguely connected with the subject of plagiarism (see *N*, 1673 and *n*).

14. *BL*, I, 18 *n*.   15. *PW*, II, 959.

16. *N*, 625, No. 18, and *n*. Sara Coleridge, not too discreetly, dropped this poem from her 1852 edition. E. H. Coleridge, in his *apparatus criticus,* cited all the verse in the *Biographia* with the exception of this (*PW*, II, 959). Coleridge found this story sufficiently amusing to apply it also to one of his "Nehemiah Higgenbottom" sonnets (*BL*, I, 18-19). Joseph Cottle, who ought to have been less gullible, cited these yarns as indicative of Coleridge's alleged penchant for self-satirization (*ER*, I, 292-293*n*); David Erdman, however, provides a sensible analysis of the facts (*BNYPL*, LXI [1957], 618).

17. *BL*, I, 19.

18. This was one of Coleridge's many promised but unfulfilled projects. This failure, however, has considerable significance. See *post* "Shakespearean Criticism."

19. *BL,* I, 22.   20. *BL,* I, 26.

21. Shawcross, I, 215. For similar charges see his letter of 5 June 1817 (*CL,* IV, 737).

22. *BL,* I, 31.   23. 29 August; 7, 9, 10, 11 September 1816.

24. *BL,* II, 205-206. Respecting these articles, Coleridge wrote in a letter of 31 August 1816 that he had "furnished a friend" with a single paragraph, while noting at the same time, "I have an exceeding reluctance to write in *any* Review entirely from motives of Conscience, conducted as *all* the Reviews are at present" (*CL,* IV, 664-665. STC's underscoring). On 17 September, to a different correspondent, he wrote, "The Essays on Bertram were in great measure dictated by me: but I was not able to revise them or correct the style" (*CL,* IV, 670). To a third correspondent, some seven months later, Coleridge denied authorship, and attributed the articles to his friend Morgan, from "Thoughts, that had been collected from my conversation years before the Bertram was in existence" (*CL,* IV, 720). Despite these protestations, Griggs is surely right in confining Morgan's role, if any, to that of an amanuensis. Except for some heavy cuts in the first *Courier* article, all the rest appear in Chapter XXIII of *Biographia* almost verbatim. Two years later, Coleridge had so far forgotten the *Courier* (and other) articles that he could write to Allsop (18 December 1818) that only in the critique of Wordsworth in the *Biographia* may he have appeared to deviate from his rule respecting genial criticism. Coleridge, of course, regularly condemned reviewing of any kind as "utterly immoral." See, for example, *CL,* III, 272, 275, 316-317. Less than four months after the *Courier* articles, he wrote: "I have never reviewed or in any other way criticized any man's work" (*CL,* IV, 699).

Two months later, an extremely laudatory review of Coleridge's second *Lay Sermon* appeared in the *Courier.* The review was submitted by Coleridge himself to T. G. Street, the editor of the *Courier,* and Coleridge pretended that it had in fact been written by a nameless friend. The review, "open and manly," according to Coleridge himself, is well worth study. David Erdman, who far more than most scholars does not flinch in the presence of the estecean labyrinth, has written of this review that "it is fascinating to observe the ingenuity with which praise is lavished yet, as much as politic, avoided. The *anonymous* reviewer is glad to afford to Mr. Coleridge, 'an old and valued Correspondent,' a fair analysis of his work—such as 'he is little likely to receive' otherwise, 'in the present state of anonymous criticism'! The nature of fair anonymity is then explained. Since the whole review consists of a fair analysis plus 'a few extracts,' 'any partiality we may feel, can have no influence on the reader, who is completely left to his own judgement.' " ("Coleridge on Coleridge." *SIR,* I [1961], 59. Italics in text.) A few extracts from this "impartial" review follow: "We have seldom seen a problem of political economy solved with so much elegance and perspicuity. . . . he proves irrefragably. . . . he has ably detailed. . . . We are particularly pleased . . . with the clearness with which Mr. C. has explained the operation of taxes. . . . respect both for the head and heart of the author" (quoted from "Coleridge on Coleridge," p. 63).

Three weeks after publishing this review of his own book, apparently still concerned over the rumor that the *Courier* articles attacking Maturin had been written by himself, Coleridge wrote that they had been Morgan's work. As for himself, "that man knows little of me (who can affirm with strictest truth that to this hour I know the meaning of the word Envy only by the interpretation given in the Dictionaries) who would look *out* of the Bertram itself for any cause of my abhorrence of that piece" (*CL,* IV, 720. STC's underscoring).

25. *BL,* I, 32. Almost the exact words were entered by Coleridge into his journals for 1802 (*N,* 1248 and *n.*), and sent in a letter to Poole the following year.

26. Also used, sometimes verbatim, in *CL,* II, 1011; III, 126, 131, 133, 145. See also "Opus Maximum," note 6.

27. In this chapter some errors of fact should be noted. On page 35 Coleridge says that although he has published nothing for years he has during all that time been abused, "year after year, quarter after quarter, month after month." This does not cause him any anger, only sur-

prise. But during those years (presumably between 1798 and 1815), Coleridge had published *The Friend* (1809-10), and *Remorse* (1812), "both of which had been reviewed in not unfavourable terms" (Shawcross, I, 217). Besides these two works one may cite the large number of political essays and poems published between 1798 and 1802 in the *Morning Post,* Coleridge's contributions to Southey's *Annual Anthology* and *Omniana,* and the publication of the third edition of his poems in 1803. This does not begin to exhaust the list of Coleridge's appearances in print during these years. A few pages later Coleridge curiously forgets his *Conciones ad Populum, Watchman,* and *Friend* when citing the works which "constitute my whole publicity" (*BL,* I, 38). Thus the first sentence of the *Biographia* reads very oddly: "It has been my lot to have had my name introduced, both in conversation, and in print, more frequently than I find it easy to explain, whether I consider the *fewness,* unimportance, *and limited circulation of my writings, or the retirement and distance in which I have lived, both from the literary and political world."* It is unnecessary to explain how misleading a picture of Coleridge's actual literary career this sentence conveys. Coleridge himself in Chapter X of the *Biographia,* defending himself against the charge of idleness, writes: "if the compositions which I have made public, and that too *in a form the most certain of an extensive circulation,* though the least flattering to an author's self-love, had been published in books, *they would have filled a respectable number of volumes"* (*BL,* I, 148-149). The juxtaposed passages indicate the peculiar selectivity of Coleridge's mind when he is anxious to establish a point. However, Coleridge's memory on this subject really does seem to have been amazingly treacherous. In 1808 he was actually able to write that he hadn't published anything in thirteen years! But in writing to Lord Byron in 1815, he boasted that "if my published Works, omitting too all that is merely temporary, were collected, they would amount to at least 8 considerable Octavo Volumes" (*CL,* III, 116; IV, 604). Among other false statements in Chapter III are several concerning Jeffrey. (See Shawcross, I, 217.)

28. *BL,* I, 38, 218.

29. *HCR,* I, 62. In 1804 Coleridge had threatened to square accounts with Mrs. Barbauld for writing a bad review of Lamb: "if I do not cut her to the Heart, openly & with my name, never believe me again" (*CL,* II, 1039; see also *CL,* III, 343, n. 3, and N, 1848*n*).

30. *BL,* I, 49. STC's italics. It would be tedious to enlarge on all of Coleridge's deviations from fact or sincerity. Nevertheless, it should be noted that Coleridge's high praise for Southey in this chapter is at sharp variance with the opinions expressed in his letters and conversations.

31. *BL,* I, 64-65. Italics in text. This justaposition of ideas may well derive from the Preface to the first edition of Kant's *Critique of Pure Reason:* "As to *certainty,* I have prescribed to myself the maxim, that in this kind of investigation it is in no wise permissible to hold *opinions. . . .* the objective deduction with which I am here chiefly concerned retains its full force even if my subjective deduction should fail to produce that complete conviction for which I hope." Coleridge's specific phrasing may owe something to a passage added in the second edition, namely, Kant's declaration that his method "consists in looking for the elements of pure reason in *what admits of confirmation or refutation"* (Kant, pp. 11-12, 23. Italics in text).

It is significant that Coleridge could reject with such confidence anything that smacked of mere *opinion,* when in the very first chapter of *Biographia* he had said that "no authority could avail in opposition to . . . the LAWS OF UNIVERSAL GRAMMAR" (*BL,* I, 14), as if these "laws" were more than another one of the eighteenth century's many post-Newtonian chimeras.

32. *BL,* I, 70, 231.

33. Pages 296-297. Ferrier, a professor of philosophy at Edinburgh, was also the first to point out that Coleridge was "not contented with purloining Schelling's philosophy, but he must also plunder him of his Aesthetics." He demonstrated part of the debt to Schelling in Coleridge's famous essay "On Poesy or Art," and also identified unacknowledged borrowings from Schiller and Stolberg. Ferrier's article remains a formidable one, but its effect is weakened by an intensity of moral indignation which does not sit well in the world of polite learning. For

example, he closes his indictment with the ringing cry: "Let all men know and consider that plagiarism, like murder, sooner or later *will out"* (p. 297. Italics in text).

Henry Crabb Robinson's immediate reaction to this article was that it was "perfectly just." Six years later, however, when Sara Coleridge's new edition of the *Biographia* was in the press, he noted: "She is perplexed by the charge of plagiarism from Schelling. I gratified her by the assurance of my belief that he was unconscious of it" (*HCR,* II, 581, 659). Here is the model for so much subsequent reaction to the plagiarism problem: the evidence itself is overwhelming for deliberate intent, but with the passage of time the facts grow fuzzy, and the wish to lean upon the dubious support of the treacherous unconscious grows irresistible.

34. Both Sara Coleridge and Shawcross cite this sentence as an instance where Coleridge was probably quoting from "imperfect" memory. But there is no basis for this seriously misleading assumption. Sara Coleridge observes that in the passages immediately preceding this sentence Maass had pointed out that "in the sixteenth century the spirit of inquiry took a new turn, and that men came forth who knew the value of empirical psychology" (Shedd, III, 215). She translates Maass as follows: "Among the first to whom this merit belongs were Melanchthon, Ammerbach, and Lud. Vives. . . . But far the most was done by Vives." It is not easy to see in what way Coleridge's sentence implies imperfect recollection of this passage. Both Sara Coleridge and Shawcross seem to assume that deviation from verbatim transcription implies that Coleridge was quoting from memory. Since Coleridge was translating out of a foreign language, and since he was giving his source no acknowledgment, there was no reason whatever why he could not alter the words before him—as here, very slightly—to suit his own style and purposes.

35. Coleridge's debts are much more easily followed in the edition of Sara Coleridge, reprinted in the third volume of Shedd, than in Shawcross. She also gives some of STC's marginalia in Maass.

36. *BL,* I, 71, 72. 37. Shedd, III, 221.

38. Coleridge confused other statements by Maass with Aristotle (Shedd, III, 221*n*). It was doubtless for these and related reasons that Sir William Hamilton called this chapter of the *Biographia* "a plagiarism, and a blundering plagiarism from Maass; the whole chapter exhibiting, in fact, more mistakes than paragraphs" (*The Works of Thomas Reid,* 2nd ed. [Edinburgh, 1849], II, 890). Ferrier credits a friend with pointing out to him the Maass debts (JCF, p. 296); the friend was quite possibly Hamilton.

I. Newell, in pointing out a probable connection between Maass and one of Coleridge's lectures on Shakespeare, goes out of his way to minimize the debt in the *Biographia:* "There is no question of plagiarism here. Coleridge merely turned to Maass, an authority; indeed, he sometimes dissented from his views." In some strange way, dissenting from one's source seems to justify failure to acknowledge use of it. See "Coleridge and J. G. Maass," *N & Q,* N S, VIII (1961), 218-219.

39. Coleridge repeated this statement in still more sweeping form in the *Philosophical Lectures,* p. 189.

40. *BL,* I, 73. Italics in text.

41. *Dissertation on the Progress of Ethical Philosophy,* Note S. (Originally prefixed to the seventh edition of the *Encyclopedia Britannica.*)

42. Sara Coleridge concluded that her father "must have had in his mind, not merely the short section on the Association of Ideas, but generally whatever relates to the subject in the Inquiry concerning Human Understanding" (Shedd, III, 222). Even if this were true, as she herself shows, the charge would be baseless. But the difficulties are not to be mitigated in this way.

Soon after the publication of the *Biographia* an article appeared in *Blackwood's* challenging Coleridge "to produce from it [Aquinas' *Commentary*] a single illustration, or expression of any kind, to be found in Hume's essay" ("Hume charged with Plagiarism from Acquinas" [1818], p. 657). Coleridge remained silent, but repeated the accusation in the mass of manuscript left unfinished at his death: "Mr. Hume . . . borrowed without acknowledgment a much more correct statement of the laws of association from Aquinas' commentaries on the 'parva Naturalia' of Aristotle'' (*CLL*, pp. 92-93).

There is no evidence that Coleridge ever spoke of this matter to his "literary acquaintances." The recently published notebooks show that in 1801 he had Sara Hutchinson copy out a portion of the very work in question, but there is nothing about any relation to Hume, though Hume was sufficiently abused in the letters of the period.

It seems odd that Miss Coburn should speak of Coleridge as merely having "suggested" that Hume used Aquinas, when in fact there is a vigorous assertion (*N*, 973A and *n*; *CL*, II, 746). For a devastating discussion of the subject see John Hill Burton, *Life and Correspondence of David Hume* (Edinburgh, 1846), I, 288.

43. *BL*, I, 65.   44. *BL*, I, 74.   45. Shawcross, I, 234.

46. Yet James V. Baker seizes upon the single appearance of the name in the *Biographia* which, as has been shown, is the opposite of a citation of debt, to argue that Coleridge's lack of acknowledgment was not complete but a matter of degree. "Now, it is regrettable, of course, that Coleridge was not all times accurate," Baker writes, "and we could have wished that he had been more honest in making a *completer* acknowledgment of indebtedness to Maass. But Coleridge, after all, made no pretense of attention to scholarly minutiae. He had a creative mind, and if he makes minor or even major slips in accuracy, he compensates us with positive insights. His sins, therefore, are easily forgiven, for we have an abundance of scholars who can set right his inaccuracies, but we do not have an abundance of minds with insights like his" (*The Sacred River: Coleridge's Theory of the Imagination* [Baton Ronge, La., 1957], p. 33). The point at issue is distortion of facts. Coleridge's lack of acknowledgment to Maass was not a question of degree, but absolute, and Coleridge *did* pretend, repeatedly, that acknowledgments were sacred obligations to him. Intellectual integrity is surely not merely a matter of fussily attending to scholarly minutiae.

47. *BL*, I, 80 and *n*.

48. In the Appendix to the essays called "On the Principles of Genial Criticism,' published in 1814, Coleridge had withdrawn from penetrating further into another abstruse subject in almost identical works: ". . .I discourse not now, waiting for a loftier mood, a nobler subject, a more appropriate audience, warned from within and from without, that it is profanation to speak of these mysteries. . . ." (*BL*, II, 246). The sentence is completed by the same quotation from Plotinus. Essentially the same devices are employed to terminate a discussion in *Aids to Reflection*, where the solution of many doctrinal difficulties is referred to a work which had been the "principal labour" of the author's life since manhood. The statement appears in all the editions of *Aids* I have consulted as the last paragraph of "Aphorism on that which is indeed Spiritual Religion," immediately preceding Aphorism I. Shedd, however, deletes the paragraph (!), perhaps because he knew that no such work was ever completed.

49. *BL*, I, 89. "Spinoza nowhere clearly formulates this doctrine" of a "pre-established harmony." Further, "it is doubtful . . . whether this doctrine [animal machines] furnished any hints to Spinoza" (Shawcross, I, 238). On matters of this sort, STC is not to be taken seriously without specific evidence.

50. Shawcross rarely prints the Schelling passages used by Coleridge. In this respect Sara Coleridge's 1847 edition is again far more useful.

51. *BL*, I, 89-90. Italics in text. Coleridge used this passage and some fifty lines following, all from Schelling, in the *Philosophical Lectures* of 1818, again without acknowledgment. See *PL*, pp. 351-352, 456, 31-32.

52. Shedd, III, 241*n*. Italics in text.   53. *BL*, I, 91-92.

54. *BL*, I, 92, 93. The line is actually from John Brown's *Essay Occasion'd by the Death of Mr. Pope.* See *Biog. Lit.* (Everyman ed.), p. 78, n. 2.

55. *BL*, I, 93.

56. For a realistic appraisal of this and other claims by Coleridge to having read widely in these philosophers at any early age, see Richard Haven, "Coleridge, Hartley, and the Mystics,"

JHI, XX (1959), 477-494, esp. pp. 488 ff. This is one of the sanest and most perceptive articles ever written on the subject of Coleridge's early reading in philosophy. See discussion *post*.

57. *BL*, I, 95. Italics in text.

58. "Now, how Coleridge could reconcile with ordinary faith his statement, that a paragraph, consisting of forty-nine lines, to which his own contribution was six, was only *in part* translated from a foreign work—how he could outrage common sense, and the capacities of human belief, by saying that he might have transcribed 'the substance of it from memoranda of his own, written many years before Schelling's pamphlet was given to the world'—how he could have the cool assurance to tell us that he 'prefers another's words to his own'—not, mark you, because these words belong to that other man, and not to him—but *as a tribute due to priority of publication*—and how he could take it upon him to say that in this case nothing more than coincidence was *possible*, (except on the ground that it was impossible for any human being to write any thing but what he had written before!)—how he could do all these things, entirely baffles our comprehension" (JCF, p. 294. Italics in text).

These three pages constitute one of several Schellingian passages from *Biographia* which were also used in the *Philosophical Lectures* of 1818. At that time, however, Coleridge said not a word about either Schelling or a "writer of the Continent." The omission is all the more glaring in view of the tributes paid to Boehme ("I have felt my own mind much indebted to him") and to Bruno, both of which immediately precede the word-for-word, silent borrowing from Schelling. Miss Coburn refers to this lengthy passage as "a piece of self-plagiarism from the B. L." and dismisses the problems raised with the curious statement that "Those who are interested in questions of plagiarism may make what they like of Coleridge's use of this material in the lecture" (*PL*, pp. 327-329; 453, n. 26).

59. *BL*, I, 98.   60. *BL*, I, 99.

61. *CL*, I, 284n. This letter, to John Thelwall, is replete with pretensions to first-hand knowledge of German letters and philosophy. Earlier that year Thomas Beddoes had written a brief article in the *Monthly Magazine* (May 1796, pp. 265-267) on Kant's system, which STC probably saw.

62. *N*, 1517n.

63. *BL*, I, 102. Ferrier has sensibly argued that "so long as human nature and the laws of evidence remain what they are, 'an identity of thought and similarity of phrase,' occurring in the case of two authors, must be held as very *strong* proof that one of them has borrowed from the other. But in the present case it is not *similarity*: it is absolute *sameness* of phrase that we are prepared to bring forward against Coleridge" (JCF, p. 289. Italics in text).

64. *BL*, I, 102-103.   65. *N*, 2375.   66. *CL*, II, 673.   67. *CL*, I, 209.

68. *CL*, III, 387.   69. *CL*, III, 411.   70. *HCR*, I, 185.

71. *CL*, IV, 792-793.   72. *CL*, IV, 561.   73. *BL*, I, 202.

74. *Letters*, II, 735. STC's underscoring.

75. For example, see R. L. Brett, "Coleridge's Theory of the Imagination," *ES* (1949), 75-90. Brett treats this extraordinary claim as absolute fact. More recently, Daniel Stempel has done the same in "Coleridge and Organic Form: The English Tradition," *SR*, VI (1967), 89-97. It seems worth stating at this point that English-speaking critics overwhelmingly tend to deny the influence of Germany on Coleridge as *indispensable*. Prodigious research has been directed to the end of demonstrating that Kant, Schelling, and other German thinkers only confirmed what Coleridge had already learned from his allegedly exhaustive reading in world philosophy, especially in the Cambridge Platonists. One of the almost ludicrous effects of these studies is to reduce Kant to a kind of synthesizer of obscure English philosophers. So Walter Jackson Bate can write in an extremely influential book that "Kant rarely inspired Coleridge except with his own ideas or with those which he had imbibed, as a youth, from the Christian Platonists" (*From Classic to Romantic* [New York, 1961], p. 181). Leslie Stephen is among the very few English scholars to take a dim view of Coleridge's philosophical pretensions; he writes, for example: "it is undeniable that Coleridge was guilty of a serious theft of metaphysical wares.

. . . The simple fact is that part of his scheme was to establish his claims to be a great metaphysician" (*Hours in a Library* [London, 1899], III, 356). Stephen's "simple fact," however, seems to be widely accepted only by European scholars. In Harald Höffding's classic *History of Modern Philosophy*, trans. B. E. Meyer (New York, 1950), Coleridge is treated in a way which must surely seem grotesque to English and American students; for example: "Consecutive thought, however, was never Coleridge's *forte*. . . . All he had to give was transcendental moonshine. . . . Coleridge never got beyond intuition and prophecy" (II, 375-376). The three pages Höffding devotes to Coleridge make for astonishing reading today.

76.   *IS*, p. 252. STC's underscoring. The almost alarming confusions inherent in this statement are only partly accounted for by the editor's note, p. 420.

77.   *DQW*, X, 77. Italics in text.   78.   *TT*, p. 207.   79.   *HCR*, I, 107, 108.

80.   "Coleridge on a Distant Prospect of Faust," *E & S*, X (1957), 89.

81.   *Ideen zu einer Philosophie der Natur [Ideas Toward a Philosophy of Nature]*.

82.   *CL*, I, 137. As late as 1811, Coleridge still referred to Hartley as one of the three greatest metaphysicians (*CT*, p. 173).

83.   *PW*, I, 123, ll. 368-369.

84.   *PW*, I, 110, n. 2. See H. N. Fairchild, "Hartley, Pistorius, and Coleridge," *PMLA*, LXII (1947), 1010-1021.

85.   *CL*, I, 295. STC's underscoring.

86.   *CL*, I, 335*n*. STC's underscoring.

87.   See the lengthy headnote in *CL*, II, 677-678. By 1803, however, STC was projecting a *History of Metaphysics in Germany* (*N*, 1646).

88.   *Jerrold, Tennyson, and Macaulay* (Edinburgh, 1868), p. 202. The chapter called "De Quincey and Coleridge upon Kant" was originally published in the *Fortnightly Review* (October 1867). Stirling is infrequently mentioned in Coleridge studies, despite the considerable value of his work, possibly because his view of Coleridge is so uncompromisingly harsh.

89.   *CL*, III, 360.

90.   ". . . Coleridge criticized Kant from a point of view which is substantially identical with that of the early, rather Fichtean Schelling. Still accepting a great deal of the frame-work, Coleridge sees the fundamental weaknesses of Kant with the eyes of Schelling" (*KE*, p. 80).

Shedd uses essentially the same argument to account for the "very striking" resemblance he finds between Coleridge and Jacobi:

> The coincidence in this case, it is very plain to the reader, does not arise, as in the case of Coleridge's coincidence with Schelling, from a previous study and mastery of a predecessor, but from sustaining a similar relation to Kant, together with a deep sense of the vital importance and absolute truth of Theism in philosophy. The coincidence in this case is not a mere genial reception, and fresh transfusion, of the thought of another mind, but an independent and original shoot in common with others, from the one great stock, the general system of Theism. Add to this, that both Coleridge and Jacobi were close students of Plato, and by mental constitution, were alike predisposed to the moulding influence of this greatest philosophic mind of the Pagan world, and we have still another ground and cause for the resemblance between the two. (Shedd, I, 26-27)

91.   *BL*, I, 106. Italics in text.

92.   *BL*, I, 103. In 1810, however, Coleridge had written that "I never brought away from his Works any thing I did not bring to them" (*CL*, III, 278). By 1825, Boehme was listed among the "poor bewildered enthusiasts" of Church history (Shedd, I, 197).

93.   *KE*, p. 278, n. 63. The spellings of such names as Boehme and Maass vary considerably. I have adopted what seems to be the prevalent usage in the text while giving names as they appear in quotations.

94.   *BL*, I, 104-105. Italics in text.   95.   *BL*, I, 104.   96.   *HCR*, I, 70, 88.

97. *PL*, p. 390.   98. *PL*, p. 391.

99. Coleridge continued making this statement privately, for example: "He metaphysicized *á la* Schelling while he abused him, saying the atheist . . ."; "He . . . complains of the Catholicism of Schlegel and Tieck, etc." (*HCR*, I, 307, 200); "Schelling is a zealous Roman-Catholic, and not the first Philosopher who has adopted this sort of Plotinised Spinozism for the defense of the Polytheism and Charms of the Church of Rome" (*CL*, IV, 883).

100. James Stirling seems to be the only writer who has ever dared challenge the universal belief that as to matters pecuniary Coleridge was either an utter innocent or a saintlike incompetent. Characteristic of Stirling's contemptuous tone is the following passage, which nevertheless makes some penetrating observations on features of the *Biographia* and of Coleridge neglected to this day.

> Now, we must say that, let his peculiarities have been what they may, ignorance of "the market"—want of "mechanic understanding"—was not among them. Of this—and in its most mechanic and market application to pounds, shillings, and pence—Coleridge must be pronounced to have possessed a very fair share. Writing his *Biographia Literaria*, after the lapse of many years, he can still tell us in it all the particulars about the commercial unsuccess of the *Watchman*, the *Friend*, etc., as about his subscribers, his canvassers, what he lost, and how he lost it, etc. He can talk as acutely as any tradesman of the stock of paper left upon his hands, "each sheet of which *stood* him," he assures us, "in fivepence previous to its arrival at his printer's." He forgets not his "postages," or how he had to buy paper and pay for printing," at least fifteen per cent beyond what *the trade* would have paid." As little does he forget that he had to give "30 per cent, not of the net profits, but of the gross results," etc. Towards the end of the last volume, again, we find him able to use such expressions as these:—
>
>> "On the 200 which Parsons in Paternoster Row sells weekly he gains eight shillings more than I do. . . . To be sure, I have been somewhat *fleeced* and overreached by my London publisher. . . . I rather think that the intention is to employ me as a mere *hackney*, without any *share of the profits.*"
>
> Surely there is no want of "the mechanic understanding"—no ignorance of the ways of "the market" here. . . . (*Jerrold, Tennyson and Macaulay,* pp. 216-217. Italics in text.)

101. *CL*, IV, 665. Italics in text.

102. This is another example of the strange fatality which dogs Coleridge studies. Though several letters from Coleridge to the Boosey firm have been carefully preserved, this perhaps most important one of all seems to have disappeared.

103. Despite STC's presumably straitened finances, Boosey had orders to buy for him anything of Schelling (and Steffens) that he didn't already own (*CL*, IV, 738).

104. *PL*, pp. 464-465, n. 36; Beach, p. 598, n. 13.

105. As far back as November 1813, Coleridge was borrowing a variety of German books from Robinson, notably "Schelling's Methodologie . . . for I have a plan maturing, to w[hich] that work would be serv[iceable]" (*CL*, III, 461-462).

106. *HW*, XVII, 113. *Hazlitt: Selected Essays*, ed. George Sampson (Cambridge, 1950), p. 157*n*; p. 9, 1. 8. Sampson notes that the literal Latin "Let the Jew Apella believe it," is better rendered by our "tell that to the Marines."

107. *CL*, II, 768; *CL*, IV, 554. Italics in text.   108. *CL*, II, 676, 699. Italics in text.

109. See, for example, *CSC*, pp. 98-99, where the language is strong: "all that is true or ingenious in the Essay [Locke's] is stolen." See also pp. 93, 102-103.

110. *HW*, XVII, 111.

111. *CL*, II, 675. Mackintosh was another of Coleridge's persistent aversions. In a letter of May 1800, Coleridge had referred to him as "the great Dung-fly" (*CL*, I, 588). We find a related image in a letter of 1801 to William Godwin, in which Mackintosh's "Lectures & Conversations" are described as "but the Steam of an Excrement" (*CL*, II, 737). (Years later Coleridge

wrote that one of Herder's works was "mere steam from a heap of man's dung"—see Helen Zimmern, "Coleridge's Marginalia Hitherto Unpublished," *Blackwood's Edinburgh Magazine*, CXXXI [1882], 120). Clement Carlyon, who travelled with Coleridge in Germany in 1799, reports that Coleridge always spoke slightingly of Mackintosh (Carlyon, I, 68-69). This aversion may in part explain the savage poem Coleridge wrote on Mackintosh, which contains the line, "I trust, he lies in his Grave awake!" (*CL*, I, 633). This poem, "The Two Round Spaces on the Tombstone," was mentioned in one of Coleridge's most brilliant and obscurantist performances, the "Apologetic Preface to 'Fire, Famine, and Slaughter,' " in which Coleridge airily disposed of the charge that his brutal attacks on such figures as Pitt had been harshly intended. When "The Two Round Spaces" was published in 1834, Coleridge prefixed a note asserting that, "This is the first time the author ever published these lines." But the verses had appeared in the *Morning Post* of 4 December 1800 (*Poems*, p. 625, No. 158).

The letters reveal an appalling attack on Mackintosh's personal honor (*CL*, II, 1041), and on his intellectual integrity (*CL*, III, 316); but the most unguarded expression of personal hate appears in the privacy of his notebooks: "the Scotch simper, or grin castrate of managed malignity in a Mackintosh, *Scotch*!" (*N*, 2618). It has been suggested that Mackintosh committed the unpardonable sin of interrupting one of Coleridge's monologues, but such suggestions obscure a baffling problem with an amusing anecdote. To understand Coleridge's detestation of Mackintosh would require a more arduous investigation of sources than the subject warrants, fascinating as it is in some ways. Mackintosh was a brother-in-law of Daniel Stuart, and an intimate of the Wedgwoods and other important figures in Coleridge's life. This partly explains the almost fulsome public praise of Mackintosh in the *Biographia* (I, 67), and the occasional profoundly respectful mention of him in the letters (for example, *CL*, III, 403).

112.   *CSC*, p. 282.

113.   See "The Years of Apprenticeship," pp. 240-242, for evidence of Coleridge's own borrowings from Taylor.

114.   *CT*, p. 324.   115.   *CL*, II, 947.   116.   *CLL*, p. 105. Italics in text.

117.   Ed. Seth B. Watson (London, 1848), p. 61*n*. I cannot say whether there is anything to this charge, which might bear looking into.

118.   *CL*, I, 379. Whatever STC's vaguely unnamed book was, none such has ever come to light.

119.   *CL*, I, 569.   120.   *CL*, III, 531.   121.   *CL*, IV, 715. STC's underscoring.

122.   *BL*, I, 148. I. A. Richards confidently cites this passage in a discussion of Coleridge's journalism as evidence of the quality and influence of his work, without inquiring at all into the factual basis of these claims (*The Portable Coleridge*, ed. I. A. Richards [New York, 1950], p. 29).

123.   *A Lay Sermon* (1817), p. 112*n*.

124.   *CT*, pp. 211-212. For Coleridge's indebtedness to Darwin, especially the celebrated theory of dramatic illusion, see E S, pp. 91-106, 319, 322-326.

125.   Quoted from *TT*, p. 458. The misty reference to "a German book published at Leipzig" is typical of estecean charges of this kind.

126.   *CL*, III, 97, n. 1.   127.   *CL*, III, 474.

128.   *HW*, XIX, 198. Italics in text. See also pp. 208-209, where Hazlitt repeats the charge.

129.   *HCR*, I, 31.   130.   *CT*, p. 176.   131.   *CL*, III, 510.

132.   *CL*, III, 524. Italics in text.   133.   *CL*, III, 530, 532. Italics in text.

134.   *CL*, IV, 560.

135.   *CL*, IV, 603. Wordsworth had written a preface acknowledging Coleridge's priority, but Coleridge had importuned him in the strongest terms not to publish it, in part for fear of creating a scandal in connection with Sir Walter Scott. See *CL*, III, 111-112; IV, 585; and *post*, "The Shakespearean Criticism."

136.   *CSC*, p. 489.

137. *CL*, IV, 667. Mme. de Staël had, in fact, acknowledged substantial obligations to A. W. Schlegel. (See *HW*, XVI, 58.) Among other French writers similarly charged were Voltaire and Volney, "mere but mischievous plagiaries," according to Coleridge (*CSC*, p. 138).

138. Quoted from P. P. Howe, *The Life of William Hazlitt* (London, 1949), p. 145.

139. *DQW*, V, 187-188, n. 1. I think, however, that one must be most cautious as to these particular allegations, behind which are some ominous shadows that should be exposed to light. In 1823 De Quincey had published in *The London Magazine* a short paper on Malthus in which he had failed to acknowledge that its central idea had been drawn from Hazlitt. The latter at once publicly pointed out the "rather striking coincidence" in De Quincey's paper to some of his own ideas, but refrained from "any charge of plagiarism." De Quincey's reply to Hazlitt is lamentably obscurantist (*DQW*, IX, 20, 23-31). Both Hazlitt and Coleridge were dead by 1838, when De Quincey wrote that the former's early book on Malthus had been drawn from the latter's conversation. In these charges and countercharges, we find one of those impasses before which certainty must pause. Although it was altogether characteristic of Coleridge to claim that his conversation had been plagiarized, De Quincey may here possibly be inventing, or unconsciously distorting through resentment against Hazlitt catching him out in an improper borrowing.

In 1965 appeared a book which severely damages De Quincey's reputation for encyclopedic learning. Albert Goldman's *The Mine and the Mint: Sources for the Writings of Thomas De Quincey* (Carbondale, Ill.) establishes beyond reasonable doubt the following "general rule": "namely, that in any matter requiring merely intellectual ability De Quincey is not likely to have plagiarized; but when it is a question of special knowledge, facts and ideas that can only be obtained by thorough research, then in almost every instance he is dependent on a single source" (p. 81). In essay after essay where De Quincey seems to demonstrate a minute and far-ranging scholarship he is in fact slavishly dependent upon an *unstated* authority. For example, in his immensely impressive and widely praised review of the life and works of Richard Bentley, the great English classicist, De Quincey was actually appropriating with both hands from the author of the very life of Bentley under review which he so airily dismissed as of little worth. These furtive borrowings extend to numerous learned allusions, details of obscure legal processes, and so forth. Goldman shows that this was *characteristic* of the whole range of De Quincey's writings on factual matters, and that one shadowy *German* authority after the other stands behind De Quincey's learned essays.

Now these disclosures are important in themselves and immensely suggestive as to the Coleridge-De Quincey relationship (and perhaps to the real nature of many polyhistoric reputations). The two men (so often linked as "opium-eaters") were simultaneously mining the same veins of foreign ore and hinting darkly about the other's literary character. But it was not until Coleridge was (safely?) dead that De Quincey delivered himself of concrete charges of plagiarism against his former friend.

Whatever effect all this may have on De Quincey's general reputation, Professor Goldman's disclosures ought not to discredit De Quincey's portraits of his contemporaries, which after all depended not upon learning but upon his own insight and intelligence. "The only compositions that are wholly original," Professor Goldman writes, "are those works of a personal nature in which he had drawn on his own experience—his dreams, his fantasies, his adventures, and *his impressions of his friends and acquaintances*" (p. 160). As a fellow plagiarist and self-proclaimed polyhistor, De Quincey may in fact now be seen to have had special insight into Coleridge's mind.

Inherent in these disclosures, however, are the means by which to discredit De Quincey altogether, and these have already been seized upon by Coleridge's latest biographer:

> By calling attention to Coleridge's borrowings (which incidentally reinforced De Quincey's own reputation as an erudite journalist) and then by implying that these were not very important anyway, De Quincey . . . was attempting to insure himself against the future. His hope was to point the way, in any future discovery of his own sources, to the excuse that

shakiness of memory and confusion in the use of materials could be both expected and pardoned in an opium addict.

De Quincey is anatomized as "one of the arch-plagiarists of modern times." But as for those who hold such a view of Coleridge:

> Their strategic error lies in a militant, heady refusal to distinguish between "plagiarism" in any ordinary sense of the word and Coleridge's general use of ideas, premises, concepts, vocabulary, from German writers of the time. The latter may be taken for granted. It is in fact much to Coleridge's credit. (Bate, pp. 132-133)

Thus it seems possible that one of the effects of Goldman's book will be to undermine still further De Quincey's testimony and analysis of Coleridge, much of which was dismissed long ago by Lowes as "petty rancors."

140. *CL*, III, 441. Italics in text. In 1821 Coleridge wrote to Allsop that "the number of my printed works bears witness that I have not been idle, and the seldom acknowledged, but strictly *proveable*, effects of my labours [in various newspapers and lecture series] (add to which the unlimited freedom of my communications in colloquial life), may surely be allowed as evidence that I have not been useless to my generation" (Allsop, I, 159. STC's underscoring). Coleridge's letters to Allsop are studded with charges and innuendoes concerning improper borrowing from his writings and conversation (see, for example, Allsop, I, 153).

141. *HCR*, I, 200.   142. *CL*, IV, 686, and n. 3. Italics in text.

143. *CL*, IV, 798. The phrase appears in *The Friend* (Shedd, II, 216). In a review of Coleridge's *Stateman's Manual* in 1816, Hazlitt had used the phrase "Mob-Sycophancy" and placed it within inverted commas. In two articles dealing with STC published in 1818, however, the phrase appears without inverted commas (*HW*, XVI, 110; XIX, 203, 208).

144. Conversely, Hazlitt said that Lamb had furnished STC with many a text to preach upon. The causes of the bitterness between Hazlitt and Coleridge are too complex to discuss here. Hazlitt's articles on Coleridge after 1816 are brutally and startlingly frank. He wrote that "Truth is to him [Coleridge] a ceaseless round of contradictions: he lives in the belief of a perpetual lie, and in affecting to think what he pretends to say" (*CL*, IV, 669, n. 2). "He [Coleridge] offends others without satisfying himself, and equally by his servility and singularity, shocks the prejudices of all about him" (*CL*, IV, 700, n. 1). Hazlitt also called Coleridge "a great quack" who "never troubles himself about facts or dates" (*HW*, VII, 181). Of the *Biographia* itself Hazlitt wrote that the author indulges "his maudlin egotism and his mawkish spleen in fulsome eulogies of his own virtues, and nauseous abuse of his contemporaries" (*HW*, XVI, 138). Coleridge in the meanwhile was attacking Hazlitt both in his conversation and correspondence on the grounds of Hazlitt's alleged immorality. For comment on Coleridge's charges of plagiarism against Hazlitt, see P. P. Howe, *The Life of William Hazlitt* (Penguin Books), pp. 145, 168, n. 1, and Elisabeth Schneider, *The Aesthetics of William Hazlitt* (Philadelphia, Pa., 1933), p. 88, n. 8.

145. *CSC*, pp. 663-664, 659, 668, 646. Italics in text.

146. *CSC*, p. 434, 443, 372. Coleridge's disapproval of Johnson was also long standing. As far back as 1804 he had projected an essay "on the supposed Genius, Style, critical powers, & morals of Dr. S. Johnson" (*CL*, II, 1054).

147. Shedd, II, 437, 440.   148. *IS*, p. 251.   149. MS. letter, *N*, 646n.

150. *PW*, I, 255, n. 1. My former student, Mr. Fred Zimmerman, in some work in progress, has pointed out that the unnecessary vagueness of this note is perhaps explained by the fact that the image Coleridge says was borrowed does not appear in Joanna Baillie's *Basil*. Moreover, *Basil*, like "Lewti," was published in 1798, though Coleridge "mis-dated" his poem as 1795 in *Sibylline Leaves* (1817). Mr. Zimmerman goes on to give some impressive evidence for Coleridgean borrowings *from* Miss Baillie.

151. Coleridge's daughter, Sara, seems not to have known this. In her edition of the *Bio-*

graphia, she dates "Lewti" as a 1795 poem and says nothing of Wordsworth, though she was meticulous in citing sources wherever she could find them (*Shedd*, III, 677).

152. *HCR*, I, 185. It is relevant to notice that Coleridge set down in his notebook (in 1797) an insightful observation: "Plagiarists suspicious of being pilfer'd—as pickpockets are observed commonly to walk with their hands in their breeches-pockets" (*N*, 224). Startlingly, this observation was made by Coleridge twenty-six years later, *almost word for word*, as reported by his nephew in *Table Talk* (p. 41): "Plagiarists are always suspicious of being stolen from— as pickpockets are observed commonly to walk with their hands in their breeches' pockets." As if this example of Coleridge's tenacious memory were not sufficiently surprising, we are confronted with a genuine puzzle in this connection. For the notebook entry immediately preceding the remark on plagiarists reads: "A dunghill at a distance sometimes smells like musk, & a dead dog like elder-flowers." The *Table Talk* entry of 4 January 1823 immediately preceding the one just given above also reads: "A dunghill at a distance sometimes smells like musk, and a dead dog like elder-flowers." As mere coincidence this is extremely baffling. Of course it is possible for a man's associations to bring forth in succession the ideas set down in his notebooks as long as twenty-six years before. But the ideas seem utterly unrelated, and HNC provides no bridge to show how these statements came up in conversation at all. Not even so great a monologuist as Coleridge would be likely to confront his auditors with wholly unrelated observations in no particular context. Coleridge more than once was suspected of "getting up" his evening conversations, and this could be an example. But it is also possible that HNC, without so stating, used notebook material in preparing the *Table Talk*.

153. *CL*, IV, 979. STC's underscoring. In this letter appears one of the two other references to the Divine Ventriloquist I have found in Coleridge's works; the other appears in *The Friend* (Shedd, II, 178).

154. *PL*, pp. 413-414. See also *TT*, p. 88.

155. *Essays towards a Critical Method* (London, 1889), pp. 128-129, n. 3. See also *TT*, 10 May 1830.

156. *BL*, I, 61.

157. Quoted by the kind permission of the Librarian of New York University. Tooke's *Diversions of Purley* seem anything but diverting today, at least to one not trained in the history of linguistic theory. A detailed study of this work and Coleridge's ideas on language might prove a worthwhile project.

158. *BL*, I, 103. Italics in text.   159. Shawcross, I, 247-248.

160. *BL*, II, 114.

161. *BL*, I, 103-104. Coleridge seems to have been nothing less than addicted to finding forerunners for all current ideas. In the *Philosophical Lectures*, he said: "And I here make a challenge, I would almost say, to point me out an opinion that has taken place since the fifteenth century which I will not shew as clearly stated and supported in some one or other of the Nominalists or the Realists" (*PL*, p. 278).

162. It has not been observed, so far as I know, that a somewhat similar disclaimer appears in the Conclusion of *Aids to Reflection*. Ever hypersensitive to criticism, Coleridge anticipates and dismisses a variety of possible objections to his work. "There is, however, one objection," he writes,

> which will so often be heard . . . that I owe it both to my own character and to the interests of my readers, not to leave it unnoticed. The charge will probably be worded in this way:— There is nothing new in all this (as if novelty were any merit in questions of revealed religion!) It is mysticism, all taken out of William Law, after he had lost his senses, in brooding over the visions of a delirious German cobbler, Jacob Böhme. . . .
> Of William Law's Works I am acquainted with the Serious Call; and besides this I remember to have read a small Tract on Prayer, if I mistake not, as I easily may, it being at least six-and-twenty years since I saw it. He may in this or in other tracts have quoted the

same passages from the fourth Gospel which I have done. But surely this affords no presumption that my conclusions are the same with his; still less, that they are drawn from the same premises; and least of all, that they were adopted from his writings. (Shedd, I, 350-351)

If a study of Law and Coleridge (a desideratum) were to show that Coleridge used not only many of Law's quotations, but also some of his arguments, and several pages of his very words, *verbatim*, would not this passage of explanation be seen as hopelessly insincere and obscurantist?

163. *BL*, I, 105.   164. *BL*, I, 107.

165. *BL*, I, 114. Italics in text. This chapter is especially checkered with false assertions. Some may be followed in Shawcross' notes. Since it would carry us too far from our central purposes, we have left almost wholly without comment Coleridge's account in *Biographia Literaria* of his Bristol years and youthful political loyalties. Coleridge's retrospective accounts of these matters are systematically misleading and thus provide a hopelessly askew portrait of himself as a young man. For some discussion of these and closely related matters, see *post*, "Some Miscellaneous Prose," n. 3.

166. *BL*, I, 120.   167. *BL*, I, 145, 146.

168. *BL*, I, 149. It is suggestive that De Quincey should have described Coleridge as "too self-indulgent, and almost a voluptuary in his studies; sparing himself all toil. . . . Neither as a boy nor as a man had he submitted to any regular study or discipline of thought. His choice of subjects [was] never amongst those which admitted of *continuous* thinking and study" (*DQW*, X, 17. Italics in text).

169. *BL*, I, 150.

170. *CBG*, p. 43. Italics in text. Since Beach's logic seems irrefutable, the disturbing question arises: Why was not the conclusion of so eminent an authority accepted a long while ago? Beach took few pains to hide his scorn for the "many distinguished scholars who have pronounced upon the subject with insufficient knowledge" (p. 50), but this can scarcely account for the persistent neglect of his findings. Perhaps the main problem was that Beach confined himself to Coleridge's borrowings from the *German*, and in the space of a scholarly article could hardly address himself to an analysis of Coleridge's complex personality and moral character. In refusing to hedge his conclusions with such qualifications as, "The evidence tends . . . suggests . . . appears," and so forth, he made it almost certain that his work on Coleridge would be viewed as extreme, and therefore unsound, an aberrant episode in a great scholar's otherwise brilliant career.

171. *BL*, I, 160.   172. *BL*, I, 162.

173. These are the *System des transcendentalen Idealismus* (1800), and *Abhandlungen zur Erläuterung des Idealismus der Wissenschaftslehre* (1796-97). The year after piecing together this disquisition, Coleridge was able to address his publisher, Rest Fenner, thus: "I can not write, no, not even for a newspaper, the commonplaces of the age, or what is supplied to me by *memory*, by passive recollection of other men's writings. It must be my *own* to the best of my consciousness. . . . I have for so many years rejected from my mind every shallow and commonplace thought and phrase, that I have induced a kind of barrenness on my faculties. . . . it is not in my *power* to write by mere dint of memory and volition" (*CL*, IV, 677, 679. STC's emphasis). In such passages Coleridge seems continually to be defending himself against inner accusations. In previous letters we find him writing urgently for books because he can't compose anything new (*CL*, III, 388, 455).

174. *BL*, I, 163.   175. *BL*, I, 164n.

176. *BL*, I, 165n. For a fragment of a Greek grammar which Coleridge prepared for his son Hartley, see *Poems by Hartley Coleridge*, ed. Derwent Coleridge, 2 vols. (London, 1851, 2nd ed.), I, xxxiv-xxxvi, and II, ccix-ccxviii. Twenty years before, while composing "Religious Musings," Coleridge had borrowed freely from Wakefield's Unitarian pamphlet *The Spirit of Christianity compared with the Spirit of the Times . . .* (1794). See *post*, pp. 243-245.

177. *BL*, I, 169.   178. JCF, p. 295. Italics in text.

179. Shedd, III, 332, 335*n*. In Shawcross' edition this passage extends from the sentence beginning "All knowledge" on p. 174 to the sentence ending "mechanism of the heavenly motions" on p. 176. Shawcross' note is vague at this point and is made still less helpful by a misprint of "bodily" for "heavenly." See *BL*, I, 268, note to page 174.

180. JCF, p. 295. 181. Shedd, III, 337. Italics added by Sara Coleridge.

182. *BL*, I, 176. 183. Shawcross, I, 269. 184. *BL*, I, 179-180.

185. Shawcross, I, 269. It was Ferrier, however, who first identified the borrowing (JCF, p. 295). The translation is that of George Watson in the Everyman *Biographia* (1960), p. 149, n. 3.

186. *BL*, I, 269, 182, 270; Shedd, III, 346; JCF, p. 295. 187. Shedd, III, 352.

188. *BL*, I, 194. 189. *BL*, I, 195.

190. Shedd, III, 359. For a detailed account of the similarity between Schelling's and Coleridge's criticism of Kant, see *KE*, p. 95.

191. *BL*, I, 198.

192. *CL*, IV, 728. Shawcross (I, 271) mistakenly gives the date as 1816.

193. *BL*, I, 199. 194. *BL*, I, 202.

195. *Coleridge on Imagination* (London, 1934), pp. 5-6.

11. *THE PHILOSOPHICAL LECTURES*

1. *The Philosophical Lectures of Samuel Taylor Coleridge* (New York, 1949).

2. *PL*, p. 17.

3. John Henry Green, a friend and disciple of Coleridge, brought eleven of these volumes home with him from Germany in 1817. In July of that year Coleridge requested the whole set from him, two at a time. These volumes, copiously annotated by Coleridge, now rest in the British Museum (*CL*, IV, 870 and n. 2).

4. *PL*, p. 18. An English translation of these tables may be found in Tennemann's *A Manual of the History of Philosophy*, trans. Arthur Johnson (Oxford, 1832), pp. 473 ff. The *Manual* was an abridgment by Tennemann himself of his twelve-volume history.

5. "S. T. Coleridge's Philosophical Lectures of 1818-19," *RES*, X (1934), 428-437.

6. *Ibid*. All quotations are taken from p. 431.

7. At the end of the fifth essay of the third volume of the *Friend* (1818), Coleridge condensed this *Assistant* and used verbatim a portion of the Prospectus, again without acknowledgment (*PL*, p. 19). Not atypically, when borrowing silently (elsewhere in this essay there are debts to Kant and Schelling), Coleridge draws attention to the originality of his own thinking. The essay begins with a quotation from Bacon dealing with the transfer of original ideas into the minds of others; Bacon advises the thinker (here Coleridge) "to review your own scientific acquirements, re-measuring as it were the steps of your knowledge . . . and at the same time to transplant it into the minds of others, just as it grew in your own" (Shedd, II, 417-418, but see also the Bohn *Friend*, p. 305, where Bacon's Latin is translated). Coleridge introduces the borrowed material with the statement, "I can conceive no better remedy for the overweening self-complacency of modern philosophy than the annulment of its pretended originality" (Shedd, II, 421). Drawing attention to the presumed independence of his own thought was at times almost a compulsion with Coleridge, a fact which is in itself as revealing as it is suggestive. A typical example of Coleridge's indirect method is his quotation from Plato at the beginning of Essay IV in Section II of the *Friend*. The translation reads: "Hear then what are the terms on which you and I ought to stand toward each other. If you hold philosophy altogether in contempt, bid it farewell. Or if you have heard from any other person, or have yourself found out a better than mine, then give honor to that, whichever it be. But if the doctrine taught in these our works please you, then it is but just that you should honor me too in the same proportion" (Shedd, II, 408).

8 . *PL*, p. 18.   9 . *PL*, p. 401, n. 22.   10. *PL*, p. 401, n. 23.

11. *PL*, p. 401, n. 25.   12. *PL*, p. 406, n. 14.   13. *PL*, p. 408, n. 31.

14. *PL*, p. 411, n. 16.   15. *PL*, p. 411, n. 21.   16. *PL*, p. 411, n. 22.

17. *PL*, p. 412, n. 2.   18. *PL*, p. 414, n. 13.   19. *PL*, p. 417, n. 2.

20. *PL*, p. 418, n. 12.   21. *PL*, p. 419, n. 22.   22. *PL*, p. 419, n. 25.

23. *PL*, p. 419, n. 29.   24. *PL*, p. 420, n. 35.   25. *PL*, pp. 424-425, n. 18.

26. *PL*, p. 432, n. 14.   27. *PL*, p. 435, n. 25.

28. The interested reader who cannot consult Tennemann's German volumes will find his translated *Manual*, cited above, useful in assessing his formidable learning and his general treatment of philosophic problems.

29. *PL*, p. 67. Italics in text. Miss Coburn uses complex typography for various editiorial purposes. I have normalized the text throughout.

30. *PL*, pp. 115-116. Miss Coburn observes: "The limits of the compliment are obvious enough" (*PL*, p. 405, n. 7).

31. *PL*, p. 117. There is a fascinating passage at this point in the notebook Coleridge was using to prepare his lectures: "The arguments on which Tennemen[n] decides undoubtingly on their being a . . . Forgery (namely, the improbability that these great men would not but in the form of quotation have borrowed several passages) weigh but little with me" (*PL*, p. 117*n*). Needless to say, Coleridge did not make this statement at his lectures.

32. *PL*, p. 118.   33. *PL*, pp. 237-238.   34. *PL*, p. 270.

35. *PL*, p. 270*n*; p. 432, n. 13. The discussion in Tennemann is at VIII, 67. In Tennemann's sixth volume is a lengthy note in Coleridge's hand, addressed to his disciple J. H. Green. It reads in part: "I need not inform *you*, my dear Sir! that *I* am no Schellingian; but I am intolerant of unfair dealing, from or against whomever it proceeds. . . . the most extraordinary thing and I fear to be accounted for only by personal or sectarian hostility to Schelling, is Tennemann's frank and cordial eulogies of so many other Founders or Revivers of the different Schools, and his ready acknowledgment of their philosophic Genius . . . and yet cold, praiseless, fault-finding spirit, with which he quotes passage after passage from Plotinus" (*PL*, pp. 427-428, n. 20. STC's emphasis). This incredible note ought not to raise questions about hypocrisy but rather Coleridge's state of mind when he wrote it. For what he accuses Tennemann of here is *precisely* his behavior not only toward Schelling himself, and also to Tennemann (who is of course much less important), but to several other writers.

36. Compare the "contemporary writer of the Continent" (Schelling) in *BL*, I, 95; the "continental critic" (Schlegel) in *SC*, I, 198; and the vague "continental philosopher" (Jacobi) in the *Friend* (Shedd, II, 143).

37. *PL*, pp. 205-206.   38. *PL*, p. 418, n. 18.   39. *PL*, p. 158.

40. *PL*, p. 411, nn. 20-24.   41. *PL*, pp. 206-207.   42. *PL*, p. 418, n. 19.

43. *PL*, p. 189; Kant, p. 17.

44. *BL*, I, 71. Other borrowings from Kant appear in Lecture XII, immediately after a lengthy appropriation from Schelling (*PL*, p. 355; p. 457, n. 37).

45. See *PL*, pp. 327-329, 348, 351-352, and p. 456, nn. 20, 28, 31, 32. Coleridge's specific debt to Schelling for the formulation of the distinction between an imitation and a copy, which he used frequently, appears also in these lectures (pp. 291-292, and p. 442, n. 7).

46. *CL*, IV, 911.   47. *PL*, pp. 54-55.

48. *PL*, pp. 54-55. Italics in text. The idea appears also in *TT*, p. 118 (2 July 1830).

49. *PL*, p. 55. For Professor Coburn's whole discussion, see pp. 53-55; for other Goethean influences in the lectures, see p. 405, n. 4; p. 415, n. 20; p. 428, n. 21; p. 458, n. 44.

50. *BL*, I, 149, 150.   51. Bate, p. 181.   52. *LW*, II, 43. Italics in text.

53. *UL*, II, 274.   54. Haven, p. 491, n. 57.

55. *CL*, IV, 750-751. STC's underscoring.

56. *BL*, I, 94. In the *Omniana* (1812) Coleridge quoted from portions of *De Innumerabilibus* for the purpose of suggesting that Bruno had anticipated later scientific discoveries concerning the circulation of the blood. Ever alert to intellectual priority, Coleridge also commented on Bruno's pioneering suggestion that the universe was infinite. See Alice Snyder, "Coleridge on Giordano Bruno," *MLN*, XLII (1927), 429.

57. On this slim foundation has the subsequent fantastic edifice of speculation been built connecting Cudworth and the early Coleridge. R. L. Brett asserts that "in the *True Intellectual System* Coleridge would have met with a theory of perception very much like Kant's," and proceeds to argue for Coleridge's fundamental independence from the Sage of Königsberg ("Coleridge's Theory of the Imagination," *E & S*, NS, II [1949], 78). Some obscure jottings from Cudworth appear in the Gutch memorandum book, but as for any impact this work had on Coleridge, the record is blank. See Albert Guerard, "Counterfeiting Infinity: The Eolian Harp and the Growth of Coleridge's Mind," *JEGP*, LX (1961), 411-422. W. Schrickx, in "Coleridge and the Cambridge Platonists," *REL*, VII (1966), 71-91, argues for an important influence from Cudworth in "The Eolian Harp" and "Reflections on Having Left a Place of Retirement." The hard evidence shows a tiny snatch of language imported from Cudworth. Like many other scholars, Professor Schrickx seems to exaggerate Coleridge's knowledge and close reading of the many authors whose works he had had in his possession. Obviously, the subject is treacherous, but certain matters of emphasis can be discussed. For example, Schrickx notes that Coleridge's borrowings from the Bristol Library began with a volume of poems in March 1795. ". . . it is sufficient here to say," Schrickx continues, "that his subsequent borrowings reflect his great interest in theology and philosophy, and that he had followed Southey's lead in devoting part of his time to the study of William Enfield's *History of Philosophy* (1791), an abridged version of J. J. Brucker's *Historia Critica Philosophia* (1766-7)" (p. 72). That Coleridge's borrowings from the Bristol Library reflect a "great interest in theology and philosophy" is very much a matter of opinion. See George Whalley, "The Bristol Borrowings of Southey and Coleridge, 1793-8," *The Library*, 5th Ser., IV (1949), 114-132. The first volume of Enfield's *History of Philosophy* (Borrowing 43) was taken out of the library by Coleridge in March 1795. We do not know that Coleridge "studied" the volume. We do know that when he returned it to the library ten days later he did not take out the second volume.

58. Haven, pp. 489-490.

59. *The Portable Coleridge*, ed. I. A. Richards (New York, 1951), p. 15.

60. On 26 October 1793, when he was not yet 21 years old, Southey wrote: "You must not be surprised at nonsense, for I have been reading the history of philosophy, the ideas of Plato, the logic of Aristotle, and the heterogeneous dogmas of Pythagoras, Antisthenes, Zeno, Epicurus, and Pyrrho, till I have metaphysicized away all my senses" (quoted from George Whalley, "Samuel Taylor Coleridge and Robert Southey in Bristol," *RES*, NS, I [1950], 327). Whalley, who like most contemporary scholars finds Southey not only a much less interesting but much less attractive human being than Coleridge, writes:

> Taking his departure from much less bookish surroundings than Coleridge's, Southey was already in 1794 a *helluo librorum* in his own right. His account (written in 1823) of discovering *Gerusalemme Liberata, Orlando Furioso*, and *The Fairie Queen* reads like a passage from *The Road to Xanadu*, and even if the four large published volumes of Southey's *Commonplace Book* look a little too much like the work-books of a professional polymath, they reflect "an hydroptic, immoderate thirst of human learning" comparable with Coleridge's. (p. 326)

Why, one asks wearily, do Southey's commonplace books smack too much of the "professional polymath," but not Coleridge's?

61. *Memoir of the Life and Writings of William Taylor of Norwich*, ed. J. W. Robberds (London, 1843), I, 215; quoted from Lawrence Hanson, *The Life of S. T. Coleridge: The Early Years* (London, 1938), p. 295.

62. *Reason and Imagination: A Study of Form and Meaning In Four Poems* (Oxford, 1960), pp.80-81.

63. See p. 84 and *BL*, n. 74 for this letter and a note to the entire passage.

64. *RX*, p. 41. See Lane Cooper's assault on this assumption, a passage that makes for amazing reading today ("Coleridge, Wordsworth, and Mr. Lowes," *PMLA*, XLIII [1928], 584-585).

65. Haven, p. 490, n. 50. See also *RX*, pp. 230-231, 235 (Coleridge "certainly knew the *Chaldaean' Oracles,* for he jots down in his Note Book a fragment of one of the most magnificent of them"); and *N*, 180 and *n.* Haven's study of Coleridge's early reading, and writing, emphasizes his *divergence* from the mystics whom he read (p. 488) and concludes with the statement that "far from providing Coleridge with the kind of language and logic which he needed, the Neoplatonists and mystics seemed to him to lack precisely such a language and logic. . . . It is a mistake, then, to see Coleridge's early years as a sort of Battle of the Books from which Plotinus or Boehme or Cudworth emerges as victor and Hartley, Priestley, and Berkeley as losers" (p. 494). The extreme overemphasis on the importance of the Neoplatonists on Coleridge's intellectual development would be utterly inexplicable were it not for the necessity of justifying Coleridge's assertions of independence from the Germans.

12. *THEORY OF LIFE* AND COLERIDGE'S WRITINGS ON SCIENCE

1. (London, 1848), pp. 7, 16. For the circumstances surrounding publication see E. L. Griggs, *Coleridge Fille* (Oxford, 1940), pp. 162-165. There was, for a time, the groundless allegation that James Gillman had written part of the work. Dr. Seth B. Watson had been a member of that group of Coleridge disciples which had met on Thursday evenings in Highgate.

2. Shedd, I, 373, 374.   3. Shedd, I, 387.

4. Shedd, I, 408. Italics in text.

5. Shedd, I, 413. Italics in text.   6. Shedd, I, 415.

7. *Praeliminarien zur Neuausgabe der Abhandlung über die Lebenstheorie (Theory of Life) von Samuel Taylor Coleridge* (Basel, 1926). A resumé was published by Nidecker in the *Bericht der philologisch-historischen Abteilung der philosophischen Fakultät* (Basel, 1927). Nidecker has published the marginal notes in the Steffens volumes possessed by Coleridge in the *Revue de litterature comparée*, XI (1931), 274-285, and XII (1932), 856-871. The latter article contains a list of parallel passages, pp. 870-871. Nidecker finds the whole theory in Steffens' *Bëytrage zur innern Naturgeschichte der Erde* (1801) and *Grundzüge der philosophischen Naturwissenschaft* (1806). Nidecker also finds several substantial passages literally translated by Coleridge from the latter work and also from Schelling's *Allgemeine Deduktion des dynamischen Processes* (1800). Beach is "inclined to think that Coleridge took hints for his treatise also from Schelling's *Ideen zu einer Philosophie der Natur* (1797) and *Erster Entwurf eines Systems der Naturphilosophie* (1799), and possibly also from his *Von der Weltseele* (1798)" (Beach, p. 333).

8. Steffens was a year younger than Coleridge. Though he is remembered primarily for his speculations in science, he was also the author of novels and poetry.

9. *CBG*, p. 45.   10. *CBG*, p. 46.

11. *CBG*, pp. 46-47. The passage is in Shedd, I, 414. On 15 June 1827 Coleridge said: "Perhaps the attribution or analogy may seem fanciful at first sight, but I am in the habit of realizing to myself Magnetism as length; Electricity as breadth or surface; and Galvanism as depth" (*TT*, p. 64). Apart from the complete erroneousness of the concept, what is of interest is the pretentiousness inherent in the way Coleridge puts his notions forward: the ideas may seem "fanciful," but he is in the "habit of realizing to" himself such and such ideas, as if these were genuinely independent ideas based on some practical experimentation. Much needs to be done by way of establishing the sources of Coleridge's *Table Talk*. Here and elsewhere he was continually dazzling his auditors with the contents of books he had been reading.

12. *CBG*, p. 47.

13. Conversely, Coleridge does not seem to have thought that light "truly" existed, but only *"visibility* under given conditions" (*CL*, IV, 750. STC's emphasis).

14. *Of Human Freedom*, trans. James Gutmann (Chicago, 1930), p. 32. In 1818, Coleridge refers to Schelling as responsible for the modern concept of "Magnetism, Electricity, and constructive Galvanism, or the Powers of Length, Breadth, and Depth" (*CL*, IV, 883), but, characteristically, sometime during the next decade he apparently forgot that these now curious beliefs had not originated in himself. For a typical example of Coleridge's handling of borrowed material, see Shedd, I, 404, and *CBG*, pp. 47-50.

15. *CBG*, pp. 48-49. Italics in text.

16. Shedd, I, 381, 382, 383, 387, 416.

17. *CL*, IV, 750-751. Italics in text. J. B. Beer, accepting this last sentence as literal fact, is led into systematic misreading of several of Coleridge's early poems (Beer, p. 163). Coleridge's claim to have "conjured over" so complex and difficult a work as Boehme's *Aurora* in his schoolboy days is very widely quoted, and in a variety of contexts, as firm evidence of Coleridge's early grappling with science and metaphysics.

Coleridge's remarks about light in this letter to Tieck have inevitably brought forth several articles. Duane B. Schneider's "Coleridge's Light-Sound Theory," *N & Q*, NS, X (1963), 182-183, and Beer's "Coleridge and Boehme's 'Aurora,' " *ibid.*, pp. 183-187, both take an important early influence from Boehme for granted. Richard Haven, however, has convincingly demonstrated how improbable this assumption is. First, there is "nothing in Coleridge's writing before 1798 to show that during that early period he held such a theory as is described in the 1817 letter." Haven shows that Coleridge's annotations in a copy of Boehme date from about 1817, and that Coleridge's allusion to Boehme in the letter to Tieck "was not so much the recollection of a study of Boehme before 1798 as one of the more recent readings, perhaps even that during the spring and early summer of 1817. . . ." Finally, "when we remember that he had been rereading Boehme during the month or so preceding this letter, and had furthermore studied him repeatedly during the past ten years, largely in connection with speculations about natural philosophy, it is difficult to avoid the conclusion that his association of the sound-light-colour theory with an early reading of Boehme is a projection into the past of an idea which in fact belonged to a more recent date" ("Coleridge and Jacob Boehme: A Further Comment," N & Q, NS, XIII [1966], 176-178). That Coleridge again and again threw back to very early years the work and ideas of his adult life is one of the key facts of his psychological portrait.

18. In marginal comments upon L. von Oken's *Erste Ideen zur Theorie des Lichts* (Jena, 1808), Coleridge violently attacked Oken's noisy promises to refute Newton's theory of light. And although Coleridge expressed himself as mightily displeased with "Oken's mountebank Boasting and Threatening [which] alone make me skeptical as to his own ability to perform the promise," he never himself carried out what in the same note he thought, "so very easy a task!" Elsewhere in these notes he attacked Oken's originality: "Oken follows them [Goethe, Schelling, and Steffens]—but stop! He waits till they are out of sight, Hangs out a new Banner (i.e. metaphor) and becomes a Leader himself" (*IS*, pp. 250-251). Coleridge also berated Schelling in a marginal note for his use of the title "Natur-Philosophie," and gave as a reason that it was "selected to make the difference between his own system and that of his old master Fichte greater than it is" (Shedd, III, 262).

19. *CL*, IV, 760.

20. *CL*, IV, 773. It may be argued that the damaging effect of such quotations derives from their being crudely torn out of a supporting context. The reader is invited to read the complete letters. See, for example, *CL*, IV, 768-769.

Among Coleridge's numerous absurdities on the subject of color was the "analogy" he professed to find between "natural grammar and colour" (T. C. Grattan, *Beaten Paths and Those who Trod Them* [London, 1865], p. 111, n. 1).

21. In one of his many notes to Tennemann's volumes, Coleridge, ever alert to the origin of ideas, wrote: "Whatever is excellent in the *Natur-philosophie* of Schelling and his Disciples and

offsets, is anticipated therein [Heraclitus' system], without the aberrations of the German School" (*PL*, p. 407, n. 23).

22. Cf. "Spinozism in its rigidity could be regarded like Pygmalion's statue, needing to be given a soul through the warm breath of love: but this comparison is imperfect, as Spinozism more closely resembles a work of art which has been sketched only in its most general outlines and in which, if it were endowed with a soul, one would still notice how many features were lacking or incompleted" (Schelling, *Of Human Freedom*, trans. J. Gutmann, p. 23).

23. *CL*, IV, 775. Italics in text. Schelling's *Einleitung zu seinem Entwurf eines Systems der Naturphilosophie* [*Introduction to the Sketch of a Philosophy of Nature*], which Coleridge was rereading in 1818 (*CL*, IV, 873), was published in 1799, when Coleridge was twenty-seven years old. The letters and journals of Coleridge and all his immediate friends are innocent of any reference to Schellingian conceptions. In November 1803 Coleridge set down in his notebooks the works he then planned to write. In this incredibly grandiose list, which includes works on contemporary politics, a prose epic, a history of logic, a history of metaphysics in Germany, a comic epic, etc., there is not the slightest suggestion of any projected works in science (*N*, 1646).

24. *CL*, IV, 775. Italics in text.   25. *CL*, IV, 874. STC's emphasis.

26. *CL*, IV, 883. Italics in text. Coleridge's comments on Steffens constitute another thicket of contradictions. Certain marginalia extol Steffens in the most exalted terms, while in others Coleridge denounces his writings as "incomprehensibly vague," or "abominable trash" (Helen Zimmern, "Coleridge's Marginalia Hitherto Unpublished," *Blackwood's Edinburgh Magazine* CXXXI [1882], 118). Shedd, III, 711, 712.

27. See, for example, Shedd, I, 166-167, 180. Coleridge's credulity is evident in his suspicion that "there may be some truth in the Spurzheimian scheme"—and this at a time when Spurzheim's phrenology with its weird maps of the human skull demarking areas of "Benevolence," and so forth, was falling into the limbo of scientific quackery. For two specimens of STC on this subject, see Shedd, I, 202*n*, and II, 381-382*n*. The long note in Shedd, I, 217-219 can only be described as amazing.

28. Shedd, II, 427. This passage appears a single page after a long and weighty footnote which is taken without acknowledgment from Kant (Beach, pp. 598-599, n. 21). Essay 6 of Section 2 of the *Friend* is wholly given over to a disquisition in the mode of the *Naturphilosophen*. Coleridge's cogitations and observations are again presented as original thoughts and experiments. There are learned references to Linnaeus, Caesalpinus, Ray, Gesner, Tournefort, Hedwig, Jussieu, and Mirbel, among other scientists, known and hopelessly obscure, but no mention of Kant, who is under immediate tribute, or to Schelling and the other German philosophers of nature who stand behind almost every line. Essay 7 in this section is in a similar vein. And here, characteristically, there is a lofty tribute to creative genius—this time to the Italian poet Chiabrera. In Essay 8, which again elaborates, without hinting at his specific sources, his theory of science, Coleridge pauses to chastise even his beloved Lord Bacon for his "studied depreciation of the ancients, with his silence, or worse than silence, concerning the merits of his contemporaries" (Shedd, II, 437-438). This is soon followed by a noble tribute to Bacon for his generous acknowledgments to Brahe (Shedd, II, 440).

29. *CL*, II, 706. STC's underscoring.   30. *CL*, II, 670-671.   31. *CL*, I, 260.

32. *HCR*, I, 215. Thomas Manning, Lamb's close friend, was a mathematician.

33. This is one of the key passages, together with the space/time passage quoted above, on which I. A. Richards erects the complex edifice of *Coleridge on Imagination*, 2nd ed. (London, 1950), p. 14. The study of Coleridge's intellectual development in Richards' first chapter is based almost entirely on Coleridge's own statements, and at no point does Richards show the slightest skepticism.

34. *CL*, II, 671. Italics in text.

35. *CL*, II, 707. STC's emphasis. Coleridge proposed instead to write a book on the "originality and merits of Locke, Hobbes, and Hume. . . . I am *confident* that I can prove the reputation of these three men wholly unmerited" (STC underscoring).

36. (London, 1743), I, 34-50. See Herbert Piper, "The Pantheistic Sources of Coleridge's Early Poetry," *JHI*, XX (1959), p. 51. Coleridge's note may be found in the Appendices of the Oxford edition of his poetry, *PW*, II, 1112-13. As usual, close analysis of Coleridge's way with sources is instructive. Almost the whole of Coleridge's first two paragraphs (more than half the whole note) comes from the first four pages of Baxter on the subject (I, 34-37). We find the phrase "It appears to me," which reinforces the belief that the ideas expressed are original, when in fact the surrounding passages are Baxter's. After a reference to David Hartley we come upon the name of Andrew Baxter, who "well observes, it doth not appear sufficient to account how the fluid may act with a force proportional . . ." Would any reader suppose from this that Baxter was being acknowledged for the entire note? And yet this is a recurrent pattern in Coleridge, here shown very early in his career, at twenty-four years old: reference to the man who is responsible for the *whole*, but in such a way that the reader has no suspicion of the debt. And yet, when the obligation is found out, a kind of excuse is already prepared: surely there was no intention to withhold acknowledgment when the man to whom he was indebted is specifically mentioned!

37. *CL*, II, 709, 1013-14, 1046-47. Scholars who think that Coleridge's letters, notebooks, and marginalia were intended as wholly private writings always blink evidence like this. Stephen Potter, for example, writes: "It is obvious that he never has in mind the possibility of the post-humous publication of his letters. . . . all is written with the spontaneity of the notes and marginalia (*Coleridge and S.T.C.* [London, 1935], p. 121). In fact, the notes and marginalia are quite often directed at an audience, both contemporary and future. In a similar vein, George Whalley maintains that "even when they were written on request the marginalia seem to have little or no outward-directed emphasis" ("Coleridge Unlabyrinthed," *UTQ*, XXXII [1963], 333).

De Quincey, however (whose comments on matters of this sort are consistently insightful and consistently ignored by contemporary scholars), has written:

> Wordsworth, in his marginal notes, thought of nothing but delivering himself of a strong feeling, with which he wished to challenge the reader's sympathy. Coleridge imagined an audience before him; and, however doubtful that consummation might seem, I am satisfied that he never wrote a line for which he did not feel the momentary inspiration of sympathy and applause, under the confidence, that, sooner or later, all which he had committed to the chance margins of books would converge and assemble in some common reservoir of reception. (*LP*, pp. 197-198)

The ingathering of those scattered comments will soon be published "in a common reservoir of reception," accompanied by the full panoply of modern scholarly resources. The volume will conclusively demonstrate, I think, that Coleridge's marginal notes were consistenly directed at an audience, both contemporary and future.

38. *CL*, III, 41. Pontifical statements on the relative stature of the great scientists appear several times in the *Table Talk*. In 1833 he repeated his early conviction that "it would take many Newtons to make one Milton." Three years before that it would have taken "two or three Galileos and Newtons to make one Kepler." It is fascinating to find Coleridge, in the process of giving Newton grudging praise, insisting that in fact Kepler had "fully conceived" the idea of gravitation. Coleridge continued: "We praise Newton's clearness and steadiness. He *was* clear and steady, no doubt, whilst working out, by the help of an admirable geometry, *the idea brought forth by another* (*TT*, pp. 257, 133. Emphasis added to last phrase). The notion that Newton "perfected" the ideas of Kepler, who had "fully conceived" the law of gravity, appears with surprising frequency and suspicious confidence in Coleridge's later writings and conversation: for example, CSC, pp. 397, 400, 401, 403, 406, 407. It has not hitherto been noted that this idea also derives from Schelling who, in distinguishing art from science, put forward the hypothesis that in science "the very problem whose solution can be discovered by genius is also soluble mechanically. Of such a sort, e.g., is the Newtonian system of gravitation, which could have been a 'genial' discovery—*and in its first discoverer, Kepler, really was*. . . ." (*STI*, p. 370).

39. *SC*, I, 78. In the edition of the Shakespeare Lectures prepared by Sara Coleridge, the first

sentence begins, "This is so far true *to appearance . . .*" (Shedd, IV, 107). Raysor does not comment on the words I have italicized, which do not appear in his own text. Were they additions by Sara to modify her father's apparent credulity?

40.   The distinguished biologist P. B. Medawar has recently written: "The advances of molecular biology have withdrawn [many] problems from the agenda of *Naturphilosophie*, which flourishes only upon what is not yet understood; and this process of attrition will continue until nothing of it remains except the good old days when, because no one could say anything conclusive, almost everyone could have his say. It seems to me hopeless to expect working biologists to take nature-philosophy very seriously. If it is to survive it must recruit a new audience from literary intellectuals who feel guilty about knowing next to nothing about biology. . . ." ("The Molecular Shadow," *New York Review of Books*, 23 October 1969, p. 23).

41.   *CL*, IV, 574-575. The significance of this is buttressed by the following passages:

> And here once for all, I beg leave to remark that I attach neither belief nor respect to the Theory, which supposes the human Race to have been gradually perfecting itself from the darkest Savagery, or, still more boldly tracing us back to the bestial as to our Larva, contemplates the Man as the last metamorphosis, the gay *Image*, of some lucky species of Ape or Baboon.
>
> . . . The History, I find, in my Bible, is in perfect coincidence with the opinions I should form on Grounds of Experience and Common Sense. (Alice Snyder, "Coleridge on Giordano Bruno," *MLN*, XLII [1927], 431. Italics in text.)

42.   Craig W. Miller, "Coleridge's Concept of Nature," *JHI*, XXV (1964), 77-96. The quotations in the previous discussion are on pp. 85-86. Miller finds "ample evidence" that Coleridge had read "every important scientific work, ancient and modern" (p. 78), which adds the vast realms of science to Coleridge's reputation for encyclopedic knowledge. We are told that Coleridge "borrows gratefully when he finds an appealing idea" (p. 79), but Miller's long article has scarcely a word to say about the sources of Coleridge's scientific conceptions.

43.   Notably by W. J. Bate, who refers the reader to Miller's article.

44.   For a valuable discussion of the general context of evolutionary discussion during Coleridge's time, and of his part in it, see Beach, especially pp. 288, 331, 333, and 593, n. 16.

45.   See James Guttman's Introduction to *Of Human Freedom* (Chicago, 1936), especially pp. xxiii, xxxvii, and 9 (where Schelling's odd use of the word "death" may be compared with *CL*, IV, 575, 760), and pp. 19-21. As *On University Studies* provides a comparatively brief, overall view of Schelling's approach to the whole range of university studies, it serves as an excellent introduction to his thought. See especially pp. 6, 23, 27, 36, 121, 128-129, 139. For further discussion of Schelling's concept of individuation, see E. D. Hirsch, *Wordsworth and Schelling* (New Haven, Conn., 1960), p. 44.

46.   *CL*, IV, 686; *Of Human Freedom*, p. 49. Here is another example of Coleridge's striking ability to pick up a vivid phrase. Equally characteristic, however, is that in using the phrase in an attack upon Hazlitt, he should immediately go on to attack Hazlitt's originality: "Almost all the *sparkles & originalities* of his Essays are, however, echoes from poor Charles Lamb—and in his last libel the image of the Angel without hands or feet was stolen from a Letter of my own to Charles Lamb, which had been quoted to him" (*CL*, IV, 686. STC's emphasis).

47.   The use of the particular philosophy of nature put forward by Schelling and Steffens was not confined, as we have seen, to *Theory of Life*. Shedd printed it as an Appendix to *Aids to Reflection* because, as he saw, it was a fuller account of some of the ideas therein (Shedd, I, 373). Another presentation of these views on the evolution of life is in *On the Constitution of the Church and State*, so that "direct borrowing of ideas from the German idealists of the Schelling school is found in at least four of Coleridge's philosophical works, instead of merely in *Biographia Literaria*, as formerly supposed" (*CBG*, p. 44). To these must be added the *Friend*, because throughout Essay VI and VII of "The Second Landing Place" (Shedd, II, 422-436), Coleridge discusses various theories of nature, takes up the ideas of Hunter, Abernethy, and others, and

repeatedly makes great claims for his own originality as a thinker in this field (see Beach, Ch. XI). Still further use of these ideas was made in the *Philosophical Lectures* (Ch. XII), where some five pages (pp. 339-344) are almost verbatim from *Theory of Life* (Shedd, I, 378 ff.).

48. (Oxford, 1953), p. 170.   49. *SP*, LV (1958), 501-502, 514.   50. RW, II, 153.

51. Bate, pp. 134, n. 4; 192-194.

52. In the same year that Coleridge's *Theory of Life* was published in England (1848), a volume devoted to an explication and eulogy of the principles of the *Naturphilosophen* was published in Boston. It is not surprising, therefore, that the author, J. B. Stallo, a young American student of German thought, should have been ignorant of Coleridge's work. Stallo's book is almost one long paean of praise, and its language sounds precisely like what one finds in Coleridge. Indeed, part of the Romantic philosophy of nature which was by 1848 taken for granted in the poetry of English and American poets, now appears in language which could easily have been written by Coleridge:

> The Schellingian philosophy has, perhaps, little absolute merit; its formal incoherence in many respects is glaring enough, and has even been acknowledged by the author in latter years. It has not rent the veil of nature; but to have earnestly announced, that there is a veil to be rent, that nature is symbolical,—this is its eternal merit. Formerly philosophers and men of science investigated but the *external* relations of the different forms of nature; now they stand before it in the attitude of interpreters. To use a comparison of Schelling; before him, in turning over the leaves of Nature's *Iliad*, they compared the forms of the letters, traced the resemblance of their shape, and examined their technical composition; now they endeavour to *read*. And now, too, does man first become *familiar* with nature, in recognizing there the same life which animates him. (*General Principles of the Philosophy of Nature.* . ., pp. 226-227. Italics in text.)

This is Coleridge to the letter, so characteristic that one is startled. And indeed, as one reads Stallo, much of it is the *Theory of Life* at a very near distance.

Stallo, however, was very young when he wrote the book. In his later work he frankly repudiated his youthful enthusiasm for transcendental science. In the Preface to his *Concepts and Theories of Modern Physics*, Stallo said that his earlier book had been written "when he was barely of age, while he was under the spell of Hegel's ontological reveries, and therefore while he was infected with the 'metaphysical malady, which seems to be one of the unavoidable disorders of intellectual infancy' " (ed. Percy W. Bridgman [Cambridge, Mass., 1960], p. xiii). Scholars who systematically comb Coleridge's scientific writings for nuggets of gold would do well to meditate on Stallo.

13.   THE "OPUS MAXIMUM"

1. *CL*, I, 519.   2. *CL*, p. 8, n. 7.   3. *CL*, IV, 589, 591, 635, 703, 706, 736.

4. See "Comment" to Aphorism XLIII among the "Moral and Religious Aphorisms." The full text reads: "What conscience is, and that it is the ground and antecedent of human (or self-) consciousness, and not any modification of the latter, *I have shown at large in a work announced for the press and described in the chapter following.*" Professor Shedd, however, seems on his own authority to have *altered* Coleridge's text by leaving out the clause I have italicized and rearranging the sentence thus: "I rather think that conscience is the ground and antecedent of human (or self-) consciousness, and not any modification of the latter" (Shedd, I, 185). Of course the announcement of unwritten works as ready, or almost ready, for publication was a persistent eccentricity of Coleridge's. See, for example, *CL*, II, 877: "[I] shall in a very few weeks go to the Press with a Volume on the Prose writings of Hall, Milton, & Taylor—& shall immediately follow it up with an Essay on the writings of Dr. Johnson, & Gibbon"; II, 1053: ". . . I have now completed my materials (and three months will enable me to send them to the Press) for a work, the contents of which you will conjecture from the Title—'Consolations & Comforts from the exercise & right application of the Reason, the Imagination, and the Moral Feelings'. . . . & I

may venture, dear and honored Friends! to say to you, without dreading from you the Imputation of Vanity, that what I have written is to my own mind a pure Strain of Music"; III, 133: "I publish my Greek Accidence, Vocabulary of Greek Terminations, Greek & English Lexicon, and philosophical Greek Grammar in Spring"; III, 279: "If it please God, I shall shortly publish . . . a work of considerable size & very great Labor—the toil of many years—entitled, The Mysteries of Religion grounded in or relative to the Mysteries of Human Nature: or the foundations of morality laid in the primary Faculties of Man." The number and particularity of references to the "Opus Maximum," however, remain a special problem in Coleridge biography.

5. *CL*, III, 533.

6. Allsop, I, 154-155. Italics in text. The "Logosophia" was the last of *five* major works of which Coleridge wrote to Thomas Allsop, his young admirer. The others included major studies of (1) Shakespeare and the Elizabethans; (2) the major European writers; (3) the History of Philosophy; and (4) Letters on the New and Old Testament.

> To the completion of these four works [Coleridge wrote], I have literally nothing more to do than *to transcribe*; but, as I before hinted, from so many scraps and *Sibylline* leaves, including margins of books and blank pages, that, unfortunately, I must be my own scribe, and not done by myself, they will be all but lost; or perhaps (as has been too often the case already) furnish feathers for the caps of others; some for this purpose, and some to plume the arrows of detraction, to be let fly against the luckless bird from whom they had been plucked or moulted." (Allsop, I, 153. STC's underscoring.)

Apart from material he had already given in public lectures, there is little evidence that any of these works was beyond the project stage at his death more than a decade later. Once again, it will be observed, Coleridge expresses his concern with unacknowledged borrowing, and uses the same figure as in the *Biographia* (I, 32).

7. *TT*, pp. 310-311.

8. "The language of Coleridge's will, together, no doubt, with verbal communications which had passed, imposed on Mr. Green what he accepted as an obligation to devote so far as necessary the whole remaining strength and earnestness of his life to the one task of systematising, developing, and establishing the doctrines of the Coleridgian philosophy. Accordingly, in 1836, two years after his master's death, he retired from medical practice [Green was a surgeon and a fellow of the Royal Society], and thenceforward, until his own death, nearly thirty years afterwards, he applied himself unceasingly. . . . 'Theology, ethics, politics, and political history, ethnology. language, aesthetics, psychology, physics, and the allied sciences, biology, logic, mathematics, pathology, all these subjects,' declares his biographer, 'were thoughtfully studied by him, in at least their basial principles and metaphysics . . .' At an early period of his labours he thought it convenient to increase his knowledge of Greek; he began to study Hebrew when more than sixty years old, and still later in life he took up Sanscrit. It was not until he was approaching his seventieth year and found his health beginning to fail him that Mr. Green seems to have felt that his design, in its more ambitious scope, must be abandoned" (J. D. Traill, *Samuel Taylor Coleridge* [New York, 1884], pp. 173-175).

Green died at seventy-two without publishing any part of his lifelong labors. James A. Greig cruelly takes this touching example of humble discipleship as evidence that "[Coleridge's] lack of grip upon actuality was infectious" (*Francis Jeffrey of the Edinburgh Review* [Edinburgh and London, 1948], p. 271).

9. *CLL*, p. 68. The unpublished philosophical mss will comprise several volumes of the *Collected Works* now in preparation. The materials are now generally known as the "Opus Maximum" and the "Logic."

10. "Coleridge's Reading of Mendelssohn's 'Morgenstunden' and 'Jerusalem,'" *JEGP*, XXVIII (1929), 505, n. 6. Again and again in Coleridge studies we encounter the same stern caveat: since Coleridge did not prepare such and such a manuscript for the press, he cannot be held accountable for any untoward absence of proper acknowledgments. We have already seen

how misleading this caution can be. But as to the mass of manuscript here being discussed, Wellek is considerably more specific about the absence of acknowledgment:

Some phrases in the MS sound almost like attempts to hide the true derivation of his ideas. Coleridge speaks frequently of himself as of a discoverer, even when he is merely taking Kantian terms, for instance, of the "primary mental act which we have called the synthetic unity, or the unity of apperception," or that of the term category, "the different meaning of which in Aristotle and in our Logic does not appear to warrant to me a change in the name" or of "truths of reason alone and those I have termed principles." Coleridge uses also such an impersonal reference as to "some Logicians" who have spoken of the "Synthetic Function of the Understanding" and refers innocently to the "writers above mentioned," though no name is pronounced before. Or Coleridge combines the impersonal passive voice with some, scarcely verifiable or defensible historical reminiscence leading away from the actual source. So he starts to explain the "universal forms of our pure sense." "This knowledge," he says, "has been borrowed from a fragment attributed to Palema, the successor of Sceucippus who succeeded Plato." (*KE*, pp. 117-118)

We should not be misled by the handsome *general* tributes and acknowledgments Coleridge paid Kant; *specific* debts were rarely noticed, and Coleridge regularly obscured the whole question of sources, as we have repeatedly seen. In the long discussion on the "momentous distinction" between the reason and the understanding in *Aids to Reflection*, Coleridge hails as intellectual kin almost everyone imaginable before he at last names Kant. We are assured that Bishop Leighton anticipated Kant on reason almost word for word, but we are not directed to specific texts (Shedd, I, 241). Elsewhere we are told that as a logician, Kant "completed and systematized what Lord Bacon had boldly designed and loosely sketched out in the Miscellany of Aphorisms, his Novum Organum" (*Letters*, II, 735). This is another of Coleridge's strange assertions which has puzzled later scholars. Among Coleridge's published writings is the statement that much in Kant comes from Richard Baxter (Shedd, V, 355), and in the unpublished "Logic" is the statement that Baxter had seen more deeply into the nature of tripartite divisions than Kant, a statement repeated elsewhere. Only Wellek, however, seems to have followed up on Coleridge's lead:

An examination of these [Baxter's] ample folios shows, however, that Baxter had not the slightest glimpse into the dialectic. . . . Coleridge himself does not seem to have understood the actual principle of the dialectic, though his own use is obviously derived from Schelling rather than from anywhere else. His own reconstruction of Dialectic along the lines of a Pentad strikes me as singularly unfortunate and its application to all sorts of subjects without any apparent principle shows that Coleridge never properly understood the inner principle of every dialectic which is far more than an empty mysticism of numbers. (*KE*, pp. 84-86, 279, n. 91)

11. *CLL*, p. vii.   12. *TT*, p. 157.

13. *CLL*, p. 13. As will be seen later, such views of Coleridge are today distinctly heretical.

14. *CLL*, p. 79, n. 7.   15. *CLL*, p. 80, n. 12.   16. *CLL*, p. 82.

17. *CLL*, p. 83 and n. 21. This practice can be seen as merely an extension of what was commonplace in *Theory of Life*,

18. *CLL*, p. 85.   19. *CLL*, p. 91.   20. *CLL*, pp. 92-93.

21. "Coleridge's Reading of Mendelssohn's 'Morgenstunden' and 'Jerusalem,' " *JEGP*, XXVIII (1929), 505. In a footnote Miss Snyder informs us that the "fourth instance" from Mendelssohn above was also used without acknowledgment in *Omniana* (1812), II, 10, and *On the Constitution of the Church and State* (1830), p. 217.

22. *CLL*, p. 95.   23. *CLL*, p. 101.   24. *CLL*, pp. 102-103.

25. Quoted from *CLL*, p. 155.   26. *CL*, III, 534.

27. The works were published at Princeton (1931) and Leipzig (1933), respectively.

28. *ERP*, p. 113.   29. Page 67.   30. *CBG*, p. 38, n. 3.

31. *Coleridge as Philosopher* (London, 1930), p. 15.

32. *Coleridge as Philosopher,* p. 117. Also quoted in RW, II, 151. The manuscript materials just discussed are at long last to be published in the first complete edition of Coleridge's works. Thus it is certain that the whole question of their value and originality will be fully reexamined. Apart from Wellek, almost every contemporary commentator treats Coleridge's achievement as a philosopher with great respect, and sometimes he is credited with philosophical gifts of the highest order. Former views of this subject are regularly attacked. In Professor Bate's recent biography, those with skeptical estimates of Coleridge as a philosopher are coldly dismissed. Professor Whalley complains that "we have been told repeatedly that Coleridge is a Kantian. I reply that Coleridge was Coleridge" ("Coleridge Unlabyrinthed," *UTQ,* XXXII [1963], 338). J. A. Appleyard's much less enthusiastic appraisal of his subject's stature in *Coleridge's Philosophy of Literature* (Cambridge, Mass., 1965) has been—on the whole—coolly received.

33. The pain and anguish present in some of Coleridge's best poems, especially "Ode to Dejection," make Coleridge a tempting subject for study from the existential point of view. But such work can only achieve philosophical weight if it can be shown that the author was not merely crying out against the world's wretchedness, but rather had an integrated view of suffering as part of man's ontological fate. Schelling has been used as a subject for just such reexaminations and his work affords numerous examples of the tone and flavor of the existential spirit. Schelling refers to "the veil of sadness that is spread over all Nature, the deep indestructible melancholy of all life." Consider the following passages: "Certainly it is a painful way the Being which lives in Nature traverses his passage through it; so that the line of sorrow, traced on the countenance of all Nature, on the face of the animal world testifies. . . . Who will trouble himself about the common and ordinary mischances of a transitory life that has apprehended the pain of universal existence and the great fate of the whole?" "Anguish is the fundamental feeling of every living creature." "Pain is something universal and necessary in all life. . . . All pain only comes from being." "The unrest of unceasing willing and desiring, by which every creature is goaded, is in itself unblessedness" (quoted from Eduard von Hartmann, *Philosophy of the Unconscious,* trans. W. C. Loupland [London, 1931], III, 3-4).

In this and similar connections it is well to remember Father Coppleston's wise caution: "the desire to find anticipations of later ideas in illustrious minds of the past should not blind us to the great differences in atmosphere between the idealist and existentialist movements" (*A History of Philosophy* [New York, 1965], VII, 182).

14. THE SHAKESPEAREAN CRITICISM

1. See, for example, Augustus Ralli, *A History of Shakespearean Criticism* (Oxford, 1932): "The first and greatest of the romantic critics, he [Coleridge] has transformed his subject. . . . The greatest of the others—Dryden, Pope, Johnson—are but shooting stars across the darkness" (I, 142). See R. H. Fogle, *The Idea of Coleridge's Criticism* (Berkeley, 1962), p. 177, n. 3, for quotations from various celebrations of Coleridge's Shakespearean writings.

2. *SC,* I, 194-196 and notes.   3. *BL,* I, 22.

4. *SC,* 11, 184; *N,* 224*n.* The letter itself is at *CL,* III, 354-361.

5. Of verbal parallels, the only one seems to be "Jesu Maria, shield her well!" But Southey, who pointed this out, seems not to have remembered that "Jesu Maria!" is exclaimed in Schiller's *Ghost-Seer* and *Robbers.* The extremely harsh attitude of the age toward unacknowledged borrowings, especially from living writers, is shown in the way Scott referred to his youthful "piracy" from Taylor's translations of German ballads (*Poetical Works of Sir Walter Scott,* ed. J. Logie Robertson [Oxford, 1906], pp. 650-651).

6. *CL,* II, 1191. See Professor Griggs's notes 1 and 2 for information on the background of this controversy.

7. CL, III, 39, 42, 111, 291-294. STC's underscoring. In 1813 Coleridge wrote to his wife: ". . . I must try to *imitate* W. Scott (who has set me the example in a less honorable way, in con-

tempt of the 8th commandment) in making Hay while the Sun shines." E. H. Coleridge expunged the parenthetic clause in his 1895 edition of the letters (*CL*, III, 431 and n. 2. Italics in text). As is true of STC's relations with so many other men, his attitude toward Scott was a bewildering mixture of gross insult and excessive praise. See, for example *N*, 2075n, 2599f89v, n., and *The Friend* (Shedd, II, 265n, 381n). Over the signature "S.T.C." appeared an attack on Scott's originality in the *London Courier* for 15 September 1810. Coleridge, on 20 September, publicly denied writing it (*CL*, III, 290, n. 2). In 1827, Coleridge wrote of Scott in a letter: "when I think of the wretched trash, that the Lust for Gain enduced him to publish for the last three or four years . . . even my feelings assist in hardening me. . . . I have enough to feel for without wasting my Sympathy on a Scotchman suffering the penalty of his Scotchery" (*UL*, II, 402).

8. The letter exists only in draft form. It is not certain to whom the letter was addressed. Was it ever sent? Was it intended as a public or wholly private statement?

9. *MC*, pp. 334-335. Italics in text. 10. *CL*, III, 355. 11. *CL*, III, 358.

12. *CL*, III, 358-360. STC's emphasis. Donald Sultana observes: "There is no evidence of this translation by Schlegel in his notebooks or of any reading by him in Spanish poetry" (*Samuel Taylor Coleridge in Malta and Italy* [Oxford, 1969], p. 387).

13. *SC*, II, 126.

14. This unusually mendacious letter begins: "If *any* one has a right to join in the every-day declamation against the hollowness or duplicity of the world, the man who is constitutionally open-hearted and both constitutionally and morally *single*-hearted, has the most reason to claim the right, and the most frequent temptation to assert it" (*CL*, IV, 829, 831. STC's underscoring).

15. *CL*, IV, 839. 16. Shedd, IV, 457. 17. *CL*, IV, 839, n. 1. Italics in text.

18. *CL*, IV, 924.

19. For still other assertions of priority over Schlegel, see *SC*, I, 16-17; II, 126, 245; *BL*, I, 22n, 102; and *CL*, IV, 898-900, n. 3.

20. *CL*, III, 360. 21. *CL*, III, 360.

22. See *ante*, pp. 86-87. T. M. Raysor, however, accepts Coleridge's explanation: "it is almost certain that the great influence of Schlegel confirmed and developed rather than suggested many of Coleridge's ideas. They had both studied Kant, Lessing, Herder, Schiller, and perhaps Richter, and had both been students at Göttingen under Heyne. . . . Their common background and common subject made coincidences not merely probable but inevitable" (*SC*, I, xxvi).

23. Wellek considers the form "Krusve" a misreading by Raysor of "Kruse," a more likely name (RW, II, 155n). However, it is at least possible that the name is Coleridge's invention.

24. *HCR*, I, 55. Italics in text.

25. Mrs. Phelan, despite the evidence, takes Coleridge at his word that he did not see Schlegel's work till after this lecture and thus she is inevitably led into massive difficulties in accounting for certain parallels. She finds a decisive change in Coleridge's 1812 lectures, beginning with the ninth, and accounts for this as follows: "The knowledge that another held views similar to his own, and expressed them with firmness, causes a perceptible change in the tone of his criticism, and a difference in his method of procedure" (H-P, p. 310. See also pp. 297, 309). Similarly, Griggs considers Coleridge's "own testimony" on the subject decisive (*CL*, III, 359, n. 1). Raysor finds some "coincidences" between Schlegel and Coleridge's lectures before 12 December 1811 "marked enough to raise the question of an influence from Schlegel for the earlier lectures of 1811, but this is impossible, unless one is willing to set aside entirely Coleridge's own account of his first acquaintance with Schlegel's lectures" (*SC*, I, xxvii).

26. *CL*, III, 343. 27. RW, II, 155n. 28. *HCR*, I, 21.

29. *CL*, III, 359, n. 1. 30. *Letters*, II, 670. 31. RW, II, 155-156n.

32. "Shakespearian Criticism: I. From Dryden to Coleridge," in *A Companion to Shakespeare Studies*, eds. H. Granville-Barker and G. B. Harrison (New York, 1960), p. 296. See also p. 299.

33. See *SC*, I, Raysor's Introduction, esp. Pt. II.

34. *DL*, p. 361.

35. *Shakespeare in Germany* (Cambridge, England, 1937), pp. 27-28. The only English translation of Schlegel's essay on *Romeo and Juliet* seems to be the one that appeared in the first issue of *Ollier's Literary Miscellany* (London, 1820). Obviously, the lengthy essay was considered important enough to launch a new magazine. In the present context, the anonymous introductory "Remarks upon the Character of German Criticism" are almost of greater interest than the essay itself. Regrettably, no copy of *Ollier's* seems to exist in the United States. Quotations are therefore from the rare British Museum copy. At the outset of his prefatory remarks, the writer describes the publications of the Schlegel brothers at the turn of the century as having "laid the foundations of the art of criticism, which they may almost claim to themselves the honour of having raised from a collection of dogmatical or empirical maxims unto the dignity of a scientific art" (p. 4).

36. *SC*, I, 10 and n. 1.   37. *SC*, I, 6, n. 1.

38. *CL*, IV, 839; *SC*, I, 16. Italics in texts.   39. *BL*, II, 182.

40. See "Lessing" in the Index to *SC* for a guide to the general subject. Of particular interest in Lessing's *Hamburg Dramaturgy* are Nos. 11, 12, 15, and 73.

41. It is instructive to study Shawcross' desperate note on this point in which he finds that "the text need not necessarily be construed as an admission of his own debt to Lessing" (*BL*, II, 299).

42. *WLC*, pp. 178-179 and n. 1. In fact, the two volumes of STC's Shakespearean criticism are devoid of even a syllable of discussion on the sonnets, a startling gap which may have something to do with the fact that Schlegel was equally silent on the subject. This omission especially irritated Crabb Robinson when he found Coleridge repeating himself to fill unelapsed lecture time: "He certainly might, with a little exertion, have collected enough matter for *one* lecture on the poems of Shakespeare. But he utterly passed over the *Sonnets*" (*HCR*, I, 53. Italics in text).

43. *HCR*, I, 193-194, 195. Italics in text.

44. 21 May 1805. *The Letters of William and Dorothy Wordsworth, The Middle Years*, ed. Ernest de Selincourt (Oxford, 1937), I, 130.

45. *SC*, I, 17, n. 1; II, 189, 245.

46. *SC*, I, 17. Analysis of Hamlet *as a character* could not, per se, revolutionize the study of Shakespeare, since psychological analysis of character was a familiar procedure. What was profoundly original in the German contribution to the subject was precisely the emphasis on a complex and perfect *dramatic form* in Shakespeare.

47. *SC*, I, 17, n. 4.

48. *HW*, IV, 171-172. This is followed by a three-page excerpt from Schlegel's "general account of Shakespear."

49. Elisabeth Schneider observes that throughout *The Characters of Shakespeare's Plays* Hazlitt never mentions Coleridge, but Schlegel many times, and that this was "an omission which is not likely to have been accidental" (*The Aesthetics of William Hazlitt* [Philadelphia, 1933], p. 89).

50. *HCR*, I, 178. Most apropos here is the opinion of the anonymous writer in the 1820 issue of *Ollier's*. He insisted that to A. W. Schlegel "belongs the honour of having first duly asserted the claims of Shakespeare to the entire supremacy in art, which is his unquestioned right" (p. 4).

51. H-P, p. 351. The intensely enthusiastic celebration of Shakespeare as master poet and dramatist, the quintessential manner of the later Coleridge, is not to be found in the younger one. Even if one did find a frenzy of enthusiasm in the young Coleridge for Shakespeare, this would matter much less than the *reasons* assigned for approval. In fact, such evidence as exists does not remotely suggest that the young Coleridge found Shakespeare's genius beyond the

reach of limiting criticism. When Coleridge first read Schiller's *Robbers* in 1794, he wondered in a letter to Southey, "Why have we ever called Milton sublime?" (*CL*, I, 122). His bedazzlement was typical of the critical opinion of his time. A youthful foible, perhaps, and a reference in any case to Milton, not Shakespeare; but two years later, in a footnote to his sonnet celebrating Schiller, Coleridge wrote: "Schiller introduces no supernatural beings; yet his human beings agitate and astonish more than all the *goblin* rout—even of Shakespeare" (*PW*, I, 72-73, n, 2. STC's emphasis). The same note was printed in the edition of 1797, but ever afterwards during his lifetime disappeared from Coleridge's works. That Coleridge could compare Shakespeare to Schiller unfavorably in *any* department of dramaturgy is, of course, unthinkable in the later utterances.

In 1797 Coleridge was able to write of Wordsworth's play, *The Borderers*: "There are in the piece those *profound* touches of the human heart, which I find three or four times in 'The Robbers' of Schiller, & often in Shakespeare—but in Wordsworth there are no *inequalities*" (*CL*, I, 325. STC's underscoring). This hardly demonstrates critical awe of the Bard of Avon. Hazlitt's report of the early Coleridge's opinion of Shakespeare as a "mere stripling in the art," surprising as it seems, should be taken seriously on several grounds. In December 1796 Coleridge wrote to Thelwall that "Collins' Ode on the poetical character—that part of it, I should say, beginning with—'The Band (as faery Legends say) Was wove on that creating Day,' has inspired & whirled *me* along with greater agitations of enthusiasm than any the most *impassioned* Scene in Schiller or Shakespere" (*CL*, I, 279. STC's underscoring). Again, a remark like this is simply unimaginable in the later Coleridge.

In August 1800, Charles Lamb, who was to become one of the great nineteenth-century critics of Shakespeare, could write that George Dyer had called Shakespeare "a great but irregular genius, which I think to be an original and just remark." Since he repeated the remark approvingly in a letter to Coleridge a few days later, it does not seem likely that he had as yet heard a contrary opinion from Coleridge (*LL*, I, 208, 211). Indeed, Lamb seems scarcely to have been aware of the history of Shakespeare criticism, for Dyer's remark was itself a commonplace, just as was Coleridge's "stripling in the art" judgment.

A careful analysis of all Coleridge's references to Shakespeare in his published notebooks through 1808 provides no evidence to support the contention that his central ideas on Shakespeare were independent of Schlegel. The references to Shakespeare, as to Milton, are enthusiastic enough, but Coleridge's post-Schlegellian style is suggested only by entry 2396: "Shakespere is not a 1000th part so faulty as the 000 believe him." This comment of 1805 hardly encourages the belief that the "judgment equal to genius" approach to Shakespeare was as yet beyond an embryonic state. The remark is essentially defensive. There is no *fundamental* attack on the conventional idea that Shakespeare was a faulty writer. It is still a matter of degree.

In November 1803 Coleridge set down an impressive list of works he hoped to write. Among a bewildering variety of topics appears what seems to be a history of English literature. Shakespeare's name is included, but no special attention is given to him nor does he indicate any fresh ideas on the subject.

In writing to Humphry Davy in September 1807 of a projected series of lectures, he referred to Shakespeare's "merits and defects" (*CL*, III, 29); the phrase reappears as late as the Prospectus to the Lectures of 1811-12 (*SC*, II, 23). But of the bard's defects in the lectures themselves we hear nothing, nor do any of the later Prospectuses qualify the genius of Shakespeare in any way.

Thus if Coleridge read Schlegel's early work around the turn of the century, which (to repeat) must be accounted as uncertain, it would seem to have made little impression on him. It was doubtless Schlegel's *Vorlesungen* that revolutionized his thinking. Coleridge's exaggerated tribute to Lessing in *Biographia Literaria* may therefore be taken as a red herring, diverting attention from the real source.

52. *CL*, III, 108.   53. H-P, pp. 297-300.

54. Such reports as we have of these lectures, however, are of great interest in demonstrating

Coleridge's general use of German ideas. Robinson reported on Coleridge's lectures in a letter of 7 May 1808: "Everything he observes on morals will be as familiar to you as all he says on criticism is to me; for he has adopted in all respects the German doctrines." A week later Robinson commented on two further lectures. His letter includes a list of the topics Coleridge touched upon. Raysor notes: "Brandl pointed out in his *Life of Coleridge* (Eng. trans. by Eastlake), p. 297, that these notes of Robinson's read almost like the index of Herder's *Kalligone*. . . . The plagiarism is obvious, for Coleridge certainly knew this work of Herder. His own copy, with marginalia, now rests in the British Museum" (*SC*, II, 9, 13, n. 1).

55.   *SC*, II, 28.

56.   *DL*, pp. 471-472. A. W. Schlegel's *Lectures on Dramatic Art and Literature* (1809-11) was first translated into English by John Black (1815) from Schlegel's third edition. All quotations are from this translation as revised by A. J. W. Morrison (1846). Many relevant passages in the original German may be found in Mrs. Phelan's study. I have chosen to use the standard translation of Schlegel, rather than the passages in German, to make the indebtedness clearer to an English-speaking audience. There is of course some slight danger in this, but the risk seems well worth taking. Black's translation has the advantage of having been made long before Coleridge's Shakespearean writings were published. Thus there is no possibility—as is the case with later comparisons between Schlegel and Coleridge—that the translator has been influenced by his knowledge of Coleridge's text.

57.   *SC*, II, 28, n. 1.   58.   *SC*, II, 29.   59.   *DL*, pp. 363-364.

60.   *SC*, II, 29-30.   61.   *DL*, pp. 468-470.   62.   *SC*, II, 30, n. 1.

63.   *BL*, I, 22.   64.   *DL*, pp. 21-22. Italics in text.

65.   Raysor notes: "This bit of false learning is partly due to Coleridge's misunderstanding of Schlegel . . . partly to Schlegel himself. . . . Coleridge repeats this remark elsewhere (Cf. ii. 216)" (*SC*, I, 175, n. 2).

66.   *DL*, pp. 341-342.   67.   *SC*, I, 175.   68.   *DL*, p. 19.

69.   *SC*, II, 212. This comes from the lecture called "General Characteristics of Shakespeare," which is particularly heavy with Schlegel borrowings. It is interesting to compare the lecture as given in *SC*, II, 211-219, with Coleridge's preparatory notes in *SC*, I, 194-196. For the passage above Coleridge wrote: "Augustan ages—children's garden. *Centos*—plucked here and there—but rootless" (*SC*, I, 196). In notes for a lecture delivered at Bristol in 1813, Coleridge wrote: "the difference between mechanical . . . and *living* forms. The former [may be] compared to a child's garden of plucked flowers stuck in the earth" (*SC*, I, 204. Italics in text).

Hazlitt was aware of this particular borrowing, for in his sharply satirical "Conversation on the Drama with Coleridge," printed in the *London Magazine* in December 1820, he has Coleridge say, "But a French play (I think it is Schlegel who somewhere makes the comparison, though I had myself, before I ever read Schlegel, made the same remark) is like a child's garden set with slips of branches and flowers, stuck in the ground, not growing in it" (*Hazlitt on Theater*, eds. William Archer and Robert Lowe [New York, n.d], p. 181). Elsewhere in this neglected essay Hazlitt has Coleridge remark of the French: "their style of dancing is difficult; would it were impossible." To this Hazlitt appends the footnote: "This expression is borrowed from Dr. Johnson. However, as Dr. Johnson is not a German critic, Mr. C. need not be supposed to acknowledge it" (*Hazlitt on Theater*, p. 182 and n.3).

70.   *DL*, pp. 400-401.   71.   *SC*, II, 216.   72.   *DL*, p. 395.

73.   *SC*, I, 120.   74.   *DL*, p. 401.   75.   *SC*, I, 49.   76.   *DL*, p. 410.

77.   *SC*, II, 223.   78.   *SC*, I, xxvi.

79.   Mrs. Phelan's text is pre-Raysor and not every parallel adduced will convince all readers equally. Nevertheless, direct examination of the passages produces a far clearer understanding of the debt than is likely to emerge from general discussion of the problem.

80.   *SC*, I, 69-70 and n. 1; *DL*, p. 367. Since both men were wrong, we may be permitted to think otherwise. Schlegel, of course, would be far less aware of the nuances of English, but how

did Coleridge miss, amid much other word play, Lady Macbeth's "I'll *gild* the faces of the grooms withal, for it must seem their *guilt*" (II, ii, 56-57) ? (Noted also in WJB, p. 418, n. 2.)

81. *SC*, I, 70.

82. *DL*, p. 367. This passage was quoted by Hazlitt in his Preface to *Characters of Shakespeare's Plays* (*HW*, IV, 173). It is possible that more than coincidence is involved.

83. In this passage Schlegel remarked upon the "affecting play of words of the dying John of Gaunt on his own name" (*DL*, p. 367). Coleridge specifically called attention to the puns in John of Gaunt's deathbed speech (*SC*, I, 135-136, 138; II, 143-144, 231).

84. *SC*, I, 70 and n. 3.   85. Shedd, IV, 458.

86. See *SC*, I, 204-206 and notes. The disappearance in this century of Coleridge's copy of Schlegel's *Vorlesungen*, containing his own unpublished marginalia, is another example of the bad luck that dogs certain aspects of Coleridge studies. See *CL*, III, 359, n. 1.

87. The parallel passages are given, with some slight modification, as printed by Orsini, in his admirable article, "Coleridge and Schlegel reconsidered," *Comparative Literature, XVI* (1964), 101-102. Professor Orsini observes:

> The reader can see for himself that Coleridge was following Schlegel step by step, sentence by sentence, and finally word for word. The all-important definition of organic form in the last paragraph is a faithful translation from Schlegel, with the alteration of only one word of the original; "soft mass" (*weichen Masse*) in Schlegel is replaced by "mass of wet clay." No doubt the change from the abstract to the concrete is a stylistic improvement. But, if the argument for Coleridge's independence from Schlegel is to rest upon this single and unimportant word, it rests on thin ground indeed. Can it honestly be doubted that Coleridge here had Schlegel's text in front of him and made a translation of it?

88. *SC*, I, 198, n. 2. In the Preface to his edition of the Shakespeare material, HNC had written:

> In many of the books and papers, which have been used in the compilation of these volumes, passages from other writers, noted down by Mr. Coleridge as in some way remarkable, were mixed up with his own comments on such passages, or with his reflections on other subjects, in a manner very embarrassing to the eye of a third person undertaking to select the original matter, after the lapse of several years. The Editor need not say that he has not knowingly admitted any thing that was not genuine. (Shedd, IV, x)

How is this deliberate omission to be explained, if not on the ground that HNC must have felt keenly the necessity to protect his father-in-law's reputation from the charge of gross insincerity in denying in so many detailed statements any intellectual obligations at all to Schlegel?

89. Raysor's footnote at page 131 of volume two of the *Shakespearean Criticism* is misleading. Coleridge had once again used the formula, putting forward the idea as his own. Raysor comments: "In making this important distinction between mechanic and organic regularity, Coleridge acknowledged his indebtedness to Schlegel," and we are invited to look at the earlier page. But Coleridge had not acknowledged indebtedness to *Schlegel*. He had referred vaguely to "a Continental critic," without even specifying nationality.

90. *CBG*, pp. 52-53.   91. *SC*, I, 197, n.2.

92. In *Criticism: The Foundations of Modern Literary Judgment*, eds. Mark Schorer et al. (New York, 1958, rev. ed.) the passage is quoted as a "useful supplement to Coleridge's remarks about Shakespeare" (p. 256*n*). No reference is made to Schlegel. The same is true of *Criticism: The Major Texts*, ed. W.J. Bate (New York, 1952), p. 392. Both these are widely used college texts. Walter Pater quotes the passage without mentioning Schlegel (*Appreciations* [London, 1915], p. 80). Gordon McKenzie in his *Organic Unity in Coleridge*, University of California Publications in English, Vol. VII, No. 1 (Berkeley, 1939), p. 45, analyzes the language of the distinction in detail without mention of Schlegel or translation. George Watson quotes a portion of this verbatim translation and calls it "paraphrasing" (GW, p. 33). Orsini, pp. 102 ff., provides additional examples of such neglect, omission, or distortion.

93. Apart from the range of learned reference which contributes to the sense of intellectual solidity in the Shakespearean criticism, there is the fact that Coleridge drew upon many sources other than Schlegel. In the second volume of Raysor's edition there are unacknowledged borrowings from Herder, Richter, Schiller, Kant, and the *Mishnah* (pp. 13, 202; 75, 167, 248, 254; 229, 248; 39).

94. *DL*, p. 360.

95. *BL*, I, 15. Schlegel is much more rational on the subject: "Let no man venture to lay hand on Shakespeare's works thinking to improve anything essential: he will be sure to punish himself" (*DL*, p. 407).

96. *TT*, p. 296.   97. *SC*, I, 212-214.   98. *SC*, I, 214.

99. *Samuel Taylor Coleridge* (New York, 1884), p. 156.

100. As does Leslie Stephen in *Hours in a Library*, III, 356. Normally hard-headed, and especially about Coleridge, Stephen here simply refuses to believe that an Englishman would find it necessary to borrow from a German on a subject like Shakespeare, any more than a man could be charged with stealing "a pair of breeches from a wild Highlandman."

101. Traill, p. 157.

102. Coleridge's character analyses are undoubtedly immensely influential, but it is a mistake to suppose that this work constituted a new departure in *method*. Nichol Smith, among many others, has shown "that the method of character-studies was well established by the end of the eighteenth century." Maurice Morgann's study of Falstaff is, of course, a central document in this development. See *SC*, I, xviii-xix.

103. Traill, p. 158.   104. *DL*, p. 411.   105. *DL*, p. 373.

106. *Coleridge's Writings on Shakespeare*, ed. Terence Hawkes (New York, 1959), p. 7 Ignoring or depreciating Schlegel remains commonplace in articles dealing with Coleridge as a critic. M.M. Badawi, as a typical example, never says that anything is directly borrowed from Schlegel but rather that there was "probably" some influence, or that a particular passage "seems to be derived," when there is no need for doubt ("Coleridge's Formal Criticism of Shakespeare's Plays," *EIC*, [1960], 148-162). What Ferrier wrote of any new edition of *Biographia Literaria* back in 1840 applies equally well to editions of the Shakespearean criticism, though his admonition has been little heeded by recent editors: "we think it would be highly discreditable to the literature of the country, if any reprint . . . were allowed to go abroad, without embodying some accurate notice and admission of the very large and unacknowledged appropriations it contains from the writings of the great German" (JCF, p. 287).

107. *Coleridge's Writings on Shakespeare*, ed. Terence Hawkes, p. 21.

15.   SOME MISCELLANEOUS PROSE

1. Professor Shedd's incomplete seven-volume edition, for example, goes back to 1853-54. Sara Coleridge's three volumes of her father's scattered lectures and essays on public affairs were published in 1850. A modern edition of the latter, with much new material, has been prepared for publication by David V. Erdman.

2. The full title is *The Statesman's Manual; or, the Bible the Best Guide to Political Skill and Foresight*. Its relevance to any of the practical problems facing England in 1817 (or since) is difficult to fathom. The work occasioned a revealing outburst of anger by Sarah Wedgwood, Josiah's younger sister:

> I have been reading a pamphlet by Mr. Coleridge [she wrote on 26 February 1817], which he calls "The Statesman's Manual, a Lay Sermon." It would quite have killed us if it had come out some years ago, when we were fighting in his cause against his despisers and haters. I do think I never did read such stuff, such an affectation of the most sublime and important meaning and so much no-meaning in reality. I can't see how any human being could possibly learn anything either about their duties, or anything else, by the whole ser-

mon. The notes I like much better, but he has the vilest way of writing that ever man had; he is as insolent as his brother-lakers, takes the same high ground, no mortal can tell why, except that it pleases them to think that their proper place is on a throne, and he writes more unintelligibly, more bombastically than any of them. (*Emma Darwin, A Century of Family Letters, 1792-1896*, ed. Henrietta Litchfield [New York, 1915], I, 109-110)

3. How treacherous the record of Coleridge's own testimony is on the subject can be partly glimpsed by the following. To the radical John Thelwall he wrote in 1796, when he was not yet twenty-four years old: "The real source of inconstancy, depravity, & prostitution, is *Property*, which mixes with & poisons every thing good—& is beyond doubt the Origin of all Evil" (*CL*, I, 214. STC's underscoring). Two years earlier Southey had written to his brother Tom that he and Coleridge had "preached Pantisocracy and Aspheterism everywhere. These, Tom, are two new words, the first signifying the equal government of all, and the other the generalisation of individual property" (quoted from *Life*, p. 35). In a footnote to "Religious Musings," dropped after 1803, Coleridge wrote: "I am convinced that the Babylon of the Apocalypse does not apply to Rome exclusively; but to the union of Religion with Power and Wealth, wherever it is found" (*PW*, I, 121, n. 1). Coleridge was sufficiently revolutionary during these early years to advocate the abolition of individual property rights so as to prevent its accumulation in individual estates (*N*, 81*n*). The whole pantisocratic program was based, Coleridge said, "on the scheme of abandonment of individual property" (*PW*, II, 1137).

In a long letter of 1 October 1803 to Sir George and Lady Beaumont, Coleridge provided a retrospective account of his earlier political enthusiasms, and expressed himself, surely without displeasure to Sir George, as "sick of Democrats & Democracy" (*CL*, II, 1001). In this letter we discover that tone of religious fervor and theological hope which was to remain constant in Coleridge's writings for the rest of his life. By 1809 he could assert in *The Friend*:

From my earliest manhood, it was an axiom in politics with me, that in every country where property prevailed, property must be the grand basis of government; and that government was the best, in which the power of political influence of the individual was in proportion to his property, provided that the free circulation of property was not impeded by any positive laws or customs, nor the tendency of wealth to accumulate in abiding masses unduly encouraged. (II, 27)

Coleridge had changed his mind, which is hardly cause for comment. What is extraordinary, however, is the urgency of his refusal to grant any conflict between his early and late political opinions. Perhaps equally surprising are the gyrations performed by many of his commentators to account for apparent inconsistencies in his writings so that "no deliberate misrepresentations" may be urged (for example, John Colmer, *Coleridge: Critic of Society* [Oxford, 1959], p. 2 and following discussion). Coleridge wrote to Daniel Stuart in 1817: "There is not a single political Opinion, which I held at the age of five and twenty which I do not hold now" (*CL*, IV, 719). Why Coleridge should have thought such consistency a virtue is a separate question; that these and similar statements should still be taken seriously is absurd.

Coleridge's early letters reveal a champion of the French revolution, an enemy of Burke, Pitt, property, and in general of the established order. No one can be certain of precisely what Coleridge said in his early political lectures because most of our texts are the versions prepared for publication by Coleridge who, for prudential and other reasons, made changes. When he reprinted the 1795 Bristol address called *Conciones ad Populum* in *The Friend*, he assured readers that it was identical with its original version but for the omission of a few names. But a comparison of this text with that printed in 1795 discloses many changes, and it would be of some value to collate the versions to determine what Coleridge later wished to suppress. The essay as it now stands discloses little that could embarrass the later conservative. References to "the childish titles of aristocracy," or statements like "vice originates not in man, but in the surrounding circumstances," would hardly be found alarming in any society.

There is much reason to believe, however, that Coleridge was vastly more radical in his Bristol period than he ever cared to admit afterwards. Again, there is nothing surprising in a man's wishing to dissociate himself from earlier political views. What makes Coleridge different from many others was his adamant refusal to admit that he *ever* had been a genuine radical, although there was no personal or social danger in such an admission. One of Coleridge's early acquaintances—who signed himself "Q"—was so incensed by the account in *Biographia Literaria* of his Bristol period that he addressed a lengthy and acidulous letter on the subject to the *Monthly Magazine* (1 October 1819, pp. 203-205). "Q" states that he knew Coleridge "well" during 1794 and 1795, and takes up the confident assertion in *Biographia Literaria* that those who knew him during those years "will bear witness for me, how opposite, even then, my principles were to those of jacobism, or even democracy." "I, sir, for one," "Q" goes on, "can bear him no such witness; for, on the contrary . . . he, Southey, Lovell, and some others . . . were, both by word and writing, positively and decidedly democratic." We are then treated to an extract from a Coleridge lecture of early 1795, in which "Mr. C. talked of 'preparing the way for a revolution in this country, bloodless as Poland's, but not, like her's, to be assassinated by the foul hands of——.' This, sir, Mr. Coleridge said,—this I heard him say. So much for his not being a favourer of a revolution in 1795." Geoffrey Carnall, who takes this lecture to have been the *Conciones ad Populum*, observes that the extract will not be found in the pages of "the authorized text" (*Robert Southey and his Age: The Development of a Conservative Mind* [Oxford, 1960], pp. 29-30). The former Bristol Jacobin reminds Coleridge that far from having held "in abhorrence" the "revolutionary principles" espoused by English supporters of the French Revolution, he had in 1794 brought his *Fall of Robespierre* "down to Bristol from Cambridge almost wet from the press, which obtained some circulation and credit for him amongst the hot-headed and youthful democrats of Bristol, amongst whom, I am not, like Mr. Coleridge, ashamed to say, that I was one." Mr. Carnall notes that the *Monthly Magazine* article "closes with a threat which was unhappily never carried out. 'It is my intention, if I have leisure to commit to paper, as matter of history, not only the piquant sayings, the amusing metaphors, and other *bonae*, of several wits and politicians, who had temporary residence in Bristol in the years 1794, 5, and 6, but also many facts which these *Pantisocrats*, as they were pleased to call themselves, think are quite forgotten. . . .' " (Carnall, pp. 29-30).

Coleridge's desire to obliterate the existence of his former political views is aptly demonstrated by his various postures towards William Pitt. Cottle, who was certainly in a position to know, wrote that all of Coleridge's early lectures were anti-Pittite (*ER*, I, 20). "Fire, Famine, and Slaughter," a violent assault on Pitt, was in later years dismissed by Coleridge as a mere joke. (See *PW*, I, 237, the "Apologetic Preface," *PW*, II, 1097, and *ER*, I, 29, 202.) Clement Carlyon, whose observations on Coleridge's manner in the "Apologetic Preface" are both shrewd and just, makes several telling points relative to his hypocrisy on the whole subject of William Pitt (Carlyon, I, 71 ff.). That the young Coleridge was anti-Pittite is wholly unremarkable. Many of his early associates were; Thomas Poole called Pitt "pernicious" (*TP*, I, 132). Similarly, in Crabb Robinson's diary for 4 March 1811 we find that "Hazlitt spoke of Coleridge with the feelings of an injured man. Hazlitt had once hopes of being patronized by Sir George Beaumont. Coleridge and he were dining with him when Coleridge began a furious attack on Junius. Hazlitt grew impatient at Coleridge's cant and could not refrain from contradicting him. A warm and angry dispute arose. The next day Coleridge called on Hazlitt and said: 'I am come to show you how foolish it is for persons who respect each other to dispute warmly, for after all they will probably think the same.' Coleridge produced an interlined copy of *Junius* full of expressions of admiration, from which it appeared that Coleridge himself really agreed with Hazlitt. 'But,' added Hazlitt to me, 'Sir George Beaumont is a High Tory and was so offended with me, both for presuming to contradict and interrupt Coleridge and for being so great an admirer of Junius, that in disgust he never saw me afterwards. And I lost the expectation of gaining a patron' " (*HCR*, I, 24).

"Coleridge usually adapted his sentiments," Carl Woodring has observed, "to what he thought his correspondents would be pleased to have him write." One example of this is the "outrageous discrepancy [that] divides Coleridge's statement to William Taylor on 25 January 1800 concerning Fox and other leaders of his party, that 'more profligate and unprincipled men never disgraced an honest cause,' from his assurance to Josiah Wedgwood ten days later that

'Fox possesses all the full & overflowing eloquence of a man of clear head, clean heart, & impetuous feelings' [*CL*, I, 565, 568]" (*PPC*, p. 85).

These examples reinforce the conviction that Coleridge's own testimony as to his intellectual life must always be studied in its specific context. Taking Coleridge's statements at face value on any subject where his self-image was involved again and again leads into insoluble difficulties.

4. *Coleridge: Critic of Society*, p. 29.   5. *MP*, LVI (1959), 254-263.

6. *Ibid*, pp. 254-256.

7. *Essays on His Own Times*, ed. Sara Coleridge (London, 1850), I, 75.

8. A similar pattern may be observed in Coleridge's early review of "Bishop Horsley's Tract on Greek Metres," which appeared in the *Critical Review* for February 1797. Coleridge borrowed from the Bristol Library a copy of John Foster's *Essay on . . . Accent and Quality* on 25 October 1796 and again on 13 December. This work was then used freely—without the necessary acknowledgments—in the review of Horsley's tract, thus assisting Coleridge to that air of far-ranging learning characteristic of even his earliest performances. Charles I. Patterson, in "An Unidentified Criticism by Coleridge Related to *Christabel*," *PMLA*, LXVII (1952), 973-988; and George Whalley in "Coleridge on Classical Prosody: An Unidentified Review of 1797," *RES*, NS, II (1951), 238-247, discuss in detail the value of this review. Coleridge paraphrased one of Horsley's remarks as follows: "We indeed of this country read the Greek and Latin as we read the English, which differs in the powers of the vowels from every other language upon earth" (Whalley, p. 243, n. 3). Patterson hails this sentence as one of Coleridge's "significant utterances," and one of "three significant positions" bearing upon what is alleged to be Coleridge's theory of metrics (p. 976). Perhaps Bishop Horsley had the universal linguistic knowledge necessary for so sweeping a generalization; the twenty-five-year-old Coleridge had no such command of languages, then or later. And should a paraphrase of Horsley be termed one of Coleridge's "significant utterances"? Disputing these minute points is intended only to put some cautionary brake on the ever-accelerating attributions of encyclopedic knowledge and original thought to Coleridge.

9. Shedd, IV, 482.

10. To Raysor, "The central ideas and frequently the very words of the lecture are derived from Schelling's oration" (*MC*, p. 204). Wellek observes that although the essay "has been used by several expositors of his [Coleridge's] aesthetics as the key to his thought, [it] is with the exception of a few insertions of pious sentiments little more than a paraphrase of [Schelling]" (*RW*, II, 152). Far more characteristic of contemporary views, however, is that of R. L. Brett, who notes that Sara Coleridge pointed out "the resemblance to Schelling. But fundamentally the notion advanced here is one which Coleridge had entertained from very early years" (*Reason and Imagination*: *A Study of Form and Meaning in Four Poems* [Oxford, 1960], p. 84). One wonders whether those who argue in this way can ever have compared the two essays line by line. When whole paragraphs are straightforward or free translation, can one properly speak merely of "resemblance"?

11. CBG, pp. 54-55. The reader should consult Beach's unusually blunt reply in these and the two previous pages to A. C. Dunstan's attempt to minimize the debt to Schelling in favor of a remoter one by both Coleridge and Schelling to Schiller ("The German Influence on Coleridge," *MLR*, XVII [1922], 272-281).

12. *BL*, II, 258; "Concerning the Relation of the Plastic Arts to Nature," trans. Michael Bullock, in Herbert Read's *The True Voice of Feeling* (New York, 1953), pp. 331-332. The availability of Bullock's translation at long last makes it possible for students unable to read Schelling's difficult German to make their own comparisons.

13. In the often reprinted and widely disseminated set of *Harvard Classics*, "On Poesy or Art" appears in the volume of *English Essays: From Sidney to Macaulay*; no reference to Schelling is provided. An example of a recent reprinting of "On Poesy or Art" which ignores mention of the source in Schelling is the collection of Coleridge's poetry and prose edited by Carlos Baker for Bantam Books.

14. See W. K. Pfeiler, "Coleridge and Schelling's Treatise on the Samothracian Deities," *MLN*, LII (1937), 162-165. In Schelling, research—in this case anthropological—all too often leads to hypothesis scarcely distinguishable from fantasy. A statement such as, "The modern world has behind it a vanished world of the most magnificent scientific and artistic achievements," is in itself unexceptional, though one would wish particulars before assenting. Schelling's vanished world, however, proves to be *pre-historic*. In setting forth this conviction, Schelling again reveals his contempt for empirical processes: "This is not the place to prove in detail that all sciences and arts of the present generation of man have been bequeathed to us," he writes in his *On University Studies* (p. 18), as if he could prove this incredible assertion elsewhere.

15. *SC*, I, 150-151. Raysor adds, somewhat dubiously, "it was, of course, legitimate for Coleridge to draw from various sources for his oral lectures, and careful acknowledgments of his sources, although desirable, would by no means be considered necessary to escape the charge of plagiarism." This seems to beg the essential question, and the word "careful" is wholly inappropriate in this context.

16. Shedd, IV, 459.   17. *MC*, p. 12, nn. 1 and 2; *SC*, I, 196-198 and Raysor's notes.

18. *MC*, pp. 148-150 and notes. A. C. Dunstan was the first to point out this parallel in "The German Influence on Coleridge," pp. 274-275. The key passage from Schiller can be found in his *Essays* (Bohn translation), pp. 282-284. Though Dunstan unfortunately depreciates the influence of Schelling to insist upon a major one from Schiller, it is nevertheless true that the relevance of Schiller's work to Coleridge, and especially the essay "On Naive and Sentimental Poetry," has been insufficiently stressed. That Coleridge actually had some of the latter essay by heart is proved by a notebook entry of 1803. See *N*, 1705 [i] and editor's note.

19. *CL*, IV, 793.

20. "So says Jean Paul Richter." Henry Nelson Coleridge expunged this reference when printing the lecture notes, most unwisely, to be sure, but demonstrating in the most unequivocal way his anxious concern to defend his uncle's reputation against the charge of excessive and improper use of German materials. See *MC*, pp. 117-120 and notes.

21. WJB, p. 364, n. 1.   22. *CL*, III, 520. STC's emphasis.

23. Shawcross (*BL*, II, 308) lists numerous logical blunders in these essays, self-contradictory definitions, and the use of words in a manner so strange that it can only be concluded that Coleridge was searching for English equivalents to Kant's thorny terminology. This discussion should be augmented by that in *KE*, pp. 111-112.

24. *BL*, II, 222. In arguing that all previous aestheticians had fallen back upon the law of association, Coleridge simply ignored "Hutcheson, Shaftesbury, Burke, and Hogarth, none of whom adopted the theory of association" (Shawcross, II, 306). But of course, neither Coleridge nor anyone else, not even the most rapacious of library cormorants, had "perused all the works on the Fine Arts known to him," let alone "carefully." It was the sort of phrase Coleridge easily slid into, and afterwards his commentators. Whatever Coleridge's abstract interest in the fine arts, his mundane attachment to them seems to have been small. Like most of those in his immediate circle, he knew next to nothing of music, despite some large generalizations on the subject. His notebooks and conversations—for a poet and aesthetician—are surprisingly thin in reference to particular paintings or sculptures, and he displayed a singular lack of interest in architecture throughout his life.

25. *BL*, II, 241 and n., 229, 230, 246.   26. *BL* I, xlix.   27. Shedd, II, 420.

28. Beach, p. 321.

29. Beach, p. 322. Beach has here provided a clue which, I think, can help clear up a long-standing puzzle. In 1825 Coleridge wrote to his nephew John Taylor Coleridge: "And Immanuel Kant I assuredly do value most highly; not, however, as a metaphysician, but as a logician who has completed and systematized what Lord Bacon had boldly designed and loosely sketched out in the Miscellany of Aphorisms, his Novum Organum" (*Letters*, II, 735). Wellek notes that

"this rather curious idea of Bacon as a forerunner of Kant recurs again and again in Coleridge" (*KE*, p. 74). I suggest that Coleridge extrapolated this proposition from the reference to Bacon in Kant's preface.

30. Beach, p. 599, n. 21. 31. Shedd, II, 425. 32. *PL*, p. 19.

33. *PL*, p. 19.

34. Shedd, II, 143; J. H. Muirhead, "Metaphysician or Mystic?" in *SSH*, p. 194.

35. Thus Professor Wellek criticizes J. H. Muirhead for denying, in *Coleridge as Philosopher* (London, 1930), the overriding influence in *The Friend* of Kant's teaching: "Kantian thought is determining the essentials of Coleridge's theoretical doctrines and coloring even the minutest tags of his terminology" (*KE*, p. 102).

This seems an appropriate point at which to cite an unpublished doctoral dissertation by Hardin McD. Goodman, *The German Influence on S. T. Coleridge* (University of Florida), the most extensive study of Coleridge's relations with Germany I know of. It has been highly praised by the distinguished scholar Richard Harter Fogle in the foreword of his book *The Idea of Coleridge's Criticism* (p. x). Goodman's conclusion, namely, that Coleridge owed nothing worth mentioning to any German, permits Fogle to ignore Coleridge's relations with Germany and to treat passages of translation as if that fact made not the slightest difference in interpreting Coleridge's ideas. "What Coleridge took," writes Fogle complacently, "we may well think, was in the public domain" (p. xi).

The extraordinary nature of Dr. Goodman's dissertation is only partially indicated in the following summary of some of his more important assertions: "Coleridge generously gave Kant credit for almost all that is in his works that may be paralleled in those of Kant" (p. 78); Coleridge's debt to Kant was small, as he had earlier formed the main points of his philosophy from reading the Cambridge Platonists (pp. 67, 80); Arthur Lovejoy's contention that Coleridge "learned from Kant and Jacobi" with respect to the distinction between reason and understanding is challenged because Goodman objects to the expression "learned from" (p. 94); as to alleged borrowings in *Theory of Life*, Coleridge had earlier formed these conceptions—in any case, "every use of Schellingian thought or term has been carefully and explicitly acknowledged" (p. 141); the "direct influence of Maass, then, may be termed almost negligible" (p. 162); no debt to Goethe (p. 325); Coleridge's "So says Jean Paul Richter" permits Dr. Goodman to conclude that the material in the lecture on "Wit and Humor" is "explicitly and generously acknowledged" (p. 372); STC is independent of the influence of Schiller's essay on "Naive and Sentimental Poetry" (p. 443); Coleridge owed nothing to the Schlegels (p. 475); Coleridge's indebtedness to Brun's poem "at first glance apparently great, is in the final analysis of the very slightest degree" (p. 550); and finally, "His critical doctrines themselves owe nothing to German thought" (p. 643).

Since detailed reasons for holding contrary views have already been provided, it seems neither necessary nor wise to dispute these (or a multitude of other) conclusions.

36. Surprisingly, a lengthy and substantive borrowing from an English source, identified only in recent years, proves to be from a contemporary work—the once-notorious *An Enquiry Concerning Political Justice*, by Coleridge's old friend William Godwin. See Lucyle Werkmeister, "Coleridge and Godwin on the Communication of Truth," *MP*, LV (1958), 170-177. Mrs. Werkmeister points out that the essay was "rewritten and considerably augmented for the third (1818) edition" (p. 170, n. 1).

37. Shedd, II, 126 (coincidentally, the same volume and page number as Coleridge's reference) unaccountably omits the note after "Eisenach," which can be found in the Bohn edition of the *Friend*, p. 82.

38. "Die Geschichte der Maria Eleonora Schöning und die Charakteristik Luthers in Coleridges *Friend*," *Englische Studien*, XLVII (Leipzig, 1913-14), 219-225. Hereafter cited as Eimer.

39. Shedd, II, 129.   40. Eimer, p. 224.   41. Shedd, II, 311-312.

42. See, for example, the passages cited by Eimer, pp. 221-223. Anyone reading Eleonora's tale without knowledge of Hess could only be astonished at the retentiveness and particularity of Coleridge's memory. Of course, this is precisely one of the effects he wished to achieve. Lowes is far too confident when he writes thus sweepingly of Coleridge, "We have to do, in a word, with one of the most extraordinary memories of which there is record" (*RX*, p. 43).

43. *CL*, II, 814. Wordsworth had earlier, in "Guilt and Sorrow" (Stanza XII), written of the bustard's "thick, unwieldly flight."

44. The foregoing review deals only with some of the more relevant borrowings in *The Friend*. As the long-awaited new edition of this work, edited by Barbara Rooke, will soon be available, no purpose would be served in providing here a bibliography of source studies. Of particular interest, however, is Dudley Bailey's "Coleridge's Revision of *The Friend*," *MP*, LIX (1961), 89-99. Bailey argues convincingly that between the versions of 1809 and 1818 there is little evidence of change in Coleridge's opinions.

16. COLERIDGE AS CRITIC AND AESTHETICIAN

1. *CL*, I, 277. STC's emphasis.

2. *CL*, I, 320-321. STC's emphasis. It seems not to have been noticed that the last paragraph just quoted (dated by Griggs as early April 1797) was used in the verse epistle "To the Rev. George Coleridge," which Coleridge specifically dated as 26 May 1797:

> . . . not unhearing
> Of that divine and nightly-whispering Voice,
> Which from my childhood to maturer years
> Spake to me of predestinated wreaths,
> Bright with no fading colours! (*PW*, I, 174)

Coleridge surely intended the voice to be "*nightly*-whispering," and if the "*rightly*-whispering" of the letter to Cottle is not a printer's error in Griggs's edition, the slip is a most interesting one. (*ER*, pp. 192-193, shows "nightly-whispering.")

Coleridge was usually extremely guarded about praising his intellectual gifts, or expressing grandiose aspirations directly. Nevertheless, his suppressed hopes did on occasion break through. At Cambridge he wrote a "Greek Ode on Astronomy." Its concluding stanza, as translated by Robert Southey, reads:

> I may not call thee mortal then, my soul!
> Immortal longings lift thee to the skies:
> Love of thy native home inflames thee now,
> With pious madness wise.
> Know then thyself! expand thy wings divine!
> Soon mingled with thy fathers thou shalt shine
> A star amid the starry throng,
> A God the Gods among.

The Ode may be found conveniently in Beer, p. 175.

3. *CL*, II, 706. STC's emphasis.   4. *CL*, II, 671.   5. *N*, 886n.

6. *Boswell's Life of Johnson*, ed. G. B. Hill, revised by L. F. Powell (Oxford, 1934), IV, 189.

7. *UL*, II, 392.   8. *CL*, IV, 925.   9. Page 149.

10. *BL*, I, 202. Italics in text.

11. *RX*, p. 103; M. H. Abrams, *The Mirror and the Lamp* (Oxford, 1953), pp. 161-162, 168-169, 175-176; F. L. Lucas, *The Decline and Fall of the Romantic Ideal* (Cambridge, England, 1963), pp. 157-180; I. A. Richards, *Coleridge on Imagination* (London, 1950), pp. 31-43.

12. Wordsworth, normally sensible in matters of this sort, actually organized his collected works under headings which included "Poems of the Fancy" and "Poems of the Imagination," besides several other categories. It is baffling to find "To a Sky-Lark" ("Up with me! up with me into the clouds!") listed under "Poems of the Fancy," but "To a Sky-Lark" ("Ethereal minstrel! pilgrim of the sky!") as one of the "Poems of the Imagination."

13. *CL*, II, 865-866. STC's underscoring. Coleridge may have meant to confine his strictures to Greek *religious* poetry, a reading which the text readily supports, but the dismissal of it all as "at best fancy" is in any case not helpful. See also Piper, pp. 140-141.

14. See Piper, pp. 126-127, 129; John Bullitt and W. J. Bate, "Distinctions Between Imagination and Fancy in 18th-Century English Criticism," *MLN*, LX (1945), 8-15; and Earl Wasserman, "Another 18th-Century Distinction Between Fancy and Imagination," *MLN*, LXIV (1949), 23-25, where will be found the work of Arthur Browne, discussed in the text.

So commonplace was a general distinction between Imagination and Fancy that a reviewer of *Lyrical Ballads* referred to one class of poems as deriving from the "power of imagination," as in "Ruth," but "The Fragment of the Danish Boy" "is a mere creation of fancy" (quoted from *Lyrical Ballads*, eds. R. L. Brett and A. R. Jones [London, 1963], pp. 323-324).

15. Browne reviews earlier discussions of the subject, argues that Ben Jonson's definitions of Fancy and Imagination are inadequate, and states that he is going to investigate "whether there are not two distinct powers in the human mind called Fancy and Imagination" (I, 16, 20). In reading Coleridge, one would hardly think that many others had indulged in similar reflections; for example: "Repeated meditations led me first to suspect . . . that fancy and imagination were two distinct and widely different faculties" (*BL*, I, 60).

16. I, 21-22. Italics in text.   17. *Decline and Fall*, p. 163, n. 3.

18. The latter part of the definition may suggest that the organization of sense data into coherent mental impressions is an imaginative act. But this is not followed up, nor does it seem useful, in any sense, to characterize the sensation, say, of pain as an act of *imagination*.

19. Kant, p. 61. Wellek finds the distinction between the primary and secondary imaginations in both Schelling and Schlegel (RW, II, 46-47, and 391, n. 38).

20. *BL*, II, 12. Italics in text.   21. Pages 40 ff.

22. London, 1934; 2nd ed. 1950, pp. xv, 184.

23. V, 100 ff.   24. No. 419.

25. Shedd, II, 286.

26. *Werke*, VI, 540 f. Quoted from *US*, p. 154, note for p. 12.   27. *BL*, I, 14.

28. *STI*, pp. 374-375. See also Schelling's related statement that the "contradiction" between conscious and unconscious activity in "aesthetic production . . . sets into motion *the whole man with all his powers*" (p. 365).

Schiller is also in the general background. In the 18th of his *Aesthetic Letters*, he said that material things do not involve the "whole personality," and elsewhere that "Poetry acts on the whole of human nature." Now any of these statements makes more sense than Coleridge's. Bernard Bosanquet notes that the passage from Schelling just quoted in the text is "plainly a reminiscence of Schiller's Aesth, Br., 27 near the end on art as addressing the *whole* man" (*A History of Aesthetic* [New York, 1957], p. 319). Bosanquet did not observe the relation to Coleridge. It may also be noted here that the passage beginning "The poet, described in ideal perfection" is reminiscent of the opening words of a very important and loosely related passage in Schiller (to be dealt with later): "Man conceived in his perfection . . ." (*Aesthetic Letters*, No. 11).

29. *Wordsworth: A Re-Interpretation* (London, 1956), p. 15. Later critics have been unable to locate this principle in Wordsworth either.

30. *STI*, pp. 364, 365, 365-366, 369. Italics in text.

31. The ordinary reader confronted with such ideas in Schelling's writings would quickly suspect that the terms have special meaning, for they make no sense to the uninitiated. "Genius is differentiated from everything that is mere talent or skill by the fact that it resolves a contradiction which is absolute and resolvable by nothing else." An honest man opening a volume of Schelling to such a sentence would either throw down the book or begin to look toward the beginning for definitions. If he read on he would encounter only more obscurity: "In all production, even in the most ordinary everyday variety, an unconscious activity works together with conscious activity; but only a production whose condition was an infinite opposition of both activities is aesthetic and is possible *only* through genius" (*STI*, p. 371. Italics in text). No one untrained in philosophy would dream of accepting the statement following the semi-colon. In Schelling's *On University Studies* one finds more oracular declarations on the subject: "Every genuine work of art, created by the imagination, is a unity of the same opposites as those unified in the Ideas" (p. 62). Shawcross (*BL*, II, 278) notes that the idea of the reconciliation of opposites in art can be found in Schiller's *Aesthetic Letters* (No. 14). I find the concept all through Schiller. In the 18th letter, for example, Schiller writes: "Beauty, it is said, links together two conditions which are *opposed to each other.* . . . It is from this opposition that we must start." Gordon McKenzie makes the point that the reconciliation of *discordant* qualities offends against the principle of organic unity (*Organic Unity in Coleridge*, in University of California Publications in English. VII [Berkeley, 1939], p. 105). This objection is a pointed one from a strictly logical point of view. But it ought to be clear that Coleridge was not thinking of defending the phrase against subsequent logicans, but was using a kind of poetic shorthand.

32. *BL*, II, 10. Italics in text.

33. M. H. Abrams has observed that "by defining a poem as a means to an 'object', 'purpose', or 'end' (terms which he employs as synonyms), Coleridge, quite in the tradition of neoclassic criticism, establishes the making of poems to be a deliberate art, rather than the spontaneous overflow of feeling" (*The Mirror and the Lamp*, p. 117). Wordsworth, however, said that poetry "takes its *origin* from emotion recollected in tranquillity," and he always insisted that the making of poetry was a deliberate art. Coleridge, on the contrary, is a mass of confusion on this subject. In the present passage he is certainly neo-classic; elsewhere he makes large claims for the unconscious. This confusion is surely a by-product of his eclecticism.

34. Kant, p. 42.   35. *DL*, p. 416.

36. M. H. Abrams, in an introduction to a collection of critical articles dealing with Milton's *Lycidas*, writes of the wide variety of approaches to Milton's poem: "With equal finality they [the critical articles] refute the opinion . . . that a literary work contains within itself everything needed for its interpretation and will yield its full and unequivocal meaning to any reader who will approach it with a lively sensibility, unimpeded by critical prepossessions or by historical knowledge of poetic kinds and conventions" (*Milton's Lycidas*, ed. C. A. Patrides [New York, 1961], p. iv). Except for the immense prestige of Coleridge (who is not mentioned), it is unthinkable that this opinion could ever have taken hold.

37. *WPW*, II, 403. Italics in text. Coleridge borrows Wordsworth's language almost exactly in disposing of Johnson's quatrain: "To such specimens it would indeed be a fair and full reply, that these lines are not bad, because they are unpoetic; but because they are empty of all sense and feeling." But all he can oppose to Wordsworth's argument about "Babes in the Wood" is the patronizing statement that we enjoy it because "we all willingly throw ourselves back for a while into the feelings of our childhood," but that it certainly does not satisfy our mature judgment (*BL*, II, 60). Elsewhere, however, Coleridge will celebrate the preservation of the feelings of childhood into adult life (again following the Germans) as the unique gift of creative genius—another example of his loose eclecticism.

38. So great is the force of tradition and prestige that Aristotle's definition continues to be broadly applied when (1) it is not at all certain whether the emotions to be purged were pity and terror or something allied, and (2) what precisely was meant by "purged."

39. *N*, 218*n*, Italics in text.

40. *CT*, p. 324. Another example of extreme critical overevaluation in Coleridge is his acclaim of Thomas Burnet's *Telluris Theoria Sacra* as "poetry of the highest kind" (*BL*, II, 11).

41. Shedd, II, 131.

42. In later years Coleridge referred to Charles Matthews, the comedian, as "the comic poet acting his own poems" (Gillman, p. 72). This idea is obviously related to the description of Luther which, as we have seen, was an unacknowledged borrowing.

43. *BL*, II, 8. STC's emphasis.

44. James A. Greig, *Francis Jeffrey of the Edinburgh Review* (Edinburgh and London, 1948), p. 182.

45. *BL*, II, 13.

46. *BL*, II, 30. Coleridge considerably distorts, no doubt unintentionally in most cases, one after another of Wordsworth's points, so that he is in effect continually knocking down straw men. Shawcross' notes draw attention to several instances. Yet even where Coleridge seems to score a direct hit, as when he disagrees with Wordsworth's "assertion, that from the objects with which the rustic hourly communicates the best part of language is formed" (*BL*, II, 39), he makes no attempt to understand what Wordsworth was struggling to express. And of course Coleridge was right to say that rustics have no special virtue (on the contrary!), but it was a petty and misleading point to make in the actual historical situation.

47. *BL*, II, 28, 39-40. Coleridge reinforces this incredible statement in his handling of Wordsworth's analysis of artificial and natural diction in a Gray sonnet. After denying that Wordsworth has in fact demonstrated anything, he goes on to say: "But were it otherwise, what would this analysis prove, but a truth, of which no man ever doubted? Videlicet, that there are sentences, which would be equally in their place both in verse and prose" (*BL*, II, 57).

48. *BL*, II, 53.   49. *BL*, II, 33-34. Italics in text.

50. *BL*, II, 38-39. Coleridge carries these rigid convictions into Chapter XXII, where "nothing, but biography, can justify" the use of local and transient detail:

> If it be admissible even in a *Novel*, it must be one in the manner of De Foe's, that were meant to pass for histories, not in the manner of Fielding's. . . . Much less then can it be legitimately introduced in a *poem*, the characters of which, amid the strongest individualization, must still remain representative. The precepts of Horace, on this point, are grounded on the nature both of poetry and of the human mind. (*BL*, II, 106-107. Italics in text.)

It is wearisome to be told again and again that what is only opinion is *grounded* in the "nature of the human mind." And it is dismal to find Coleridge completely failing to grasp the *psychological power* of the concrete fact (he leaned upon an *oaken* staff).

51. Greig, p. 180. (See n. 44 above.)   52. Greig, p. 182.   53. *BL*, II, 107-108.

54. Greig, p. 221.   55. MM, I, 387.   56. *BL*, 37-38.

57. Quoted by permission of the Librarian of New York University.

58. *BL*, II, 97.   59. *BL*, II, 115, 118, 121, 122, 124.

60. *BL*, II, 97, 101, 109. Italics in text.

61. *HW*, XI, 87-89. Italics in text.

62. *STI*, p. 355. Italics in text.

63. George Whalley, "Coleridge Unlabyrinthed," *UTQ*, XXXII (1963), 340.

64. Bate, pp. 149-150. Italics in text.   65. *BL*, II, 258.

66. "Concerning the Relation of the Plastic Arts to Nature," trans. Michael Bullock, in Herbert Read's *The True Voice of Feeling* (New York, 1953), pp. 331-332.

67. But this exaggeration is to be found in Goethe, Schiller, Carlyle, and many others. It is

self-contradictory, mere enthusiasm, for elsewhere in these writers the judgment is seen as equal to genius.

68.   The unconscious is a central concept in Schelling's *System of Transcendental Idealism* (1800). I believe, however, that Schelling's unconscious is very much less a forerunner of Freud's than generally supposed. The *idea* of an unconscious, of course, had a long previous history, and little purpose would be served in trying to trace it here. Except for its use as a technical term in philosophy, the basic meaning of unconscious to the Romantic critics was simply—for all the elaborate terminology—*mental activity of which the thinker was unaware*. An immense gulf exists between this and Freud, who provides a theory as to *why* there is an unconscious at all, and elaborated the concepts of repression, censorship, ego, id, superego, and so forth. Nothing is easier than to quote passages from Schelling which *sound* as if a modern unconscious were spoken about. But this is quite misleading. When in the *Transcendental Idealism* he writes that "conscious and unconscious activity are to be absolutely one in the product, just as they are to be one in a different way—both are to be one *for the ego itself*" (STI, p, 363. Italics in text), the reader will suspect that he is in the presence of the technical jargon of transcendental philosophy and not of an unconscious essentially *psychological* in nature. With the following passage, there is no doubt: "this unknown, which here brings objective and conscious activity into unexpected harmony, is none other than that Absolute which contains the universal ground of the pre-established harmony between the conscious and the unconscious" (*STI*, p. 364). If only there were a "pre-established harmony between the conscious and the unconscious," how much emotional grief would be absent from the world! But we are not here in a world of psychological speculation, but of philosophical system-building.

69.   Shedd, I, 437-438. From *The Statesman's Manual*, Appendix B.

70.   "Coleridge's Critical Theory of the Symbol," *TSLL*, VIII (1966), 25. The Schlegel passage may be found in *DL*, p. 88.

71.   *The World's Great Classics* (New York, 1900), p. 265.

72.   *CSC*, p. 131.   73.   *Ollier's Literary Miscellany* (London, 1820), pp. 11-12.

74.   See JAA, pp. 81, n. 44; 101, 112. Also *CL*, I, 625-626.

75.   Quoted from WJB, p. 241.   76.   Kant, p. 33.

77.   Pages 146,148. The reader is surely inclined to consider Dostoevsky, Baudelaire, Joyce, and Kafka as great and very independent artists. But simple and serene? These terms in Schelling come not from any examination of the actual facts of artists' lives (or works), but from the supposed ultimate reality of nature, of which the great artist must be an analog in his creative power. But who, in this age of billions of solar systems and exploding stars, is still likely to describe nature as either serene or simple?

78.   Ennead V. In *Philosophies of Art and Beauty*, eds. Albert Hofstadter and Richard Kuhns (New York, 1964), p. 151.

79.   *CL*, III, 360.   80.   RW, II, 73.   81.   *DL*, pp. 342-343.

82.   *DL*, pp. 353, 355, 358, 359, 368-369.   83.   *BL*, II, 16.   84.   *BL*, II, 19.

85.   *DL*, p. 18.   86.   *BL*, I, 59.   87.   *SC*, II, 112.   88.   *BL*, II, 14.

89.   *DL*, p. 362.

90.   *DL*, p. 375. Schlegel may appear even in such an unlikely place as the Preface to "Christabel." Coleridge wrote: "occasional variation in number of syllables (per line) is not introduced wantonly, or for the mere ends of convenience, but in correspondence with some transition in the nature of the imagery or passion" (*PW*, I, 215). Cf. Schlegel: "Even the irregularities of Shakespeare's versification are expressive; a verse broken off, or a sudden change of rhythmus, coincides with some pause in the progress of the thought, or the entrance of another mental disposition" (*DL*, p. 376). The sublety and precision of artistic intent and control implied by Coleridge's statement is the very bread and water of much modern literary criticism. The tendency is found even in Humphry House, one of the sanest and most intelligent of those who have written on Coleridge. An otherwise brilliant discussion of "Frost at Midnight" is disfigured by the

sort of oversubtle analysis so favored by Coleridge; for example: "the descriptive passages are more intricately and closely knit to their psychological effects; the description is more minute, delicate and various *in correspondence with the more minute and various states of mind on which it bears*" (HH, p. 73).

91. "This is so." Professor Wilkinson continues, "for instance, in the case of his dramatic fragment, *The Triumph of Loyalty*. The names and the setting point to Spain, but the draft of it we find in his *Notebooks* is modelled on the excerpts he made from the section on Spanish drama in Lessing's *Hamburgische Dramaturgie* (869 and 871).

"All this is not to reflect on Coleridge's originality. . . . There is an originality of taking as well as of making" (*N*, 1, Appendixes, pp. 453-454).

92. RW, II, 156-157. 93. RW, II, 156.

94. *PQ*, XXXVI (1957), 107. Although Raysor agrees that Coleridge's "eclecticism never attains a real synthesis, as Wellek says . . . it is more than random, I think, and includes at times many of the most profound insights in European criticism," which remain unstated. It is true this is a short review, but these insights, so far as I know, have not been demonstrated elsewhere. Raysor does not deny Coleridge's debts to Schlegel, Herder, etc., but he finds the Germans "obviously inferior" to Coleridge "in the intuitive perceptions of taste and the clarity and delicacy of style which the great critic must have in some degree." To attempt to meet such arguments is to enter upon quite a different subject.

95. *BL*, I, 4. 96. *Idea of Coleridge's Criticism*, p. ix. 97. *CL*, II, 864.

98. Coleridge's widely quoted remark, "Poetry, like schoolboys, by too frequent & severe corrections, may be cowed into Dullness!" is a paraphrase of Young's "A poem, like a criminal, under too severe corrections, may lose all its spirit, and expire." I find it most suggestive that Coleridge should take jottings from works probably right before his eyes in such a form. See *N*, 33, 34, 35, 36. Miss Coburn's assumption, in the note to entry 34, that Coleridge was jotting down a sentence from Young from memory need not necessarily be true. Barbara Hardy has noted the similarity between entry 36, based on Young, and a famous passage from *BL*, II, 13 ("The Natural Man," *EIC*, IX [1959], 314).

99. *Organic Unity in Coleridge*, p. 74. 100. Page 120.

101. *Coleridge on Imagination*, pp. 1, 2, 5-6.

102. *CL*, II, 676, 679. STC's emphasis. 103. *CL*, II, 679-680, 683.

104. *CL*, II, 686, 700-701. STC's underscoring. 105. *CL*, II, 702, 703, 701.

17. THE YEARS OF APPRENTICESHIP

1. *Rasselas*, Ch. xxx.

2. George McLean Harper has performed this task with his characteristic sensitivity for poetic values in "Gems of Purest Ray," in *SSH*, pp. 133-147. In 1934 Harper could begin an essay on Coleridge with the statement that "only three of Coleridge's poems are widely known."

3. *BL*, I, 8 ff.

4. "Wordsworth Sources: Bowles and Keate," *The Athenaeum*, London, 22 April 1905, pp. 498-499. Reprinted in *Late Harvest* (Ithaca, N. Y., 1952), pp. 42-46. The above quotation is taken from the latter, p. 42.

5. *Life*, p. 17. 6. *CL*, I, 287, 259. 7. *Poems*, p. 542. 8. *Life*, p. 18.

9. *A Wiltshire Parson and his Friends* (Boston and New York, 1926), p. 20. Coleridge probably used not the first edition of Bowles's poems, which was privately printed, but the second, published at Bath in 1789, which contained the 21 sonnets he later wrote of so often. Greever refers to Bowles's poems by the titles given in the final collected edition. In all Bowles's editions, from the second through the eighth (1802), "The Bells, Ostend" was titled "Sonnet XIII: Written at Ostend, July 22, 1787." Bowles's many revisions in his numerous editions

create, as we shall see, vexing difficulties. P. M. Zall has most usefully reprinted the 21 sonnets of Bowles's second edition together with Coleridge's "Sonnets from Various Authors" (Glendale, Calif., 1968). The standard edition of Bowles's *Poetical Works* was edited by George Gilfillan, 2 vols. (Edinburgh, 1855).

10. *LL*, I, 18.

11. Thus in all editions from the second (1789) to the eighth (1802). Bowles later changed "wan" to "pale."

12. *PW*, I, 17, *app. crit.* In 1796 Bowles published his *Elegiac Stanzas Written During Sickness at Bath, December 1795.*

13. *PW*, II, 1124.

14. *Poems*, p. 474. Campbell erroneously gives the title as "Monody On Henry Headley."

15. Thus in all Bowles's editions from 1794 to 1802. In Gilfillan the punctuation is very different.

16. While at college Coleridge wrote to his brother George: "An Epitaph for Howard's tomb on the Banks of the Dneiper. N. B. I have got great credit by this." Griggs notes that Coleridge's Greek epitaph "was probably prompted by Bowles's poem, *The Grave of Howard.*" As the attitude taken towards Howard and the details of the epitaph were all available in Bowles's poem, this seems probable indeed (*CL*, I, 35 and n. 1).

17. "Coleridge's 'Anthem': Another Debt to Bowles," *JEGP*, LVIII (1959), 270-275. In the following discussion this article is referred to as LW. Bowles's *Verses* first appeared in a small pamphlet published at Bath in 1790. Thus EHC's conjectural date of the poem as 1789 now proves to be impossible. (See *PW*, I, 5, and LW, p. 275, n. 5.) Mrs. Werkmeister, however, seems not to have been aware that the 1790 text of Bowles's *Verses* varies considerably at some points from later versions. As I have been unable to locate a single copy of Bowles's 1790 pamphlet in the United States, there seems little point in referring the reader to it, since he would then be unable to follow up on any part of the comparisons made. I have therefore cited Mrs. Werkmeister's text of the *Verses*, which can be found in Gilfillan's edition, and have where necessary referred to the scarce 1790 pamphlet I have consulted in the British Museum. Although this decision obviously leaves room for some confusion, it seems better to permit the reader to compare Coleridge's "Anthem" with a version of Bowles's *Verses* he can consult than to refer to a text that for the overwhelming majority of readers is for all practical purposes inaccessible.

18. *CL*, I, 34.

19. Mrs. Werkmeister suggests that the poem "is not a transcription of Bowles' *Verses*, but may be fairly called an adaptation. Coleridge has made alterations, but alterations must be made if one is to convert a poem such as Bowles' *Verses* into an anthem" (LW, p. 271). In this context the meanings of the terms "transcription" and "adaptation," to this reader, are not clear. In music one may speak of a transcription, as when a piece written for the violin is rescored for the piano. Adaptation, properly so called, is the fitting of one thing to another. Yet, if a poet uses another's poem for such a purpose, without stating that he is so doing, alters and in fact so disguises the model that any debt eludes detection for one hundred fifty years, it would seem proper to speak neither of adaptation nor transcription, but of disguise.

20. LW, p. 271. In several other of Coleridge's unacknowledged borrowings he followed the same pattern. The first three lines of the "Elegy" (*PW*, I, 69) are original while the rest of the poem puts into rime a blank verse inscription by Akenside. The last five lines of "Fancy in Nubibus" are from Stolberg, and the last three stanzas of "Separation" are from Cotton's *Chlorinda* (*PW*, I, 397, n. 1).

21. LW, pp. 271-272.

22. *LW*, p. 273. Cf, Bowles, ll. 105-106, 113-114 with STC, ll. 16-20.

23. LW, p. 273.

24. Mrs. Werkmeister correctly asserts that Bowles used this idea at four points (ll. 121-122, 135, 137-140, 164-176), but this is only true of the later texts. LW, p. 274.

25. The passage is on p. 25 of the 1790 *Verses*.

26. LW, p. 275. Coleridge quoted six lines of "The Philanthropic Society" in a letter to Southey of 1794 (*CL*, I, 86), but did not mention Bowles.

27. *CL*, II, 855. On a manuscript of the poem "Melancholy," Coleridge wrote, "Bowles borrowed these lines unconsciously, I doubt not. I had repeated the poem on my first visit" (*PW*, I, 73, n. 2). Considered without regard to Coleridge's whole literary career, a note like this would certainly imply a sober concern with the niceties of unacknowledged borrowings, and the question of authorial intent.

28. R. D. Havens, *The Influence of Milton on English Poetry* (Cambridge, Mass., 1922), p. 473, cites only Coleridge's "Music," "Inside the Coach," and "To Disappointment" as under strong Allegro-Penseroso influence.

29. How a poet learns his craft is his own business. Still, it is noteworthy that Coleridge should have claimed this rough-hewn imitation of Milton as a particularly spontaneous creation. Though the poem was originally sent to George Coleridge in 1791, three years later Coleridge sent a part of it, including all the lines given above, to Southey, with the comment that they had been written when "I unwarily fell into Poetry" (*CL*, I, 85). He also conveyed the impression that the occasion of the verses had been his thinking about the capabilities of pleasure in a mind like Southey's!

30. *PW*, I, 38, n. 1.

31. "Imitated from Ossian" was reprinted in the collected editions of 1828, 1829, and 1834, but after 1803 Coleridge did not include the note giving the lines in *Ossian*. As we have seen, Coleridge's use of the word "imitated" in a title or subtitle is extremely ambiguous, so that without his provision of the note an interested reader would have had no way of knowing how much of an "imitation" this was, without carefully searching through the lengthy *Ossian*. In the case of "Imitated from the Welsh," Coleridge did not specify a source, and none has been found to this day. He sent it to Southey without any title at all as "a little Song of mine," without reference to imitation, Welsh or otherwise (*CL*, I, 137). Thus there is no way of knowing whether the poem is a paraphrase of some as yet unknown text or a completely independent composition. Since Coleridge published many poems closely based on models, tracing the development of his mind and craft is beset with special difficulties. "Imitated from Ossian" was one of the poems in the manuscript collection Coleridge presented to Mrs. Estlin around 1795. On this occasion Coleridge dropped the note and changed the title simply to "Ode," which obliterated all debts.

32. *PW*, I, 39, n. 1.

33. *Ossian's Poems* (London, 1773), II, 199. See also Lucyle Werkmeister and Paul Zall, "Coleridge's 'The Complaint of Ninathoma.' " *N & Q*, NS, XVI (1969), 412-415.

34. The last few lines of this poem, not considered above, also derive from *Ossian*, but less directly. Here again Coleridge dropped the identifying note after 1803. He sent the poem to Mary Evans in 1793 (*CL*, I, 52) several years before it was first published, and mentioned neither *Ossian* nor Macpherson. The epistolary version is a little closer to *Ossian*, substituting "dark-tressed Maid" for "dark-haired Maid" instead of the "white-bosom'd Maid" of the published version.

35. *PW*, 49, ll. 23-24. "Hope" is the title of the poem as printed in Gilfillan. However, it was not among the 21 sonnets of Bowles's second edition which so impressed Coleridge. It seems to appear for the first time in the third edition (1791) with the title "Sonnet XVIII," and so remains through the eighth edition. Immediately before the "matin bird" lines just quoted, Bowles had used the rime "his weary *frame* / thy holy *flame*" (ll. 17-18). In the famous opening stanza of Coleridge's "Love" is the rime "this mortal *frame* / his sacred *flame*." Was there a connection? "Love" was printed in 1799. Sometime after his eighth edition (1802), Bowles

changed his "holy flame" to a "sacred flame." Had he seen Coleridge's poem and thought the younger poet's modification an improvement?

36. Quoted from Bowles's third edition (Bath, 1794).

37. *PW*, I, 71-72.

38. It seems curious (and perhaps suggestive) how often Coleridge seems to borrow from the beginning and end of books. The very first Duan in *Ossian* furnishes the commonplace image cited, but also a "floating beard," which may be added to the long list of possible sources for the "floating hair" in "Kubla Khan." In the first two printings of the "Ode to the Departing Year," the first strophe contained the lines "far onwards waving on the wind / I saw the skirts of the DEPARTING YEAR" (*PW*, I, 160, *app. crit.*) The second Duan of *Ossian* contains this image no less than three times: "from the skirt of his squally wind!"; "with squally winds in their skirts"; and, finally, "the skirts of winds." The two imitations of *Ossian* cited above both come from "Berrathon," the last episode in the work. Apart from these, the only other certain borrowing in all of the lengthy *Ossian* is the sleeping hunter image from the first paragraph of "The War of Inis-thona."

39. So in the early editions, where "The Dying Slave" is titled "The African." In later revisions "Heaven's beauteous bow" became a "radiant bow." "Recollection" may be found in *PW*, II, 1023.

40. *PW*, I, 16, 87, 85.   41. *PW*, I, 92.

42. *CL*, I, 136.   43. *PW*, I, 85, n. 2; *LL*, I, 19 (where Lamb claims it as his).

44. *PW*, I, 29, ll. 5-8. The phrase "wonder at the tale" appears at line 67 of Blair's "Grave," in a context Coleridge was to use in "The Ancient Mariner."

45. Coleridge used the notebook mainly between 1795 and 1798, but Professor Coburn shows that he used it later also (*N*, xix-xx).

46. *RX*, pp. 5, 12, 34.   47. *N*, 259*n*.

48. Miss Coburn gives Psalm 43:5 as the source: "Why art thou cast down, O my soul? and why art thou disquieted within me?" But Coleridge's consecutive phrases come from the consecutive and identical word clusters of Psalm 38:8.

49. *RX*, p. 233. 50. See *N*, 256-305 and notes.   51. *CL*, I, 289.

52. See *N*, 264-269 and notes.

53. The "cloudy seat" may derive from Milton's "cloudy Chair" in *Paradise Lost*, II, 930.

54. Miss Coburn has omitted from her note from Ecclus, 40:6 the phrase, "as if he were escaped from battle," which inadvertently makes it seem as if Coleridge had added the phrase to the verse, whereas he added only the phrase "but even now," through which he subsequently drew an X, probably because in this instance he preferred the original text.

55. *N*, 267*n*. Entry 175 consists of four brief paragraphs which come almost verbatim from Ps. 76:8-10 (*N*, 175*n*, doubtless by accident, confines the source to 76:8-9); Wisdom of Solomon 5:21; and Ecclus. 39:28, another very strange collocation of sources. The entry deals with the vengeance of God. Miss Coburn suggests that the entries were made "possibly for the *Ode to the Departing Year*, see especially stanza v." Such resemblances as may be seen, however, are not, I think, to be found in the final text but in the version published by the *Cambridge Intelligencer*, which can be found in the *apparatus criticus* of *PW*, I, 164-165.

56. *N*, 272*n*.

57. *N*, 180*n*. Although it is widely assumed that knowledge of sources and origins cannot legitimately influence evaluation of any poem considered as such, here as elsewhere knowledge of source and origin often illuminates aspects of the work not previously noticed. In Coleridge's poem, "God's image" seems to have no antecedent and thus to stand simply for itself, which makes its apposite clause, "sister of the Seraphim," somewhat odd, if not altogether jarring, since God's image would be thought of as *brother* to the Seraphim, if any connection were seen at all. In Taylor, however, the *soul* "is of an angelic substance, sister to a cherubim, an image

of the Divinity." Although Coleridge twice mentions his soul in the final stanza of the Ode, there is no connection between it and the final line which, resonant as it is, taken as a single line, is discordant in context. Knowledge of the source throws considerable light on this jaggedly sewn seam of the poem.

58. Coleridge thought it worth alleging that Sir James Mackintosh (whom he detested) had in a recently published lecture imitated Jeremy Taylor, "rather copying his semi-colon punctuation —as closely as he can" (*CSC*, p. 282). Coleridge also affirmed that Young's *Night Thoughts* could be compared with Taylor's *Holy Dying* "in all its particulars, even the rhythm" (*CT*, p. 324). Both remarks are quintessential STC. *Credat Judaeus Apella!*

59. *PW*, I, 112, n. 1; II6, n. 2.   60. *PW*, I, 168, *app. crit.*

61. In 1803 Coleridge also altered "with inward stillness, and a bow'd mind," which had come from the Psalms, to "with inward stillness, and a *submitted* mind," a change which he himself recognized as bad in a marginal note in a copy of *Sibylline Leaves (The Poems of Samuel Taylor Coleridge*, ed. Richard Garnett [London and New York, 1898], p. 293). All this suggests that Coleridge, at least generally, knew his sources perfectly well and used them quite consciously.

Into the detail of the "bowed mind" now enters Charles Lloyd, Coleridge's gifted and intensely unstable young friend. In 1796 Lloyd had published *Poems on the Death of Priscilla Farmer*. The volume contained an epigraph from Bowles and poems by both Coleridge and Lamb. In Lloyd's sixth sonnet is the line, "How She doth keep in thankful quietness / Her bowed soul. . . ."

In the Henry E. Huntington Library at San Marino, California, is Charles Lloyd's personal copy of this handsomely printed volume, and it contains numerous revisions in his own hand. Through the word "bowed" Lloyd drew a line and wrote in "patient." Was he too trying to take a step away from the Psalms, or had Coleridge's Ode in the meanwhile appeared, containing the same phrase? It is certainly odd that two friends should use the same phrase in poems published the same year, and that both should then alter it.

Another unexpected connection between Coleridge and Lloyd eddies around the conclusion of the Ode where, as we have seen, the poet is cleansed from vaporous passions and recenters his immortal mind "In the deep Sabbath of meek self-content." In Charles Lloyd's notorious *Edmund Oliver*, the novel heavily based on Coleridge's college and army experiences, the publication of which led to a crisis in the relations of Coleridge with both Lamb and Southey, we find the hero writing: "my spirit has ever been agitated with fervors unnatural and almost fatal; but *the sabbath, the quiet sabbath of a tranquil and subdued mind*, is at length come . . . ," language which combined lines 6 and 159 from the Ode. (*Edmund Oliver* was published in Bristol in 1798, by Coleridge's own publisher, Joseph Cottle. The quotation is from II, 288.)

The "Dedicatory Lines" by Charles Lloyd in the *Priscilla Farmer* volume contains the phrase "manhood's maze," which appears in "Ode to the Departing Year" as "Love illumines Manhood's maze" (l. 18). Two of Coleridge's most famous images may actually derive from these forgotten sonnets by Lloyd. In Sonnet VII there is "the lone leaf on the wintry bough," which is as good a source for "The one red leaf, the last of its clan" in "Christabel" (l. 49) as can be found outside Dorothy Wordsworth's *Journals*. Far more significantly, Lloyd's Sonnet IX contains the line "Oft did I look to Heaven, but could not pray," which powerfully suggests the Ancient Mariner's "I looked to Heaven, and tried to pray . . ." (l. 244).

62. *PW*, II, 990, No. 20; and 994, Nos. 42-45 (*N*, 179, 272 [g], [h], [l], [t], and notes). Another group of entries that has caused editorial error is the long series Coleridge copied into his notebooks in 1804, derived from William Cartwright's poems (*N*, 1914 ff. and notes). Among the "Metrical Experiments" printed by EHC from STC's notebooks (*PW*, II, 1014 ff.), No. 10, with some changes, is from Cartwright. O. Ritter identified No. 4 as actually from Sir John Beaumont's "Ode of the Blessed Trinitie," and No. 7 as the first stanza of a poem by Parnell ("Coleridigiana," *Englische Studien*, LVIII [1924], 377). Professor E. R. Wasserman identified No. 12 as a seventeenth-century song ("Coleridge's 'Metrical Experiments,' " *MLN*, LV [1940], 432-433; LXIII [1948], 491-492). Morchard Bishop has shown more particularly that No. 12 is "made up by joining two halves of different stanzas" of an anonymous poem, ca. 1650 (*The

Complete Poems of Samuel Taylor Coleridge, ed. Morchard Bishop [London, 1954], p. 632).

This seems the appropriate place to note that among the "Fragments" printed as an appendix to EHC's edition (*PW*, II, 996 ff.), No. 11 proves to be from *Paradise Lost*, IX, 309-312 (Bishop, p. 635). No. 29 ("Fragment of an Ode to Napoleon") is, according to Carl Woodring, merely transcribed from another poet; unaccountably, Woodring does not specify whom (*PPC*, p. 255, n. 15). No. 32 is adapted from *Paradise Lost*, IX, 227-228, 288-289, and has been printed by STC's editors by garbling two entries (Bishop, p. 635); No. 53 ("Napoleon") is actually from Phineas Fletcher's *The Purple Island*, Canto iii, Stanza 1 (Bishop, p. 635).

Several of the entries from Cartwright found their way into the most excellent edition of Dykes Campbell, who was more scrupulous than most later editors in excluding from the Coleridge canon works known not to be his; for example: "A few 'Epigrams' which had gained a place in Coleridge's collected works have been omitted, being found not to belong to him" (*Poems*, p. 443). In the section of Campbell's edition called "Fragments From Various Sources," it is now known that No. 64 is from Cartwright (STC added an opening line); No. 96 is also from Cartwright, and had been printed as "The Second Birth" in *PW*, I, 362. EHC noted the error (*PW*, I, iv), and the poem does not appear in the 1957 reprint.

In *Poems*, Nos. 98, 111, 113, and 118 are also from Cartwright, and in almost every instance STC has altered the orginal text. Of these Cartwright entries, one seems to appear in "Alice du Clos" (*N*, 1915n).

In the midst of the Cartwright entries Coleridge wrote, "Gray's Orient Forms from Small-wood's Verses." In STC's own Cartwright volume is a memorial poem by Matthew Smallwood in which appears the phrase "Bright orient formes live here." STC was misremembering line 120 from Gray's "The Progress of Poesy"; "With orient *hues* unborrow'd of the Sun" (*N*, 1919 n). Had Gray written "orient forms," STC might have been right in conjecturing a relationship, though "orient" was one of the eighteenth century's most commonplace poetic adjectives; but when we remember Coleridge's own silent use of Gray, and his attack on Gray in the *Biographia* for alleged borrowings from Shakespeare, it does not seem altogether unreasonable to suspect that an uneasy conscience towards Gray caused him, characteristically, to fire from the hip at the appearance of unacknowledged borrowing in others.

For more evidence of Coleridge's free adaptations of books he was reading, the culling of learned references, and other practices suggesting the purposeful gathering of materials, see *N*, 2164-67 and notes.

63.   *TT*, p. 110, n. 1. In one of his marginal notes Coleridge wrote: "In order to form a style worthy of Englishmen, Milton and Taylor must be studied instead of Johnson, Gibbon, and Junius" (*CSC*, p. 282). These opinions are strikingly similar to those recorded by Southey: "I prefer the sober stateliness of Lord Bacon and the mighty strength of Milton and Jeremy Taylor to our later writers. They cut their sentences into epigrams. Johnson's I utterly disapprove—and would have mine a well of English undefiled. . . . Gibbon's is French. . . ." (*Journals of a Residence in Portugal: 1800-1801, and a Visit to France: 1838*, ed. Adolpho Cabral [Oxford, 1960], p. 162). It is probably impossible to know who influenced whom, but it should not be taken for granted that the benefits were conferred solely in one direction.

64.   *PW*, I, 108-125.

65.   *The Influence of Milton on English Poetry* (Cambridge, Mass., 1922), p. 553, n. 2, Humphry House sees a somewhat larger passage (ll. 9-22) as "a positive pastiche from Milton" (*HH*, p. 64, n. 2).

66.   House's useful discussion of certain aspects of Milton's influence on the early Coleridge, especially in the political sonnets of December 1794 and January 1795, is unfortunately blemished by his assertion that Coleridge's "Miltonising [in the political sonnets] is not a mere matter of political echoes, such as might be found at any time through the eighteenth century; it is part of a conscious political act" (*HH*, pp. 65-66). No evidence is offered for this now fashionable approach to the problem of literary borrowings. By terming the sort of borrowings that only a scholar or fellow poet would recognize "a conscious *political* act," Coleridge's failure to achieve an independent voice is transformed into the supposed virtue of deliberate ironic

allusiveness, in the manner of Eliot and other moderns. The improbability that poetical echoes could effectively be used for political purposes (unless they were of the order of "To be or not to be") is suggested by the fact that House himself did not notice in his discussion of this small number of political sonnets that the image used in the first four lines of the sonnet to Burke (*PW*, I, 80), in which, as the poet "lay in Slumber's shadowy VALE . . . I saw the sainted form of Freedom rise," is directly based on the famous dream image in Milton's sonnet on his blindness ("Methought I saw my late espoused Saint"), a connection noted by Woodring (*PPC*, p. 95). Woodring otherwise argues that Coleridge's sonnets are "woefully indebted to Charlotte Smith and William Lisle Bowles" (p. 92), but gives no evidence apart from directing the reader to Havens' book on the influence of Milton (cited above). Coleridge's sonnets are not in themselves worth all this attention, since they are poetically of minimal value.

67. *PW*, I, 110, n. 2. Italics in text.

68. Quoted from H. N. Fairchild, *Religious Trends in English Poetry* (New York, 1949), III, 279. Coleridge's celebration of Hartley's genius in this poem is well known:

> . . . he of mortal kind
> Wisest, he first who marked the ideal tribes
> Up the fine fibres from the sentient brain. (ll. 368-370)

"The poem as a whole," in Arthur Beatty's words, "has many Hartleian features, and has several passages which have the appearance of being little more than paraphrases from this 'wisest of mortal kind,' or are written in the spirit of associationism and Hartleian optimism." Beatty cites "Lines 28-45, which show the discipline of Fear and the growth of the soul to its identity with God; lines 88-104, an account of the transmutation of the Passions to higher forms; lines 198-259, which depict the 'unsensualizing' of the mind through Imagination. Lines 395-401 are avowedly Berkeleian in proclaiming 'the final happines of all men;' but this is also Hartley." Unfortunately, Beatty does not specify precise passages in Hartley with which to compare the lines given from Coleridge. This leaves the interested reader with the forbidding task of hunting through Hartley's two weighty volumes to determine whether the more than one hundred lines in Coleridge "which have the appearance of being little more than paraphrases" are indeed that. (See Arthur Beatty, *William Wordsworth: His Doctrine and Art in their Historical Relations,* 3rd ed. [Madison, Wisc., 1960], p. 101 and n. 6).

69. *PW*, I, 119, n. 1; *RX*, p. 495, n. 31.   70. *JHI*, XX (1959), 47-59.

71. Piper, pp. 47-48. Kathleen Coburn had somewhat earlier noted that "there are some fairly close similarities of phrase in Wakefield's earlier anti-war sermons (e.g., 'The Spirit of Christianity . . .') and *Religious Musings*" (*N*, 104n).

72. *CL*, I, 201.

73. Wakefield, p. 14. Italics in text. Carl Woodring in PPC, p. 115, notes this point also, and writes: "Either Wakefield influenced Coleridge, or they shared the same mind in some other way." This supposition is perhaps ironic, in view of Coleridge's known eclecticism, and more especially insofar as Woodring himself writes: "The *Conciones* of 1795 and other early works by Coleridge parallel rather closely the expressed thought of Wakefield."

74. *PW*, I, 112, n. 1; 120, n. 1; 123, n. 2.   75. Wakefield, p. 24. Italics in text.

76. Wakefield, p. 37. Italics in text.

77. *PW*, I, 115, ll. 170-173. Iniquities perpetrated against Poland are deplored also in "Ode to the Departing Year" (*PW*, I, 162, n.2), and in Coleridge's "A Moral and Political Lecture" as published in Bristol, 1795 (p. 7). The latter reference is deleted from later editions.

78. Piper, p. 50. Piper cites *Botanic Garden,* I, i, 387-388, but I find the passage at I, ii, 407-408. Relevant lines not quoted by Piper occur just ten lines earlier in Darwin: "Long had the Giant-form on GALLIA'S plains / Inglorious slept . . ." The lines from "Religious Musings" are 317-322. Piper also invites comparison between *Botanic Garden,* I, ii, 361-394 and "Religious Musings," ll. 224-237.

79. Piper, pp. 49-50.   80. *CL*, I, 205.

81. *RES*, XVIII (1942), 49-71. In the following discussion this article is cited as "Gordon." Quotations are from the various texts as printed by Gordon. E. H. Coleridge's *apparatus criticus* contains some small errors.

82. Gordon, pp. 52-54.

83. These lines are missing from later versions. I suspect, however, that they surface in the description of the

> Youth of tumultuous soul, and *haggard eye*
> Thy wasted form, thy hurried steps I view,
> On thy wan forehead starts the lethal dew . . . (ll. 74-76)

84. Interestingly, the image cluster appears also in Wordsworth's "Peter Bell" (l. 1077): "In agony of silent grief."

85. Gordon, pp. 54, 55.   86. Gordon, pp. 55, 57.   87. Gordon, p. 57.

88. Gordon does not consider this line, but I think it significant in showing the same end-rime as in Coleridge.

89. In the *Biographia Literaria* (I, 12), it will be remembered, Coleridge censured Gray for allegedly borrowing from Shakespeare in "The Bard." *"The Bard* once intoxicated me," Coleridge wrote in 1799, "& now I read it without pleasure" (*N*, 383).

90. Gordon, p. 58.

91. I am convinced that Gray's "The Progress of Poesy" figures still more largely in Coleridge's early verse. A canceled passage from "Absence: a Poem" (which eventually became "Lines on an Autumnal Evening") reads:

> Float round my *lyre*, while Nesbitt's charms I sing,
> And with light fingers touch each *trembling string!* (ll. 35-36)

The opening lines of "The Progress of Poesy" read:

> Awake, Aeolian *lyre*, awake,
> And give to rapture all thy *trembling strings* . . .

(See W. Braekman, "The Influence of William Collins on Poems Written by Coleridge in 1793," *Revue des Langues Vivantes* [Brussels], XXXI [1965], 239.) The "wildly-cinctur'd" young singer from other cancelled lines (ll. 85-86) may derive from Gray's savage youth who sings "In loose numbers *wildly* sweet" of "feather-*cinctured* chiefs" (ll. 61-62). I suspect also a connection between Gray's Ode and Coleridge's "Greek Ode on Astronomy," which was written for a prize at Cambridge in 1793, the same year as "Absence: A Poem."

92. Quoted from the third edition of Bowles's *Sonnets* (1794).

93. Elsewhere in Coleridge's "Monody," the personified "Affection" is described as "pale" (ll. 82-83). Bowles has a "pale Affection" (l. 10).

94. *CL*, I, 104.

95. *PW*, I, 68, n. 2.

96. *CL*, I, 134.

97. As already noted, in the Preface to his *Poems* of 1796 Coleridge said he was indebted to Samuel Favell for a "rough sketch" of the sonnet "Pity" (*PW*, II, 1137).

98. Much of "The Destiny of Nations" originally appeared in Book II of Southey's *Joan of Arc* (1796). The collaborative relations between Coleridge and Southey in this composition (and perhaps several others) have never been untangled and probably never can be. George Whalley's "Coleridge, Southey and 'Joan of Arc,' " *N & Q*, CXCIX (1954), 67-69, is a valuable introduction, and Carl Woodring's long note on the subject (*PPC*, p. 253, n. 2) is indispensable. Woodring emphasizes that the evidence of Southey and Coleridge is "a tangle of contradictions," and that Coleridge's notes on the poem "do not always agree with each other, much less with his collaborators' or other evidence."

99. The passage (*PW*, I, 138, ll. 195-217) is italicized as in RX. Quotations from Lowes in the following pages are from *RX*, pp. 106-109, unless otherwise noted.

100. This line did not appear in the first publication of the poem. David V. Erdman's discovery of a 1797 printing of 148 lines of the poem later titled "The Destiny of Nations" brings to light many interesting variants. See "Unrecorded Coleridge Variants," *SB*, XI (1958), 151-153.

101. *Coleridge: Poetry and Prose*, ed. H. W. Garrod (Oxford, 1925), p. vii.

102. *RX*, p. 493, n. 6. Coleridge's image of mankind early in the poem:

> in this low world
> Placed with our backs to bright Reality,
> That we may learn with young unwounded ken
> The substance from its shadow . . . (ll. 20-24)

is from Plato's parable of the cave. So famous a locus hardly required citation; the same could not be said of Bryan Edwards.

103. Piper, p. 41. Note 3 should cite "The Destiny of Nations" ll. 47-59 instead of 61-81. The relevant passages from *The Botanic Garden* are all from Book I: i, 115-116; ii, 228; iii, 522-524.

104. *RX*, pp. 96-98. I have not followed Lowes exactly in his use of italics. Apart from the debts to Darwin noted above, Piper (p. 42, n. 2) invites comparison of "The Destiny of Nations" (ll. 283-291) and *Botanic Garden*, I, i, 101-104.

105. For the background of *Osorio* and related information, see P. M. Zall, "Coleridge's Unpublished Revisions to 'Osorio,' " *BNYPL*, LXXI (1967), 516-523.

106. *RX*, p. 243; 540, n. 7. *Der Geisterseher* had been translated into English in 1792 and 1795, and it was undoubtedly through one of these versions (for reasons to be given later) that Coleridge knew the work. Among the more interesting connections cited by Lowes is the presence in *Der Geisterseher* of the recently invented glass harmonica, an instrument in which Schiller had been "greatly interested"; in *Osorio* "Coleridge had the following stage direction: 'Here a strain of music is heard from behind the scenes, from an instrument of glass or steel— the harmonica or Celestina stop, or Clagget's metallic organ.' " *The Robbers*, as Lowes also observes, is also present in *Osorio*, but much less directly. See also *PPC*, pp. 199-203 and notes. Curiously, the most substantial verbal borrowing (some half-dozen lines) is not from Schiller but from Voltaire's *Désastre de Lisbonne (PW*, II, 559, n. 1).

107. (New York, 1932), pp. 61-62. The extraordinary dependence upon a model here shown is repeated in the autumn of 1800, when Coleridge began and abandoned a play he entitled *The Triumph of Loyalty*, a fragment of which was published in 1817 (*PW*, I, 421-423). An extant twelve-page draft of the play itself, Miss Coburn has convincingly shown, "seems to draw its plot, down to small details, on a play by the Spanish dramatist Coëllo . . . " (*N*, 869, 871).

108. *EL*, p. 188.

109. Émile Legouis, *The Early Life of William Wordsworth: 1770-1798*, trans. J. W. Matthews (London, 1897), p.356. C. J. Smith puts the matter as follows:

> *Osorio* and *The Borderers* are remarkably parallel in structure, in plot incident, in the philosophies and attitudes of the characters, and in verbal echoes. This is partially explained by Coleridge's being so impressed with *The Borderers* that he imitated it in the second half of his play, adopting in particular Oswald's deterministic reasoning, but the surprising thing is the similarity of theme arising out of each man's independent effort. ("Wordsworth and Coleridge: The Growth of a Theme," *SP*, LIV [1957], 57)

Without, however, the similarity between Oswald and Osorio, and the general tendency of the second half of Coleridge's play, the two themes would not seem nearly so similar.

A much revised version of *Osorio* was successfully produced in 1814 under the title of *Remorse*. In a letter to Southey dealing with the play, Coleridge wrote:

> As to my Thefts from the Wallenstein [which Coleridge had translated in 1800], they were on compulsion from the necessity of Haste—& do not lie heavy on my Conscience, being partly thefts from myself, & because I gave Schiller 20 for one I have taken. I shall, however, weed them out as soon as I can: & in the mean time, I hope, they will lie snug.

—'*The obscurest* Haunt of all our Mountains' I did not recognize as Wordsworth till after the Play was all printed" (*CL*, III, 435, and nn. 1, 2. A list of borrowings from *Wallenstein* may be found in *Poems*, pp. 650-651.)

This letter to Southey is not necessarily a specimen of Coleridge's candor as to his borrowings. It may well have been provoked by some observation of Southey's. In the privacy of his own notebooks, Coleridge had in 1804 complained of Southey's failures of character and sympathy, among which had been his censure of Coleridge's "poetic thefts and trivialities, and whatever is incongruous and not any too decent." This last is a translation of Coleridge's Latin (*N*, 1815 and n.).

110.   *CL*, I, 84.

18.   SPASMS AND STAGNATION

1.   These poems have been discussed previously, especially in "Souvenirs of Germany." The exceptions are "Tell's Birth-Place," "On an Infant," and "The Picture, or the Lover's Resolution" (*PW*, I, 309, 312, 369). EHC's note to "The Picture" states that "the conception of the 'Resolution' that failed was suggested by Gessner's Idyll *Der Feste Vorsatz* ('The Fixed Resolution')." But apart from the conception, Coleridge adopted large blocks of language from Gessners' forty-five-line poem. See Garold N. Davis, *German Thought and Culture in England: 1700-1770* (Chapel Hill, N. C. 1969), pp. 105-106. "On an Infant" is identified at *N*, 625, No. 20*n*, where the text unfortunately credits Coleridge with making "a poem" out of the "epigram" *Wenn ich ein Vöglein war'*, which is in fact a well-known eighteen-line folk song.

2.   Elisabeth Schneider has noted that the resemblances to "Kubla Khan" in "Hymn to the Earth" derive mainly from Coleridge's additions to Stolberg (ES, p. 203).

3.   This poem comes to us in the *Biographia* as an incidental illustration of the author's activities as a diligent student in Germany:

> my chief efforts were directed towards a grounded knowledge of the German language and literature. From Professor TYCHSEN I received as many lessons in the Gothic of Ulphilas as sufficed to make me acquainted with its grammar, and the radical words of the most frequent occurrence; and with the occasional assistance of the same philosophical linguist, I read through OTTFRIED'S metrical paraphrase of the gospel, and the most important remains of the THEOSTICAN, or the transitional state of the Teutonic language from the Gothic to the old German of the Swabian period. (*BL*, I, 138-139)

We need not quote further from this impressive passage. An asterisk directs us to Coleridge's translation of Ottfried. But are we really to believe that Coleridge labored from the Gothic or shall we more reasonably suppose that he actually construed from the Latin translation of Ottfried, conveniently supplied in the margin of the volume Coleridge possessed? The matter is of consequence only because Coleridge's linguistic claims are so often false, and too often taken seriously. See L. A. Willoughby, "Coleridge as a Philologist," *MLR*, XXXI (1936), 181.

As to the putative date of the poem, 1799, neither notebooks nor letters give any hint of the existence of this work. Coleridge rarely lost an opportunity to impress others with his linguistic progress, and we have seen how desperate he was at times for any poetic scrap to send off to the newspapers. The sudden appearance of the Ottfried paraphrase in the *Biographia* therefore suggests that it may have been provided for the occasion.

4.   *PW*, I, 306, 311, 326, 392, 427, 433, 436.

5.   *PW*, I, 397, n. 1.

6.   *PW*, I, 402 and n. 1. The poem was published in Campbell's 1893 edition without comment. The source in Greville might still be unknown but for the fact that Coleridge inscribed the poem in the margins of Lamb's copy of Greville's works. See also Coleridge's "alteration" of Greville's Sonnet 93 (*PW*, II, 1116).

7.   The journal entry can be found at *PW*, II, 1110-11. I have, however, quoted from Kathleen Coburn's more accurate text in "Reflections in a Coleridge Mirror: Some Images in His

Poems," in *From Sensibility to Romanticism*, eds. Frederick W. Hilles and Harold Bloom (New York, 1965), pp. 423-425. EHC invites the reader to compare "Work Without Hope" with the last stanza of Herbert's "Praise" (*PW*, I, 447, n. 2), but the major source is Herbert's "Employment," I, stanza 5.

19. THE *ANNUS MIRABILIS* BEGINS

1. In commenting upon Coleridge's early emotional life, George Whalley notes that "just before his twentieth birthday he claimed that 'Hope itself was all I knew of Pain' " (*Asra*, p. 131), which shows how much mischief is caused by taking poetry too seriously as an autobiographical record, especially where Coleridge is concerned.

2. Quoted from WJB, p. 216.

3. *New Essays towards a Critical Method* (London, 1897), pp. 187, 138.

4. See *RX*, pp. 414-425 for the non-medical aspects of this controversy. Since Lowes, a great deal more information about Coleridge's early use of opium has come to light.

5. See ES, *passim*, but especially pp. 21-109. "There is no doubt that his range of dream experience was largely due to opium," writes House (HH, p. 153), thus taking for granted what there is much reason to doubt. Nor should it be automatically accepted that Coleridge's dream experience was of an unusual range.

6. F. W. Bateson, "Wordsworth and Coleridge," in *From Anne to Victoria*, ed. Bonamy Dobrée (New York, 1937), p. 554.

7. *New Essays towards a Critical Method*, p. 140.   8. *CL*, I, 325. Italics in text.

9. *CL*, I, 391.   10. *CL*, I, 410. STC's underscoring.   11. *CL*, I, 623.

12. *DWJ*, p. 137: " . . . Coleridge came in—his eyes were a little swollen with the wind. I was much affected with the sight of him, he seemed half stupefied."

13. Dorothy's journal entry for 27 March, laconic as usual, reads: "*Saturday*. A divine morning. At Breakfast Wm. wrote part of an ode." The previous day's entry reads: "While I was getting into bed, he wrote *The Rainbow* ['My heart leaps up']" (p. 139). According to Wordsworth, "two years at least passed between the writing of the first four stanzas [of the Intimations Ode] and the remaining part" (*WPW*, IV, 463).

14. As the original draft of the "Ode to Dejection" is cast in the form of a letter to Sara Hutchinson and very carefully dated "April 4, 1802.—Sunday Evening" (*CL*, II, 790), critics have, with customary alacrity, accepted that the poem was therefore composed on a single evening, and it has thus become another example of Coleridge's powers with the hot fit of composition upon him. Griggs calls this version a "first draft" (*CL*, III, xxxv). Undeterred by its immense length of 340 lines (as compared to 139 in the published poem), Moorman (I, 528) states that it was written between "sunset and midnight," as does Watson (GW, p. 77); the evidence for this is presumably that the poem begins by describing a sunset and ends with a post-midnight scene. There is no external evidence of the poem's existence until 21 April, when Dorothy records that Coleridge (who had arrived the previous afternoon) "repeated the verses he wrote to Sara."

So far as the poem's *worth* is concerned, it makes not the slightest difference whether it was written in one night or twenty, but since critics are constantly making a point of its swiftness of composition, it is relevant to try to get at the hard facts. The holograph manuscript of this "letter" is in Dove Cottage. Apart from its title, "A Letter to—," surely a common bit of poetic license, there is no reason whatever for including it among Coleridge's collected *correspondence*. The "letter" proves to be a carefully written *fair copy* of an earlier, unknown manuscript. Can one be sure of this? First, in 340 lines there are just ten words canceled and replaced. The poem is carefully divided and spaced into stanzas, which are in turn indented at various points to clarify rime patterns. Of course, for the man who wrote "Kubla Khan" in a dream, this kind of near perfection is perhaps child's play. Nevertheless, the poem is neatly written on one side of the page into the center leaves of a string-sewn notebook from which the outer leaves, front and rear, may have been removed so that the notebook's covers serve as a binding for the poem. If Coleridge wrote a 340-line poem in one night, he might finally have had several score worksheets, from which at last he made a fair copy. If the poem was finished on 4 April he seems to have said not a word about it to anyone until 17 days later, when he read it to the Wordsworths. The matter would not really be worth arguing except that, as we have seen, the Ode is regularly cited as an example of rapid composition. For example: "after *The Ancient Mariner*, most of the poems he completed, like the first version of *Dejection: An Ode*, were written at a single sitting, in a burst of inspiration or spasm of intense effort" (M. H. Abrams in *Norton Anthology of English Literature* [New York, 1968], II, 180). Incidentally, Coleridge soon wrote Poole that "on the 4th of April last I wrote *you* a letter in verse; but I thought it dull & doleful—& did not send it" (*CL*, II, 801).

15. *BL*, II, 5-6.   16. *HW*, XVII, 120.   17. *CL*, I, 631.

18. *WPW*, I, 361.

19. Those who assign Coleridge a major share in the conceptual framework of the 1800 Preface have not attempted to account for the absence of any discussion of the kind of poetry represented by "The Ancient Mariner," "Christabel," or "Kubla Khan." Coleridge's poems are, in fact, acknowledged only in an excessively spare note (*WPW*, II, 385, n. 2).

20. *WPW*, I, 360-361. Wordsworth was wrong in assigning these events to the spring of 1798. Dorothy Wordsworth's journal gives 13 November 1797 as the precise date "The Ancient Mariner" was begun, and Coleridge's letters and voluminous other materials confirm the year as 1797.

21. The idea of *collaboration* may have provided the associative link, since after the seeming digression of the Mariner recollections Wordsworth returned to note that the original first stanza of "We Are Seven" had been provided, after the rest of the poem was written, by Coleridge:

> A little child, dear brother Jem,
> That lightly draws its breath,
> And feels its life in every limb,
> What should it know of death?

Dr. David Beres suggests that in dictating the Fenwick note "thoughts of death and their denial remained in Wordsworth's mind in association with the crime of murder in 'The Ancient Mariner' " (Beres, p. 113).

22. *WPW*, II, 336-337.

23. These criticisms, graceless as they are, are almost precisely those he made of his own early poem, "Guilt and Sorrow": "the incidents . . . do only in a small degree produce each other, and it deviates accordingly from the general rule by which narrative pieces ought to be governed" (*WPW*, I, 330).

24. In the note where this acknowledgment is found, Coleridge reported only that the poem was planned during a "delightful walk" in the autumn of 1797, "and in part composed" (*PW*, I, 196, n. 1).

25. "Wordsworth's Conception of the 'Ancient Mariner,' " *Archiv für das Studium der Neueren Sprachen und Literaturen*, CXXV (1910), 89-92; reprinted in *Late Harvest* (Ithaca, N. Y., 1952), pp. 96-100. The quotation given is from the latter, p. 96.

26. Quoted from *Poems*, p. 594. Italics in text. STC changed the navigation of the ship by the dead men for the 1800 version, and much else followed from this excellent decision.

27. *RX*, p. 223.

28. *RX*, pp. 223-224. This approach to Wordsworth's contributions to the poem (and to his influence generally) is characteristic of Lowes's handling of many source problems in Coleridge. To Lowes, the Wordsworth who dictated the Fenwick note in question was a "prosy septua-

genarian" (p. 420). The hard evidence would certainly seem to sustain C. J. Smith's argument that

the figure of the Ancient Mariner most probably was born in Wordsworth's imagination, not Coleridge's. Although John Livingston Lowes assigns him to Coleridge, somewhat gratuitously, it is not likely that Wordsworth would make such fundamental contributions to the story as mentioned above without a figure to attach them to. That figure was waiting, ready-made, in his own imagination. The old sailor appears as early as in The Gothic Fragment, which de Selincourt dates 1791. He reappears, more fully developed, as the central character of "Guilt and Sorrow," where he is referred to more than once as "the Mariner," and even "the impatient Mariner," a phrase close in sound to its final form. As he wanders the wasteland, full of remorse, pursued by demons and the very rocks of the moor, he is not far in imagination from the Ancient Mariner. ("Wordsworth and Coleridge: The Growth of a Theme," *SP*, LIV [1957], 58)

29. *RX*, p. 224.

30. In *Late Harvest*, pp. 96-97. In a notorious (and unforgivably harsh) review of *The Road to Xanadu*, Cooper was particularly impatient with Lowes's "smouldering conception," and emphasized the crucial role Wordsworth played in "The Ancient Mariner" (*PMLA*, XLIII [1928], 585-586).

31. *CHCR*, I, 402.

32. *WPW*, I, 374.

33. Quoted from the Quarto Text of 1796, which may be found in *LL*, p. 79, or laboriously reconstructed from EHC's critical apparatus. These lines not only show the quality of Coleridge's diction during the closing days of 1796, but reveal again the compulsive refashioner of already used materials. The passage continues:

> Hither, in perplexed *dance*,
> Ye WOES, and young-eyed *JOYS, advance*!
> By *Time's wild* harp, and by the *hand*
> Whose indefatigable sweep
> Forbids its fateful strings to sleep,
> I bid you haste, a mix'd tumultuous band!

In "Lines to a Friend in Answer to a Melancholy Letter," which Coleridge had published in his edition of 1796 (both EHC and JDC suggest 1795 as the date of composition), appear these lines:

> *Wild*, as the autumnal gust, the *hand* of *Time*
> Flies o'er the mystic lyre: in shadowy *dance*
> The alternate groups of *Joy* and Grief *advance*
> Responsive to his varying strains sublime! (*PW*, I, 90)

The emphases provided above are confined to identical words, but the relationship between the passages is much closer. The original "shadowy dance" becomes "perplexed dance"; the hand which "flies o'er the mystic lyre," now comes to "sweep" over a "wild harp," which has "fateful strings." Where "groups of Joy and *Grief*" had advanced, now "*Woes*, and young-eyed Joys" do so. As can be seen, practically every change is for the worse, which suggests the mechanical forcing of old ideas into new molds. In a volume of the edition of 1828 annotated by Coleridge himself, he wrote of this latter poem that it was "very like one of Horace's odes, *starched*" (*Poems*, p. 576, n. 74. STC's underscoring). The *OED* gives one meaning of "starch" as "to compose . . . to a severe or formal expression." Sara Coleridge thought there were some debts here to Casimir's thirteenth Ode (Shedd, III, xxxviii).

34. Lines 28-33. *WPW*, II, 241, and *app. crit.*

35. Lines 37-43. *PW*, I, 180. Coleridge read Wordsworth's "Lines Left upon a Seat" to Lamb in July, when we find the latter writing for a copy and adding, "You may believe that I will make no improper use of it" (*LL*, I, 112).

36. *BL*, II, 16-17. "Corrupted by a classical education," writes F. L. Lucas acidulously, "I find myself perversely giving the preference, if any, to the quieter tone of the first passage" (*The Decline and Fall of the Romantic Ideal* [Cambridge, England, 1963], p. 172).

37. *The Portable Coleridge* (New York, 1950), pp. 8, 35, 37.

20. THE BACKGROUND OF *LYRICAL BALLADS, WITH A FEW OTHER POEMS*

1. *WLC*, p. 120.

2. See Grosart, III, 438-439.

3. In Émile Legouis' influential early study it is simply assumed that Coleridge gave Wordsworth his general philosophy (*The Early Life of Wordsworth: 1770-1798* [London, 1897], p. 331). George McLean Harper took for granted Coleridge's primacy in conceptual discussions. Harper asks, in a typical instance, "When Wordsworth, in *Tintern Abbey*, speaks of

> '. . . all the mighty world
> Of eye and ear,—both what they half create
> And what perceive',—

is he not employing, although with a curious and significant reservation, the language of philosophical idealism, and who but Coleridge has been his teacher?" ("The Wordsworth-Coleridge Combination," *SR*, XXXI [1923], 269). To the second question we may confidently answer that not Coleridge, but Edward Young's old-fashioned *Night Thoughts* had been Wordsworth's teacher, as he acknowledged in a note in the original *Lyrical Ballads*. As to whether the language of philosophical idealism is employed, the answer seems certainly to be no, in the sense that Harper means. The purely philosophical aspects of what is perceived and what projected is central in Locke, whom Wordsworth had studied at Cambridge. We do not have to run into the labyrinths of philosophical idealism to account for the unsettling problem which is at the very heart of Wordsworth's security about the moral investitures of nature.

A more recent example of how the relative intellectual powers of the two men are now judged is to be found in Graham Hough, who finds that Coleridge's influence "was in the first place intellectual, and showed Wordsworth another road to travel than the Godwinian one. The enormous reading of Coleridge's studious youth had given him a mind far more richly stored, of far greater range and variety than Wordsworth's" (*The Romantic Poets* [London, 1958], p. 40). Such opinions seem simply to be handed on from one commentator to another. In the Introduction to the widely disseminated Modern Library edition of Coleridge's poetry and prose (New York, 1951), Donald Stauffer assures the reader that "Coleridge read everything and forgot nothing," and that "essentially Coleridge gave Wordsworth a mind, and Wordsworth gave Coleridge a will" (pp. xi, xxi).

In a similar vein we find F. W. Bateson writing that Wordsworth did not "generally absorb ideas directly from books, but at second-hand through the conversation of his friends. His intellectual mentors, such as Taylor, Beaupuy and Coleridge, took the place of books. What Wordsworth went to books for were for facts and for poetry" (*Wordsworth: A Re-Interpretation* [London, 1956], p. 121). Surely this is a dangerous statement. What is known of Beaupuy's conversation? And the conventional opinion about Coleridge needs examination.

Lane Cooper is one of the few who has ever argued for Wordsworth's greater knowledge of poets and his systematic reading (*PMLA*, XLIII [1928], p. 585). Whatever may be the truth of this matter, is it relevant? Breadth of learning is precisely the kind of argument the Baconians are continually advancing in favor of their cause.

4. *WLC*, p. 250.

5. Thus, at about the time when the work of John Livingston Lowes and I. A. Richards had had about a decade to take hold, we find in a long article by Florence Brinckley on R. P. Knight's *Inquiry Into Taste* (*HLQ*, I [1937], 63-99) that the marginalia by Wordsworth and Coleridge in a copy of that work are mostly in Wordsworth's handwriting. "Certainly, however," we are

assured, "the ideas are those of Coleridge . . ." (p. 609, n. 140). That may be, but one asks for more substantive evidence.

6. *DQW*, X, 48; XI, 55.   7. *LP*, p. 113, n. 1.

8. "Wordsworth, Coleridge, and the 'Plan' of the *Lyrical Ballads*," *UTQ*, XXXIV (1965), 239, 241.

9. "Coleridge, Wordsworth, and the 1800 Preface to *Lyrical Ballads*," *SEL*, V (1965), 619, 625. Six years before, James Reeves, without pausing to argue the question, had simply asserted in the preface to a collection of Coleridge's poems: "It is impossible to doubt that, in the intimacy between him and Wordsworth which produced *Lyrical Ballads*, and the Preface to the second edition, it was he who was the guiding intelligence, the leading force. Much of the credit for Coleridge's seminal ideas went to Wordsworth . . ." (*Selected Poems of Samuel Taylor Coleridge* [New York, 1959], p. xxxi). It is revealing that it has now become "impossible to doubt" that which was undreamt of in the nineteenth century.

10. (London, 1963), pp. 111, 114, 117. In Watson's later *Coleridge the Poet*, those portions of the Preface presumably of little value are naturally assigned to Wordsworth; for example: "It is not surprising if Coleridge handled Wordsworth's jejune theories of poetic language with such aplomb in the later chapters of *Biographia Literaria*" (p. 37). As to the relative powers of the two men, Watson puts the matter bluntly: Wordsworth was "conceptually much the less intelligent of the two . . ." (GW, p. 69).

11. *N*, 787. The entry comes from the inside cover of a notebook, "is faded and rubbed, stained with damp; all is scribbled over in pencil by a child." A photograph (Plate III) is provided on the facing page to entry 787 in the text volume.

12. See Miss Coburn's note to entry 787. She accepts that the Preface is "practically a joint product," and dates the entry in August in the absence of firm evidence because this was "close to the time when Coleridge must have been trying to write it [the Preface], before he abandoned it to Wordsworth." Yet this disjointed entry comprises just about the total evidence from the journals, or letters of the period, that Coleridge was trying to write an essay! As if the stated extrapolations were not sufficiently daring, this entry is held to bear out "another contention, that much of what he later found in Schelling was a 'genial coincidence' with his own views."

13. M. F. Schulz ("Coleridge, Wordsworth, and the 1800 Preface to *Lyrical Ballads*," p. 636) discloses that on a proof sheet of the Preface there is a phrase in Coleridge's hand. It occurs in the middle of the long paragraph beginning, "I cannot, however, be insensible to the present outcry against the triviality . . ." After the phrase "till at length," Coleridge added, "if we be originally possessed of much organic sensibility." The passage deals with the moral growth of the poet and reader (*WPW*, II, 388).

14. "The Wordsworth-Coleridge Combination," p. 268.

15. *PW*, II, 1144-45. In the 1815 "Essay Supplementary" Wordsworth wrote:

> Having had the good fortune to be born and reared in a mountainous country, from my very childhood I have felt the falsehood that pervades the volumes imposed upon the world under the name of Ossian. From what I saw with my own eyes, I knew that the imagery was spurious. In nature everything is distinct, yet not defined into absolute independent singleness. In Macpherson's work, it is exactly the reverse; everything (that is not stolen) is in this manner defined, insulated, dislocated, deadened,—yet nothing distinct. It will always be so when words are substituted for things. (*WPW*, II, 423)

But of course scores of Macpherson's admirers had also grown up in the country, so that Wordsworth's casual assumption collapses. In fact, his prescience more probably derived from his capacity to look at nature with a freshness of perception given only to those few geniuses who see things as they are and not how they have been conditioned to see them. Legouis (*The Early Life of Wordsworth*, p. 123) has observed that Wordsworth was the only poet of his time not to imitate *Ossian*.

Worthy of note also is the typical attitude of the age towards unacknowledged borrowing in the harsh reference to Macpherson's "stealing." And a few pages earlier Wordsworth wrote that at one time Milton's early poems were so neglected that "Pope in his youth could borrow from them without risk of its being known." About the *Ossian* controversy he wrote that it was not necessary to call all resemblances *conscious* plagiarism; it was enough that "the coincidences were too remarkable for its being probable or possible that they could arise in different minds without communication." One can't help wondering what Coleridge felt upon reading these lines, especially after the Schlegel problem. It is possible that there is more here than meets the eye relative to the relationship between the two men.

16. *CL*, I, 279.

17. *HW*, XVII, 120. Lamb had sent Coleridge the year before a poem addressed to Cowper, "of England's Bards, the wisest & the best" (*LL*, I, 36. 6 July 1796).

18. *WPW*, II, 425. Three pages earlier Wordsworth had shrewdly identified Percy as the main source of the German balladists.

19. *WPW*, II, 428.

20. The context of Coleridge's disclosures regarding the genesis of the Preface to *Lyrical Ballads* has never been closely examined. They appear in a letter of 13 July 1802, two years after the publication of the Preface, written to a very recent and influential acquaintance, William Sotheby, a literary figure of some consequence. Six days later Coleridge wrote Sotheby again. Both letters are immensely long, comprising twelve closely printed pages in the published text (*CL*, II, 808-819). Some 5,000 words to a single correspondent within the space of a week is impressive, and in fact the letters are among the most brilliant he ever wrote.

The first letter begins with a long and anxious apology to Sotheby for having been "unpardonably loquacious" during a recent meeting. (The present very long letter may, however, be retrospectively seen as deriving from the same need to impress.) A smooth and affectionate transition takes us to a beautiful description of nature, a brilliant metaphor about Milton, and a couple of lines in Latin from Cicero (pp. 808-809).

The second paragraph proceeds to discuss Coleridge's thoughts of translating Gessner, mentions "poor Giordano Bruno," by the by, and takes the opportunity to quote from "his strange yet noble Poem De Immenso et Innumerabili." Coleridge finds Gessner's *Der erste Schiffer* too silly to translate, but its "first conception is noble—so very good, that I am spiteful enough to hope that I shall discover it not to have been original in Gesner [*sic*]." We proceed at length to several lines of Latin (from Lucretius, unidentified), reflections on poetry and metaphysics, and a reference to his reading in French and German. Then appears a "malicious Motto, which I have written on the first page of Klopstock's Messiah." The clever Latin motto, however, comes from Virgil's fifth Eclogue, which Sotheby may or may not have known (pp. 809-811 and notes).

After stating "I read a great deal of German," Coleridge passes on extremely affectionate regards from Wordsworth, and flatters Sotheby's "description of Wordsworth's character." From this we come to the famous passage: "It is most certain, that that Preface arose from the heads of our mutual Conversations &c—& the first passages were indeed partly taken from notes of mine / for it was at first intended, that the Preface should be written by me." Coleridge quotes from Drayton, apropos, condemns "Bowles's *execrable Translation* of that lovely Poem of Dean Ogle's," and proceeds to identify differences of opinion with Wordsworth on the nature of meter. As to these friendly differences between comrades, Coleridge quotes a passage from St. Augustine, "who said more good things than any Saint or Sinner, that I ever read in Latin" (pp. 811-812. STC's underscoring). The letter concludes with graceful regards and praise of Sotheby's poems and translations.

Surely Sotheby was impressed with this letter, as well he might be. And just a few days later he was to receive a far more brilliant letter, which included long extracts from the "Ode to Dejection," carefully identified as a "Letter written Sunday Evening, April 4" (p. 815). His next letter to Sotheby, dated 26 August, is almost as impressive, and it is in his very long fourth letter to Sotheby, of 10 September 1802, after all sorts of intellectual dazzlements, that he writes that on Scafell "I involuntarily poured forth a Hymn"—in fact the Chamouni poem based on Brun (p. 864).

These letters are of a piece with many Coleridge wrote to new acquaintances whom he wished to impress. If, to say the least, Coleridge exaggerated the spontaneity of the "Hymn Before Sun-Rise," what reason do we have to credit his retrospective account of the genesis of the Preface to *Lyrical Ballads*, here given to a comparative stranger, but no claim to even one word of it breathed in the previous two years to such confidants as Lamb or Poole or the Wedgwoods or Southey?

21.   Coleridge's limitations in dealing poetically with ordinary human experience is probably related to his crippling emotional deprivation as a child. Yet it is relevant in the present discussion to observe how little Coleridge has given us by way of manifest human insight in his poems. However profound and intense the emotional experiences contained in poems like "The Ancient Mariner" and "Christabel," few readers feel themselves participating in a shared and recognizable world. Conversely, Wordsworth, a lover of solitude in a way Coleridge never was, much less gregarious, more arrogant and self-assured, nevertheless has given the world many deeply affecting poems about *others*. In his love for his family and deep interest in his neighbors, Wordsworth contrasts strikingly with STC, who always detested his family and whose friendships were ardent but stormy. Poems like "Michael," "The Brothers," "The Ruined Cottage," those about Lucy, the heartbreaking "Surprised by Joy," and literally dozens of others, leave Wordsworth without a rival in the whole eighteenth and nineteenth centuries as the poet of family experiences.

22.   "Johnson's 'London' and 'The Vanity of Human Wishes,' " in *Twentieth Century Critical Essays, First Series*, ed. Phyllis M. Jones (Oxford World's Classics), p. 302.

23.   *Wordsworth*, p. 156. Wordsworth's prose is so little known that it is relevant to add that his "letter to Charles James Fox, a sociological masterpiece, followed in January 1801 . . . and the long letter to John Wilson, a critical supplement to the Preface, dates from June 1802" (pp. 156-157) . In 1802 Wordsworth added to the Preface what Coleridge wrote Southey was a "valuable appendix . . . & in the Preface itself considerable additions, one on the Dignity & nature of the office & character of a Poet, that is very grand, & of a sort of Verulamian Power & Majesty," all this written without any assistance from Coleridge. It is in this letter of 1802, however, that Coleridge wrote that the original Preface was "half a child of my own Brain" (*CL*, II, 830).

24.   *Wordsworth and Schelling* (New Haven, Conn., 1960), p. 1.

25.   *LL*, I, 55, 59.

26.   *LL*, I, 93, and "Religious Musings," *PW*, I, 113, ll. 105-116. George Whalley, in "Coleridge's Debt to Charles Lamb" *E & S*, XI, (1958), 68-85, argues for an important influence. Lamb was a very brilliant critic, and in fact his letters, in my opinion, show a practical critical judgment superior to Coleridge's. But Lamb's analyses of poetry, though sensitive and shrewd, are not in advance of his time from any theoretical point of view. If he was perhaps the only member of the immediate circle to appreciate "The Ancient Mariner" at anything like its true value, he also consistently overrated Coleridge's early poetry. With Southey's *Joan of Arc* he had been "delighted, amazed. . . . the poem is alone sufficient to redeem the character of the age we live in from the imputation of degenerating in Poetry." He had found, in June 1796, Southey's "Fierce and terrible Benevolence!" a phrase "full of grandeur and originality." And he found that "Southey's personifications in this book are so many fine and faultless pictures" (*LL*, I, 13-14). In judging all this, let us remember that Lamb was at this time just 21 years old.

27.   *LL*, I, 84.   28.   *LL*, I, 240. Italics in text.

29.   *LL*, I, 247.

30.   *Selections from the Letters of Robert Southey*, ed. J. W. Warter (London, 1856), I, 216. Southey also wrote: "The fault of Coleridge has been a too-swelling diction. . . ."

The self-originating nature of Wordsworth's art seems to have been apparent to almost everyone. Crabb Robinson said that "Southey was only a collector of other men's thoughts: Wordsworth gave forth his own. Wordsworth was like the spider, spinning his thread from his own substance" (Ellis Yarnall, *Wordsworth and the Coleridges* [London, 1899], p. 90).

As late as 1831, the young John Stuart Mill wrote: "When you get Wordsworth on the subjects which are peculiarly his, such as the theory of his own art, no one can converse with him without feeling that he has advanced that great subject beyond any other man, being probably the first person who ever combined, with such eminent success in the practice of the art, such high powers of generalization and habits of meditation on its principles" (*Letters*, ed. Hugh S. R. Elliott [London, 1910], I, 11-12).

31. *Edinburgh Review*, I (1802), 65; review of Southey's *Thalaba*. A writer for the *Monthly Review*, LXXVI (1815), 129, noted: "It is true that the poetical world talked much some years ago about the *Loves of the Plants* . . . and that, in the bold language of eastern metaphor, the little hills are represented as dancing with joy: —but Mr. Wordsworth disdains metaphor and fable. *That which he describes is set forth in the colours of reality, not of fiction*" (quoted from J. Scoggins, "The Preface to *Lyrical Ballads*: A Revolution in Dispute," in *Studies in Criticism and Aesthetics, 1660-1800*, eds. H. Anderson and J. S. Shea [Minneapolis, Minn., 1966], p. 390).

But Robert Mayo's "The Contemporaneity of the *Lyrical Ballads*," *PMLA*, LXIX (1954), 486-522, appears to annihilate a century and a half of received opinion on the subject. Toward the close of his formidable article, Mayo writes: "whatever aspect of *Lyrical Ballads* we examine, whether it be the meters, the lyrical and narrative kinds, the subjects, attitudes, and the themes of individual poems or groups of poems, we are struck by the great number of particulars in which *the volume conforms to the taste and interests of some segments of the literary world in 1798*" (p. 517). Those segments prove to be not an *avant-garde*, or another coterie of sophisticates, but, surprisingly, the readers of the poetry columns of popular magazines. Mayo compares these long-forgotten pieces to what has always been thought to be the revolutionary work of *Lyrical Ballads*, and finds that one poem after another in the famous volume "conforms strictly to type," is "modish," "very much in fashion," or among the "recognized minor modes in popular poetry." "Wordsworth's lonely and forsaken women are in some degree stereotypes . . . perfectly in line with contemporary taste. . . . Bereaved mothers and deserted females were almost a rage in the poetry departments of the 1790's" (pp. 495-496). Poems like "Lines Written in Early Spring" are "obviously not experimental in subject; nor in *form* either, as a matter of fact. Considered as a species of poetry the 'nature' poems of the *Lyrical Ballads* were anything but surprising in 1798" (p. 490. Italics in text).

And so this devastating article goes on. The works Mayo cites are completely forgotten now, leaving scarcely a wrack behind. If the major literary antecedents of *Lyrical Ballads* are not to be found in any of the still-remembered poets of the eighteenth century, but rather in the yellowing columns of dusty journals, then it would at least have to be said that Wordsworth identified in the dreary ephemera of contemporary magazine verse just those qualities through which English poetry was to be shortly resurrected.

But Mayo's evidence, weighty as it is, does not compel so drastic a revision of former belief. The gravest weakness of this article is the failure to take account of how time alters our conceptions so that we consistently distort the past. "The new poets of the day were everywhere striving for artless expressions of sensibility," Mayo writes, without citing any instance of a "new poet" stating such a desire. "Both Southey and Coleridge were well-known magazine poets of 1797, and recognized masters of 'simplicity' " (p. 494). Recognized by *whom*? We have seen what "simplicity" actually meant to a contemporary like Lamb. The very language Mayo employs derives from Wordsworth's Preface, which defined the linguistic sensibility that has become our common heritage.

Mayo has performed a genuinely valuable service in setting *Lyrical Ballads* against the now-shadowy background from which it emerged and in demonstrating how much in the volume can be firmly linked to the stream of poetry appearing in the journals. But the differences remain decisive. Mayo has, I believe, consistently minimized the testimony of Wordsworth's contemporaries in favor of his own reconstructions of the period. Thus he notes that Charles Burney "in the *Monthly Review* [1799] questioned whether verses so unembellished as some of the *Lyrical Ballads* could properly be ranked as poetry." But these poems, Mayo comments, "were merely the fulfillment of a tendency which a great number of contemporary poets, without the benefit of Wordsworth and Coleridge's esthetic and psychological theories, were already showing. *To most readers* this feature of the volume would seem less a revolution, therefore, than the excess of a new orthodoxy" (p. 495). Who is in a better position to judge what *Lyrical Ballads* seemed like to most readers in 1798, a distinguished contemporary musician and man of broad culture like Charles Burney, or a scholar one hundred fifty years later? Contemporary evidence is not always decisive, but when it massively points in a given direction—on a matter of this sort—it is almost never wrong.

It should be borne in mind that original work almost always seems less so as time passes. (And the minute scrutiny of backgrounds always produces "precursors.") If it is nearly impossible for us to hear the dissonances that so appalled the contemporaries of Beethoven (born the same year as Wordsworth), how are we to discriminate between carefully selected passages of "simple" verse from the 1790's and the poems in *Lyrical Ballads*, which so startled most of the critics who wrote on the subject *at the time*?

32. *LP*, p. 152. *DQW*, II, 139; III, 204, 206.

33. *HW*, XVII, 121. Since these remarks, and those given above from De Quincey, were published after *Biographia Literaria*, there would appear to be as pointed a slight as in the refusal of both Hazlitt and Wordsworth to acknowledge Coleridge as the originator of the new principles of Shakespearean criticism.

34. *CL*, IV, 572. Italics in text.

35. Warter, *Selections from the Letters of Robert Southey*, I, 216.

36. *Wordsworth*, p. 200. 37. *CL*, IV, 564.

38. *BL*, II, 70; *N*, 1702n. There is no reason to suppose that Coleridge's mistranslation was deliberate; his knowledge of German was far from exact. Yet it is psychologically suggestive that he should make so serious a mistake on a matter of such importance.

39. Addison, for example, in praising a medieval ballad, felt it necessary to "caution the reader not to let the simplicity of the style, which one may well pardon in so old a poet, prejudice him against the greatness of the thought" (*Spectator*, No. 70). Thomas Gray's letter to Richard West (April 1742) is germane here: "As to the matter of style, I have this to say: the language of the age is never the language of poetry . . . [which] has a language peculiar to itself." For an excellent summary of critical opinion on the subject before Wordsworth, see W. K. Wimsatt and Cleanth Brooks, *Literary Criticism: A Short History* (New York, 1957), pp. 342-343.

40. *BL*, I, 5. Italics in text.

41. *CL*, I, 278. 17 December 1796. Coleridge had, by the previous March, carefully read and interleaved with observations the manuscript of Wordsworth's "Guilt and Sorrow" (p. 216, n. 1).

42. *PW*, I, 145, *app. crit.* Italics in text.

43. *PW*, I, 3, n. 1. This is surely another example of the way Coleridge sometimes put his own views into the mouths of others. See also Gillman, p. 35.

Brandl observes that the "youthful hymns of other pupils of Boyer's; namely, by Middleton and Leigh Hunt," brimmed over with "the same superfluity of personifications and metaphors" to be found in Coleridge's "Anthem for the Children of Christ's Hospital" and other Christ's Hospital poems (*Samuel Taylor Coleridge and the English Romantic School*, pp. 26-27).

44. "To An Unfortunate Woman at the Theatre" (*PW*, I, 172).

45. "On the Christening of a Friend's Child" (*PW*, I, 176).

46. David V. Erdman, "Lost Poem Found: The cooperative pursuit and recapture of an escaped Coleridge 'sonnet' of 72 lines," *BNYPL*, LXV (1961), 249-268. The discovery by Lucyle Werkmeister of this poem in a newspaper of January 1798 requires the redating of the shorter (and somewhat different) version called "The Snow Drop" in *PW*, I, 356-358, where it is given as 1800. Erdman points out that we must think of this poem, therefore, as being close in time to "Frost at Midnight," "Fire, Famine and Slaughter," and the first part of "Christabel." "I leave it to others," he writes, "to make anything of these juxtapositions" (p. 261). One point that

can surely be made is that Coleridge's gift was highly unstable, and that his poetic style in early 1798 was in a state of mercurial change. Even in the middle of "France: An Ode," as we have seen, we come upon such examples of poetic *rigor mortis* as:

> Alike from Priestcraft's harpy minions,
> And factious Blasphemy's obscener slaves. (ll. 95-96)

In "Fears in Solitude," written in April 1798, we espy "the owlet Atheism, / Sailing on obscene wings athwart the noon" (ll. 82-83).

47. *CL*, I, 327-328.

48. *CL*, I, 333. STC's underscoring.

49. Both Lamb and Leigh Hunt were aware of Coleridge's encomiums to Boyer and neither provided a supporting word. Lamb's detailed description of Boyer reveals only a stern pedant. "His English style was crampt to barbarism," Lamb writes. "His Easter anthems (for his duty obliged him to those periodical flights) were grating as scrannel pipes" (*LW*, II, 19). Leigh Hunt, however, was actually Boyer's student. "The merits of Boyer," he writes in his *Autobiography* (ed. J. E. Morpurgo [London, 1948]), "consisted in his being a good verbal scholar, and conscientiously acting up to the letter of time and attention. I have seen him nod at the close of the long summer school-hours, wearied out; and I should have pitied him if he had taught us to do anything but fear" (p. 67). Hunt scornfully opines that "his natural destination lay in carpentry," and that he "had no imagination of any sort" (pp. 67-68). The rest of this detailed portrait deserves to be read, if only as a counterweight to the almost universal conviction that Boyer was a major influence on Coleridge's theory and practice of poetry. For example, the astute W. L. Renwick supposes that Coleridge "taught to Wordsworth, the constructive 'inner logic' which he had learned in Christ's Hospital to be an essential condition in the making of poetry" (*English Literature: 1789-1815* [Oxford, 1963], p. 156). G. Watson cites Boyer's instruction as evidence of Coleridge's early preoccupation with poetic theory (GW, p. 11), and J. A. Appleyard identifies Boyer, "this wise teacher," as one of the three most important figures in Coleridge's intellectual development (JAA, p. 204). M. H. Abrams hails Boyer's instruction as one of the three "milestones" in Coleridge's "development of . . . theory of poetry and poetic diction" ("Wordsworth and Coleridge on Diction and Figures," *EIE* [1952], p. 192). In his famous essay "The Correspondent Breeze: A Romantic Metaphor," in *English Romantic Poets* (Oxford, 1960), Abrams identifies Boyer as "Coleridge's schoolmaster and pre-Wordsworthian reformer of poetic diction" (p. 38).

Finally, for this list could be extended indefinitely, J. A. Greig cites Coleridge's recollections as proof that Boyer, among others, had long anticipated Wordsworth in freeing "English poetry from the thraldom of Augustan phraseology" (*Francis Jeffrey of the Edinburgh Review*, p. 233). Obviously, if one proceeds on such assumptions as these, the development of Coleridge's thought, and especially his relationship to Wordsworth, becomes hopelessly muddled.

50. *PW*, I, 267-268. Characteristically, Coleridge finds space to remark in the first sentence of his Preface that he has been "encouraged" to publish the poem "by the decisive recommendation of more than one of our most celebrated living Poets," but nowhere does he mention that the story was provided by Wordsworth, who had also written substantial portions of the work.

51. *PW*, I, 101. This is a treacherous poem to discuss as an early specimen of either Coleridge's thought or art because of the crucial later additions. Thus the central passage of eight lines quoted again and again as proof of Coleridge's early pantheism, beginning "O! the one Life within us and abroad," did not appear anywhere until as late as 1817 (*PW*, I, 101 and *app. crit.*).

52. C. G. Martin, "Coleridge and William Crowe's 'Lewesdon Hill,' " *MLR*, LXII (1967), 400-406. Coleridge singled out this poem for praise in *BL*, I, 11.

53. *PW*, I, 107. Italics in text. Martin compares the content of this passage down to line 42, "Blest hour! It was a luxury—to be!" with a similar passage in Crowe, and concludes: "Coleridge's thought is, of course, more complex, and he recounts a past decision, where Crowe recalls the content of his 'meditation.' But the general outline of the experience ('Blest hour!' for Coleridge, 'A blest condition' for Crowe), and the moral claims which oblige each poet to forego its

pleasures are very similar; while the spirit in which each returns to the world's battles is identical" (p. 404).

54. Pages 7, 15-16. The full title of Hucks's rare book is *A Pedestrian Tour Through North Wales in a Series of Letters* (London, 1795). I believe there is a connection between Hucks's Preface and the Preface to Coleridge's *Poems on Various Subjects* (1796). Coleridge wrote: "Compositions resembling those of the present volume are not unfrequently condemned for their querulous egotism. But egotism is to be condemned then only when it offends against time and place, as in an History or an Epic Poem. To censure it in a Monody or Sonnet is almost as absurd as to dislike a circle for being round" (*PW*, II, 1135). Hucks had, the year before, claimed "the indulgence of his readers for the tautology and egotism, almost inseparable from works of such description [that is, accounts of personal travels]" (pp. 6-7).

55.   *LL*, I, 68. 9 December 1796.   56.   *PW*, I, 106, *app. crit.*   57.   *CL*, II, 864.

58.   *CL*, I, 197.   59.   *PW*, I, 257, *app. crit.*

60. What we really find in such poems as "The Eolian Harp" and "Reflections" is the fitful influence of Bowles and Cowper and Collins, all "precursors" of the Romantic Movement. T. S. Eliot's dictum that every work of literature rearranges the literature of the past is perhaps nowhere better vindicated than in our view of eighteenth-century poetry as seen with post-Wordsworthian eyes. Here, for example, is a passage from Cowper's *The Task*, published in 1785, when Wordsworth was fifteen years old and Coleridge thirteen:

> Mighty winds,
> That sweep the skirt of some far-spreading wood
> Of ancient growth, make music not unlike
> The dash of ocean on his winding shore,
> And lull the spirit while they fill the mind;
> Unnumber'd branches waving in the blast,
> And all their leaves fast flutt'ring, all at once.
> Nor less composure waits upon the roar
> Of distant floods, or on the softer voice
> Of neighb'ring fountain, or of rills that slip
> Through the cleft rock, and, chiming as they fall
> Upon loose pebbles, lose themselves at length
> In matted grass, that with a livelier green
> Betrays the secret of their silent course. (I, 183-196)

There are many passages like this in Cowper, and Coleridge and Lamb after all did think that Cowper was the best of the modern poets. Coleridge, as we shall soon see, used a portion of this very *Task* in his "Frost at Midnight." We would hardly have to look further than here if what we are seeking is excellent blank verse, an essentially natural word order (far better than anything Coleridge was to write before his *annus mirabilis*), sharp and precise observation of nature, and, indeed, a conviction of nature's soothing powers:

> . . . scenes that sooth'd
> Or charm'd me young, no longer young, I find
> Still soothing and of pow'r to charm me still. (*Task*, I, 141-143)

But how crucially different is the smooth transition between youth and age in Cowper, and the *cri de coeur* in Wordsworth on precisely the same subject!

> The Rainbow comes and goes,
> And lovely is the Rose,

> The Moon doth with delight
> Look round her when the heavens are bare,
>> Waters on a starry night
>> Are beautiful and fair;
> The sunshine is a glorious birth;
> But yet I know, where'er I go,
> That there hath passed away a glory from the earth.

And just as an emotional chasm separates the intensity of Wordsworth's view of nature and Cowper's, so is there a profound difference between the comparative chasteness of Cowper's diction and the severe simplicity and compression of Wordsworth's early poems.

61. *CL*, I, 397-398. Precisely when these lines were written is uncertain. And since they *may* have been added to "The Ruined Cottage" after June 1797, it is possible to argue that they reflect the influence of Coleridge. Needless to say, this has been done. How does it happen that the theme seems essential Wordsworth and that Coleridge was unable to find in his own poetry a passage to quote to his brother? We are asked to believe that Coleridge, "the most humble of men," ceded the theme of the "One Life" to his new friend!

62. "Fears in Solitude," l. 24, *PW*, I, 257.

63. *CL*, I, 354. STC's underscoring. This famous passage should be related to a neglected one in Crabb Robinson's diary. During a conversation in 1811 on German metaphysics with Coleridge, the latter

> related some curious anecdotes of his son Hartley, whom he represented as a most remarkable child—deep thinker in his infancy; one who tormented himself in his attempts to solve the problems that would equally torment a full-grown man. . . . Hartley, when about five, was asked a question by someone concerning himself calling him "Hartley." "Which Hartley?" asked the boy. "Why, is there more than one Hartley?" "Yes," he replied, "there's a deal of Hartleys." "How so?" "There's Picture Hartley" (Hazlitt had painted a portrait of him) "and Shadow Hartley, and there's Echo Hartley, and there's Catch-me-fast Hartley," at the same time seizing his own arm with the other hand very eagerly, an action which shows that his mind must have been led to reflect on what Kant calls the great and inexplicable mystery, viz. that man should be both his own subject and object, and these should yet be one. At the same early age, says Coleridge, he used to be in an agony of thought, puzzling himself about the reality of existence. . . . Hartley when a boy had no pleasure in *things*; they made no impression on him, till they had undergone a sort of process in his mind, and become thoughts of feelings. (*HCR*, W, 44. Italics in text)

The last sentence confirms the suspicion that has been mounting throughout the passage, namely, that we are confronted with another Coleridgean fantasy. Coleridge's identification with his son Hartley was very strong (as will be seen hereafter), and here we see him projecting onto Hartley that which he so urgently wished to have believed of himself: that it was as a preternaturally gifted child that he had come to grapple with the abstruse problems of his mature meditations.

64. *PW*, I, 102.

65. "Lines Written in the Album at Elbingerode," ll. 16-18. *PW*, I, 315-316.

66. "Ode to Dejection," of course, is the key document in this matter. I do not think it can be doubted that, from a philosophical point of view, he has far the better of the dispute (if it is a dispute) between himself and Wordsworth. He is surely right in saying that "we receive but what we give" in our relations with nature. This, however, is irrelevant to our present concerns. Usually it is said that Coleridge's personal unhappiness led him to this discovery. But we have seen that from 1795 to 1799, presumably in the very intensity of his flush of love for nature, there were always doubts—and, I believe, always a sufficient distance between himself and his subject to be aware that the "symbolic language" of nature was just a useful poetic myth.

By 1803, Coleridge seems to have become fully aware of the danger of these beliefs to orthodox Christian doctrine. In his notebooks he warns Wordsworth against the danger of becoming "a Pedant yourself in a bad cause. . . . surely, always to look at the superficies of Objects for the purpose of taking Delight in their Beauty, & sympathy with their real or imagined Life, is . . . deleterious to the Health & manhood of Intellect . . ." (*N*, 1616).

The idea of nature as speaking a mysterious, symbolic language, however, always had its intellectual attractions, especially in connection with cosmological system-building. It was in 1805 that he entered into his notebooks the following often-quoted passage:

> In looking at objects of Nature while I am thinking, as at yonder moon dim-glimmering thro' the dewy window-pane, I seem rather to be seeking, as it were *asking*, a symbolical language for something within me that already and forever exists, than observing any thing new. Even when the latter is the case, yet still I have always an obscure feeling as if that new phaenomenon were the dim Awaking of a forgotten or hidden Truth of my inner Nature. . . . What is the right, the virtuous Feeling, and consequent action, when a man having long meditated & perceived a certain Truth finds another, [?&/a] foreign Writer, who has handled the same with an approximation to the Truth, as he ⟨had previously⟩ conceived it? Joy! Let Truth make her Voice *audible*! (*N*, 2546, STC's underscoring)

Coleridge has not vouchsafed to tell us in which "foreign writer" the "truth" is to found. It might have been any one of several, since the general idea was becoming a commonplace. In Schelling's *On University Studies*, for example, we find:

> Nature is like some very ancient author whose message is written in hieroglyphics on colossal pages, as the Artist says in Goethe's poem. Even those who investigate nature only empirically need to know her language in order to understand utterances which have become unintelligible to us. (p. 40)

And elsewhere in Schelling we read: "What we call nature is a poem encoded in secret and mysterious signs, but if the riddle could be solved, we would recognize in nature the Odyssey of the mind" (*Werke*, III, 628. Quoted from *US*, p. xv).

The instability of Coleridge's views on all these matters appears clearly in *Biographia Literaria*, where he chides Wordsworth for choosing in the daffodil too mean a vessel for such great thoughts, thus turning his back upon, or misunderstanding, one of the primary springs of Wordsworth's power as a poet. If the daffodil cannot provoke thoughts too deep for tears, what in nature can? Is not all of creation part of "One Life"?

The later years show a violent reaction against earlier doctrinal errors. The criticism of Wordsworth in *Biographia* is trifling compared to that leveled against his "nature poetry" a few years later in one of Coleridge's letters to Allsop (I, 107). And it is melancholy that anyone who had ever loved nature and found it so beneficent, could later have attacked the whole idea of Pantheism as "a handsome Mask that does not alter a single feature of the ugly Face it hides." The doctrine of "Deus omnia et omnia Deus" is "incompatible with moral responsibility. . . . Pantheism is but a painted Atheism and . . . the Doctrine of the Trinity is the great and only sure Bulwark against it" (*PL*, p. 433. Miss Coburn suggests a date of around 1818 for this entry).

Coleridge's poetry, letters, and notebooks of 1797-98 (to confine ourselves solely to that) testify amply and eloquently not only to the author's intense but presumably long-standing love of nature. Yet it is a curious and revealing fact that Coleridge, in any practical sense, seems rarely to have gone out of his way to enjoy those beauties and feelings so sweet to remembrance. Of course, this in itself may mean no more than the pious Coleridge's singular indifference to church attendance, but it is suggestive. In Ernest Hartley Coleridge's edition of his grandfather's letters appears the following note, worth pondering:

> Coleridge will never lose his title of a *Lake Poet*, but of the ten years during which he was nominally resident in the Lake District, he was absent at least half the time. Of his greater poems there are but four, the second part of "Christabel," the "Dejection: an Ode," the "Picture," and the "Hymn before Sunrise," which take their colouring from the scenery of Westmoreland and Cumberland.

He was but twenty-six when he visited Ottery for the last time. It was in his thirty-fifth year that he bade farewell to Ṣtowey and the Quantocks, and after he was turned forty he never saw Grasmere or Keswick again. Ill health and the *res angusta domi* are stern gaolers, but, if he had been so minded, he would have found a way to revisit the pleasant places in which he had passed his youth and early manhood. In truth, he was well content to be a dweller in "the depths of the huge city" or its outskirts, and like Lamb, he "could not *live* in Skiddaw." (*Letters*, I, 404-405, n. 2. Italics in text)

Was it about the earlier or the later Coleridge that Wordsworth said "he was not under the influence of natural objects" (Grosart, III, 442)?

67. Lines 54-55. *PW*, I, 365. *WPW*, IV, 279 (Intimations Ode, l. 4).

68. Piper, in a minute and lengthy analysis of the development of Wordsworth's and Coleridge's ideas, concludes that Wordsworth "had come to some of his most important beliefs long before Coleridge visited Alfoxden in June 1797." I believe him mistaken when he adds, "Those beliefs had a good deal in common with the ones which Coleridge had reached on his own account" (p. 79). For while Piper demonstrates convincingly Wordsworth's development, the same cannot be done *from Coleridge's poetry*, but must be pieced together from statements he made in letters *after* he met Wordsworth or long afterward.

In Jonathan Wordsworth's often brilliant *The Music of Humanity: A Critical Study of Wordsworth's Ruined Cottage* (New York, 1969), the influence of Coleridge is asserted as crucial from one end of the book to the other, again without proof. The fact that the documentary record of Wordsworth's works and thoughts between 1794 and 1796 is abysmally meager permits every kind of supposition to flourish as fact with respect to the influence of Coleridge. But the record of Coleridge's letters and notebooks from 1794 onwards is of almost unparalleled richness. And *nowhere* do we find those beliefs which, at the middle of 1797, flow so abundantly from his pen. Everybody knows that Coleridge was almost compulsively communicative about his ideas; it was deeply ingrained in his nature to speak and write of ideas that interested him. We have seen how often he seemed compelled to enunciate ideas as his own which derived from recent reading. The absence of any *record* of an idea in Coleridge's writings is strong presumptive evidence of its nonexistence. But this is not true of Wordsworth, who was not communicative about his ideas and did not keep a journal.

The absence of manuscript evidence in Wordsworth has, therefore, a very different meaning from the same fact in Coleridge. Furthermore, the early Wordsworth manuscripts remain, despite the heroic efforts of scholars (including Jonathan Wordsworth), in a most uncertain state. For example, one of Wordsworth's early works, *The Sometshire Tragedy*, is now destroyed. If a passage of ten lines can provide scholars with opportunity for seemingly endless commentary (as is true of one of the 1794 "Windy Brow" alterations), should we not continually remind ourselves that the manuscript record, after all, represents only a small part of any artist's aesthetic activity? When we recall that the records of the Wordsworths were picked over by generations of scholars before it was learned that William had had a French mistress and an illegitimate daughter by her, should we not be extremely cautious as to how far manuscripts tell the whole story of anything? When Jonathan Wordsworth writes that "under the influence of Coleridge [in 1797], Wordsworth had become interested in the spiritual basis of his own experience," (p. 17) he substitutes supposition for fact. And because he sees Coleridge's influence as so decisive, he practically obliterates the existence of any significant poetic activity in Wordsworth between *An Evening Walk* and *The Borderers*, a two-year period which may well have been the decisive one in Wordsworth's aesthetic development. One awkward result of this procedure is that Wordsworth has to be credited with a tremendous amount of poetic activity in the three months just preceding the arrival of Coleridge: "Yew Trees," the original "Ruined Cottage," and "The Old Cumberland Beggar" are all assigned to April-June 1797. As to "The Ruined Cottage": "Before he [Wordsworth] came under the influence of Coleridge at Alfoxden there was no total scheme of things into which Margaret's life and death could have been fitted" (p. 108). And what is this "total scheme of things," which is asked to bear so heavy an intellectual burden? We are continually brought back to the now fashionable phrase, "One Life." "Wordsworth had taken over from Coleridge the doctrine of the One Life because it gave a firm basis for his intuitions, and in doing so had no doubt convinced himself that he perceived the life-force directly" (p. 209). The particularity of these specific claims—for which, be it remembered, there is no documentary evidence—could simply not have been made by otherwise careful scholars before the ascension of Coleridge to his present commanding position in the literary firmament. But let us look past the dazzle of reputation to the simple realities. Could Wordsworth really have reached maturity without having heard the doctrine that all animated nature is instinct with common life? Let it be emphasized that there is no such doctrine as the One Life in Coleridge *before* meeting Wordsworth, and if some lines can be interpreted so as to imply such a construction, we may certainly say that there is no *emphasis* on the doctrine in Coleridge before 1797. (The whole heretical idea was anathema to him later when he reverted to his earlier orthodoxies.) But *all* of Wordsworth's work in 1797-98 either implies or firmly states some version of this belief. Coleridge *may* have urged Wordsworth to express the idea concretely and in a broad philosophical setting—a dubious blessing, as Wordsworth's later history was to show. But we need not accept any of this as a true account of the intellectual relations of Wordsworth and Coleridge. There is *no reason* to believe that all these ideas were not explicitly in Wordsworth's head before he met Coleridge.

Intellectual relations between geniuses are inevitably complex, and those between Wordsworth and Coleridge far more so than most. The influence of Coleridge on Wordsworth is beyond our present concerns, but I hope to deal with the subject elsewhere. To state two of my conclusions summarily, Coleridge's influence on *The Prelude* is very great, and in part quite destructive, for it enmeshed Wordsworth in an ever-more-grandiose, self-centered, intellectual project (to which his egotism was all too susceptible) and set him voyaging through ever stranger seas of thought, quite alien to his natural genius.

21. MIRACLES AND RARE DEVICES

1. *Pliny's Letters*, trans. William Melmoth, revised by W. M. L. Hutchinson (Loeb Classical Library, 1915), pp. 57-58. Quoted from *N*, 1944n, where the information about the appearance of the quotation in the *Friend* is also given.

2. *BL*, I, 129. Italics in text. One of the most sharply observed details in "This Lime Tree Bower" is that of the rook that "Flew *creeking* o'er thy head" (l. 74). In a note to all editions Coleridge drew attention to this phenomenon as follows: "Some months after I had written this line, it gave me pleasure to find that Bartram had observed the same circumstance of the Savanna Crane" (*PW*, I, 181, n. 1). The quotation that follows from Bartram uses the word "creek" to describe the sound of the crane's wings in flight. Precisely when Coleridge first read Bartram has been much debated. Lowes devoted one of his longest notes to the problem and concluded, after mistakenly rejecting the possibility that "Lewti" was based on a Wordsworth poem, that Coleridge must have read Bartram as early as 1794-95 (*RX*, pp. 513-516). Miss Coburn concludes that the numerous entries from Bartram in Coleridge's Gutch memorandum book must all be dated *after* "This Lime Tree Bower" (*N*, 218n), the overwhelming reason for which would seem to be Coleridge's statement that he read Bartram "some months after" he had written the line about the rook's creeking wings. But surely Coleridge's memory could have been wrong, as it so often was in these matters. Or Coleridge might have picked up the detail about the creeking wings directly from Bartram (whom he used in several other poems without acknowledgment) and have written his note as a bit of obscurantism, which is not uncharacteristic. The earliest of Coleridge's journal entries from Bartram, No. 218, need not, therefore, be dated as no earlier than June 1797, the more so as No. 211 is dated by Miss Coburn as "close to 19 Nov 1796." For Coleridge to have written just six brief entries into his journals in the seven months between November 1796 and June 1797 would be most unusual.

3. *BL*, I, 128.

4. House cites these lines on pages 78-79. But in using a Cowper text of 1803 or after, he prints "brittle *toils*" at l. 307, instead of "brittle *toys*," a much closer link with "Frost at Midnight." See *Cowper's Poetical Works* (Oxford, 1934), p. 189, *app. crit.*

5. HH, p. 79.   6. *PW*, I, 240, n. 2.

7. *PW*, I, 241, *app. crit.* After all this was written, I learned that everything had been pointed out long ago by the indefatigable A. Brandl, who not only anticipated the connections thus far stated, but my later observation about the derivation of "The Frost performs its secret minstry"! See "Cowpers 'Winter evening' und Coleridges 'Frost at Midnight,' " *Archiv für das Studium der Neueren Sprachen und Literaturen*, XCVI (1896), 341-342.

8. Italics in text.

9. Allsop, I, 107. Italics in text. Coleridge continued: "the odd introduction of the popular, almost the vulgar, religion in his later publications (the popping in, as Hartley says, of the old man with a beard), suggests the painful suspicion of worldly prudence. . . ."

10. *CL*, I, 328. The passage finally appeared many years later in Book I of *The Excursion*, ll. 900-907.

11. *CL*, IV, 572. Italics in text.   12. *CL*, I, 351. STC's emphasis.

13. *CL*, I, 396-398.

14. Cowper, however, differs from the Romantics in not overevaluating the *moral* meaning of nature, and in seeing, like Johnson, just how the city is necessary to high civilization. Of so temperate and measured a position, obviously, passionate poetry is unlikely to emerge. In this sense, no matter what Coleridge believed about nature, the Wordsworthian myth was indispensable.

15. *CL*, I, 333-334. STC's emphasis. The following June, Coleridge told one of his traveling companions in Germany that when he had written his college Greek Ode on Astronomy, "he first conceived the idea and afterwards hunted thro' the several poets for words in which to clothe those ideas." The remark occurs in a discussion of the authenticity of Chatterton's Rowley poems, during which extremely suggestive remarks are put forward as to the methods Chatterton may have used to confuse later investigators (Edith J. Morley, "Coleridge in Germany (1799)," in *Wordsworth and Coleridge*, ed. E. L. Griggs [New York, 1939], p. 231).

16. *CL*, IV, 571. Italics in text.

17. Beer, p. 175.

18. In Germany during 1798-99, away from the immediate influence and example of Wordsworth, Coleridge's verse experiments and imitations commence again in extraordinary profusion. We find specimens of "Hexameters," "Catullian Hendecasyllables," "The Homeric Hexameter," "The Ovidian Elegiac Metre," and more, much, much more by way of translation and paraphrase in the following months. The notebooks throughout Coleridge's life show many "experiments for a metre."

19. Lowes seems quite right in cautioning against exaggerating Taylor's influence. Chaucer and Spenser were, after all, nearer to hand. See *RX*, pp. 335 ff. For possible connections between *Lenore* and "The Ancient Mariner," see *RX*, pp. 545-546, n. 52.

20. Pages 147-148.

21. Upon the publication of the second edition of *Lyrical Ballads*, Lamb wrote Wordsworth a long and deservedly famous letter. He was sorry that Coleridge had added "A Poet's Reverie" as a subtitle to "The Ancient Mariner." Far more important, Lamb courageously took exception to Wordsworth's strictures against the poem. "For me," he wrote, "I was never so affected with any human Tale. After first reading it, I was totally possessed with it for many days. . . . I am hurt and vexed that you should think it necessary, with a prose apology, to open the eyes of dead men that cannot see" (*LL*, I, 240).

22. Quoted from *Lyrical Ballads*, eds. R. L. Brett and A. R. Jones (London, 1963), p. 314.

23.   A passage in one of Wordsworth's juvenile poems reads:

> Perhaps my pains might be beguil'd
> By some fond vacant gazing child;
> He the long wondrous tale would hear . . . (*WPW*, I, 281, ll. 490-492)

24.   *RX*, pp. 140-141. Italics in text.

25.   *CL*, I, 297. In February Coleridge said that Lamb's criticisms had been so severe that he did not have the "heart to finish the poem" (*CL*, I, 309).

26.   "The Destiny of Nations" (ll. 64-69, 79-80). *PW*, I, 133-134, and *RX*, p. 96, where the italics are supplied. Among the omitted lines we find the Laplander

> Guiding his course or by Niemi lake
> Or Balda Zhiok, or the mossy stone
> Of Solfar-kapper . . .

Lamb had written that the simile of the Laplander here "will bear comparison with any in Milton for fullness of circumstance and lofty-pacedness of Versification" (*LL*, I, 13). It seems worth stressing that Lamb was capable of praising lines like these in such exalted terms on 10 June 1796, and much later, because it is important not to overemphasize his influence on Coleridge in the direction of a purer diction. "Monody on the Death of Chatterton," "Religious Musings," and "Ode to the Departing Year" were all highly praised by him. This was still more true of the Wedgwood circle, whose conventional judgments could not have influenced Coleridge in other directions. See R. S. Woof's "Coleridge and Thomasina Dennis," *UTQ*, XXXII (1962), 37-54, for much valuable information about the aesthetic judgments of this group, especially pp. 41, 43, and 44. Shortly after meeting Wordsworth, Coleridge praised some lines of Thomasina Dennis thus: "These have the freshness of nature on them, they are not taken from Books" (p. 47).

27.   *RX*, pp. 96-97.

28.   *PW*, I, 86 and n. 1. In 1811 Coleridge said that he had written this sonnet to Godwin on Southey's recommendation, without as yet having read Godwin (*CL*, III, 315)!

29.   *RX*, p. 41. See Lowes's further discussion, p. 509.

30.   Quoted from *Poems*, p. 598. Mrs. Humphrey Ward, in Ward's *English Poets* (1880), I, 550, had originally identified the borrowing from Davies (*RX*, p. 604*i*).

31.   Lines 6-10, 19-20. *PW*, I, 252 and *app. crit.*

32.   Quoted from *RX*, pp. 333-334. Lowes's italics.

33.   Lines 347-355. *PW*, II, 1040.

34.   *RX*, p. 334. In a copy of *Sybilline Leaves*, at the foot of the page containing the lines "Nodding their heads before her goes/The merry Minstralsy," Coleridge wrote: "Chaucer. Squire's Tale—v. 260. Beforne him *goth* the loude minstralsie." Beneath this line he added: "Till he come to his chamber of paraments,/Ther as they *sounden* divers instruments" (*RX*, p. 604*g*). The italics are Coleridge's. "Divers instruments" suggests a possible origin of the phrase "And now 'twas like all instruments."

35.   That our fates are in our stars is, of course, an idea almost as old as man. Still, Coleridge just possibly was remembering the phrase "shedding sweet influence" from *Paradise Lost*, VII, 275.

36.   *PW*, I, 101 and *app. crit.*

37.   A typical example of such work is H. F. Watson's " 'The Borderers' and 'The Ancient Mariner,' " *TLS*, 28 Dec. 1935, p. 899. Watson cites the passage below from Wordsworth's early play for its obvious similarities with "The Ancient Mariner" and notes also the strong parallels in the character of Oswald and the Mariner.

Oswald:

   The wind fell;
We lay becalmed week after week, until
The water of the vessel was exhausted;
I felt a double fever in my veins,
Yet rage suppressed itself;—to a deep stillness
Did my pride tame my pride;—for many days,
On a dead sea under a burning sky,
I brooded o'er my injuries, deserted
By man and nature;—if a breeze had blown,
It might have found its way into my heart,
And I had been—no matter—do you mark me?

Marmeduke:

Quick—to the point—if any untold crime
Doth haunt your memory,

Oswald:

Patience, hear me further!—
One day in silence did we drift at noon
By a bare rock, narrow, and white, and bare . . . (IV, 1692-1706)

38. ES, pp. 210-211. Italics in text.   39. *CL*, I, 318.
40. Lines 181, 195-196. *PW*, I, 195, *app. crit.*
41. Lines 330, 337-339. WPW, I, 368; 277-278.   42. Lines 275-276. *PW*, I, 198.
43. Lines 5-6. *WPW*, I, 42.

44. The nature and value of originality in the arts are among the least understood and consistently ignored problems in aesthetics. Only a substantial work could possibly do justice to the difficulties involved. Fortunately, it is not obligatory to undertake such a task to understand the broad shape of Coleridge's poetic achievement, or to draw sound inferences about his creative procedures. I hope elsewhere to deal comprehensively with the general subject, but I would here predict that the present dogmatic insistence on the self-contained inviolability of the aesthetic object will collapse. In practice, origins are almost always central to the evaluative process. A hallowed painting that proves to be a fake, forgery, or copy, at once plunges precipitously in esteem. The canvas and colors have not changed, yet their value has. Few critics possess the courage or authority to assign this process to mere philistinism. Overwhelmingly, critics revise their former judgment of the false work, thereby preserving the shaky dogma which holds that only an original genius can produce a great work.

Coleridge himself, in a revealing remark that has been ignored by critics, wrote in a volume of Barry Cornwall's poems: "There are poems of great merit, the authors of which I should yet not feel impelled so to designate" (*MC*, p. 343). Does this not imply that there are works, taken in themselves, that are greater than their creators? Coleridge's beloved Casimir, for centuries revered as one of the brightest luminaries of Poland's Renaissance literature, has in recent years been shown to have "stolen *en bloc* and without acknowledgment from a contemporary Italian" the world-famous series of poems called the *Silviludia* (John Sparrow, "A Polish Plagiarist," in *Controversial Essays* [New York, 1966], p. 89). It is barely possible that the poems themselves will retain their former reputation, but there is no doubt whatever that Casimir's reputation, which has already suffered grievously, will not recover.

Because every artist's work is to some extent derived from predecessors, it is very easy to confuse the novice as to the central issues involved. Part of the problem is that our critical instruments are so imprecise that we frequently admire a poem or an artist for the wrong reasons. Some years ago an eight-line poem by Hugh MacDiarmid was printed in *TLS* as a "small imagist masterpiece." The following week Glyn Jones wrote to say that with the exception of the first line, all the rest were his own words, rearranged in the form of a poem from one of his short stories. Then followed an alternately brilliant and excruciatingly silly series of letters, during which MacDiarmid's unacknowledged borrowings were widely extended, while other correspondents wrote to insist upon the importance of what MacDiarmid had achieved by rearranging the words of others into, allegedly, more emphatic visual patterns. Whatever the *theoretical* problem, everyone (except certain critics) will concede that MacDiarmid in future years will not be praised for having written a "small imagist masterpiece," in which only one line was his own invention. The art *object* remains the same, but knowledge of origins *has* made a change in our view of the words. (The controversy will be found in *TLS* under the title "Mr. MacDiarmid and Dr. Grieve," 31 Dec. 1964, p. 1178; 21 Jan. 1965, p. 47; 28 Jan., p. 67; 4 Feb., p. 87; 11 Feb., p. 107; 18 Feb., p. 127.)

Between extreme dependence and the most subtle influence there is, obviously, an unbroken chain of gradations. Because literary criticism, especially in recent decades, has either steered clear of the problem of originality, or scornfully exiled the matter from the courts of evaluation, critics must insist dogmatically that the distinction between a seemingly completely independent work, and one that has been subtly influenced by another, or a third that is a gross imitation, can have no bearing on a poem's *inherent worth* (another vague term that struts about as an objective reality).

45. *RX*, pp. 53-54. Italics in text.   46. *RX*, p. 249.

47. That Coleridge *did* identify the Mariner and the Wandering Jew would seem to be proven by a direct statement in a portion of his *Table Talk* which Henry Nelson Coleridge did not publish. It is a very curious fact—and one which bears investigation—that HNC omitted from the *Table Talk* passages of immense interest to students of his uncle's poetry, while admitting all sorts of dull and inconsequential passages.

48. F. Schiller, *Aesthetical and Philosophical Essays and The Ghost-Seer*, ed. N. H. Dole (Boston, 1902), II, 224-225.

49. *RX*, p. 113.   50. *RX*, p. 92.

51. *CL*, I, 320-321.

52. "Coleridge and *The Ancient Mariner*," *Nineteenth Century Studies* (Ithaca, N. Y., 1940), pp. 15-16. In the following discussion this article is cited as "Bald." The first journal entry has subsequently been published in its entirety and may be found in *N*, 1616.

We have seen how carefully Coleridge was on the hunt for materials during his years of apprenticeship, how often he read with pen in hand, making notes from the books he was reading for future poems. In his letter of July 1797, referred to several times already, he invites Southey to visit Wordsworth's home at Alfoxden: "so divine and wild is the country that I am sure it would increase your stock of images" (*CL*, I, 336). Somewhat later he said, "I attend Davy's lectures [on chemistry] to increase my stock of metaphors" (Shedd, IV, 468).

53. This subject may be studied in detail by consulting the indexes in *RX*, and Arthur Nethercot's *The Road to Tryermaine* (Chicago, 1939), a less successful attempt to relate "Christabel" to Coleridge's reading.

54. Bald, p. 16.

55. Bald, pp. 19-21. Italics in text. See also *HCR*, I, 87 and Grosart, III, 487. In October 1795 Southey wrote that Coleridge "did me much good—I him more." Whalley suggests that one can go far in justifying this claim by recognizing a previously unnoticed contribution of Southey to the formation of Coleridge's mind. Southey, Whalley suggests, "stimulated Coleridge's interest in the poetic possibilities of travel literature and the twilight materials of nascent science" ("Samuel Taylor Coleridge and Robert Southey in Bristol, 1795" *RES*, NS, I [1950], 330).

56. *WLC*, p. 243. Italics in text.

57. *CL*, I, 379. Coleridge did not indicate to Wordsworth that "wherever Mr. Lewis has borrowed, he has acknowledged his obligations," which comes from a review of *The Castle Spectre* that appeared in 1798 and which D. V. Erdman has attributed to Coleridge on the basis of circumstantial evidence. It seems impossible to doubt the hand of Coleridge when one finds such

observations as that there is "scarcely an original incident in the piece"; and, "Mr. Lewis has frequently imitated the styles of Schiller" (See *BNYPL*, LXIII [1959], 584-585).

58. *CL*, III, 469-470.

59. Determining the probability of an asserted parallel is one of the most frustrating problems in all literary scholarship. Unless a considerable verbal identity exists between two passages, it is not only possible that two readers will disagree sharply as to the asserted connection between one work and another, but it seems in fact to be probable. A sufficient number of pennies will eventually become a fortune, but an almost infinite number of slight or problematical "parallels" will not add up to certitude.

Anyone who has followed controversies among scholars as to literary influences must, at least intermittently, feel deeply skeptical that source studies will ever be governed by clear, controlling, and sensitive principles. For the present, it remains sadly true that one scholar's certainty is another's vague possibility, if not utter absurdity.

The truth of these remarks is sharply underscored by the problems raised by the work of W. W. Beyer, whose several articles on the influence of C. M. Wieland's *Oberon* on Coleridge culminated in his book *The Enchanted Forest* (New York, 1963). Beyer's main propositions, that Coleridge in several of his major poems, especially "The Ancient Mariner," and to a lesser extent "Kubla Khan" and "Christabel," drew in detail upon the plot, images, ideas, and words of *Oberon* have been widely accepted.

Needless to say, a convincing demonstration of these assertions would not be unwelcome to those students of Coleridge who are frustrated at the apparent lack of clear and direct sources in some of the major poems of the *annus mirabilis*. If "The Ancient Mariner" derived from a single source as clearly as Coleridge's early "Anthem for the Children of Christ's Hospital" was reconstituted from Bowles's *Verses on the Philanthropic Society*, a substantial advance could be hoped for in our understanding of the creative mind. And, in fact, this is what Beyer's work claims to establish. Arthur Nethercot's work on the supposed diverse sources of "Christabel" (in *The Road to Tryermaine*) is dismissed as of small value. As for Elisabeth Schneider's *Coleridge, Opium, and Kubla Khan*, "to more than one reader her 'parallels' virtually without exception seemed *no* parallels and hence utterly unconvincing" (pp. 122, 145. Italics in text). The fifty-page chapter in *The Enchanted Forest* called "A Matrix for the *Ancient Mariner*?" summarizes a large portion of Wieland's *Oberon* as follows:

> Cantos V, VII-X, and the last of Canto XII of *Oberon*—the central, daemonically motivated portion which begins with the weirdly interrupted wedding feast—tell of the departure of a ship, a moment's misdeed on shipboard (a crime against divine ordinance) and, immediately, protracted daemonic vengeance and a lengthy spiritualizing penance. On a circular voyage, under natural then daemonic propulsion, the crime having been committed, its sinful wanderer-hero finds all nature turned against him, and experiences an awful sea storm and imminent shipwreck, his shipmates' condemnation, and gambling for his fate. He undergoes desert wanderings and hunger and thirst, agonized remorse and delusive spectral persecution. At length sympathy and love bring saintly intervention and a visitation of angelic voices. He undergoes gradual spiritualization and finally atonement; and, ultimately, after a welcoming at a daemonic pageant of lovely lights, he returns with the aid of benevolent spirits of the air to his own country. (p. 72)

As if this similarity—identity, rather—of plot were not sufficiently astounding, we soon read: "*that central choral element of two aerial voices which Lowes quite failed to trace*, is pervasively similar to the daemonic machinery of *Oberon*, even as step for step the patterns are basically and consistently akin" (p. 74. Italics in text). To these connections, Beyer adds still more, so that in fact it appears that there is scarcely an event or image in "The Ancient Mariner" which Coleridge had not drawn from *Oberon*.

Let us pause, however, and examine the relevant portion of the lengthy *Oberon*. Huon, a Christian hero, rescues the lovely Moslem girl Rezia from her intended bridegroom during their wedding festivities. The supernatural Oberon appears and bids the two lovers hasten to Rome to be wed with the Pope's blessing. Until then, they are strictly forbidden to trespass against the laws of chastity. Through the better part of two cantos the lovers resist their powerful inner promptings, but one night, thinking Huon ill, Rezia enters his cabin, and then, scarcely conscious of what they are doing, their love is consummated. At this point, Beyer writes, "by this *shipboard sin of a heedless moment* the daemon king [Oberon], their benevolent guardian, is at once transformed into his other phase: a baleful, dread avenger. For *the sin (or fall) releases the daemonic vengeance and spectral persecution, and all Nature turns against them*" (p. 76. Italics in text). From this point on in Beyer's discussion of the relations between Coleridge and Wieland, the illicit moment between the two young lovers who resisted long and hard their powerful physical desires is referred to as "the shipboard sin." Since the Mariner's unmotivated killing of the albatross is also *a shipboard sin of a heedless moment*, the persistent substitution of this phrase for the concrete events eventually creates the effect that there is a deep and significant bond between the two stories.

But these events are not to be equated. The fatal moment in *Oberon* is not, in Beyer's sense, heedless. The description of the event in this way seems to derive from the pull of the Mariner's *unpremeditated* act, which is not at all the same thing. *A* may equal *B*, and *B* may equal *C*, but it does not then follow *in poetry* that *A* equals *C*. The "crime" of the lovers in *Oberon* is experienced as something totally different from the Mariner's killing of the albatross. Huon and Rezia are tormented by desire before they at last succumb to ungovernable passion. Their act is entirely comprehensible. And they were forewarned of what their fate would be if they consummated their love before a formal marriage in Rome.

In Beyer's summary of the action, the "wanderer-hero," after committing his shipboard sin, experiences "his shipmates' condemnation, and gambling for his fate," which is the Mariner's tale completely. But in *Oberon* the fate of Huon ("the wanderer-hero") is never gambled for in this sense at all. The event put forward as a parallel to the specter-bark sequence is the casting of lots by the ship's crew to find out who has offended the gods, which is very different.

We are told that the wanderer, after suffering hunger and thirst, agonizing remorse and delusive spectral persecution, "undergoes gradual spiritualization." No two readers are likely to assign emphases the same way in describing a plot; nevertheless, it is much to be doubted that many readers of *Oberon* will recognize this description of the events. Huon does not seem in any sense to undergo "spiritualization." His character can hardly be said to change at all. He undergoes protracted abstinence solely to appease Oberon; there is never any psychological change, no spiritual crisis, no "sympathy and love" which bring angelic intervention—certainly not in the sense that this can be said of the Ancient Mariner.

Still more convincing, initially, than the plot parallels seem to be are the numerous verbal connections Beyer finds. But here, too, intimate knowledge of Coleridge's poem seems powerfully to influence Beyer's reading of the German tale. We are told that "the central action of Wieland's romance occurs in Canto V, significantly soon after *the lordly guests having met* and the *wedding feast being set*" (p. 75. Italics in text). But these are Coleridge's operative words: "The guests are met, the feast is set" ("Ancient Mariner," l. 7), and thus the wedding scenes, so very different in both poems, come to seem distinctly alike, especially as Beyer at once goes on to describe the stately entrance amid blaring trumpets of the "rosy bride." Rosy is not underscored, nor does the word appear in Wieland, but it does in Coleridge: "The bride hath paced into the hall / Red as a rose is she." Similarly, Beyer consistently describes Rezia as "the dark lady" (for example, pp. 75, 78), thus endowing the Moslem girl with all the subtle Coleridgean associations of "the dark ladié."

Beyer's verbal and ideational parallels are so numerous and apparently so close that it may well seem that a great many could be denied and that a very strong case would still remain. But this, I feel, is not true. Again and again parallels are asserted which could only be refuted by being tediously minute. Let a few further examples, therefore, suffice. One of Beyer's most convincing parallels is that at a certain point, "realizing his helplessness to aid *his companion*, 'wonder of nature, *so* loving and *beautiful*,' he [Huon] *cries out* and '*bites his* lips in wild anguish.' " Beyer invites us to compare "the helpless and remorseful Mariner, who not long after he bites his arm and cries out at the sight of the illusory spectre ship, pities *his* companions, 'the many men, so beautiful' " (p. 78 and note). We may perhaps wish to quarrel with assigning as the source of Coleridge's unusual phrase the completely trite word *beautiful* applied to a nubile young woman. That Coleridge should describe ordinary sailors, and dead men at that, as *beautiful* is utterly different. More important, Beyer tells us, outside quotation marks, that the wanderer "*cries out*," but in fact Huon merely makes a speech. He does indeed bite his lips in a frenzy, but this is very different from the Mariner's extraordinary act of deliberately *biting his arm and sucking the blood* so that his throat will be sufficiently moist to cry out to the specter ship.

Analysis of parallels can often induce a sense of frustration. One can easily feel niggardly in disputing this or that connection. But to concede "possible" connections, however grudgingly, can soon lead to the concession of a substantial connection, since a multitude of connections could hardly be "accidental." The gravest problem to deal with is the accuracy of translation from a foreign language when the words of an English poem are very powerfully in one's mind.

A reasonable test in such an instance is to consult a translation made by someone with no knowledge of what one hopes to prove. It happens that a translation of *Oberon* in two volumes by William Sotheby appeared in London in 1798. This translation seems to agree at hardly any point with the crucial verbal parallels adduced in *The Enchanted Forest*.

Now the entire chain of links between *Oberon* and Coleridge's great poems—for Beyer establishes a multitude of verbal, structural, and ideational parallels not only to "The Ancient Mariner," but also to "Christabel" and "Kubla Khan," and practically all of "The Wanderings of Cain"—all this rests of course on the assumption that Coleridge could read German before he went to Germany in late 1798. We have seen how contradictory are Coleridge's own statements on this particular subject. Later in life he maintained repeatedly that he could not read a word of German before going abroad and had formulated his philosophy long before he had read the German philosophers or could have understood them had their works been available to him.

Beyer, however, would seem to have proved the contrary. So convincing is his evidence that Carl Woodring, in a review of *The Enchanted Forest*, writes that he "demonstrates except to the strongest doubter that Coleridge's knowledge [of German] developed earlier than has been generally believed" (*PQ*, XLIII [1964], 450). To George Watson "it is now clear" that Coleridge had a substantial command of the language before going to Germany (GW, p. 55). As Beyer's case, however, rests almost entirely on Coleridge's own statements, they should be carefully scrutinized. On 5 May 1796 Coleridge wrote Thomas Poole, "I am studying German, & in about six weeks shall be able to read that language with tolerable fluency" (*CL*, I, 209). This looks like a "categorical" statement; nevertheless, it may not be true. A year and a half later, he wrote to Cottle:

I am translating the Oberon of Wieland—it is a difficult Language, and I can translate at least as fast as I can construe.—I pray you, as soon as possible, procure for me a German-English Grammar—I believe there is but one—*Widderburne's*, I think [actually Wendeborn's]—but I am not certain. I have written a ballad of about 300 lines—the Sketch of a Plan of General Study:—and I have made a very considerable proficiency in the French Language, and study it daily—and daily study the German—so that I am not, & have not been, idle. (*CL*, I, 357)

Taken at face value, this is indeed persuasive evidence. But let us remember that Coleridge at that very time had criticized Petrarch's sonnets and delivered himself of various opinions as to the strengths and limitations of Italian, before he could read or speak a word of it. Need we now rehearse the multitude of similar false claims Coleridge had made? To write Poole or Cottle or Wedgwood about his linguistic proficiency means, in itself, alas, next to nothing. In fact, on 1 April 1796, a few days *before* he wrote Poole that he *would* have a tolerable proficiency in German in about six weeks, he wrote to Benjamin Flower, an editor, about one of Lessing's infidel books "not yet translated." "I had some thoughts of translating it," Coleridge complacently goes on. "It unites the wit of Voltaire with the subtlety of Hume and the profound erudition of *our* Lardner" (*CL*, I, 197. STC's underscoring). The young Coleridge's scattershot, scholarly pretentions are marvellously in evidence here. Beyer does not take note of this letter, which ought to induce extreme caution in anyone approaching Coleridge's early linguistic claims.

If Coleridge was studying German at any time before going to Germany, his notebooks betray no sign of it. Precisely how he was studying German, when he had no grammar, is difficult to understand, but we may let that pass. Beyer notes that in a letter of December 1796 to Thelwall Coleridge wrote: "I will translate literally a passage from a German Hexameter Poem Voss's *Luise*" (*CL*, I, 283), and proceeded to deliver some 30 lines of free translation. If Coleridge in fact translated the given passage from *Luise*, it would testify, I think, to quite remarkable proficiency in a beginning student.

But did he actually read *Luise*, and does the passage in English represent his own translation? Beyer points out (p. 43) that the one howling mistranslation from Voss was not really Coleridge's fault but derived from a misprint in a number of the *Critical Review* of some months before, in which this very passage from *Luise* was published! It seems clear, *me judice*, that Coleridge picked up his passage from the journal and not from the original source. It is possible that he puzzled out the meaning with the aid of a dictionary, but it may well be doubted. It seems as likely that he simply asked any one of his wide acquaintance who knew German to translate it for him. (Beyer notes [p. 43] that a sentence from this translation surfaced, unacknowledged, in "The Wanderings of Cain.")

"It is clear from these early notebooks," writes E. M. Wilkinson in an appendix to Kathleen Coburn's edition, "that when Coleridge arrived in Germany he was linguistically ill-equipped for the literary and philosophical tasks he had set himself" (*N*, I, p. 451). Coleridge's journal entries vividly flesh out this too general statement, for in October 1798 we find Coleridge studying the language as a beginner would. He begins to keep lists of nouns and verbs and a variety of basic linguistic forms. Of one word list Miss Coburn writes: "This list is inaccurate at times to the point of incomprehensibility. There seems to be little point in laboriously correcting the mis-hearings and mis-spellings and misunderstandings of one hearing a language for the first time" (*N*, 353*n*). Quite. But as late as May 1799, after eight months in Germany, we find Coleridge entering into his notebook under the heading "German Sounds" what he took to be their English equivalents. "If Coleridge pronounced German according to this description of the sounds," writes Miss Coburn, "it is small wonder that Schlegel begged him to speak English. . . . The vowel equivalents given in this entry are for the most part inadequate or wrong, and there are other mistakes . . ." (*N*, 433 and n).

In the circumstances, what weight are we to give to Coleridge's statements before going to Germany that he was diligently studying the language, that he was translating Voss and Wieland? The answer would appear to be, "Very little." It is curious that in Wilkinson's appendix, "Coleridge's Knowledge of German as Seen in the Early Notebooks," no mention is made of Beyer's well-known work or the quotations from Coleridge on which it rests.

Let us suppose that Coleridge did in fact know some German before 1798, enough even to construe with the aid of a dictionary and grammar. How likely would it be that a beginner would undertake to translate a lengthy and complex German poem, in which the difficulties of comprehension would be enormously complicated by poetic constructions? Would even so gifted an intelligence as Coleridge's struggle along for hundreds of pages translating from a language he had never heard? What would be the aesthetic pleasure in that?

When we observe that the notebooks are devoid of any hint of German study before his arrival in Germany, and then loaded with entries of the sort one would expect a gifted student to enter into a workbook, we are forced to the conclusion—surely not a difficult one to accept in itself— that Coleridge was "romancing" when he wrote that he was translating *Oberon*, and that his general comments as to his study of German are merely bravado. Coleridge, after all, wrote that he was groping his way through Malebranche when we know that he later took out an English translation. And let us not forget the bold etymological speculations a few years later to Wedgwood, which come straight out of a German dictionary.

It would seem, therefore, that with respect to Coleridge's knowledge of German before going to Germany the safest position we can take is that he knew very, very little, certainly not enough to translate either a complex poem or any of the German philosophers he was eventually to study with such diligence.

60. *CL,* IV, 616.

61. *The Use of Criticism and the Use of Poetry* (London, 1944), p. 175. The remark is especially interesting as coming from so ecletic and free-borrowing a poet as Eliot.

62. *CL,* I, 326.

63. Coleridge was even able to put to good use the suggestions of his early publisher Joseph Cottle. See the latter's *ER,* I, 219-224, and *Reminiscences of Samuel Taylor Coleridge and Robert Southey* (London, 1847), pp. 88-95 for an account of Coleridge's acceptance and rejection of Cottle's suggestions for changes in the text of "To an Unfortunate Woman at the Theatre" (*PW,* I, 171).

64. *EL,* p. 239.

65. *CL,* I, 462; *"tinkle"* underscored in text. Coleridge did not mention Wordsworth's letter to his wife, but a decade later, in reprinting passages from his German letters in the *Friend,* he carefully acknowledged Wordsworth, a persuasive example of how retentive his memory could be as to origins. (See also *BL,* II, 122.) For many reasons it is most regrettable that so many of the letters between Wordsworth and Coleridge in Germany have not survived. (See MM, I, 443, n. 1.)

An important bit of evidence bearing upon this and closely related problems is found in Charles S. Bouslog's "Coleridge's Marginalia in the Sara Hutchinson Copy of *Remorse,*" *BNYPL,* LXV (1961), 335. *Remorse* (1814), it will be remembered, was a revision of *Osorio* (1797), the last half of which had been written after he and Wordsworth became neighbors. At the bottom of the page on which I, i, 116-117 appears, Coleridge wrote: "Till then the Play was printed off, I never remembered or rather never recollected, that this phrase was taken from Mr. Wordsworth's Poems! Thank God! it was not from his MSS Poems—& at the 2nd Edition I was afraid to point it out, lest it should appear a trick, to introduce his Name." In a footnote Professor Bouslog writes: "The resemblance between Coleridge's 'It is the obscurest haunt / Of all the mountains' and Wordsworth's 'It is the loneliest place in all these hills' does not seem close enough to justify Coleridge's self-criticism; the point may be that he is thinking of the line as it may have first been written by Wordsworth."

On the contrary, the point is precisely that "It is the loneliest place in all these hills" is ideationally *an exact equivalent* of Coleridge's "It is the obscurest haunt / Of all the mountains." The substitution of "obscurest haunt" for "loneliest place" is almost an object lesson in the difference between the poetic styles of the two men.

Surely Coleridge's note is over tense. Why such extreme emphasis on so trifling a matter? Can we escape the inference that the whole subject was extremely painful to him? As early as 1794 we find him writing to Southey, "In 'Fayette' [*PW,* I, 82] I *unwittingly* (for I did not know it at the Time) borrowed a *thought* from You" (*CL,* I, 137. STC's underscoring).

66. *RX,* pp. 495-496, n. 8.   67. *CL,* I, 493.

68. The first line of the very first poem Coleridge wrote in Germany begins, "William, my teacher, my friend!" ("Hexameters," *PW,* I, 304). W. L. Renwick has noted the implications of line 81 in "Dejection," in which Coleridge, recalling happier days, writes: "Fruits and foliage, not my own, seemed mine." Renwick supposes that the line "can only be acknowledgment of his debt to Wordsworth, for he was a good enough critic to realize that his poems of 1797-8 were different from anything he had written before, and better, and his letters at this time were full or Wordsworth's praise" (*English Literature: 1789-1815* [Oxford, 1963], p. 175).

69. *CL,* I, 623.

70. *CL,* I, 632. By "nature's Lady" Coleridge almost certainly meant "Three Years She Grew in Sun and Shower."

71. *Memoirs of William Wordsworth* (London, 1851), II, 306. See n. 76 below.

72. *LL*, I, 66.

73. *CL*, I, 634, 656, 658. Cf. Alexander Pope: "What we call a Genius, is hard to be distinguished by a man himself, from a strong inclination . . ." ("The Preface of 1717," p. 1).

74. *CL*, II, 714. This whole context is one of the most often quoted and misunderstood in Coleridge's writings. Just a few lines before, Coleridge declared:

> The Poet is dead in me—my imagination (or rather the Somewhat that had been imaginative) lies, like a Cold Snuff on the circular Rim of a Brass Candle-stick, without even a stink of Tallow to remind you that it was once cloathed & mitred with Flame. That is past by!—I was once a Volume of Gold Leaf, rising & riding on every breath of Fancy—but I have beaten myself back into weight & density, and now I sink in quicksilver. . . .

Appleyard observes that this "brilliant series of metaphors . . . paradoxically invokes the imaginative gift he is denying" (*JAA*, p. 72). But the juxtaposition is less paradoxical than deliberate. I. A. Richards has here shrewdly observed that we ought not to take this letter to Godwin too "tragically": it contains too much humor (*The Portable Coleridge*, p. 16).

75. *CL*, II, 959. Italics in text.

76. *CL*, II, 831. STC's emphasis. A few months later he wrote to Mary Robinson, the poetess, "Poetic composition has become laborious & painful to me" (*CL*, II, 903).

77. *N*, 2407. STC's underscoring. Four months later (May 1805), he wrote into his notebook: "Pretended Originality / the Hydnora Africana on the roots of the Euphorbia Mauritanica, & others, that seem to grow out of the ground, having their roots below the surface yet always fastened to the roots of some other Plant / these are the Hypocrite-Parasite plants" (*N*, 2580). Do not such observations suggest how deeply the subject nagged him?

78. *TT*, p. 425. Italics in text.

79. For example: "[Chapman's] moral poems are not quite out of books like Jonson's, nor yet do the sentiments so wholly grow up out of his own natural habit and grandeur of thought, as in Milton" (*CSC*, p. 504).

80. *CSC*, pp. 562-563. STC's emphasis.

81. In the twentieth century the relative popularity of the poetry of Wordsworth and Coleridge has undergone a radical change, a fact which tells us much about how great a shift in aesthetic and moral values has taken place in our time. Both Wordsworth and Coleridge, during the years when their major poetry was being written, placed far more emphasis on the moral and intellectual effects their poetry, especially Wordsworth's, might have upon sympathetic readers than upon the revolution in poetic form and technique which they were accomplishing. When Coleridge praised poems like "Ruth" and "The Brothers" in such exalted terms, he was testifying to their assumed profound moral and characterologically formative content. And when he wrote that "Christabel" was only a "common fairy tale," he was, we may be sure, testifying to his actual original conception of the poem.

Yet few readers today place anything like as high a value on "Ruth" or "The Brothers" as did Wordsworth's contemporaries (and most of the nineteenth-century public). Contemporary critics in fact neglect these poems, while "Christabel" is considered one of the great works in the language, although it is a poem without a discernible content. Critics have, to be sure, discovered in its depths all sorts of misty meanings. But the contemporary reader feels the power of the poem without necessarily articulating to himself any particular significance. If the theme of lesbianism is brought forward, he will listen respectfully. As to "Kubla Khan," our pleasure is not likely to be spoiled by reflections that we do not understand it, or that it is a fragment. The tormented and isolated Mariner was from the beginning sailing in the wrong historical latitudes.

The very weaknesses of Coleridge's poems, as seen by his contemporaries and most of the nineteenth century, their alleged dreaminess, inconsequence, fragmentariness, dreariness, or self-pity, are today perceived from wholly different perspectives. A comparison of the way Coleridge and Wordsworth separately handle the problems of despair, dejection, the loss of zest or intensity, is itself most instructive as to the way time has altered our judgments.

In Wordsworth the theme of dejection actually appears far more often than in Coleridge, whose Ode on the subject is an isolated handling of the theme. Dorothy Wordsworth's journals testify repeatedly to the instability of William's moods. There is good reason to believe that Wordsworth was for most of his life a prey to despondency, against which he fought doggedly, with a kind of silent heroism. Two key poems in this connection are "The Leech Gatherer" and the Intimations Ode. In the first we are introduced to a despondent poet on a sunny morning after a storm. He thinks of Chatterton and Burns, poets dead in their youth. These reflections are a *result* of his mood, not a cause of it. And in fact in this poem the reasons for the poet's despondency are never given and seem irrelevant. It is taken for granted that dejection is part of every man's experience. Wordsworth introduces us to a heroic old man eeking out a scanty livelihood by gathering leeches from cold ponds on lonely moors. Yet this stooped and rugged old man is cheerful, wise—despite the harshness of his yoke. In the face of this, the poet finds that "he can laugh himself to scorn to find so firm a mind" in this ancient man, and so despondent a one in himself.

The lesson is clear, but it is not the kind of lesson many readers today care about. Wordsworth's whole conception of poetry as a healing power in the almost literal sense in which he meant it is essentially rejected today. Remember that he complained of the way Coleridge had handled the story of "The Three Graves," which he himself had supplied, because Coleridge had, with respect to the bitter tale, "failed to sweeten it with any healing views." To today's "Theatre of Cruelty," Wordsworth would have wished to oppose a "Theatre of Kindness"—we can imagine with what opportunities for critical hilarity. And we should remember that in the Preface to *Lyrical Ballads* Wordsworth had declared that in all his poems, however disguised it might be, there was a moral purpose.

The theme of dejection culminates in the Intimations Ode. Too often the poem is treated as if its theme is confined to the loss of intensity towards the wonders of nature. And the Platonic fable of coming from another world trailing clouds of glory does in fact contribute to the unnecessary narrowing of one of the major experiences in human life, namely, that of the irrevocable loss of certain kinds of organic sensibility. This can be the most dreadful passage in life, the loss of youth, the dimming of physical intensity, the steady diminution of one's vivid sensual apprehensions. Despondency, madness, even suicide may follow upon the realization that though much charm may remain in the life of the senses, the glory and wonder and power are gone.

Wordsworth does not evade the bitterness of his feelings, but he does not overdraw them either. The rose is still lovely. Waters on a starry night are beautiful and fair. But there was a time when the universe was appareled in celestial light. Had Wordsworth ended his poem at the end of the fourth stanza, with the poignant cry that the glory and the freshness of the dream was past, it would be a poem wholly to modern taste. But Wordsworth could not leave the poem at that. Probably it never even occurred to him that the four stanzas might be published as a bitter cry of pain over what has been lost. Poetry never was to him merely the overflow of powerful emotions, though it took its *origin* from such a state of mind. The poet did not walk the earth to dispirit other men. Wordsworth undoubtedly always viewed those great four stanzas as the introduction to a longer work.

And what does the remainder of the poem tell us of Wordsworth's way of handling tragic human experience? (The loss of organic sensibility for a poet like Wordsworth can be seen as almost comparable to the loss of hearing in a musician.)

> Though nothing can bring back the hour
> Of splendour in the grass, of glory in the flower;
>   We will grieve not, rather find
>   Strength in what remains behind:
>   In the primal sympathy

> Which having been must ever be;
> In the faith that looks through death,
> In the soothing thoughts that spring
> Out of human suffering;
> In years that bring the philosophic mind. (ll. 181-190)

How typical of Wordsworth, and how antithetical to the modern spirit, for which despair, *Angst*, the fact of death and the absurdity of aspiration are articles of faith. Yet it is useless to argue with a *Zeitgeist*. Wordsworth's grim stare into the fearful pit of cosmic processes does not destroy him. If we cannot have joy, we can at least have wisdom. Of such dogged determination are the images of Daddy Wordsworth made.

As to Coleridge, however, time has added the most attractive kind of patina to what were always brilliant poems. Coleridge's inability in "Ode to Dejection" to find any solace in a world from which joy has fled is much more acceptable testimony to man's fate. In this sense "Dejection" is a far more modern poem than Wordsworth's Ode. Coleridge allows himself to be personally overwhelmed by fate. If he cannot have his heart's desire, he will obliterate what remains of the "natural man." The poem is a kind of farewell to poetry; henceforth he will turn to abstruse researches. Wordsworth, conversely, will keep watch o'er man's mortality. For him the setting sun is lovely yet. He will not submit to a cosmic calculus of extremes. Though much is lost, much remains. Coleridge's grief is "without a pang, void, dark, and drear." To see, but not *feel* how beautiful the forms of nature are is intolerable.

> My genial spirits fail;
> And what can these avail
> To lift the smothering weight from off my breast?

This can profitably be compared with the cry in *Samson Agonistes*:

> I feel my genial spirits droop,
> My hopes all flat, nature within me seems
> In all her functions weary of herself. (ll. 594-596)

The despair of the blind Samson is all too tragically *caused*. But in "Dejection" there is so little that is clear about why Coleridge feels despair that critics have been explicating the poem in this regard for generations. Wordsworth's Ode offers no such interpretive difficulty.

But whatever the interpretive difficulty, "Dejection" suffers no loss of power in one's actual *reading* of the poem. The very confusions and uncertainties in themselves add to the credibility of the experience. Indeterminacy of motive, a break between mood (or action) and the stated causes of it are major features of Coleridge's poetry and wear extremely well in an uncertain and irrational age.

22. "KUBLA KHAN"

1. T.S. Eliot, for example, has written:

The faith in mystical inspiration is responsible for the exaggerated repute of *Kubla Khan*. The imagery of that fragment, certainly, whatever its origins in Coleridge's reading, sank to the depths of Coleridge's feeling, was saturated, transformed there—'those are pearls that were his eyes'—and brought up into daylight again. But it is not *used*: the poem has not been written. . . . Organisation is necessary as well as 'inspiration'. The re-creation of word and image which happens fitfully in the poetry of such a poet as Coleridge happens almost incessantly with Shakespeare. (*The Use of Poetry and the Use of Criticism* [London, 1933], p. 146. Italics in text)

Eliot here speaks for a miniscule minority of critics. It is noteworthy that he takes it for granted that the poem is a fragment and written in a dream.

2. For example: "Havelock Ellis mentioned *Kubla Khan* as having the best claim as an exception to his general statement that, although the creative mind undoubtedly receives many valuable suggestions from dreams, 'it is more doubtful whether the creative activity of normal dreams ever reaches a sufficient perfection to take, as it stands, a very high place in a master's work' " (quoted from Phyllis Bartlett, *Poems in Process* [New York, 1951], p. 65). More recently, Brewster Ghiselin has dedicated his popular book of readings on *The Creative Process* (Mentor Books) to "The Man from Porlock."

3. *RX*, p. 104. Italics in text.

4. *PW*, I, 295-296. Italics in text.

5. See the chapter on dreams in Phyllis Bartlett, *Poems in Process*, and Alethea Hayter, *Opium and the Romantic Imagination* (London, 1968), pp. 67-83.

6. ES, p. 231.   7. *RX*, p. 363.

8. ES. p. 173. Miss Schneider's major source on this point is Clement Carlyon's *Early Years and Late Reflections*, 4 vols. (London, 1836-1858). To her evidence we may add that Carlyon's first volume repeatedly deals with matters where mention of "Kubla Khan" might naturally have been made, had Carlyon—whose memory on many other matters of less consequence is minute—known of the poem's existence, or had Coleridge referred to it in opportune contexts. Thus Carlyon mentions that Darwin's *Zoonomia* contains much valuable information on dreams (I, 210); he reports a long conversation on dreams in 1803 with Coleridge, Humphry Davy, and others: in neither instance is "Kubla Khan" mentioned. A long passage (I, 199-235) reports many stories and anecdotes about dreams and ghosts, and again nothing is said of "Kubla Khan." Finally, and most significantly, during the long conversation about dreams, Davy recited a poem on the subject and Coleridge reciprocated with "The Devil's Walk" (I, 239), *not* with the dream poem which was to become the most famous of all time.

Miss Schneider's masterful *Coleridge, Opium, and Kubla Khan* (1953) was the first work seriously to attack the almost universal conviction that "Kubla Khan" had been written in an opium dream. A great cry of pain and protest at once was heard on both sides of the Atlantic. A reviewer in the *New Statesman and Nation* (NS, XLVII [1954], 710) complained, "On this showing . . . Coleridge must appear as a shameless, almost a pathological, liar; and the most disturbing thing about this book is that it belittles Coleridge not just in this way, but in general."

M. H. Abrams declared of the book that "all the major propositions it offers must be graded on a scale ranging from barely possible to (at best) somewhat probable; and it can be gloomily predicted that the book will stimulate further contention on every point" (*MLN*, LXX [1955], 219).

There seems to have been no such result. On the single problem of the dream origin of "Kubla Khan," however, there is evidence of slowly spreading skepticism. But the overwhelming majority of critics, scholars, and editors of college anthologies of literature go right on accepting Coleridge's account as fact. And the older authorities, almost to a man, never doubted it.

9. *RX*, pp. 352-355. Neither Dykes Campbell nor E. H. Coleridge was quite certain of the pristine purity of the text. Campbell believed that

> some changes must have been made in the draft before it was printed, for in the lines "To S. T. Coleridge, Esq.," Mrs. Robinson. . . writes:—

> 'I'll mark thy "sunny dome," and view
> Thy "caves of ice," thy *"fields of dew,"* '

the phrase italicized not being found in the published text. (*Poems*, p. 583)

E. H. Coleridge quoted the same lines and remarked: "It is possible that she [Mrs. Robinson] had seen a MS. copy of *Kubla Khan* containing these variants from the text (*PW*, I, 298, n. 2). Lowes proved that the quotation marks around "fields of dew" did not exist in Mary Robinson's text, thereby destroying any inferences about an early version of "Kubla Khan" containing this variant.

It is suggestive that the two chief editors of Coleridge's poetry were ready enough to admit the possibility of variants on the basis of evidence which proved false. Had they been as convinced of Coleridge's absolute veracity as Lowes and many other scholars, they might have looked at Mrs. Robinson's poem more closely. E. H. Coleridge, indeed, seems merely to have copied Campbell's note without verifying an extremely important point. It is worth remembering his clear-eyed view of some of his grandfather's anecdotes: "The scene is laid in Arcadia" (*SSH*, p. 15).

10.   The manuscript was first exhibited at the National Portrait Gallery in London in 1934. On 2 August 1934 Alice Snyder's description of textual variants (including several errors and omissions) appeared in the *Times Literary Supplement* (p. 541). So little stir was created in the world of scholarship by these events that, seventeen years later, E. W. H. Meyerstein published in the same journal (12 January 1951, p. 21, and 9 February 1951, p. 85) his own list of variants (also including errors), unaware that the work had already been done. At last, in 1962, the British Museum acquired the elusive manuscript and made it generally available to scholars. One result was the discovery of still more variants noted by neither Snyder nor Meyerstein. A photographic reproduction of the autograph manuscript may be found in *The British Museum Quarterly*, XXVI, Nos. 3-4, pp. 77-83, plates XXX and XXXI. A very faint pencil note suggests that the document was once owned by Robert Southey, for whom Coleridge presumably wrote his explanatory note.

11.   Thus M. H. Abrams writes of Miss Schneider's analysis of the conflicting evidence of the Crewe MS and the 1816 Preface:

> I do not feel the force of Miss Schneider's claim that these accounts are contradictory. The second can be interpreted as an elaborated analysis of the peculiarly deep reverie, often attested in the literature of opium, in which the dreamer, rendered oblivious to his surroundings by what Coleridge called "a profound sleep, at least of the external senses," is lost in the inner world of his phantasy. To claim that Coleridge's published Preface was a lie is to bring a moral indictment against the poet far graver than the earlier charges—many of them ill-founded—of his "plagiarism." To present this new claim as virtually proved, on little more basis than the variance between Coleridge's two accounts and a depth-analysis of Coleridge's temperament, seems, to say the least, ill-advised. (*MLN*, LXX [1955], 217)

Among those scholars who now have doubts about the 1816 Preface, few seem to take so serious a view of the matter. Warren U. Ober cheerfully agrees that the famous Preface is a "Coleridgean hoax, albeit a harmless one" ("Southey, Coleridge, and 'Kubla Khan,' " *JEGP*, LVIII [1959], 414). Professor Ober locates some suggestive parallels to "Kubla Khan" in Sir William Jones's "The Palace of Fortune," but more especially in Southey's commonplace books.

George Watson, in arguing for the "rigorous logic" of "Kubla Khan," seems to admit that it is "not a dream-poem," but at once insists: "This is not to say that Coleridge's own account of how the poem came to be written, in the 1816 preface, is mendacious or mistaken. It is only to assert that the dream-hypothesis does not help" ('The Meaning of Kubla Khan" *REL*, II [1961], 21-22).

Most commentators have not been harassed by the problem offered by Coleridge's Preface to such Orwellian Newspeak extremities.

12.   *Purchas his Pilgrimage* (1617), p, 472.

13.   De Quincey has referred to Coleridge's "demoniac inaccuracy in the statement of facts. . . . inaccuracy as to facts and citations from books was in Coleridge a mere necessity of nature" (*DQW*, III, 227-228). Still, he acted deliberately far more often than is realized. The effect of the garbled quotation from Purchas is to place the opening lines of "Kubla Khan" further from

their source than they really are; e. g. , "In Xamdu did Cublai Can" is certainly much closer to "In Xanadu did Kubla Khan" than "Here the Khan Kubla commanded," which he gave as coming from Purchas. If obscurantism was Coleridge's intention—and he was abnormally devious in these matters—his anxiety seems to us grotesque, in view of the bewitching transmutation he has in fact wrought.

14. At line 29 Coleridge originally wrote, "And mid this Tumult Cubla heard from *fear*"; he crossed out the last word and substituted the present "from far." This point will be discussed later.

15. For the influence of William Collins, see *RX*, pp. 399-400, where Lowes has pointed out similar lines in Collins' "The Passions: An Ode for Music," a poem much admired by Coleridge.

16. *MP*, III (1906), 327-332.   17. *RX*, p. 373.

18. *RX*, pp. 373-374. Italics in text.

19. *RX*, p. 396 and note.

20. There is no certainty on this point among authorities.

21. See *N*, 4. But it is possible that Coleridge wrote "Amora" before "Amara." This is the reading of John Shelton, who has published a photograph of the Crewe MS in his article "The Autograph Manuscript of 'Kubla Khan' and an Interpretation" (*REL*, VII [1966], 32-42; see especially p. 33, n. 2). I have examined the original document in the British Museum and find the problem impossible to resolve. Even in Shelton's photograph it is obvious that many letters were formed with heavy strokes of the pen, so that it is not certain that the heavy middle *a* of "Amara" is an attempt to establish precedence over an original *o*. Supposing it to be so, however, we can conjecture that Coleridge initially wrote "Singing of Mount Amora" either as a slip of the pen, or by momentarily misremembering—both acts prompted by the pull of poetic considerations. The change to "Amara" is then explained by his remembering the real place-name. But if he deliberately wrote "Mount Amara" and then changed it to "Amara," it was probably because he thought so obvious a submission to technical pressures unacceptable and preferred to settle for the more awkward, if forthright, "Amara." In view of all this, the change to "Abora" is still more satisfying.

22. Not uncharacteristic of J. B. Beer's influential *Coleridge the Visionary* is his discussion of the question, "why had Amara been changed to Abora?" Beer continues:

> Two reasons may be suggested. The first is that the word "Abor" appears on the second page of Holwell's mythological dictionary with the comment that "the Sun was called Abor, the parent of light". The second is that Beth-Abara was the place where Christ was baptized in Jordan by John the Baptist, and where the spirit descended upon him "like a dove". Milton used it in *Paradise Regained*, and Coleridge used it as a symbol for the place where Truth is revealed to man. After his discussion of Arctic superstitions in *The Destiny of Nations*, he continued:

> > Wild phantasies! yet wise,
> > On the victorious goodness of high God
> > Teaching reliance, and medicinal hope,
> > Till from Bethabra northward, heavenly Truth
> > With gradual steps, winning her difficult way,
> > Transfer their rude Faith perfected and pure.

> The change from Amara to Abora thus adds to the Abyssinian paradise the further symbolism of the sun, the descending dove, and the revelation of divine Truth. (p. 256)

Little purpose would be served in providing a bibliography of articles, mostly ephemeral, where explications of this point may be found. What is important, however, is that the *kind* of analysis cited above is commonplace. Deriving from such studies is a view of the creative process which is in some respects quite fantastic. Thus G. Wilson Knight in a discussion of the place-names in "Kubla Khan" conjures with the idea that the "x" in "Xanadu," and the "a" of "Abyssinia-Abora" and the "k" of "Kubla Khan" may represent first, middle, and last things (*The Starlit Dome* [London, 1941], p. 97).

23. Nevertheless, we may well ask, "How early is the Crewe MS?" This question is so complex that a monograph would be required to arrive at an answer, which would in any case be circumstantial. The testimony of watermarks, paper, ink, handwriting—all this and much more can never lead to a conclusive answer. The spellings "Xannadù" and "Cubla" seem to suggest an early date, but this belief rests more on intuition than fact. The unresolved poetic problems offer more weighty evidence of fairly early composition.

But the poem already displays a dazzling technical virtuosity. The manuscript itself is very neat, and carefully indented and spaced. Surely this indicates that Coleridge had written out the poem before. Though it cannot be proved, at least at present, that the note at the end of the manuscript was not written long after the accompanying poem, it does not appear to be. Ink, handwriting, margins—these are sandy foundations on which to build; nevertheless, both poem and note seem to have been written at the same time. The note concludes with the information that the fragment was composed "in the fall of the year, 1797." This seems to me to imply a backward glance of at least several years. Coleridge was not averse, as we have repeatedly seen, to providing *exact* dates for the composition of poems, especially those allegedly written spontaneously. I cannot imagine Coleridge writing "in the fall of the year, 1797" during 1797 itself, unless he thought he was making a statement for posterity. But the frankness about the opium (as compared to the 1816 "anodyne") shows that he was writing for an intimate. The absence of any other manuscript of "Kubla Khan" can be seen as highly suspicious. Did they bear the all too obvious testimony of worksheets and were thus destroyed?

In view of Coleridge's continual revisions of his other poems, there is no reason whatever to suppose that he did not make changes between the original composition of "Kubla Khan," whenever that was (between 1797 and 1800), and its eventual publication in 1816. We have seen how many variants the Crewe MS contains. There is other, much less certain, evidence of textual changes. Leigh Hunt printed "Kubla Khan" in his *Imagination and Fancy* (London, 1844), p. 288, and commented in a note: "I think I recollect a variation of this stanza, as follows:—

> In Xanadu did Kubla Khan
> A stately *pleasure-house ordain*,
> Where Alph the sacred river ran
> Through caverns measureless to man,
> Down to a sunless *main*."

Hunt actually thought this superior to the published version!

"Perdita" Robinson's references to "Kubla Khan" in her lines "To the Poet Coleridge" prove nothing conclusive. As Lowes has shown, only "sunny dome" and "caves of ice" seem to be orthographically identified as direct quotations from Coleridge. Still, fanastic as it seems, she did describe the pleasure-dome as a "flaming temple, studded o'er/With all Peruvia's lus'trous shore" (*RX*, p. 355).

24. The most systematic study of the sources is, of course, Elisabeth Schneider's *Coleridge, Opium, and Kubla Khan*. As she assigns a date of 1799 to the poem, both Southey's *Thalaba* and Landor's *Gebir* become possible influences. Southey's impact on Coleridge, a subject too little regarded, has partially been studied in a long, unpublished doctoral dissertation by Warren U. Ober ("Lake Poet and Laureate: Southey's Significance to his own Generation" [Indiana University, 1958]). Ober argues that Southey's influence on Coleridge "might well have been an important factor in the conception and shaping of 'The Rime of the Ancient Mariner,' 'Christabel,' and especially, 'Kubla Khan.' Certainly the evidence that Coleridge in these poems borrowed from Southey's poetry, notes, and reading is so great as to justify a thorough re-examination of Coleridge and Southey's relationship" (p. 371). That reexamination remains to be done.

25. See "Years of Apprenticeship," n. 65. On 4 July 1796 Coleridge wrote to Estlin: "You rejoice that the Prince & Princess are reconciled—altho' I fear 'that never can true Reconcilement grow Where wounds of deadly Wrong have pierced so deep' " (*CL*, I, 223). These lines, as Griggs notes, are from the fourth book of *Paradise Lost* (ll. 98-99). Coleridge, with the exception of changing "hate" to "Wrong" and beginning the quotation with "that" instead of "for," quoted the lines perfectly. An allusion to this same book appears in "The Devil's Thoughts" (*PW*, I, 321 and n. 1). We must conclude, therefore, that Coleridge had a minute knowledge of Milton's epic (which no one has ever doubted), and particularly with the fourth book, which contains a roll call of paradises.

26. Lines 216-218, 223-225, 227-231, 239-240. I. A. Richards, in *Principles of Literary Criticism* (London, 1928), pp. 31-32, has pointed out some of the above parallels in slightly different form. He took it for granted that Coleridge was dreaming and that the parallels were the result of unconscious recollection (p. 227).

As the description continues, Milton refers to "Hill and Dale" (l. 243), "Groves whose rich Trees wept odorous Gums and Balm" (l. 247), "Grots and *Caves* / Of cool recess" (ll. 257-258). Elsewhere in the fourth book we find: "Not distant far from thence a murmuring sound / Of waters issu'd from a *Cave*" (ll. 453-454). There is a description of the "Garden of Bliss" in the eighth book of *Paradise Lost* which may also have played a part in "Kubla Khan." A "woody mountain" is seen:

> A Circuit wide, *enclos'd*, with goodliest *Trees*
> Planted, with Walks and Bowers, that what I saw
> Of Earth before scarce pleasant seem'd. Each Tree
> Load'n with fairest Fruit, that hung to the Eye
> Tempting, stirr'd in me sudden appetite
> To pluck and eat; *whereat I wak'd, and found*
> *Before mine Eyes all real, as the dream*
> *Had lively shadow'd* . . . (ll. 299, 303-311)

27. In Milton's *Arcades*, for example, there is a likely source for Coleridge's river "Alph": "Divine *Alph*eus, who by secret sluse,/Stole under Seas to meet his Arethuse" (ll. 30-31). Howard Parsons finds many other connections to Milton, but mostly from *Paradise Lost*, Book IV ("The Sources of Coleridge's 'Kubla Khan,' " *N & Q*, CXCVI [1951], 233-235). Beer finds still another echo from *Paradise Lost*, IX, 69-75 (Beer, p. 236). The list of such sources seems endless.

28. The belief that the kings of Abissinia kept all sons but the first born under luxurious but firm isolation from the throne appears in Johnson's *Rasselas*, where Coleridge could conceivably have seen it. In the very first chapter of *Rasselas* we read: "The place which the wisdom or policy of antiquity had destined for the residence of the *Abissinian* princes, was a spacious valley in the kingdom of *Amhara*, surrounded on every side by mountains, of which the summits overhang the middle part." Elsewhere in this chapter appears the following description: "This lake discharged its superfluities by a stream which entered a *dark cleft of the mountain* on the northern side, and *fell with dreadful noise* from precipice to precipice till it was heard no more." (Cf. "that deep romantic chasm which slanted down the green hill," and "sank in tumult to a lifeless ocean.") See also ES, pp. 263 and 355, n. 28.

Anyone who has long worked with "Kubla Khan" eventually comes upon clusters of "parallels." Wordsworth's early *Descriptive Sketches* contains "a spot of *holy ground*" (l. 1); would it not be fatuous to urge this as a source for Coleridge's "holy and enchanted" savage place? But what of Oswald's speech in *The Borderers*, in which he describes a walk

> . . . through woods of gloomy *cedar*,
> Into *deep chasms* troubled by *roaring streams*;

Or from the top of Lebanon surveyed
The *moonlight* desert, and the *moonlight sea.* (ll. 1804-7)

Even here, in a cluster that involves links with Coleridge's *"deep* romantic *chasm* . . . athwart a
cedarn cover," beneath a "waning *moon"* and noisy waters ("sank in tumult," "ceaseless turmoil"), one is simply not convinced that there is a connection. These are, after all, common
words to describe common facts of nature. If the elements of "Kubla Khan" are to be found
everywhere in earlier poetry, we can also work forwards and "prove" that everybody after Coleridge was influenced by the poem.

29. *LL,* I, 94-95.   30. *LL,* I, 104-106.   31. ES, p. 247.

32. *N,* 240 and n. The Empress Elizabeth of Russia's "ice-palace" had created a stir in England
and was commented upon disapprovingly in Cowper's *Task,* Book V.

33. *N,* 1804.

34. *LL,* II, 190. The whole nineteenth century (and most of the twentieth) took "Kubla Khan"
to be a dream. Lowes was anything but alone in his adamant certainty that he was dealing with a
fragment created in a dream. H. J. Grierson's and J. C. Smith's *A Critical History of English
Poetry* (London, 1946) offers a typical instance of how the poem was conventionally read:

> [Kubla Khan] was composed in a sleep induced by "an anodyne," theme and rhythm sug-
> gested by a sonorous sentence of Purchas, which Coleridge was reading when he fell asleep.
> It has all the earmarks of a dream—vividness, free association, and inconsequence [!]. Short
> as it is, it runs off the rails before the end: the "Abyssinian maid" has nothing to do with
> the subject. (p. 341)

Recent years, however, have witnessed a startling reversal of such attitudes. "Kubla Khan" may
still be a dream, but it is nevertheless a poem of "rigorous logic," "fully formed and spontaneous," a "complete poem in the profoundest sense," a work exhibiting "full unity of conception,"
and so forth. A fantastic "Jungian Reading of 'Kubla Khan' " (*JAAC,* XVIII [1960]) concludes
with the incredible statement, "The poem is a finished whole. Greater logicality or economy is
difficult to conceive" (p. 367). The doctrine of Unity has now become the idol before which even
common sense prostrates itself, and many interpretations of "Kubla Khan" seem to bring to
birth deformed offspring by the too-often rude forceps of close reading. It would be egregious
here to cite individuals.

35. Shedd, II, 130. The whole context is relevant.

36. It is difficult enough to remember more than a few words from dreams, and Coleridge's
recorded dreams are no exception. To have remembered fifty-three lines of prose, let alone verse,
would be without parallel in dream literature. See Havelock Ellis, *The World of Dreams* (Boston, 1911), pp. 275-276.

37. Quoted from Lawrence Hanson, *The Life of S. T. Coleridge* (Oxford, 1938), p. 483, n. 60.
Italics in text. The publication of Coleridge's later notebooks may throw light on this difficult
entry.

38. It is important to emphasize that the famous farmhouse may have nothing to do with
"Kubla Khan." The quarrel with Lloyd here referred to took place in 1798. The note certainly
seems to imply that this was Coleridge's *first* retirement to the farmhouse for the purpose of
imbibing opium. But the 1816 Preface dates the poem as having been written "in the summer of
1797," and the Crewe MS "in the fall of the year, 1797." Note that if the Crewe MS is wrong,
then its note (and therefore probably the accompanying poem) must have been written down
considerably after that year.

How to resolve this vexatious problem? The date of "Kubla Khan" is one of the most debated
problems in literary scholarship, and the evidence is staggeringly complex. On the whole it
seems easier to discount the almost hysterically defensive note of 1810 about Lloyd (which in any
case does not mention "Kubla Khan") than to ignore both the 1816 Preface and the Crewe MS.

However, Coleridge's datings are so often wrong that we cannot feel much confidence in any conclusion based on the evidence thus far presented.

Intensive study of Coleridge's movements during 1797-98 has failed to produce many dates on which it is probable he might have been at the farmhouse. Professor Griggs summarizes some of the evidence in the headnote to a letter written by Coleridge on 14 October 1797, which mentions a brief absence from home and contains the sentence, somewhat reminiscent of "Kubla Khan": "I should much wish, like the Indian Vishna [Vishnu], to float about along an infinite ocean cradled in the flower of the Lotos, & wake once in a million years for a few minutes" (*CL*, I, 349-350). Most scholars take the date of 1798 as more likely; Miss Schneider is almost alone in arguing for 1799. One of the gravest difficulties here is the assumption that "Kubla Khan" was written at one particular time. It need not necessarily be so. The poem that we know might have begun with a single cluster of lines and been elaborated in the next year or so, without doing violence to the basic idea that the original images may all derive from a single experience. He might have made notes on a particularly vivid train of ideas or images, though in the absence of documentary evidence we must be cautious about such assumptions.

Despite the complexities of the problem, I am inclined to believe that Professor Griggs is essentially correct. The *origin* of "Kubla Khan" would seem to derive from an experience in October 1797, though the actual writing of the poem that we know almost certainly took place later. Evidence to be provided hereafter involving the meaning of "Kubla Khan" also happens to point to a date close to the two painful autobiographical letters Coleridge wrote to Poole on 9 October and 16 October 1797, precisely when Coleridge had the opportunity to be away from home, and closest to "the fall of the year, 1797" given in the Crewe MS, which certainly seems to stand much closer to the actual composition of the poem than the statements of 1810 and 1816.

39.   Did Coleridge really visualize an Abyssinian maid playing a *dulcimer*? Alethea Hayter is surely right in stating that "most of us . . . have a mental picture of the damsel flitting about with something in the nature of a lyre or a lute. . . ." But in fact a dulcimer is

> a flat box up to three feet wide, standing on a table or on its own legs, most definitely not portable, and played with two hammers. If Coleridge really knew what a dulcimer was, and did not simply choose an instrument with a beautiful name, we must imagine the Abyssinian maid warbling away while wielding a couple of padded hammers, a set concert performance which is not at all what one had imagined or wished for in *Kubla Khan*. (*Opium and the Romantic Imagination*, p. 220)

The point is not a trivial one. If "Kubla Khan" were a true dream, the radical incongruity of an African girl playing so European an instrument as a dulcimer would suggest that the maid is really a disguise for someone much closer to Coleridge's genteel English surroundings.

23.   THEMES

1.   *TT*, 31 May 1830. Italics in text. Humphry House fairly summarizes the story of the Merchant and the Genie in *The Arabian Nights*, and attempts to undermine Coleridge's apparent meaning. Since almost all recent commentators agree "that the poem has a very serious moral and spiritual bearing on human life," it is obviously necessary to demonstrate that the statement to Mrs. Barbauld does not mean what it says, but rather that Coleridge meant only to emphasize as a fault "*the obtrusion* of the moral sentiment *so openly* . . . in a work of such pure imagination" (HH, pp. 90-92. Italics in text). It is unthinkable to most of Coleridge's present critics that as late as 1830 he could have used the word "imagination" so loosely, without intending it to bear the great weight of his earlier critical theory, in which, among many other functions, the poetic imagination "brings the whole soul of man into activity." If Coleridge's nephew has reported his words to Mrs. Barbauld correctly, Coleridge's memory played him false in a suggestive way. The Genie's son was not only struck in the eye by a date-stone but was in fact killed. That Coleridge's Genie at once condemns the Merchant to death for an act of much lesser gravity makes the relationship between an unintentional crime and its punishment

still more outrageous. This strongly suggests that Coleridge meant to establish the *irrationality* of the *Arabian Nights* story.

Now it is true that the Merchant, during the year of respite he wins from the Genie to arrange his personal affairs, behaves with such justice and honor that it comes to matter very much to us that he should escape the Genie's vengeance. In fact he does escape through the assistance of three old men, who appear and disappear without explanation. House provides the following as a possible summation of the moral meaning of the story: "The arbitrary character of fate may be overcome by human honour and goodness; and there may be mysterious powers in the world which aid these virtues" (HH, p. 91). We certainly do feel some dim connection between the Merchant's goodness and his happy escape, and we rejoice in it. But it is a radical misreading of the story, and of "The Ancient Mariner," to build upon such sandy foundations profound spiritual meanings. This is not at all to suggest that either "The Ancient Mariner" or the *Arabian Nights* story is morally meaningless. It is, however, to insist very strongly that moral meanings in art can be, and regularly are, fractional, contradictory, illusory, logically just but emotionally unsatisfying or, conversely, logically unjust but morally quite satisfying—and so forth. The need to impose the morality of the later Western Church on all the world's literature would seem to be very great.

2.   *PW*, I, 169. "The Raven" is another poem attended by generations of editorial error due to Coleridge's misdatings, in this case surely deliberate. The poem was first collected in 1817, where it appeared prominently in a small section headed "Juvenile Poems." Thomas Ashe, undoubtedly taking his cue from this, wrote that "The Raven" was "decidedly the earliest poetical production of Coleridge," probably written at thirteen or fourteen (Ashe, I, 87). Dykes Campbell proposed 1791 (*Poems*, p. 18), but there is no doubt whatever that the poem was written in 1796 or 1797. When STC published it in the *Morning Post*, he referred to Spenser's *Shepherd's Calendar* and signed himself "Cuddy." Woodring has cited debts to Spenser's *Second Eclogue*, where a "Cuddy" appears (*PPC*, p. 134). Coleridge's use of such archaisms as "ne more mote you spy," "Wel-a-day," and "auld" suggests further links with those "elder poets" whose diction figured so largely in the first version of "The Ancient Mariner." Lamb wrote that the first nineteen lines of "The Raven" were a "most happy resemblance of Chaucer" (*LL*, I, 94). In view of all this, it is not surprising that "The Raven" does not appear in either MS. O or E, the two collections of "juvenile" poems Coleridge wrote in his own hand before 1796.

3.   E. E. Bostetter, with typical acuity, has observed connections between "The Raven" and "The Ancient Mariner" (*The Romantic Ventriloquists* [Seattle, Wash., 1963], pp. 108 ff.) Another baffling connection between this poem and others of the great period is the recurrent detail of the "old oak tree." "The Raven" begins with the line, "Underneath an old oak tree." The "Hermit good" in the last part of "The Ancient Mariner" prays upon a "rotted old oak-stump" (l. 522.) which is covered with moss. Christabel kneels to pray in the woods "beneath the huge oak tree," also covered with moss (ll. 34-36), a detail repeated several times (ll. 42, 281, 297). The abandoned baby boy in "The Foster-Mother's Tale" is found "wrapt in mosses" beneath a huge tree (ll. 21-24). The abandoned royal orphan, Bethlen, in *Zapolya*, is found "in the hollow of an oak" (II, i, 347). Whatever the ultimate significance of this repeated image, it is notable that it is so often connected with the theme of the abandoned child, the personal significance of which to Coleridge can hardly be doubted.

4.   To Allsop he wrote: "If I should finish *Christabel*, I shall certainly extend it and give new characters, and a greater number of incidents. This the 'reading public' require. . . . I had the whole of the *two cantos* in my mind before I began it" (quoted from *TT*, p. 425). But a year before he died he said that he had always had the plan of the poem "*entire* from beginning to end in my mind"; the reason he gave for not finishing it was doubt as to his ability to carry on the idea of the poem with equal success, an idea which was "an extremely subtle and difficult one" (*TT*, p. 259). In *Biographia Literaria*, however, he said that "expressions of admiration [for Christabel"] . . . (I can truly say) appeared to myself utterly disproportionate to a work, that pretended to be nothing more than a *common Faery Tale*" (*BL*, II, 210-211).

5. Gillman, p. 283.   6. Gillman, pp. 301-302.

7. Many critics have found this synopsis so disappointing that they have refused to believe Coleridge was serious. Nethercot finds it "totally at variance with the first two cantos and all that they imply" (*The Road to Tryermaine*, p. 27). Dante Gabriel Rossetti felt otherwise (HH, p. 128 and n. 3). I myself do not doubt that this synopsis accurately reflects Coleridge's intentions as to the overt *action* of the poem. For reasons given hereafter, I believe that Coleridge remained uncertain as to the character of Geraldine.

8. This passage is almost always quoted from EHC's handsome 1907 edition of "Christabel"; he in turn was quoting from Derwent Coleridge's *The Poems of Samuel Taylor Coleridge* (London, 1870), an edition based essentially on the work of Derwent's sister, Sara. The famous note occurs on p. xlii. Immediately after the paragraph cited, Derwent continued: "Certain is it that he [Coleridge] would not, could not, have produced anything out of harmony with the commencement, or which did not satisfy his own taste and judgment,—which perhaps may be taken as one reason why he produced nothing. If any reader of 'Christabel' be displeased with this explanation, let him impute it to mistaken apprehension or imperfect recollection on the part of the writer—and forget it." This is in fact what most commentators have done.

9. Lines 206, 192-193, 221. Geraldine and the Mariner both have "glittering" eyes. The fratricidal Osorio, a "crazy-conscienced man," also has a "frightful glitter" in his eye (*Osorio*, V, 150-151).

10. The unresolved problem of what overall plan for "Christabel" was in Coleridge's mind is entirely different from that of how much of the poem was ever actually written, about which there are also many conflicting statements. The poem that we know, including the conclusion to Part II (which some scholars consider a tacked-on afterthought), contains 677 lines. On 9 October 1800 Coleridge wrote Humphry Davy that the reason the poem was not to be included in the second edition of *Lyrical Ballads* was that it "was running up to *1300 lines*" (*CL*, I, 631). Griggs notes that this is a "puzzling statement," and that "Chambers's suggestion is as good as any: 'conceivably part remained only in Coleridge's head' " (*CL*, I, 631, n. 1). Is Chambers' suggestion really as good as any? Can we believe that Coleridge had over 600 lines of "Christabel" in his head which he never at any time wrote down? In a letter postmarked *one day* after the letter to Davy, Coleridge wrote Poole that "Christabel" had "swelled into a Poem of *1400 lines*" (*CL*, I, 634). In 1815 he wrote Byron that after returning from Germany he finished the second part of "Christabel" and part of a third (*CL*, IV, 601). Of this maze of contradictions Nethercot observes: "The conclusion seems perfectly clear: Coleridge actually composed a 'Christabel' which, fragmentary as it was, was nevertheless more than twice as long as the version which was finally printed" (*The Road to Tryermaine*, p. 13). Since no one has ever reported having *heard* any portion of "Christabel" apart from what we now have, and since not a line further has been found among Coleridge's many fragmentary manuscripts, is it really "perfectly clear" that any such continuation ever existed? This critical impasse derives from failure to assess Coleridge's character realistically. On the subject of his own work he is never to be automatically trusted. It must always be remembered that Coleridge sometimes spoke of works as *"ready for the press"* which had not even been outlined.

11. *PW*, I, 290.   12. *N*, 2368. Italics in text.   13. *N*, 2998.

14. *CL*, II, 782. This letter was written to William Godwin in 1802.

15. *CL*, I, 260. 19 November 1796, to John Thelwall.

16. *CL*, II, 797. This is from the original version of the "Ode to Dejection."

17. *CL*, II, 1203. Circa 3 December 1806 to the Wordsworths.   18. *N*, 2090.

19. *PW*, I, 451. In this self-portrait, the problems of originality and plagiarism appear as follows:

> Behind another's team he stept,
> And plough'd and sow'd, while others reapt;

> The work was his, but theirs the glory,
> *Sic vos non vobis*, his whole story.
> Besides, whate 'er he wrote or said
> Came from his heart as well as head. (ll. 43-48)

The Latin phrase (from Virgil) means, "Thus you do, but not for yourselves," or, "You do the work, but others take the credit."

20. Coleridge's "Something Childish, But Very Natural" (*PW*, I, 313) begins:

> If I had but two little wings
> And were a little feathery bird,
> To you I'd fly, my dear!

This is a translation of *Wenn ich ein Vöglein wär'*.

A suggestive cluster of ideas—bird, death, murder—appears in "The Destiny of Nations":

> . . . that Giant Bird
> Vuokho, of whose rushing wings the noise
> Is Tempest, when the unutterable Shape
> Speeds from the mother of Death, and utters once
> That shriek, which never murderer heard, and lived. (ll. 93-97)

21. In the lines of poetry identified with "The Wanderings of Cain," there is a little child lost in a wilderness, silent and wild: "Has he no friend, no loving mother near?" (*PW*, I, 287). And almost precisely the same image appears in "Dejection," where

> a little child . . .
> Not far from home, but she hath lost her way:
> And now moans low in bitter grief and fear,
> And now screams loud, and hopes to make her mother hear. (ll. 121-125)

22. "And all his hospitality . . . Brought thus to a disgraceful end" (ll. 644, 647). The "Argument" of "The Ancient Mariner" for 1800 contains the following description: "how the Ancient Mariner cruelly and *in contempt of the laws of hospitality* killed a Seabird and how he was followed by many and strange Judgements" (*PW*, I, 186, n. 3).

23. Beres relates the slaying of the albatross after it has been welcomed by the sailors, who gave it "the food it ne'er had eat," to Coleridge's "oral character" (Beres, pp. 104-105). He then cites the following passage from a letter of 1797:

> The mice play the very devil with us. It irks me to set a trap. By all the whiskers of all the pussies that have mewed plaintively, or amorously, since the days of Whittington, it is not fair. 'Tis telling a lie. 'Tis as if you said, "Here is a bit of toasted cheese; come little mice! I invite you!" when, *oh, foul breach of the rites of hospitality*! I mean to assassinate my too credulous guests. (*CL*, I, 322)

The emphasis on food and drink in Coleridge's letters, and at key points in the great triad (for example, "He on honey-dew hath fed, And drunk the milk of Paradise") is heavy enough to justify speculation as to its unconscious meaning.

24. III, i, 326. Usurpation is not only a dominant theme in *Osorio*, but also in *Zapolya* (1817), which is divided into sections subtitled "The Usurper's Fortune" and "The Usurper's Fate." There are, however, more subtle perspectives from which this theme can be considered. Geraldine at the end of Part II of "Christabel" has succeeded in at least partially usurping the af-

fections of the old Baron, upon whose arm she marches out of the "presence-room," leaving the rightful daughter behind in disgrace. Perhaps it is significant also that one of the effects of Geraldine's fearful power is that she gains control over the *words* of Christabel:

> "In the touch of this bosom there worketh a spell,
> Which is *lord of thy utterance*, Christabel!" (ll. 267-268)

Is there a connection between this and the Mariner's crime, one of the results of which is that he has "strange power of speech" (l. 587)?

25.   *CL*, I, 352-353. Italics in text.

26.   Direct evidence abounds as to Coleridge's bitter hatred of his brothers, and much indirect evidence of his hatred for his mother. We have seen how violently hostile he felt towards his brother Frank, and in his retrospective accounts to Poole of his childhood at Ottery St. Mary there is not a single word of genuine affection about any of his many other siblings. During his years of dependency on his family—when he was a lonely ward of Christ's Hospital—his letters home, and especially to his brother George, are affectionate enough. But once he is on his own and independent, difficulties with his family thicken. Of the first forty-eight letters of Coleridge extant, thirty-five are to George. After 1794 the proportion, understandably, drops off sharply. But it is not easy to account for a gap of six months (from which twenty-one letters to other correspondents remain) before he writes to George again. And this letter, to all appearances, brims with undiminished affection. Yet three years and three months, plus 162 letters to other correspondents, were to pass before he wrote to George again. From the next five years just six letters to George remain, though of letters to other correspondents during this period there are 292. The last of these was written on 2 October 1803 (two days before his own wedding anniversary and the date he thought of as the anniversary of his Father's death): "You I have always loved & honored as more than mere Brother: & it was not my fault, that the mere names of Brother & of Kindred were of necessity less powerful in my feelings, than in those of other men who with perhaps vastly less Sensibility have had the good fortune to have been more domestically reared. But what I am is in consequence of what I have been." Just before closing with "affectionate Esteem & grateful & rememb'ring Love" for George, he wrote, "present my best Duty to our venerable Mother—my kindest Love to your Wife" (*CL*, II, 1008-9). Thus to his mother, "my best Duty," to his sister-in-law, "my kindest Love," eloquent testimony to the coolness of his feelings for his mother. After this, Coleridge did not write George again for three years.

Before departing for Malta in 1804, in the desperate hope of regaining his health and strength of purpose, Coleridge wrote to Sir George Beaumont: "I was hardly used from infancy to Boyhood; & from Boyhood to Youth, most, MOST cruelly" (*CL*, II, 1053). (Thus Coleridge has bitter memories even of the years at Ottery St. Mary *before* his father's death.) Three years later he wrote Humphry Davy that he was "releasing my conscience wholly from all connection with a family, to whom I am indebted only for misery" (*CL*, III, 31). Just a few months later he recalled a woman at Christ's Hospital from whom he had "received the greatest tenderness, a tenderness, which God knows! I had never received before, even from my own family" (*CL*, III, 44). We may well believe this true. In his recollections to Gillman he said that at school he met a kind, widowed mother of one of his classmates: she "taught me what it was to have a mother. I loved her as such" (Gillman, p. 28). Upon the death of Thomas Poole's mother in 1801, Coleridge wrote: "She was the only Being whom I ever *felt* in the relation of Mother" (*CL*, II, 758. STC's underscoring). As David Beres has pointed out, "There is not in any of his writings . . . any note of the death of his own mother, a strange omission when we consider how easily and volubly he wrote on all that touched and moved him" (Beres, p. 102).

Relations with his brothers for most of his life were either frigid or stormy. "God be my witness!" he wrote to George on 18 October 1809, "I never uttered a disrespectful word concerning you to another person, nor even for a day together ever thought—much less spoke of you—without gratitude and remembrance of former times" (*CL*, III, 250). Yet but two days later he was able to write to one Samuel Purkis, a mere acquaintance, that when he had recently asked his brother George for assistance, "for the first time since I became of age, having never received either accommodation or present from any one of my family during all my hard struggle thro' Life, and I received a refusal so couched that it would require an Oedipus to determine whether the baseness, the inhumanity, or the insolence of the answer was the greater." Just a few sentences later on the "Revd G. Coleridge" is called "my Brother by accident of Midwifery"; and a few years after the whole family were merely "Relations by Gore" (*CL*, III, 252, 507). The reference to Oedipus in relation to hatred of an older brother, sometimes thought of as a father surrogate, is in itself suggestive.

27. *N*, 1698.
28. Characteristic of one aspect of Lowes's handling of source problems in Coleridge centers on the following stanza from "The Ancient Mariner":

> Like one, that on a lonesome road
> Doth walk in fear and dread,
> And having once turned round walks on,
> And turns no more his head;
> Because he knows, a frightful fiend
> Doth close behind him tread. (11. 446-451)

"That this stanza," Lowes wrote, "which is sheer, inimitable Coleridge, was nevertheless suggested by a bit of Dante at his most Dantesque, I learned, long after this chapter was written, from a pencilled scrawl in Coleridge's own copy of *Sibylline Leaves*." That certainty derives from the pencilled words opposite the quoted passage, "From Dante," *not* in STC's hand. But supposing they were? The English translations of Dante Coleridge might have seen do not resemble Coleridge's lines. "Did Coleridge read Italian before 'The Ancient Mariner' was written?" Lowes asks, and then embarks upon a prodigious analysis of the question, which nevertheless ignores STC's later embarrassing admission that he was unable to read a word of Italian when he first undertook (in 1796) to criticize Petrarch and Italian sonnet patterns. Though Lowes cannot produce a shred of evidence that Coleridge knew Italian at the time, the force of the words "from Dante" is so great that he concludes by leaving the question open, and reminds the reader that Coleridge was able to put his "imperfect knowledge" of French and German at this period to "good account" (*RX*, pp. 217n, 525-528).

Below is a passage from Blair's "The Grave." It begins with a description of a schoolboy whistling his way past a "lone churchyard at night," when of a

> Sudden he starts, and hears, or thinks he hears,
> The sound of something purring at his heels;
> Full fast he flies, and dares not look behind him,
> Till out of breath he overtakes his fellows;
> Who gather round, and wonder at the tale
> Of horrid apparition, tall and ghastly,
> That walks at dead of night . . . (ll. 63-69)

Is this not a far more likely source than Dante, especially when we remember that the phrase "wonder at the tale" appears in Coleridge's early "Sonnet on Quitting School for College"? (See "Years of Apprenticeship," n. 44). And after all, where so common a human experience is involved, need we go a-hunting for any source?

29. *RX*, p. 400n. In the Preface Lowes said that his book was "not a study of Coleridge's theory of the imagination. It is an attempt to get at workings of the faculty itself" (p. x). And yet in trying to unravel the mystery of Coleridge's creative process, the poet's personal life is almost

entirely left out of account. Surely the artist's imagination is nourished by food other than books, even when we are dealing with a library cormorant.

"I have not included 'Christabel,' for the reason that 'Christabel' has failed completely to include itself," Lowes wrote at the beginning of his study. "Wherever the mysterious tracts from which it rose may lie, they are off the road which leads to 'The Ancient Mariner' and 'Kubla Khan'. . . . I wish I did know in what distant deeps or skies the secret lurks, but the elusive clue is yet to capture" (*RX*, p. 4*n*).

Nethercot supposes that he has found those clues, in a very much less convincing book. We see here the limitation, and it is a very important one, in Lowes's method. For in confining his attention to literary source hunting he has made "Christabel" somehow seem off the beaten track from where "The Ancient Mariner" and "Kubla Khan" lie. But to the extent that great poetry is always in some sense a projection of the artist's deepest and most abiding concerns, it would not be psychologically possible for "Christabel" to be so oblique a product. And of course it is not.

24. DREAMS

1. The origin and significance of all dreams, and especially nightmares, are among the most hotly debated subjects in twentieth-century thought. All investigators seem agreed, however, that true nightmares are very much rarer than anxiety (*Angst*) dreams, that nightmare in adults is much less common or intense than in children, and that regular, *repeated* nightmares in an adult, over long periods of time, are quite rare. The almost universal conviction among the early psychoanalysts that nightmares were related to suppressed incestuous longings has been, of course, fiercely disputed. That repeated nightmares are a manifestation of severe emotional distress, however, is almost never doubted. The student who supposes that Coleridge's nightmares resulted primarily from opium addiction or poor digestion will find little support in the standard literature of dreams. On the contrary, he is likely to be startled by such passages as: "the affection [nightmare] is frequently met with in various forms of mental alienation, particularly manic-depressive insanity and dementia praecox" (Ernest Jones, *On the Nightmare* [New York, 1959], p. 53).

2. *CL*, I, 347. Here is the whole passage:

> At six years old I remember to have read Belisarius, Robinson Crusoe, & Philip Quarle— and then I found the Arabian Nights' entertainments—one tale of which (the tale of a man who was compelled to seek for a pure virgin) made so deep an impression on me (I had read it in the evening while my mother was mending stockings) that I was haunted by spectres, whenever I was in the dark—and I distinctly remember the anxious & fearful eagerness, with which I used to watch the window, in which the books lay.

As to the probability that at six years Coleridge read Belisarius, Robinson Crusoe, and Philip Quarll, besides a volume of the *Arabian Nights*, the reader may be at this point left to his own surmises. (These claims have, of course, produced the expected effect upon some later commentators. The young T. S. Eliot was sufficiently impressed to begin a one-paragraph biography of Coleridge for a National Portrait Gallery picture-postcard with the sentence: "When five years old [he] had read the *Arabian Nights*." Quoted from Kathleen Coburn's Introduction to *Coleridge: A Collection of Critical Essays* [Englewood Cliffs, 1967] p. 1.) In any case, what meaning could the idea of seeking for a pure virgin have for a six-year-old boy? (I cannot find any tale in the *Arabian Nights* that answers even remotely to Coleridge's summary. Professor Joseph Campbell, who has edited the collection and is, of course, one of the world's greatest authorities on folktales, informs me that he is unable to suggest another source.) But however distorted or even fabricated the specific details may be, the idea of being compelled to embark upon a long search, with the implication of far-ranging travels, seems to have had deep and forbidding meanings for Coleridge.

3. *C.L*, I, 63, 104, 187.   4. *PW*, I, 43, 77, 158.

5. *PW*, I, 166. Quoted from the quarto text of 1796 as given in *app. crit.*

6. I, 60, 276, 285. In one of the climactic scenes of the play, Albert asks his fratricidal brother, whose pride, cunning, and sophisms he has just exposed:

> Have they given thee peace?
> Cured thee of starting in thy sleep? or made
> The darkness pleasant, when thou wakest at midnight? (V, 191-193)

A moment later, Osorio, thinking he has seen a ghost, exclaims:

> Ha!—my brain turns wild
> At its own dreams—off—off, fantastic shadow! (V, 222-223)

The 1801 "Ode to Tranquillity" contains several passages of self-portraiture. In one we find:

> Idle Hope
> And dire Remembrance interlope,
> To vex the *feverish slumbers of the mind:*
> *The bubble floats before, the spectre stalks behind. (ll. 13-16)*

The final couplet of the poem describes the "present works of present man" as

> *A wild and dream-like* trade of blood and guile,
> Too foolish for a tear, too wicked for a smile!

7. *PW*, I, 290.

8. Similarly, genuinely restful sleep appears in "Christabel" as something extraordinary:

> For she belike hath drunken deep
> Of all the blessedness of sleep! (ll. 375-376)

Perhaps the extreme familiarity of

> O sleep! it is a gentle thing
> Beloved from pole to pole!

blinds us to the realization of how much intense longing is held within those lines.

9. *CL*, II, 989-990.

10. *CL*, II, 1009. Two days before he had written that against the advice of Sir George Beaumont he was still reading at night "only from the *dread* of falling asleep; & I contracted the Habit from awaking in terrors about an hour after I had fallen asleep, & from the being literally afraid to trust myself again out of the leading-strings of my Will & Reason" (*CL*, II, 999. STC's underscoring).

11. *CL*, II, 1021.

12. *N*, 2398.

13. *N*, 2666. Italics in text. Just a year before, Coleridge had confided the dreaded secret in plainer language to his journal, but disguised to prying eyes by a number cipher which, decoded, reads: "no night without its guilt of opium and spirit!" (*N*, 2387 and n).

14. For example, in a letter to Southey: "what my dream was, is not to tell" (*CL*, II, 804); and even into the supposed privacy of his notebooks: "part of my Dream is too strange & the feelings connected with the images in sleep too different from those which have been connected with the same awake to mention" (*N*, 2539).

15. *CL*, II, 982. STC's emphasis.

16. "Base Men my vices justly taunting," in a letter to Poole three weeks later (*CL*, II, 1009). The process of emendation and modification continued, and when Coleridge published the poem, this line, and several others doubtless considered too explicit, were excised.

17. Four years later, in one of his most shattering journal entries, Coleridge wrote: "O great God! Grant me grace truly to look into myself, & to begin the serious work of Self-amendment. . . . Let me live in *Truth*—manifesting that alone which *is*, even as it *is*. . . ." (*N*, 2091). The underscorings are Coleridge's and would seem to emphasize that *is* means *truth, reality*—so that we can take Christabel's "Dreaming that alone, which is," as proof that the maiden's virtue is such that despite the horror of the dream, it does not embody *imaginary* terrors—the sort, presumably, only visited upon more fallen specimens of humanity. Without some such gloss it is difficult to understand the odd emphasis of the lines:

> Fearfully dreaming, yet. I wis,
> Dreaming that alone, which is—

In a copy of the *published* "Christabel" (1816), Coleridge underscored the last word, "*is*," in his own hand, to provide the needed emphasis. (See EHC's edition of the poem [1907], p. 81, n. ii.)

18. All quotations from "The Pains of Sleep" are from the 1803 letter to Southey (*CL*, II, 982-984. Italics in text). The published version may be found at *PW*, I, 389-391. STC's later changes for publication are almost all away from the candor of concrete statements toward general ones. Thus "crimes" becomes "deeds"; "for all was guilt" becomes "all seemed guilt," and so forth. A collation of the several versions, with particular emphasis to excised lines, would be revealing.

19. Quoted from Beer, p. 126. Related statements abound in the notebooks. "Wurde, Worthiness, VIRTUE consist in the mastery over the sensuous and sensual Impulses," he wrote in 1805 (*N*, 2556—the whole context should be studied); and sometime later he condemned "the Nadir of Love, appetite" (N, 3154) in another revealing passage.

20. The same cluster appears in a rejected stanza of the "Ode to Tranquillity": "Half-thinking, sensual France, a natural Slave" (*PW*, I, 360, *app. crit.*).

21. *CL*, I, 213-214. Italics in text. The previous month he had written: "I do consider Mr. Godwin's Principles as vicious; and his book [*Political Justice*] as a Pander to Sensuality" (*CL*, I, 199). It is worth noting that the word "pleasure" comes in for almost as great a perjorative barrage as "sensual." "A hideous hag th' Enchantress Pleasure seems," and "painted Pleasure . . . the Enchantress vile" (*PW*, I, 25, 31) are typical sentiments from the early poems. All the ideas and attitudes under discussion are combined in a single line from a poem written in his twenty-first year, "To Fortune": "Unholy Pleasure's frail and feverish dream" (l. 8. *PW*, I, 55).

22. *CSC*, p. 444. Italics in text. This is a marginal comment upon Browne's *Religio Medici* and begins with a reference to his love for Sara Hutchinson.

23. *CSC*, p. 445. Italics in text.   24. *N*, 2595. Italics in text.

25. *CL*, I, 458. STC's emphasis. For more on his reaction to the waltz, see *CL*, I, 506. It should be emphasized that such matters are never far from his mind. He always views any kind of irregular connection in the worst possible light. "Why is it that studies of Music and Painting are so unfavorable to the human Heart?" he asks Southey in 1799, and goes on to find that both painters and musicians "both alike are almost uniformly Debauchees" (*CL*, I, 539-540).

26. *N*, 2556.

27. *CL*, IV, 905-906. Italics in text. The whole letter, dealing with qualities he considered desirable in a wife, is important.

28. A letter from Humphry Davy had prompted Coleridge to think back over the names of all the women he had known. Having completed the roster of *"virtuous* Women," Coleridge wrote:

> Then (& verily I, a Husband & a Father, & for the last seven years of my Life a very Christian Liver, felt oddly while I did it) then, I say, I went as far as memory served, thro' all the loose women I had known, from my 19th to my 22nd year, that being the period that comprizes my Unchastities; but as names are not the most recollectible of our Ideas, & the name of a loose Woman not that one of her adjuncts, to which you pay the most attention, I could here recollect no *name* at all—no, nor even a face nor feature. I remembered my vices, & the times thereof, but not their objects. (*CL*, II, 73, STC's emphasis.)

Coleridge was 28 when he wrote this letter. It seems significant that he could remember neither names, faces, nor features of any of the "loose women" he had known.

29. *CL*, III, 514-515.   30. *N*, 2398.

31. *CL*, I, 145. Italics in text. The tone of this famous letter seems never to have been accurately assessed. Though there is much truth in what Coleridge says, the letter is consistently falsified by staginess, insincerity, and the self-image he is anxiously projecting.

32. One of the journal entries for 1805 is significant in this regard. Coleridge describes how he rose from bed at half past two in the morning and made "*a vow* aloud / O me! that I ever should have had need to make such a Vow!" Two coded words follow that have not been deciphered, so that we have only the vaguest clue as to what this vow may have been. The note goes on to attack those who argue that human nature is either all good or all bad. Such reasoners "destroy the Unity of H[uman]. N[ature]. —& make the Association without *will* or *reason*, fantasms and fantastic feelings, the concupiscent, vindictive, and *narcissine* part of our nature one separate, dividuous being. . . ." Like the dream, then, thoughts which come to mind unbidden are not truly part of one's character. One is not *accountable* for them. The note goes on:

> Merciful God! grant that this Rising out of my Bed may be a Resurrection to my better Spirit!—rose for this cause/ I felt myself in pleasurable bodily feeling half-asleep and interruptively *conscious* of being sweetly half-asleep/ and I felt strongly, how apart from all concupiscence . . . I felt strongly how apart from all impurity if I were sleeping with the Beloved [Sara Hutchinson] these kind and pleasurable feelings would become associated with a Being *out of me*, & thereby in an almost incalculable train of consequences increase my active benevolence. . . . [The note goes on to argue that physical love can be virtuous] yea, that the Pressure of the Husband's Hand or swelling chest on the bosom of the beloved Wife shall appear as strictly and truly virtuous, as *Actively* virtuous, as the turning away in the heat of passion from the Daughter of Lust or Harlotry. . . . But I, Sara! But I am not worthy of you/ I shall perish!—I have not goodness enough to hope enough/ and tho' I neither game nor ever connect myself with Woman ⟨even by a Thought⟩, yet my bodily infirmities conquer me, and the cowardice of pain, or rather of danger of Life, drives me to stimulants that cannot but finally destroy me. O me/ let me return!—Awake! awake!—(*N*, 2495. STC's underscoring).

The two undeciphered words are given as *Mss σε'τκο9*. Miss Coburn notes that "the last letter, the numeral 9, is a clearer reading than *σε'τκοο* which, however, may be the intention. *M[i]ss Sehtkonine*, an anagram for some name? Or *Mss*=hands, *sehtkoo*=she took? The concealment had not been deciphered" (*N*, 249*n*). In Coleridge's cryptogram, however, the number 9 stands for the ninth letter of the alphabet: "I". May not the difficult reading therefore be, "I took hands"? And would this not point to the masturbatory conflict suggested by the whole entry?

33. None of this, of course, is intended to deny the influence of physical stimuli on mental states. As any kind of discomfort may affect our conscious moods, so may bad digestion or a torn sheet invite a bad dream. But the specific *character* of the dream would remain decisive. Thus it is one thing for a cold draught to provoke a dream of shivering in a snowstorm and quite

another for the same stimulus to lead to a dream of fleeing naked over frozen tombs while being pursued by ravenous wolves.

34. *N*, 848.   35. *DWJ*, p. 70.   36. *N*, 848*n*.   37. *N*, 1998.

38. *PW*, I, 289, 285.   39. *CL*, I, 647.   40. *CL*, II, 914-915.

41. For example: "My eye is so inflamed that I cannot stir out" (*CL*, I, 189; 12 March 1796); "the Lid of my left eye is still swolln & red" (*CL*, II, 1127; 16 April 1804).

42. *N*, 2780*n*.

43. *N*, 1250. Italics in text. Miss Coburn notes that "the absence of surprise in sleep was noticed by Coleridge's favourite author on dreams, Andrew Baxter. . . . The idea also appears in Erasmus Darwin's *Zoonomia* I 215-17." In Darwin I also find the following: "Two other remarkable circumstances of our dreaming ideas are their inconsistency, and the total absence of surprise" (*Zoonomia*, i, 166).

44. *N*, 1726.

45. He was to write of Dorothy in his journal: "deep ⟨hearted⟩ & wide ⟨hearted⟩ Dorothy, my Sister! my Sister! so like to myself in the forms of our Hearts. . . ." (*N*, 2531). Other journal entries testify to more mysterious associative links. In a long note of 1804, Coleridge reflected rather murkily on his dreams, and suspected that almost all of them seemed to involve or refer to Sara Hutchinson. See also *N*, 2061.

46. *PW*, I, 32, *app. crit.* Coleridge's wretched self-image is one of the most destructive of the several forces contributing to his feeble self-confidence, especially with women. In 1792, in a letter to Mrs. Evans, the mother of the girl forever identified as his first true love, he referred to "that ugly arrangement of features, with which Nature has distinguished me" (*CL*, I, 22). Four years later he wrote to Thelwall that his face expressed "great Sloth, & great, indeed almost ideotic good nature. 'Tis a mere carcase of a face: fat, flabby, & expressive chiefly of inexpression" (*CL*, I, 259). Almost twenty years later the description is, if anything, worse: "my face is not a manly or representable Face. . . . The face *itself* is a *feeble*, unmanly face. . . . The exceeding *weakness*, strengthlessness, in my face, was very painful to me—not as my own face but as *a* face" (quoted from Kathleen Coburn, "Reflections in a Coleridge Mirror: Some Images in His Poems," in *From Sensibility to Romanticism*, eds. F. W. Hilles and Harold Bloom [Oxford, 1965], p. 418. Italics in text). As if this were not bad enough, one of the later notebook entries describes the body as the "Eternal Shadow of the finite Soul / The Soul's self-symbol / its image of itself, Its own yet not itself" (*ibid.* p. 419.) It is possible, of course, to have a perfectly objective and unflattering view of one's own physiognomy without destructive consequences to one's self esteem, but this is surely not true when a man considers himself decidedly *unmanly*. And this, we shall see, is a recurrent haunting fear of Coleridge's. Even in the description of the face above there is an emphasis on it as *unmanly, feeble, weak.* (The final qualifying clause is typically Coleridge: the face causes him pain not because it is *his* face, which might be egocentric, but because it is so poor a face considered as such!)

47. Miss Coburn notes that "*smokelike* is a somewhat doubtful word. It could be *snakelike*" (*N*, 1250*n*). If indeed "snakelike," the association is much intensified with the "lofty lady" Geraldine, who is several times identified as a serpent. But I do not myself find the reading doubtful. The formation of the m's and n's in the phrase "dim & indefinite & smokelike" points with seeming certainty to the reading "smokelike," which, after all, reinforces the meaning of the whole phrase.

48. *CL*, I, 348. In the nursery rime, Coleridge wrote, "two at my *bed*" instead of *head*. Curiously, in the Malta notebooks he made the reverse error: "I am perfectly calm tho' well for my body that there are the Doric Columns to my ~~Head~~ Bed!" (*N*, 2078).

49. *N*, 1214.   50. *N*, 1681. STC's underscoring.

51. Personal communication. Dr. Levy is a psychoanalyst, a former member of the New York University faculty, and presently the Executive Director of the Research Institute of Personality, Psychotherapy, and Education.

52. *N*, 1577.

53. *N*, 1620. Italics in text. It had been a terrible night for Coleridge. He had gone to bed the night before after tea "& in about 2 hours absolutely summoned the whole Household to me by my Screams, from all the chambers—& I continued screaming even after Mrs. Coleridge was sitting & speaking to me!—O me! O me!—" (*N*, 1619). The dream about Hartley is especially interesting because Coleridge related it to the physical stimulation of a watch ticking close to his ear, so that the dream's "Hum & Ha, & the Ticking of the Watch were each the other." But Hartley's christening had not yet taken place, so that the dream, as Miss Coburn suggests, is anticipatory. But does not that fact suggest a major underlying meaning of the dream? If we accept that Coleridge identified very deeply with his son, does not the dream reveal deep self-dissatisfaction? The willful child's fumbling over a simple moral truth, even when perfectly well known, is thus a disguise for the dreamer's angry self-criticism.

54. *N*, 1647. Italics in text.

55. *N*, 1649. Italics in text.

56. Orphans and property figure again and again in Coleridge's writings. One wonders how much bitterness Coleridge felt at his own hard lot in life, that as an orphan and a youngest son he had inherited nothing. Upon failing to win a coveted scholarship at Cambridge he wrote to Mrs. Evans that he could not help regretting "that Nature had not put it into the head of some *Rich* Man to beget *me* for his *first born*—whereas now I am likely to get bread, just when I shall have no teeth left to chew it" (*CL*, I, 48. STC's underscoring). Three years later he wrote to Thelwall that property was the "real source of inconstancy, depravity, & prostitution . . . beyond doubt the Origin of all Evil" (*CL*, I, 214). In a bitter letter of 1808 to his brother George, he referred to himself as a "deserted Orphan" (*CL*, III, 103). A notebook entry shows the following reflections:

> O the impudence of those who dare hold Property to be the great binder up of the affections of the young to the old, &c. . . . Two Brothers in this Country fought in the mourning Coach, & stood with black eyes & their black Clothes all blood over their Father's Grave. (*N*, 1636)

The above follows immediately upon an unpleasant story dealing with "the foul lust for gold!— PROPERTY." Needless to say, these were not the sentiments he expressed publicly in later life.

In reflecting upon his own lack of egotism, he employed the following odd metaphor to explain his reaction to expressions of esteem and admiration from others: "I feel as a man whose good dispositions are still alive feels in the enjoyment of a *darling* Property on a doubtful Title" (*N*, 2726. STC's underscoring).

57. Allsop, II, 85. This page discloses Coleridge's statement that "neither awake nor asleep have I any other feelings than what I had at Christ's Hospital."

58. *N*, 1698.

59. *CL*, II, 1021 and n. 1. Immediately after a journal entry date of 22 October 1801, Coleridge wrote: "Account of the climate of Madeira by Adams—from Longman [a publisher]" (*N*, 1000). And just four days before this another entry reads: "Laudanum, Friday, Septem. 18. 1801. Poem, dream from Dor.—both dead—feelings after death—seeking the children" (*N*, 990). It seems odd that the ideas of death and children and Madeira should appear so close together in journal entries, and to reappear in an apparently wholly different context two years later. Miss Coburn's note cites difficulties in reading entry 990: " 'Dor,' Dorothy?, is not beyond doubt." Examination of Notebook 21 confirms the suspicion that the reading is "Der.," surely for Derwent, thus unifying the entry around the dream of the poet's children.

60. *CL*, II, 1020-21.

61. Lamb's famous essay "On Witches and Other Night Fears" exhibits the same process of rationalization when confronted by such baffling phenomena as intense fears in young and innocent children. What was incomprehensible to Lamb, and Coleridge, was that the frightful

demons peopling the dark could possibly have resulted from *their own experience*. Thus Lamb writes after an account of his childhood terrors: "That the kind of fear here treated of is purely spiritual—that it is strong in proportion as it is objectless upon earth—that it predominates in the period of sinless infancy—are difficulties, the solution of which might afford some probable insight into our ante-mundane condition, and a peep at least into the shadow-land of pre-existence." In the same essay is a passage which can easily be taken for a pre-Jungian insight: "Gorgons, and Hydras, and Chimaeras . . . may reproduce themselves in the brain of superstition— but they were there before. They are transcripts, types—the archetypes are in us, and eternal." But the crucial point missed in all this is that these images are creations from within, resulting from post-natal experience. Lamb, like Coleridge, never came close to grasping this central point, and thus his own fear-laden childhood was never related to concrete causes. When his sister, Mary, killed their mother with a kitchen knife, the appalling act could be seen as another example of demonic visitation. "I was dreadfully alive to nervous terrors." Lamb wrote of his childhood. "The night-time solitude, and the dark, were my hell. The sufferings I endured in this nature would justify the expression. I never laid my head on my pillow, I suppose, from my fourth to the seventh or eighth year of my life—so far as memory serves in things so long ago— without an assurance, which realized its own prophecy, of seeing some frightful spectre" (*LW*, II, 67-68). We see here some of that mutually shared body of experience which lay behind the lifelong friendship of Lamb and Coleridge.

62. *N*, 2061. Coleridge's emphasis.

63. Quoted from *RX*, p. 543. Another quotation from Lowes's long note is most apropos the present discussion. In Germany Coleridge had summarized for Clement Carlyon an old German play

> in which Eve is represented as telling Cain and Abel to take care to have their hair combed, and their faces and hands well washed, for that the Almighty was about to pay them a visit. Upon His approach, Eve scolds Cain for not taking off his little hat to Him, and for not giving Him his little hand to shake. Cain is represented as making a very bad hand of the Lord's Prayer; upon which Eve apologizes. In conclusion, God pays Abel the compliment of hoping to see his descendents Kings and Bishops; but that as for Cain's children he forsees very plainly that they will be nothing better than tinkers and shoemakers.

This was Coleridge's summary *before* either of the dreams we have been discussing.

Amazingly, several of these details coalesce in letters Coleridge wrote to his own young children containing advice as to behavior and moral duties. These few letters are especially important in that they provide a chilling reflection of the kind of stern upbringing Coleridge had at Ottery St. Mary, and of the fear-inducing moral training he had at Christ's Hospital (together, of course, with his own convictions). In February 1807, having determined upon a separation from his wife, Coleridge took the ten-year-old Hartley with him to join the Wordsworths, and wrote a long letter (the first so far as is known) to his son Derwent, who had remained behind with his mother. The letter begins with expressions of great love and longing and then moves to an account of what the boy's duties towards his parents should be. As for the mother, Coleridge writes:

> she gave *you* nourishment out of her own Breasts for so long a time, that the Moon was at it's least and it's greatest sixteen times, before you lived entirely on any other food, than what came out of her Body; and she brought you into the world with shocking pains, and yet loved you the better for the Pains, which she suffered for you; and before you were born, for eight months together every drop of Blood in your body, first beat in HER Pulses and throbbed in HER Heart. So it must needs be a horrible wicked Thing ever to forget, or wilfully to vex, a Father or a Mother: especially, a Mother. God is above all: and only good and dutiful Children can say their Lord's Prayer, & say to God, 'OUR FATHER', without being wicked even in their Prayers. . . . *always to tell the Truth* . . . to tell a Lie . . . is such a base, hateful, and wicked Thing, that when good men describe all wickedness put together in one wicked mind, they call it the Devil, which is Greek for a *malicious Liar*. . . . Never, never, tell a Lie—even tho' you should escape a whipping by it: for the Pain of a whipp[ing]

does not last above a few minutes; but the Thought of having told a Lie will make you miserable for days—unless, indeed, you are hardened in wickedness, and then you must be miserable for ever. (*CL*, III, 1-2. STC's emphasis)

These are strong words to a child not yet six and a half years old. It may also be added that Coleridge had the amazing tactlessness to conclude the letter with the sentence, "Your dear friend, Sara Hutchinson, sends her Love to you!"—surely certain to infuriate Mrs. Coleridge, whose feelings over the separation were bitter and whose resentment toward the Wordsworths and her rival are understandable enough.

The following month Coleridge provided Hartley with a character analysis which, as he said, might equally be applied to himself:

nothing gives you pain, dwells long enough upon your mind to do you any good. . . . this power, which you possess, of shoving aside all disagreeable reflections, or losing them in a labyrinth of day-dreams, which saves you from some present pain, has on the other hand interwoven into your nature habits of procrastination, which unless you correct them in time (& it will require all your best exertions to do it effectually)—must lead you into lasting Unhappiness.

You are now going with me (if God have not ordered it otherwise) into Devonshire to visit your Uncle, G. Coleridge. He is a very good man, and very kind; but his notions of Right and of Propriety are very strict; & he is therefore exceedingly shocked by any gross Deviations from what is right and proper. I take therefore this mean of warning you against those bad Habits, which I and all your friends here have noticed in you—And be assured, I am not writing in anger, but on the contrary with great Love, and a comfortable Hope, that your Behaviour at Ottery will be such as to do yourself, and me and your dear Mother, *credit.*

First then I conjure you never to do anything of any kind when out of sight which you would not do in my presence. What is a frail and faulty Father on earth compared with God, your heavenly Father? But God is always present.

Specially, never pick at or snatch up any thing, eatable or not. I know, it is only an idle foolish Trick; but your Ottery Relations would consider you as a little Thief—and in the Church Catechism *picking* and *stealing* are both put together, as two sorts of the same Vice—'and keep my hands from picking and *stealing*.' And besides, it is a dirty trick; and people of weak stomachs would turn sick at a dish, which a young FILTH-PAW had been fingering. . . .

Among the lesser faults I beg you to endeavor to remember, not to stand between the half opened door, either while you are speaking or spoken to. But come *in*—or go out—& always speak & listen with the door shut.—Likewise, not to speak so loud, or abruptly—and never to interrupt your elders while they are speaking—and not to *talk* at all during Meals.

I pray you, keep this Letter; and read it over every two or three days. . . .

P. S. I have not spoken about your mad passions, and frantic Looks & pout-mouthing; because I trust, that is all over. (*CL*, III, 9-11. STC's underscoring)

Coleridge's plans to keep the two boys with him after separating from his wife came to nothing. He went back to London alone and after 1812 never visited Stowey or the Quantocks again. For ten years he did not write a single letter to any of his children, nor did he in fact see them more than two or three times. That they grew up to honor and respect him must be accounted to the credit of the much-abused wife, who could so easily have poisoned their feelings toward their absent and seemingly neglectful father.

64. *N*, 1726. STC's underscoring.

65. It is worth remembering that Christabel goes into the woods to pray because she had dreamed the night before of her bethrothed knight: "Dreams that made her moan and leap, / As on her bed she lay in sleep" (*PW*, I, 216, *app. crit.*). These lines appeared only in the first edition of the poem. It seems probable that Coleridge struck them out when he perceived their jarring sexual implications.

66. In a brilliant article on Geraldine and Coleridge's dreams (*UTQ*, XXV [1956], 121-130), Kathleen Coburn suggested that "Christabel" was a projection of his own experiences, and that he "could not finish it because it was too closely a representation of his own experience; that experience was screened through a female figure but this figure was none the less, perhaps even more so, significantly one side of his own nature" (pp. 128-129). Miss Coburn further saw the connection between Geraldine's pursuit of Christabel and his own dreams, "in which one gathers he was frequently pursued by unpleasing female figures . . ." (p. 129). Regrettably, Miss Coburn did not seek to relate either the poem or the dreams to Coleridge's conscious life.

67. *PW*, I, 224, *app. crit.*

68. *N*, 1646. As late as 4 September 1833, Coleridge was still talking about this project. See *TT*, p. 278.

69. *N*, 1214.

70. *SC*, II, 6. Relevant to Coleridge's thoughts about Bacchus and his personal fantasies and identifications is the following passage from the 1808 lecture itself:

> with the ancients Bacchus, or Dionysus, was among the most awful and mysterious deities. In his earthly character [he was] the conqueror and civilizer of India, and allegorically the symbol, in the narrower and popular notion, of festivity, but worshipped in the mysteries as representative of the organic energies of the universe, that work by passion and joy without apparent distinct consciousness, and rather as the cause or condition of skill and contrivance, than the result. . . . aided by his traditional history as an earthly conqueror, Bacchus was honored as the presiding genius of the heroic temperament and character, this being considered not as an acquisition of art or discipline, but something innate and divine, a felicity above and beyond prudence; and hence, too, the connection with the same deity of all the vehement and awful passions and the events and actions proceeding from such passions. (*SC*, I, 165)

The phrase that Bacchus was "allegorically the symbol" of festivity shows how loosely in practice Coleridge used these key terms.

Patricia M. Adair observes of the passage quoted above that Coleridge's language about Bacchus is very close to that in Maurice's *History of Hindostan*, a work with which Coleridge was very familiar; Maurice wrote that Bacchus was "the first conqueror, and not the conqueror, but the reformer and legislator of India" (*The Waking Dream*, [London, 1967], p. 127). Coleridge's "conqueror and civilizer of India" brings to mind his notebook statement that "if ever I imagined myself a conqueror, it was always to bring peace" (*N*, 1214). Thus the links with Bacchus would seem to be very strong. Curiously, Coleridge was later to be described by Charles Lamb as looking and *acting* like Bacchus: "Damn Temperance and them that first invented it, some Anti Noahite. Coleridge has powdered his head, *and looks like Bacchus, Bacchus ever sleek and young*. He is going to turn sober, but his Clock has not struck yet, meantime he pours down goblet after goblet, the 2nd to see where the 1st is gone, the 3rd to see no harm happens to the second, a 4th to say there is another coming, and a 5th to say he's not sure he's the last" (to Dorothy Wordsworth, 13 Nov. 1810. *LL*, II, 108).

71. *CL*, I, 347.

72. Kathleen Coburn, "Coleridge, Wordsworth and 'the Supernatural'," *UTQ*, XXV (1956), 127.

73. The encounter with the "biting" prostitute is followed immediately thus: "I sit down on a broad open plain of rubbish with rails & a street beyond . . . wanderings thro' the Hall . . . wanderings thro' Streets." This cluster of events may possibly be related to the sequence of thoughts Coleridge set down slightly more than three years later in relation to Asra:

> Could I fearel for a moment the supremacy of Love suspended in my nature, by accidents of temporary Desire; were I conscious for a moment of an Interregnum in the Heart, were the usurper Rebel to sit on the *Throne* of my Being, even tho' it were only that the rightful Lord of my Bosom were sleeping, soon to awake & expel the Usurper, I should feel myself as

much fallen & as unworthy of her Love in any ⟨such⟩ tumult of Body indulged toward her, as if I had roamed,⟨like a Hog⟩in the rankest ~~Stews~~ Lanes of a ~~prostitute~~ city, battening on the loathesome offals of Harlotry / yea, the guilt would seem greater to me. . . .(*N*, 2984)

74. The first is to "wanderings thro' Streets, the noticing *the Complex side of a noble Building*." This may foreshadow a detail remembered in a moment from a former dream: "*the slight pain in my side* produced a fellow knuckling me there." The previous August Coleridge had written Southey that he was "in serious dread of a paralytic Stroke in my whole left Side" (*CL*, II, 974). How far physical pain in dreams results from outside stimuli is, of course, a much debated point. If we allow ourselves completely free associative rein, we may wonder whether the phrase "*noble* Building" does not hint at a personal projection here also. Coleridge was nothing if not complex. Remembering now the dream of the two sons of the Noblemen, and asking pity for a Nobleman's orphan, we may wonder whether the deformed side ("lean and old and foul of hue") of the noble Geraldine is not in some way connected with the maimed and deformed characters of Coleridge's dreams.

75. Similar threats may be implied in a letter to Southey written four months before: "three times I have wakened out of these frightful Dreams, & I found my legs so *locked* into each other as to have *left* a bruise" (*CL*, II, 976. STC's underscoring). I am aware that the image of the male "wretch" grasping the dreamer's scrotum may also point to homosexual or perhaps masturbatory conflicts, but it seems unwise to pursue these points here.

76. Hallucinatory passages in Coleridge's notebooks can always be attributed to opium. Obviously, this creates great difficulties of interpretation. In general, I believe, commentators are far too quick to assume a drug influence when confronted with distortions of reality in Coleridge's fantasies or semi-somnolent states of mind.

77. It is much to be suspected that nightmares and difficult breathing coexist in Coleridge from the beginning. References to panting in sleep are common in his poetry. In the nightmare described in "Ode to the Departing Year" we find "my thick and struggling breath / Imitates the toil of death!" (ll. 111-112. *PW*, I, 166). Coleridge's asthma may be as much a cause as a result of these phenomena. Nor is it probably entirely accidental that the Mariner's torments are confined to the mouth and throat ("throats unslaked, black lips baked"); that a sign of the Mariner's crime is an albatross hung around his *neck*; that Christabel's speech is affected; that the experience forbidden to the poet in "Kubla Khan" is oral ("He on honey-dew hath fed, and drunk the milk of paradise"). Even the blissful experiences of slumber in both "The Ancient Mariner" and "Christabel" are clothed in oral metaphor:

> Sure I had drunken in my dreams,
> And still my body drank. (ll. 303-304)

> For she belike hath drunken deep
> Of all the blessedness of sleep! (ll. 375-376)

This subject is worth a monograph in itself.

78. ". . . but what wonderful wanderings thro' the Hall, with bad Portraits of the Emperor of Russia, the Hall belonging to the E." This whole passage is baffling and especially rich in associative links. There is no suggestion of who "the E," the owner of the hall, might be. Since so many proper names appear in the dream, the single initial may either be a disguise, or a simple abbreviation for a name Coleridge would not forget no matter how long afterwards he looked at the dream. Almost eight years before, Coleridge had written while on a business trip:

> . . . I am quite home-sick—aweary of this long absence from Bristol.—I was at the *Ball*, last night—and saw the most numerous collection of handsome men & Women, that I ever did in one place—but alas! far from my comfortable little cottage I feel as if I were in the long damp Gallery of some Nobleman's House, amused with the beauty or variety of the Paintings, but shivering with cold, and melancholy from loneliness. (*CL*,I, 179. STC's underscoring)

Loneliness, homesickness, and cold were three of Coleridge's constant afflictions at Christ's Hospital. The recipient of this letter was a Rev. John Edwards, who had been introduced to Coleridge by another acquaintance whose name began with E, John Prior Estlin. But the most likely E identified with Christ's Hospital belonged to the Evans family. The word "Hall" is repeated just before the appearance of the university harlot, Sal Hall.

79. On 23 October 1802 Lamb had sent Coleridge the news that Samuel Le Grice was dead (*LL*, I, 325). But as there was also a brother, Charles Le Grice, it is impossible to identify the dream-figure absolutely.

80. This is the *OED* definition.

81. *LL*, I, 172 (8 February 1800). On the Le Grice brothers, see *N*, 979*n*.

82. *N*, 1403.

83. For notes on "*Obsonant* . . . one of the words used by the young [? Fowos/Forward]," see *N*, 1726*n*.

84. *N*, 1824. Italics in text.

85. *N*, 1824*n*.

86. *CL*, II, 746.

87. See Vera Watson, "Coleridge's Army Service," *TLS* (9 July 1950), p. 428. (Related material may be found in E. L. Griggs, "Coleridge's Army Experience," *English* [Summer 1953], 171-175, and *CL*, I, 75-6). It is just possible that there is more than meets the eye in the obscure problem of how Coleridge managed his army discharge. Watson begins her discussion thus: "It may well be asked how Coleridge, a perfectly rational being (if a little conscience-stricken about his conduct, as his letters of that period prove) was able to obtain his discharge on the grounds of insanity. The answer can only be—by the connivance of the military authorities, particularly that of his commanding officer." That seems plausible, but the matter is not settled. This article repeats several of the famous tales concerning Coleridge's army service which figure so largely in biographies. Watson notes that EHC, the poet's grandson, "expresses some doubts" about accounts circulated by Bowles and Mary Russell Mitford, but she does not understand why EHC was so much a skeptic. Here are EHC's own words:

In the various and varying reminiscences of his soldier days, which fell "from Coleridge's own mouth," and were repeated by his delighted *and credulous* hearers, this officer plays an important part. Whatever foundation of fact there may be for the touching anecdote that the Latin sentence, "*Eheu! quam infortunii miserrimum est fuisse felicem*," scribbled on the walls of the stable at Reading, caught the attention of Captain Ogle, 'himself a scholar,' and led to Comberbacke's detection, he was not, as the poet Bowles and Miss Mitford maintained, the sole instrument in procuring the discharge. He may have exerted himself privately, but his name does not occur in the formal correspondence which passed between Coleridge's brothers and the military authorities. (*Letters*, I, 63, n. 1)

EHC was vastly more clear-eyed about his grandfather than most subsequent scholars. Perhaps his inability to finish his biography of Coleridge had something to do with this.

Enough has been said of Coleridge's general distortion of his past life. But there is something special about his Cambridge and army experiences. His reminiscences to Gillman on both subjects are systematically misleading. There is reason to suppose that Coleridge's family never got over his behavior between entering college and marrying. In 1808 Coleridge was still defending himself to George on the subject: "even the Errors of my Youth have been most grossly exaggerated . . . yet since my leaving the university, what deviation from honor or rectitude can be fairly charged to me?" (*CL*, III, 102).

88. Lamb wrote to Coleridge on 5 February 1797: "I have a dim recollection that, when in town, you were talking of the Origin of Evil as a most prolific subject for a long poem" (*LL*, I, 95).

89. *N*, 1770. STC's underscoring. Just two weeks later, in a long note on association and behavior, Coleridge wrote:

... I saw great Reason to attribute the effect wholly to the streamy nature of the associating Faculty and especially as it is evident that *they most* labor under this defect who are most reverie-ish & streamy—Hartley, for instance & myself.... (*N*, 1833. STC's emphasis)

Hartley was then two years and three months old.

That these disturbing dissonances in the stream of consciousness were long-standing is suggested by a passage in "The Eolian Harp" (1795):

> Full many a thought uncall'd and undetain'd,
> And many idle flitting phantasies,
> Traverse my indolent and passive brain,
> As wild and various as the random gales
> That swell and flutter on this subject Lute! (ll. 39-43)

90. For example: "frightful Dreams with screaming—breezes of Terror blowing from the Stomach up thro' the Brain / always when I am awakened, I find myself stifled with wind / & the wind the manifest cause of the Dream / frequent paralytic Feelings—sometimes approaches to Convulsion fit" (*CL*, II, 976. STC's underscoring). "The wind the manifest cause of the Dream" is another example of psychological contents supplied by supposed physical stimuli.

But the record is by no means devoid of *aperçus* which show that he sometimes was aware of psychological deception in himself. In a journal entry of April 1805 we find: ". . . Evil produces Evil—One error almost compels another/ tell one lie tell a hundred/ O to shew this, a priori by bottoming it in all our faculties/ & by experience of touching Examples." Several lines of Greek letters follow, which when translated produce words in several languages. (The page immediately following has been cut out of the notebook.) The whole, as translated by Miss Coburn, reads: "He praises a deception and cerebelline fantasies through the night; awakening into con[ciousness] in the morning early, and sometimes so as not to remain awake, he hopes for a delusion—Then anxiety, stifling—breath" (*N*, 2535 and n). There are an unusual number of heavy excisions in the notebooks around this time. See also the extremely important entry at *N*, 2543.

91. *CL*, II, 1203. Italics in text.   92. Shedd, I, 195-197.

93. Coleridge's interest in, and fear of, madness is one of the most neglected chapters in his biography. "Madness is not simply a bodily disease," he said in one of the late *Table Talk* entries. "It is the sleep of the spirit with certain conditions of wakefulness; that is to say, lucid intervals. During this sleep, or recession of the spirit, the lower or bestial states of life rise up into action and prominence. *It is an awful thing to be eternally tempted by the perverted senses.*" The last sentence, to which emphasis has been added, is a stark stare into what agonies Coleridge's reveries and dreams led him. "I think it was Bishop Butler," he concluded, "who said, that he was all his life struggling against the devilish suggestions of his senses, which would have maddened him, if he had relaxed the stern wakefulness of his reason for a single moment" (*TT*, pp. 84-85). Until some such passage is located in Butler (most improbable in view of Butler's known biography), Coleridge's remarks should be taken as another example of ventriloquism: putting into the mouths of others his own thoughts.

In the *Friend* Coleridge quoted approvingly the following from Giordano Bruno: "Pay particular attention, I beseech you, to these things; in that way you may understand me, a person who may perhaps seem mad—or at least see why I am mad" (Shedd, II, 117). This key passage appears in a letter (*CL*, III, 133), in the notebooks (*N*, 927), and as the motto of the *Statesman's Manual* (and in an appendix to it). In most cases the contexts are significant. In a late letter Coleridge proposed that the government fund an asylum "for lunacy and idiocy of the *will*." "Had such a house of health been in existence," he continued, "I know who would have entered himself as a patient some five and twenty years ago" (*Letters*, II, 767-768). See also the famous letter of 14 May 1814, in which Coleridge attributed "*all* his vices" to the effects of opium and argued that "a man, whose moral feelings, reason, understanding, and senses are perfectly sane and vigorous, may yet have been *mad*" (*CL*, III, 489-490. STC's emphasis).

The whole question of Coleridge's state of mind, at least at various times in his life, with respect to contemporary knowledge of psychological states, remains largely *terra incognita*. Why the relevance of such investigations to literary matters is so often and so hotly disputed is in itself a separate and vexed question. Without venturing into that mare's nest, however, we may at least remind ourselves that fear of madness, severe distortions of reality, and states of extreme hallucination appear repeatedly in Coleridge's dreams and notebooks. Relevant in this connection is a passage from Sara Coleridge's vindication of her father's character in connection with the charges of plagiarism raised by De Quincey:

> At all times his incorrectness of quotation and of reference, and in the relation of particular circumstances, was extreme; it seemed as if the door betwixt his memory and imagination was always open, and though the former was a large strong room, its contents were perpetually mingling with those of the adjoining chamber. I am sure that if I had not had the facts of my Father's life at large before me, from his letters and the relations of friends, *I should not have believed such confusions as his possible in a man of sound mind.* (Shedd, III, xxxvi, *n*)

94.   *CL*, I, 385. STC's underscoring.   95.   *CL*, I, 626.   96.   *PW*, I, 153-154.

97.   *CL*, II, 728-729. Thoughts of his children's deaths appear in a heartbreaking stanza from the original "Dejection":

> My little Children are a Joy, a Love,
>   A good Gift from above!
> But what is Bliss, that still calls up a Woe,
>   And makes it doubly keen
> Compelling me to *feel*, as well as KNOW,
> What a most blessed Lot mine might have been.
> Those little Angel Children (woe is me!)
> There have been hours, when feeling how they bind
> And pluck out the Wing-feathers of my Mind,
> Turning my Error to Necessity,
> I have half-wished, they never had been born!
> *That* seldom! But sad Thoughts they always bring,
> And like the Poet's Philomel, I sing
> My Love-song, with my breast against a Thorn. (CL, II, 797)

98.   *N*, 1645. STC's emphasis. Derwent's "filthy Pawlets" and the "young FILTH-PAW" in a later letter to Hartley (*CL*, III, 10) reflect Coleridge's growing horror of dirt (*N*, 2531).

99.   *N*, 2468. The entire entry should be read. For other comments relating to dreadful fears for the lives of his (and others' children), see *CL*, II, 728, 1084, 1139, 1144, 1162, 1184. The obscure dream at *N*, 990 may also be related to this problem. In 1805 he wrote: "my feeling, in sleep, of exceeding Love for my Infant/ seen by me in the Dream/ yet so as that it might be Sara, Derwent or Berkley/ and still *it was an individual Babe and mine.* Of Love in Sleep, the seldomness of the Feeling . . ." (*N*, 2441. STC's underscoring). Again, the whole context should be consulted. It seems to me very odd that Coleridge refers to his three children as "Sara, Derwent or Berkley." But the infant Berkeley had died when Coleridge was abroad in Germany (a fact which may have great bearing on his subsequent dreads). The substitution of the dead child's name (Coleridge had never seen him) for the living Hartley is ominously suggestive.

This seems an appropriate place to lay to rest a long-standing misconception regarding Wordsworth's "A Slumber Did My Spirit Seal." The poem is regularly published with the note that Coleridge suspected that the epitaph had perhaps been composed with the thought in mind of Dorothy Wordsworth's possible death. The conjecture appears in a long letter from Coleridge to Poole, written from Germany in reply to news that Berkeley had died. After a series of complex and (in the circumstances) somewhat strange reflections on the death of a child, Coleridge wrote: "Some months ago Wordsworth transmitted to me a most sublime Epitaph/ whether it had any reality, I cannot say.—Most probably, in some gloomier moment he had fancied the moment in which his Sister might die" (*CL*, I, 479). It ought to be perfectly obvious that this is altogether a projection and that there is no basis whatever for believing that Wordsworth's epitaph has anything to do with Dorothy, or any other member of his family, for that matter.

100. This has been observed by Kathleen Coburn, who cites articles by herself on the subject ("Coleridge, Wordsworth and the 'Supernatural,'" *UTQ*, XXII [1956]), and E. E. Bostetter, "*Christabel*: The Vision of Fear," *PQ*, XXXVI (1957), 183-194. Miss Coburn's note at *N*, 2468 should be consulted.

101. In one of the journal entries Coleridge made aboard vessel bound for Malta he noted: "Light of the Compass & rudderman's Lamp reflected with forms on the Main Sail" (*N*, 2001), which ties the "Ancient Mariner" stanza closely to an observation of 1804, a year before the dream about the fiendish child. Furthermore, entry 2001 is obscurely linked by "SICKLY Thoughts" about the death of Mary Wordsworth, who was of course very much alive.

102. *N*, 2470.

103. Coleridge seems to have been close to his sister Anne (Nancy), who died in 1791. He had three much older half-sisters, one of whom was at Ottery when he was growing up, but Coleridge himself says he somehow never felt towards her as he did towards Nancy (Gillman, p. 10). Not a single letter is extant to any of these half-sisters, nor any mention of them outside of Gillman, so far as I know.

104. *CL*, I, 348-349. Miss Schneider has pointed out to me that Coleridge may have been in Bristol on 13 October 1797, for the two volumes of Nash's *Worcestershire*, which had been borrowed from the Bristol library the previous August, were returned on that date. Now Coleridge's famous letter to Thelwall, which begins, "I have just received your letter—having been absent a day or two—," is headed "Saturday Morning" [14 October 1797]. Bristol is fifty miles from Nether Stowey, and Porlock is some twenty miles in another direction. If, therefore, he was in Bristol on the 13th, and made a detour to a lonely farmhouse, he would have had to travel some 140 miles in "a day or two," while lugging about the heavy and rare folio of Purchas' *Pilgrimage* and for about half his journey the two volumes of Nash, meanwhile finding time to write "Kubla Khan"—all of which is most improbable. Griggs's assertion that "The brief absence mentioned in the opening sentence [of the letter to Thelwall] probably refers to the solitary retirement near Porlock, where *Kubla Khan* was composed" does not take note of the complexities of the problem. On balance, however, the case for Coleridge's presence in Bristol on the preceding day or two seems very slim. STC is the least likely of men to have made a 100-mile journey for the sole purpose of returning books to a library, from which he did not borrow anything further on that date. He would hardly have gone to Bristol without giving himself time to spend with his many friends in that city. Furthermore, the Nash volumes had been signed out of the library the previous August not in Coleridge's hand, but apparently in that of his sister-in-law Mrs. Lovell, who borrowed a book herself on that date. The fact that Coleridge's volumes were returned on 14 October is recorded only by a librarian's initials. Since the borrowing was not made personally by Coleridge, there is no compelling reason to believe that he personally returned them. (See Paul Kaufman, "The Reading of Southey and Coleridge: The Record of their Borrowings from the Bristol Library, 1793-1798," *MP*, XXI [1924], 319. I am grateful to Mr. W. S. Hough, the City Librarian of Bristol, for providing me with xerox copies of the relevant pages of the 1797 ledgers and for answering related questions.)

105. *CL*, I, 348.

106. On 3 November 1796, Coleridge wrote to Cottle: "A devil, a very devil, has got possession of my left temple, eye, cheek, jaw, throat, and shoulder. I cannot see you this evening. I write in agony." Two days later he wrote: "I am seriously ill. The complaint, my medical attendant

says, is nervous—and originating in *mental* causes. I have a Blister under my right-ear—& I take Laudanum every four hours, 25 drops each dose." Thus an early medical opinion (Coleridge was just twenty-four years old) finds his illness psychological. The same day Coleridge wrote to Poole, and built his description of his sufferings on the metaphor of being attacked by a monster:

> . . . I took between 60 & 70 drops of Laudanum, and *sopped* the Cerberus just as his mouth began to open. On Friday it only *niggled* . . . but *this morning* he returned in full force, & his Name is Legion!—Giant-fiend of an hundred hands! with a shower of arrowy Death-pangs he transpierced me, & then he became a Wolf & lay gnawing my bones.—I am not mad, most noble Festus!—but in sober sadness I have suffered this day more bodily pain than I had before a conception of. (*CL*, I, 248-250. Italics in text)

107. *RX*, p. 593, n. 128.

108. *N*, 1718 and n. The passivity of this reverie is notable. It differs sharply from most notebook entries on the subject in that Coleridge's "Reason [is] at the Rudder," keeping his mental bark well away from the dangerous *stream* of association.

109. *The Waking Dream*, pp. 108-143. The author, I should hasten to add, does not suggest that Bacchus is a dream-projection, or note the appearance of the fat, sturdy boy, "like a young Bacchus," in the Christ's Hospital dream.

110. Adair, p. 131.

111. The whole passage, of course, has long been related to passages in Bartram. See *RX*, pp. 368-370. What is notable is that the key images here discussed stand apart from the general source. G. Wilson Knight impressionistically sees in the erupting fountain passage a "riotous impression of agony, tumult, and power: the dynamic enginery of birth and creation" (*The Starlit Dome* [Oxford, 1941],p. 92).

112. *RX*, pp. 396-397. Italics in text. Adair, p. 113, accepts this juxtaposition as the source of the lines.

113. John Shelton ("The Autograph Manuscript of 'Kubla Khan' and an Interpretation," *REL*, VII [1966], 33, n. 1.) accepts this reading.

114. *CSC*, p. 445. The extremes of fire and frost were used by Coleridge to describe his wife's temperament (*N*, 2398*n*). In a passage of 1801 not quite obliterated by later hands, he wrote of Sara: "I have dressed perhaps washed with her, & no one with us—all as cold & calm as a deep Frost . . ." (*N*, 979). Both these comparatively obscure passages have been often quoted to emphasize Sara Coleridge's limitations as a woman and as a wife. The voluminous evidence bearing upon the husband's parallel limitations is consistently ignored.

115. Those who seek still richer Empsonian ambiguities can conjure with "*Abyss*-inian maid," which combines references to the abyss of the unconscious and the caverns measureless to man.

116. A considerable critical controversy exists as to the tone and meaning of the concluding lines. The traditional reading holds that they express the poet's frustration at his inability to finish the poem. With the now widespread view that "Kubla Khan" is a perfectly ordered and completed work of art, no such interpretation, of course, is possible. Humphry House finds the concluding lines "a triumphant positive statement of the potentialities of poetry" (HH, p. 116), and Patricia Adair agrees that the poem has a "triumphant climax" (*The Waking Dream*, p. 138). There seems to me no question about the intensity and exaltation of the closing lines: they are among the most marvellous in English poetry. But they express what the poet *would* achieve, if only he could restore a previous state of mind. House and Adair seem fundamentally to misread the last eighteen lines, which clearly state that something has been *lost*. There is no hint of tragic despair, nor should there be. To express the triumphant potentialities of poetry is not the same as writing a triumphant climax. Those who argue for "Kubla Khan" as a perfectly ordered whole, and a song of affirmation, simply ignore the publishing history of the poem. After all, it is not irrelevant that Coleridge didn't publish it for some twenty years after it was written, and that he twice called it a fragment.

117. *CL*, I, 355. Italics in text.

118. Douglas Angus writes of this memory:

It would be hard to find a more classic bit of evidence for a strongly developed Oedipus complex than this. Waking out of a deep sleep, at a moment when the unconscious would be in the ascendant, he announces the fulfillment of the repressed wish. But how darkly mysterious and sinister the world must have seemed when the wish turned out to be true. It would be a world perhaps too sinister, one that must be covered with another world, a world dominated by love, the kind of world Coleridge, in his philosophy and poetry, tries to persuade himself exists. ("The Theme of Love and Guilt in Coleridge's Three Major Poems," *JEGP*, LIX [1960], 657)

Angus also notes that "Coleridge was violently jealous of his older brother Francis, a situation often referred to as a secondary Oedipus complex," and suspects that the demon-lover may be an "unnatural lover" (pp. 657, 665).

119. This image, conventional in itself, appears often in Coleridge. In the sonnet called "On Receiving an Account that his only Sister's Death was Inevitable," we find:

> Say, is this hollow eye, this heartless pain,
> Fated to rove thro' Life's wide cheerless plain—
> Nor father, brother, sister meet its ken—
> My woes, my joys unshared! Ah, long ere then
> On me *thy icy dart, stern Death*, be prov'd:—
> Better to die, than live and not be lov'd! (*PW*, I, 20)

Anne Coleridge (Nancy) died in March 1791, and the poem's title suggests that it was written soon afterwards. The earliest known text of the poem, not published till 1834, is MS. O, which dates from about 1793. There, instead of the line "Nor father, brother, sister meet its ken," Coleridge actually wrote, "Nor *Mother*, brother, sister meets its ken" (*PW*, I, 20 *app. crit.*). Since his mother was still alive at the time, we seem here to have one of those astounding slips of the pen which reveals so clearly Coleridge's hatred for his mother.

120. *N*, 1649.   121. *N*, 2489.   122. *LL*, I, 136.

123. Yet in practice Coleridge might deny such evil in man, if it touched too close to home. One of the Malta voyage journal entries reads:

Hawk with ruffled Feathers resting on the Bow-sprit—Now shot at & yet did not move— how fatigued—a third time it made a gyre, a short circuit, & returned again/ 5 times it was thus shot at/ left the Vessel/ flew to another/ & I heard firing, now here, now there/ & nobody shot it/ but probably it perished from fatigue, & the attempt to rest upon the wave! —Poor Hawk! O Strange Lust of Murder in Man!—It is not cruelty/ it is mere non-feeling from non-thinking. (*N*, 2090)

The relation of this to the Mariner and the albatross would seem so obvious that it is almost astounding to find that Coleridge himself makes no connection. That such "Strange Lust of Murder" is "not cruelty" but "mere non-feeling from non-thinking" is another example of Coleridge's need, in particular instances, to deny the relation between external act and inner life.

124. *PW*, I, 193-194, *app. crit.* Italics in text.

125. The interpretive problems raised by this whole sequence has been observed by many critics (and ignored by still more). I quite agree with Professor E. E. Bostetter, who has argued very powerfully that the Mariner's tale takes place in an irrational universe. "The most disturbing characteristic of this universe is the caprice that lies at the heart of it; the precise punishment of the Mariner and his shipmates depends upon chance. The spectre crew of Death and Life-in-Death gamble for them. . . . Surely, [the dice game] knocks out any attempt to impose a systematic philosophical or religious interpretation . . . upon the poem." See "The Nightmare

World of 'The Ancient Mariner'," *SR*, I (Summer 1962), 241-254, and the chapters on Coleridge in *The Romantic Ventriloquists*. Both are among the most perceptive things ever written about Coleridge.

126.   Beres's discussion of Coleridge's fear of dying in his sleep, and of sleep itself, should be read by anyone interested in the subject.

> God forbid that my worst Enemy should ever have the Nights & the Sleeps that I have had, night after night—surprized by Sleep, while I struggled to remain awake, starting up to bless my own loud Screams that had awakened me. . . .

Beres observes of this portion of one of Coleridge's letters:

> The fear of sleep was the fear of his anxiety-laden dreams. Only opium in ever-increasing doses could give him the peace of dreamless sleep. To a lesser degree also the pains of his illness, which may have served as a bribe to his super-ego, a punishment for his unconscious crimes, also brought him some relief. In the letter just quoted, after a listing of his symptoms, he wrote:
> "No Bridegroom ever longed for Rapture more impatiently than I for Torture—It is wonderful, how this has relieved me! how balsam-sweet & profound my Sleep has been—how freely I breathe—how freely my Spirits seem to move within me!"
> The need for punishment was as much a theme of his life as it was of the *Ancient Mariner*. (Beres, p. 110)

I have quoted Coleridge's letter from the more accurate text at *CL*, II, 1009-10. The letter, which contains a portion of "The Pains of Sleep," was written to Poole on 3 October 1803, exactly one year after one of his most frightful dreams, and one day before the anniversary of becoming a bridegroom himself.

127.   Beres, pp. 103, 105. Coleridge's profound emotional insecurity and appalling dependency appear startlingly in two very touching, agonizing, truly hysterical letters of 1796 to Thomas Poole. It appeared as if the young Coleridge's plans to live in Nether Stowey (near Poole) had fallen through. Coleridge could not believe that Poole's most sensible reasons for discouraging him from making the move (which in the event proved all too true) were sincere.

> Surely, surely, my friend! something has occurred which you have not mentioned to me. Your Mother has manifested a strong dislike to our living near you—or some thing or other —for the reasons, you have assigned tell me nothing except that there are reasons, which you have not assigned. Pardon me if I write vehemently—I meant to write calmly; but Bitterness of Soul came upon me. Mrs. Coleridge has observed the workings of my face, while I have been writing; and is intreating to know what is the matter—I dread to shew her your Letter—I dread it. My God! my God! what if she should dare to think, that my most beloved Friend is grown cold towards me! (*CL*, I, 273)

The fear that affection has been withdrawn throws Coleridge into an emotional paroxysm. And it is revealing that he instantly supposes that Poole's *mother* has taken a "strong dislike" to the plan. How untrue this suspicion was is shown by the fact that Coleridge came to view Mrs. Poole as a surrogate mother, and wrote tenderly about her death (though he never mentioned, either in letter or notebook, his feelings upon the death of his own mother).

128.   *On Being Creative And Other Essays* (Boston, 1932), p. 71.

129.   Beres, p. 107. The view of the lofty Geraldine as "devouring mother" may be seen as receiving considerable support from Coleridge's dreams (few of which had been published when Beres wrote his article). The "biting" prostitute, the tall woman who tries to pluck out Coleridge's eye, both point to the female as a destructive monster. And the dream of the "frightful pale woman" who turns first into a stool, and then into some other "common thing," and who repeatedly changes her physical location when the dreamer rushes up to her—all this suggests how undependable and treacherous women can be.

130.   *N*, 1649. STC's underscoring.

131.   There are other reasons to identify Coleridge with Geraldine. The lofty lady says she has been kidnapped from her home far away. She is found in the woods beneath an old oak tree, like so many other orphans in Coleridge's poetry. Coleridge and Geraldine are very similar names, a point which may not be mere accident. Coleridge played anagrams with names regularly. Asra, for Sara Hutchinson, is well known. In journal entries she appears in various nomenclatures, once in a cipher anagram as "asra Schonthinu," with Samuel Taylor Coleridge transformed to "musaello rita gelocedri" (*N*, 3222 and n). He very often published under pen names, sometimes remotely connected with himself. So it ought not to be altogether surprising if *Gerald*ine's name—rooted in a male stem—has unconscious identifications with his own. It happens that Coleridge had written upon one Joseph Gerald in an early political and moral lecture, and with particular emphasis in a letter to Thelwall of 1796:

I have been informed by a West-Indian . . . that *to his knowledge* Gerald left a *Wife* there to starve—and I well know that he was prone to intoxication, & an *Whore*monger. I saw myself a letter from Gerald to one of his FRIENDS, couched in terms of the most abhorred Obscenity, & advising a marriage with an old woman on account of her money—Alas! alas! Thelwall—I almost wept—& poor Lovell (who read it with me) was so much agitated that he left the room. (*CL*, I, 215. STC's underscoring)

The reason for this extraordinary agitation is that Gerald had fallen from the grace in which he had appeared as so sympathetic a political and moral figure in Coleridge's *Conciones ad Populum*. (See *Essays on His Own Times*, I, 18 for the context.) Gerald therefore was an example of a divided personality, with much good and much evil.

Coleridge himself insisted that his name was to be pronounced as "a Trisyllabic Amphimacron —⏑—!" (EKC, p. 2). These are the accents on Geraldine but also on Christabel. All three names contain ten letters composing three syllables. The names Coleridge and Geraldine, however, have eight letters in common. Only the *a* and *n* of Geraldine are unmatched in C-o-l-e-r-i-d-g-e. So far as pronunciation goes, only the *n* is without a parallel letter or sound. Geraldine's supposed home is Tryemaine. Coleridge was raised in Ottery St. Mary. *All* ten letters of Tryermaine are matched in O-t-t-e-r-y S-a-i-n-t M-a-r-y (and vice-versa, but for an *o* and *s*). The reader will have to decide how far this seems like coincidence.

132.   The context shows several memory distortions:

I forget whether it was in my fifth or sixth year [according to the letter to Poole he was at least seven] . . . in consequence of some quarrel between me and my brother, *in the first week of October*, I ran away from fear of being whipped, and passed the whole night . . .

In my seventh year [he was actually nine], *about the same time, if not the very same time, i.e. Oct. 4th*, my most dear, most revered father, died suddenly. (Gillman, p. 11)

133.   This date is repeated through the entire range of Coleridge scholarship, with the exception of Bernard Lord Coleridge in *The Story of a Devonshire House*, where a date of 14 October 1781 is assigned. I suspect that 14 is merely a typographical error for 4. If Lord Coleridge had intended to disagree with his illustrious ancestor, he would surely have underscored the point. The Ottery parish register records that the "Revd. John Coleridge, Vicar of Ottery St. Mary, died suddenly at 3 o'clock on the morning of Saturday, the 6th of October 1781. He was buried in the Chancel of the Church on Wednesday, the 10th of October." I am indebted to Mr. John A. Whitham, the historian of the church of St. Mary of Ottery, for supplying this information and to Miss Jennifer Kinley, who solicited this information for me when visiting Ottery.

134.   *CL*, I, 160. STC's underscoring.

135.   This was also the date on which "Ode to Dejection" was published for the first time. In fact the whole month of October is studded with dates of powerful emotional significance, most of them mournful—which reinforces the unconscious meanings of "Kubla Khan." Just ten days after his own wedding on 4 October, Mary Evans was married, the girl forever identified as the "young Lady, whom for five years I loved—almost to madness" (*CL*, I, 121, and 130, n. 1).

136.   ". . . Mr. Cruikshanks [sic], an old acquaintance, who married on the same day as I, & has got a little girl a little younger than David Hartley. Mrs. Cruikshanks is a sweet little

woman, of the same size as my Sara—& they are extremely cordial" (*CL*, I, 301). Cruikshank. was also the first Treasurer of a group pledged to give £5 a year to assist STC (*CL*, I, 210n).

137.   *PW*, I, 284. Edward's "hard quick pants" in the grip of nightmare (with its sexual overtones) is reminiscent of the "fast thick pants" of "Kubla Khan."

138.   *PW*, I, 18, *app. crit.*, and 295, l. 53. This is an instance of a brilliant image becoming mechanical by repetition.

139.   In "Frost at Midnight," the lonely bluecoat boy longs to see the face of "Townsman, or aunt, or *sister more beloved,/My play-mate when we both were clothed alike!*" (ll. 42-3). The charming image now takes on a more complex significance. Still more suggestive is the following passage Coleridge copied into his notebooks: "O that thou wert as my Sister, that sucked the Breasts of my Mother! Should I find thee without, I would lead thee and bring thee into my House!" But the passage from the Song of Songs reads, "O that thou wert as my *brother*," not sister—and the sibling would be brought not "into my house," but into "my *mother's* house" (*N*, 2427 and n). The variants suggest how intricate were Coleridge's attitudes in these matters.

140.   Similar to the theme of the demon masquerading as lover in "Christabel" is a passage in "Love," dealing with a knight, crazed with unrequited love:

> There came and looked him in the face
> An angel beautiful and bright;
> And that he knew it was a Fiend,
>   This miserable Knight! (ll. 49-53. *PW*, I, 333)

141.   "The Ancient Mariner" has been one of the language's most admired and widely anthologized poems since at least the middle of the nineteenth century. Of the work's intense emotional power there has never been any doubt. But the precise grounds on which the poem (and "Christabel" and "Kubla Khan") was to be rationally admired has always been a massive embarrassment to critics. If it was difficult to give one's heart away completely to Shakespeare so long as the doctrine of the formal unities held sway, so it was—and is—difficult for some critics to accept Coleridge's most popular poems as specimens of great art because of the pull of the ancient injunction that great art should instruct as well as delight. What instruction the mystery poems of Coleridge could be said to promulgate was not even a matter that could be discussed. "The Ancient Mariner's" nominal moral—

> He prayeth best who loveth best
> All things both great and small;
> For the dear God who loveth us,
> He made and loveth all—

is not only inadequate to the action of the poem, it makes nonsense of it. Considered thus grossly, the poem would have to be shunned as a moral document because of its blasphemous mixture of Christian and pagan deities. It is not absurd to say that taken at this literal level it would be impossible for a man after reading this poem to sit down with a clear conscience to a roasted fowl. If two hundred men can die horribly for approving of the death of a single albatross, without being given any chance to expiate their crimes, it is nonsense to speak of Christian morality. Despite all this, multitudes of readers, including subtle ones, continued to value the poem highly if for no other reason—and it is a good one—than that it is intense, that is gives rise to states of mind which seem to be their own reward. Most apropos is a neglected passage from one of Coleridge's letters: "The truth is, that Images and Thoughts possess a power in and of themselves, independent of that act of the Judgement or Understanding by which we affirm or deny the existence of a reality correspondent to them. Such is the ordinary state of the mind in Dreams" (*CL*, IV, 641). It remained for the twentieth century, however, to revolutionize both the aims and methods of literary criticism. In the process it is seriously to be doubted that any poem has been so violently misinterpreted as "The Ancient Mariner." Robert Penn Warren's *A Poem of Pure Imagination: An Experiment in Reading* (New York, 1946) is perhaps the most influential single work ever written on Coleridge's poem. Coming from so widely respected a critic, poet, and novelist, this lengthy essay was at once widely discussed and the object of far-ranging controversy. All the essay's major propositions—that the poem embodies a "sacramental vision" of the universe, that the shooting of the albatross represents "a crime against the imagination," that there is a consistent and integrated light symbolism in the poem, whereby the moon represents a "beneficent" force and the sun the opposite—all this would not only seem strange to readers of the poem, but incredible. The fact that Warren's arguments, even in his own terms, have been cogently and repeatedly refuted (notably by Bostetter), seems to make no difference whatever to droves of subsequent scholars. That light symbolism functions not only in "The Ancient Mariner," but throughout the range of Coleridge's poetry, is now a commonplace of criticism. The notion that there is a "sacramental vision" in the poem has not done much harm, since the idea can readily be accommodated, if erroneously, at one remove from that of God making and loving all his creatures. However, to symbolize the slaying of the albatross as a crime against the imagination is far more serious, since it fastens onto the poem an artistic purpose which, if it were really there, would radically alter all our notions of what kind of artist Coleridge was—or anybody else in his time, for that matter. That no evidence can be brought forward to show that Coleridge thought in this way has made little difference. Nor does it seem to matter that Coleridge began writing "The Ancient Mariner" when his imaginative powers were in triumphant ascendancy, with almost all his great poetry still to be written. Perhaps the most serious consequence of interpreting "The Ancient Mariner" (or any other of Coleridge's poems) in these arbitrary and abstract symbolic modes is that it divorces the artist's work from the known facts of his life, or from what is known about the symbol-making powers of the unconscious mind.

25.   THE UNRECONCILED OPPOSITES

1.   *The Letters of William and Dorothy Wordsworth, The Middle Years*, ed. E. de Selincourt (Oxford, 1937), I, 321. Italics in text.

2.   *HCR*, I, 11.

3.   Mrs. Catherine Clarkson to Henry Crabb Robinson, 5 December 1811. Quoted from *Diary, Reminiscences, and Correspondence of H. C. Robinson*, ed. Thomas Sadlier (London, 1872), p. 182.

4.   From an unpublished letter of 10 April 1812, as printed in the Sotheby auction catalog of 23 June 1969, p. 88.

5.   EY, p. 189.

6.   See n. 1, above, p. 367. "Burn" italicized in text. On the previous page of this long and searing letter, Dorothy wrote:

As to Coleridge, if I thought I should distress you, I would say nothing about him; but I hope that you are sufficiently prepared for the worst. . . .If he were not under our roof, he would be just as much the slave of stimulants as ever; and his whole time and thoughts, (except when he is reading and he reads a great deal), are employed in deceiving himself, and seeking to deceive others. He will tell me that he has been writing, that he *has* written, half a Friend; when I *know* that he has not written a single line. This Habit pervades all his words and actions, and you feel perpetually new hollowness and emptiness. Burn this letter, I entreat you. I am loath to say it, but it is the truth. (Italics in text)

Coleridge was extremely fond of the recipient of this letter, Mrs. Clarkson. "Had she been my

Sister," he once wrote, "I should have been a great man" (*CL*, III, 307). But Mrs. Clarkson, barely a year later, was to describe him as "worthless as a friend" (*CHCR*, I, 71).

7. *CL*, II, 489-490. To J. J. Morgan, 14 May 1814. STC's underscoring. The letter of the next day is extremely important in this connection and should be read in its entirety.

8. *CL*, III, 274. STC's emphasis.

9. *Emma Darwin: A Century of Family Letters, 1792-1896*, edited by her daughter Henrietta Litchfield (New York, 1915), I, 249. Italics in text.

10. *HW*, XVII, 113.

11. Crabb Robinson to Mrs. Clarkson, 7 May 1808. Quoted from *Blake, Coleridge, Wordsworth, Lamb, etc.*, ed. Edith J. Morley (London, 1922), pp. 105-106. It is perhaps from statements like this that Wordsworth later attributed both Coleridge's and Lamb's "incorrectness in talk . . . to a *school habit*. Lamb's veracity was unquestionable in all matters of a serious kind," Wordsworth added immediately. "He never uttered an untruth either for profit or through vanity." But this qualification is notably absent in his reference to Coleridge, whose "incorrectness" was "far more equivocal" (HCR, II, 487. Italics in text).

12. I, 353. *PW*, II, 895.   13. *CL*, I, 34.

14. *Anima Poetae*, p. 197. The note was recorded on 18 May 1808, years after the experience.

15. *CL*, II, 1074.

16. Orlo Williams, *Life and Letters of John Rickman* (Boston and New York, 1912), pp. 88, 151.

17. *HCR*, II, 501; I, 26.   18. *HCR*, I, 77.   19. *CT*, p. 388.

20. *CT*, p. 42. See also p. 49.   21. *CL*, II, 959.

26. SHIPWRECK AND SAFE HARBOR

1. *N*, 2398.   2. *CL*, II, 1028.

3. In the letter to Southey just cited, Coleridge wrote: ". . . I have swellings, with moveable Fluid, in my knees or ancles, & am *bed-ridden* / if by means of opiates I revivify the actions of the Absorbents, I have no swellings nor eruptions—no bad knees, no Boils in my neck, & Thighs, no little agony-giving ulcers in my mouth, et super Scrotum . . ." (*CL*, II, 1029). Among many other grim details, Coleridge mentioned one affliction of awful skin rashes. Two days later he referred to his "Caterpiller Skin which I believe, the Butterfly Elect is wriggling off, tho' with no small Labor and Agony" (*CL*, II, 1032). This image combines many recurrent metaphors in Coleridge which have psychological implications: ugly self-image, uncertain identity, identification with women, desire for beauty and freedom.

4. *CL*, II, 1199-1200. Shortly before embarking for Malta, Coleridge wrote to the Wordsworths of a certain bookseller named Mottley, who though the father of six children and possessed of a "nice sweet-tempered Wife [was] nevertheless, alas! alas! addicted to almost promiscuous Intercourse with women of all Classes. At first, he was actually *astonished* at my principles & practice . . ." (*CL*, II, 1119. STC's underscoring).

5. *N*, 2600. Italics in text. "In the Dream," Coleridge continued, "I supposed myself in a state of Society, like that of those great Priests of Nature who formed the Indian Worship in its purity, when all things, strictly of Nature, were reverenced according to their importance, undebauched by associations of Shame and Impudence, the ⟨twin-⟩children of sensuality. . . ." These thoughts seem more likely to have been occasioned by the dream, rather than to have been experienced *in* it.

6. *CL*, I, 145.   7. *N*, 1770.

8. *CSC*, p. 454. STC's emphasis.

9. *N*, 2398 and n.

10. *N*, 520, 1552. The appearance of the name Tiberius is suggestive. Tacitus writes of the tyrant thus:

> So completely had his crimes and infamies recoiled, as a penalty, on himself. With profound meaning was it often affirmed by that greatest teacher of philosophy that could the minds of tyrants be laid bare, there would be seen gashes and wounds; for, as the body is lacerated by scourging, so is the spirit by brutality, by lust and evil thoughts. Assuredly Tiberius was not saved from his elevation or his solitude from having to confess the anguish of his heart and self-inflicted punishment. (*Annals* 6.6)

The relationship between this and Coleridge's own psychic sufferings as a result of sensual promptings would seem to be self-evident.

11. *N*, 2998. STC's underscoring.

12. *N*, 2542. STC's underscoring. See the editor's notes. I suggest that *Vossius* may refer less to the German classicist and theologian Gerhard Johann Vossius, than to Johann Heinrich Voss, the poet whose poems Coleridge once carried in his pocket (*N*, 1207*n*) and from whom he took a few silent borrowings.

13. *CL*, II, 1038 and n. 1.   14. For example, *N*, 1646, 2019, 2086, 3148.

15. *N*, 3148. This nexus of autobiographical confession appears in a revealing stanza of the "Asra" poem "Separation," written two years before. (The last three stanzas of this poem, it will be remembered, were appropriated from Cotton.) In the second stanza, Coleridge wrote:

> The dazzling charm of outward form,
> The power of gold, the pride of birth,
> Have taken Woman's heart by storm—
> Usurp'd the place of inward worth. (*PW*, I, 398)

16. *N*, 3148. STC's underscoring. "Awakened from a dream of Tears, & anguish of involuntary Jealousy," Coleridge wrote immediately afterwards. Jealousy towards Wordsworth, natural enough in the circumstances, appears often in the notebooks of this period. And so rigid are the moral demands Coleridge makes on himself, that each appearance either throws him into a frenzy of guilt or, as here, is made "involuntary Jealousy."

17. *PW*, I, 450-451, where the title "Love, A Sword" is given.   18. *N*, 2531.

19. To Coleridge, "awe of womanhood" was "a heaven-sanctioned" characteristic of England (*PW*, I, 483). These attitudes toward women seriously mar his analyses of Shakespeare's heroines, whom he regularly idealizes or desexualizes into the image of his own fantasies.

20. *CL*, II, 1054-55.   21. *CL*, I, 269-276.

22. *CL*, I, 249-251. STC's underscoring.

23. *CL*, I, 490. STC's underscoring. Coleridge wrote to Poole as his "dearest friend" over a period of seven years (1796-1803), which suggests how deep the attachment was (*CL*, I, 273, 302, 345, 358, 381, 491, 556, 619; II, 1009). Then there was, at least for a time, an unpleasant break. Just before leaving for Malta, admittedly one of the more trying periods in Coleridge's life, he became severely angry with Poole. The cause seems to have been Coleridge's conviction that Poole had become tightfisted towards him. In an unusually affectionate letter to Southey, Coleridge wrote that Poole

> denied me once a Loan of 50£ when I was on a Sickbed—I never dreamt of asking him. Wordsworth did it without my knowledge—& it would have been against my Consent. Poole *answered* not *W* but me, and proposed to have a subscription of 50£ raised for me, to which *he* would contribute 5£ ; but wondered, that I had not applied to my Brothers! ! !—and 3 years long did I give my mind to this man/ exclusive of introductions &c &c. (*CL*, II, 1124. STC's underscoring.)

Untangling this thicket of semi-truths, distortions, and falsehoods would require a small essay. The main points are that Coleridge knew quite well that Wordsworth was going to write to Poole for a loan or gift on his behalf. Poole responded by sending not £5 but £20, at a time when Coleridge was already in debt to him for £52. Coleridge's letters to Poole over the following months contain some amazing passages on his own lofty indifference to money and Poole's stained moral purity arising from his wealth. (See *CL*, Nos. 403, 411, 412, and 416). In October 1801, three months after the unpleasantness began, the friendship had mended sufficiently for Coleridge to write Poole that he was desperately in need of some £20 and would be grateful for a loan of any part of that amount. Poole responded by sending him £25 (*CL*, II, 770-771). Griggs's headnote to letter No. 441 is, I believe, extremely misleading and excessively partial to Coleridge. The reader inclined to follow up this affair should also consult *TP*, I, 22-73.

24.   Coleridge was to some extent aware of the feminine side of his personality. "The truth is," he said in the closing years of his life, "a great mind must be androgynous" (*TT*, p. 201). Oddly, in recalling some few pleasant memories from his early youth, he wrote: "To be feminine, kind, and genteely (what I should now call neatly) dressed, these were the only things to which my head, heart or imagination had any polarity, and what I was then, I still am" (Allsop, II, 86).

All this may help explain the origin of certain of Coleridge's phobias. For example, one of the most painful consequences of opium addiction for Coleridge proved to be agonizing costiveness. The usual treatment was enema, but as Coleridge wrote to Southey, "my silly horror of having an Enēma performed on me, greatly increased the sum of my sufferings." Repeated submission to necessity only increased his dread of the instrument: "& strange it is!—but tho' the pain is so trifling that it is almost a misnomer to call it pain, yet my dread of and antipathy increased every time" (*CL*, II, 1176-77). A terrible experience of this kind is described in the Maltese voyage journals, where in the immediate aftermath of an enema Coleridge describes "pains & sore uneasinesses, & indescribable desires" (*N*, 2085). "An enēma is not attended with the slightest pain," he wrote in an amazingly graphic letter to Crabb Robinson in 1811, "—and yet such is the force of thought & intellectual repugnance that I am convinced, I should submit to a Lithotomy with less revulsion and less fortitude—" (*CL*, III, 347). Just three years before, however, Coleridge had thought himself suffering from some "morbid Affection of the Bladder. If it prove to be so—," he wrote to De Quincey, "(and I CANNOT bring myself to the shocking operation of being examined for it, from the *same* kind of feeling or false shame, but greater in degree, that brought my Life twice or more in Hazard on board Ship, from the encreasing Horror on my mind of submitting to the Clyster . . ." (*CL*, III, 52. Italics in text). In 1814 the problem appears in almost identical form. Coleridge wrote to J. J. Morgan of a dreadful fear preying on his mind, that he was afflicted with a stricture of the urethra. To ascertain the truth, a probe was to be made the next day:

Tomorrow morning this is to be done: & you may well imagine the state of my mind at present, in expectation of the Event, the distressful feelings ιοφ μοδεστι and a crowd of indefinite sensations connected with ΜΟΔΕΣΤΥ put out of the Question: tho' God knows, they now agitate me so as to overwhelm the Dread of having the Worst, I suspect, ascertained. (*CL*, III, 515)

Surely any man might look forward with extreme agitation to such trials, but the fear in Coleridge is not of physical pain, but of intolerable affront to his *modesty*.

25.   *N*, 2598.

26.   Shedd, II, 168; *N*, 1998.

27.   *N*, 2471. Italics in text. What Coleridge was here trying to achieve is what too many biographers shirk, namely, to see their subjects whole, with all the warts. Coleridge wrote of our "dislike that a bad man should have any virtues, a good man any faults," and this crippling prejudice runs through Coleridge studies.

28.   The Maltese voyage journals record the following:

abomination! The full moon came thundering down from Heaven, like a Cannon Ball; & seeing that nothing could be done went quietly back again! Dreamt these words before day light, May Morning, 1804. Put 'em into a Mrs. Jordan's mouth, ridiculing some pompous moral or political Declaimer. (*N*, 2059)

Miss Coburn's notes identify Dorothea Jordan as "a famous talker as well as a popular actress. In her early days she played many male-impersonation parts." These sparing details are in themselves extraordinarily suggestive. The rough rule that single speakers in dreams often are surrogates for the dreamer would seem to hold true here. Mrs. Jordan (to whom Coleridge sent a copy of *Lyrical Ballads*[*CL*, I, 654]) was "a famous talker," which Coleridge always was. She played many "breeches" parts, which points to Coleridge's own mingled self-identity. The long DNB article describes her as "Indolent, capricious, imprudent, and at times refractory, she made less way than might have been expected"—which might also be said of Coleridge. The meaning of this dream is especially elusive, but the first word, "abomination!" is ominous.

29. *N*, 2091. STC's emphasis.

30. During Hartley's crisis at Oxford, where he lost his scholarship because of repeated "intemperance," Coleridge wrote as follows to his son Derwent:

Last night . . . I screamed out but once only in my sleep, and my stomach felt but in a very slight degree sore after I woke—the exceeding order and wild *Swedenborgian* rationality of the Images in my Dreams, whenever I have been in any great affliction, so that they haunt me for days—and the odd circumstance that these dreams are always accompanied with profuse weeping in my sleep towards morning, and probably not long before I wake—for my pillow is often quite wet: (or the screaming fits take place in the first sleep, and from dreams that are either frightful or mere imageless sensation of affright and leave no traces)—these are problems which I encourage myself in proposing and trying to solve, were it only to divert my attention from the occasion of them. O surely if Hartley knew or believed that I love him and (hunger) after him as I do and ever have done, he would have come to me. (*UL*, 270. Italics in text)

But Hartley had many reasons to believe that his father did not love him, chief among them the fact that he had seen so little of him. But in view of Hartley's reverential respect for his father, it is doubtful that such thoughts ever rose to consciousness. Among Hartley's bitter thoughts upon having to leave Oxford was that he had disgraced the name of Coleridge, "the one scabby sheep turn'd out of an immaculate flock," he wrote to his father at the time, "the sole jarring note in the concert of the Coleridges" (*Letters of Hartley Coleridge*, eds. G.E. Griggs and E.L. Griggs [Oxford, 1937], p. 43). I can find no evidence that there was any irony in Hartley's words, or that STC ever suggested to his suffering son that he had had his own troubles at college, or related difficulties thereafter. Indeed, Derwent thus reported the effect of the news on his father: "I was with him at the time, and have never seen any human being, before or since, so deeply afflicted: not as he said, by the temporal consequences of his son's misfortune, heavy as those were, but for the moral offense which it involved" (*Letters of Hartley Coleridge*, p. 33). It is perhaps against such a background that Coleridge's sanctimonious letter to Derwent about the proper behavior of a college student, quoted earlier ("The Parched Roots," n. 24), should be understood.

31. Gillman, p. 257, n. 19. While at Highgate, Coleridge wrote Derwent to pursue his

classical studies under the guidance and in the light of *Philology*, in that original and noblest sense of the term, in which it *implies* and is the most *human* practical and fructifying Form, and (what is of no small moment in the present state of society) the most popular *Disguise*, of Logic and Psychology—without which what is man? (The last 5 words I wrote with the line "Without black velvet Breeches what is man?" running in my head). (*UL*, II, 280. STC's underscoring)

It is suggestive that the previous last five words are "*Disguise*, of Logic and Psychology."

32. Gillman, p. 19.   33. Gillman, p. 303.   34. *CSC*, p. 446.

35. Gillman, pp. 116-117. Italics in text. The full name was "Satyrane, the Idoloclast, or breaker of Idols." But the root, which Coleridge seems not to have perceived, is *satyr*: half-man, half-beast, of lustful propensities.

Index

Index

Material in the notes that continues discussion obviously implied by a reference in the text is not normally indexed. Initials C and W represent Coleridge and Wordsworth; A.M. and K.K. identify "The Ancient Mariner" and "Kubla Khan."

Aaron, R. I., on C's reading of Locke, 457 (n.16).

Abernathy, J. 134.

Abora, form of the word, 342-3; unconscious significance of, 400.

Abrams, M. H., 134, 181, 498 (nn. 33, 36); on C's rapid composition of poems, 512 (n.14); emphasizes Boyer's formative influence, 520 (n.49); review of Schneider's *Opium, Coleridge, and Kubla Khan,* 538 (n.8).

Abyssinian Maid, her presence in K.K., 343; incest and, 399-400.

Adair, Patricia M., on Bacchus, K. K., and C., 396-7, 558 (n.70); on completeness of K.K., 564 (n.116).

Adams, Dr., possible relation to C's dreams, 380.

Addison, Joseph, on "faculties of the mind," 185; on poetic diction, 519 (n.39).

Adelung, J. C., his German *Dictionary* and C's "etymological fancies," 62-3.

Ainger, Alfred, on a "handsome apology," 456 (n.8).

Akenside, Mark, his blank-verse "Inscription" "imitated" by C., 38-40, 168, 502, (n.20); 287, 292.

Allegory (*See* "Symbol").

Allen, Robert, in C's dreams, 381.

Allsop, Thomas, 93, 98, 136, 307, 330, 417, 461 (n.24).

Allston, Washington, and "objective correlative," 460 (n.5).

Ammerbach, Vitus, on association, 76-7.

"Ancient Mariner, The," genesis of, 269-71; W's account of, 271-2, 274, W's contributions to plot, 271-6, 312-3, and to figure of Mariner, 510 (n.28), and to diction of, 277-281, 312-3, 315, 320, 327; influence of ballads on, 311-2; and travel books, 313-4; C's use of "The Romaunt of the Rose," 316-8; Gothic elements in, 320; its wedding scene and Schiller's *Ghost-Seer,* 322-3; Lowes on C's creative process in, 320-2, 324, and Bald's criticisms of, 324-5; other objections, 325-6; theme of crime in, 353; Mrs. Barbauld's criticism of its moral, 353-4; morally confused universe of, 353-4, 565 (n.125); C's childhood recollections in background of, 362-4, 402-3; Cruikshank's dream, 403-4; the "Nightmare LIFE-IN-DEATH," and C's own nightmares, 404-5; links between marriage and death